The Communist and the Revolutionary Liberal in the Second American Revolution

Historical Materialism
Book Series

Editorial Board

Loren Balhorn (*Berlin*)
David Broder (*Rome*)
Sebastian Budgen (*Paris*)
Steve Edwards (*London*)
Juan Grigera (*London*)
Marcel van der Linden (*Amsterdam*)
Peter Thomas (*London*)
Gavin Walker (*New York*)

VOLUME 326

The titles published in this series are listed at *brill.com/hm*

The Communist and the Revolutionary Liberal in the Second American Revolution

Comparing Karl Marx and Frederick Douglass in Real-Time

By

August H. Nimtz
Kyle A. Edwards

BRILL

LEIDEN | BOSTON

The Library of Congress Cataloging-in-Publication Data is available online at https://catalog.loc.gov
LC record available at https://lccn.loc.gov/2024029284

Typeface for the Latin, Greek, and Cyrillic scripts: "Brill". See and download: brill.com/brill-typeface.

ISSN 1570-1522
ISBN 978-90-04-70637-8 (hardback)
ISBN 978-90-04-70638-5 (e-book)
DOI 10.1163/9789004706385

Copyright 2024 by August H. Nimtz and Kyle A. Edwards. Published by Koninklijke Brill BV, Leiden, The Netherlands.
Koninklijke Brill BV incorporates the imprints Brill, Brill Nijhoff, Brill Schöningh, Brill Fink, Brill mentis, Brill Wageningen Academic, Vandenhoeck & Ruprecht, Böhlau and V&R unipress.
Koninklijke Brill BV reserves the right to protect this publication against unauthorized use. Requests for re-use and/or translations must be addressed to Koninklijke Brill BV via brill.com or copyright.com.

This book is printed on acid-free paper and produced in a sustainable manner.

Contents

Acknowledgements VII

Introduction 1

1 Two Biographies – or, Two Routes to the Quest for 'True Democracy' 16
   1 From Chattel Slave to Revolutionary Liberal 17
   2 From Radical Democrat to Communist 33

2 Prelude to the Conflagration: From Paris to Fort Sumter 54
   1 The European Spring 55
      1.1 *Marx in the Cauldron* 56
      1.2 *Douglass: a Wary Cheerleader from Afar* 63
   2 The Coming American Spring 68
      2.1 *'Let the Battle Come': Douglass Considers Extra-Constitutional Measures* 68
      2.2 *Douglass, Weydemeyer, and the Republicans in 1856* 74
      2.3 *The Crisis Deepens* 77
      2.4 *King Cotton* 83
      2.5 *John Brown – Agent Provocateur Extraordinaire* 84
      2.6 *Lincoln's Election* 92
      2.7 *The Secession Crisis* 97

3 Toward the Convergence of Douglass and Marx: From Fort Sumter to the *Trent* Affair 104
   1 The 'Fall of Sumter' 105
   2 Douglass Gets on Board 111
   3 Marx's Return 117
   4 Marx and Douglass Converge 131
   5 'What's Happening at Manassas Junction?' 137
   6 'Complications with Foreign Powers': The *Trent* Affair 148

4 From a Constitutional to a Revolutionary Civil War: 'the Cruel and Apocalyptic War Had Become Holy' 160
   1 'A *Turning Point* in the War Policy Had Been Reached' 161
   2 'At Last the Tide of Battle Seems Fairly Turned' 167
   3 Two Real-Time Assessments of 'the Tremendous Conflict' 171
   4 Slouching Toward Redemption 180

  5 Redemption Time 185
  6 The Preliminary Emancipation Proclamation 199
  7 The Slave's Appeal to Great Britain 211

5 **The End of the War and the Rise and Fall of Radical Reconstruction** 216
  1 The Long Grinding Road to Appomattox 217
  2 'That the Paper Proclamation Must Now Be Made Iron, Lead and Fire' 220
  3 The Reality of Recruitment 228
  4 Toward Lincoln's Re-election and Union Victory 236
  5 'A Missed Revolutionary Opportunity' 249
  6 Weydemeyer's 'On the Negro Vote' 252
  7 Douglass and Marx on the Same Political Page – Almost 262

Conclusions 275
  1 The Key Takeaways of the Comparison 277
  2 'What Is to Be Done?' – Today 300

Appendix A: Douglass and Marx on the Paris Commune and the Labour Question in the United States 317
Appendix B: Marx and Engels on the Race Question: A Response to Critics 352
Bibliography 382
Index 402

Acknowledgements

Projects like this, as always, are indebted to lots of people, especially because neither of us claims Civil War or Douglass expertise. Thus, there isn't enough thanks we can give to all who took the time to patiently respond to our inquiries, point out errors, and engage with our arguments.

Two Douglass scholars who deserve special mention are John Kaufman-McKivigan and Peter Myers. The spirit of collegiality both demonstrated in reading the manuscript, offering correctives and incisive inquiries, and, in John's case, searching the Frederick Douglass Papers whenever we requested help, unquestionably strengthened the factual accuracy of the manuscript while sharpening our arguments.

Others who read the entire manuscript or large portions of it while providing invaluable feedback include Kevin Anderson, Bob Braxton, Adam Dahl, Mary Dietz, Gregory Downs, Benjamin Fagan, Allan Kulikoff, Robert Levine, James Mahoney, and Angela Zimmerman. Fagan's work and feedback on Douglass and the 1848 Revolutions were especially galvanising. Dahl's close reading and comments helped us develop and enhance our arguments on Douglass and political violence. Our portrait of Radical Reconstruction would have been incomplete without the observations Downs was willing to share with us. Bob Braxton's research into post-war Georgia is indispensable for claims we make about Reconstruction and the importance of the property question.

More scholars who graciously and forbearingly engaged with our arguments and questions about their scholarship include Charisse Burden-Stelly, Don Doyle, Bruce Levine, Stephanie McCurry, Peter Rachleff, David Roediger, Gregory Slack, Igor Shoikhedbrod, and Sara-Maria Sorentino.

David Samuels organised a joint colloquium attended by graduate students and faculty at the University of Minnesota from the political theory, comparative politics, and American politics sub-fields and the African and African-American Studies Department. This opportunity to present our work and receive probing comments and interrogation from discussants Anuja Bose and John Wright, in addition to Samuels's own challenging and constructive critique, undoubtedly strengthened our work. Conversations with Nancy Luxon on democracy's reconstruction, a product of this colloquium, are illuminating and ongoing.

Blake Fitzgerald and Bonnie Horgos, over the five-plus years of work that went into this project, continually offered much-needed encouragement and friendship while reading early drafts of research on the John Brown and Frederick Douglass relationship and Douglass's views on the Paris Commune, respectively.

Jonathan Eig, author of the new authoritative biography of Martin Luther King Jr., took time out of what must have been a jam-packed schedule and email box in the wake of publishing *King: A Life* to share with us a copy of King's Frogmore speech that kicks off our introduction.

The editorial assistance early in the project of Joseph Towns IV raised important considerations while making the prose more readable. But without the team at Historical Materialism, beginning with Sebastian Budgen, and then the crucial work of Danny Hayward, this book could not have seen the light of day. We're forever grateful.

A less direct, but equally essential contribution was the opinion of historian Allen Isaacman, who opined more than a decade ago that comparative real-time analysis would be an original contribution to historical inquiry and encouraged its application – this book being the latest example. Alongside Isaacman's comments, David Blight's *Prophet of Freedom* was the direct inspiration for the conversations that eventually resulted in this book. Blight's book is one of the pillars of scholarship upon which our book, as the reader can verify, stands.

Last but not least, the debt incurred by our companions, Katie Pederson and Natalie Morrison – for their patience, indulgence, and support – is unlikely to be repaid. But we hope this work makes them proud. And the same for Ellie when she's old enough to read it.

Introduction

In the last year of his life, Martin Luther King, Jr. revealed an epiphany that is often forgotten or ignored. Two years after the two legislative conquests of the Civil Rights Movement, the 1964 Civil Rights Act and the 1965 Voting Rights Act, unmistakable evidence confirmed that formal political equality for African Americans did not mean social equality. It took only a week, in fact, after the signing of the second piece of legislation for that truth to hit home – the social explosion in the Black neighbourhood of Watts, Los Angeles. Both before and after Watts, similar upheavals took place in scores of Black communities in the North where their residents had enjoyed for decades the rights that their kin in the South had just won. At a leadership meeting of his Southern Christian Leadership Conference in May 1967, King urged his organisation to acknowledge its new challenge and rethink tactics. 'Now, if we are to recognize that we are in this new era where the struggle is for genuine equality', and no longer just for civil rights, 'we must recognize that we can't solve our problems until there is a radical redistribution of economic and political power'.[1] King repeated the point on a number of occasions before his assassination the next year, even at one point suggesting the nationalisation of certain industries and a guaranteed income.[2] The urban rebellions, in other words, soberly taught the limits of the two legislative victories. King, tragically, didn't live long enough to elaborate on the solution he envisioned.

The question that King offered an answer for, how to realise racial equality in America, is as current as ever; hence the debate, as this is being written, about the decision of the United States Supreme Court in June 2023 to end racial affirmative action in higher education.[3] But it is also a question as old as ever. The first time it was posed in a meaningful way, that is, when the possibility of an apparent solution was at hand, was during the Civil War. We argue

---

[1] Southern Christian Leadership Conference leadership meeting at Frogmore, South Carolina, May 1967: King 1967b and online at https://kairoscenter.org/mlk-frogmore-staff-retreat-speech-anniversary/. See also King's interview with NBC News in May 1967, King 1967a and online at: https://www.youtube.com/watch?v=2xsbt3a7K-8. As well, his speech to the SCLC Convention in Atlanta in August 1967, Washington 1991, pp. 245–52, and talk to the American Psychological Association in September 1967 which addresses, amongst other issues, the political science literature on the limits of voting and was printed the next year in the *Journal of Social Issues*: King 1968. Both Douglass and Marx, apparently, make an appearance in the full May speech.

[2] Halberstam 1967, p. 48. Eig 2023, p. 525.

[3] For a Marxist analysis of the decision, see Evans 2023, p. 1.

that a revisit to that moment clarifies what is at stake with the question – aiding and abetting an assessment of what King offered and, thus, the quest for a still needed answer.

No one from the Civil War era for whom an extensive paper trail exists devoted as much time and energy to thinking about and answering the question as did Frederick Douglass. For the one-time escaped slave, the personal was indeed political. A European contemporary of Douglass also addressed the question. Though less well known for doing so – the fact will be a surprise to many – Karl Marx devoted both pen and ink and organisational time to providing an answer. For Marx, unlike for Douglass, however, the issue was not personal. Rather, it was a major item on a larger agenda. But, as the facts reveal, Marx's more encompassing concerns allowed him to see the world-historical significance of what was taking place on the other shores of the Atlantic in a way Douglass could not.

This book is a comparative real-time political analysis of the responses of Douglass and Marx to America's Second Revolution, the struggle to end chattel slavery. It compares how the two made and *acted* on judgments about what needed to be done in the moment, not after the fact. In hindsight, we can all look smart – the proverbial Monday morning quarterback. Historians, someone once quipped, are like vultures; they feed off the past. The test for political beings, rather, what both Douglass and Marx claimed to be, is knowing what to do next – the essence of politics. The years-long sanguinary fight to end the millennial-old practice of chattel slavery, the essence of the Civil War, was, as well, the nineteenth century's test for the democratic credentials of anyone who had the opportunity to live through it.

Comparing Douglass and Marx on their responses to the Civil War isn't just an interesting intellectual exercise. It's an opportunity to examine how two still competing political perspectives, liberalism and Marxism, performed when the biggest breakthrough for the millennial-old democratic quest after the French Revolution occurred – whose consequences continue to reverberate. Marx, though a co-founder of modern communism, might not seem an obvious choice for the test. But he was more than an influential theorist as commonly assumed. Less well known is that he was first and foremost a revolutionary activist – a fact that one of us has documented in detail.[4] His epiphany in 1845 that 'the educator must himself be educated' by *'revolutionary practice'* was instantiated by virtually everything he did afterward.[5]

---

4 Nimtz 2000.
5 Marx and Engels 1975–2004d, p. 4.

Douglass's activist credentials, on the other hand, are better known owing especially to David Blight's award-winning 2018 biography *Frederick Douglass: Prophet of Freedom*.[6] But the escaped slave had also been an enthusiastic devotee of the liberal agenda for almost two decades prior to the War – about the same number of years that Marx had been a communist – an agenda he actively promoted in the cause to abolish chattel slavery. Thus, why Douglass can be legitimately touted now as the liberal alternative to the particularistic 'trap' of identity politics.[7] Douglass scholars debate what kind of liberal – classical or reform.[8] We characterise him as a revolutionary liberal for the period of our focus because he advocated for and enabled revolutionary methods to realise liberal ends. When the War began in April 1861, our two revolutionary activists with two very different political perspectives found themselves on the same political page, making for a fair and potentially significant comparison.[9] There were certainly other better-known nineteenth-century liberals who related to the War, for example, John Stuart Mill. Unlike Mill, however, Douglass put in the requisite time and effort to advance the liberal cause for emancipation – an activist and, thus, a better comparison with Marx.[10] Both Douglass and Marx were born in the same year, 1818, a control for advantages that might – but not inevitably – come with age.[11]

---

[6] Blight 2018.

[7] Mounk 2023, pp. 54, 69.

[8] For the best concise treatment of Douglass as a liberal, see Myers 2008. We are indebted to Myers for enlightening us via communications on Douglass the thinker. Other important contributions to the study of Douglass's political thought include Martin 1984 and Buccola 2012. Sandefur 2018 argues for Douglass's libertarian bona fides. Nick Bromell offers a philosophical basis for Douglass's activism and argues that liberalism is inadequate to describe his Black political philosophy that is action-based and anchored in his slave experience. See Bromell 2021 and his 2019 presentation: https://www.youtube.com/watch?v=eeStz97ahv4. Roberts 2015 argues against a 'tendency to endorse a form of liberal political theory' and cautions against reading Douglass 'through the framework of liberalism'. Instead, Roberts emphasises the influence of British Romanticism on Douglass's conception of republicanism. See especially pp. 73–4. Roberts, Myers, and Buccola continue to flesh out their disagreements on Douglass in Roberts 2018. On Douglass's place in the American liberal tradition, see Kloppenberg 2016, pp. 15–16.

[9] Kevin C. Black argues, correctly, that by putting Douglass in conversation with European 'contemporaries' on reform and revolution, Douglass's politics are clarified. But for Black that means Adam Smith, Edmund Burke, Montesquieu, and Alexis de Tocqueville. Marx, we argue, would have been more relevant. We'll return to Black in the Conclusion. Black 2021, pp. 209–20.

[10] As for Mill's response to the Civil War, see Nimtz 2019b, Chapter Three.

[11] A comparison of Lenin with two older liberal figures, Max Weber and Woodrow Wilson, reveals that the younger Lenin proved to be the more efficacious politician exactly because

There is an even more important justification for our comparison owing to another underappreciated side to Marx. 'No other major thinker of his time', in the recent assessment of three Marx scholars, 'wrote so variously on slavery when his whole body of work is taken into account, and perhaps none, except Frederick Douglass, commented so profoundly on U.S. slavery'.[12] This book does exactly what the three scholars at best only suggest. Two contemporary historically consequential figures with two very different theoretical/political perspectives who expertly examined arguably the most contentious issue of the nineteenth century – and one that continues to resonate – offer a unique opportunity for comparative analysis.

To make comparisons and to learn from them is an analytical tool that Marx, as the reader will learn, employed almost from the beginning of his research and until the end. Douglass too, benefitted from thinking beyond the borders of the United States, specifically, to learn that criteria other than skin colour could be employed by ruling elites to justify the subjugation of peoples. By the end of the book, the reader, we think, will also have a better appreciation of the comparative method.

In his better-known speech, 'Where Do We Go From Here', in August 1967 in Atlanta, King did make clear, to the approval of his Ebenezer Baptist Church audience, according to the full transcript, what his call for a 'radical redistribution of economic and political power' *did not* mean – an embrace of Marx.

> Now, don't think you have me in a bind today. I'm not talking about communism. What I'm talking about is far beyond communism. (Yeah) My inspiration didn't come from Karl Marx (Speak); my inspiration didn't come from Engels; my inspiration didn't come from Trotsky; my inspiration didn't come from Lenin. Yes, I read [the] *Communist Manifesto* and *Das Kapital* a long time ago (Well), and I saw that maybe Marx didn't follow Hegel enough. (All right) He took his dialectics, but he left out his idealism and his spiritualism. And he went over to a German philosopher by the name of Feuerbach, and took his materialism and made it into a system that he called 'dialectical materialism.' (Speak) I have to reject that.[13]

---

of what might be called the 'head-start' programme he inherited from Marx and Engels. See Nimtz 2019b.

12   Foster et al 2020, p. 97.

13   https://kinginstitute.stanford.edu/where-do-we-go-here. This seems to be the transcript of the entire speech. Other versions omit the details reproduced here as, for example, Howard-Pitney 2004, p. 154. The speech is conspicuously absent in Peniel E. Joseph's *The*

But what if King's responsive listeners had actually read what Marx and Engels had written and done to abolish chattel slavery, the successful victory upon which all subsequent struggles to end the oppression of Black people rest? And had, then, been able to compare and contrast what Marx wrote and did with arguably the Martin Luther King, Jr of that era, Douglass? Would they have so quickly rejected 'communism' as he did? That, of course, is impossible to know. But what awaits readers of this book is the opportunity to answer the question for themselves. They'll be able to judge whether King – or any of his followers who continue to subscribe to what he said – got Marx right, or whether he too quickly dismissed the founder of modern-day communism.[14] And for those who are truly convinced of the need for a 'radical redistribution of economic and political power', knowing how Marx responded to the decisive fight to abolish slavery could be invaluable.

The comparison is rewarding in many ways. It makes it possible for readers long familiar with Douglass and Marx to see, we think, aspects of them not usually seen in either their autobiographies, in the case of Douglass, or in their biographies – that certainly was our experience in doing the research and writing for this book. Comparing Douglass to Marx requires knowing, for example, his views on revolutionary developments in Europe such as the European Spring and the Paris Commune and, thus, his opinion of the socialist project. The discovery about the Commune is quite rich as well as instructive, warranting separate treatment in an appendix.[15] The reader, most importantly, learns about Douglass's opinion of the working class not only in Europe but also in the United States, along with the consequential political implications of those opinions. The detailed attention that Marx gave to military matters in the Civil War requires discovering if Douglass did the same. Lastly, Marx, living in London during the War, viewed the conflagration not only from a British and European proletarian lens but a global one as well. And Douglass? Could he, from afar, have been able to do the same? And with which class lens? This book answers those and related questions.

What about Marx? Comparing him to Douglass requires knowing what he knew and thought about chattel slavery in the United States and how the peculiar institution figured into his assessment of the country's broader historical/political reality, as well as his communist project more generally. What

---

Sword and the Shield: The Revolutionary Lives of Malcolm X and Martin Luther King Jr, but it provides evidence that King did read what he claimed when a student at Crozer Theological Seminary in Chester, Pennsylvania, Joseph 2020, p. 60.
14 For a critique of King's reading of Marx, see Douglas and Loggins 2021, pp. 22–3.
15 For a detailed study, see K. Edwards 2022.

about the Enlightenment/natural rights philosophy that informed the founding documents of the US polity that Douglass fervently embraced, especially, the Constitution? Did Marx view them similarly? Those answers also await the reader. Once the Civil War began, did Marx, four thousand miles away, follow it as closely as did Douglass who was closer to the scene? Because his biographers largely ignore the longest revolutionary moment that Marx ever lived through and responded to, readers of this book will have a better appreciation of Marx's better known epiphany in 1845 that 'the philosophers have only *interpreted* the world in various ways; the point is to *change* it'.[16] The War also required him to make judgments about the 'humbug', as he called it, of US politics, such as elections and the presidency. Probably no one frustrated Douglass as much in his lifetime as Abraham Lincoln – would he or would he not do the proverbial 'right thing'? Did Marx wax and wane over Lincoln as did Douglass? Another answer that awaits the reader.

Finally, this comparison helps to avoid an all-too common pitfall when it comes to historical analysis – the fallacy of presentism. In the era of political correctness or, dare we say, 'woke' sensibility, it is easy to fall into both traps when it comes to Marx, subjecting him, namely, to present-day norms, particularly with regard to race. By having Douglass in the picture with his own real-time understanding of race, the presentist/politically correct treatment of Marx can potentially be avoided – another topic that merits special attention in an appendix.

A brief note regarding the much discussed – as this is being written – *New York Times' 1619 Project* and Critical Race Theory. Never have the founding documents of the United States received as much public attention and debate in the last half-century as since the publication of the *Times' Project* in August 2019. In dispute, briefly, is what constitutes the founding moment of the Republic: the 1776 project,[17] namely, the issuance of the Declaration of Independence and

---

16   Marx and Engels 1975–2004d, p. 5. For the most recent examples of the Civil War lacuna in Marx biographies, see Sperber 2013; Stedman Jones 2015; and Liedman 2018. The latter volume reveals that even sympathetic biographers ignore the War. Admirable journal articles and chapter-length attempts to fill the Civil War gap include K. Anderson 2010, pp. 79–114, K. Anderson 2017, and Battistini 2021. Raya Dunayevskaya included a short chapter in her book on Marxism and freedom where she showed that Marx was deeply impacted by the U.S. Civil War. That impact found its way into the structure of *Capital*, most obviously in his chapter on the working day. This chapter was written late in the drafting of *Capital* because of the struggle for a shorter workday in the United States which emanated from the Civil War. See Dunayevskaya 1958, pp. 81–91.
17   Our conceptualization of the 1776 project – the American movement, initiated in the 1760s, to throw off the yoke of the British monarchy and establish a united democratic

victory in 1783, or the institution, apparently, of racial slavery in 1619 in colonial Virginia? Motivating the attention the *Times* project has garnered is the still unanswered question that King grappled with in 1967 – how to realise racial equality in the United States. Advocates of what is called Critical Race Theory also seek an answer and agree to one degree or another with the *1619 Project* proponents – maybe for different reasons – that racial inequality is baked into the DNA of the American Republic. Though Douglass had a lot to say about the founding documents of the Republic, the Declaration and the Constitution, he is virtually absent in the essays the *Times* commissioned to be written. So too, regrettably, is the abolitionist movement that he belonged to. In the Conclusion, we'll revisit the two attention-getting projects and offer an answer that both claim to seek – an answer that a comparison of Douglass and Marx makes possible.

In our comparison we treat Marx and Frederick Engels as a political team.[18] Collaborators from 1844 to the end of their lives in respectively 1883 and 1895 – the latter being the same year of Douglass's death – their partnership was tellingly on display during the Civil War. The division of labour they adopted in analysing the War, Marx on the political side of the conflict and Engels on the military side – indispensable for Marx – revealed the only documented political difference in their four-decade long collaboration. Their methodology, the reader learns, the 'materialist conception of history' as they called it, or historical materialism, was a tool for political analysis and not a template for reaching political conclusions. In many ways, as the reader will see, Engels and Douglass were more in accord about the course of the War than Engels was with his partner. Employing their historical materialist method, in other words – and this is something Martin Luther King, Jr. probably did not know when he delivered his 1967 critique of it – required a degree of nuance that Marx proved in the end to be more adept at. Not unimportant in their collaboration was Engels's financial support to the Marx household, without which his partner could have in no way been as productive as he was, responding not only to the War but also completing his magnum opus, *Capital*, Volume I. The closest to that kind of partnership Douglass had was with the long-time wealthy backer of the abolitionist movement, Gerrit Smith. While both his financial and editorial contributions to sustaining Douglass's newspapers were significant,

---

republic – differs from the organisational agenda of the Trump Administration's 1776 Commission and the 1776 Project PAC. This movement's high-water mark was the issuance of the Declaration of Independence and the inauguration of gradual abolition movements in the North.

18   See Nimtz 2000, pp. x, 280–3.

Smith, being twenty years Douglass's senior, served more as a mentor whereas the Marx-Engels relationship was one of political equals. Their correspondence reflected that fact in a way that doesn't appear to be the same with Douglass and Smith.[19]

This book, as suggested above, complements an earlier comparison that one of us made in 2019 – comparing and contrasting how Marx and John Stuart Mill responded to the Civil War.[20] That comparison originated in a key claim in a 2000 book, also by one of us, that Marx and Engels did more to advance the millennial-old democratic quest in the nineteenth century than any of their liberal contemporaries. Evidence for the claim rested on a real-time comparison of the performance of Marx and Engels, on one hand, and Alexis de Tocqueville, on the other, in response to the European Spring of 1848–9. Though persuasive, what about the other leading liberal light of that century? Thus, the reason for the 2019 Marx-Mill comparison regarding the Civil War. But Mill, it could be objected, never pretended to be the activist that Marx was – or, for that matter, Tocqueville. The 'investigation of abstract truth, & the more abstract the better' is what Mill decided early in life he was 'really fit for'.[21] Except for a brief stint as a Member of Parliament after the Civil War that had politicised him, Mill remained to the end a thinker/theorist. The central conclusion of the comparison, that Marx had better democratic credentials than Mill because unlike Mill he was willing to put in the necessary time and energy to advance the democratic quest, might, therefore, be questioned. A comparison of Marx and Mill, in other words, wasn't a fair test of liberalism – the apples and oranges or false equivalence fallacy. Employing Douglass for the test, to compare how liberalism and Marxism performed in relation to the Civil War, helps, albeit not perfectly, to solve that potential methodological problem. Readers of this volume will, thus, be able to determine if the claim one of us advanced in 2000 – that Marx and Engels did more than any contemporary liberal figure to advance the democratic quest in the nineteenth century – is valid.

There is an apples and oranges issue for the comparison that we recognise – the documents we utilise. For the years that we prioritise, Douglass's eponym-

---

19 McKivigan 1990, pp. 205–32. Blight 2018, especially pp. 202–22, 252, 265, 268, 275–6, 293–4, 322. See also, McKivigan 2013, pp. 141–64. Before Smith's mentorship and financial backing, Douglass had a similar relationship with William Lloyd Garrison. Marx acknowledged Smith as one of the principal leaders of the abolitionist movement. Marx and Engels 1975–2004j, p. 233.
20 Nimtz 2019b, Chapter Three.
21 Nimtz 2019b, p. 79.

ous newspaper, *Douglass' Monthly*, is our primary source; in order of authority, his unsigned editorials, his transcripts of his speeches, and transcripts of his speeches from other sources that he republished in his newspaper. After August 1863, Douglass no longer had a newspaper until 1870. For that period, in addition to the pre-war period, we rely on the authoritative collections of Douglass's works in volumes edited by John W. Blassingame, John R. McKivigan, and Philip S. Foner.[22] Douglass's three autobiographies, most authoritative, of course, but written before and after the period of our focus are, therefore, of minimal importance for our real-time political analysis. There is yet no complete works of Douglass that would include all of his correspondence – as is true for Marx.[23] We have, therefore, a better sense of the quotidian and personal context in which Marx responded to real-time developments. An invaluable tool is Hal Draper's *The Marx-Engels Chronicle*, indispensable for any serious political treatment of the two.[24] Hopefully, a Douglass scholar will one day do the same for him. Along the way in our comparison, we acknowledge the possible significance of that deficit in the record for reading Douglass – the possibility of being more sensitive to the personal challenges that Marx had to deal with. The English-language fifty-volume *Marx-Engels Collected Works* is our primary source for the Marx and Engels texts, which includes their correspondence with each other and their replies to others.[25]

Unlike Douglass, Marx, except for one year during the 1848–9 German Revolution, did not have his own newspaper. For the period of our focus, he wrote articles for the pro-abolitionist *New York Daily Tribune*, arguably the nation's most influential newspaper, and the liberal Viennese daily *Die Presse*. Both newspapers, Marx well understood, were, however liberal they may have been,

---

[22] Blassingame 1979, 1982, 1985; Blassingame and McKivigan 1991; McKivigan 2009, 2018, 2021; P. Foner 1950a, 1950b, 1952, 1955, 1975.

[23] The published correspondence of the Frederick Douglass Papers, while invaluable, is a selection of Douglass's letters, unlike the *Marx and Engels Collected Works* or *Gesamtausgabe*. Currently two volumes of Douglass's correspondence are published, through 1865. A third volume is currently in production which will bring the volumes through 1880.

[24] Draper 1985.

[25] Except for a couple of references, we do not make use of the *Marx-Engels Gesamtausgabe* [MEGA²], projected to be 114 volumes when completed; as of this date, sixty-seven have been published. The MEGA², unlike the MECW, includes the correspondence to which Marx and Engels replied. Angela Zimmerman has performed an invaluable service in having edited and republished *Karl Marx and Friedrich Engels, The Civil War in the United States*, ed. Richard Enmale (New York: International Publishers, 1937) in 2016, also with International Publishers, where many of the documents we employ were first published in English. Zimmerman's edition includes documents not in the original and, as well, her introduction – the subject of one of our appendices.

capitalist organs. The former, as he explained to Engels in 1853, 'represent[s]' the 'industrial bourgeoisie of America'.[26] But as a correspondent for the paper, a source of desperately needed income, Marx could only challenge its politics in his articles in a 'clandestine' manner.[27] As for his *Die Presse* articles, 'I always', also to Engels in 1862, 'write them in such a way that they can print them'.[28] Marx, in other words, unlike Douglass who had his own newspaper, had to be more circumspect in his articles in bourgeois publications, sometimes pulling his punches. The reader, hence, needs at times to read between the lines of a Marx article for its full political meaning.

In the period we focus on, only four of Marx's writings qualify as or come close to pure and unadulterated communism – the most notable after *Capital* being his congratulatory letter on behalf of the International Workingmen's Association to Abraham Lincoln on his re-election in 1864.[29] In a number of instances, luckily, Marx commented on his articles in his correspondence with Engels – thus, an opportunity to understand their full meaning. Yet Marx enjoyed an advantage Douglass did not have – at least until November 1862. Despite not writing for his own newspaper, Marx wrote for dailies and his articles, word for word, are often richer in content, as the reader will see, than a Douglass speech reproduced in his monthly. Rendering many dense ideas was not an option for Douglass the orator when speaking to a live audience and trying to keep their attention. Douglass's insights come with a lot of rhetorical flourishes while those of Marx are more bare-boned and, thus, proportionately more per printed word.

This is the appropriate place to address Marx's and Engels's occasional usage of the 'n-word'. The editors of the *Marx-Engels Collected Works* noted in 1987 that in the nineteenth century the word did not have the 'more profane and unacceptable status' it did in later history, particularly in the United States.[30] In her Introduction to the 2016 new edition of *Karl Marx & Friedrich Engels, The Civil War in the United States*, Angela Zimmerman points out that the 'racial epithet "nigger"' appears 'nine times in the texts reproduced in this volume. They used this term ironically, however, to highlight a racism that they criticized rather than endorsed. Marx and Engels opposed racism at every turn, and the communist movements they inspired have remained some of the most power-

---

26 Marx and Engels 1975–2004s, p. 346.
27 Ibid.
28 Marx and Engels 1975–2004u, p. 351.
29 In ranking the importance of Marx's and Engels's texts, we employ to some degree Hal Draper's list of their writings 'in descending order of reliability'. See Nimtz 2000, p. xi.
30 Marx and Engels 1975–2004v, p. xi.

INTRODUCTION 11

ful and consistent anti-racist and anti-imperialist forces in the world, including in the United States'.[31] Here is what one of us wrote in 2003 about the issue:

> Marx began to use 'nigger' during the Civil War as he was familiarizing himself with the U.S. reality. In published writings he always employed quotation marks; in letters often without. Only once, it seems, did he use it in a derogatory sense, in a diatribe against Ferdinand Lassalle ... in 1862, that is, in the year when he first used the word.[32] ... Marx and Engels, like all mortals, were products, clearly, of the world in which they lived. Their comments in personal correspondence that were unambiguously racist, sexist or anti-semitic must be seen in context and in relation to their entire corpus of writings and actions. For what it's worth, Marx was fondly known by close friends and family as 'Moor' owing to his dark features and had a son-in-law, Paul Lafargue, a mulatto, who was also fondly called in family circles, 'African', 'Negro' and 'Negrillo'. This suggests that one should be cautious and not rush to judgment based on the vapid criteria of 'political correctness'.[33]

Missing in the list of family sobriquets for Lafargue is 'nigger'.[34] Almost always, it should also be added, Marx and Engels employed the original English term – apparently, there was no German equivalent. 'Negro', more often than not, appeared in Marx's publications.[35]

The point made earlier about the value of a Douglass-Marx comparison in avoiding the pitfalls of presentism and political correctness is all so relevant for this issue. The n-word is sprinkled throughout Douglass's speeches and writings, never, as far as we can determine, in a derogatory way, but often 'ironically', as Zimmerman argues for Marx's and Engels's usage, or when quoting its racist

---

31 Marx and Engels 2016, p. xxvi.
32 Marx and Engels 1975–2004u, pp. 389–90. In the diatribe, as the reader will see, Marx calls him the 'Jewish NIGGER' and then later draws attention to 'his head and the way his hair grows also testify – that he is descended from the negroes who accompanied Moses' flight from Egypt ... The fellow's importunity is also niggerlike'. Yet, when Lassalle lost his life in a duel two years later, Marx was sincerely grief-stricken. Marx and Engels 1975–2004u, p. 556. On the complicated Marx-Lassalle relationship, see, Draper 1990, pp. 241–69, and Avineri 2019, pp. 124–7.
33 Nimtz 2003, pp. 131–2fn35.
34 Derfler 1991, p. 46.
35 For a tendentious treatment of Marx's usage of both terms, see Hund 2021, pp. 80–2. We address Hund's charges in Appendix B: Marx and Engels on the Race Question: A Response to the Critics.

usage. A search for 'nigger' in the database for his newspapers yielded 92 results and it seems always within quotation marks.[36] Douglass's take on the Emancipation Proclamation, for example, is instructive: 'Give them a chance; stop calling them "niggers", and call them soldiers'.[37] Yet, also like the two communists, Douglass too was a product of the same era and voiced on occasion the then en vogue prejudices – as Douglass called them – such as those against Irish Americans and Native Americans. Caution is also advised, therefore, in making similar judgements about Douglass regarding matters of race (to be revisited in Appendix B).

One last method issue. Although we call our comparison real-time political analysis, we recognise that real-time is always relative – in this case, the time it took news to get from one side of the Atlantic to the other. For most of our time period, it took about twelve days for letters and newspapers to get from New York to London and vice versa. That time difference should be kept in mind in reading about the events we report on. Only in 1866 did the transatlantic telegraph become available.

In 1961, Marxist historian George Novack wrote: 'Just as American historians have ignored the organic affiliation between the First American Revolution and the Second, so they usually overlook the affinity between the revolutionary movements in the United States and Europe during the mid-nineteenth century'.[38] Though neither of us claims to be a Civil War scholar, or to be writing a history of that modern world-defining moment, this book adds to a growing body of literature that now situates the War in world-history, specifically, in the transatlantic theatre.[39] It argues, as Novack presciently did, that the War actually began with the European Revolutions of 1848–9, the European Spring. Douglass, as the reader will see, instantiates that claim. A notable veteran of those Revolutions was certainly aware of the connection. 'As in the 18th century', Marx wrote in the Preface to *Capital*, 'the American War of Independence sounded the alarm bell of the European middle class, so in the 19th century the American Civil War sounded it for the European working class'.[40] Written just two years after Appomattox, little wonder the War was still on Marx's brain, just as it was for other veterans of the European Spring who were now Civil War vet-

---

36 A search performed on 18 July 2022 of the issues of Douglass's papers included in the American Historical Newspapers database (https://www.readex.com/products/americas-historical-newspapers).
37 Blassingame 1985, p. 567.
38 Novack 2013, p. 319.
39 See, for example, Doyle 2015; Fleche 2012; Levine 1992.
40 Marx and Engels 1975–2004p, p. 9.

erans. We return to Marx's insightful point in the Conclusion. It confirms the value of having not just an Atlantic world perspective but a global one as well. The reader by then, we think, will agree.

Bringing Marx into the picture will build upon and add the important focus on class and the labour question to other published comparisons. There have been three comparisons of the lives and politics of Abraham Lincoln and Douglass, two of Lincoln and Marx, and one recent book contrasting Andrew Johnson and Douglass.[41] We hope this real-time comparison of Douglass and Marx will help clarify aspects of Douglass's political philosophy and offer fruitful lessons to those who wish to change the world as Marx and Douglass both did.

Following this Introduction, Chapter 1, 'Two Biographies – or, Two Routes to the Quest for "True Democracy"', distils the lives of our two protagonists to the beginning of 1848, the European Spring. What in their backgrounds explains how they responded to the guns of April 1861? We begin with Douglass's biography because chattel slavery, what Douglass personally knew, was the raison d'etre for the Civil War, the backdrop for our comparison. His first three decades serve as the basis for interrogating the comparable years in Marx's life. With Marx's biography, we make our initial comparisons with Douglass, mostly occasional and cursory.

Chapter 2, 'Prelude to the Conflagration: From Paris to Fort Sumter', with an eye on April 1861, the Confederate attack that initiated the Civil War, begins with the European Spring Revolutions of 1848 and the two very different responses of Marx and Douglass. The bulk of the chapter then shows how the growing power of the slave oligarchy obligated Douglass to rethink his pacifist perspective and begin to converge with Marx on the revolutionary methods he defended. It ends with the increasingly fraught situation following Abraham Lincoln's election in November 1860, especially the six weeks after his Inaugural Address.

Chapter 3, 'Toward the Convergence of Douglass and Marx: From Fort Sumter to the *Trent* Affair', begins with Douglass's and Marx's initial responses to the slavocracy's attack on Fort Sumter, posing the questions of why it happened and what was at stake. The exigencies of the War brought Douglass and Marx closer politically, not only on the domestic side of the conflagration but in terms of its international repercussions as well. The reader learns along the way how Marx, at a critical moment in the War, may have both aided eventual Union victory and caused Douglass to rethink a prior political view.

---

41 Oakes 2007; Stauffer 2008; Kendrick and Kendrick 2008; Blackburn 2011; Kulikoff 2018; R. Levine 2021.

Nine months into the conflict, when the chapter ends, he and Douglass were in objective if not conscious collaboration with one another in the promotion of the Union cause.

Chapter 4, 'From a Constitutional to a Revolutionary Civil War: "the cruel and apocalyptic war had become holy"'. How Douglass and Marx read, reacted to and – in Douglass's case – tried to impact Lincoln's uncertain and hesitant path to emancipation constitutes the substance of the chapter. Details about how Marx and Douglass read the battlefield are highlighted. The centrepiece is the prelude to and issuance of, first, the Preliminary and then, second, the Final Emancipation Proclamation – the moment that tested the best of our protagonists' political analytical skills. Lincoln's executive orders put Douglass and Marx on the same political page as never before.

Chapter 5, 'The End of the War and the Rise and Fall of Radical Reconstruction'. With a thinner paper trail for both Douglass and Marx for the last twenty months of the War, brevity characterises the comparisons of this chapter. The first part ends with the Confederate surrender at Appomattox in April 1865. From then, Marx and Douglass increasingly went their separate political ways. No post-War issue distinguished Douglass and Marx partisans more from one another than land for the former slaves. In hindsight, the failure of a real land reform signalled the end of Radical Reconstruction, the focus of the second and concluding part of the chapter.

In the Conclusion, we evaluate the performance of Douglass and Marx; how did the two revolutionaries, one a liberal and the other a communist, respond to the opportunity to end racial slavery when this was posed in April 1861? Was one more perceptive and, thus, a more effective actor than the other? We then return to the question that introduces this inquiry; does a comparison of the two protagonists in that historical moment when the question of how to realise racial equality was first posed offer any answers for a still needed resolution?

Two appendices are effectively extended footnotes with valuable complementary details that would otherwise clutter the text. The first, 'Douglass and Marx on the Paris Commune and the Labour Question in the United States', supplements Chapter 5, how Douglass's and Marx's responses to the Commune anticipated their response to the overthrow of Radical Reconstruction. The second, 'Marx and Engels on the Race Question: A Response to the Critics', updates an earlier essay that one of us wrote on the topic in 1985.

There are admittedly many details in the narrative that the reader might get lost in, as one of our reviewers noted. A suggestion for our readers: beginning with the first part of the Conclusion which distils the comparison can be a way to avoid that potential problem. Also of value are the epigrams that introduce Chapters 1 to 5. Far from decorative, they preview the key issues in the comparison. The reader is advised to return to the epigrams after reading the chapter to ensure that they understand what the chapter tries to convey.

This project began, unbeknownst to us at the time, when one of us, Kyle Edwards, who was reading David Blight's *Prophet of Freedom*, began asking the other, August Nimtz, for his opinions about issues raised in Blight's volume – questions, more specifically, about Marx's position on such and such a matter. Also, was Douglass different from the liberals examined in the *Marxism versus Liberalism* project?[42] As the 'I don't knows' began to pile up, the latter suggested that both of us should try together to find the answers and, hence, this book. Again, the inquiry has been a learning experience for both of us. We think we've answered all our questions and even more.

We are not disinterested investigators – hopefully, honest ones – interested in history for its own sake. Not that long after Marx's death, Engels, thinking back on his deceased partner's life and the political responsibilities he now shouldered, opined: 'Not one of us possesses the breadth of vision that enabled [Marx], at the very moment when rapid action was called for, invariably to hit upon the right solution and at once get to the heart of the matter … at a revolutionary juncture his judgment was virtually infallible'.[43] For those who might be inspired by Marx's example and seek a solution to the deepening political crisis that confronts humanity today, who are not content to wait until all the documents have been discovered and poured over, and all the data have been analysed, but are motivated *to act* for its realisation, this book may be of some use. Comparing and contrasting, to wit, the best that liberalism and communism had to offer in addressing, in real-time, arguably the nineteenth century's most pressing political issue could actually prove invaluable.

---

[42] Nimtz, 2019b.
[43] Marx and Engels 1975–2004aa, p. 202.

CHAPTER 1

Two Biographies – or, Two Routes to the Quest for 'True Democracy'

> Was it political action that removed your prejudices, and raised in your minds a holy zeal for human rights? No one will say this.
> DOUGLASS, 1842

∴

> … making criticism of politics, participation in politics, and therefore *real struggles*, the starting point of our criticism. …
> MARX, 1843

∴

Even though they were born in the same year, 1818, nothing would immediately suggest that Frederick Douglass and Karl Marx had enough in common to warrant a comparison. But to think so means to operate, as Marx might have said, at the level of appearances. Birth years can be determinative and fortuitous opportunities to participate in history-making events. Only three decades separated 1818 from the curtain-raising uprisings of the nineteenth century's contribution to the age-old democratic quest – the 1848 Revolutions, the European Spring – more than enough time for the birth class of 1818 to be prepared to seize the opportunity. The European upheavals, in hindsight, foreshadowed the nineteenth century's foremost and only victory in that quest, the defeat of the North American slave oligarchy in April 1865. The biographies of the protagonists of momentous historical events often disclose the seeds of their realisation. What, if anything, in Douglass's and Marx's backgrounds, therefore, might explain why and how they evaluated the historic epoch that began in 1848, its central task, and the ways they could influence its unfolding? Presented here is a highly distilled and selective reading of both biographies involving a comparison of the motivations of Marx and Douglass in anticipation of 1848 and afterward.

1   From Chattel Slave to Revolutionary Liberal

'I had been treated as a pig on the plantation. I was treated as a *child* now'.[1] So tellingly and poignantly did Frederick Douglass (1818–95) describe his early years on a slave plantation in his second and more informative autobiography, *My Bondage and My Freedom* (1855). He was referring to arguably the luckiest development in his life, from being raised as a slave on a rural plantation to becoming a house-slave in a major urban community – 'a special interposition', as he later described it, 'of Divine Providence in my favor'. The wife of his new Baltimore slave-master, Sophia Auld, treated Douglass with kindness, taught him the alphabet, and before long Douglass was able to spell words three or four letters long. Douglass's temporary escape from the worst brutalities of slavery did not last long. By the time he was eleven years old, his owner, Hugh Auld, 'suddenly forbade with stern anger any further instruction in reading'. 'To use his own words', as Douglass recounted: '"if you give a nigger an inch, he will take an ell ... he should know nothing but the will of his master, and learn to obey it ... Learning would spoil the best nigger in the world ... if you teach that nigger"', pointing to the eleven year old Douglass, '"how to read the bible, there will be no keeping him ... it would forever unfit him for the duties of a slave"'. With Douglass's love of the written word already in bloom, this all too instructive admonition was, he wrote, the 'first decidedly anti-slavery lecture to which it had been my lot to listen'. David Blight, author of the recent magisterial biography of Douglass, contends that no other turning point or battle in Douglass's life 'was ever more important than his ascent to literacy and knowledge'.[2] It more than anything enabled him to realise his life's 'mission of deliverance to my enslaved people'.[3] Shaped by his birth into chattel slavery, Douglass, in the words of George Novack, was 'bent on destroying the slave power in order to get justice and equality for the Negroes and fulfill the democratic ideals of the Republic'.[4]

Douglass spent the first eight years of his life on the eastern shore of Maryland, which he later described as 'thinly populated ... worn-out, sandy, desertlike ...' and 'dull, flat, and unthrifty ... surrounded by a white population of the

---

1   Douglass 2014, p. 115.
2   Douglass 2014, pp. 113–18. Blight 2018, pp. 38–40. P. Foner 1950a, p. 17. Preston 2018, p. 107. The great grandmother of one of the authors of this book (AN) was one of those fortunate houseslaves who was taught to read and write by the children of the slave-master, explaining in part why this book could be realised.
3   P. Foner 1952, p. 374.
4   Novack 2013, p. 335.

lowest order, indolent and drunken to a proverb'.[5] As a young child, his owner, Aaron Anthony, separated him from his grandmother, Betsey Bailey, who had raised him, and sent Douglass to the Wye plantation where Anthony worked as the general overseer.[6] After two years, Anthony decided to send him to Baltimore to live with Hugh Auld, Anthony's son-in-law, husband of Sophia – the intervention of 'Divine Providence'.[7]

Material exigency, according to Philip Foner, motivated Douglass's owner to send him to Baltimore: 'Slave labor in Maryland agriculture had ceased to be profitable. Consequently, after 1820 it was common to farm slaves out to townspeople where they could be employed as house-servants and mechanics' – conditions that worked in Douglass's favour. Baltimore was a massive trading centre, had a booming shipbuilding industry, and a population of almost eighty thousand people, and, when Douglass arrived, approximately three thousand slaves compared to more than seventeen thousand free Blacks. The European immigrant population, mostly Irish and German, was in the midst of a boom, while the free Black population was increasing at the expense of the slave population.[8]

Douglass employed a variety of strategies to become fully literate after slave owner Auld's injunction forbade further instruction by his wife. When Douglass was 11, Auld sent him to work at the Auld & Harrison shipyard, where he was initially assigned to run errands and keep fires kindled. He watched carpenters mark a ship's timber with letters to indicate for which part of the ship it was intended. By listening to the conversations of the workers, he learned the names of the letters and then practised writing them with chalk or sticks when no one was looking. Douglass would then copy the letters onto a fence or board and dare other neighbourhood children to do better, thus learning more letters in the process.[9]

Douglass made friends with several white boys Blight describes as 'struggling and hungry immigrant kids'. He utilised them as teachers, seeking help and lessons from them with a discarded *Webster*'s spelling book. Sometimes Douglass would pay the hungry boys with pieces of bread that amounted to his

---

5 Douglass 2014, pp. 29–30.
6 Preston 2018, pp. 43–6.
7 Preston 2018, p. 93. Douglass 2014, p. 113.
8 P. Foner 1950a, p. 17. Blight 2018, p. 37. Allan Kulikoff points out that on Maryland's western shore, unlike the eastern shore where Douglass was raised, the economic realities differed, and slaves were more likely to be engaged in tobacco production rather than hired out as a house-servant or mechanic.
9 Preston 2018, p. 109.

'*tuition fee*'. These educative conversations with his young white friends nurtured a sense of 'natural rights' that grew inside Douglass, encouraging him as he struggled with the damaging psychological effects of enslavement. 'The boys took him into their secret emotional havens and supported their enslaved friend', writes Blight. 'They told him slavery was unfair and that he would be free one day'. Douglass later wrote, 'they believed *I* had as good a right to be free as *they* did … they did not believe God ever made anyone to be a slave'.[10]

The most important piece of literature Douglass stumbled upon during this time was *The Columbian Orator*. The book was the creation of Caleb Bingham, a man 'of decidedly anti-slavery sympathies, determined to democratize education and instill in young people the heritage of the American Revolution, as well as the values of republicanism'. This was no doubt Douglass's introduction to the founding of the Republic that would forever inform his core political beliefs. Bingham's anti-slavery impulses found their way into multiple stories in the *Orator*, such as one in which a slave reasoned with his owner and argued successfully for his freedom. By reading and rereading *The Columbian Orator*, Douglass learned the art of oratory, gained confidence in himself, and developed his abolitionist beliefs. Reading this book, and any other texts that he could get his hands on, also led him to feel 'very discontent', Douglass wrote in 1855, a discontentment 'so graphically predicted by master Hugh … The revelation haunted me, stung me, and made me gloomy and miserable. As I writhed under the torment of this knowledge, I almost envied my fellow slaves their stupid contentment'. Yet the book also increased Douglass's vocabulary and knowledge of language, helping him to articulate thoughts that had crossed his mind but had died because of his lack of an ability to express them.[11] The *Orator* was also decisive in Abraham Lincoln's intellectual development. That both Lincoln and Douglass were of humble backgrounds and had both been cultivated politically by the same book probably helped in some way to cement their friendship.[12]

At about the same time Douglass was learning to read, he underwent a spiritual awakening. A Methodist minister, identified by Douglass as Hanson, preached, 'that all men, great and small, bond and free, were sinners in the sight of God'. Having felt 'wretched' for weeks, 'a poor, broken-hearted mourner', without 'means of making myself otherwise', Douglass experienced 'that change of heart which comes by "casting all one's care" upon God, and by

---

10   Blight 2018, pp. 42–3. Douglass 2014, pp. 125–6.
11   Blight 2018, pp. 43–7. Douglass 2014, pp. 126–9. P. Foner 1950a, p. 18.
12   Stauffer 2008, pp. 62–5, and Chapter Five.

having faith in Jesus Christ, as the Redeemer, Friend, and Savior of those who diligently seek Him'.[13] He'd experienced a 'born-again moment' as Christians sometimes call it.

Douglass also met Charles Lawson, an old beer cart driver in Baltimore and the most devout man he had ever met. That Lawson's 'life was a life of prayer, and his words ... were about a better world' attracted Douglass. Douglass spent many Sundays with Lawson. Because Lawson struggled with reading, Douglass 'could teach him *"the letter"*, but he could teach me *"the spirit"*'. Lawson was Douglass's 'chief instructor, in matters of religion' and his 'spiritual father', telling him that 'the "Lord had a great work for me to do", and I must prepare to do it ... I must preach the gospel'. Lawson also bestowed upon Douglass the 'advice and the suggestions' that 'were not without their influence upon my character and destiny'. When Douglass shared his despair about being a slave for life, Lawson replied, 'the Lord can make you free, my dear. All things are possible with him, only *have faith in God*'.[14] This, Douglass's earliest spiritual awakening, prepared him for a second spiritual awakening in the late 1840s when he perceived Divine Providence to be the main force in history, as we shall see later. Speaking in 1846, he said, 'I remembered that God was God still, I took courage again, and resolved to continue to pray to that God who has the destinies of nations in his hand to change their hearts'.[15] Being religious, therefore, was for Douglass a core coping strategy.

Because of a disagreement between Hugh Auld and his brother Thomas, Douglass, now 15 years of age, was recalled from Baltimore and moved to St. Michaels, Maryland to work for Thomas. There Douglass became rebellious, due in part to his eye-opening and thought-transforming experience with literacy in Baltimore – what Hugh Auld had feared. To break him, Thomas sent him to work for overseer Edward Covey, who had a reputation for making uppity slaves submissive. Covey ordered Douglass to work as a field-hand for the first time in his life, and by beating him, succeeded for a time in forcing Douglass to cower and grovel. When Douglass's attempt to convince Thomas to intervene failed, he resolved to *'stand up in my own defense ... I was resolved to fight'*.[16]

The fight turned into the pivotal moment in Douglass's life as a slave. Defending himself physically 'rekindled in my breast the smouldering embers of liberty; it brought up my Baltimore dreams, and revived a sense of my own manhood ... A man, without force, is without the essential dignity of human-

---

13   Douglass 2014, pp. 134–5.
14   Douglass 2014, pp. 135–7.
15   Blassingame 1979, p. 124.
16   Douglass 2014, pp. 140–5, 162–4, 187–94.

ity'. As important as learning to read and write, Douglass's courage to fight back demonstrated 'the physical force necessary for male', or human, 'dignity and power'. Douglass wrote, 'I was *nothing* before. I was a MAN NOW'. The spirit that energised Douglass after defeating Covey made him 'a freeman in *fact*', while he 'remained a slave in *form*'. Masters sold many slaves to the Deep South for much lesser transgressions. Douglass claimed Covey never laid a hand on him again. It is possible that Covey told no one because it would have hurt his reputation as a breaker of slaves.[17]

Douglass's first attempt to escape slavery was in 1836, at age 18. He convinced five others to join him and wrote them forged passes, but one withdrew and betrayed the plot. Thomas Auld jailed Douglass but opted not to sell him south, even promising to emancipate him at age 25 for good behaviour. 'This moment', Blight writes, 'may easily have been the greatest stroke of luck in Douglass's life' – not only for him but for all of us who have since stood on his shoulders.[18] History, to paraphrase Luther, sometimes staggers along like a drunk on horseback and sometimes it runs on a determined line like a fugitive slave riding the rails north.

Back in Baltimore, Douglass established a place for himself within the growing free Black community. He learned a trade as a caulker, and for a while he was able to hire himself out and keep a portion of his wages. But he also received racist taunts from white workers that sometimes turned violent. Douglass worked in the Gardiner shipyard for eight months, acting as an assistant to the seventy-five or so carpenters employed in the yard. He answered to 'Say darkey' and 'Halloo nigger' in the normal course of workplace interactions. After standing up for himself on Covey's farm, Douglass was less likely to back down from a fight. Douglass was accused by white workers of taking 'white men's jobs,' and after one cursed him, Douglass responded by throwing him into the water. But he was not always victorious. Four white men, apprentices in the shipyard, ambushed and brutally beat him. Blight describes this time as one when Douglass 'learned even deeper lessons about the natural struggle between labor and capital' and how this struggle intersected with skin colour.[19] It would probably be more accurate to say that this firsthand experience was when the seeds were planted that enabled Douglass, a decade or so later –

---

17 Douglass 2014, pp. 193–9. Blight 2018, pp. 65–6. P. Foner 1950a, pp. 19–20. Wilson Jeremiah Moses doubts Douglass's explanation of Covey's 'strangely restrained behavior'. Instead, Moses believes Douglass's 'family connections', that is, pressure from his master, were more likely the cause. Moses 2004, pp. 25–6.
18 Douglass 2014, pp. 216–41 Blight 2018, pp. 69–73.
19 Blight 2018, pp. 75–7.

this will be discussed in the next chapter – to acquire an almost Marxist-like understanding of the divide-and-rule strategy that the slavocracy employed to pit workers of different skin colours against one another. This divide-and-rule strategy was the means by which a minority could rule over a majority.

Douglass, as it became increasingly clear, was no longer willing to accept his slave status. Another rebellious act on his part, plus a threat from Auld to sell him south, convinced Douglass to work with the free Blacks he knew, including his future wife Anna Murray, on a new plan for self-emancipation.[20] Through cunning intrigue and the crucial assistance of abolitionists like David Ruggles in New York, Douglass eventually ended up in New Bedford, Massachusetts.[21] Prevented from caulking on the docks by white workers, he survived by taking a variety of manual jobs that allowed him to bring home wages without having to turn any money over to a master who claimed him as property. He became a proletarian for the first time. Conditioned to view slave ownership as the core of private property, Douglass was astonished at the accumulation of wealth in the industrial whaling town of New Bedford and the high standard of living of its workers. This is when the former slave first learned about the advantages of the capitalist mode of production.[22]

Because Douglass's owners in Baltimore were Methodists, he tried to join the Elm Street Methodist Church in New Bedford. His time at the Elm Street Church didn't last long. Forbidden from sitting in the main pews and thinking that it was because he was not a member or a convert of the church, he soon realised that he was denied seating because of his skin colour, so he never returned. Racism, he quickly learned, was not unique to the slave-owning South. Having faced the discrimination of the white church, the African Methodist Episcopal Zion (AMEZ) Church later became his place of faith and community. Founded on the principles of abolitionism, the AMEZ ministers were active in the anti-slavery movement and encouraged their congregations to speak out against chattel bondage. Douglass soon became a leader among the small congregation, serving as a steward, sexton, and Bible class leader. The classes he taught, the sermons and tutorials he gave, and his exhortations inspiring congregants' faith in the Gospel 'launched him in his new vocation'. Instead of a labourer, Douglass was now listed in New Bedford as a 'Reverend'.[23]

Now actively involved in anti-slavery agitation, on 12 March 1839, Douglass spoke publicly, probably for the first time outside of church, against colonisa-

---

20 Douglass 2014, pp. 251–2. Blight 2018, pp. 79–81. P. Foner 1950a, pp. 21–2.
21 Blight 2018, pp. 81–6. P. Foner 1950a, pp. 22–3. See also, E. Foner 2015, pp. 1–4.
22 Blight 2018, pp. 90–1. Lampe 1998, pp. 35–6.
23 Lampe 1998, pp. 38–40. Blight 2018, pp. 92–8.

tion at an abolitionist meeting. Colonisation was the movement led primarily by whites that promoted the resettlement of free North American Blacks in West Africa or elsewhere. He and other New Bedford free Blacks looked to the Declaration of Independence and its enunciation of their 'natural, inherent, just, and inalienable rights' to secure support for their resolution to oppose colonisation. By June 1841, Douglass was chairing and motivating assemblies to pass similar resolutions.[24]

William Lloyd Garrison, the foremost white figure in the abolitionist cause, visited New Bedford in April 1839, and Douglass made sure to attend the antislavery meeting where he was scheduled to speak. Garrison's charge that the United States was a 'nation of liars', in clear violation of the abolitionist rendering of the Declaration of Independence, rang all too true for the ex-slave. The principle 'that all men are created equal and endowed by their Creator with certain inalienable Rights, that among these are Life, Liberty and the pursuit of Happiness', the most remembered lines in the document, would forever inform Douglass's politics. Garrison's condemnation of the nation's pro-slavery churches, and his 'steadfast ... insist[ence] upon the immediate, unconditional emancipation as the right of the slave and the duty of the whole county', also deeply resonated with Douglass.[25]

Garrison's supporters had their eyes on Douglass for some time. In August 1840, Ellis Gray Loring wrote to a colleague explaining that he wanted to employ Douglass as a lecturer. Exactly a year later, William Coffin, 'a local bookseller, Garrisonian devotee, and member of a prominent antislavery family', invited Douglass to an abolitionist convention on Nantucket Island. This is when Douglass rose and 'astonished' his audience of 'as many as a thousand abolitionists' with his 'personalized version of a slave's travail'. The 'great power' with which Douglass spoke inspired Garrison, in turn, to give 'one of his sublimest speeches'. Garrison and John A. Collins immediately extended an offer to Douglass to join the Massachusetts Anti-Slavery Society on a paid speaking tour. Within a week, Douglass was expounding on his life as a slave before audiences in Massachusetts and southern New Hampshire.[26] From thereon, he was able to sustain himself and his household on the earnings that came from those speeches. Never again would he have to depend on manual labour for survival.

Between late 1841 and 1845, Douglass threw himself into the Garrisonian abolitionist movement. Among its demands was the call for the North's secession from the United States. The Republic's founding document, the Constitu-

---

24 Lampe 1998, pp. 45–7. Blight 2018, pp. 97–8.
25 Blight 2018, p. 96. Lampe 1998, pp. 42–3.
26 Blight 2018, pp. 93, 98–101.

tion, was a compromise with slavery and, Garrison charged, a violation of the Declaration of Independence. The 'free labor' North should leave the Union and part company with the slave-holding South. Garrisonians advocated for non-violent moral suasion to achieve their goals, including abolition and civil rights for Blacks, and they objected to electoral participation of any kind such as voting and supporting political parties. To do so, they held, would legitimise an illegitimate political system. And for any church not to agitate as they did was to be hypocritical. Douglass embraced every tenet of the movement.

In his first recorded speech, in Lynn, Massachusetts in October 1841, Douglass argued for moral suasion by telling his audience about a speech he had read by John Quincy Adams when he was still a slave. The speech, he reported, produced 'joy and gladness'. It showed that 'there was a large and growing class of people in the north called abolitionists, who were moving for our freedom'. Their 'agitation' had built up the hopes of slaves like him, helping to obviate, he claimed, the need for slave rebellions that he said he would have opposed. 'There will be no outbreaks, no insurrections', Douglass added, 'whilst you continue this excitement: let it cease, and the crimes that would follow cannot be told'.[27] Douglass, apparently, saw – at least then – no contradiction between promoting abstention from politics while celebrating the actions of an elected official, a Member of Congress. Given his subsequent trajectory, this may have been an early sign of Douglass the tactician playing the threat of violence card for strategic ends.

At the Plymouth County Anti-Slavery Society quarterly meeting in November 1841, Douglass defended Garrison's position in support of the North seceding from the Union. The Fugitive Slave Clause of the Constitution in Article Four, which required non-slave holding states to return runaway slaves to their southern slave owners, deeply implicated the North in upholding the peculiar institution – 'the bulwark of slavery', he alleged. No provision in the document was dearer to the hearts of slave owners than this Clause that convinced South Carolina and Georgia to sign on to the new republic in 1787. 'This is the union whose "*desolation*" we want to accomplish', Douglass explained, 'and he is no true abolitionist, who does not go against this union'.[28]

In January 1842, Douglass rose to speak at the Massachusetts Anti-Slavery Society in opposition to both electoral politics and the newly founded anti-slavery Liberty Party. Turning to his audience, Douglass asked, 'Was it political action that removed your prejudices, and raised in your minds a holy zeal for

---

27   Blassingame 1979, p. 4.
28   Blassingame 1979, p. 6.

human rights? No one will say this'. During the debate a Liberty Party supporter expressed disagreement with the Garrisonian tactic of asking candidates running for office what their views were on abolition. To do so, he claimed, would only tempt them to lie. Douglass, in defence of the tactic, responded that he was willing to 'take my chance about that ... [rather] than be obliged to take a man I know nothing about' simply because of 'the mere nomination of the third party'.[29] Behind Douglass's retort to the Liberty Party supporter was the fact that the party had been founded by a faction that split from the American Anti-Slavery Society in 1840 in opposition to Garrison's leadership.

In an instructive letter to Garrison in October 1844, Douglass distilled his views on how to deal with the Liberty Party issue and politics in general. While he had 'frequently deprecated, in public and in private, the continued controversy between Old Organization [Garrisonians] and [the] Liberty Party', he told Garrison, 'I have ever felt little disposition to say or do anything in opposition to what is called the Liberty party'. Douglass preferred to *'let it alone –* if it could live, let it; if it would die, let us have as little to say or do about it as possible'. He reaffirmed his opposition to political action and his support for moral suasion. 'The real, and only-to-be-relied-on movement for the abolition of slavery in this country', Douglass wrote, 'is a great moral and religious movement', which would enlighten the public mind and help bring about a determination to end the slave system. But as long as the Liberty Party did not attack the moral suasionists, he would prefer to use his time attacking slavery instead of those engaged in securing votes. And though Douglass did attend a Liberty Party convention in New Bedford in 1844, he nevertheless defended opposition to voting – to do so, again, would legitimise an illegitimate system owing to the pro-slavery Constitution – endorsed moral suasion, and accused Liberty Party leaders of corruption.[30]

Antislavery activists often debated the scope of their reform efforts. Some advocated for a narrow focus on emancipation while others broadened their reform efforts or had other causes in mind. In late July 1843, Douglass debated John A. Collins, one of his earliest mentors in the anti-slavery movement and a utopian socialist. The quarrel was provoked by the question of whether or not Collins could schedule an 'anti-property' meeting after an anti-slavery convention Douglass had just led in Syracuse, New York. According to Douglass, Collins had described abolitionists as narrow-minded, eschewing universal reform. Moreover, in Douglass's opinion, Collins was mistaken for thinking that some

---

29   Blassingame 1979, pp. 14–15.
30   McKivigan 2009, pp. 33–8.

form of slavery would remain even after the abolition of chattel slavery, that property in the soil was worse than property in man, and that the universal reform movement would do more for the slave than the anti-slavery movement itself. Charles Lenox Remond, a Black abolitionist, also opposed Collins and charged him 'with making the antislavery cause, a mere stepping stone to his own favorite theory of the right of property'. Douglass did not, he said, oppose Collins for participating in 'anti-property' agitation in general, but he accused him of slandering the anti-slavery movement and working for its destruction.[31] Three years later, Marx and Engels would bring a communist perspective to the debate in America about the relationship between land ownership and abolition.

Douglass's embrace of Garrison's non-violent moral suasion position was publicly on display in 1843 when he cast a decisive vote to not publish the speech of Black leader Henry Highland Garnet that provocatively called for a slave insurrection in the South. Though only tactically opposed to violence – the numbers were not on the side of the enslaved he contended – it would take Douglass about another half decade to do as other leading Black figures like Garnet were then doing, putting distance between themselves and Garrison's principled pacifism.[32]

Between December 1844 and May 1845, Douglass, according to Blight, mostly remained at home in Lynn, Massachusetts writing his first autobiography, *Narrative of the Life of Frederick Douglass, an American Slave, Written by Himself*. Douglass joined what Manisha Sinha calls an 'extraordinary group of fugitive slaves ... whose narratives comprised the best-selling literature of the day ... [The] foremost among them was Douglass'. In order to counter racist suspicions that his African heritage and enslavement were incompatible with his exemplary oratory and literacy skills, he wrote the first of his autobiographies, 'in multiple editions and to rave reviews', full of names and facts to verify its authenticity. Sinha credits Douglass's narrative with 'making the slave's indictment of slavery the most effective weapon in the abolitionist arsenal and for popularizing the genre'.[33]

Garrison wrote the preface to Douglass's *Narrative*, giving him a ringing letter of endorsement. That fateful convention meeting between a 23-year-old

---

31 Buccola 2012, pp. 41, 52–3. McKivigan 2009, pp. 10–12. See also, Manisha Sinha 2016, p. 354. Root 2016 provides some useful details about the broader context for Douglass's debate with Collins.
32 Jackson 2019, pp. 38–41. Blight 2018, pp. 132–3.
33 Blight 2018, p. 137. Sinha 2016, p. 426. For an example of the success of the *Narrative* verifying Douglass' status as an escaped slave, see his public letter to A.C.C. Thompson, McKivigan 2009, pp. 84–5.

Douglass and the abolitionists in Nantucket in August 1841, was, as he put it, 'fortunate for the millions of his manacled brethren ... fortunate for the cause of negro emancipation, and of universal liberty! – fortunate for the land of his birth, which he has already done so much to save and bless!' Douglass was an 'intellect richly endowed – in natural eloquence a prodigy – in soul manifestly "created but a little lower than the angels"'. As a public speaker, Douglass 'excels in pathos, wit, comparison, imitation, strength of reasoning, and fluency of language'. As exhibited in the *Narrative*, Douglass wrote with 'great eloquence and power' and was 'an ornament to society and a blessing to his race'.[34]

Douglass had been contemplating a trip abroad for some time after joining the organised abolitionist movement. Outed now as a fugitive, owing to his published autobiography, and, therefore, vulnerable to recapture and re-enslavement, travelling abroad would make practical sense. A visit to Great Britain, specifically, became an opportunity to promote abolition and the Garrisonian current to which he belonged. His approximately eighteen-month trip, beginning with the sea voyage itself, gave him the opportunity to defend his brand of abolitionism, to interact with other social activists and think beyond the United States about the broader global, temporal, and institutional context for the fight against slavery. Four issues took centre stage during his sojourn in the British Isles: a comparison of the advantages and disadvantages of republics versus constitutional monarchies for advancing social justice; the oppression of the Irish nationality; a comparison of the advantages and disadvantages of using violence versus nonviolence in advancing social justice; and lastly, the Chartist movement, or, the fight for working-class suffrage in England.

Shortly after arriving in Ireland, Douglass received the news that Kentucky abolitionist Cassius Clay's printing press had been sacked by a racist mob. This event prompted an angry and sarcastic response from Douglass. Not lost on him was the irony of the moment: his presence in a constitutional monarchy that according to advocates of republican government was an inferior form of rule. Yet the racist attack on free speech had taken place in republican America with its 'free and noble institutions ... where freedom of the press means freedom to advocate slavery, and where liberty regulated by law means slavery [is] protected by an armed band of bloody assassins!' Furthermore, on his trip Douglass noticed a glaring difference between his experience of the British Isles and his experience back home – he had not encountered any discrimination based on

---

34   Gates 1994, pp. 3–10.

the colour of his skin. 'In this country, I am welcomed to the temperance platform, side by side with white speakers, and am received as kindly and warmly as though my skin were white'.[35]

In Ireland, Douglass witnessed and was deeply impressed by a speech given by Daniel O'Connell, the Irish nationalist and Catholic leader. In addition to advocating for Irish self-determination, O'Connell addressed, much to Douglass's delight, American slavery. O'Connell's internationalist perspective was especially noteworthy in Douglass's report to Garrison. In his attack on 'Negro slavery', O'Connell, according to Douglass, said 'I am an advocate of civil and religious liberty, all over the globe, and wherever tyranny exists, I am the foe of the tyrant; wherever oppression shows itself, I am the foe of the oppressor; wherever slavery rears its head, I am the enemy of the system ... My sympathy is not confined within the narrow bound of my own green island ... It extends itself to every corner of the earth'.[36] Douglass's own horizons were broadening.

Before an audience in Limerick, Ireland on 10 November 1845, Douglass denounced American slavery and in doing so compared the plight of the Irish with what American slaves endured. 'But there was nothing like American slavery on the soil on which he now stood', Douglass said. 'Negro-slavery consisted not in taking away any of the rights of man, but in annihilating them all – not in taking away a man's property, but in making property of him, and in destroying his identity – in treating him as the beasts and creeping things'. Douglass's intent was not to condemn republicanism in general, 'but the slavery that was identified with it; but it was not a true democracy, but a bastard republicanism that enslaved one-sixth of the population'. He referred to the southern slave owners encroaching on northern Mexico in order to annex it to the United States as 'free booters', that were 'appropriating [Mexican] territory to themselves in order to make it a hot bed of negro slavery. Mexico with all her barbarism and darkness had wiped away the stain of slavery from her dominions, and now the enlightened, Christian United States had stained again what was washed'.[37] Even 'backward' Mexico (Douglass wasn't immune to the Eurocentric prejudices en vogue about the Latin American country) had a better record than the 'bastard' republic when it came to chattel slavery.[38]

---

35 P. Foner 1950a, pp. 119–21.
36 P. Foner 1950a, p. 121. Bradbury 1999, p. 175.
37 Blassingame 1979, pp. 77–8, 80–1.
38 Douglass knew better than Marx and Engels about the real reason for Washington's annexation of northern Mexico, to advance the pecuniary interests of the slavocracy. Compare and contrast Douglass's explanation for the creation of Texas with what they thought to be

Despite his empathy for the plight of the Irish, the longer Douglass stayed in Britain, the more he began to sound like an admirer of the preeminent British constitutional monarchy. A few months after his visit to Limerick, Douglass declared that 'Liberty is commensurate with and inseparable from British soil'. Speaking seemingly for all humans of any skin colour, Douglass wrote that 'No matter in what language his doom may have been pronounced; no matter what complexion incompatible with freedom an Indian or an African sun may have burnt upon him; no matter in what disastrous battle his liberties may have been cloven down; – no matter with what solemnities he may have been devoted upon the altar of slavery; the first moment he touches the sacred soil of Britain ... he stands redeemed, regenerated, and disenthralled, by the irresistible genius of Universal Emancipation'.[39] And then later for an article in Garrison's organ *The Liberator*, from 30 January 1846, Douglass wrote: 'Whatever may be said of the aristocracies here, there is none based on the color of a man's skin. This species of aristocracy belongs pre-eminently to "the land of the free, and the home of the brave"'.[40]

Five months later, Douglass wrote to Garrison that the constitutional monarchy of Great Britain was preferable to the 'tyrant many' or the tyranny of the majority in the United States. This tyranny of the majority was, in his opinion, 'even more tyrannical than the tyrant few', i.e., the tyranny of the minority. Also to Garrison, Douglass wrote that 'Liberty in Hyde Park is better than democracy in a slave prison – monarchial freedom is better than republican slavery'.[41]

In seeming to prefer constitutional monarchy to American republican government during his tour of the British Isles, it is not clear if Douglass ever resolved in his mind the Irish question of self-determination when he compared republicanism to the ruling system in imperialist Great Britain. Though he made the unsubstantiated claim that Great Britain was free of skin colour discrimination, how did he account for the national discrimination and subjugation of the Irish by the British? Why would Irish nationalists like O'Connell desire self-rule in Ireland? A February 1846 letter published in *The Liberator* revealed that Douglass felt conflicted and concerned about Great Britain's oppression and exploitation of the Irish people. Touring Ireland had 'filled him

---

the reason; Blassingame 1979, pp. 71–4, 118–24; Marx and Engels 1975–2004e, p. 527; Marx and Engels 1975–2004f, p. 365.
39   Blassingame 1979, p. 185.
40   P. Foner 1950a, pp. 125–9. Blight 2018, p. 154.
41   P. Foner 1950a, pp. 168, 171–2. Some may argue that Douglass was being sarcastic in his comparison of monarchical freedom and republican slavery, but McKivigan and Silverman 1999 demonstrate that the praise of Great Britain's monarchy was earnest and enthusiastic.

with pain'. Before the trip, he had prepared himself to witness 'the misery and wretchedness of the Irish people', but he now realised 'the half has not been told'. Douglass told Garrison that though he had founded the *Liberator* for the overthrow of slavery, the newspaper should also publicise the conditions of 'the oppressed of every class, color, and clime' and boldly vindicate their rights. 'I am not only an American slave', Douglass continued, 'but a man, and as such, am bound to use my powers for the welfare of the whole human brotherhood'. He accused some in both England and America of being just as willing to 'sell on the auction-block an Irishman, if it were popular to do, as an African'. Douglass described the incredible poverty of the Irish working class, including women and children among the beggars, in heart-wrenching terms. His visits to the 'huts of the poor' in Dublin led him to compare their living conditions to the 'degradation of the American slaves'.[42] Douglass clearly struggled with the topic. To his Irish and British audiences, he often told his own story to try to make the case that however much exploited wageworkers and peasants were, to be a chattel slave was worse – the most degraded of the toilers.[43]

As for the question of using violence or non-violence in the quest for social justice, a visit to an ancient Scottish battlefield prompted Douglass to take a stance. After learning about the extent of the carnage that had taken place, 'I see in myself', he wrote to an American abolitionist, 'all those elements of character which were I to yield to their promptings might lead me to deeds as bloody as those at which my soul now sickens and from which I now turn with disgust and shame'. He thanked God that there is another way, 'one which hurls defiance at all the improvements of carnal warfare. It is the righteous appeal to the understanding and the heart – with this we can withstand the most fiery of all the darts of perdition itself'. Douglass believed that the 'gnawing of a guilty conscience', brought on by nonviolent abolitionists, was superior to America's 'naval, and military power'. To a peace meeting in May 1846, he said that if asked 'whether I would have my emancipation by the shedding of one single drop of blood, my answer would be in the negative'.[44]

While advocating for pacifism during his tour, Douglass acknowledged on at least two occasions that should there be war in America, it would be an opportunity for slave emancipation. 'If', he said in March 1846, 'a foreign enemy were to land in America and plant the standard of freedom, the slaves would rise to a man, they would rally round that standard'. 'But', as he wanted to make clear to his audience, 'you are not to infer from this that I am an advocate for war, no, I

---

42 P. Foner 1950a, pp. 138–41. Bradbury 1999, p. 174.
43 For example, Blassingame 1979, pp. 77–9.
44 P. Foner 1950a, pp. 135–6. Blassingame 1979, p. 262.

hate war'.[45] To a London audience in May, Douglass declared: 'You may think it is somewhat singular that I ... should stand forth at this time as an advocate of peace between two countries situated as this [country] and the United States are, when it is universally believed that a war between them would eventuate in the emancipation of three millions of my brethren who are now held in most cruel bonds in that country. I believe this would be the result'.[46] Douglass could be forgiven for not seeing the exact opposite fifteen years later when the Civil War broke out. The constitutional monarchy proved to be no friend of America's enslaved, contrary to what he might have thought by the end of his visit.

Working-class men in Britain, unlike in republican America, lacked the right to vote – the disadvantage of 'the tyranny few'. Thus, the Chartist movement was founded in 1836 in Britain to achieve universal male suffrage. The movement was given its name by its Charter, a list of six demands for basic liberal-democratic political rights and civil liberties compatible with bourgeois rule. While in London in May 1846, Douglass spoke to a meeting of the Complete Suffrage Union, a moderate wing of the movement. As Douglass explained to Garrison, the Union was 'called in contradistinction from the Chartist party, and differing from that party, in that it repudiates the use of physical force as a means of attaining its object'. After describing the meeting, Douglass confidently told Garrison that 'the next great reform will be that of complete suffrage', a time 'when people and not property shall govern' and 'people will cease to be subordinate to property'.[47]

Douglass seems to have been attracted more to the moderate wing of Chartism than its more militant working-class component. The Moral Force Chartists, as they were known, advocated for temperance and education while discouraging militant mass confrontations during the downturn in the movement in the early 1840s. One of its leaders, 'did not believe that workers were yet ready for political power'. Instead, workers needed to raise their levels of education, self-discipline, and culture before they could be trusted to govern.[48] A middle-class abolitionist who had Douglass's ear urged him to 'avoid radical working-class politics' and to 'stop hammering at the churches'.[49] Like Douglass, Garrison was also attracted to Moral Force Chartism. He met with

---

45   Blassingame 1979, p. 187.
46   Blassingame 1979, p. 262.
47   P. Foner 1950a, p. 167. Blight 2018, p. 174.
48   Bradbury 1999, p. 178. As Richard Bradbury writes, 'Frederick Douglass's visit to Britain, then, coincided with a point in the history of Chartism at which the strategic thinking of those dominant in the movement was closest to Douglass's at that time'. Bradbury 1999, pp. 183–4.
49   McFeely 1991, pp. 153–4.

Moral Force Chartists when he joined Douglass in England that summer.[50] Both shared the stage with Moral Force leaders on 17 August 1846, at the public launch of the Anti-Slavery League.[51] This new organisation served as an 'affront to the British and Foreign Anti-Slavery Society' which had no interest in reform movements other than abolition.[52]

Other Garrisonians like Wendell Phillips were taken with Moral Force Chartism, evidence that they viewed acquiring bourgeois democratic rights as an end in itself. Moral Force leader William Lovett's writings that claimed the Charter could secure 'to all classes of society their just share of political power' and guarantee 'equality of political rights' impressed Phillips. Aforementioned utopian socialist and abolitionist John A. Collins argued that the wage-system itself, and not only a lack of suffrage, was to blame for the grievances and suffering of workers. However, the popularity of 'self-reform' causes among Garrisonians like Douglass, such as the promotion of temperance and industrious habits among workers, revealed their preference for individual over systematic solutions to social problems, obviously with the exceptions of slavery abolition and Chartist reforms.[53] Despite, however, the differences between the moderate and militant wings of Chartism, both advocated for working-class suffrage. Not long after Douglass's return to the United States, he began to reconsider Garrisonian opposition to voting. His encounter with the Chartists was probably determinant in his reconsideration.[54]

Back in America, Douglass's recent international experiences made him more disposed than ever before to think globally and temporally about everything, including slavery. 'Human nature', stretched across time, space, and economic circumstances, appeared to provide an answer. 'Douglass believed', as Nicholas Buccola writes, that 'the phenomenon of slavery was a manifestation of the spirit of selfishness in human nature'. But humans, clearly, were not written in stone. Douglass celebrated West Indian Emancipation on 2 August 1847, to mark abolition day in the British West Indies in 1834, an event he 'justly regarded [as] the greatest and grandest of the nineteenth century'. In a speech

---

50   McDaniel 2015, p. 147. Blight 2018, p. 173.
51   Bradbury 1999, p. 179. Sinha 2016, p. 351 notes the launch of the Anti-Slavery League by William Lovett and Henry Vincent, among others – the Moral Force Chartists Douglass worked most closely with in Britain.
52   McFeely 1991, p. 151.
53   McDaniel 2015, pp. 147–50, 153. Douglass described intemperance as 'the immediate' and possibly 'the main cause of extreme poverty and beggary in Ireland'. P. Foner 1950a, pp. 141.
54   Finley 2020, pp. 45–6, argues that Douglass's trip to the United Kingdom was 'the start of Douglass's investment in political abolitionism'. Finley's essay, however, does not mention the Chartists or their potential influence.

before a mixed-race audience of thousands in Canandaigua, New York, Douglass explained that, 'From the earliest periods of man's history, we are able to trace manifestations of the spirit of selfishness, which leads one man to prey upon the rights and interests of his fellow-man'. Selfishness overrides the better aspects of human nature and 'cursed the world with Slavery and kindred crimes'. Deep in the human heart lies the love of 'ease, love of power, a strong desire to control the will of others'. He also, during his England trip, blamed this subordination of the better aspects of human nature on 'the love of money ... the root of all evil – with this lust for gold has England too been contaminated, and hence the result we witness'.[55] Events slowly unfolding in America would begin to test the explanatory power of Douglass's thesis and many of his beliefs – not the least of which was pacifism.

2 From Radical Democrat to Communist

Karl Marx (1818–83), unlike Douglass, was the product of developments mainly on the other side of the Atlantic. No historical event impacted him more than the French Revolution of 1789. Trying to realise the promise of that cataclysmic upheaval is what, in a fundamental sense, led him to communist conclusions. But his political biography reveals an often-underappreciated truth: the American reality – its exceptionalism – aided and abetted that trajectory.

Even with its democratic deficit, Restoration France offered more political liberties than its neighbour to the east. Only in Germany's most western provinces, where Napoleon's armies had been, were there traces of what 1789 had promised. Coming of political age in that part of Germany forever marked Marx: 'No region of Germany produced so many revolutionary radicals as the Rhineland'.[56] Also, unlike and in stark contrast to Douglass, Marx came from an intellectual/professional middle class milieu. For class cohorts of his generation, the burning question was: how could liberal democracy be planted on German soil? The proximity of relatively more liberal France was determinant in his quest for an answer.

That Marx was a Jew is of no little importance given that 1789 opened new opportunities for those who so identified and were identified by the majority Christian society as such. His family, rabbis on both sides, deeply understood what it meant to be Jewish in late eighteenth- and early nineteenth-century,

---

55 Buccola 2012, p. 20. Blassingame 1982, pp. 69, 72–3. Blassingame 1979, pp. 123–4. See also, Buccola 2018, pp. 64–6.
56 Avineri 2019, p. 8.

largely anti-Semitic Europe. His father, especially, was his most direct link to that consciousness. Though needing to obfuscate his family's Jewishness by converting them to Lutheranism in order to protect them from systemic German anti-Semitism and ensure them opportunities for upward social mobility, there is much to suggest that Marx's father instilled, maybe unconsciously, liberal anti-status quo values in his only son that would survive childhood.[57] Marx too, like Douglass, had, if not consciously – apparently – a personal interest in contesting the socially unequal order of the day. His lifelong nickname that close friends employed, 'the Moor' (a term used to refer to Africans and Middle Easterners in Europe by the fourteenth century and a synonym for 'negro' by the seventeenth century), suggests their awareness of Marx's outsider status as a Jew in Germany, instead of simply his swarthier-than-typical skin tone for a German. Whether his Jewish identity motivated him to contest social inequality, as did Douglass's Black identity for him, continues to be an interesting subject of speculation that cannot be resolved here.[58] We may never know the answer to that question, particularly as it pertains to his childhood, because Marx, owing to his 'aversion to the personality cult' – as if in anticipation of Stalin – could never be convinced to write an autobiography, so strikingly in contrast to Douglass.[59] Nevertheless, an extant high school graduation essay and college-years correspondence with his father provide invaluable real-time glimpses into his youth for which nothing comparable exists in the Douglass corpus of writings.[60]

As a newly minted PhD in philosophy in 1841, earned with a very erudite and maybe esoteric dissertation on ancient Greek philosophy, Marx hoped that he could get a teaching post at one of the German state universities.[61] That would be unlikely, he quickly realised, given his radical democratic politics that he was unwilling to compromise. Thus, he decided to become a cub reporter for a liberal organ in his home province of Rhineland-Palatinate, the *Rheinische Zeitung*. He got the job owing in part to a remarkable letter of recommendation from Moses Hess, six years Marx's senior and author, at that point, of two books on philosophy.

---

57 For details, see Heinrich 2019, pp. 76–83.
58 While willing to defend political rights for Jews, Marx made clear his 'dislike [of] the Jewish faith' (Marx and Engels 1975–2004a, p. 400). More recently, in addition to Avineri and Heinrich, see Stedman Jones 2013, pp. 9–18; and Sperber 2013, pp. 496–502, 548–9, 553–6.
59 Marx and Engels 1975–2004y, p. 288.
60 For the most informed discussion of these materials, see Heinrich 2019, pp. 33–120.
61 About the significance of the dissertation for Marx's later political trajectory, see Heinrich 2019, pp. 292–321.

> Be prepared to meet the greatest, perhaps the only real philosopher living now ... Dr. Marx ... is still a young man, barely 24 years old, but he will give the final blow to all medieval religion and politics; he combines the deepest philosophical seriousness with a cunning wit. Can you imagine Rousseau, Voltaire, Holbach, Lessing, Heine, and Hegel combined – not thrown together – in one person? If you can – you have Dr. Marx.[62]

Except perhaps for John Stuart Mill, no other influential figure of the nineteenth century began their career with such a sterling intellectual endorsement.

Despite his scholarly credentials, 'I first found myself', Marx later admitted about his first job, 'in the embarrassing position of having to discuss what is known as material interests'.[63] Douglass, his cohort in age, on the other hand, knew viscerally about 'material interests', especially those of his slave owner. Marx soon learned firsthand in 1842, after becoming the editor of the *Rheinische Zeitung*, about the heavy hand of absolute monarchy, i.e., the Prussian Hohenzollern dynasty that ruled over the province. State censorship of his articles about the oppression of the peasantry was evidence for him of the 'essence' of the regime. 'There is no confidence in the intelligence and goodwill of the general public even in the simplest matter ... This fundamental defect is inherent in all our institutions'.[64] How to explain and how to rectify the defect?

Marx's starting point towards an answer, the quest for freedom, informed his first recorded comment about slavery on the North American continent. He critiqued the claim of an unnamed Rhinelander legislator about the value of censorship, according to whom: 'Truth ... cannot be suppressed for long. The more obstacles are put in its way, the more keenly it pursues its goal, and the more resoundingly it achieves it'. To which Marx sarcastically replied: 'A fine argument for slave traders – to bring out the Negro's human nature by flogging ...'.[65] By at least age twenty-four, Marx assumed, therefore, that enslaved Black Africans were human beings – an assumption not to be taken for granted given the ubiquity of chattel slavery in the Atlantic world in that era – and that their humanity did not depend on the slave owner's lash. He was aware, apparently, that slave owners, like Douglass's master, preferred illiterate slaves. Four thousand miles away, Marx knew rationally what Douglass knew experientially – their first but not their last trans-Atlantic mind-meld.

---

62 Avineri 2019, p. 56.
63 Marx 1989, p. 19.
64 Marx and Engels 1975–2004a, p. 130.
65 Marx and Engels 1975–2004a, p. 160.

Two pages later, slavery was still on Marx's mind. Armed with a Hegelian normative notion of law, with which he would soon part ways, Marx maintained that 'censorship, like slavery, can never become lawful, even if it exists a thousand times over as a law' – as was the case in the United States.[66] Yet, as he noted in his next article on 15 May, in his transnational survey of press laws, 'You find the natural phenomenon of freedom of the press in *North America* in its purest most natural form'.[67] Marx was aware, therefore, at least as early as 1842, of the glaring contradiction about the republic on the other side of the Atlantic. It combined one of the best features of freedom, for the press, with the very unfree system of slavery – not unlike Douglass's 1845 critique of America 'where freedom of the press means freedom to advocate slavery'. But if Douglass may have sounded equivocal about freedom of the press – at least in that moment – Marx, a victim of state censorship, was unequivocal. Such democratic rights were valuable tools in the fight against semi-feudal patriarchal social relations not only in Central and Eastern Europe but also in slave-holding North America.

After about a year, the regime grew tired of Marx's criticisms; it pulled the plug on the *Rheinische Zeitung*. To make sense of the paper's banning, and how to realise freedom in Germany, Marx turned to Georg Wilhelm Friedrich Hegel (1770–1831), the towering figure of German philosophy for Marx's generation. Hegel stood on the shoulders not only of Germany's best thinkers, including Immanuel Kant for sure, but also upon those of France and England – especially English philosophers like John Locke and political economists like Adam Smith and David Ricardo. Amongst other topics, Marx was informed by Hegel's critique of the individual-centric doctrine of natural rights and law, which was foundational for all three, especially Locke and, in turn, owing to the latter's impact on the Declaration of Independence and the Constitution, for Douglass.[68] For Hegel's progeny, society rather than the individual was the likely starting point for analysis. Marx's political quest, in other words, was cultivated by the kind of intellectual milieu that was not only unavailable to Douglass but also virtually anyone else in the US in that era, regardless of skin colour or class position. Hegel, let alone his critique of the natural rights/law philosophical position that undergirded Douglass's politics, appeared on almost no one's

---

66 Marx and Engels 1975–2004a, p. 162. To fully understand Marx's language, see Shoikhedbrod 2020 for valuable commentary, pp. 24–7.
67 Marx and Engels 1975–2004a, p. 167. A college course on comparative jurisprudence no doubt informed Marx's critique.
68 See Shoikhedbrod 2020, pp. 24–8, for details.

radar in the United States before the Civil War.[69] The advantages, therefore, of an elite European education, and not only race and class privilege, to employ current parlance, distinguished Marx from Douglass at this comparable stage in their careers.

In addition to the problem of press censorship, Marx reported on the plight of landless peasants and impoverished grape growers at the mercy of the wealthy – with whom Douglass could have easily identified – an issue that required him to address the legal and thus political framework within which these developments unfolded. This journalistic research obligated him to take on Hegel's defence of constitutional monarchy – which Marx opposed and Douglass defended, at least in the case of Britain – and, therefore, Hegel's theory of constitutions as well.[70] The twenty-four year old's interrogation of Hegel's thought on constitutions is of major importance for a comparison with Douglass who, as we will see later, spilled a lot of ink and spoke extensively on the meaning of the United States Constitution.

Hegel's basic problem, Marx argued, is that he began with 'the idea' or 'the spirit' of the state and its constitution. 'If Hegel had set out from real subjects as the bases of the state he would not have found it necessary to transform the state in a mystical fashion into a subject'.[71] Marx therefore dismissed as a 'trivial truth' Hegel's point that a constitution could be out of sync with the 'customs and consciousness of any given people' at any determinant moment, and 'a heavy fetter on an advanced consciousness'.[72] The solution, Marx proposed, 'would be simply the demand for a constitution which contains within itself the designation and the principle to advance along with consciousness, to advance as actual men advance, [and] this is only possible when 'man' has become the principle of the constitution'.[73] Therein lay the premise of Marx's alternative theory.

The 'man' Marx had in mind was the 'sovereignty of the people', 'the democracy' in the parlance at that time. 'Democracy', he argued, 'is the solved *riddle* of all constitutions'. If understood that way, he continued, 'the constitution is constantly brought back to its actual basis, the *actual human being*, the *actual people*, and established as the people's *own* work'. To get the attention of the audience of his time, Marx asserted: 'Just as it is not religion which creates man

---

69   Easton 1966, Chapter One.
70   Avineri 2019, Chapter Two is a useful introduction to Marx's critique. Draper 1977, Chapter Three, is still the best summary.
71   Marx and Engels 1975–2004b, p. 23.
72   Marx and Engels 1975–2004b, p. 19.
73   Ibid.

but man who creates religion, so it is not the constitution which creates the people but the people which creates the constitution'. The basis of all constitutions, in other words, were 'the people', either their consent for democratic ones, in both 'content and form', or their passive compliance with and subjugation by constitutional monarchies or even tyrannies.[74]

As for constitutional change, Marx rejected Hegel's category of *'gradual transition … it explains nothing … Posed correctly, the question is simply this: Has the people the right to give itself a new constitution? The answer must be an unqualified "Yes", because once it has ceased to be an actual expression of the will of the people the constitution has become a practical illusion'.*[75] But 'for a *new* constitution', as France 1789 taught, 'a real revolution has always been required'.[76] Given the world in which he lived and his experience as a cub reporter, Marx had no illusions about 'the people' vis-à-vis the constitution. 'The political constitution at its highest point is therefore the constitution of private property', especially 'landed property'. Being no friend of private property given its 'barbarism … against family life', Marx emphasised 'the power of *abstract private property* over the *political state*'.[77] The oppression of landless peasants and small grape growers by the propertied class, the landed elite in the Rhineland, no doubt informed Marx's harsh judgement.[78]

Marx also criticised Hegel for not calling for 'the *extension* and greatest possible *generalization* of *election*, both of the right to *vote* and the right to *be elected*. This is the real point of dispute concerning political *reform*, in France as in England'.[79] On this score, the pre-communist Marx sounded like Douglass in 1846 who asserted that with 'complete suffrage … people will cease to be subordinate to property'. Toward clarification and differentiation, Marx offered his first criticisms of liberals in the democratic quest. That liberal opponents to the regime embraced Hegel's political premises was evidence that they were 'by no means equal to the task' to defend either freedom of the press or any other civil liberties. The failure of the liberal owners of the *Rheinische Zeitung* to put up a fight when the newspaper was banned was further evidence for Marx of liberal

---

74   Marx and Engels 1975–2004b, p. 29.
75   Marx and Engels 1975–2004b, p. 57.
76   Marx and Engels 1975–2004b, p. 56.
77   Marx and Engels 1975–2004b, pp. 98–9.
78   The currency of this judgement was 'recently captured by a picket sign carried by locked-out dockworkers in Quebec last fall [2022], one that rings true to tens of millions of workers and their families facing the bosses' relentless drive for profits: "Longshore worker wanted. No spouses. No kids. No friends. Available 24/7, 365"'. Clark and Evans 2023, pp. 8–9.
79   Marx and Engels 1975–2004b, p. 120.

vacillation. Within a year, he would argue, without being specific, that the only answer to Prussian despotism was the 'impending revolution'.

Some of Marx's final comments on Hegel have to do with the emergence of private property, its legalisation, and as 'the guarantee of the political constitution'. Roman law took the lead as seen in the institution of slavery: 'the human being (as slave), as amongst the peoples of antiquity generally, is object of private property ... the manner in which slavery is explained is through military law, the law of occupation; they are slaves precisely because their political existence has been destroyed'.[80] Marx's analysis of the self-interests and political effects of private property recalls Douglass's point in 1847 about slavery having its origins in 'selfishness, which leads one man to prey upon the rights and interests of his fellow man'. What Marx did was to explain the political consequences for a society based on private property, a society that Douglass defended – as in his debate with John Collins the utopian socialist in 1843 – except for property in persons.

In criticising the regime, Marx also engaged in a debate with the left, specifically, the Young Hegelians. One of their favourite topics was the critique of religion that Marx found unsatisfactory. 'I requested ... that religion should be criticized in the framework of criticism of political conditions rather than that political conditions should be criticized in the framework of religion ... for religion in itself is without content, it owes its being not to heaven but to the earth, and with the abolition of distorted reality, of which it is the *theory*, it will collapse of itself'.[81] For Douglass, on the other hand, religious belief came to be his lodestar – revealing very early in their lives the profound epistemological/methodological difference between the two protagonists. Douglass's critique of religious America for not condemning slavery would have been for Marx beside the point because religion did not explain anything. For the scion of a family of rabbis, it was rather religion that had to be explained within the socio-economic 'political conditions' which framed it.

Marx soon realised that criticism was unconvincing if it was not accompanied by a solution. To do so required, as he chided the Young Hegelians, 'less vague reasoning, magniloquent phrases and self-satisfied self-adoration, and more definiteness, more attention to the actual state of affairs, more expert knowledge'. More concretely, as he explained two years later in *The German Ideology*: 'one has to "leave philosophy aside" ... one has to leap out of it and devote oneself like an ordinary man to the study of actuality, for which there

---

80   Marx and Engels 1975–2004b, pp. 108–10.
81   Marx and Engels 1975–2004b, pp. 394–5.

exists also an enormous amount of literary material, unknown, of course, to the philosophers'. In pursuit of his new course, Marx made clear that he was burning bridges: 'Philosophy and the study of the actual have the same relation to one another as onanism and sexual love'.[82]

On the road to ending relations with the Young Hegelians, in 1843 he criticised then collaborator Arnold Ruge for his pessimism about the way out of the increasingly despotic situation in Germany and his failure to see 'the impending revolution'. There was, alas, 'nothing political about' Ruge's plaintive pessimism. 'No people wholly despairs, and even if for a long time it goes on hoping merely out of stupidity, yet one day, after many years, it will suddenly become wise, and fulfill all its pious wishes'. Marx's revolutionary optimism about the oppressed began to set him apart from former colleagues. But his idealism about 'thinking beings, free men, republicans' meant that he was not yet a communist.[83] Nevertheless, he told Ruge, 'nothing prevents us from making criticism of politics, participation in politics, and therefore *real struggles*, the starting point of our criticism, and from identifying our criticism with them'.[84] Nothing from Marx's early career best anticipated why America's Civil War so captivated his attention for almost four years than this perspective. The Marx-Ruge partnership, as it turned out, proved to be short-lived, if not stillborn. Marx would soon, however, be more successful – spectacularly so – in his second such venture.

The US 'actuality' taught the most important lessons about politics. If America, as Marx would conclude, was the best that political democracy had to offer, then clearly something else was required for 'human emancipation'. Alexis de Tocqueville's *Democracy in America* was informative. A footnote pointed out that *Marie, or Slavery in the United States*, the volume of Tocqueville's travel companion Gustave de Beaumont, would be more appealing to 'those readers who above all else, desire a true picture of actual conditions' in America. Also published in 1835, Beaumont's novel provided just the kind of 'expert knowledge' and 'literary material' to which the young Marx was referring, and not just for the reality of race in America. Almost a third of the book consisted of appendices with valuable observations about race – concerning both Blacks and Indians – as well as about class, religious, and gender issues.

The US case revealed its importance for the analytical-cum-political breakthrough he was about to make in his 1843–4 articles on 'The Jewish Question'.[85]

---

82   Marx and Engels 1975–2004d, p. 136.
83   Marx and Engels 1975–2004b, pp. 133–4.
84   Marx and Engels 1975–2004b, p. 144.
85   The first two of the five articles, the most well-known, were written in 1843 (Marx and

In addition to Beaumont's *Marie*, and Tocqueville's *Democracy*, the articles were informed by the two-volume account of an English traveller to the US published in 1833, Thomas Hamilton's *Men and Manners in America*. Despite their title, Marx's articles are basically about the requisites for political democracy and, thus, the lessons he learned from America. Though Tocqueville's *Democracy* gets only minor billing in them, one of its major findings figured significantly in Marx's argument. Marx discovered and was impressed by the exceptional religiosity of America, a religious fervour that Tocqueville noted and explained was unlike anything in Europe. Not the least important, 'North America' taught that 'the *preaching of the gospel* itself and the Christian ministry have become articles of commerce and the bankrupt businessman deals in the gospel just as the gospel preacher, who has become rich, goes for business deals'.[86] What Douglass blamed on 'mammon', churches that defended slavery, Marx would later diagnose as the logic of capitalism – the commodification of everything.

Religion for Marx, like for the Young Hegelians, was a 'defect' in a society because it fostered sectarianism, 'the separation of man from man'. That widespread religiosity, with its accompanying sectarian practices that both Hamilton and Beaumont reported on, particularly with regard to race, not only existed within the most politically democratic state in the Atlantic world but seems also to have been fostered by that state, was instructive. That was probably the first sign for Marx that the US was no paragon of 'human emancipation'.[87] Douglass's rude awakening to the racialisation of religion in more politically liberal, non-slave holding New Bedford exemplified Marx's point. Clearly, again, for the young radical democrat, something was amiss on the other side of the Atlantic. And it was not just about the 'peculiar institution'.

Marx's notebooks reveal his close reading of Hamilton's volumes that, with many details about class and racial inequality, offered a more sober portrait of America than Tocqueville's text. Contra Tocqueville's problematic claim, for

---

Engels 1975–2004b, pp. 146–74). Less referenced, but just as important for understanding Marx's argument, are the three in *The Holy Family*, written in 1844 (Marx and Engels 1975–2004c, pp. 87–90, 94–9, 106–18). Because of what might be interpreted as anti-Semitic comments in the articles, a long-standing debate has taken place about Marx's views regarding Judaism and Jews. A recent example of the 'anti-Semitic Marx' is Montgomery and Chirot 2015, p. 82. See Shoikhedbrod 2023; Avineri 2019, Chapter Three, 'Zur Judenfrage', for the most persuasive recent defence of Marx. See also, Draper 1977, pp. 591–608.

86 Marx and Engels 1975–2004b, p. 171.
87 Tocqueville's insight also found its way into the first collaborative writing of Marx and Engels, *The Holy Family*: 'religion develops in its practical universality only where there is no privileged religion (cf. the North American States)'. Marx and Engels 1975–2004c, p. 116.

example, that 'universal suffrage has been adopted in all the states of the Union', Hamilton's account made clear that was not the case; Virginia's electoral laws had fairly high property qualifications for who could vote and be elected. Yet his data on the states that had abolished property qualifications allowed Marx to make one of his key observations about the significance of private property for political democracy. The prohibition of property qualifications did not, however, abolish private property; it 'even presupposes it'. The secular state, therefore, 'allows private property, education, occupation, to *act* in *their* way ... to exert the influence of their *special* nature. Far from abolishing these *real* distinctions, the state only exists on the presupposition of their existence'.[88] As long as inequalities in wealth – as well as education and occupation – persisted, Marx noted, there would be inequalities in access to the electoral process including the 'right to be elected'. The US case revealed, again, that 'political emancipation was not human emancipation' or 'true democracy'. Four thousand miles away, Marx, in effect, offered an explanation for the oligarchical rule of the slave owners that Douglass, a defender of private property, either denied or ignored.

Another topic that captured Marx's attention in Hamilton's account was the recently formed Workingmen's Party (1829–1831) in New York City, the first of its kind anywhere. Their demand for 'equal and universal education' is noteworthy: 'It is false, they say, to maintain that there is at present no privileged order, no practical aristocracy, in a country where distinctions of education are permitted ... There does exist then – they argue – an aristocracy of ... knowledge, education and refinement, which is inconsistent with the true democratic principle of absolute equality'.[89] Could this have been the inspiration for Marx's above-cited point about how social distinctions and privileges such as education '*act* in *their* way ... to exert the influence of their *special* nature'? Marx's soon to be taken path to find in the proletariat the solution to the democratic quest may have had its origins in what Hamilton reported.[90]

In pointing out the limitations of political democracy in the US, Marx was in no way dismissive of what was in place on the other side of the Atlantic. To the contrary. Political democracy was far superior, he knew, to what existed in Hohenzollern Germany. His main point about the US was that its democracy, 'political emancipation', was not 'true democracy' or 'human emancipation'. Rather the US was a work in progress instead of the 'absolute democracy' that

---

88 Marx and Engels 1975–2004b, p. 153.
89 Hamilton 1833, pp. 226–7.
90 For details of Marx's reading of Hamilton, Beaumont, and Tocqueville see Nimtz 2003, Chapter One.

Tocqueville claimed. The combination of what Tocqueville, Beaumont, and Hamilton reported revealed that something else was required for 'true democracy'. That something else is what his attention would then turn to. In other words, Marx was still on his way to reaching communist conclusions.[91]

Nevertheless, Marx's description of the US, at least then, was not that different from Douglass's characterisation: 'not a true democracy, but a bastard republicanism that enslaved one-sixth of the population'. For Marx, even before he pointed it out to Abraham Lincoln two decades later, the existence of slavery in the US was 'to defile [the] republic' – exactly why he and Douglass could be on the same political page when the Confederacy fired on Fort Sumter in April 1861. Yet, a fundamental issue divided the two. Douglass thought that 'a true democracy' could be realised in the United States once chattel slavery had been abolished. For Marx, the soon to be communist, it would require the abolishment of the private ownership of the means of production. That was the claim that allowed Marx to look beyond what Douglass desired, specifically the end to chattel slavery, and to see its overthrow as a necessary means to an end. 'True democracy' for Marx, unlike for Douglass, could only be realised with the overthrow of class society. The difference went to the very heart of what distinguished the communist Marx from the liberal Douglass.

Like Marx, Frederick Engels (1820–95), two years younger, was also a Rhinelander, raised a few hours away from Marx's hometown. But Engels came to radical democratic and communist conclusions by a different route from that of his future partner. He too had to wrestle with Hegel, but he did so as a self-taught scholar. Telling about the bourgeoisie in that era is that his father, a factory owner, saw no need for his son to get a university education. Being a bookkeeper, a career to be learned on the job, was deemed more practical. Engels, essentially a high school dropout, had to pursue his intellectual proclivities on his own time by hanging out with the university crowd and attending lectures to learn what they were absorbing. Having been raised in a pious Protestant family, Engels had, unlike Marx, a personal stake in the debates with the Young Hegelians on the religion question. And like Marx he thought German liberals, or at least some of them, vacillated in the fight for liberal democracy; he too would begin to question their resolve.

Most consequential for his partnership with Marx is that Engels knew firsthand about the other major historical development that influenced Marx – the

---

91   Losurdo 2011, pp. 318–22, suggests that Marx ignored the institution of racial slavery in making a case for political democracy in the US. The reader of this book knows by now that's not true.

Industrial Revolution. Because his family had part ownership in a textile factory in Europe's industrial heartland, Manchester, England, Engels's apprenticeship as a clerk there for two years from 1842 to 1844 gave him the opportunity to experience industrial capitalism par excellence, which his cohorts in more backward Germany could only read about. An essay Engels had published in 1843, 'Outlines of a Critique of Political Economy', is what convinced Marx to turn his attention to literature about industrialisation in order to understand the basis of civil society and how it related to the secular state. On his way back from Manchester, Engels met with Marx in Paris where he was now in self-exile. Their ten-day meeting, during August/September 1844, to discuss what they had in common, resulted in what is arguably the most influential political partnership in modern history; with due apologies to John Reed, those were the actual 'Ten Days That Shook the World'. It is no coincidence that the subtitle of Marx's magnum opus a quarter century later, *Capital* (1867), was essentially the same as the title of Engels's 1843 article.

In their first collaborative writing in 1844, *The Holy Family*, Marx and Engels declared that the proletariat

> cannot emancipate itself without abolishing the conditions of its own life [and, thus,] ... without abolishing *all* the inhuman conditions of life of society today which are summed up in its own situation ... It is not a question of what this or that proletarian, or even the whole proletariat, at the moment *regards* as its aim. It is a question of *what the proletariat is*, and what in accordance with this *being*, it will historically be compelled to do. Its aim and historical action is visibly and irrevocably foreshadowed in its own life situation as well as in the whole organization of bourgeois society today. There is no need to explain here that a large part of the English and French proletariat is already *conscious* of its historic task and is constantly working to develop that consciousness into complete clarity.[92]

Only the working class, namely, had the interest and capability to bring about 'true democracy' or 'human emancipation' – the thesis that would distinguish Marx and Engels from others who called themselves communists.

The other key issue in *The Holy Family* addressed the all-important question in modern politics – the role of intellectuals in liberatory movements of the masses. They criticised the Young Hegelians for thinking, as Marx and Engels had also once believed, that as philosophers they were 'the spiritual weapon'

---

92 Marx and Engels 1975–2004c, p. 37.

of the masses – the brain or mind of their movements. The problem with such a perspective is that the 'brain' begins to 'see itself incarnate not in a *mass*, but exclusively in a *handful* of chosen men'. But history revealed, particularly during the French Revolution, that it was the 'great mass' that was the true mover of human change and advancement. The 'great mass' now was the proletariat as made evident by the 'French and English workers'. Intellectuals who thought like the Young Hegelians could never be the source for real transformation. 'Ideas', Marx emphasised in making his point, 'can never lead beyond an old world order but only beyond the ideas of the old world order. Ideas *cannot carry out anything* at all. In order to carry out ideas men are needed who can exert practical force'.[93] At the very beginning of his joint venture with Engels, Marx was, therefore, sceptical about any liberatory project that relied on the goodwill of 'a handful of chosen men' such as intellectuals.

Of the two now self-proclaimed communists, only Engels had had direct experience and contact with organised workers, and this contact allowed them to make the above-quoted claim that the 'large part of the English ... proletariat [is] already *conscious* of its historic task'. Engels's two years in Manchester brought him in contact with the Chartists, the first working-class political organisation in Europe, and his familiarity with the Chartists is what primarily informed their declaration about the revolutionary potential of the proletariat. Composed in 1838, the aforementioned Chartist six-point programme for political and civil rights for the working class, including universal male suffrage, was key to their decision to privilege the proletariat as the most potentially revolutionary class above and beyond any other social layer.

Engels's *The Condition of the Working Class in England*, published in 1845, described the indigent, downtrodden and wretched reality of England's proletariat – not unlike Douglass's description of the impoverished Irish proletariat – and brought the working-class Chartists to the attention of aspiring German communists. Not only did Engels write about the Chartists, but he sought to forge ties between them and workers movements on the continent. Douglass, as already noted, seemed to be more impressed with the moderate liberal component of Chartism during his visit to England. Through his articles in their organs, Engels introduced more militant Chartists, even before the formation of their partnership, to 'Dr. Marx', a member of the German 'communist party'. Engels, hence, took the lead in what would later be called proletarian internationalism.

---

93 Marx and Engels 1975–2004c, pp. 84–6, 119. Marx, as later revealed, authored most of the book.

When the Prussian army brutally suppressed a strike of silk weavers in Silesia in June 1844, it laid bare the class nature of the state, and from this event Marx and Engels drew their most important political conclusion. Only if the proletariat organised itself politically and took state power could it liberate itself. That was the only piece still missing in their road to communism. Just as Douglass was defending the apolitical stance of the Garrisonians, Marx was concluding that politics was the sine qua non for 'true democracy', i.e., 'human emancipation'.

Marx and Douglass came within a few weeks of being in England at the same time, the only time they could have met at that moment. Marx's six-week visit to Manchester and London with Engels in July–August 1845 preceded Douglass's arrival in Liverpool at the end of August. The visit reinforced Marx's decision to prioritise the working class. He could now put faces on his claims about the revolutionary potential of the workers. Not only was this visit an opportunity to see advanced capitalism with his own eyes but, even more important, to meet the proletarian fighters about whom Engels had been writing and talking. And among them were the proletarian Irish nationalists, the sisters Mary and Lydia Burns, both of whom were long-term romantic partners of Engels.[94] The radical sisters introduced the two young German communists, especially Marx, to the Irish nationalist struggle for self-determination shortly before Douglass learned during his visit to Ireland that the Irish were an oppressed nationality within the British Empire. Meetings and discussions between Marx and Engels, the militant Chartists, and German workers from the League of the Just resulted in the establishment in September 1845 of the first, though short-lived, international worker's organisation, the Society of Fraternal Democrats, though Marx and Engels were unable to attend its premier assembly. Also during this momentous visit to England, Marx had an opportunity to use the libraries there to do research for what would eventually become his magnum opus. It was Engels, by the way, more than anyone, who insisted that Marx get down to writing *Capital*, which would be completed almost a quarter of a century later.

All the aforementioned practical experiences and theoretical insights were distilled in Marx's famous three-page 'Theses on Feuerbach' of 1845. They are a critique of the best that philosophy had to offer Marx at that stage in his trajectory – the materialist perspective of German philosopher Ludwig Feuerbach

---

[94] Mary, four years older than Lydia, was Engels's partner initially until she died in 1863 and was replaced by Lydia, whom Engels married hours before her death to appease her Christian faith.

(1804–72). The thread that runs through all of Marx's kernels of wisdom is the need to bring human actions into 'the materialist doctrine', particularly, *'revolutionary practice'* for both the 'educator' and 'society' as a whole – the fourth thesis. And, as if in summation of his argument – an actual line precedes this unlike the other theses – he gave his famous eleventh and last thesis: 'The philosophers have only *interpreted* the world in various ways; the point is to *change* it'.[95] Nothing captures better what would distinguish the once postdoctoral philosophy student from the world in which he had come of age intellectually than the fourth and eleventh of the theses.

The overall problem with Feuerbach, as Marx explained to one-time colleague Arnold Ruge a year earlier, was that he 'refers too much to nature and too little to politics. That, however, is the only alliance by which present-day philosophy can become truth'.[96] Yet to be determined who 'present-day philosophy' had to ally with, the real world of politics and political activity were now Marx's calling. The 'Theses on Feuerbach' were for him like a divorce settlement with philosophy.[97] While Douglass had concluded by 1841 that joining Garrison's movement would make him a more efficacious abolitionist, it wasn't until four years later that Marx concluded that he too needed to join a movement, the workers movement. Unlike Douglass, Marx arrived at that conclusion through intellectual reasoning informed by his readings and analyses of history, from which he deduced that there was the need for a political party to build the workers movement – another key difference from Douglass.

When Douglass's *Narrative* appeared in 1845, Marx and Engels were writing *The German Ideology*, a more collaborative project than *The Holy Family*. It was both a final settling of accounts with German intellectual traditions as well as, more significantly, a detailed declaration of what the Marx-Engels team stood for. Though never published in their lifetime, they wrote it, as Engels later said, 'for self-clarification'. A detailed review of its content would take this presentation too far afield for present purposes. Suffice it to say that its key claims would soon find their way into subsequent publications such as Marx's 1847 critique of

---

95 Marx and Engels 1975–2004d, pp. 3–8.
96 Marx and Engels 1975–2004a, p. 400.
97 I am indebted to Sergio Valverde who reminded me (private communication) that Hegel continued to exercise a major influence on Marx, especially in *Capital*, such as in his analysis of value. For a defence of Hegel's speculative method, see Valverde 2017. Marx's aforementioned 'onanism' jab was probably a polemical excess as often happens in such debates. Yet, Marx failed to complete his magnum opus exactly because of the priority he gave, unlike the world of philosophy that he critiqued, to 'revolutionary practice' as detailed in Chapters 3, 4 and 5; hence the significance of the fourth and eleventh Feuerbach theses.

the two-volume tome of the French anarchist Joseph Proudhon, *The Poverty of Philosophy*. Two points are worth noting about that critique for the Marx/Douglass comparison.

First, the topic of slavery. Five years after his brief comments in 1842, Marx offered a more informed opinion that registered his deep dive into the political economy literature. He took issue with what he considered Proudhon's simplistic understanding of Hegel's dialectic, specifically that all economic categories have 'two sides – one good, the other bad ... The problem to be solved: to keep the good side, while eliminating the bad'. If this was true, then what about slavery?

> *Slavery* is an economic category like any other. Thus it also has its two sides. Let us leave alone the bad side and talk about the good side of slavery. Needless to say, we are dealing only with direct slavery, with Negro slavery in Surinam, in Brazil, in the Southern States of North America.
>
> Direct slavery is just as much the pivot of bourgeois industry as machinery, credits, etc. Without slavery you have no cotton; without cotton you have no modern industry. It is slavery that gave the colonies their value; it is the colonies that created world trade, and it is world trade that is the precondition of large-scale industry. Thus slavery is an economic category of the greatest importance.
>
> Without slavery North America, the most progressive of countries, would be transformed into a patriarchal country. Wipe North America off the map of the world, and you will have anarchy – the complete decay of modern commerce and civilization. Cause slavery to disappear and you will have wiped America off the map of nations.[98]

Marx, of course, was not defending the institution of slavery but, rather, illustrating the inadequacies of Proudhon's method and the superiority of the perspective that he and Engels were promoting, namely 'the materialist concep-

---

98 Marx and Engels 1975–2004e, p. 167. Engels, for the 1885 German edition, added the following note: 'This was perfectly correct for the year 1847. At that time the world trade of the United States was limited mainly to import of immigrants and industrial products, and export of cotton and tobacco, i.e., of the products of southern slave labour. The Northern States produced mainly corn and meat for the slave states. It was only when the North produced corn and meat for export and also became an industrial country, and when the American cotton monopoly had to face powerful competition, in India, Egypt, Brazil, etc., that the abolition of slavery became possible. And even then this led to the ruin of the South, which did not succeed in replacing the open Negro slavery by the disguised slavery of Indian and Chinese coolies'.

tion of history', i.e., the modern communist theoretical perspective. A more informed understanding of Hegel taught that 'the good' – and also 'the bad' – is often riddled with contradictions. Proudhon's 'good and bad' distinction resembled the normative 'good and evil' character of natural rights and law that Douglass subscribed to – inadequate in Marx's view for explaining social reality. Prior to Marx, no one had offered a rational explanation for the origins of modern capitalism via 'the peculiar institution', and, thus, why so many would be willing to defend it, even with their lives – and, more consequentially, the lives of others. These were the premises Marx brought to the table when Fort Sumter was fired upon.[99] For Douglass, again, the 'peculiar institution' owed its existence to age-old 'selfishness, which leads one man to prey upon the rights and interests of his fellow-man'. For Marx, on the other hand, the very logic of the capitalist mode of production, and not just personal greed, explained why the ancient institution was alive and profitable on the other side of the Atlantic. More importantly, the 'slave-economy', he predicted five months later in 1847, would 'provoke the most fearful conflicts in the southern states of republican North America'. This was Marx at his prescient best.[100]

Marx complemented his critique of Proudhon's faulty understanding of the dialectic with another take on slavery a few months later in a lecture in Brussels, later published under the title 'Wage Labour and Capital'. That slavery was still on Marx's brain is of significance for this book. To explain what capital consists of, he offered an example. 'What is a Negro slave? A man of the black race. The one explanation is as good as the other. A Negro is a Negro. He only becomes a slave in certain relations. A cotton-spinning jenny is a machine for spinning cotton. It becomes *capital* only in certain relations. Torn from these relationships it is no more capital than *gold* in itself is *money* or sugar the *price* of sugar'.[101] Marx was interrogating the concept 'Negro'. By the mid-nineteenth century, in the Atlantic world at least, the category 'Negro' had become increasingly synonymous with servitude. This was especially true in the slave states in the United States where with each succeeding decade of the century the laws and courts made the condition of 'free Blacks' increasingly impossible – what visitors like Gustave de Beaumont and Thomas Hamilton had taught Marx.

---

99   Defenders of chattel slavery had long argued, à la John Calhoun, that without slavery no civilization. Marx's unique contribution was to link the nefarious institution to capital's Industrial Revolution. John Stuart Mill's discussion of the topic in his 1848 *Principles of Political Economy* did not make the connection; see libertyfund.org/title/mill-principles-of-political-economy-ashley-ed#lfo199_label_651.
100 Marx and Engels 1975–2004e, p. 325.
101 Marx and Engels 1975–2004g, p. 211.

In that historical context – in which 'race' meant something similar to ethnicity (see the next chapter) – Marx, therefore, challenged the racist conclusions about Blacks that derived from their oppression and exploitation. That in the very next sentence he employed the example of the 'cotton jenny' is not coincidental.[102]

Engels, meanwhile, in what proved to be the second draft for the *Communist Manifesto*, made definitional distinctions on the topic. '*Slaves* ... in the southern parts of the United States', along with '*serfs*' in then central Europe and Russia, were members of 'the working classes' that could be traced back to antiquity. What distinguished the slave from the modern 'proletarian' is that the 'slave is sold once and for all, [while] the proletarian has to sell himself by the day and by the hour ... The slave frees himself by abolishing, among all the private property relationships, only the relationship of slavery and thereby only then himself becomes a proletarian; the proletarian can free himself only by abolishing private property in general'.[103] This difference between the chattel slave and the proletarian 'wage slave' was crucial in distinguishing the project of Engels and his partner from that of Douglass. Nota bene the matter of 'private property in general', the abolition of which was so essentially determinative for the Marx-Engels team. Douglass, on the other hand, a fierce opponent of ownership of persons, proclaimed in a letter published in his newly founded newspaper, *The North Star*, about a year later in 1848 and contra 'Mr. Inglis', the land reformer who spoke at the Rhode Island Anti-Slavery Society, that to

> own the soil is no harm in itself. It was given to man. It is right that he should own it. It is his duty to possess it – and to possess it in that way in which its energies and properties can be made the most useful to the human family – now and always. There is therefore no wrong in the fact of holding property in the soil itself.[104]

Douglass, in other words, instantiated exactly Engels's point. Ending slavery implied nothing about ending 'private property in general'. Peter Myers, in an

---

102 For a tendentious reading of what Marx sought to convey, see Hund 2021, p. 80. We address Hund's claims in Appendix B: Marx and Engels on the Race Question: A Response to the Critics.
103 Marx and Engels 1975–2004e, pp. 343–4. Engels's distinction, most relevant for our book, didn't make it into Marx's final version of the *Manifesto*, Marx and Engels 1975–2004e, p. 495.
104 Foner 1975, p. 105. See Buccola 2012, p. 53. In April 1849 Douglass gave a defence of the Lockean theory of property in the soil. See Blassingame 1982, p. 165.

article praising Douglass for rebuffing revolutionary excesses writes, 'He rejected as "arrant nonsense" the socialists' conflation of one illegitimate property claim with all private property claims'.[105]

The other point worth noting about Marx's critique of Proudhon was the latter's assumption, according to Marx, that *'Providence* is the locomotive' that drives society towards what Proudhon considered to be the default position of social organisation – 'equality'. This resembled Douglass's natural rights/law understanding of individual and social reality in general. 'Providence, providential aim, this is the great word used today to explain the march of history. In fact, this word explains nothing', Marx countered. 'It is at most a rhetorical form, one of the various ways of paraphrasing facts'.[106] Again, the clear epistemological/theoretical divide between Marx and Douglass revealed itself long before the Civil War.

Marx's critique of constitutional monarchy took on new meaning when the Louis-Philippe regime, due to pressure from Berlin, expelled him, wife Jenny, and daughter Jenny from France in February 1845. His writings, even from afar, increasingly alarmed the Hohenzollern absolutist monarchy of Frederick William IV. After relocating to Brussels, Marx set out to do, with the assistance of both Jenny and Engels, what was implicit in the eleventh of the Feuerbach theses – build a political party. Toward that goal, Engels, unlike Marx who was still a persona non grata in Germany, went on a speaking tour there in spring 1845 to make a case for their new project. Effective party building, Engels explained in a letter to his new partner, entailed more than literary production: 'standing up in front of real, live people and holding forth to them directly and straightforwardly, so that they see and hear you is something quite different from engaging in this devilishly abstract quillpushing with an abstract audience in one's mind's eye'.[107] Engels's insightful epiphany about a unique feature of modernity resonates even more so in the all so alienating world of virtual hypertext – 'quillpushing' on steroids. Douglass, 'the Reverend', knew firsthand the truth Engels discovered even before he joined Garrison's movement.

Marx's and Engels's party building activities first bore fruit with the Committees for Communist Correspondence, formed in 1846 with Brussels as its headquarters inside Marx's home. Its purpose was to foster communication between communist currents in various countries – including in the United States – and to build a communist party in Germany. A German émigré in New

---

105 Myers 2013, p. 125.
106 Marx and Engels 1975–2004e, p. 173.
107 Marx and Engels 1975–2004r, p. 23.

York, Hermann Kriege, who claimed to be a representative of German communism, was the target of a critical circular that Marx and Engels wrote in 1846 on behalf of the Committees. Basically, they charged him with promoting land reform as the primary aim of the communist project. Communists, they argued, did indeed support land reform in America but as a means, not as an end, which they acknowledged two years later in their *Communist Manifesto*. They accused Kriege of acting opportunistically by pandering to the increasingly popular homestead movement. Their circular helped to clip Kriege's pseudo-communist wings, an intervention which in hindsight stood the future German communist movement in America in good stead. The reason for this is that the land reform movement never truly embraced abolition; many land reformers abstained from taking a position on the question of slavery's abolition, and some, in fact, were hostile to abolitionism.[108] What came to be called 'the Marx party' in America had never, therefore, been misguided by abstentionism on the slavery question – nor for that matter, as noted earlier, by 'socialists' like John Collins who Douglass had criticised for minimising the abolition question. To the contrary, Marx party members were fully primed – as will be seen in subsequent chapters – to step forward and play a vanguard role when the opportunity presented itself to put a dagger into the heart of America's 'peculiar institution'.

The Committees of Correspondence brought the young duo to the attention of the League of the Just, a German worker's current in exile in London, Paris, and Brussels. The League invited them to join their fraternity, to which the two agreed. Both sides had conditions for the union: the Marx-Engels team insisted that the League abandon its semi-clandestine mode of operation and change its name to the League of Communists; and the League insisted that the two intellectuals draft a document that stated the program and aims of the new organisation. Thus, the birth of the *Manifesto of the Communist Party*.[109] Marx, working with two drafts by Engels, finally finished composing the forty-odd page document on 24 January 1848. Exactly a month later, it came off the press in London, the same day that Louis-Philippe was dethroned by the force of a mass uprising that erupted two days earlier in Paris, the uprising which ignited the European Spring. Seldom in history has a text been so timely. Never to be forgotten is how Engels in late 1847, in response to the charges of an opponent, described the project he and his partner had just helped to launch. 'Communism is not a doctrine but a movement; it proceeds not from principles but from

---

108 For details, see Nimtz 2003, pp. 52–8.
109 For an overview of Marx and Engels' party building activities see Nimtz 2016b.

facts ... Communism, insofar as it is a theory, is the theoretical expression of the position of the proletariat in this struggle and the theoretical summation of the conditions for the liberation of the proletariat'.[110] That's the frame which informed his partner's response to the events recovered in this book.

∵

Just as Marx was laying the groundwork for his party building activities, Douglass was wrapping up his visit to Britain. Like Marx, Douglass was also impacted by the meetings he had with the Chartists, causing him, again, to rethink Garrisonian opposition to politics. But there was a big difference between what Marx and Douglass took away from the encounters, especially because Marx had already concluded a few years earlier that politics was necessary. Specifically, they differed about which class to look to for effective agents of radical social change. For Douglass, owing to his American experience, moderate middle-class liberal reformers seemed to be the answer. 'Socially', in the opinion of one biographer, 'Douglass reached upward, rather than outward to the laborers, one of whom he had been not so long ago'.[111] No wonder he gravitated to the non-militant Moral Force wing of the Chartist movement. For Marx, however, only the proletariat, that new social layer modernity had brought into existence, had, owing to its class position, an inherent interest in abolishing and, more importantly, the capacity to abolish social inequality, the prerequisite, as his 'materialist conception of history' posited, for 'human emancipation'. His meetings with working-class Chartists steeled his determination to prioritise history's newest toilers for the communist project to abolish not only chattel slavery but all forms of social oppression, in order to realise 'true democracy'.

Nothing distinguished the two subjects of this comparison more from one another than what they desired as a final goal: one of them sought only to abolish chattel slavery in North America, while the other sought the same but as the necessary means to the end of abolishing class society. This key difference anticipated how both would view and respond to the approaching history-changing conflagration and its aftermath.

---

110 Marx and Engels 1975–2004e, pp. 303–4. The opponent, Karl Heinzen, eventually found his way to Boston where he sought, unsuccessfully, to influence abolitionists like Wendell Phillips. See Honneck 2011, Chapter Five.
111 McFeely 1991, p. 152.

CHAPTER 2

Prelude to the Conflagration: From Paris to Fort Sumter

> The revolution of France ... has aroused the world from its stupor.
> DOUGLASS, 1848

∴

> Their battle cry must be: Revolution in Permanence.
> MARX AND ENGELS, 1850

∴

> The car of emancipation is advancing gloriously ... the shouts of millions ... go up in joy over the freedom of the Russian serf.
> DOUGLASS, 1860

∴

> ... the most momentous thing happening in the world today is the slave movement ... on the one hand in America, started by the death of Brown, and in Russia, on the other ... the signal has now been given.
> MARX TO ENGELS, 1860

∴

In the second sentence of his 1863 Gettysburg Address, Abraham Lincoln declared: 'Now we are engaged in a great civil war, testing whether that nation, or any nation so conceived and so dedicated, can long endure'. As the first sentence made clear, 'that nation' referred to the 1776 project: 'conceived in Liberty and dedicated to the proposition that all men are created equal'. The bloodletting at Gettysburg, Lincoln resolved, was not 'in vain' but for 'a new birth of freedom – and [so] that government of the people, by the people and for the people', that is, republican government, 'shall not perish from the earth'. Less clear is what Lincoln meant by 'can long endure'.[1]

We argue that the 'new birth of freedom', the Civil War, actually began with the European Spring, the 1848 democratic republican revolutions – not unlike how 1848 itself was a 'new birth of freedom' for the French Revolution of 1789, the most consequential echo of 1776. Lincoln was a 'republican internationalist', like so many of his colleagues, and it was from that vantage that his point in the second sentence, 'can long endure', is to be understood.[2] Like the Arab Spring of 2011–12, the mid-nineteenth century democratic opening did not 'long endure'.[3] Lincoln, like other champions of republicanism, was all too aware of the sobering fact that radical egalitarian projects had slim chances for survival. Despite that history, the democratic breakthroughs in Europe between 1848 and 1849 heartened democratic forces in the Americas to emulate likeminded activists on the other side of the Atlantic. The United States Civil War was not only a 'new birth of freedom' or an extension of what began in 1776, it was also a belated echo of the 1848 European Spring, the second edition of 1789, as well as the Haitian Revolution of 1791 – all intertwined. Frederick Douglass, like Lincoln, took hope in the upheavals in Europe in which Karl Marx was one of several prominent protagonists.

This chapter, with an eye on April 1861, the Confederate attack on Fort Sumter, begins with the European Spring Revolutions of 1848 and the responses of Marx and Douglass. The bulk of the chapter then distils from that moment their responses to the key events in the decade-long lead-up to Lincoln's election in November 1860. It ends with the especially fraught situation six weeks after Lincoln's Inaugural Address.

1   The European Spring

Suffering from the first transnational economic depression of the modern era, the Parisian working class rose up and took to the streets at the end of February 1848, forcing France's last monarch Louis-Philippe to flee to England.

---

1 Fehrenbacher 1989, p. 536.
2 For a concurring interpretation, see Potter 2011, p. 16. On Lincoln and his cohorts' republican internationalist credentials, see Doyle 2015, pp. 281–4. On the impact of the 1848 upheavals on Lincoln, see Mason 2013 and Honeck, 2011. One of the first monographs to argue for the transatlantic character of the mid-nineteenth century abolition movement is Roberts, 'Epilogue', 2009.
3 Weyland 2012.

Their demands for economic relief and social benefits quickly fused with the already active liberal-democratic bourgeois campaign in Western Europe to extend voting rights and expand civil liberties – i.e., to restore in France and to institute for the first time in Germany the republican project. Thus began the 1848 Revolutions which, as a result, gave birth to the modern movements for social democracy as well as, concomitantly, communism. Almost fifty similar uprisings took place in Europe in the first four months of 1848, with subsequent echoes in the Americas.[4]

1.1   *Marx in the Cauldron*

Like many other politicos at the time in Western Europe, Marx and Engels accurately anticipated the upheavals – what their just published *Manifesto of the Communist Party* registered. The facts and events outlined in the previous chapter prepared them for this insurrectionary period both programmatically and organisationally, as is well documented.[5] Distilled here are the key reasons why and the main ways how Marx would respond to America's 'new birth of freedom'.

Marx was dead serious about his conclusion three years earlier that philosophers need to change the world. He threw himself into the revolts at personal risk to life, limb, and family but as part of a collective, the Communist League. After a few nights in prison in Brussels and a move to Paris, family in tow, the Central Authority of the organisation, its executive, elected Marx as its chair, conferred with 'full discretionary power for the temporary central direction of all League affairs'.[6] From revolutionary Paris he organised and led in early April the return of the exiled League members to revolutionary Germany. Its plebeian masses in Berlin, inspired by their cohorts in Paris three weeks earlier, had taken to the streets on 18 March and forced the Prussian regime to appear to be willing to make republican concessions. The primary task, therefore, of 'communists' in Germany, as explained in the last paragraphs of the *Manifesto*, was to 'fight [in alliance] with the bourgeoisie as long as it acts in a revolutionary way against the absolute monarchy, the feudal squirearchy, and the petty bourgeoisie'.[7] No instructions, to be seen later, better explain the actions of the exiled Marx party in the United States a decade later than that directive.

---

[4]   Christopher Clark's *Revolutionary Spring*, 2023, now constitutes the most comprehensive account.
[5]   See especially, Nimtz 2000, Chapters Two to Five.
[6]   Nimtz 2000, p. 62.
[7]   Nimtz 2000, p. 60. We employ here the qualifier 'as long as', in the original document, as

The most impactful action Marx took, with Engels's indispensable assistance, was to begin to publish in Cologne on 1 June 1848 a communist party newspaper inside Germany – the New Rhineland Newspaper (*Neue Rheinische Zeitung*, or NRZ), the first of its kind. Noteworthy was its subhead – 'Organ of Democracy'. Its raison d'être, Marx explained two years later, was 'its daily intervention in the [democratic] movement and speaking directly from the heart of the movement, its reflecting day-to-day history in all its amplitude, the continuous and impassioned interaction between the people and the daily press'.[8] Such a publication testified to the new political space now available in Prussian Germany, so unlike the scene in 1843 when the original Rhineland Newspaper that Marx briefly edited was forced to shut down.

The NRZ became a communist teaching tool to inform, amongst other things, about the democratic movement elsewhere. For example, its readers were rewarded with news from the United States in the 6 July 1848 issue, specifically a report by an unnamed correspondent in Boston about a recent antislavery convention there. It criticised the gathering: 'the members and speakers took to the field with taunts against the planters and the system, but took no practical step to abolish it. They contented themselves with scolding, moral persuasion and collecting more and more money in order to pay 'lecturers' (wandering speakers) and newspaper publishers. All of this will undoubtedly be just as effective in reforming and softening the hearts of men of the South as a short rain shower in summer'.[9] Because Douglass had not yet broken with Garrisonian 'moral persuasion' abolitionism, did he exemplify that brand of abolitionism that Marx's newspaper had criticised, feckless abolitionism characterised by 'wandering speakers' and 'newspaper publishers'?[10] The extant record, unfortunately, is inconclusive.

With Marx as its editor, the NRZ effectively became the organising centre for the Communist League's activism during Germany's iteration of the European Spring. With a readership of six thousand and 'one of the largest and most passionately read newspapers in Germany', the NRZ put Marx in the crosshairs of

---

opposed to 'whenever' in the subsequent edition now widely recognised as the standard version. See Draper 1994, pp. 320–1, for the significance of the change.

8   Nimtz 2000, pp. 70–1.
9   *Neue Rheinische Zeitung*, https://www.deutschestextarchiv.de/nrhz/?d=nn_nrhz036_1848.txt.xml
10 By 1855 Douglass would agree with the critique from the correspondent of the NRZ. The Garrisonians and their slogan '*no union with slaveholders*' were a 'mere expression of abhorrence of slavery, the sentiment is a good one; but it expresses no intelligible principle of action, and throws no light on the pathway of duty'. P. Foner 1950b, p. 351. See also Jackson 2021, p. 158.

Prussian authorities.[11] 'Herr Marx (!)', wrote the Cologne military commander in a memo in February 1849, 'is becoming increasingly more audacious ... He takes the Liberty ... in his increasingly popular paper ... to promote even greater feelings of discontent and indirectly calling on the people to revolt'.[12] Not for naught were Marx and other League members charged with 'incitement to rebellion' along with 'defamation of character'. Marx's expert familiarity with Prussian law, however, and his display of that fact in testimony before a jury trial led to his and his comrades' acquittal.

The renown of the NRZ and its editor came to the attention of Charles Dana, managing editor of Horace Greeley's influential *New York Daily Tribune*, a publication that was representative, as Marx put it, of the 'industrial bourgeoisie of America'.[13] During a tour of revolutionary Europe in 1848, Dana hired Marx to be a regular correspondent. As one of the most popular newspapers in the US, if not the world, from 1852 to 1862 the NYDT provided Marx with the kind of broadcast platform he hadn't had before or after his employment with the periodical. Greeley 'introduced his new European correspondent by saying Marx had "very decided opinions of his own", but he was "one of the most instructive sources of information on the great questions of current European politics"'.[14]

Marx's *Tribune* articles brought him to the attention of Henry Carey, the first major economist in the US and an admirer of the communist's NYDT articles. Carey's admiration was evidence for Marx, the historical materialist, of the then still underdeveloped character of US capitalism.[15] 'In the United States', he noted in a March 1852 letter to Joseph Weydemeyer, a recent League émigré there, 'bourgeois society is still far too immature for the class struggle to be made perceptible and comprehensible' – which is why Carey, Marx inferred, could laud his political writings. Economic categories like 'capital', 'wages', and 'profit' for Carey were 'rather than being conditions of struggle and antagonisms ... conditions of association and harmony' – exactly the opposite of Marx's position.[16] Another avid reader of Greeley's paper was the future sixteenth president, Abraham Lincoln and, no doubt, Douglass as well – the significance

---

11   Nimtz 2000, p. 78.
12   Nimtz 2000, p. 99.
13   Marx and Engels 1975–2004s, p. 346.
14   Doyle 2015, p. 150. See also, Borden 1957. 'Marx's columns brought forth more responses, favorable as well as unfavorable, than those of any other foreign correspondent of the *Tribune*' (p. 457n3).
15   Carey later went on to be a major figure in the Republican Party, including an economic advisor to Lincoln. See Rossi 2019.
16   Marx and Engels 1975–2004s, p. 62.

of which will be discussed shortly. Both of them shared Carey's reverence for class harmony, symptomatic of capitalism's low level of development in America.[17]

Though Marx escaped jail time, the charges against him, particularly 'inciting rebellion', signalled the ebbing and eventual demise of Germany's participation in the 1848 revolutions; political space was beginning to shrink. Forced to shut down the NRZ, Marx with panache published on 19 May 1849 twenty thousand copies of the famous final issue of the newspaper, known as 'the red issue' because it was printed all in red ink to highlight the injustice of its brutal suppression by the tyrannical German monarchy. Marx and family soon went into involuntary exile for the second time while Engels, with Marx's encouragement, went on to participate in the final months of the armed struggle.[18]

Germany's chapter in the European Spring was dependent from the beginning on developments in France. The bloody defeat of the uprising of the Parisian proletariat in June 1848 was in hindsight the beginning of the end of the mid-nineteenth-century democratic quest. Its winter became official after Louis Napoleon Bonaparte orchestrated a coup d'état in December 1851, bringing an end to France's Second Republic, and crowned himself emperor a year later. Germany's brief moment in the republican sun also came to an abortive end. The task for communists was to draw a balance sheet on the events in order to prepare for an expected resurgence of the revolutions.

Revolution and Counter-Revolution in Germany, the first of their balance sheets on the events that had just transpired, was written by Engels though attributed to Marx. It was serialised in the NYDT in 1851–2 and was thus the first Marx party document to be published originally in English. Publishing in the US was easier for them than publishing in Germany owing to newly imposed censorship laws there. The publication of the most famous balance sheet, Marx's *Eighteenth Brumaire of Louis Bonaparte*, was facilitated by Weydemeyer who was in New York City. Slightly more than a hundred pages, it was Marx's summary analysis on the ascent and descent of the 1848 French

---

17 Douglass's embrace of Carey's position was most pronounced after the War as he sought to convince workers through his newspaper and in the Colored National Labor Union of the harmony of interests between capital and labour. As he editorialised in 1871, 'Capital and labor meet and part as friends in these columns'. 'Position of the New National Era', *New National Era*, 30 March 1871. More on Douglass and his shift to reformism and class collaborationism in Appendix A: Douglass and Marx on the Paris Commune and the Labor Question in the United States.

18 The details are unknown because Marx, Engels and other League members destroyed much of their correspondence and related documents when they fled to prevent German authorities from knowing.

Revolution. Like *Revolution and Counter-Revolution*, it was required reading for Communist League members and supporters who not only remained in Europe but were regrouping on the other side of the Atlantic.

The political message at the heart of both narratives was that the 1848 European democratic quest had been aborted due not only to the cowardice of the liberal bourgeoisie but also to that of the petit bourgeois democrats. Both social classes proved to be far more fearful of the increasingly assertive proletarian masses – as exemplified by the Paris uprising in June 1848 – than of the retrogressive, suppressive and reactionary manoeuvrings of the still extant *ancien régimes*, i.e., monarchy, aristocracy, and theocracy. Both bourgeois and petit bourgeois liberals feared that the republican overthrow of the *ancien régimes* would be, as the *Manifesto* proposed, 'the prelude to an immediately following proletarian revolution'. They weren't alone, as we will see shortly, in their trepidation.

Less well known is Marx's and Engels's eleven page 'Address of March 1850 of the Central Authority of the Communist League'. Forced into exile in London, the third for him and his family, Marx now had breathing room to assess the two previous years. A rare self-criticism in their arsenal, the 'Address' sought to correct Marx's decision to suspend the Communist League and merge it into the larger democratic movement. Enabling that policy was the position he took at the meeting of the Cologne Workers' Association in January 1849 about the upcoming elections to the Prussian Diet: 'Citizen Marx is also of the opinion that the Workers' Association ... would not be able to get candidates elected now ... [P]lain common sense demands that if we realise that we cannot get our own view of principle accepted in elections, we should unite with another party, also in opposition, so as not to allow our common enemy, the absolute monarchy, to win'.[19]

The 1850 Address directed League members to act differently in the expected revival of the revolutionary movement in order to make sure that the next time it would be a 'Revolution in Permanence'. Place no trust, it advised, in the petit bourgeois liberals; alliances with them were permitted but unity must be refused, unlike the previous strategy. Instead, the workers' movement should pursue independent working-class political action. In the next elections, contrary to what Marx had once advised, the worker's party should run its own candidates 'even where there is no prospect whatsoever of their being elected ... in order to preserve their independence, to count their forces and to lay before the public their revolutionary attitude and party standpoint'. They

---

19   Marx and Engels 1975–2004f, p. 514.

PRELUDE TO THE CONFLAGRATION: FROM PARIS TO FORT SUMTER 61

should have no fear that by doing so 'they are splitting the democratic party and giving the reactionaries the possibility of victory'. The advantages of 'independent action' for the proletariat, the 'Address' advised, far outweighed the disadvantages 'that might be incurred by the presence of a few reactionaries in the representative body'.[20] When anti-slavery activists on the other side of the Atlantic like Douglass decided almost at the same moment to engage in electoral politics for the first time, they too, like the Marx party, had to grapple with the choice of forming alliances to support the 'lesser evil' candidate or party versus 'splitting' the progressive vote by prioritising independent political action.

But of utmost importance for Marx and Engels – and in stark contrast to Douglass, as will be seen – elections were not an end in themselves but rather a useful means to the end of making a proletarian revolution.[21] A term Engels coined in the heat of the German Revolution articulated that orientation. The affliction of 'parliamentary cretinism' was to believe, as the liberals typically did, that the legislative arena, and, thus, being elected to legislatures, was the be-all and end-all of politics. Politics was ultimately decided, Marx and Engels countered, outside parliaments on the barricades, in the streets, and on the battlefields.

Contrary to Marx's and Engels's expectations, there was no immediate revival of the revolutionary movement. For that reason, many League members eventually left Germany, voluntarily or involuntarily, and the Communist League was formally put to rest by Marx and Engels in 1852. The United States became the destination of many, such as Weydemeyer, along with other participants in the German revolution, who eventually came to be referred to as the 'Forty Eighters'. Marx considered doing the same but realised he had leadership responsibilities in Europe because it was there that the possibility existed, and not in America, for the first successful proletarian revolution.

Marx continued to direct what was left of the League until it was clear that chapter in the history of the modern communist movement had ended. An ersatz party through informal contact, one in waiting until the next major upsurge in the class struggle, was all that needed to be maintained.[22] In the meantime, 'I hope', Marx told Weydemeyer, 'to win a scientific victory for our party'.[23] The research and writing for what would become his magnum opus in

---

20   Marx and Engels 1975–2004i, p. 284. Of significance, the document became Lenin's playbook for the drama of 1917; see Nimtz, 2017.
21   See Nimtz 2019a, Chapter One.
22   See Nimtz 2000, Chapter Six for how that was done.
23   Marx and Engels 1975–2004t, p. 377.

1867, *Capital*, took precedence. Along the way, Marx, with Engels's assistance, continued to pump out pieces for the *NYDT*, employment that was needed, literally, to keep food on the table for him and his family. Worth noting are the first articles that Marx wrote on the English elections in 1852, with particular focus on the Chartists, a topic that would have been of interest to at least one reader of the *NYDT* – Douglass.[24]

With Engels having recently moved to Manchester, Marx's correspondence with him became even more important. Most noteworthy in that era for our purposes here was Marx's comment about a book by the aforementioned economist Henry Carey entitled *The Slave Trade, Domestic and Foreign* (1853), a copy of which Carey had just gifted to Marx.

> The only thing of definite interest in the book is the comparison between Negro slavery as formerly practiced by the English in Jamaica and elsewhere, and Negro slavery in the United States. He demonstrates how the main STOCK of Negroes in Jamaica always consisted of freshly imported BARBARIANS, [Carey's language] since their treatment by the English meant not only that the Negro population was not maintained, but also that ⅔ of the yearly imports always went to waste, whereas the present generation of Negroes in America is a native product, more or less Yankeefied, English speaking, etc., and hence *capable of being emancipated* [italics in original].[25]

Within a decade, events on the ground would verify Marx's assessment. No one would epitomise 'capable of being emancipated' more than Douglass. Not their first trans-Atlantic mind-meld.

Once permanently settled in America, Weydemeyer, along with another Communist League member, Adolph Cluss, began doing the spadework for what would become the Marx party in the US. The significance of that initial groundwork, with little direction from Marx owing to his preoccupation with 'scientific work', would reveal itself at the end of the decade as the coming conflagration approached. Not to be ignored is the fact, discussed briefly in Chapter 1, that Marx had made clear that abstention on the slavery question was impermissible for a communist. Cluss and Weydemeyer were able to build upon that directive.

---

24 Marx and Engels 1975–2004i, pp. 327–53.
25 Marx and Engels 1975–2004s, p. 346. In the MECW small caps designate the original English rendering employed by Marx and Engels. Regarding 'Barbarians' see, Slack 2023.

1.2   Douglass: a Wary Cheerleader from Afar

If Marx's relationship to the European Spring is almost self-evident, for Douglass that's not the case. Yet, recent scholarship reveals that the upheavals inspired him. Douglass's nineteen-month visit to Great Britain in 1845–7 primed him to be attentive to political developments in Europe. The Chartist movement in particular, specifically the moderate Moral Force wing rather than the militant wing, taught Douglass the importance of electoral political work, moving him to rethink the Garrisonian rejection of voting. Not long after his return to the US, he resettled in Rochester, NY, no longer in Garrison's orbit in Boston, and founded his own weekly newspaper in late 1847. Whether the Chartist *Northern Star* newspaper was an inspiration for Douglass's *North Star* is uncertain. More certain is that his encounter with them convinced Douglass that for the abolitionist movement to be effective it needed to engage the electoral arena. His newspaper, along with his public speaking, would be the means for doing so. Marx's NRZ, a daily, founded nine months after the *North Star*, also existed for political ends not limited to the electoral arena. Not to be forgotten, the Chartist movement also had a major impact on Marx, but tellingly, unlike for Douglass, its militant wing was what inspired Marx. Their example confirmed what had been until then only a theoretical construct for Marx – the political potential of the working class, in its broadest sense.

So when the Parisian masses took to the streets in February 1848 to force France's monarch to flee, thereby establishing France's Second Republic while inspiring cohorts elsewhere in Europe to do the same, Douglass and likeminded liberals elsewhere were elated.[26] But something else beyond the republican cause came with the February Revolution that was no doubt more decisive for Douglass – namely, the abolition of slavery. After all, he was still an admirer of the foremost constitutional monarchy in the world, the United Kingdom – the kind of regime the young Marx criticised Hegel for endorsing. Douglass continued to laud the UK monarchy because Britain had ended chattel slavery on 1 August 1834.

When the two-month-old Second Republic government abolished slavery in the French West Indies on 27 April 1848 – the first Republic had done the same in 1794 three years after the Haitian Revolution had begun, but Napoleon revived the institution – Douglass took heart: 'hopeful aspects of the time'. He heaped praise on the new government's Justice Minister for greeting 'the black and mulatto men that come to congratulate them', addressing them as 'friends! brothers! men!' Maybe, he wondered, the conditions that existed in France for

---

26   Clark 2023, p. 469. On the impact on other abolitionists, see Honeck 2011, Chapter One.

overthrowing Louis Philippe existed in America, enabling the 'uniting into one mighty phalanx of freemen to bring down the haughty citadel of slavery with all of its bloody towers and turrets'.[27] To an audience of 'working-men and mechanics of Rochester' in early May, Douglass extolled the 'Provisional Government of France' for having 'made and set in operation', so unlike the US republican government, 'measures which must bring about the entire overthrow of Slavery in all her dominions'.[28] For Douglass, abolition of slavery was paramount, the lens he employed, in evaluating the merits of a political system. Revolutionary France taught him that, once again, a government could be employed to that end. The 'grand movement of France' was encouraging. Benjamin Fagan examines Douglass's jubilant reaction:

> In an editorial on the Paris uprising of February 1848, Douglass argued that a 'revolution now cannot be confined to the place or the people where it may commence, but flashes with lightning speed from heart to heart, from land to land, till it has traversed the globe, compelling all the members of our common brotherhood at once, to pass judgment upon its merits ... The revolution of France, like a bolt of living thunder', he concluded, 'has aroused the world from its stupor'.[29]

Because Marx employed a more encompassing, wide-angle, and telescopic lens, the February Revolution for him was only the beginning of a much more comprehensive abolitionism involving the abolition of all social classes and with them wage slavery. Douglass, like his compatriot economist Carey, was the product of a society that lacked what was indispensable for Marx's historical materialist breakthrough – a millennial old class-based society. American chattel slavery for Marx was a species of the far older genus of class exploitation. The relationships between social classes rather than types of government, republican or not, determined the persistence of class exploitation and the form it took.

When Douglass learned that a Chartist remonstration in London on 10 April 1848, inspired by the republican movement on the continent, sought to peacefully deliver petitions with millions of signatures to parliament demanding universal male suffrage, he was livid. The protestors, never more than twenty-five thousand, had attempted, in his opinion, to 'overawe the government' in

---

27   Blassingame 1982, pp. 122, 127.
28   Blassingame 1982, p. 116.
29   Fagan 2021, p. 111. See also Fagan 2018, pp. 76–84.

a 'wild and wicked measure'.³⁰ There was no justification, he claimed, for the protest. 'While the liberty of speech is allowed – while the freedom of the press is permitted, and the right of petition is respected, and while men are left free to originate reforms without, and Members are left free to propose and advocate them within the walls of Parliament, no excuse can be valid for resorting to the fearful use of brute force and bloodshed'.³¹

One can only speculate as to why Douglass responded the way he did given the absence of any evidence to support his claims that the mass remonstration had been violent. It sounds like he relied on sources who violence-baited the protest, which was widely considered by friend and foe alike to have been feckless. His scepticism about the militant wing of the working-class Chartist movement during his visit to England, the organisers of the 10 April action, was likely also determinant in his misinformed evaluation that the peaceful protest had been violent. Whatever the case, he revealed probably for the first time his criteria for permitting the 'use of brute force and bloodshed'. Violence for Douglass was only valid when the oppressed were denied all civil liberties, as was the case with chattel slaves. When the oppressed possessed some civil liberties, they should use only peaceful means to press for social justice. This obvious inching away from a hitherto pacifist position on his part would become in a few years a full gallop for Douglass.

Engels, on the other hand, was hoping – Marx the same, no doubt – for exactly what Douglass feared. About the inept 10 April mass action, it 'was a mere bagatelle', just a trifling, non-violent prelude to the real thing. 'In a couple of months, my friend, *G. Julien Harney* [leader of the militant wing of the Chartists] … will be in [Prime Minister] Palmerston's shoes. I'LL BET YOU TWO PENCE AND IN FACT ANY SUM'.³² Never would Engels be so spectacularly wrong about the revolutionary process. Nonetheless, these two starkly different responses to 10 April reveal, we argue, the first moment in real-time politics that the fundamental political differences between Marx and Douglass became evident. If Douglass gave special place to what took place 'within the walls of Parliament', Marx and Engels took to task exactly that viewpoint, captured best in their soon to be coined 'parliamentary cretinism'.

Two months later this fundamental difference was on stark display once again. Angered by the termination of the national workshops by the liberal social democratic government that issued from the February Revolution, the

---

30 About the demonstration, see https://www.historytoday.com/archive/failed-chartist-demonstration-london
31 Fagan 2014, p. 61. See also, Fagan 2018, pp. 86–90.
32 Marx and Engels 1975–2004r, p. 171.

Parisian proletariat took to the streets. In hindsight, the 22–6 June uprising in Paris was the world's first working-class revolution. More than three thousand workers lost their lives at the hands of government organised forces which defeated that revolution. Douglass was not sympathetic. Denouncing the 'wild and wicked means of anarchy and bloodshed' of the insurgents, he told *North Star* readers that 'the communists of Paris are chiefly responsible for this last confused scene of human slaughter. They have been the agents if not the principals in the concern, and to them must attach the glory or shame of the foul undertaking'.[33] One of the early instances of red baiting in the US press. Two inches backward for Douglass.

Helping to lead the bloody charge against the workers was one of the leading liberals of the nineteenth century, the author of *Democracy in America*, Alexis de Tocqueville. Another major liberal light, and friend of Tocqueville, John Stuart Mill, also disparaged the insurgents.[34] Douglass, hence, was in good liberal company in siding with the Second Republic government against the Parisian proletariat. Yet, the former slave distinguished himself from the two other liberals with an observation that neither, given their very different class origins and sympathies, could make about the insurgents. 'The people', he wrote, 'however mistaken and eluded, evidently felt that they were fighting for their just rights. They regarded themselves deceived and defrauded by the government, and whether correct or incorrect, they acted upon their belief'.[35] Three inches forward for Douglass.

Marx, not surprisingly, had a very different opinion about the uprising that he explained, in real-time, to *NRZ* readers. The abolition of the capitalist world's first programme for the unemployed was a direct provocation. 'The workers were left no choice, they had to starve or let fly ... The Paris proletariat was forced into the June insurrection by the bourgeoisie. This sufficed to mark its doom'.[36] The insurgents, angered by severe government austerity and violence, did not have time to organise their rebellion. Of greater import is what Marx, with the advantage of hindsight three years later, argued in his *Eighteenth Brumaire of Louis Bonaparte*. The drowning in blood of the Parisian proletarian uprising in June 1848 paved the road to the end of the Second Republic in 1851 and, thus, the European Spring – what liberals like Douglass, Mill, and Tocqueville could not or did not want to see. The demise of the European Spring

---

33 P. Foner 1975, pp. 86–7.
34 See Nimtz 2019b, Chapters Two and Three, for details.
35 P. Foner 1975, pp. 86–7. See Clark 2023, pp. 564–5, on the contrast between the reactions of other liberals and Marx to the insurgency.
36 Marx and Engels 1975–2004h, pp. 67–8.

is what Lincoln's 'long endure' words in his Gettysburg address referenced. But no liberal, Lincoln included, understood or agreed with what the incipient communist, the young Marx, along with his partner, Engels, had concluded about a half decade earlier: only with the working class in power could actual democracy, i.e., 'the sovereignty of the people' and 'human emancipation', be instituted.

Despite his abhorrence of violent resistance to oppression, Douglass, in a speech in May 1849, suggested that the French events had caused him to rethink such opposition. To probably a majority US liberal white audience he confessed that he would welcome any news that 'the slaves in the South ... were engaged in spreading death and devastation there'. What provoked such a comment from the hitherto pacifist Douglass? As he explained: '... you welcomed the intelligence from France, that [King] Louis Philippe had been barricaded in Paris ... and should you not hail, with equal pleasure, the tidings from the South, that the slave had risen, and achieved for himself, against the iron-hearted slaveholder, what the republicans of France achieved against the royalists of France'.[37] Events on the ground in France emboldened Douglass. The Parisian masses had given him licence to speak to such audiences as never before. Toward a gallop.[38] But – an important qualification – violence for Douglass was permissible only for advancing the liberal and not, as his reaction to the events in London and Paris in respectively April and June of 1848 demonstrated, the proletarian cause. The distinction anticipated not only the radical but also, later, the more conservative Douglass.

The European Spring emboldened other progressives in America. Think of the Seneca Falls Convention in 1848, the founding moment of the women's equal rights movement in the US, which Douglass attended.[39] For the oppressed, under the foot – or, perhaps, more au courant, the knee – of the oppressor, stable ground, stability, is the least desirable. A shaky terrain is a potential ally, the possibility that your oppressor may stumble and actually

---

37   Blassingame 1982, pp. 216–17.
38   In a speech a month earlier, Douglass juxtaposed his pacifist principles with support for a slave uprising, maybe for the first time: '... unless the American people shall ... let the oppressed go free, that spirit in man which abhors chains ... will lead those sable arms that have long been engaged in cultivating, beautifying and adorning the South, to spread death and devastation there. Some men go for the abolition of Slavery by peaceable means. So do I; I am a peace man; but I recognize in the Southern States at this moment ... a *state of war* ... I want [slaveholders] to know that at least one colored man in the Union, peace man though he is, would greet with joy the glad news should it come here to-morrow, that an insurrection had broken out in the Southern States'. Foner 1975, p. 115.
39   B. Anderson 1998. Fought 2017, pp. 152–6.

fall to the ground. Anything that 'arouses the world from its stupor' and suggests that business as usual is threatened is encouraging. For Douglass, the 1848 upheavals seemed like the trembling earth of a seismic event even four thousand miles away. A new era had begun.

2   The Coming American Spring

The unfinished business of 1776 – postponed, kicked down the road, and compromised – proved increasingly unavoidable. Cascading political events, including the Mexican-American War, the Compromise of 1850, the Kansas-Nebraska Act, presidential electoral politics and the Supreme Court's Dred Scott decision, forced, ineluctably, the elephant in the room onto the centre-stage not just of the American but the world political theatre. What had once seemed inconceivable – non-constitutional means to abolish slavery – became increasingly thinkable and acceptable.

2.1   'Let the Battle Come': Douglass Considers Extra-Constitutional Measures

Once Marx and Engels concluded that the European Spring had ended, they were obligated as communists to draw balance sheets on the events that had just transpired. Marx's 1852 and most famous account, *The Eighteenth Brumaire*, began with a thesis: 'Men make their own history, but they do not make it just as they please ... not ... under circumstances chosen by themselves, but under circumstances directly encountered, given and transmitted from the past'.[40] The human inability to choose the circumstances within which choices are made describes precisely the dilemma Douglass faced in the decade preceding the Civil War.

Circumstances beyond Douglass's control obligated the once apolitical Garrisonian to dive into politics. Three presidential elections, two major congressional actions, and a Supreme Court decision suggested unlike ever before that there was the possibility of a constitutional solution to America's 'original sin'. During that epoch Douglass also began to consider a more radical abolitionist tactic – armed struggle. Even before the February Revolution in Paris in 1848 legitimised that alternative for him, a white abolitionist actively sought, beginning in 1847, to recruit the avowed pacifist to a plan for staging a slave rebellion – John Brown's project.[41] But first, Douglass would try to exhaust the constitutional options.

---

40   Marx and Engels 1975–2004i, p. 103.
41   A short and useful introduction to Douglass's abolitionism points out: 'His breaking point,

On the road to breaking with Garrison, Douglass came to believe, contrary to his one-time mentor's view, that the Constitution was not essentially or irretrievably a pro-slavery document. It embodied, rather, a 'fundamental contradiction' between 'Liberty and Slavery' – the position, in fact, of much modern scholarship.[42] Within a short period of time he came to believe that it could become an abolitionist document that could be wielded to defeat the slavocracy. 'Almost no one else in the abolitionist movement', according to historian James Oakes, 'held that position'.[43]

Marx, as noted in Chapter 1, also knew, as early as 1842, of the contradiction in the US polity – advanced freedoms, such as for the press, combined with laws protecting slavery. But what most struck Marx about the US, as he read deeper a year later, was a more basic contradiction – the combination of advanced political liberties with laws that allowed owners of private property, including slaves, 'to act in their own special way', such as property qualifications in voting. The 'sovereignty of the people', in other words, was unachievable in a society that privileged owners of private property. If the US was the best that political democracy had to offer, then clearly something else was required for human emancipation. That's the realisation, again, that brought Marx to communist conclusions.[44] To repeat what Engels explained in his second draft for the *Communist Manifesto*, 'the proletarian', unlike a slave, 'can free himself only by abolishing private property in general' – a distinction that Douglass never made or agreed with. Douglass, from the perspective of a slave and not a worker, only opposed 'property in persons', not 'private property in general'. The latter, as Marx and Engels argued in their *Manifesto*, was indispensable for a less obvious but just as, or even more, exploitative form of bondage: wage slavery.

When Douglass discovered the 'fundamental contradiction' in the US Constitution, Marx too, almost at the same time, pointed to the 'fundamental contradiction' in another constitution – the new one that issued from the founding of the Second Republic in February 1848. Universal male suffrage made France's male proletariat political citizens for the first time. But as long as, Marx argued, the constitution protected ownership of private property – a feature of both bourgeois documents that Douglass the liberal endorsed – it would 'perpetu-

---

the point at which he moved beyond self-defense to political violence, may have come in 1847 after he met John Brown in Springfield Massachusetts'. Jackson 2021, p. 153.

42 P. Foner 1950b, p. 118. Blight 2021.
43 Oakes 2015.
44 On the significance of the U.S. experience for the communist conclusions Marx reached, see Nimtz 2003, pp. 3–21.

ate' 'social slavery', specifically, wage slavery.[45] Only if the working class took power in France and, therefore, abolished private property could the contradiction be resolved. In anticipation of what would be on the political agenda on the other side of the Atlantic once chattel slavery ended, workers there, in all their skin colours, would have to do something similar – a transformation even more revolutionary than the overthrow of the slavocracy. Douglass's and Marx's key differences on the property question would be on stark display in post-Civil War America.

The 1848 presidential election – with the outcome of the Mexican-American War as context – is what convinced Douglass to test the American political waters for the first time. That anti-slavery parties of varying degrees competed in the election appealed to him. Though the outcome itself proved to be mostly irrelevant for the abolition movement, Douglass's interest in the Liberty Party, especially its Eastern wing personified by Gerrit Smith – which eventually led to an almost decade-long loyalty – had been piqued. Before the Civil War it was the only party in favour of slavery's abolition and equal rights for Black men. Also kindled during the 1848 election campaign was Douglass's interest in a political party based on a broader coalition – as his vacillating support of the Free Soil Party displayed.[46]

Of major significance was the congressional Compromise of 1850 between slave states and 'free' states; it deeply disappointed and angered Douglass. Nothing embittered him more than the Fugitive Slave Act, one of the components of the agreement. A previous congressional compromise in 1820, that allowed Missouri to enter the Union as a slave state, created a path-dependent scenario that limited Douglass's choices. Despite his recent claim that the Constitution could be an abolitionist document, the Act gave new teeth to its Article Four that required free states to return runaway slaves to their owners. The Compromise, he admitted, was an attempt 'to secure quiet in the nation'. But 'instead of quiet, they have produced alarm; instead of peace, they have brought us war' – one of the first public signs that the 'John Brown project' inspired by Nat Turner, the enslaved preacher from Virginia who led a violent rebellion in 1831, had found, perhaps, a receptive listener in Douglass.[47] In hindsight, the Compromise of 1850 was decisive in setting Douglass on a course of considering extra-constitutional measures to end America's peculiar institution.

---

45   Marx and Engels 1975–2004i, p. 79.
46   Martin 1984, p. 34. Blight 2018, p. 200. Brooks 2016, p. 150. For examples of Douglass's early political commentary, see P. Foner 1950a, pp. 280–97. An example of Douglass's vacillating support for the Free Soil Party is P. Foner 1975, pp. 87–93.
47   P. Foner 1950b, p. 139.

If revolutionary France had once inspired Douglass, the news from Paris at the end of 1851 must have been dispiriting, especially in the aftermath of the Compromise of 1850. Louis Bonaparte's overthrow of the Second Republic in December 1851 and restoration of the Empire a year later were exactly what Lincoln's 'can long endure' words in his Gettysburg Address alluded to. 'Americans who initially had been supportive of the popular insurgencies of 1848–9 did not hide their disappointment that the ancient regime had not collapsed but was alive and kicking'.[48] Though none of his public utterances are revealing, we assume the same about Douglass.[49] Communists, on the other hand, were obligated to explain unfulfilled expectations – lessons needed by the toilers for the next round expected in the class struggle. Thus, the elucidative balance sheets by Marx and Engels on the course of the European Spring are accounts that still have shelf life.[50]

On 5 July 1852, Douglass gave one of his most oft-quoted speeches. The occasion, to celebrate the 1776 project, was not, he told his largely white audience, something in which he could partake. Although Douglass celebrated the Declaration of Independence, often as a foil to the hypocritical Constitution, he had announced the year before his changed views on the Constitution – now a document to be used as a weapon for abolition. Given his changed position, his tone, midway into the speech, struck a surprisingly sour chord. 'I do not hesitate to declare, with all my soul, that the character and conduct of this nation never looked blacker to me than on this 4th of July! ... This Fourth of July is *yours*, not *mine*'.[51] The Fugitive Slave Act, he told the audience, explained his mood: 'it stands alone in the annals of tyrannical legislation'. Could the demise of the Second Republic have also contributed to Douglass's bitter tone? Perhaps.

But what modern day fans of Douglass's 4 July speech conveniently ignore is how he ended it on an optimistic note.[52] Despite the abominable Fugitive Slave Act, 'there are forces in operation', he told his audience, 'which must inevitably work the downfall of slavery ... The arm of commerce has borne away the gates of the strong city. Intelligence is penetrating the darkest corners of the globe ... Thoughts expressed on one side of the Atlantic are distinctly heard on

---

48 Honeck 2011, p. 15.
49 A much-appreciated fruitless search by Douglass scholar, John Kaufman-McKivigan, gives us reason for believing that such utterances don't exist. Private communication, 24 August 2021. Another liberal who had been heartened by February 1848, John Stuart Mill, also had writer's block about the demise of the Second Republic; see Nimtz 2019b, p. 82.
50 For an overview, see Nimtz 2000, pp. 102–12.
51 Blassingame 1982, p. 368.
52 Charles Mills also notes the optimistic ending to the speech but not the one we focus on here but rather the hope for a 'nonracial America'. See Mills 1998, p. 171.

the other ...'[53] To look to 'the arm of commerce' and 'thoughts' in Europe for hope that the end of American chattel slavery was on the horizon put Douglass in close intellectual company with Marx. Four years earlier, the *Communist Manifesto* proclaimed that the 'bourgeoisie has through its exploitation of the world market given a cosmopolitan character to production and consumption in every country ... [W]e have ... universal inter-dependence of nations. And as in material, so also in intellectual production. The intellectual creations of individual nations become common property'.[54] And for Douglass to note that the 'Celestial Empire', the 'iron shoe, and crippled foot of China', could not escape this development is also noteworthy. As the *Manifesto* explained: 'The cheap prices of its [the bourgeoisie's] commodities are the heavy artillery with which it batters down all Chinese walls, with which it forces the barbarians' intensely obstinate hatred of foreigners to capitulate'.[55] Not for nothing did he celebrate the Taiping Rebellion in 1850 which was the product of British commercial penetration into China's coastal areas.[56]

If Douglass looked to global developments for hope, so too did Marx and Engels. By the end of 1848, even before, therefore, the demise of the European Spring, they had concluded that the fate of the German revolution depended on the successful outcome of a worldwide revolutionary process that combined national liberation, anti-feudal and anti-capitalist revolts 'waged in Canada as in Italy, in East Indies as in Prussia, in Africa as on the Danube'.[57] Also like Douglass, Marx had his eyes on the future. He prefaced his *Eighteenth Brumaire* with the prescient point that unlike bourgeois revolutions of the past, 'proletarian revolutions, like those of the nineteenth century', seldom succeed in their 'first attempts'. And while 'the prodigiousness' of their tasks might prompt them to 'recoil again and again', sooner or later the 'situation' demands otherwise – it 'makes all turning back impossible'. 'Conditions', in a word, compelled the proletariat to try again. For Douglass to have claimed in July 1852 that ideas inspired by movements on the other side of the Atlantic would be determinant in ending slavery suggested that he too had not given up hope on the European Spring. But his reasons were very different from those of Marx, who concluded that the bourgeoisie's pusillanimity in 1848 cleared the way for the proletariat to do something far more radical than Douglass was prepared to embrace.

---

53   Blassingame 1982, pp. 386–7.
54   Marx and Engels 1975–2004e, p. 488.
55   Ibid.
56   Marx and Engels 1975–2004h, p. 267.
57   Marx and Engels 1975–2004f, p. 215.

Fast forward to 1854 – the tipping point. Another congressional decision, the Kansas-Nebraska Act, allowed the Kansas Territory to enter the Union as a slave state if its citizens, via 'popular sovereignty', voted to do so. Because the 1820 Missouri Compromise had restricted slavery to below the 36°30′ north parallel, the admission of Kansas, about one and a half degrees north of the parallel, as a slave state would effectively tear up the 1820 agreement. This Compromise, Douglass recognised in early 1854 as the debate on the Kansas-Nebraska Act was underway, was a 'demoralizing bargain, and has done more to debauch the moral sentiment of the nation than any other legislative measure we know of'.[58] Yet, all was not lost. The Kansas proposal, made by his 'namesake', Senator Stephen A. Douglas, a Democrat of Illinois, had thankfully opened up a needed national debate 'with all its violence and excitement'. Passage of the bill would 'turn to ashes in the hands of the slaveholders'. A pyrrhic victory, in other words. Douglass welcomed the coming contest 'with joy', for the anti-slavery party now had the 'freedom to fight slavery over a line, hand to hand, man to man'.[59]

The German Forty-Eighters also mobilised to fight the Kansas-Nebraska proposal, including Weydemeyer, Marx's closest contact in the US. Since his arrival from Germany in November 1851, Weydemeyer had been arguing in print and in public presentations against German figures in the US (like the aforementioned Hermann Kriege, the one-time target of Marx's and Engels's ire) who argued that the 'abolition of wage slavery was the primary issue' and that 'Negro slavery' was a 'side issue'. Weydemeyer 'insisted that wage workers could not advance further in American society until chattel slavery was eliminated, that they must play an important role in hastening its downfall, and that its demise would in turn strengthen their organisation for the subsequent fight against capital'[60] – all positions consistent with the basic arguments of the *Manifesto*. At a meeting of his chapter of the *Amerikanische Arbeiterbund* (American Workers' League) in New York City on 1 March 1854, he introduced and successfully motivated a resolution that denounced the proposed Kansas legislation. 'Whereas, this bill authorizes the further extension of slavery, we have protested, do now protest and shall continue to protest most emphatically against both white and black slavery'.[61] If Marx's and Engels's rejection of Hermann Kriege's pseudo-communism six years earlier had not explicitly

---

58 P. Foner 1950b, pp. 276–9; Blight 1991, pp. 42–3.
59 Blassingame 1982, pp. 465, 468.
60 P. Foner 1977, p. 14.
61 Obermann 1947, pp. 78–80. Also, Efford 2013, p. 63.

addressed the slavery question, the Marx party in the US, led now by Weydemeyer, left little doubt about their position.[62]

Once Congress passed the Kansas-Nebraska bill, a new era, Douglass contended, had opened. The principle of 'popular sovereignty' had replaced the immoral Missouri Compromise. 'Woe! Woe! Woe to slavery! Her mightiest shield is broken ... in the name of God, let the battle come'.[63] 'Bring it on,' Douglass seemed to be saying. Whether what then happened constituted what Douglass actually wanted is uncertain.

If armed resistance to end slavery had only been an idea until then, the violent contest between the settlers in Kansas over whether it would be a free or slave state, namely, 'popular sovereignty', made it real for the first time. Not for naught do many historians consider the battles called 'Bloody Kansas' to be the beginning of the Civil War. John Brown's proposal to Douglass in 1847 now had flesh, bones, and blood. Brown's sons, followed by their father, helped lead the vanguard abolitionist forces that went to Kansas to determine popular sovereignty – by arms if necessary. These struggles proved that 'Democracy', as the young Marx wrote in 1843, 'is the solved riddle of all constitutions'. The more than decade long debate amongst abolitionists, including Douglass with his rare interpretation, about what the framers of the Republic's founding document meant about slavery was now in the only arena where the issue could be resolved – the 'Democracy' of the masses in conflict, struggle, and motion. Douglass, with the Fugitive Slave Act on his brain, revealed why John Brown's project would be increasingly attractive: 'Every slave-hunter who meets a bloody death in his infernal business is an argument in favor of the manhood of our race'.[64] The militant struggle that Brown had initiated on behalf of the abolitionist cause in Kansas was not only met with Douglass's passionate approval, it also anticipated precisely how and where the masses would provide an answer to their debate about the constitution – on the battlefield.

2.2 Douglass, Weydemeyer, and the Republicans in 1856

But Douglass was not ready to completely abandon a constitutional solution to end slavery. He continued to hedge his bets especially because the Kansas-Nebraska Act provoked a realignment of national party politics. The old and venerable Whig Party of Henry Clay had been in terminal decline at least since

---

62 Weydemeyer and the American Workers' League is briefly mentioned in Sinha 2016, pp. 369–70.
63 P. Foner 1950b, p. 283.
64 P. Foner 1950b, p. 287. Jackson 2019, pp. 69–70, identifies the Fugitive Slave Law as the act which 'compelled him [Douglass] to abandon the moral suasion camp completely'.

the Compromise of 1850. Peaceful coexistence with the slavocracy, its raison d'etre, ended with the Kansas-Nebraska Act of 1854. Into the political fallout came a new player, the Republican Party, born the same year, which provided a new possible constitutional solution to end slavery and, thus, a new temptation for Douglass.

Prior to the Republican Party, the only party of any significance that advocated for immediate, uncompensated abolition and equal rights for Black people was the Liberty Party, the one Douglass supported when he broke in 1850 with Garrison and his electoral abstentionist posture.[65] The polarising impact of the Kansas-Nebraska Act prompted it to take a more militant anti-slavery stance as its new name, the Radical Abolitionist Party, registered. That the party's convention in 1855 in upstate New York provided a platform for John Brown – as well as Douglass – and applauded what he and his sons were doing in Kansas spoke volumes about its new orientation.

The moderate wing of the new Republican Party, its main component, inherited the anti-slavery tradition of the Salmon Chase wing of the Liberty Party. Unlike the Radical Abolitionists, the moderate Republicans adhered to a position that frustrated Douglass: opposition to the extension of the abominable institution to the territories but acquiescence in the states where it already existed. Yet, Douglass reluctantly realised, the new party was vastly superior to the Democratic Party which was firmly beholden to 'the slave power'. And besides, the Republicans had the potential for putting an anti-slavery party, however limited, in the White House for the first time.

To the shock of many former Liberty Party allies, Douglass, despite a more than year-long denunciation of the Republican Party's half-hearted or – depending on one's perspective – practical position on the slavery question, announced in his eponymous newspaper on 15 August that he was endorsing its candidate for the 1856 presidential contest. Rather than support, as he had done up to that point, Gerrit Smith, the candidate of the Radical Abolitionist Party, Douglass told his readers that he intended to marshal 'whatever influence we possess, little or much, [for] John C. Frémont and William L. Dayton, the candidates of the Republican Party for the presidency and vice-presidency of the United States'. Frémont, a California senator and former military officer, was, he explained, the 'recognized antagonist of the Slave Power' and is the

---

65   Douglass, at various points, also described himself as a 'Free Soiler' and endorsed the election campaigns of the Free Soil Party, the anti-slavery expansion precursor to the Republican Party. See Foner 1975, pp. 243–4. In a speech to Ohio farmers, Douglass also said that antislavery is 'the poor man's work. The rich and noble will not do it'. In September 1852 Douglass endorsed the Free Soil ticket. See Foner 1950b, pp. 211–19.

candidate of the 'most numerous Anti-Slavery Party' that has the best chance to 'achieve a valuable victory over the Slave Oligarchy'. Gerrit Smith, he continued, had 'no chance whatever' of winning and a vote for him 'would only serve to weaken the Republican Party'. Supporting the Republicans, Douglass eventually concluded, would advance the 'more comprehensive claims' of the fight to end slavery.[66] Possibly determinant in his decision were numerous instances and reports of slave insurgencies that Douglass knew were inspired by the Frémont campaign.[67] Whatever the case, the Gordian electoral knot he grappled with continues to confuse American progressives.

If Douglass had agonised over whether to support the Republicans in the 1856 campaign, for Weydemeyer the choice was easy. As early as the 1852 presidential election, he had distinguished himself amongst the Forty-Eighters in arguing for the necessity of German émigré workers engaging in political activism.[68] Though details are lacking, it is clear that he campaigned enthusiastically for the 1856 Republican ticket through lectures and articles and not from the defensive posture Douglass adopted.[69] These actions were consistent with his half-decade old campaign to educate workers, especially those of German origin, that the fight to overthrow the slavocracy was indispensable to the workers' movement. As long as the Republicans, certainly not a workers' party, let alone a Marxist one, were willing to wage a consistent fight to advance that goal, then they deserved the support of communists.

The extant correspondence doesn't reveal what Marx and Engels may have thought of Weydemeyer's efforts, but nothing suggests that they would have opposed it. In the final section of the *Manifesto* they wrote that 'as soon as the bourgeoisie acts in a revolutionary way', German communists were obligated to fight 'together with the bourgeoisie against ... feudal landed property'.[70] The Republicans were certainly a bourgeois party and the slavocracy was clearly America's version of the feudal oligarchy. Five years later, the Republican Party would truly act 'in a revolutionary way' and a significant payoff would come from Weydemeyer's support for Frémont. For the Marx party, again, the abolition of chattel slavery was, unlike for Douglass, a means – an indispensable one – to the greater end of abolishing class society rather than an end in itself.

---

66 P. Foner 1950b, pp. 396, 398–401.
67 Egerton 2015.
68 Obermann 1947, p. 79.
69 Obermann 1947, pp. 89–90.
70 In the original text, Marx and Engels employed 'as soon as'. Engels's 1888 translation, the standard text, substituted 'whenever', his recognition that the German bourgeoisie did not act in 1848–9 as he and his partner had expected. For details, see Draper 1994, pp. 320–3.

2.3 The Crisis Deepens

The inauguration on 4 March 1857 of James Buchanan, the Democratic Party victor in the 1856 presidential election, did not augur well for the future of the anti-slavery cause. Slavery dominated the campaign unlike any previous election. Buchanan, who received forty-five percent of the popular vote but almost sixty percent of the electoral college vote, campaigned in defence of 'popular sovereignty', namely, exporting America's original sin to the territories. The official institutions of the nation, therefore, were still firmly in the hands of the slavocracy. For that reason, no doubt, Douglass became increasingly more public about considering militant, extra-constitutional methods to settle the issue.

About a month after the election, he told an audience that 'the slave's right to revolt is perfect, and only wants the occurrence of favourable circumstances to become a duty'. While he could not but 'shudder' when he thought of 'the horrors' that would come with a slave insurrection, 'the recoil, when it comes, will be in exact proportion to the wrongs inflicted; terrible as it will be, we accept and hope for it'. These words were in remarkable anticipation of Abraham Lincoln's chilling lines in his Second Inaugural Address nine years later. 'The slave holder', Douglass continued, 'has been tried and sentenced, his execution only waits the finish to the training of his executioners. He is training his executioners'.[71] A one-time leading but moderate abolitionist admirer of Douglass did in fact 'shudder' at his new tone. About your 'vengeance is mine' attitude, this moderate admirer wrote to Douglass, 'I cannot go with you'.[72] But for another long-time, militant abolitionist, John Brown, it was exactly what he was hoping to hear from Douglass – encouragement for his project.

At the end of his second autobiography, *My Bondage and My Freedom*, published in 1855, Douglass committed himself to do what he assumed his readers would want to see – 'to use my voice, my pen, or my vote, to advocate the great and primary work of the universal and unconditional emancipation of my entire race'.[73] But he was not totally transparent about his activities. In addition to the three he listed, the historical record now reveals that he was engaged in another activity – fundraising for John Brown that began at the Radical Abolition Party conference earlier that year.[74] Douglass, in other words, was hedging his bets for good reason.

---

71 P. Foner 1950b, p. 406.
72 McKivigan 2018, p. 202. Blight 1991, p. 95.
73 Douglass 2014, p. 325.
74 Reynolds 2005, p. 135. On the Radical Abolitionist convention and Douglass and Brown's participation see also Blight 2018, pp. 293–4. Stauffer 2002, pp. 8, 12–13, 15, 25. Sinha 2016, p. 546.

Buchanan's election foreshadowed the second blow that anti-slavery forces sustained in 1857, the Supreme Court's day of infamy. Chief Justice and onetime slave owner Roger Taney ruled on 6 March that the framers of the Constitution never intended for people of African descent to be citizens of the United States. The enslaved Dred Scott, who tried to sue for his freedom, therefore, had no legal standing to do so. Taney took it upon himself to pronounce on what the framers never did – the citizenship status of Americans of African descent, free or bonded. For a number of years Douglass had promoted the decidedly minority position within anti-slavery circles that the Constitution could be an abolitionist document.[75] The Taney Court's *Dred Scott* decision said otherwise.[76]

Hearing the decision momentarily paralysed Douglass with 'an aching heart'. Inherently indomitable, conceding was not his style. He appealed to a higher law two months later. The 'Supreme Court of the United States', he declared,

> is not the only power in this world. It is very great, but the Supreme Court of the Almighty is greater. Judge Taney can do many things, but he cannot perform impossibilities ... He may decide, and decide again; but he cannot reverse the decision of the Most High. He cannot change the essential nature of things – making evil good, and good, evil.[77]

Marx probably read about the *Dred Scott* decision in the *Tribune*, but there is no record of his reaction. Yet, it can safely be assumed that if Douglass looked on high for justice, Marx, informed by his insight about constitutional matters fourteen years earlier and having 'turned Hegel on his head', was more earthbound. Whether or not Black Americans were citizens – the question that the Scott case posed – could only be answered by 'Democracy', the masses in motion, and not by the alleged disagreement between the 'Most High' and Justice Taney. The question would be answered unambiguously on the battlefield beginning four years later.

With *Dred Scott* still on the brain, Douglass delivered his oft excerpted 'If There is No Struggle' speech five months later in Canandaigua, New York, in

---

75   As Eric Foner writes, 'In the mid–1850s, Douglass embraced the view that the federal government possessed the power, without any change in the Constitution, to abolish slavery throughout the nation. Few inside or outside the antislavery crusade found this last argument convincing'. E. Foner 2019, p. 9.
76   For an overview of the origins of the *Dred Scott* case, the arguments, deliberations, and opinions, and the reaction North and South, see Stampp 1990, pp. 82–109.
77   P. Foner 1950b, pp. 408, 410–11.

celebration of the twenty-third anniversary of the abolition of slavery in the British West Indies. After detailing the world-historical significance of 1 August 1834, Douglass turned to the American scene. There, he declared sarcastically, 'the first and last question' asked about the feasibility of emancipation is

> *will it pay*? ... Can money be made out of it? Will it make the rich richer, and the strong stronger? How will it affect property? In the eyes of such people, there is no God but wealth, no right and wrong but profit and loss ... [O]ur national morality and religion ... allow that if men can make money by stealing men and women, and by working them up into sugar, rice, and tobacco, they may innocently continue the practice ... Money is the measure of morality, and the success or failure of slavery as a money-making system, determines with many whether the thing is virtuous, or villainous, and whether it should be maintained or abolished ... [and, therefore,] denouncing the abolition of slavery in the West Indies a failure.[78]

Marx, as will be seen, offered at almost the same time an explanation for the money-driven basis of American slavery and, even more instructively, why Douglass would take umbrage.

Douglass then addressed 'an objection' to celebrating the 1st of August, from that of the distinguished Black doctor James McCune Smith.[79] Why should Black people, Smith asked, celebrate an event orchestrated by people who despised them? Douglass respectfully objected to Smith's criticism and then articulated what was, in his opinion, the real story behind emancipation in the British West Indies. He premised his explanation on what he called 'the philosophy of reform' – perhaps Douglass's singular and underappreciated contribution to liberal democratic theory.[80] It began with a trenchant opening thesis.

> The whole history of the progress of human liberty shows that all concessions yet made to her august claims, have been born of earnest struggle. The conflict has been exciting, agitating and all absorbing, and for the time being, putting all other tumults to silence. It must do this or it does

---

[78] P. Foner 1950b, pp. 431–2.
[79] For a succinct description of Smith's objection, see Jackson 2019, pp. 1–2.
[80] Douglass first used 'the philosophy of reform' in 1849, apparently, his own philosophy. See Bromell 2021, p. 25. For his most detailed treatment of what he meant, in 1883, see Breitenwischer 2021.

nothing. If there is no struggle, there is no progress. Those who profess freedom and yet deprecate agitation, are men who want crops without ploughing up the ground, they want rain without thunder and lightning. They want the ocean without the awful roar of its many waters.

Acknowledging, he continued, his Garrisonian moral suasion origins, he asserted that the 'struggle may be a moral one, or it may be a physical one, and it may be both moral and physical, but it must be a struggle'. Then he rounded out his argument with the all-familiar claim about 'the philosophy of reform':

Power concedes nothing without a demand. It never did and it never will. Find out just what any people will quietly submit to and you have found out the exact measure of injustice and wrong which will be imposed upon them, and these will continue till they are resisted with either words or blows, or with both ... If we ever get free from the oppressions and wrongs heaped upon us, we must pay for their removal. We must do this by labor, by suffering, by sacrifice, and if needs be, by our lives and the lives of others.

Douglass proceeded to put flesh, bones, and blood on his 'philosophy', that is, real examples from West Indian and American slave resistance history, to make clear to his racially mixed audience what he meant by 'if needs be, by our lives and the lives of others'. 'What [English abolitionist leader William] Wilberforce', to be unmistakably clear, 'was endeavoring to win from the British Senate by his magic eloquence, the Slaves themselves were endeavouring to gain by outbreaks and violence'.[81] 'Abolition', he concluded, 'followed close on the heels of insurrection in the West Indies, and Virginia was never nearer to emancipation than when General [Nat] Turner kindled the fires of insurrection at Southampton'.[82] Perhaps that's the sanguinary example that gives liberal democratic theorists pause in including this speech in their canon.[83] It

---

[81] Not unlike what one of us argues about the outcome of the Second Reconstruction in the US, namely, the Martin Luther King, Jr/Malcolm X nexus. See Nimtz 2016a.

[82] P. Foner 1950b, pp. 434, 437–9.

[83] To his credit, in Kloppenberg 2016, the introduction includes: 'Douglass had explosive significance in shaping modern democratic thought and culture', p. 15. He later cites the 4 July 1852 speech as evidence but makes no mention of the August 1857 speech. Only the 4 July speech is cited in Losurdo 2011. There isn't even an entry for Douglass in Rosenblatt 2018.

registered, nevertheless, how far the one-time pacifist had travelled over the preceding decade owing to 'circumstances', as Marx might have explained, 'not chosen by [himself]' – not the least of these being the notorious *Dred Scott* decision.

Douglass's 'philosophy of reform' brings Marx to mind more substantively. His opening claim about 'the whole of history of the progress of human liberty' recalls the opening thesis of the 1848 *Manifesto*: 'the history of all hitherto existing society is the history of class struggles'. But the similarity is superficial. Unlike Douglass, Marx was no inevitablist about the progress of human emancipation. If so, then why the need for the *Manifesto*? 'Inevitable', *unvermeidlich* in the original German, appears only once in the forty-page document, and the word is immediately followed by instructions for the proletariat. The class struggle was all that Marx and Engels promised once class society appeared in human social evolution. The outcomes of those struggles would be uncertain, such as the slave insurrections that both Douglass and Marx praised. The *Manifesto*, and the activism it called for, sought to give the toilers, the proletariat specifically, a better than even chance in the outcomes of the struggles – the kind of programme that insurgent slaves, alas, lacked. For Douglass, at that moment in his career, Providence and natural law were most decisive in the unfolding of the history of society, whereas for Marx the conscious intervention of human beings (shaped by circumstances beyond their control) was most decisive in this unfolding. This marked the fundamental epistemological difference between the two protagonists.

A year and a half after Douglass had denounced, as previously noted, the proletarian uprising in Paris in June 1848, he proposed for the first time, not coincidentally we argue, his 'philosophy of reform'.[84] Marx and Engels may have anticipated the earlier Douglass's politics of anything-but-revolution. In the too-neglected third part of the 1848 *Manifesto*, they dissected proponents of 'Bourgeois Socialism' – 'hole-and-corner reformers of the most variegated kinds'. They existed 'to remedy *social ills*, in order to safeguard the existence of bourgeois society'. Their main task was to call 'on the proletariat to … remain inside present-day [bourgeois] society … to cast off its hateful ideas about that society … [and] to make the working class disgusted with any revolutionary movement'.[85] When the Parisian proletariat rose up again in 1871 and established its Commune, Douglass denounced them once again, thus confirming that his response in 1848 was not a one-off. His limits as a liberal revolutionary,

---

84 Bromell 2021, p. 25. Martin 1984, pp. 18, 22, 80, 167–8.
85 Draper, 1994, pp. 173–5.

anticipated, as will be seen later, how he responded to the class dynamics of post-Civil War Radical Reconstruction America.[86]

Around the same time that Douglass expressed his disgust for the money-driven character of the chattel slave economy in America, Marx provided an explanation for the American ruling elite's obsession with profits. Begun in 1857, the research and writing in his notebooks known as the *Grundrisse* – that would eventually find their way into *Capital* – sought amongst many goals to distinguish between the role of labour under capitalist and pre-capitalist relations of production such as slavery and serfdom.[87] According to Marx, basically, 'slavery ... represents an anomaly in relation to the bourgeois system itself'.[88] A little later: 'That we now not only describe the plantation-owners in America as capitalists, but that they are capitalists, is due to the fact that they exist as anomalies within a world market based upon free labour'.[89] Distilled in the third volume of *Capital* from his prior research was the key point that slavery had undergone a 'metamorphosis from the patriarchal system [in which it is] mainly for home use to the plantation system [in which it is] for the world market ... Where the capitalist outlook prevails, as on American plantations, this entire surplus value [of slave labor] is regarded as profit'.[90] At some moment in the first half of the nineteenth century, American slave plantation production, in other words, became integrated into global capitalism and, from then on, was driven by the unquenchable thirst for profits. That integration required squeezing as much surplus labour as possible out of the enslaved. Marx had discovered the raison d'être for the 'money-making system' that Douglass deplored.

On the road toward clarity about the American slave economy, Marx in his notes revealed a prescient insight about slavery and its future. Capitalist relations of production, in and of themselves, engendered an 'awareness' in workers that the 'separation' of the products of their labour from themselves 'was improper and imposed by force' – and this awareness is an 'enormous consciousness ... the knell to ... [capitalism's] doom'. Such awareness about alienation and how it was produced, through exploitation, was not unlike, he continued, 'the consciousness of the slave that he cannot be the *property of another*, his consciousness of being a person, [therefore] reduced slavery to an artificial lingering existence, and made it impossible for it to continue

---

86 See K. Edwards 2022 and Appendix A in this volume.
87 For a useful overview of Marx's antebellum research on the topic, see Foster et al 2020.
88 Marx and Engels 1975–2004o, p. 392.
89 Marx and Engels 1975–2004o, p. 436.
90 Marx and Engels 1975–2004q, p. 790.

to provide the basis of production'.[91] This claim, made around 1857, possibly explains why Marx confidently posited in the opening days of the Civil War that, whatever its outcome, slavery was doomed. Not only accurate, his insight was also uncanny – as if he had Douglass in mind. Arguably no one epitomised more than the once enslaved Douglass the 'consciousness of being a person', and, later, no one contested more than him the claim that the enslaved were 'the property of another'. Nota bene the word 'consciousness' – for Marx an awareness of injustice by exploited and oppressed people was indispensable for human emancipation. His attention to consciousness exemplified not the first nor the last trans-Atlantic mind-meld he would share with Douglass.

2.4   King Cotton

The famous 'King Cotton' speech of South Carolina senator James Hammond to his colleagues on 4 March 1858 deserves mentioning in this context.[92] The speech created quite a stir. The main part of the text lauded the economic value to the nation of cotton production, confirming in many ways both Marx's and Douglass's observations about the profitability of US slavery. It was the second part of Hammond's lengthy address to the Senate that provoked debate. He unapologetically made the case that because cotton production was crucial to the nation's economic well-being, the slave labour system indispensable to said production was justified. He rested his unapologetic argument on the notion of the 'mud-sill' – the claim that 'all social systems ... progress, civilization, and refinement' required a social layer to be on the bottom, i.e., 'the mud-sill'. America, he continued, was blessed to have 'a race ... eminently qualified in temper, in vigor, in docility, in capacity to stand the climate, to answer all her purposes'. A class-based defence of chattel slavery undergirded Hammond's thesis, a defence that Marx would have easily understood (Douglass too, to be seen later) and that, once combined with the ideology of biological racism, felt all too familiar to Douglass. Most provocatively, slave labour, Hammond claimed, was preferable to 'free labour' – a claim so controversial that future president Abraham Lincoln felt compelled, even eighteen months later, to publicly dispute Hammond's thesis.[93]

The *Tribune* reported on Hammond's speech and the contentious reaction. As will be seen later in his congratulatory message to Lincoln upon his re-election in 1864, Marx referenced Hammond's points about the problematic

---

91   Marx and Engels 1975–20040, pp. 390–1.
92   https://www.americanantiquarian.org/Manuscripts/cottonisking.html
93   Fehrenbacher 1989, pp. 90–101.

role of the Northern white proletariat vis-a-vis chattel slavery. Though Douglass knew about the speech, it's unclear what he thought about it. He certainly knew, from first-hand experience during his time as a slave on the docks in Baltimore, about the contradictory consciousness of white workers as he related in his 1855 autobiography, *My Bondage and My Freedom*. Though oppressed as a part of the toiling class, the perks accompanying 'whiteness' limited white workers' ability to embrace class solidarity across skin colour lines with the enslaved. For exactly this reason, the Marx party in the US prioritised putting an end to America's race-based chattel slavery, an essential prerequisite to achieving inclusive subaltern class consciousness and, thus, the end of class oppression.[94]

Also noteworthy, Hammond's speech registered the apparent confidence that the slavocracy felt about its way of life on the eve of the coming conflagration. The Buchanan election and the *Dred Scott* decision had no doubt emboldened the Southern ruling elite. Their 'money-making', 'profit-driven' slave-based political economy was not about to die on its own. Something of near-biblical proportions would be required to destroy it – not the idealism of moral suasion but material reality in mortal combat with material reality.

2.5 John Brown – Agent Provocateur Extraordinaire

Ever since 1847 when John Brown first planted the seed of an armed underground railroad in Douglass's ear, the two abolitionists intentionally stayed in touch with one another. For Douglass the consequences of their comradery were transformative. 'There can be little doubt', in David Blight's opinion, 'that through the course of the 1850s, Douglass's acquaintance with Brown quickened his receptivity to violence'.[95] We argue that Brown's decade-long close association with Douglass, in turn, determined in part the historical figure he became. The martyr of Harpers Ferry had every reason to believe that his revolutionary project had the seal of approval from the country's most authoritative Black voice for abolition. But events beyond the control of either man were far more decisive in shaping their political trajectories – the 1854 Kansas-Nebraska Act, the 1857 *Dred Scott* decision, and Brown's execution in December 1859.

In calling for 'popular sovereignty' to determine whether the Kansas territory would enter the Union as a 'free' or slave state, the passing of the Kansas-

---

94 For an informative local level study on the racial obstacles to class consciousness for the white proletariat, see Gronowicz 1998 – the text addresses the issue of why a working-class alternative to a liberal solution to slavery in America was not available to Douglass.

95 Blight 1991, p. 95. See also, Jackson 2019, p. 43.

Nebraska Act by Congress inadvertently provoked the first battle in the Civil War. Militant pro-slavery and free-state forces began to move to the territory to decide the outcome of the far-reaching vote; both sides were prepared to use arms to advance their positions. Among the latter were first his sons and then, shortly after, Brown himself. At the aforementioned June 1855 meeting of the Radical Abolition Party, Brown made a presentation and, with Douglass's assistance, collected 'sixty dollars, an assortment of pistols, broadswords, and muskets to avenge the murder of free-state settlers' in Kansas.[96]

In retaliation in part for the May 1856 pro-slavery attack on Lawrence, Kansas, a few weeks later Brown and his sons brutally murdered five men at Pottawatomie Creek – until then Brown's most notable act. Of crucial significance, for our purposes here, is that Douglass came to his defence. 'What could be more absurd?' asked Douglass of the murder charges against Brown. 'If he has sinned in anything, it is that he has spared lives of the murderers, when he had the power to take vengeance upon them'.[97] The one-time pacifist had come a long way.

A half-year later in December 1856 the collaboration between Brown and Douglass deepened. Not content with only sharing information about his plans and accepting the funds Douglass helped raise to realise a militarised underground railroad into the South, Brown 'repeatedly tried to recruit Douglass to the cause'. Though Douglass would not commit to actually joining the military action, he continued to aid and abet the cause, which included his participation in their joint appearance at a rally in Worcester, Massachusetts in March 1857.[98]

The Supreme Court's March 1857 *Dred Scott* decision steeled Brown's long-held conviction that only armed action would end chattel slavery. But another circumstance beyond his control, 'the Panic of 1857', made fundraising for the project more difficult. Capitalism's first global crisis – anticipated in the *Communist Manifesto* – reached the United States in the fall of 1857, requiring Brown to rely no longer on public events such as the ones at which he and Douglass had shared a platform. A group of private funders, 'the secret six', including Douglass's long-time contact and financial supporter, Gerrit Smith, came to the rescue.

In January 1858 Brown arrived at Douglass's Rochester, New York, home and lived there as the Douglass family's guest for about three weeks. The result,

---

96 Reynolds 2005, p. 135.
97 Quoted in Cook 1999, p. 141. On the debate about Pottawatomie Creek, see Oakes 2007, pp. 96–7, Sinha 2016, pp. 546–8, and Reynolds 2005, pp. 139–41, 144, 148–78.
98 Blight 2018, p. 295.

Blight writes, is that 'Douglass became as well informed of Brown's ultimate aims as any abolitionist or accomplice outside his small personal band'.[99] During the stay Brown drafted a 'Provisional Constitution' that would be used to govern any liberated territory from Virginia. 'Douglass', John Stauffer believes, 'probably edited Brown's constitution, for it is more polished than almost anything else Brown wrote'.[100] The preamble rejected 'a recent decision of the Supreme Court' which 'declared' that Black people had 'no rights which the White Man is bound to respect' – i.e., it explicitly rejected the *Dred Scott* decision. To the contrary. The alternative covenant asserted that 'Oppressed People ... together with all other people degraded by the laws thereof, Do, for the time being ordain and establish ourselves, the following Provisional Constitution and Ordinances, the better to protect our Persons, Property, Lives and Liberties ...' Toward that end, the document declared that its intent was not 'in any way to encourage the ... dissolution of the Union, but simply to amendment and repeal. And our flag shall be the same that our fathers fought under the Revolution'.[101] Blight is not sure just 'how much Brown and Douglass debated political philosophy and constitutionalism', but argues that 'Douglass surely agreed wholeheartedly with Brown's preamble, most of which could have been lifted from editorials and speeches written by his host'.[102]

Shortly after his visit to the Douglass household, Brown reported in February 1858 to one of his sons that Douglass had pledged fifty dollars to him. Douglass also served as a conduit between other Black leaders and Brown. A month later Douglass helped organise Brown's meeting with Henry Highland Garnet and the Philadelphia Underground Railroad activist William Still. Blight speculates that as 'long as Brown bravely advanced the idea of funneling fugitive slaves out of the upper South and thereby politically threatened the slave system generally, Douglass was on board despite the risks. But when assaulting a large US arsenal emerged in the scheme, the writer parted ways with the warrior'.[103]

After Brown's 'most heroic and admirable feat', the liberation of a group of Missouri slaves to freedom in Michigan at the end of 1858 and the beginning of 1859, he met with Douglass in Detroit and later in Rochester in April, meetings during which he no doubt told him about his latest and boldest plan – an attack on a government military arsenal. Although non-committal about joining in the raid, Douglass continued to raise funds for Brown. To Douglass, Brown was,

---

99   Blight 2018, p. 296.
100 Stauffer 2008, p. 159.
101 https://www.famous-trials.com/johnbrown/614-browconstitution
102 Blight 2018, pp. 296–7.
103 Blight 2018, pp. 298.

as he wrote in his newspaper about the April meeting, 'a hero'.[104] The future martyr had good reason to believe he had Douglass's imprimatur.

Brown didn't give up on Douglass; until almost the very end he thought he could recruit him. In August 1859 Brown rented a farmhouse in western Maryland, only five miles from Harpers Ferry, to stage his attack on the federal arsenal. 'Douglass', Blight notes, 'was certainly informed of the location and now of its purpose'. He and Brown maintained a correspondence the months preceding the attack, and Brown's son met with Douglass on 10 August. Douglass then 'answered the Old Man's summons' to meet with him in Orangeburg, Pennsylvania near the Maryland border on 19 August. Douglass brought more money, 'a $20 contribution given him on a stop in New York City by a black couple ... as well as one significant recruit, a fugitive slave named Shields Green'. Brown tried his best to persuade Douglass to fight. 'I want you', he told Douglass, 'for a special purpose. When I strike the bees will begin to swarm, and I shall want you to help hive them'.[105] But rather than attract 'bees', i.e., the enslaved to fight, the attack, Douglass argued, would only bring the full military weight of the United States down on anything resembling a slave insurrection.[106] If Brown couldn't convince Douglass, he apparently did recruit Harriet Tubman, the next most renowned Black abolitionist for whom Brown had the highest regard, to commit to taking part in the raid. Only because of her incapacitating migraine headaches, owing to blows she once sustained as a slave, was Tubman unable to be with Brown and the eighteen other attackers at Harpers Ferry.[107]

Well-documented is Brown's raid and its failed outcome in mid-October 1859, composed of thirteen other white people and five Black people (close to the same racial composition of Union forces in the Civil War). Douglass was correct in his prediction about its chance for success. Admittedly not in keeping with real-time political analysis, we can't resist a counterfactual. By all measures Fidel Castro, almost a century later, should not have attempted something

---

104 Blight 2018, pp. 300–1. See also Reynolds 2005, pp. 278–80.
105 Blight 2018, pp. 301–3. See Balfour 2011, pp. 67–9, for a thoughtful take on how W.E.B. Du Bois treated the differences between Douglass and Brown about carrying out the raid.
106 We differ with Neil Roberts's claim that because Douglass did not join Brown at Harpers Ferry, he 'never considered actual mass revolution an option to contest the violence of the slave commodity market'. By relying solely on Douglass's 1855 text, *My Bondage and My Freedom*, Roberts ignores the subsequent facts we present about the actual Douglass-Brown relationship. More importantly, Roberts neglects Douglass's invaluable advocacy, to be examined below, for the creation of a revolutionary army that would march south and emancipate slaves – turning a war to restore the antebellum status quo into a revolutionary war for the abolition of slavery. See Roberts 2015, pp. 80–3.
107 Clinton 2005, pp. 124–36.

quite similar – an attack, with a force ten times larger than Brown's, on Cuba's second most defended military arsenal in July 1953.[108] Only for at least two lucky breaks did he live, with all of their history-making consequences. Can any of Brown's contemporary Monday morning quarterback detractors confidently deny that with a little bit of luck he, too, might have survived?[109] This leads to the next intriguing question: what if Brown, like Castro, had lived? We leave that question, hitherto ignored as far as we can tell, for others to speculate on with an answer. For Civil War students, by the way, Castro's authentic John Brown moment was not his failed attack on the military barracks but rather his appropriately titled 'History Will Absolve Me' trial speech.

More significant, therefore, than the failed raid on Harpers Ferry is what happened next. If ever the proverbial making-lemonade-from-lemons wisdom deserves application, it must surely be with Brown's decision, for whatever reason, to act as a martyr for the cause at his trial, in jail, and on the hangman's scaffold where he died on 2 December 1859.[110] His heroic comportment in the aftermath of the raid prompted figures like Ralph Waldo Emerson to compare Brown favourably to Jesus of Nazareth.[111] Hitherto pacifists like Garrison became converts to armed struggle.

The commemoration of Brown's execution in Cincinnati offers telling evidence of the impact of his post-raid conduct. The dramatic event began with 'a giant torchlight procession through the streets' headed by August Willich, a one-time comrade of Marx and Engels in the Communist League and in the German Revolution.[112] The commemoration ended with a mass interracial meeting in the German Over-the-Rhine neighbourhood, reported on by an unsympathetic 'Spectator'.

> Spectator seemed most shaken by the words of a third speaker – August Willich, leader of the city's *Arbeiterverein* [Workers' Union] and editor of its newspaper. Spectator listened in stunned disbelief as Willich not only mourned Brown and denounced slavery, the Democratic party, and

---

[108] Though not sympathetic, Cova 2007 provides valuable details. An irresistible factoid: Toussaint L'Ouverture, the Haitian leader who led the revolution, was a hero for both Brown and Castro.

[109] The most respected recent figure in the detractor camp is Oakes 2007. However, the latest scholarly assessment of Brown, Brands 2020, gives 'the zealot', Brown, in comparison with Lincoln, 'the emancipator', his due.

[110] See McGinty 2009.

[111] For the best overview of the reaction in the North and counter-reaction in the South, see Reynolds 2005, pp. 370–437.

[112] Easton 1966, pp. 22–3.

its supporters but also 'exhorted his hearers to whet their sabers and nerve their arms for the day of retribution, when Slavery and Democracy would be crushed in a common grave'. No less alarming than these speeches was the reaction of the interracial crowd. The fiery words delivered from the podium, Spectator reported indignantly, 'received the rapturous applause of the motley gathering'. Indeed, he continued, 'the fiercer the denunciations of slavery and Democracy, the more uproarious were the woolyheads and their allies'.[113]

Nicknamed the 'Reddest of the Red', Willich stood out amongst German-American working-class fighters as not only an opponent of slavery but an advocate for racial equality as well, positions which made him, ironically, more authentically democratic than the imposter 'Democracy' of the slavocracy.[114]

Other locations emulated Cincinnati. 'Northerners commemorated both the trial and the execution [of Brown] with public prayers, church services, marches and meetings'. Black-led interracial gatherings in Brown's honour took place 'from the Atlantic to the Pacific', in Boston, Pittsburgh, New York City, Cleveland, and in countless other locations – including Port-au-Prince, Haiti. Brown's example 'galvanized the nation and captured the particular imagination of blacks'. Honouring his martyrdom arguably became Black America's first national commemoration. Most significantly, whether directly inspired or not by Brown, a number of slave rebellions and conspiracies arose from Virginia to Texas in the months after Harpers Ferry.[115] As we will see shortly, such reactions in the North and the outrage they generated in the South did more than anything to provoke the slavocracy to overreact and make its fatal mistake – the firing on Fort Sumter seventeen months later.[116]

Owing to the extant paper trail that connected him with Brown, Douglass decided to flee the United States, first to Canada and then to England. Though Brown had been unable to persuade him to join the action at Harpers Ferry, Douglass came to his defence in the aftermath in print and speech. Prophetically, he declared that the raid had 'initiated a new mode of carrying on the

---

113 B. Levine 1992, p. 71. Honeck 2011, pp. 72–3, 83–90, 93–103. Efford 2013, pp. 63–4. Though Willich broke with Marx and Engels in 1852 over the prospects for the German revolution, he and Marx were on the same political page regarding the Civil War. See Easton 1966, pp. 320–5. Marx and Engels later gave Willich his due owing to his exemplary performance in the War.
114 Sikafis 1988, p. 720; Honeck 2011, pp. 96–8.
115 Finkelman 1995, pp. 45, 47. Littlefield 1995, p. 67. Aptheker 1983, pp. 352–5.
116 Reynolds 2005, pp. 488–506.

crusade of freedom' and 'has sent dread and terror throughout the entire ranks of the piratical army of slavery'.[117] Brown, the *New York Times* quoted Douglass, 'has not failed'. With the uprising in France still inspiring him, Douglass asserted that Brown 'has dropped an *idea*, equal to a thousand bombshells into the very Bastille of slavery. That idea will live and grow, and one day will, unless slavery is otherwise abolished, cover Virginia with sorrow and blood'.[118] The one-time pacifist was primed now to embrace what Brown so accurately predicted as his militancy led him gallantly to the hangman's noose: 'the crimes of this *guilty land: will* never be purged *away*, but with Blood'.[119]

Marx and Engels learned of the reaction to Brown's execution by at least the first week in January 1860. Ever conscious of the global picture, Marx – providing the epigram that introduces this chapter – commented to his partner on 11 January: 'In my view, the most momentous thing happening in the world today is the slave movement – on the one hand in America, started by the death of Brown, and in Russia, on the other'. The latter referred to Czar Alexander's recent decree to emancipate the peasantry – Russia's slaves. Given Marx's ever-present financial difficulties – 'I really don't know how I can keep my head above water' – and their consequences – 'I simply cannot get on with my work' – the likelihood that 'a "social" movement has been started both in the West and in the East' was just the tonic he needed: 'this promises great things'. 'I have just seen', he then told Engels, 'in the [*New York*] *Tribune* that there's been another slave revolt in Missouri, which was put down, needless to say. But the signal has now been given. Should the affair grow serious BY and BY, what will become of Manchester?' Not a disinterested question. Exactly sixteen months later to the date, 'the affair' indeed became 'serious', with major repercussions for the textile industry in Manchester, England – and, in turn, for the Marx household. Engels, whose own income derived from his family's textile mill in Manchester where he worked, had been providing needed funds to Marx and family. As for the 'slave revolt in Missouri', specifically in the small town of Bolivar at the end of December, it instantiated what Marx was hoping for.[120] In hindsight, it anticipated the far more consequential slave revolt at the core of the Civil War.

---

117   P. Foner 1950b, p. 460.
118   Blight 2018, p. 311.
119   Reynolds 2005, p. 395.
120   Marx and Engels 1975–2004u, pp. 4–5. In addition to the *New York Daily Tribune*, other papers reported on the revolt; see https://hd.housedivided.dickinson.edu/index.php/node/28719.

Engels's reply to Marx is also instructive.

> Your opinion of the importance of the slave movement in America and Russia is already being confirmed. The Harpers-Ferry affair, with its sequel in Missouri, is bearing fruit. Everywhere the free NIGGERS in the South are being hounded out of the states, and I have just seen from the first New York cotton report ... that the planters HURRIED their cotton ON TO THE PORTS IN ORDER TO GUARD AGAINST ANY PROBABLE CONSEQUENCES ARISING OUT OF THE HARPERS-FERRY AFFAIR.[121]

Hurrying 'cotton on to the ports'! – the first sign of the slavocracy's panicky reaction to Brown's daring action didn't quite correlate with the confident slave masters that Hammond sought to portray eighteen months earlier in his 'King Cotton' speech to the US Senate. What Engels reported to his partner testified to the global significance of the slave-based cotton trade and, thus, why 'the Harpers-Ferry Affair' would provoke the all-too-fateful response of the slavocracy in April the next year.

Of utmost importance is what caught the attention of Marx and Engels – not Brown's heroic actions per se but rather the responses to them, specifically those of the enslaved. Their agency, as the millennia-old class struggle taught, would be determinant in that movement of history. Though an initially unsuccessful agency, 'needless to say, the signal' – as events in a few years would confirm – 'has now been given'. Two decades later Engels, with the advantage of hindsight perhaps, credited Brown as having done 'more than anyone else for the abolition of slavery'.[122]

Peasant emancipation in czarist Russia also caught Douglass's eye. As he noted eight months later at the annual West Indies Emancipation celebration, even in that 'grim and terrible [land], half way between barbarism and civilization ... supremely indifferent to the good or ill opinion of mankind – with no freedom of tongue, no freedom of the press ... The car of emancipation is advancing gloriously ... the shouts of millions ... go up in joy over the freedom of the Russian serf'.[123] That Douglass and Marx drew inspiration in real-time from

---

121 Marx and Engels 1975–2004u, p. 7. See Introduction regarding the usage of the N-word by Marx and Engels.
122 Marx and Engels 1975–2004z, p. 77. As Walter Stahr writes, 'In a sense, Brown failed, for his raid on Harpers Ferry did not lead to a slave rebellion. In another sense, he succeeded, for his raid and the *reaction* to his raid did more than any other single event to lead to the Civil War'. Stahr 2021, p. 287.
123 Blassingame 1985, p. 370.

the same two events underscores the core political character they both shared as partisans of the millennial old human emancipation project. Yet again the two articulated the same global political perspective, even if for different reasons.

2.6   Lincoln's Election

The spectre of John Brown, not surprisingly, hung over the truly consequential presidential election of 1860. For at least a decade the future of slavery had dominated the national electoral arena. Harpers Ferry and what it portended, namely an armed showdown between pro- and anti-slavery forces, prompted the still new anti-slavery Republican Party to take, unlike in its 1856 campaign with the Frémont candidacy, a less intransigent stance on ending the peculiar institution with a candidate to match. Moving toward the centre of the political spectrum, a time-worn feature of American electoral politics, was the best way, the Republicans thought, to ensure victory in November. Compromise, going back to 1820, seemed to be the time and tested way to address the inconvenient issue. But Brown dramatically objected in a way no one had done before. Kicking the proverbial can down the road had to cease, a fact that even the mainstream's most anti-slavery party was unwilling to face – unless made to do so.

Douglass's response to the 1860 presidential campaign was, to put it charitably, conflicted due to, as Marx might have explained again, 'circumstances' beyond his control – the reality of bourgeois electoral politics. Not long after his return to the US from England, the Republicans, at their convention in May in Chicago, nominated on the third ballot a compromise candidate for the presidency, Abraham Lincoln. The collective thinking of the gathering was that a candidate not identified with the abolitionist movement would be more attractive to voters opposed to slavery, especially in lower north states such as Pennsylvania and Illinois, but repulsed by Brown's raid. Lincoln, compared to the alternative Republican candidates, seemed to be the best choice. The platform the convention adopted for him to run on made clear that, like the 1856 platform, it opposed slavery in territories where it did not exist. At the same time, it signalled, unlike in 1856, that a Republican administration would not interfere with the institution in those states where it existed – the sticking point for Douglass.[124]

Douglass's formula for the 1852 and 1856 presidential campaigns had been to initially endorse the candidate of the principled abolition party and then, as

---

124   For a book-length treatment of the 1860 campaign, including the Republican nominating contest, see Egerton 2010.

the election date drew closer, switch his support to the lesser-evil anti-slavery party, either the Free Soil Party in 1852 or the Republicans in 1856. For 1860, however, he took a stance, according to Douglass scholar James Oakes, 'that baffled his contemporaries and has perplexed historians ever since'. After initially expressing a liking for Lincoln but a distaste for the Republican platform, he made 'a startling announcement' in July. 'He would "sincerely hope" for a Republican victory "over all the odds and ends of slavery combined against it". But he would cast his own vote for the Radical Abolitionist candidate, knowing that the party was now a shrunken remnant of its former self. He hoped the Republicans would win, but as he wrote to his longtime friend Gerrit Smith, "I cannot support Lincoln"'.[125]

The 'baffling' conduct of Douglass in the lead-up to the November election was actually, David Blight explains, 'the searching efforts of a black leader to comprehend an amalgam of political interests and a party that seemed to both despise and champion his people'. Moreover, this conduct revealed 'the reflections of a hardened abolitionist not certain whether the impending political collisions augured the liberation or the sacrificial doom of his people'.[126] In the end he probably did vote for Smith. Why Douglass rendered ineffective his vote though clearly wanting the Republicans to win can only be a question for speculation. Whatever the reason, he vacillated on what until then was the country's most momentous election. And, unlike in the 1856 Frémont campaign, he failed to use his *Monthly* to promote Lincoln's election – not Douglass's finest political hour. In hindsight he seems to have missed an opportunity to help elect the president who did more than any other one to advance the quest for racial equality in America.

In instructive contrast to Douglass's prevarication during the 1860 election stood the minuscule but resolute Marx party – exactly because it functioned not as a conflicted individual but as a disciplined collective with political responsibilities. It too had to grapple with the reality of the 'lesser/evil' Lincoln candidacy, but once Marx's comrades decided to support the Republican nominee, they single-mindedly did just that.

Having campaigned for Frémont in the 1856 election, Weydemeyer had the wherewithal to come on board for Lincoln. To do so required a venue that Milwaukee, where he was living in 1860, didn't offer. An invitation to move to Chicago to edit the daily newspaper *Stimme des Volkes* (*The People's Voice*) of

---

125 Oakes 2007, p. 89. For Douglass's speech announcing he would vote for Smith but sincerely hope for Republican victory, see Blassingame 1985, pp. 366–87, especially pp. 381–2. For Douglass's letter to Smith see McKivigan 2018, p. 303.
126 Blight 2018, pp. 322, 324–5.

the *Arbeiterverein* (Workers' Party) got his positive reply. No doubt decisive in Weydemeyer's decision was that Chicago would be the site of the upcoming Republican national convention located in Lincoln's home state. Once in his new post Weydemeyer contacted Marx for assistance and consultation regarding 'the question of Negro slavery' especially.[127] Enthusiastically, Marx, who was deeply involved in a libel suit having to do with his involvement in the 1848 German revolution, appealed to a number of 'party' members in Europe to become correspondents for the paper: 'as party work it is *very* important. W[eydemeyer] is one of our *best* people'.[128] Being part of a transnational collective continued to mark Weydemeyer's political work in America since his arrival a decade earlier.

From Chicago Weydemeyer collaborated with another 1848 veteran, Adolph Douai, 'to mobilise support among German-American workers for the Republican party' in New York.[129] Douai had already earned well-deserved anti-slavery credentials, first as the leading abolitionist voice in Texas (during his stay in San Antonio from 1852 to 1856), and then later in Boston where he challenged the reactionary views of the renowned Harvard naturalist, Louis Agassiz. 'He attacked Agassiz not only as a reactionary but as a racist, noting that his belief in Negro inferiority – as set forth in his 1850 essay 'The Diversity of the Origin of the Human Race' – helped to provide a rationale for slavery'.[130]

On the eve of the Republican national convention in May 1860, Weydemeyer and Douai were delegates to the Deutsches Haus conference in Chicago. Organised by the German American Republican clubs around the country, it aimed to influence the outcome of the convention. Its priorities included: the convention take a strong anti-slavery position; that it oppose Know-Nothing 'Americanism' – specifically, restrictive naturalisation laws; lastly, that it support congressional passage of the Homestead Act.[131] The conference resolutions reflected all three positions.[132]

---

127 Marx and Engels 2016, p. 18. Marx and Engels 1975–2004u, p. 123, reveals that many of his letters are missing.
128 Marx and Engels 1975–2004u, p. 117.
129 P. Foner 1977, p. 26.
130 P. Foner 1977, pp. 15–23, 25.
131 For Weydemeyer and Douai, support for the Homestead Act was only one item of the Marx party's programme in America whereas for Hermann Kriege, who claimed to be a representative of German communism in the US, land reform was the primary goal and, thus, the target of Marx's and Engels's ire in 1846. See Chapter 1, pp. 51–2.
132 For the latest treatment of the conference, see Achorn 2023, pp. 202–5.

Regarding the all-important issue of slavery, the conference resolved that the founding principles of the Republican Party from the 1856 convention be 'applied in a sense most hostile to slavery'.[133] While accounts of the conference are sketchy, Weydemeyer was one of its 'forceful characters' and he 'worked closely together with Douai to realise its aims'.[134] There is some suggestion that Weydemeyer, while an active participant in the conference, didn't see it, as some apparently did, as an effort to give marching orders to the German American delegates to the Republican convention. To have done so would have meant 'usurping the rights of the people' who elected delegates to the latter – evidence that the Marx party member scrupulously observed democratic norms.[135]

The Deutsches Haus delegates 'requested' that the German-American delegates to the Republican convention make every effort to have the resolutions become part of the party's platform. Though only partially successful, in 'the end, the Republican National Convention did satisfy many of the Deutsches Haus concerns'.[136] If the platform wasn't as 'hostile to slavery' as they hoped, it did incorporate positions with which they could live – ultimately, not unlike Douglass. For other concerns – naturalisation laws and the homestead legislation – they were more successful.

Because the Deutsches Haus meeting tactically decided not to back any particular presidential nominee, it actually improved Lincoln's chances – an outcome that was apparently wanted by some delegates. Those from Baltimore, for example, had concluded by the time of the Chicago convention that Lincoln, though not as anti-slavery as they would have wished, was more electable – which Douglass also admitted.[137] Weydemeyer's *Stimme des Volkes*

> judged the ... platform 'certainly something short of a radical one, and a little lukewarm', but one nevertheless 'that in general satisfies the demands we make upon it'. It believed Lincoln was 'the choice of the conservative wing of the Republican Convention' but vowed to support him as the 'lesser of two evils'. [August] Willich's *Cincinnati Republikaner* took the party's preference for Lincoln over an outright radical as 'a stunning blow'. But at least, it noted, Lincoln was free of Know-Nothing taint ... 'If

---

133 Herriott 1928, p. 189.
134 Herriott 1928, p. 181, P. Foner 1977, p. 26.
135 Berquist 1966, p. 296.
136 B. Levine 1992, p. 248.
137 Herriott 1928, pp. 155–6, offers the example of the Baltimore delegates to the meeting.

Lincoln is not enshrined in the hearts of the people like Frémont, he has nonetheless labored among the people all his life – he is truly a self-made man!'[138]

Like Douglass, the Marx party and kindred comrades like Willich were reluctant supporters of Lincoln. But unlike Douglass, they actively campaigned for a Republican victory. An ad in Willich's *Republikaner* declared: 'Close Ranks! For Free Labor, against Slavery. Abraham Lincoln for President! Hannibal Hamlin for Vice President!'[139] Marx would have agreed. Hence his comment – the first time on record he weighed in on a US presidential contest – to a party member in Berlin shortly before the election: 'This time there seems good reason to hope that victory ... will go to the REPUBLICAN PARTY'.[140] Weydemeyer moved to New York City in August 1860, allowing him to work more closely with Douai on the campaign, activism about which he kept Marx informed.[141] Their activism proved to be of enormous help since the clothing industry bosses – right-wing Democratic partisans like most of the city's bourgeoisie – carried out a scare campaign to get their tailors to vote for the Democratic-fusion ticket that the slavocracy could live with. A vote for Lincoln, they claimed, would lead to secession, an economic crisis, and the loss of their jobs.

Because the German American vote, concentrated in New York City, could tip the state's vote in favour of Lincoln, and because the vast majority of the tailors in the city were German, Weydemeyer's presence and political interventions were significant. Through Douai's newspaper, the *New Yorker Demokrat*, the Marxist-oriented Communist Club, and his own participation in the mass movement, Weydemeyer proved to be an effective campaigner. In the end he was able to minimise the scare tactics of the right-wing bosses.[142]

Although Lincoln lost New York City – the influence of its bourgeoisie and the weight of the Irish vote were decisive – Weydemeyer and Douai's efforts were not without reward. The Republican vote in the predominantly German wards increased markedly over that of the 1856 vote. Notably the wards in Brooklyn where most of the tailors lived – precisely those German workers to whom Weydemeyer had devoted special attention – contributed to Lincoln

---

138 B. Levine 1992, p. 249.
139 http://ourworld.compuserve.com/homepages/JanHochbruck/Cincinn.html.
140 Marx and Engels 1975–2004u, p. 210.
141 Marx's letter to Engels on 1 September 1860, indicates as much. Marx and Engels 1975–2004u, pp. 184–5.
142 Obermann 1947, pp. 108–13, and Obermann 1968, pp. 367–9. The first of the Communist Clubs was formed in New York with Weydemeyer's assistance and had some contact with Marx. P. Foner 1977, pp. 5–6.

actually winning a majority of the German-American vote. In Midwest cities where a Communist Club existed, specifically Chicago and Cincinnati, Lincoln won or was nearly successful no doubt due in part to Communist Club campaigners.[143] How effective Weydemeyer's endeavours were in all this is unclear. Marx, nearly overwhelmed with a family health crisis, pressing an unsuccessful libel suit to defend his political reputation, as well as writing and publishing a book to accompany that legal project, offered little or no advice to Weydemeyer. But once able to come up for air and to appreciate the implications of Lincoln's election, he quickly prioritised developments on the other side of the Atlantic.

2.7 The Secession Crisis

Even before Lincoln's election, secessionist sentiment had been building in the South in the aftermath of Harpers Ferry, with South Carolina, the state with the highest per capita number of slave owners, in the vanguard. Brown's abortive raid provided the proponents of secession with, if not the proverbial smoking gun to make their case, something that could serve the same purpose.

On the first anniversary of Brown's execution, Douglass told an audience in Boston on 3 December 1860 that slave state secession from the Union would be propitious because the incoming Lincoln administration would not be obligated to enforce the Fugitive Slave Act. But the sixteenth president would not take office until 4 March 1861. The incumbent, James Buchanan, qualitatively more hostile to abolition, still had three months to be a protagonist. Just as Douglass was addressing the Boston audience, Buchanan issued his State of the Union message. Though opposed to secession, he declared that he could do nothing about it. 'Without descending to particulars, it may be safely asserted that the power to make war against a State is at variance with the whole spirit and intent of the Constitution'.[144]

Douglass, obligated to deal with political reality in the moment, and without knowing what Buchanan had written, declared in his Boston address that arms could be and, he hoped, would be used if slave state secession occurred. Secession under Buchanan could have unintended consequences: 'In case of such a dissolution, I believe that men could be found ... [anti-slavery filibusters] ... who would venture into those States and raise the standard of liberty there, and have ten thousand and more hearts at the North beating in sympathy with

---

143 Both Nadel 1990, p. 136, and B. Levine 1992, pp. 249–53, provide details, especially, the latter, for the national picture.

144 https://www.presidency.ucsb.edu/documents/fourth-annual-message-congress-the-state-the-union

them. I believe a Garibaldi would arise who would march into those States with a thousand men, and summon to his standard sixty thousand, if necessary, to accomplish the freedom of the slave'.[145]

Douglass wished for another Brown. The Italian revolutionary nationalist, Giuseppe Garibaldi, the Che Guevara of that era who sympathised with the anti-slavery cause, would be a godsend. What Douglass hoped for registered, again, how far the former pacifist had travelled over the course of the decade. And he clearly had, as in the case of Brown, no qualms about the skin colour of whoever could be so bold.

On 20 December, South Carolina's slavocracy granted Douglass, at least in part, his wish. Their unanimous vote to not just separate but to dissolve the Union meant that they 'can only be satisfied when Cotton is declared king'. South Carolina, and any other cotton state that followed it, could only succeed by using, he wrote prophetically, 'swords, guns, powder, balls, and men behind them to use them ... South Carolina must conquer the United States, or the United States must conquer South Carolina'.[146] Whether the Palmetto State's slave owners could get away with secession depended, Douglass cautiously or even nervously recognised, on the resolve of the president-elect.

Three weeks later the slavocracy in Mississippi followed its counterpart in South Carolina. Mississippi's Ordinance of Secession of 9 January 1861 is worth highlighting due to its utterly transparent raison d'être – the Ordinance confirmed Marx's insight about the indispensable role of slave-produced American cotton in the world capitalist economy.

> Our position is thoroughly identified with the institution of slavery – the greatest material interest of the world. Its labor supplies the product which constitutes by far the largest and most important portions of commerce of the earth. These products are peculiar to the climate verging on the tropical regions, and by an imperious law of nature, none but the black race can bear exposure to the tropical sun. These products have become necessities of the world, and a blow at slavery is a blow at commerce and civilization. That blow has been long aimed at the institution, and was at the point of reaching its consummation. There was no choice left us but submission to the mandates of abolition, or a dissolution of the Union, whose principles had been subverted to work out our ruin.[147]

---

145 Blassingame 1985, pp. 418–19.
146 P. Foner 1952, pp. 58–9.
147 https://avalon.law.yale.edu/19th_century/csa_missec.asp

What followed was a list of sixteen instances of that 'long aimed' campaign. Mississippi's declaration of secession, insufficiently cited by historians, left little doubt about the primary motive for the secession – 'commerce'.[148] Notably Mississippi's ruling elite employed the same racist ideology to rationalise chattel slavery that Hammond defended in his King Cotton/Mudsill speech three years earlier – an ideology with which Douglass, again, was all too familiar, and which was not unrelated to positions rebutted by the Marx party sympathiser Adolph Douai.

South Carolina's secession got Engels's attention – not surprising given his family's business connections in Manchester, the world's major importer of Southern cotton. Following comments about a number of potential political hotspots in Europe, he noted to his partner on 7 January 1861 that in 'North America things are also heating up. With the slaves the situation must be pretty awful if the SOUTHERNERS', South Carolina's slavocracy, 'are playing such a risky game. The least irruption of irregulars from the North might result in a general conflagration. At all events, one way or another, slavery would appear to be rapidly nearing its end and hence also COTTON PRODUCTION. What repercussions this will have on England, we shall soon see'.[149]

Engels's assumption, regardless of its accuracy, that the enslaved were the actual protagonists in provoking the slavocracy to secede, complemented what Marx had thought about the significance of Harpers Ferry and the slave insurgencies it sparked. Both of them, at least in that moment, prioritised the actions and agency of the enslaved. Like Douglass, Engels, too, thought that secession might induce anti-slavery Northern 'irregulars' to move southward – Douglass's 'filibusters' – thus provoking 'a general conflagration'. If overly optimistic at the time, Engels's prediction about 'slavery ... nearing its end' proved to be accurate, with 'repercussions' not only in England but elsewhere. Marx, still reeling from household health and financial crises, admitted that he hadn't had time to even read the *Tribune* while all of this was happening.[150] The most he could say, to a party member in Berlin on 16 January, was that 'the slavery crisis in the United States will bring about a terrible crisis in England in a year or two; the Manchester COTTON LORDS are already beginning to tremble'.[151] Once Fort

---

148 Surprisingly, Walter Johnson, in Johnson 2013 doesn't cite the Ordinance.
149 Marx and Engels 1975–2004u, p. 242.
150 Marx and Engels 1975–2004u, p. 265. Although, interestingly, he did read, 'for recreation ... Appian's Civil Wars of Rome in the original Greek. A most valuable book' – in preparation, possibly, for the 'great conflagration'.
151 Marx and Engels 1975–2004u, p. 246.

Sumter exploded almost exactly three months later, he would become as attentive as his partner had been to the history-altering events on the other side of the Atlantic.

As the secession crisis deepened, Douglass employed his *Monthly* in an attempt to embolden the president-elect as 4 March approached, Inauguration Day. He initially expected Lincoln to stand tall, but he didn't take anything for granted. Reject, he demanded of Lincoln, 'the whines for compromise' being made by too many influential voices in the North, by matching the intransigence of the slave power that 'can accept no compromise, no concession, no settlement that does not exalt slavery above every other interest in the country'.[152] Douglass wanted wrath and fire to be poured onto the South as soon as possible. 'Let the conflict come', proclaimed the *Monthly* right before the Inauguration, and 'God speed the Right, must be the wish of every true-hearted American, as well as that of an onlooking world'.[153]

The Marx party and its collaborators also sought to stiffen Lincoln's spine in the face of the growing secession movement. Douai, like Douglass, employed his pen specifically for the *New Yorker Demokrat* to do so.[154] But it was in Cincinnati once again, with Willich no doubt in the lead, that the effort was probably the most impactful. On his way to Washington, D.C. for the inauguration, Lincoln was greeted on 12 February by a delegation of two thousand German Americans workers in the city with a message:

> Sir – We, the German free workingmen of Cincinnati, avail ourselves of the opportunity to assure you, our ... sincere and heartfelt regard. You earned our votes as the champion of Free Labor and Free Homesteads. [We reject any efforts] to create an impression, as if the mass of workingmen were in favor of compromises between the interests of free labor, and slave labor, by which the victory just won would be turned into a defeat ... We Trust, that you ... will uphold the Constitution and the laws against secret treachery and avowed treason. If to this end you should be in need of men, the German free workingmen, with others, will rise as one man at your call, ready to risk their lives in the effort to maintain the victory already won by freedom over slavery.[155]

---

152   P. Foner 1952, pp. 62, 65.
153   P. Foner 1952, p. 67.
154   P. Foner 1977, pp. 28–9.
155   P. Foner and Shapiro 1994, pp. 287–8.

When Lincoln called for volunteers two months later to repel 'treason', many, if not most, of the signers of the message enthusiastically fulfilled their vow to the president-elect, including Willich.[156] Cincinnati – and no doubt some other stops on the way to Washington, DC – gave Lincoln every reason to believe that he need not rely on 'filibusters', as Douglass had hoped, or 'irregulars', as Engels had speculated, to crush the traitors in South Carolina. Though it took four bloody years, he was right.

Three weeks later Lincoln delivered his long-awaited Inaugural address. For Douglass, it was, at best, a mixed message – 'but little better than our worst fears and vastly below what we fondly hoped it might be'. Lincoln's affirmation of his long-standing position that the Constitution did not give him the right to end slavery in the states where it existed betrayed 'the inhuman coldness' of the new president. On the positive side, Lincoln explicitly rejected the *Dred Scott* Supreme Court decision by insisting that the Constitution guaranteed that free Blacks 'were entitled to all privileges and immunities of citizens in the several states'. In this regard, Lincoln had gone further than any prior president.[157]

The tone Lincoln struck convinced Douglass that it was the 'wildest nonsense' to presume 'that the people of the North will fight for the Union'. 'The bravest thing we ever did was to elect Lincoln ... and [also] our meanest thing ... as we certainly shall desert him, and leave him a potentate without power, a commander without a sword, the sport of traitors, and a hissing and byword to the surrounding world'. This sentiment clearly contradicted the opinion of the German workers in Cincinnati. Douglass's sobering but ultimately mistaken judgement may explain why he toyed with, for the first time, emigration – but only as Plan B. Yet, '[a]bolition', he also declared in that moment, 'may be postponed, but it cannot be prevented. If it comes not from enlightenment, moral conviction and civilization, it will come from the fears of tyrants no longer able to hold down their rising slaves'.[158] Engels – Marx too – would likely have agreed.

Five weeks later the slavocracy gave its fateful reply to Lincoln's peace offering. To make sense of it, know that almost immediately after Brown's failed raid and, most importantly, the positive reaction to it in the North, secessionists seized the opportunity to press their case. None of them proved to be more

---

156   On the response in Cincinnati to Lincoln's call, see Honeck 2011, pp. 98–103. Although not formally a Marx party member, Willich – Douai as well – who broke with Marx in 1851 over the course of the German revolution, was now on the same page as his former opponent. Of the significance of this political reconciliation, see Nimtz 2003, pp. 76–9.
157   P. Foner 1952, pp. 73, 78.
158   P. Foner 1952, pp. 82, 84–8. Blight 2018, pp. 337–40.

strategic and effective in advancing the campaign than Virginia slave owner Edmund Ruffin, later known as 'the father of secession'. Briefly, Ruffin tirelessly portrayed Brown's raid, execution (that he surreptitiously witnessed), and martyrdom in the North as an existential threat to the slavocracy. With creative flair he made use of the pikes that Brown had manufactured for the insurgent slaves, some of which Ruffin had obtained, to alarm and focus Southern minds. To the governors of each slave state he sent the weapons with the attached label: 'Sample of the favors designed for us by our Northern Brethren'. Each pike, he recommended, should be prominently displayed in slave state capitol buildings. Ruffin's campaign 'fell on willing ears'. Brown the bogeyman 'made even conservative Southerners think seriously about secession'.[159]

Less well known about Ruffin is that he had the honour, owing to his years-long campaign for secession, of firing the first shot that actually hit Fort Sumter on early morning 12 April 1861 – the act that sparked 'the great conflagration'.[160] Lincoln, like his predecessor Buchanan, gave no indication that he would employ arms to prevent secession during the early stages of the secession. 'Even after the firing on Fort Sumter, he declared, "I have no purpose to invade Virginia or any other state", though soon enough he would be forced to call up 75,000 troops'.[161] Ruffin's shot unintentionally but surely and singularly contributed to human emancipation. Until then secessionists like him could have exited the Union without costs. 'Slavery and racism provoked secession ... but secession did not necessarily', cautions historian Emory Thomas, 'provoke war'. That required conscious intention with a lot of hubris.[162] Whether Lincoln sought to entice the Fire-Eaters to make their fatal mistake by also saying in his Inaugural Address that he had the obligation as president to defend federal properties with arms can only be a subject for speculation.

Douglass was only two degrees removed, through Brown and Ruffin, from the most consequential action that would lead to abolition – the firing on Fort Sumter. If Brown did more than any single person, as his biographer David Reynolds persuasively argues, to cleanse America of its 'original sin', then Douglass's flirtation with Brown's militant project prior to Harpers Ferry – the hope it gave Brown that he would eventually come on board – to help 'hive' the 'bees', plus Douglass's ardent defence of the failed attack – was arguably the Black

---

159 Reynolds 2005, pp. 421–3.
160 Maloy 2020. Also, Detzer 2002.
161 Reynolds 2005, p. 272. For Lincoln's reply to the Virginia Secession Convention, see Fehrenbacher 1989, pp. 229–31. For Lincoln's vow to 'hold, occupy, and possess the property, and places belonging to the government' in his Inaugural, see Fehrenbacher 1989, p. 218.
162 Ayers and Thomas 2011.

abolitionist's most consequential contribution to abolition.[163] But someone like Lincoln was needed as president for that goal to be realised. Nothing suggests that any of the other three candidates in the 1860 election would have responded the way he did to the fire that Ruffin lit. Helping, therefore, to put Lincoln in the White House constituted the most consequential contribution to abolition made by Marx's and Engels's comrades and partisans in America – as the next four years would confirm. Unconsciously, both of our protagonists had aided and abetted each other's cause.

∴

Marx's and Douglass's two tellingly different responses to the 1848–9 Revolutions, the opening act of the Civil War, spoke to their fundamental differences – revolutionary versus reformist politics. But that difference anticipated only the far future and not the increasingly fraught situation on the other side of the Atlantic. If Douglass had once disdained the revolutionary methods that Marx and Engels defended, the growing power of the slave oligarchy in the decade afterward compelled him to reconsider his pacifism and move closer to what the two communists and their comrades in America deemed necessary to end the peculiar institution.

---

163 Reynolds 2005, pp. 438–79. For a more recent appreciation of Brown, see Brands 2020.

CHAPTER 3

Toward the Convergence of Douglass and Marx: From Fort Sumter to the *Trent* Affair

> ... by *carrying the war into Africa*. Let the slaves and free colored people be called into service.
> DOUGLASS, May 1861

∴

> ... the North ... has a last card up its sleeve in the shape of a slave revolution.
> MARX, May 1861

∴

> Of the two governments, looking at the circumstances of the [*Trent*] case, our government stands at this moment in a vastly more enviable position than that of England.
> DOUGLASS, Jan. 1862

∴

> ... simple justice requires to pay tribute to the sound attitude of the British working classes, the more so when contrasted with the hypocritical, bullying, cowardly, and stupid conduct of the official and well-to-do John Bull.
> MARX, Feb. 1862

∴

Although the Winter 1860–1 secession crisis alerted both Douglass and Marx that 'things' were 'heating up', neither realised how much. The firing on Fort Sumter took the two by surprise. Both protagonists had to reorder priorities. With access to a podium and stage and his own newspaper, Douglass could swing into action sooner. It would take Marx seven months to get into print to opine on developments in America. In the meantime he had to rely on correspondence with his partner Engels to begin making sense of the Civil War and its prospects and, most importantly, to figure out how best to politically respond – collaboration that proved, once again, to be invaluable. Though he had a publication of his own, Douglass was bereft of the kind of assistance that Engels provided to Marx. But unbeknownst to Douglass, from London Marx aided and abetted the uncompromising cause for abolition he was leading in America.

This chapter begins with Douglass's and Marx's initial responses to the slavocracy's attack on Fort Sumter, why it happened, what was at stake – to simply restore the Union or to abolish slavery? – and the likely outcome. For different reasons, our two protagonists agreed that abolition and the overthrow of the Slave Power was the fundamental issue in play and began energetically to utilise the venues available to them to advance that argument. Events on the ground then required them to opine on the Union's military conduct of the War. The exigencies of the War brought Douglass and Marx closer politically, not only on the domestic side of the conflagration, but in terms of its international repercussions as well. Nine months into the War the two were in objective if not conscious collaboration with one another in the promotion of the Union cause – as we will see at the chapter's conclusion.

1   The 'Fall of Sumter'

When the Slave Power attacked the federal fort in the Charleston, South Carolina harbour on the early morning of 12 April 1861, Douglass had expected to be on a ship bound for Port-au-Prince, Haiti – as he told an interracial audience on 21 April at the Rochester Spring Street AMEZ Church, during that Sunday's edition of the church's new speakers series. 'Mr. Douglass', according to a local newspaper, 'stated that he had intended to leave during the past week on a visit to Hayti, but that the vessel on which he had engaged passage had been taken for a better use, viz: for the service of the Government to transport troops &c, and it was uncertain now when he should'.[1] To the readers of the May issue of his *Monthly*, he added, 'We shall stay here and watch the current of events, and serve the cause of freedom and humanity in any way that shall be open to us during the struggle now going on between the slave power and the government'.

---

1   *Douglass' Monthly*, hereafter, DM, May 1861, p. 463.

Why Douglass arranged a visit to the Caribbean island has been the subject of much speculation that cannot be resolved here.[2] Far from 'uncertain', however, is that he never rebooked a trip to Haiti during the next four years. The conflagration, ignited, literally, by Fire-Eater and John Brown-hater Edmund Ruffin, required his undivided attention.

Douglass heralded what Ruffin had sparked. 'He reviewed', to the same audience on 21 April, 'the events of the past week, and considered it as a week of greater historical interest than any which has occurred in American history, if not in the history of the world ... He concluded by recommending every member of his audience to stand by the country and the Constitution and each to perform their part in inaugurating a reign of righteousness in the land'.[3] Not since the plebeian uprising in Paris in February 1848 had Douglass been so enthused.

A schadenfreude-like tone marked his first published pronouncement on the Fort Sumter attack. 'The chickens', implied in the first part of his editorial, under the title 'Nemesis', had 'come home to roost' for 'our proud Republic', owing to the many proverbial cans about 'our National Sin' that had been cowardly kicked down the road.

> The power given to crush the negro now overwhelms the white man ... [A]ny attempt to secure peace to the whites while leaving the blacks in chains ... will be labor lost ... The American people and the government at Washington may refuse to recognize it for a time: but the 'inexorable logic of events' will force it upon them in the end; that the war being waged in this land is a war for and against slavery; and that it can never be effectively put down till one or the other of these vital forces is completely destroyed.[4]

Unbeknownst to Douglass, that 'occasional correspondent' in London, whose articles in the *Tribune* he no doubt read, had reached a similar conclusion about the same time, but – as we will see – with an important clarification.

---

2   Doyle 2015, p. 156, claims that Douglass and his white companion Ottilie Assing made plans to move to Haiti owing to his disenchantment with the Lincoln presidency and the possibility that the interracial couple could have a more public relationship. Blight 2018, however, pp. 337–8, disputes such a claim, saying the long-planned trip was not for the purpose Assing's biographer, or perhaps Assing herself, suggests. Rather, McKivigan 2008 argues it was for reconnaissance at the urging of fellow abolitionist James Redpath – maybe in connection with Douglass's Plan B, p. 72.
3   DM, May 1861, p. 463.
4   DM, May 1861, p. 450.

In the second part of his editorial, 'The Fall of Sumter', Douglass listed the tactics of the secessionists in the lead up to the attack, amongst them 'planting liberty poles', the John Brown pikes that Ruffin had sent to slave state capitols to be put on display as propaganda.[5] But in Douglass's mind Ruffin and gang had overplayed their hand. 'They have completely shot off the legs of all trimmers and compromisers, and compelled everybody to elect between patriotic fidelity and pro slavery treason'. Other excerpts from the editorial reveal Douglass's mood at that moment. The attack constituted 'another instance of the wrath of man working out the purposes and praise of eternal goodness!' At stake was 'not merely a war for slavery, but ... a war for slavery domination'. But it 'remains to be seen whether they have acted wisely in transferring the controversy with the North from the halls of diplomacy to the field of battle'. Not certain, in other words, was which side would be victorious in the war. Whatever the case, 'we say, out of a full heart, and on behalf of our bleeding brothers and sisters, thank God! – The slaveholders themselves have saved our cause from ruin! They have exposed the throat of slavery to the knife of liberty ... Let the long crushed bondsman arise! ... Now is the day, and now is the hour!'[6]

Douglass admitted that until then he had been pessimistic. 'The Eagle that we left last month something like as good as dead' – an allusion to Lincoln's Inaugural Address – 'has revived again, and screams terror in the ears of the slaveholding rebels'.[7] Arguably nothing had ever heartened the abolitionist and one-time pacifist as did the attack on Fort Sumter. The cause for the first time looked winnable. A deeply moved Douglass attended Rochester's farewell ceremony on 3 May, attended by 20,000, for about 800 of the city's first contingent of fighters who answered Lincoln's call for 75,000 volunteers barely three weeks earlier. 'That departure', he told his audience at AMEZ Church two days later, many of whom had been there, 'was a thrilling spectacle. I witnessed it with feelings I cannot describe. And as I saw the tears, and heard the mournful sobs of mothers as they parted from their sons; wives – as they parted from their husbands; sisters – as they parted from their brothers, my very soul said in the depths of its bitterness, let slavery, the guilty cause of all this sorrow and sighing, be accursed and destroyed forever – and so I say today'.[8]

But 'How to End the War' concerned the third part of Douglass's editorial. 'Simple', he told his readers – 'Strike down slavery itself'. Again, how? 'This

---

5 Whether Douglass knew of Ruffin's vanguard role in the secession movement and his authorship of the ruse is uncertain.
6 DM, May 1861, pp. 450–1.
7 DM, May 1861, p. 451.
8 Blassingame 1985, p. 429.

can be done at once, by "*carrying the war into Africa*", – the epigram that introduces this chapter. 'LET THE SLAVES AND FREE COLORED PEOPLE BE CALLED INTO SERVICE AND FORMED INTO A LIBERATING ARMY, to march into the South and raise the banner of Emancipation amongst the slaves'. Boldly, Douglass claimed that 'ten thousand black soldiers might be raised in the next thirty days to march upon the South. One black regiment alone, in such a war, would be the full equal of two white ones'. Douglass ended his plea by highlighting convincing examples of Blacks in different localities who wanted to enlist in the cause but were frustratingly denied the opportunity as well as a proposal from a reader for forming 'Black regiments'.[9] The no-brainer Douglass began to argue for, namely the arming of African Americans, unceasingly occupied his *Monthly* and his public talks until Lincoln, sixteen months later – maybe with Douglass's prodding – finally decided to do just that.

In two Sunday public addresses at AMEZ, on 28 April and 5 May, Douglass reiterated and elaborated to varying degrees on what he had written in his *Monthly*. But meriting attention are a couple of exceptional points that he made at the 28 April meeting. At stake in the outcome of the War was which form of governance would prevail in America. The slavocracy, he charged, sought to impose slavery on the 'whole country'. Lincoln had said as much in his famous 'House Divided' speech in 1858.[10] That goal, Douglass continued, 'animates all their movements. The war on their part is for a government in which Slavery shall be National, and freedom nowhere, in which the capitalist shall own the laborer, and the white non-slaveholder a degraded man, to be classed, as such as men are now classed all over the South, as "poor white trash"'.[11] Here for the first time Douglass distinguished between Northern white workers and 'the white man' or 'the whites' in general, as he had called them in the May issue of his *Monthly*. Capitalist relations of production framed how race worked. The suggestion being, therefore, that Northern white workers had a class interest in the abolition of chattel slavery – certainly a claim of Marx, and one that the Marx party, with Weydemeyer in the lead, had been arguing for almost a decade.[12] Independently of Marx, most likely, the 'capitalist' was now on

---

9   DM, May 1861, pp. 451–2.
10 'Such a decision [by the Supreme Court] is all that slavery now lacks of being alike lawful in all the States', said Lincoln. Fehrenbacher 1989a, p. 432. The full House Divided speech is pp. 426–34.
11 DM, June 1861, p. 473.
12 See Appendix B: Marx and Engels on the Race Question: A Response to Critics for more details on this point.

Douglass's radar. How and to what end could only be answered once chattel slavery had been duly interred.

The other noteworthy point Douglass raised with his audience on 28 April had to do with the outcome of the just-started War – specifically how it would be resolved. 'The speaker', according to a newspaper reporter, 'proceeded to show that the only settlement that can be made will be by the destruction of the cause which has produced the difficulty – Slavery. True, the Government seems not to be doing anything to bring about this result directly; but things are working. If the Government is not yet on the side of the oppressed, events mightier than the Government are bringing about that result'.[13] – foreshadowing the conclusion that Marx had also reached and would soon publicise.

The meetings at AMEZ Church in Rochester were just as important for Douglass as what he wrote. 'We have', he wrote to the readers of the June issue of his *Monthly*, 'therefore, with others, been holding public anti-slavery meetings here every Sunday afternoon during the last six weeks, speaking to crowded houses, sowing the seed of sound Abolitionism, which, whether in peace or in war, will never rest until the slave is redeemed from his chains, and made to rejoice in the possession of his liberty'.[14] As the young Engels put it in 1845: 'standing up in front of real, live people and holding forth to them directly and straightforwardly, so that they see and hear you is something quite different from engaging in this devilishly abstract quillpushing with an abstract audience in one's mind eye'.[15] Douglass would likely have agreed – advice that present-day inhabitants of cyberspace who pretend to be political activists could benefit from.

Marx and Engels would not have been surprised to learn that 'the vessel on which' Douglass had 'engaged passage' to Haiti had been commandeered by the federal government. Marx's first opinion on the outbreak of the War, in a letter to his uncle in Holland on 6 May, is instructive – capturing the similarities and differences between his and Douglass's almost simultaneous readings of the moment. Though far briefer than Douglass's editorial – comprising a bit less than half of the letter's content that mostly deals with family related matters – it displays a degree of specificity lacking in Douglass's account. For example, Marx emphasised the distinction – all so important as events would soon demonstrate – between 'the SECEDED STATES' and 'all 8 BORDER STATES', which he listed. 'The acts of violence ... perpetrated not only' by the former but

---

13   DM, June 1861, p. 473.
14   DM, June 1861, p. 468.
15   See Chapter 1, p. ##.

'some of the latter ... have rendered *all compromise* impossible' – an observation similar to Douglass's point about the attackers having 'shot off the legs of all trimmers and compromisers'. Then, most accurately, Marx predicted that 'there can be no doubt that, in the early part of the struggle, the scales will be weighted in favour of the South, where the class of propertyless white adventurers provides an inexhaustible source of martial militia'.[16] Douglass, on the other hand, had a different perspective: 'it remains to be seen' whether the Slave Power would prevail on the 'field of battle'.

Of more significant prescience, Marx then declared: 'IN THE LONG RUN, of course, the North will be victorious since, if the need arises, it has a last card up its sleeve in the shape of a slave revolution' – the other epigram that introduces this chapter. Douglass would have agreed with Marx except that he wasn't certain that the 'need' for that option would ever arise and that a slave revolt, therefore, needed to be the 'first card'. This explains all of the ink he spilled on making a case for the Lincoln administration to recruit Blacks into the war to crush the slaveholders.[17]

If Marx and Douglass agreed about 'a slave revolution' in 'the long run', what about the immediate situation? 'For the North', Marx continued, 'the great difficulty is the QUESTION [of] HOW TO GET THEIR FORCES TO THE SOUTH' – why the federal government's commandeering of Douglass's 'vessel' was necessary. To prove his point Marx provided detailed mileage from Northern staging areas like Boston, New York and Washington D.C. to Charleston and Montgomery, Alabama, the Confederate Capitol. Because the 'use of the railways by the NORTHERN INVADERS would merely lead to their destruction ... all that remains is sea transport and naval warfare'. But the latter, he noted with remarkable foresight, 'might easily lead to complications with foreign powers' – as events would soon confirm.

Such specificity makes evident the intense reading and research Marx had been doing about the United States since Fort Sumter. 'Maps of the United States covered the Marx family's dining room table and newspapers were stacked high in every corner', reported a visitor to the Marx household about this time.[18] As precocious as she may have been, it should come as no surprise that his six-year-old daughter Tussy 'composed letters to Lincoln offering

---

16   Marx and Engels 1975–2004u, p. 277.
17   Lincoln's Treasury Secretary Salmon P. Chase, an early anti-slavery leader of the Liberty Party and founder of the Republican Party, said something remarkably similar to Marx in late June 1861, although he professed a hope to avoid drawing 'the sword which we prefer at present to leave in the sheath'. See Stahr 2021, p. 346.
18   Doyle 2015, p. 151.

him advice on the war'.[19] Those maps probably remained in the same place for the duration. Having gone through the European Revolutions of 1848–9 proved advantageous to Marx's and Engels's analysis of America's belated echo of those upheavals – something Douglass, like most Americans, had never experienced. Veterans of the European Spring played – to be seen shortly – an outsized role in the War on behalf of the Union.

Marx was not just a keen dispassionate observer of what was taking place on the other side of the Atlantic; events there, he suspected, could have personal consequences. He had just visited his uncle Lion Philips in Holland – a progenitor of the Dutch multinational Philips conglomerate – to try to solve his continuing financial woes. 'For myself personally', he wrote, 'developments in America are naturally RATHER damaging since transatlantic newspaper readers have neither eyes nor ears just now for anything save their own affairs'.[20] In other words, his 'occasional correspondent' employment for the *Tribune* was now in jeopardy and, along with it, the economic well-being of his household.[21]

2   Douglass Gets on Board

In the June issue of his *Monthly* Douglass put the War on its front page for the first time, whereas his trip to Haiti, unlike in the May issue, was relegated to the last pages. Specificity now marked the coverage of the War and covered topics such as why Maryland, a border state he intimately knew, had not seceded; the publication became a roundup of War-related news from some of the Confederate states.[22] A more immediately concerning topic, however, was the slave-as-property issue owing to a decision that Lincoln's generals would soon face: whether to return runaway slaves to their owners or not. After dismissing, in Douglass's opinion, slavers' bogus claims to the right to reclaim humans as property – because the federal government was under no obligation to return property to those who had rebelled against the Constitution – Douglass then went on the offensive. The refusal of Union military officials to return fleeing

---

19   Gabriel 2011, p. 291.
20   Marx and Engels 1975–2004u, pp. 277–8.
21   His wife Jenny, by the way, provided essential assistance in that desperately needed work by transcribing his near illegible handwriting and perfecting his English – the kind of help that Douglass lacked in a marital partner. Marx's oldest daughter Jenny also began to perform those tasks. Gabriel 2011, p. 278. Why Anna Douglass remained illiterate and whether Douglass bore any responsibility for that is one of the unanswered questions about his nearly inscrutable private life. See Blight 2018, pp. 207, 212, 632.
22   DM, June 1861, p. 468.

slaves to their masters would actually facilitate the suppression of the rebel secessionists who depended on the labour of the enslaved. Thus, the decision by the Union to refuse to help re-enslave escapees could be made 'in the light of military wisdom', namely, the logic of war. Neither, for the same reason, would it make sense for a Union army to suppress a 'slave insurrection' – 'the last card up its sleeve' option of the North that Marx foresaw. How imminent Douglass thought that option was is uncertain. Elsewhere in the same issue, in an article about 'John Brown, Jr.', he claimed that 'a note from his bugle can at once bring to him a thousand men, ready for any enterprise which shall promise liberty to the slave and humiliation to the master'.[23]

That the War might substantially increase the number of runaway slaves was no longer a hypothetical issue as Douglass informed his readers at the end of his editorial. Union General Benjamin Butler, he had just learned, refused on 27 May to return three runaways who escaped to Fort Monroe in the Chesapeake Bay area in Virginia. Douglass felt optimistic: 'progress, and that is something – The end is not yet'. A few weeks earlier in Annapolis, Douglass noted scornfully, Butler had 'offered unasked to suppress a reported rising of the slaves' elsewhere in Maryland.[24] Douglass's introductory sentence to the note at the end of his editorial – 'our Government is taking a wiser and more humane course towards those of the slaves who succeed in getting within the lines of our army' – failed to make explicit that the Lincoln administration's War Department issued a directive on 30 May that permitted Union officers to now do exactly what Butler had done. While not allowed to interfere 'with the relations of persons held to service', they could 'in respect to the negroes who came within your lines from the service of the rebels … refrain from surrendering [them] to alleged masters'.[25] Though Douglass, in real-time, could not have perceived the significance of the directive, in hindsight it effectively constituted the first official recognition of the Union Army's indispensable role in slave emancipation.[26]

Under the heading 'Danger to the Abolition Cause', Douglass complained that his comrades 'still hope and believe that by some means now inscrutable, Providence will bring freedom to the slave out of this civil war. Herein is the danger of our laying down our mighty arms of truth and love before our great work of moral regeneration has been in any measure accomplished, and the

---

23   DM, June 1861, p. 467.
24   DM, June 1861, p. 466.
25   Berlin et al. 1985, pp. 71–2.
26   Gallagher 2011 continues to be the pathbreaking narrative about the topic.

millions of our fellows are still in chains'. However much abolitionists, he continued, should be grateful to

> the Divine powers of the universe ... [O]ur faith is at once to be suspect at the moment it leads us to fold our hands and leave the cause of the slave to Providence ... No doctrine is more grateful to the heart of the slaveholder, than that which would leave slavery to Divine Providence ... He fears more from the human conscience than from the Divine conscience. A meeting for prayer gives far less alarm than a meeting for works.[27]

A faint echo perhaps of what Marx wrote in 1847 about Providence,[28] Douglass's complaint registered how far the uncompromising abolitionist had travelled intellectually. If he had once looked to the heavens to explain social reality, the exigencies of war brought him down to earth and, thus, epistemologically, closer to Marx.[29] The practical implications of his new wisdom were obvious: 'Instead of giving up anti-slavery meetings, we should increase them; instead of calling home our anti-slavery agents, we should send out more; instead of allowing anti-slavery papers to languish for support, we should earnestly labor to extend their circulation and to increase their influence'.[30]

Douglass then, with 'a little malicious pleasure', indicated that two of his misguided abolitionist comrades had gotten some well deserved comeuppance. William Lloyd Garrison, Douglass's estranged one-time mentor, and his colleague Wendell Phillips had to eat some humble pie. 'We are very glad ... [to see that] they are not above instruction. They have not been able to get slavery out of the Union', with their two-decade long call for disunion, 'and have jumped at the first chance of killing it in the Union, and by the Union' – what the attack on Fort Sumter enabled. Douglass felt, in other words, vindicated by his decade-long alternative perspective of staying in the Union. Had the North withdrawn from the Union as Garrison and Phillips had long argued, then it would not have been in a position to chastise the Slave Power when it violently bolted in April 1861.

---

27   DM, June 1861, p. 467.
28   Chapter 1, p. 51.
29   Some Douglass scholars make a lot out of his reading with Ottilie Assing in 1859 the materialist Ludwig Feuerbach, who had impacted Marx. Whether Douglass had broken with Christianity and become an atheist, see Blight 2018, pp. 514–15. See also Wallace 2021, p. 252. Nick Bromell examines Feuerbach's potential influence on Douglass's language linking 'self-consciousness to consciousness of being human'. Bromell 2021, p. 52.
30   DM, June 1861, p. 467.

Marx, meanwhile, sought other venues to get into print given the increasing uncertainty about his employment with the *Tribune*. A request in early June from a leading liberal organ in Vienna to write about the War prompted him on 10 June to ask Engels for assistance. 'Since I would like to get the 2 sample articles off this week, you must do the military part about America for me. I will then fit it into the political part'.[31] The division of labour that he proposed to his partner at that time informed their collaborative analysis of the War until its end. Marx sorely needed Engels's assistance because, as he informed his partner, 'a week ago I made a serious start on my book' – what would six years later become the first volume of *Capital*.

In the same letter to Engels, Marx called Italian revolutionary Giuseppe Garibaldi – a hero for Douglass – 'the jackass'. Why? Because the Che Guevara of the nineteenth century turned down an unauthorised offer from a holdover of the Buchanan administration to head up a Union military unit to defeat the secessionists. Garibaldi reasoned that the new president had not declared the War one to abolish slavery but only to end the rebellion.[32] Only a 'jackass', in Marx's view, could not see that the War was unavoidably about abolition. Douglass, closer to the scene, could not, perhaps, be as certain as the historical materialist in London, which explains why he was now, from Rochester, on a mission to make sure that the War was decidedly abolitionist. Garibaldi, in his view, could be forgiven for not taking up the offer as long as Union officers were expected to return runaways to their slave masters.[33]

Two days after Marx's proposal to his partner, Engels replied with a detailed overview of the military picture at that moment. About a thousand words in length (the end of the letter is missing), it distilled the big picture, based, he admitted, on newspapers he no longer had and on inadequate maps. 'The South', Engels began, 'had been quietly arming for years, particularly since the fuss over the presidential elections' of November 1860 and with the illegal assistance of figures in the outgoing Buchanan administration. Only 'after the attack on Sumter, [was] the North ... sufficiently aroused to silence all outbursts on the part of the opposition, thereby making powerful military action a possibility'. He estimated 'that ten times' the 75,000 men that Lincoln called for 'were eager to volunteer, so that there may be up to 100,000 men now serving'. For both the Union and Confederate forces, controlling Washington DC, and everything related to that objective, was key – at least at that juncture.

---

31   Marx and Engels 1975–2004u, p. 292.
32   See Doyle 2015, pp. 19–20, for details.
33   DM, September 1861, p. 514.

Very perceptively, Engels noted that the 'extent to which Kentucky's neutrality is favourable to the North or South will probably depend on circumstances and events. For the time being, at any rate, it will restrict the theatre of war to the area that lies further east' – exactly what transpired for most of the War. While Douglass began to grow impatient with Lincoln's worries about Kentucky's 'neutrality', Engels knew that the logic of war dictated Lincoln's concerns.[34]

Despite the slavocracy's head start, Engels continued, it faced a major challenge – the demographic advantage of the North. 'For every man the South can still produce, the North will produce three or four'. An analysis of the data, he then showed, explained why. 'The seceded states have about 7½ million inhabitants, of which more than 3 million are slaves'. And one telling disadvantage for the South: 'a minimum of 1 million whites must be deducted to guard the slaves, so that barely 2 ½ million are left as the aggregate of the population available for war'. Douglass, in fact, instantiated Engels's point in the June issue of his *Monthly* with a report from Louisiana about sugar plantation owners failing to send their quota of white employees to the Confederate army, precisely for the reason Engels foresaw.[35] Shortly before his letter abruptly ended, Engels concluded: 'Man for man, there is no question that the people from the North are markedly superior to those from the South, both physically and morally'.[36] Douglass would have surely agreed.

Engels's first report to his partner on 'the military part' of the War reflected not only his own participation in the actual fighting in the German Revolution in 1849 but also his subsequent detailed study of and familiarity with martial history. Not for naught did he acquire his sobriquet in the Marx household, 'the General'. Marx, too, knew enough to be able to engage in informed discourse on the topic with his partner. In his thankful response to Engels on 19 June, he revealed that he had been reading on his own and didn't think much of Lincoln's generals – a wise assessment. As for '[Union General-in-Chief Winfield] Scott – now 76, to boot ... I would expect him to make tremendous BLUNDERS – if, that is, the old jackass isn't supervised by others. Above all, slow and irres-

---

[34] Modern scholarship continues to debate Lincoln's strategy of conciliating border-state slave owners. James Oakes writes, 'Lincoln was right to be concerned about the border states. Without them the North would probably have lost the Civil War, and the slaves would have lost their only real chance for freedom'. Oakes 2007, p. 152. While confirming Kentucky's strategic importance, Elizabeth Varon provides evidence that Kentucky Unionists were more firmly in control than Lincoln thought. Varon 2019, pp. 44–5.
[35] DM, June 1861, p. 477.
[36] Marx and Engels 1975–2004u, pp. 294–6.

olute'.[37] Douglass, again, like most Americans, lacked the kind of background the two veterans of 1848–9 had to make such judgments when the War commenced. 'Incidentally', in Marx's reply to Engels, 'from the facts appearing in the *Tribune* I see that the North is now speaking openly of a slave war and the abolition of slavery'.[38] That's not the picture a reader of *Douglass' Monthly* would have acquired; instead that publication bore a slightly more pessimistic tone regarding the prospects for abolition.

Douglass's 16 June lecture at the AMEZ Church revealed the intent of his call for an 'increase' in anti-slavery meetings. Much of the talk was a merciless indictment of the slavocracy and all the evils it represented – Anti-Slavery Lecture 101. During the assembly he issued a recommendation. Penalising the rebellious slave owners required abolishing slavery. 'I think that while our Government uses its soldiers to catch and hold slaves and offers to put down slave insurrections, and subject them to the control and authority of their rebel masters, it will make precious little headway in putting down the rebels, or in establishing the peace of the country hereafter'. Union success on the battlefield necessitated abolition. Douglass had confirmed the need to convert the War from one of simply putting down the rebels to one to end slavery. Here Douglass's argument anticipated his eventual political convergence with Marx.

Then Douglass began his wrap up. 'No grander opportunity was ever given to any nation to signalize, either its justice and humanity, or its intelligence and statesmanship, than is now given to the loyal American people'. Because of the War the abolition cause had never before had such a favourable chance to realise its long-sought goal. That outcome, however, wasn't inevitable – it had to be fought for, which is why he mounted his current campaign. Douglass ended by saying: 'I have only one voice, and that is neither loud nor strong. I speak to but a few, and have little influence; but whatever I am or may be, I may, at such a time as this, in the name of justice, liberty and humanity, and in that of the permanent security and welfare of the whole nation, urge all men, and especially the Government, to the abolition of slavery ... Sound policy, not less than humanity, demands the instant liberation of every slave in the rebel States'.[39] Whether Douglass engaged in a bit of false modesty is neither here nor there. More importantly he acted as if he had a loud and influential voice – not unlike the miniscule Marx party, except that its members now employed arms in the Union Army to convey their message.

---

37 Marx and Engels 1975–2004u, p. 299.
38 This may be evidence of James Oakes's thesis in *Freedom National*, that Republicans set out to emancipate slaves and abolish slavery from the outset of the Civil War. Oakes 2013.
39 DM, July 1861, pp. 485–6.

The Lincoln administration appointed one-time Republican presidential candidate John Frémont to be Commander of the Department of the West, with its headquarters in St. Louis. Veterans of 1848–9 who lived in the area were able to prevent Missouri, a border state, from seceding when the War began. But the situation was still precarious. On his return from a European trip, Frémont stopped in New York City in July to recruit aides for his command post. As soon as Weydemeyer, an artillery officer in the 1848 Revolution and a one-time campaigner for Frémont, learned of the job search he signed on.[40] Rising eventually to the rank of Lieutenant Colonel in the Union Army, Weydemeyer's letters to Marx and Engels were invaluable in providing them with a battlefront view of the War.

Three months into the War, Douglass lamented the conduct of the North. The government, he charged, failed to understand the diabolical character of the enemy and what was needed to defeat them. 'There is no whipping the traitors without hurting them. War was made to hurt ... and the only conceivable good which can come out of war, comes because it hurts'. And nothing would be more effective toward that end than the employment, again, of 'black troops'.[41] In the same July issue of his *Monthly*, not coincidentally, Douglass reprinted an extensive article from the *Atlantic Monthly* – the longest in the issue (in fact only concluded in the next one) – about the 1822 Denmark Vesey slave conspiracy in Charleston, South Carolina. The September issue included an article on the 1831 Nat Turner revolt in Virginia. Educating his readers about the history of slave insurrections indicated Douglass's hope for something similar in that all so opportune moment. Concurrently, Douglass criticised the *Tribune* for editorialising 'against making this a war for the destruction of slavery'.[42] Relevant to our comparison, this criticism confirms that he read closely the organ that published articles of 'an occasional correspondent' in London – articles by Marx that he would have likely read.

3   Marx's Return

To get back into print in the *Tribune*, Marx had to immerse himself in both the current situation in the United States as well as its history – while writing his magnum opus. His 1 July letter to Engels is instructive. It began by asking, with remarkable foresight, about troop manoeuvres on both sides 'at Manassas

---

40   Obermann 1947, pp. 118–19.
41   DM, July 1861, p. 481.
42   DM, July 1861, pp. 481–2.

JUNCTION' in Virginia. Three weeks later the War would take its first turning point exactly at that location – getting Douglass's attention for the first time. Not on Douglass's radar but also meriting recognition was the progress Union forces were making in Missouri, involving 1848 veterans, some of whom Marx apparently knew personally.

After a deep dive into US history Marx declared, 'I have come to the conclusion that [in] the conflict between South and North – for 50 years the latter has been climbing down, making one concession after another' – just what Douglass had been complaining about since the Compromise of 1850. The conflict, in Marx's opinion, had 'been brought to a head ... by the weight which the extraordinary development of the NORTH WESTERN STATES has thrown into the scales. The population there, with its rich admixture of newly-arrived Germans and Englishmen and moreover, largely made up of SELF-WORKING FARMERS' – as distinct from slave plantation masters – 'did not ... lend itself so readily to intimidation as the gentlemen of Wall Street and the Quakers in Boston'. The armed conflict in Kansas in 1856, 'from which this war really dates', originated in the readiness of the rapidly increasing North West denizens to come 'to blows with the BORDER RUFFIANS'.[43]

Douglass, unbeknownst to him, corroborated Marx's estimation of the sentiment in the 'North Western States'. His experiences in many of them as a stump-speech campaigner for abolition is instructive. About his first visit to Ohio in 1847, he observed that the 'West is decidedly the best Anti-Slavery field in the country'.[44] Between the beginning of February and the middle of March 1859, Douglass toured the Midwest delivering more than fifty speeches in six weeks. Unlike other speaking tours, the hostility the radical Black abolitionist encountered was minimal and he never needed to fight for his life when exiting such meetings. He could recall when 'it was common to meet with church doors bolted and barred against the cause of the slave', and when he and William Lloyd Garrison had 'their lives endangered in the civilized capital of Pennsylvania, for the utterance of simple abolition sentiments'. 'But', Douglass wrote in April 1859, 'times have changed very much of late ... We, therefore, bring no discouraging news from the West – none from Michigan, none from Wisconsin, none from Illinois – the cause of freedom is onward and upward in them all'. This report anticipated what Marx would write about the 'North Western States' two years later.[45]

---

43   Marx and Engels 1975–2004u, pp. 300–1.
44   P. Foner 1950a, pp. 262–3.
45   Blight 2018, p. 303. P. Foner 1950b, pp. 447–8.

Marx's point about 'self-working farmers' in the 'North Western States' recalls something else Douglass said about the 3 May farewell ceremony in Rochester for the first contingent of Union volunteers and the impression their departure made on him. 'It is not the sturdy farmer of the west', he insisted to the audience at AMEZ Church two days later, 'who tills his broad acres with his own hard but honest hands', nor, 'the skillful mechanic of New England ... [I]t is not the hardy laborer of the North, nor of the South, who has treacherously conceived this hell-black conspiracy to destroy the Government and the Liberties of the American people'. Those who had driven the country to civil war were 'of a privileged class, who are permitted to live by stealing. We owe it to the existence of a set of respectable robbers and murderers, who work their fellow men like beasts of burden, and keep back their wages by fraud'.[46] For Douglass, as for Marx, toilers were the true nobility and emphatically not the esteemed surplus-value thieves, the slaveholders. By the end of 1861, Douglass would come to recognise what Marx had accurately understood: 'The Northern and Western Members of Congress see and understand the cause of this rebellion ... and know the true remedy'[47] – the advantage, perhaps, Marx had of looking from afar.

Marx then revealed in his 1 July letter to his partner how meticulously he'd researched the facts related to the War's prelude. 'A closer look at the history of the secessionist movement reveals that [all of its components] ... are USURPATIONS without exception. Nowhere did they allow the people *en masse* to vote. This "USURPATION" – which is concerned, not only with secession from the North, but also with consolidating and intensifying the oligarchy of the 300,000 slave lords in the South *vis-à-vis* the 5 million whites – has been the subject of highly characteristic articles which appeared in the Southern PAPERS at the time'. To prove his point, since Engels seemed sceptical, Marx's 5 July letter provided details – accompanied with extensive quotes from local newspapers – about how the 'oligarchy' in virtually every slave state engineered the 'usurpation' in 'Bonapartist' fashion. That Marx tracked down so many Southern newspapers in London – not available in the British Museum Library or in Manchester where Engels lived – is in itself remarkable.[48] After processing as many historical details as possible, he proposed an explanation for the fateful attack on Fort Sumter. Due to the hierarchical character of their decade-long secessionist movement, 'the fellows were compelled to provoke a war so that with the cry "THE NORTH AGAINST THE SOUTH" they could keep the movement

---

46 Blassingame 1985, pp. 434–5.
47 P. Foner 1952, p. 186.
48 Marx and Engels 1975–2004u, p. 429.

going".[49] But after a war begins, it tends to generate its own momentum. No one wanted more to 'keep the movement going' than Fire-Eater movement founder Edmund Ruffin, explaining why he had been granted the honour of firing the first shot to hit the fort.

Modern scholarship sustains Marx's 'usurpation' characterisation of the secession project. In her authoritative account of the politics that birthed the Confederacy, historian Stephanie McCurry concludes: 'Only a small minority of the Southern people – fewer than 2 million adult white men out of a population of 12 million – had ever been consulted about the wisdom of secession and the risk of war ... never mind secured ... If that seemed an unremarkable aspect of Southern political life at the end of the antebellum era, it would not be so for long' – exactly why Marx thought it important to know the details about the secession process, specifically, who actually gave their 'consent' to it.[50] He assumed that the answer to that question would be meaningful, as McCurry subsequently shows in convincing fashion. Marx's and Engels's 'Address of March 1850 of the Central Authority of the Communist League' – their balance sheet on the German Revolution – declared that elections could be of immense value in not only propagating ideas but also so that political contestants could 'count their forces'.[51] Knowing who did and didn't vote for something would likely be decisive in the outcome of armed struggle. Douglass, on the other hand, apparently, was not interested in details about 'who' amongst whites in the South voted for secession. No comparable data exist in *Douglass' Monthly*. Seceded states, rather than the different types of denizens in them – except of course for Blacks who couldn't vote in South Carolina – seemed to be of sufficient interest to Douglass.[52]

Marx's penchant for comparative analysis likely began with university courses that exposed him to comparative jurisprudence, as reflected in his first publication in 1842. That press censorship laws varied not only between nations but also regionally within nation states, as the US case no doubt taught the young Marx – as well as Douglass the new newspaper editor – explains why he would have been attuned to the distinction between chattel slave states and non-chattel slave ('free') states when the War broke out. Prospective German immigrants to the US – as Marx himself once was – would also likely have been conscious of the North/South, 'free' state/slave state distinction in the US. What Douglass might have taken for granted was essential for future émigrés to know.

---

49   Marx and Engels 1975–2004u, pp. 305–9.
50   McCurry 2010, p. 77.
51   See Chapter 2, p. 60.
52   Foner 1952, pp. 57–62.

Though it took Marx until October 1861 to finally get something published in the *Tribune* about the War, his article, 'The American Question in England', addressed belatedly and unknowingly a 30 June speech and an early July article by Douglass. Both texts concerned how the War was playing out in public opinion in England. Back in May, shortly after the War had begun, 'great consternation' is how Marx described the mood in London. For Douglass, as he told his listeners – again, at AMEZ Church – of great importance was 'what the *London Times* had to say – what [former Prime Minister] Lord John Russell had to say', and even, 'what Louis Napoleon had to say'. The opinions of the European ruling elite, in other words, were on Douglass's mind.

But no one should express 'surprise' and 'indignation', Douglass continued, 'that European governments have manifested so little sympathy with the Government in suppressing the slave holding rebels'.[53] Despite 'her anti-slavery history and professions', even England had every right to be unsympathetic toward the North, he argued in his July article 'The Attitude in England Towards the United States'. 'We can easily see that in the view of the British public that the question of the abolition or non-abolition of slavery was not involved in the present contest'. Furthermore, 'it was ... natural that the statesman of Great Britain, especially in view of our pernicious Northern tariff, should, for commercial purposes, assume an attitude of friendliness to the new Confederacy ... It is ridiculous for the North ... in view of its anti-abolition record and even its pro-slavery policy, to claim the sympathies of Great Britain on abolition grounds'.[54] At fault, then, in Douglass's opinion, was not the British ruling elite but rather the Lincoln administration in Washington DC. He sounded almost like an apologist for the pro-Confederacy posture of London's 'statesmen'. Perhaps he thought that faulting Washington would put pressure on the Lincoln administration to declare the War to be an abolitionist project, thereby taking away London's excuse for not supporting the Union. But Douglass's critique effectively gave Britain's dominant class a free pass to maintain its backhanded support of the slavocracy – not inconsequential support, as events would soon demonstrate.

Marx would have none of that. The press organs of the British ruling elite in London – *The Times, The Economist, The Examiner, The Saturday Review* – and 'their hostile tone against the North, and their ill-concealed sympathies with the South' were exactly what he took to task in his 11 October article in the *Tribune*. Written about two months after Douglass's July article, it reads as if

---

53   DM, August 1861, p. 501.
54   DM, July 1861, p. 482.

Marx had actually read Douglass, though that's probably unlikely. What Marx had read was a letter from Harriet Beecher Stowe, world-renowned author of *Uncle Tom's Cabin*, in the *Times* on 9 September 'urging Britons to give moral support to the North'.[55] While Douglass took at face value 'England's anti-slavery history and professions', Marx treated shallow English moralism with sarcasm by describing British patricians as 'people affecting an utter horror of Slavery'. While Douglass derided the voices of those like Stowe for their 'surprise' about British lack of sympathy with the North, Marx took it as an opportunity to expose the hypocrisy of England's 'betters' and contrast it with – in subsequent articles – the superior and nobler morality of its proletariat. Marx, incidentally, was in good company with the celebrated liberal John Stuart Mill, who also took his class cohorts to task for not supporting the North. Unlike Marx, however, Mill was unwilling to go public with his critique until he thought it politically safe to do so – an object lesson in distinguishing smart people from smart people unafraid to publicise their political beliefs. Marx, by the way, lacked citizenship rights to do so.[56]

Marx began his exposé by acknowledging that the North explained its actions only as a defence of the Union instead of as a struggle to emancipate enslaved Africans. But it was the Southern slavocracy that initiated the war, and it did so, according to its Constitution and the Confederacy's vice-president, Alexander Stephens, to defend the 'peculiar institution'. 'It confessed to fight for the liberty of enslaving other people, a liberty which, despite the Northern protests, it asserted to be put in danger by the victory of the Republican party and the election of Lincoln'. For the British bourgeois press to feign disappointment with the North for not defending its actions as a war against slavery was hypocritical. 'If Anti-Slavery and idealistic England felt not attracted by the profession of the North, how came it to pass that it was not violently repulsed by the cynical confessions of the South?' – a question for which Douglass had no answer.[57]

As for the charge that the North had never really challenged slavery, Marx then sketched out US political history to show how the slavocracy, in alliance with the northern wing of the Democratic Party, sought to impose its will on the rest of the country – 'the general formula of the United States history since the beginning of this century' – with a number of successes including the Kansas-Nebraska Act. Having already drawn a similar portrait, Douglass would have

---

55 Marx and Engels 1975–2004j, p. 368n.8.
56 For details, see Nimtz 2019b, Chapter Three.
57 Marx and Engels 1975–2004j, p. 8.

concurred with Marx. But the victories were costly because they incurred the increasing hostility of anti-slavery forces in the North. 'If the positive and final results of each single contest told in favor of the South, the attentive observer of history could not but see that every new advance of the slave power was a step forward to its ultimate defeat' – the dialectic of the class struggle. Unless abolitionism was aided by some kind of Providential intervention, perhaps, that wasn't the outcome Douglass envisioned in fall 1861. The material basis for the North's advantage was its growth in population and the influence of the 'North-West ... from 1850 to 1860'. The formation and eventual victory of the Republican Party was the concrete political expression of that material basis.

Marx then defended the Republican Party against the charge of *The Economist* that its platform, calling for limiting slavery to the states in which it was already established, was disingenuous. He reminded his readers that it was the same newspaper that had argued only two years earlier that by 'dint of an economical law' slavery would be ended if denied the power to expand. Two years later, however, it changed its tune to say that a non-expansionist policy could not guarantee slavery's 'extinction'. The *Economist*, in other words, had manufactured another pretext to slander the Republicans and give backhanded support to the slavocracy. But, as Marx pointed out, it was exactly the anti-expansionist Republican platform that provoked the threats of secession from the slavocracy in December 1860 in the immediate aftermath of Lincoln's electoral victory. The slave owners also knew that their survival depended on slavery's expansion – the workings of an 'economical law'. But unlike the editors of *The Economist* they had also understood for some time that 'keeping up their political sway over the United States' was essential for the realisation of such a 'law'. The Republican electoral victory had now threatened that 'sway'.

A most important political reason informed the expansionist agenda of 'the Oligarchy of the 300,000 slave owners'. The only way they could 'maintain their sway at home' was 'by constantly throwing out to their white plebeians the bait of prospective conquests within and without the frontiers of the United States' – Marx's explanation for why non-slave owning whites in the south didn't challenge the oligarchy but rather gave them their support.[58] Afterall, the 'swinish multitude', Fire-Eater Edmund Ruffin's label for them, had to be aware of such contempt from the oligarchs.[59] No one knew that better than

---

58   Marx and Engels 1975–2004j, p. 14.
59   Isenberg 2016, p. 382n27.

Lincoln's vice-president Andrew Johnson – of enormous consequence when he succeeded Lincoln in 1865.

Class collaborationism, to employ a modern term for Marx's explanation, came, as it always does, with possible material perks. Douglass certainly knew and criticised 'white plebeians' who kowtowed to the slavocracy, as early as in his 1855 autobiography, *My Bondage and My Freedom*. Noteworthy are his recollections about the white workers with whom he had worked as a slave in Baltimore's harbour: 'these poor, white mechanics in Mr. Gardiner's ship-yard, instead of applying the natural, honest remedy for the apprehended evil, and objecting at once to work there by the side of slaves, made a cowardly attack upon the free colored mechanics, saying *they* were eating the bread which should be eaten by American freemen, and swearing that they would not work with them'.[60] Their 'prejudices', their 'pride' in being white and not Black, he argued, was reason enough for their 'cowardly' actions. Doubtless an accurate description, Douglass's account failed, however, to explain the origins of the 'prejudices' of those 'poor, white mechanics' that enabled Mr. Gardiner's divide and rule agenda. Douglass, at least with regard to his Irish fellow-toilers, surely knew, based on his trip to Ireland in 1847, that their anti-Black views were mostly non-existent in their homeland. Obviously, the Irish dock workers acquired those 'prejudices' in America. Marx offered an explanation – 'the bait of prospective' upward mobility.

Worth noting here is Confederate Vice-President Alexander Stephens's infamous 'corner-stone speech' of 21 March 1861, two weeks after the Confederates adopted their Constitution. In a not too subtle appeal to the South's white plebeians, he threw out the kind of 'bait' Marx may have had in mind.

> Many governments have been founded upon the principle of the subordination and serfdom of certain classes of the same race; such were and are in violation of the laws of nature. Our system commits no such violation of nature's laws. With us, all of the white race, however high or low, rich or poor, are equal in the eye of the law. Not so with the negro. Subordination is his place.[61]

With the likelihood of war on the horizon, three weeks before Ruffin's fateful shot, the slave oligarchs needed to secure the loyalty of their 'swinish multitude'. If Hammond in 1858 failed to specify who solely would be confined to

---

60 Douglass 2014, p. 247.
61 Alexander J. Stephens's 'Corner-stone Speech': https://www.battlefields.org/learn/primary-sources/cornerstone-speech

the 'mudsill', Stephens, three weeks before Fort Sumter, removed, understandably, all doubt. The oligarchs needed, as always, foot soldiers to keep them in power.

Five months into the War, Douglass returned to the topic of 'poor white people' in the slave holding states, about a month prior to Marx's comment. In an article about 'the natural and necessary social philosophy of slavery' he distilled how such a society functioned.

> The submission and deference which the people see practiced toward [slaveholders] by their slaves, speedily defuses itself among the people, and they measurably imitate the behavior of the slaves. The slave pulls off his hat, the poor man touches his, and the slavemaster is thus taught by common consent to regard himself as belonging to a privileged class. The lesson is learned naturally on both sides, and is the inevitable result of the relation. The slaveholder must be master of society, otherwise he cannot be master of his slaves. There are at times when slaves must be hunted, whipped and hanged, and they always need watching. All of this must be done by the non-slaveholding, or what is called *'poor white trash'*, the common name for poor white people at the South. They must give up the thoughts, words and bearing of free men, or the dingy rafters of human bondage topples about their heads.[62]

The threat, that is to say, of being reduced to some form of subjugation akin to what Black slaves experienced explained for Douglass 'poor white' complicity in the slave enterprise. For Marx – as if in response to Douglass but unlikely – there was more involved in the dance with the devil than just a threat, something that gave agency to 'white plebeians': again, the lure of upward mobility. Marx revisited the all-important issue in a subsequent article.

If *The Economist*, to continue with Marx's critique of Britain's ruling class organs, and those who held similar views were sincere, they would now, he argued, support the North since it 'had arrived at the fixed resolution of circumscribing Slavery within its present limits, and of thus extinguishing it in a constitutional way'. Implementing the Republican programme, in other words, would lead eventually to slavery's extinction. Exactly because *The Economist* was not sincere in its demand that the North wage a '"war for the emancipation of the Negro race"' – what they counterposed to the Republican stance – they

---

[62] DM, September 1861, p. 515. Marx was aware of this role of 'the 'POOR WHITES'' in slave society. He likened it to the Berbers who were recruited by French colonial rule in North Africa known as the Zouaves. Marx and Engels 1975–2004u, p. 307.

shuddered from even considering the 'repulsive' possibility of 'summoning the slaves to a general insurrection'. When provided an opportunity to advocate for such a war, the newspaper managed to find an excuse for not supporting the North. 'Thus the English eagerness for the Abolitionist war is all cant', Marx pointedly remarked. Why Douglass, who was pushing at that very moment for a slave insurrection, didn't see what Marx accurately saw, namely the repulsion of the British ruling class for such a slave uprising, deserves an explanation. The likely reason for Douglass's myopia was his long-held admiration for Britain's elite for having abolished slavery in its West Indian possessions in 1834, even though he knew that slave uprisings led to that abolition.

Regarding Douglass's charge about 'our pernicious Northern tariff' being a legitimate grievance for the 'statesmen of Great Britain', Marx would have found that complaint odd coming from an abolitionist. It complemented the decades-old one of the slavocracy, 'tired of being robbed of the fruits of their slave labor'. If the US imposed tariffs on British manufactured goods, Britain, in turn, was obligated to do the same for US exports, slave-produced cotton being the most valuable. No friend of protective tariffs, Marx had argued at least since 1847 that the debate between free traders and protectionists was one amongst the oppressors of the toilers and never in the interest of the latter, workers as well as slaves.[63] Contrary to Douglass's claim, the tariff, thus, wasn't 'our[s]' – something the toilers should take ownership of. Besides, as Marx pointed out, what Douglass was referring to, the Morrill Tariff, only went into effect in March 1861. 'The *Examiner* ought to know that the present rebellion did not wait upon the passing of the Morrill tariff for breaking out'. Up to then 'from 1846 to 1861 a Free Trade tariff had obtained', that is, a regime of Anglo-American trade liberalisation prevailed until the secessionist movement began to grow.[64] In other words, the tariff issue was only 'a pretext for secession' – as had been true in South Carolina's dispute with the federal government in 1832 – contrary to the claims of ruling class organs in London echoed by Douglass. Modern scholarship, again, confirms Marx's critique. The 'tariff was never more than an ancillary grievance added to the litany of secessionist charges against the incoming Republican Party's positions on slavery in the territories, the weakened federal enforcement of the Fugitive Slave Act, and the South's rapidly diminishing position in the United States Senate'.[65]

---

63 Marx, 'Speech on the Question of Free Trade', January 1848, Marx and Engels 1975–2004e, p. 450.
64 Marx and Engels 1975–2004j, pp. 14–15.
65 Magness 2009.

Marx concluded by speculating on the real reasons for British ruling class duplicity. He ended with a long quote from a liberal weekly, *The Spectator*, which suggested that a victory of the North would ensure a much stronger United States, while dissolution of the Union would leave the two regions at each other's throats for some time and thus 'draw out of our side the thorn of American rivalry'.[66] Whether this quote reflected Marx's own opinion is not clear, but it certainly meant that he considered the objections of the British bourgeois press to the Lincoln administration and the Northern cause to be disingenuous at best.

In his next *Tribune* article on 14 October, Marx introduced the English working class to his American readers. 'As long as the English cotton manufacturers depended on slave-grown cotton, it could be truthfully asserted that they rested on a two-fold slavery, the indirect [wage] slavery of the white man in England and the direct slavery of the black man on the other side of the Atlantic' – a not too subtle appeal for trans-Atlantic class solidarity on the part of both groups of toilers.[67] Six years earlier, as already noted, Douglass, in *My Bondage and My Freedom*, commented on the racial dimension of class exploitation on the docks of Baltimore where he had worked as a slave.

> The difference between the white slave, and the black slave, is this: the latter belongs to *one* slaveholder, and the former belongs to *all* the slaveholders, collectively. The white slave has taken from him, by indirection, what the black slave has taken from him, directly, and without ceremony. Both are plundered, and by the same plunderers. The slave is robbed, by his master, of all his earnings, above what is required for his bare physical necessities; and the white man is robbed by the slave system, of the just results of his labor, because he is flung into competition with a class of laborers who work without wages.[68]

Like Marx, Douglass, at least in 1855, sought to make a case for a transracial class alliance amongst the toilers. Douglass's insights about the similarities and differences of exploitation under the capitalist and the slave mode of production were remarkable, ones that Marx with his historical materialist perspective could have agreed with. Whether that concurrence would be the basis for potential future collaboration remains to be seen.

---

66   Marx and Engels 1975–2004j, pp. 15–16.
67   Marx and Engels 1975–2004j, p. 20.
68   Douglass 2014, pp. 246–7.

Not long after his 11 October *Tribune* article Marx detected what he thought was a change of opinion from British Prime Minister Lord Palmerston's government toward Washington owing to articles in the *Times* and *Economist*, Palmerston's mouthpieces in Marx's view. 'From the altered tone of the London Times during the past week', he told *Tribune* readers on 21 October, 'we may ... infer that Lord Palmerston is about to recede from the extremely hostile attitude he had assumed till now against the United States'. The *Times*, Marx pointed out, reconsidered its claim of Confederate 'military superiority', and the *Economist* now admitted that '"the indisputable fact [is] that the real aim and ultimate motive of secession ... was ... to extend Slavery over a vast, undefined districts, hitherto free from that curse"'. There is no indication that Douglass noted the 'change of tone' in the British ruling-class press. But Marx was all too happy to publicise it to the pro-Northern readership of the *Tribune*. If his assessment was accurate – which he promised 'to explain in a subsequent' article – it put into sharper relief a crisis that was about to happen in relations between the two countries.

Noteworthy, also, is Marx's last sentence: 'Before concluding, I may ... add that Mr. Forster, M.P. for Bradford, delivered last Tuesday, in the theater of Bradford Mechanics' Institute, a lecture 'On the Civil War in America,' in which he traced the true origin and character of that war, and victoriously refuted the misstatements of the Palmerstonian press'. Marx thought it important, not surprisingly, to let *Tribune* readers know that a working-class venue hosted the event – another not too subtle message about which class in England to look to defend the Union cause. Tellingly, Douglass also drew the attention of the readers of his November *Monthly* to Forster's speech but without mention of the working-class location where it was delivered. Forster, in Douglass's opinion, 'arrives at the just conclusion that the war is after all, a war for slavery on the part of the South, and against slavery on the part of the North ... he nobly commends the North to the sympathy and regard of Englishmen ... Just such an advocate do we need at this moment'.[69]

Whether Douglass learned of Forster's speech from Marx or from the *Tribune* is unclear. More certain is that after Marx's exposé of the hypocrisy of Britain's ruling elite in his 11 October *Tribune* article, Douglass no longer prioritised the voices of England's 'statesmen' like Lord John Russell for taking the pulse of English public opinion.[70] Marx would have agreed with Douglass that what

---

69 DM, Nov. 1861, pp. 546.
70 That Russell, as Marx began his *Die Presse* article (Marx and Engels 1975–2004j, p. 43), now called for Northern severing of ties with the slavocracy, something Douglass could

such figures 'had to say' about the War was important as his dispatches from London testified. Of greater import for Marx, however, and not so apparently for Douglass, was what those subject to 'indirect slavery' in England 'had to say' – exactly the voices *Tribune* readers needed to hear. And to leave no doubt about whose side Marx was on, 'in this contest', he wrote three weeks later, 'the highest form of popular self-government till now realised is giving battle to the meanest and most shameless form of man's enslaving recorded in the annals of history' – till then, arguably, his highest compliment to the American polity.[71] For Douglass, the United States had yet to earn such praise. Nota bene Marx's opinion of America's 'peculiar institution' – the worst of the worst.

The *Tribune* provided Marx with an invaluable platform to promote the Union cause not only in Britain but also to English language readers elsewhere in Europe; though frustratingly for him, politically and personally, not everything he submitted was published.[72] The liberal *Die Presse* in Vienna – even more negligent than the *Tribune* about publishing all that Marx wrote for it – helped Marx promote the cause to German-language readers not only in Europe but also in the US. Notably, for a time there were, owing to the censorial character of the Prussian state, more German-language newspapers in America than in Germany itself. And some of them, Marx mentioned in 1859, 'reprint stuff from it', that is, from his *Tribune* articles.[73]

Because *Die Presse*'s readership had less familiarity with US history than the *Tribune*'s American readers, to get his German-language readers up to speed on the War Marx mostly reiterated the claims in his *Tribune* articles but more didactically. The reason he claimed 'so-called poor whites' gave support to the slave oligarchs deserves a revisit.[74] To clarify what he meant in his *Tribune* article by the slavocracy tempting the 'plebeian-like' layer of southern white society with 'the bait of prospective conquests within and without the frontiers of the United States', Marx rephrased his crucially important point for *Die Presse* readers.

---

      have read in the *Times* like Marx and vehemently opposed, may have been determinant in Douglass's deprioritising such 'betters'.

71   Marx and Engels 1975–2004j, p. 30.
72   Marx and Engels 1975–2004u, p. 323. In the 21 October article, Marx promised his readers that he would explain Palmerston's change of heart. But no such article exists, maybe one of the two that were never published.
73   Marx and Engels 1975–2004t, p. 410.
74   'Marx', according to the MECW editors, 'gives the English words 'poor whites' in parenthesis after their German equivalent' – making clear, apparently, that the label was not his.

> Only by acquisition and the prospect of acquisition of new Territories, as well as by filibustering expeditions, is it possible to square the interests of these 'poor whites' with those of the slaveholders, to give their restless thirst for action a harmless direction and to tame them with the prospect one day of becoming slaveholders themselves.[75]

The hope, again, for upward mobility and the realisation of the 'American Dream', as it would later be called, went a long way, Marx argued, in explaining why white plebeians were willing 'to square' their class interests with slave owner interests instead of contesting them and, by implication, allying with the Black toilers. Again, in Marx's view this material basis for the anti-Black 'prejudices' of white workers, that Douglass had intimate familiarity with, stood in the way of such an alliance. As long as these white plebeians dreamed of 'the prospect one day of becoming slaveholders themselves', there would be no possibility, in the opinion of Marx and his comrades in America, of white toilers organising as a class to end class society – essentially what Marx told Lincoln three years later. That sobering fact explained why Weydemeyer and other Marx party members, along with like-minded 1848 veterans in America, enthusiastically threw themselves into the battle to shut down the slave-master-route to the 'Dream' upon which the 'so-called poor whites' set their hopes.[76]

Recent scholarship sustains Marx's thesis about how the 'bait' or 'prospect one day of becoming slaveholders themselves' enticed 'poor whites' in the South to buy into the slave oligarchy's project. As Civil War historian Elizabeth Varon persuasively argues

> Secessionists had laid the groundwork of Southern nationalism by emphasizing non-slaveholders' stake in slavery as a system of economic mobility and of racial control. On the eve of the Civil War, one in four white Southern families owned slaves, but a broad majority of whites were invested in the slave system: they hired slaves, worked for slave owners, had or would own slaves, aspired to own slaves, or were tied to the slave economy through kinship, patronage, commerce, and politics. The promise of upward mobility depended on access to land and slaves, and hence on slavery's westward expansion across the continent ... Claiming that all white men benefitted from slavery since no white man had to occupy soci-

---

75   Marx and Engels 1975–2004j, p. 41.
76   Northern white workers, Marx recognized, could also be enticed to betray their class interests for short-term economic reasons. See his analysis of the Fall 1862 election returns on pp. 208–10.

ety's bottom rung, slaveholders enlisted non-slaveholders in surveilling, exploiting, and punishing slaves and in wielding censorship and mob violence against suspected abolitionists.[77]

From four-thousand miles away, Marx understood better, apparently, than Lincoln what motivated 'poor whites'. And with Marx, the expert diagnostician of the class struggle, came another insight – the oligarchy's need 'to tame' them. As the prospects diminished for the aspiring slave owners, they proved within less than three years to be increasingly unruly allies of the oligarchs.[78] Douglass too may not have grasped what Marx correctly did. Nothing in his corpus resembles Marx's point or makes for a more convincing alternative explanation.

4   Marx and Douglass Converge

In the second *Die Presse* article of 7 November, Marx dispensed with recapitulating the key points in his *Tribune* articles and introduced a number of original theses about the cause of the War, its essence, its course, and prospects – claims about which this can only be a distillation.

First, his opening premise: 'The war of the Southern Confederacy is ... not a war of defence, but a war of conquest, a war of conquest for the spread and perpetuation of slavery'.[79] After a survey of the demography of the slave holding states, the ratio of slave to non-slave populations in those states, and how the Slave Power had manipulated the votes for secession, Marx arrived at another proposition:

> It will have been observed that we lay particular emphasis on the numerical proportion of slaves to free men in the individual border states. This proportion is in fact decisive. It is the thermometer with which the vital fire of the slave system must be measured. The soul of the whole secession movement is *South Carolina*. It has 402,541 slaves and 301,271 free men. *Mississippi,* which has given the Southern Confederacy its dictatorship,

---

[77] Varon 2019, pp. 15–16. In the revised edition of *Half Slave and Half Free: The Roots of the Civil War*, Bruce Levine notes how nonslaveholders 'aspired to become slaveowners themselves one day, and some succeeded'. B. Levine 2005, p. 247. For Marx party member Joseph Weydemeyer's post-War opinion about the 'poor whites' issue, see below, pp. 252–3.
[78] For the best overview of that development, see B. Levine 2013.
[79] Marx and Engels 1975–2004j, p. 44.

Jefferson Davis, comes second. It has 436,696 slaves and 354,699 free men. *Alabama* comes third, with 435,132 slaves and 529,164 free men.[80]

That is, the ratio of slaves to free people predicted the degree of commitment to the secession project. The significance of the claim would reveal itself in the not-too-distant future.

Though absent in any of Douglass's accounts, Marx emphasised the significance of the struggles within each slave state to realise secession – in his opinion these were class struggles. The 'oligarchy of three hundred thousand slaveholders' used the secession campaign to 'reshape the internal constitutions of the slave states, to subjugate completely the section of the white population that had still preserved some independence under the protection of the democratic Constitution of the Union'. What did Marx mean?

> Between 1856 and 1860 the political spokesmen, jurists, moralists and theologians of the slaveholders' party had already sought to prove, not so much that Negro slavery is justified, but rather that colour is a matter of indifference and the working class is everywhere born to slavery. One sees, therefore, that the war of the Southern Confederacy is in a true sense of the word a war of conquest for the spread and perpetuation of slavery.[81]

'Secession, indeed, only took place', he asserted in a related claim, 'because within the Union the transformation of the border states and Territories into slave states seemed no longer attainable'. Douglass said something quite similar a month earlier. 'The very moment [the slaveholders] lost all hope of controlling and directing the Government, they set themselves logically to the work of destroying the Government'.[82]

What the Slave Power really wanted, Marx argued, based on his reading of the Confederate Constitution and the deliberations about it, especially 'the paragraph ... which leaves it open to every state of the old Union to join the new Confederacy',[83] was not a 'dissolution of the Union' but rather a '*reorganization on the basis of slavery*, under the reorganized control of the slaveholding oligarchy'.[84] Then another pithy conclusion:

---

80   Marx and Engels 1975–2004j, p. 47.
81   Marx and Engels 1975–2004j, p. 49.
82   DM, September 1861, p. 515.
83   Presumably Article IV, Sec. 3: https://avalon.law.yale.edu/19th_century/csa_csa.asp
84   Marx and Engels 1975–2004j, p. 50.

> The slave system would infect the whole Union. In the Northern states, where Negro slavery is in practice impossible, the white working class would gradually be forced down to the level of helotry [as in Sparta]. This would fully accord with the loudly proclaimed principle that only certain races are capable of freedom, and as the actual labour is the lot of the Negro in the South, so in the North it is the lot of the German and the Irishman, or their direct descendants.

Then, Marx's oft-quoted conclusion:

> The present struggle between the South and North is therefore, nothing but a struggle between two social systems, the system of slavery and the system of free labour. The struggle has broken out because the two systems can no longer live peacefully side by side on the North American continent. It can only be ended by the victory of one system or the other.

Marx then addressed 'the chief weakness of the North', the problem (to be revisited) of how to deal with the Border States.[85] How the North addressed the question of Kentucky, the key Border State, was particularly revealing. 'With the real war for the border states in the border states themselves, the question of winning or losing them is withdrawn from the sphere of diplomatic negotiations and parliamentary discussion' – deliberations that angered Douglass to no end. 'One section of the slaveholders', Marx predicted, 'will throw off the mask of loyalty; the other will content itself with the prospect of a financial compensation such as Great Britain gave the West Indian planters'.[86] Lincoln would indeed play – unsuccessfully to be seen – the 'financial compensation' card. The £20,000,000 that the British government paid to the 'West Indian planters' was conspicuously absent in Douglass's August 1857 speech, his most detailed treatment of emancipation in Britain's colonies in 1834.[87] 'The motive which led the Government to act, no doubt', he claimed, 'was mainly a philanthropic one, entitled to our highest admiration and gratitude'.[88] 'Philanthropy, however', as Marx pointedly noted in his next *Die Presse* article, 'does not make

---

85 Marx and Engels 1975–2004j, pp. 50–1.
86 Marx and Engels 1975–2004j, p. 51.
87 Douglass also failed to mention that along with the compensation the 'freed slaves' were 'forced to undergo a period of uncompensated "apprenticeship"', further enriching the former slave owners. Davis 2006, p. 238.
88 Blassingame 1985, p. 207.

history, least of all commercial history' – why Britain's dominant class had no interest in aiding and abetting, as it had done in 1834, emancipation in America.[89] Though Douglass, perhaps no longer admiring of and grateful to Britain's 'betters', had yet to publicly rebuke them, Marx never missed an opportunity to expose their hypocrisy regarding slavery in America.

To appreciate the key claims in his second *Die Presse* article, it is necessary to recognise that Marx was operating in real-time just seven months into the War. Almost two decades of thinking and writing about constitutions informed his reading of the Confederate Constitution and its deliberations. He brought, also, a world-historical perspective to his reading of Hammond's age-old class defence of Southern slavery, a perspective that comprehended that the 'mud-sill', those at the bottom of social hierarchies worldwide, came in all kinds of skin colours. Hence, the meaning of Marx's claim that 'colour is a matter of indifference' – ultimately unimportant in the world of class societies. He believed that slave oligarchs like Hammond were prepared – as revealed by his notorious 1858 King Cotton speech that Marx had read about in the *Tribune* – to reduce 'the German and the Irishman' and 'the white working class' as a whole 'to the level of helotry', that is, to the equivalent of 'Negro' slaves in the South.[90] Hammond, again, had asserted that Northern white workers were 'slaves' who happened to be 'white' – why his speech was so controversial – demonstrating that he and his class cohorts sanctioned class oppression whether it took the form of wage slavery or chattel slavery.

To the extent that Marx attributed a racist view to Hammond and the other slave oligarchs, it consisted of their self-serving and 'loudly proclaimed principle that only certain races are capable of freedom'. Whether that 'principle' constituted biological racism and/or white supremacy, as it would be later called, in Marx's view is interesting but beside the point. More important is how he saw the race/class nexus – be it race as ethnicity/nationality or as biology. Both Marx and Douglass, as we will see, employed 'race' to refer to ethnicity

---

89 Marx and Engels 1975–2004j, p. 54.
90 James Oakes, in a 1982 study, found that while slaveholders upheld the slave system based on a crude racism, at the core of their defence of slavery 'was primarily one of economics and property rights'. Oakes 1982, p. 134. A more recent work from Elizabeth Fox-Genovese and Eugene D. Genovese shows how a powerful faction of southern slaveholders defended 'Slavery in the Abstract – the doctrine that declared slavery or a kindred system of personal servitude the best possible condition for all labor regardless of race', confirming there was a 'loudly proclaimed principle', which Marx detected, that 'colour is a matter of indifference and the working class is everywhere born to slavery'. Fox-Genovese and Genovese 2008, p. 1.

and/or nationality.[91] The exploitation of labour, inherent in class society, was the basis of and rationale for racial oppression, in arguably Marx's first and until now underappreciated reference to the topic. Despite the claim that 'color is a matter of indifference', Marx soon recognised the need to point out the different skin colours of America's toilers. Skin colour there did indeed matter in the facilitation of class oppression, but that indisputable fact – at least so far – was only the beginning of wisdom instead of its end. The logic of the need to exploit labour explained why it happened to be skin colour that took on the socio-political importance it did four thousand miles away in the United States.

Was Marx's thesis credible? Douglass, we should remember, said as much in his presentation in Rochester on 28 April. At stake in the outcome of the War, to repeat, was which form of governance would prevail in America. The Slave Power, he charged – not unlike, again, Lincoln in his 'House Divided' speech – sought to impose slavery on the 'whole country'. That goal 'animates all their movements. The war on their part is for a government in which Slavery shall be National, and freedom nowhere, in which the capitalist shall own the laborer, and the white non-slaveholder a degraded man, to be classed, as such as men are now classed all over the South, as "poor white trash"'.[92] Nota bene, again, 'the capitalist'. Like Marx, Douglass also entertained the idea 'that color is a matter of indifference' when it came to the subjugation of labour. What was underway for 'poor white trash' in the South could happen in the 'whole country'.

Douglass repeated the point in the article on 'the social philosophy of slavery' in the September issue of his *Monthly*, specifically, the threat of 'poor white people' being subjugated to 'the dingy rafters of human bondage'.[93] It was as if – though unlikely – both of our protagonists were now reading one another. That independently of one another both revolutionaries claimed that the long-term goal of the slave-holding oligarchy was to enslave all toilers regardless of skin colour, gives credence to the notion of the Douglass-Marx mind-meld which had been long in the making. The idea of a universally enslaved American working class seems fantastic to contemporary minds only because Douglass and Marx didn't know what we all know today – the failed outcome of the slavocracy's sick dream. Marx, unlike Douglass, didn't think 'the capitalist' actually wanted to 'own the laborer' – only their capacity to produce, namely, their 'labor power', and, of course, the product of that labour. The significance of

---

91   At a speech in New York in February in 1862, for example, Douglass said: 'Take any race you please, French, English, Irish or Scotch ...' DM, March 1862, p. 615.
92   DM, June 1861, p. 473.
93   DM, September 1861, p. 515.

their different understandings of 'the capitalist' would only reveal itself after the overthrow of the slaveholding oligarchy.

Before the overthrow of the Slave power and chattel slavery, the cautious advice of a popular German-language guide to the United States about how German immigrants should behave when around Blacks suggests that it was not farfetched for Marx to think that his fellow compatriots in the North 'would gradually be forced down to the level' of something equivalent to the status of chattel slaves in the South. '[B]y treating black men with a certain familiarity and good nature,' the plebian immigrant 'lowers himself even more in the estimation of the [social] circle to which he belongs'. Sometimes, thus, 'in answer, "Was he a white man?" one will hear, "No, sir, he was a Dutchman".[94] The German immigrant, in other words, had to learn how to be 'white', otherwise they might end up being a uniquely Northern version of Sparta's helots, in Marx's estimation. That almost happened to a group of European migrants who found themselves in the position of virtually replacing emancipated Blacks right after the War. 'One Alabama planter brought in thirty Swedes in 1866, housed them in slave cabins and fed them the usual rations. Within a week, the labourers had departed, informing him "they were not slaves".[95] Neither Douglass nor Marx would have been surprised at the story, except for, maybe, the 'race' of the white skinned migrants, that is, their ethnicity. The Alabama planter instantiated exactly their warning about the essence of the recently defeated slave-holding oligarchy – its need to exploit labour regardless of skin colour.

Marx ended his pregnant article with a forecast. Despite the Border State problem, which caused the Lincoln administration to act 'pusillanimously ... Events themselves drive to the promulgation of the decisive slogan – *emancipation of the slaves*'.[96] Douglass had also said as much. Eleven months later Lincoln would issue the most consequential presidential executive order ever, the preliminary Emancipation Proclamation. Marx's method, 'the materialist conception of history' – historical materialism, as it would later be called – and his adroit use of it, allowed him to see what Lincoln would do before Lincoln himself could imagine such a move. Knowing the method and how to use it proved to be two different tasks, as Marx's ensuing debate with Engels about the prospects for the North would soon reveal. Of all Marx's writings on the War, his second *Die Presse* article is arguably, word for word, the most theoretically rich and prescient. With its testable claims, the article is now easily

---

94   B. Levine 1992, p. 150.
95   E. Foner 1988, p. 213.
96   Marx and Engels 1975–2004j, p. 51.

available to English-language readers and is thus, we think, a fount for a potentially seminal research project.

5   'What's Happening at Manassas Junction?'

Douglass held out little hope that anything of significance would be achieved when Congress met for the first time since the beginning of the War on 4 July 1861. His pessimism was understandable. Concerning Lincoln's message to Congress about the War, 'no mention', he told readers of his August *Monthly*, 'is made of slavery. Anyone reading that document, with no previous knowledge of the United States, would never dream from anything there written that we have a slaveholding war waged upon the Government, determined to overthrow it, or so to reconstruct it as to make it the instrument of extending the slave system and enlarging its powers'.[97] Note the second clause. It reiterated his 28 April claim, alleged also by Marx, about the long-term agenda of the Slave Power. Again, for Douglass, their goal was 'to reconstruct' the Union for 'extending the slave system and enlarging its powers'; and similarly for Marx this reconstruction referred to 'a reorganisation' so that the 'slave system would infect the whole Union'.[98]

On 1 July Marx queried Engels with a couple of questions for which he needed answers '*at once*', one about whether 'the SOUTHERNERS' position at Manassas JUNCTION [Virginia] is an offensive one?'[99] 'Your questions about the state of affairs in Virginia are easier put than answered', Engels replied two days later. He then proceeded to go into great detail about what was at stake – the ability of the Confederacy 'to maintain communications with North-West Virginia' via a railroad line: 'whether it has any tactical importance I can't say, for no conclusions at all can be drawn from the maps. All in all, the war in West Virginia will now turn on the railway junction'.[100] Four thousand miles away in the real-time of a mail carrier's ten-day trip from New York to London, Engels's prompt reply previewed the expert advice Marx could expect from his partner regarding military engagements.

Marx's concerns about a 'railway junction' in Virginia, about thirty miles southwest of Washington, DC, were prescient. On 21 July the largest military battle on North American soil until then took place between there and the

---
97   DM, August 1861, p. 497.
98   Marx and Engels 1975–2004j, p. 50.
99   Marx and Engels 1975–2004u, p. 300.
100   Marx and Engels 1975–2004u, pp. 303–4.

Bull Run tributary. About 60,000 combatants, almost equally divided between Union and Confederate forces, mobilised to engage one another. At the end of the day, Union casualties mounted to almost 3,000, with almost 2,000 for the Confederacy. The forces of the Slave Power outperformed those of the Union in the first real battle of the War. The widely held assumption on both sides that the War would be over in about three months was shattered. For the Union, Manassas, or Bull Run as it was also known, was a wakeup call.

There is no record of the immediate reaction of Marx and Engels to the defeat. Neither, probably, would have been surprised at the outcome. Marx, it may be recalled, had predicted that 'in the early part of the struggle, the scales will be weighted in favour of the South'. Douglass, apparently, thought otherwise. With the victory at Manassas 'the rebels have had a decided advantage, and are probably stronger than at the beginning of the war', suggesting that for him the Union defeat was unexpected.[101] Nevertheless, he quickly pivoted to seize the moment. The rebel victory, he told the readers of the August issue of his *Monthly*, taught an object lesson. Only if the War, as he had been arguing for months, turned into one against slavery would Union victory be assured. Toward that goal the Lincoln administration needed to emancipate those slaves 'working and fighting for slavery under the hateful flag of rebellion' – a factor that aided the rebel victory at Manassas – in order to 'break the back bone' of the Confederacy. Douglass called on abolitionists to pressure the Union government to strike against slavery: 'press this idea upon public notice. The Government should be addressed through the press, by petitions, by letters, by personal representation'. He argued that John Quincy Adams had pointed out decades earlier that 'the war power of the Government gives power to abolish slavery'.[102] And while half the North only 'a few months ago denounced coercion', they were then after Manassas united in the fight against the Confederacy. Many other voices were making similar demands on Washington to free the slaves of rebel slaveowners as well as those slaves who had fled to Union lines.

On 8 August 1861 Lincoln signed the First Confiscation Act. The bill, according to James Oakes, was 'the first federal law in American history designed to emancipate slaves in states where slavery was legal'.[103] Its limitations notwithstanding, 'the Confiscation Act', Eric Foner writes, 'represented an early turning

---

101   DM, August 1861, p. 498. His October *Monthly* estimated that 'five hundred of the Federal troops were killed at the battle of Bull Run', while 'the rebel loss can safely be put down at two thousand killed and wounded' (p. 529) – suggesting, perhaps, wishful thinking on Douglass's part.
102   DM, August 1861, p. 498. Oakes 2013, pp. 36–41.
103   Oakes 2013, p. 110.

point in the relations of the federal government to slavery'.[104] But Douglass was unsatisfied with the legislation. Composed by Lincoln's Secretary of War, it was ambiguous about how Union field officers should deal with runaway and confiscated slaves – 'a complete muddle' in Douglass's opinion; the consequences of this ambiguity soon became apparent. When Union General and Commander of the Department of the West John Frémont proclaimed martial law in the highly contested Border State of Missouri on 30 August, allowing for the confiscation and immediate emancipation of the slaves of all rebel slaveholders in the state, Lincoln rescinded the order on 11 September. This is what Marx meant at the end of his second *Die Presse* article when he said that the Border State problem had caused Lincoln to act 'pusillanimously'. That is, Lincoln had revoked Frémont's Proclamation 'solely out of regard for the loud protest of the "loyal" slaveholders in Kentucky'.[105] Marx elaborated on his point in the prior paragraph.

> Anxiety to keep the 'loyal' slaveholders of the border states in good humor; fear of throwing them into the arms of secession, in a word, tender regard for the interests, prejudices and sensibilities of these ambiguous allies, has smitten the Union government with incurable weakness since the beginning of the war, driven it to half measures, forced it to dissemble away the principle of the war, and to spare the foe's most vulnerable spot, the root of the evil – *slavery itself*.[106]

Douglass could have written these lines, leading one historian to mistakenly think that Marx had actually read the *Monthly*.[107]

Douglass's own words, probably not available when Marx penned his lines, do anticipate Marx's.[108] Douglass rejected the *New York Times*' defence of Lincoln's revocation of Frémont's order on the grounds that it 'would drive the loyal slaveholders in Kentucky and Tennessee into the arms of the rebels'. This 'assumption would have some weight did Frémont's Proclamation propose (as it does not) the liberation of the slaves of loyal masters'. Instead, it 'strikes only at slaveholding rebels'. If it is to be assumed that 'loyal masters would be

---

104 E. Foner 2010, p. 175.
105 Marx and Engels 1975–2004j, p. 51.
106 Marx and Engels 1975–2004j, pp. 50–1.
107 Stauffer 2008, p. 232. In addition to there being no evidence that Marx read Douglass, Stauffer mistakenly thinks Marx was in Vienna when he wrote this.
108 The *Monthly* had subscribers in Britain but it's not certain when issues actually reached them.

driven into disloyalty by the well-merited chastisement of slave-holding rebels', that 'implies', Douglass argued, 'that after all, there is a stronger bond existing between these loyal slaveholders and the slaveholding rebels, than subsists between the former and the Government'. Douglass wanted the Union to break any alliances with 'loyal men' who kept humans in bondage. 'The open hostility of these so-called loyal slaveholders', he continued, 'is incomparably to be preferred to their friendship ... From the beginning, these Border Slave States have been the mill-stone about the neck of the Government, and their so-called loyalty has been the very best shield to the treason of the cotton States'.[109] That both of our protagonists reached in real-time, independently of one another and four thousand miles apart, a similar opinion about the problem of the Border States is of greater import than whether either was reading the other. Not the first or last such concurrence.

Douglass characterised the conflict between Lincoln and Frémont as one about 'whether the war should be waged against traitors only by the cunning technicalities of the crafty lawyer, or by the cannon and courage of the determined warrior. Unhappily ... the lawyer has prevailed over the warrior'.[110] A month later, in regard to the revocation of Frémont's Proclamation, Marx, the one-time lawyer, commented that 'Lincoln, in accordance with his legal tradition, has an aversion for all genius, anxiously clings to the letter of the Constitution and fights shy of every step that could mislead the "loyal" slaveholders of the border states'.[111] Douglass later employed the same language as Marx to describe Lincoln's counter-order – the 'pusillanimous and pro-slavery interference of President Lincoln'.[112] His October *Monthly* devoted an inordinate number of its columns in defence of Frémont's directive, which the journal called 'by far the most important and salutary measure which has thus far emanated from any General during the whole tedious progress of the war'.[113]

In the November issue of his *Monthly*, Douglass doubled down on defending Frémont's Proclamation. The logic of war, he argued, dictated – we choose our word carefully – that stance.

> Necessity is the master over all. It has compelled our Government, much against all its wishes, to draw the sword against the slaveholding rebels,

---

109 DM, October 1861, p. 531.
110 DM, October 1861, p. 530.
111 Marx and Engels 1975–2004j, p. 87.
112 DM, November 1861, p. 546.
113 DM, October 1861, p. 530.

to suspend in different parts of the country the privilege of the writ of *habeas corpus*, placed Baltimore under martial law, abridged the liberty of speech and press, to invade the sacred soil of Virginia, to fill Fortress Monroe with slaves, to confiscate the property of slaveholding rebels, to blockade and threaten all the Southern coast. It has done ... many other things under the higher law, not of the written Constitution or, of its own inclination, but of necessity. It has been from the first, and must be to the last, borne along on the broad current of events.

It was this 'higher law' that gave Douglass hope, the 'iron necessity, which shall compel our Government to aim a deathblow at the life of slavery'.[114] Frémont's Proclamation inspired Douglass and pointed the way forward.

Two points about Douglass's defence are worth noting as we compare him to Marx. Marx and Engels also subscribed to the law of necessity but one driven by material reality, specifically, the inherently more profitable, more productive and technologically advanced nature of the capitalist mode of production vis-a-vis prior modes of production such as slavery. The demographic and economic advantages of the North instantiated that claim. Douglass's social analysis, on the other hand, operated at two levels, those of material reality and providentiality, or perhaps some version of the contemporary faith in the progressive bending of reality's moral arc towards justice. He recognised that the material necessities involved in conducting a war required particular measures such as martial law and confiscating the property of the enemy. Yet for him the long term prospects for victory depended on the ideal of a 'moral sky ... a power behind the throne, greater than the throne itself' as well as the 'broad current of events' seemingly mobilised by some benevolent spirit of history – in other words, a very different epistemology from that of Marx and Engels. Second, Douglass's enthusiastic defence of the measures the Union was forced to adopt to win suggests that he was not – at least in that moment – a civil liberties absolutist, despite his hitherto ardent defence of them. Defeating the slavocracy took precedence over the slave owners' rights to private property.

As for what Marx might have thought about Douglass's point about civil liberties in revolutionary wartime, there is a brief, but we think telling, comment he made later in connection with the *Trent* affair. 'The people of the United States having magnanimously submitted to a curtailment of their own liberties in order to save their country' should be willing, he implored in a

---

114 DM, November 1861, pp. 547–8.

Tribune article, to turn the other cheek, metaphorically, in order to settle the kerfuffle with Britain.[115] The comment suggests that he approved of the 'curtailment' because it had been done with the agreement of the northern masses to save the Union – consistent, we contend, with Douglass's meaning.

Not to be forgotten, to pursue the point, are the two years that Marx and Engels spent in a revolutionary war, the German edition of the European Spring, and the setting in which they coined the phrase, 'the dictatorship of the proletariat'. Despite the Stalinist baggage it later acquired and continues to carry – confusing readers into erroneously thinking that Marx and Engels sought to empower autocratic, demagogic tyrants – the phrase meant no more than the fact that in a revolutionary context the proletarian majority would have to impose its collective will over the oppressive and exploitative bourgeois minority and thus employ dictatorial measures in order to be victorious – no more, no less.[116] We read Marx and Engels to have understood that during the US Civil War the revolutionary class was not the proletariat but instead the bourgeoisie represented by Lincoln and the Republican Party in opposition to the retrograde slavocracy – the dictatorship of the three-hundred thousand slaveholders.[117] The measures, therefore, that Lincoln took and Douglass applauded are ones we confidently think Marx and Engels would have also endorsed.

Almost two months after rescinding Frémont's confiscation order, and despite the widespread support from Frémont's defenders like Douglass, Lincoln fired him on 2 November from the post of Commander of the Department of the West, supposedly for misuse of government funds. The actual and immediate reason, most likely, is that Frémont's martial law order caused a falling out with the influential Blair family of Missouri, a member of which was Lincoln's Post Office General Montgomery Blair.[118] Douglass had worried about Frémont's future ever since Lincoln's 11 September revocation: 'whether he will continue in his command, resign or be dismissed' was uncertain.[119] A month after he voiced his worries, Douglass lamented about 'a still more disheartening rumor to the effect that Frémont's policy had not only been condemned by

---

115   Marx and Engels 1975–2004j, p. 100. On the measures Lincoln took early in the War to limit civil liberties, including freedom of the press, see Holzer 2014, pp. 312–14, 439–40.
116   Draper 1986 remains the most authoritative exposition on the phrase.
117   The description, for example, of Lincoln's ambassador to Britain in April 1861, Charles Francis Adams: 'The Slave States always have been troublesome and dictatorial partners'. https://www.masshist.org/publications/cfa-civil-war/
118   See Keith 2020, pp. 144–7, and Denton 2008, pp. 305–11 for details.
119   DM, October 1861, p. 531.

the Government, but that the Government was seriously debating the question of his removal from his command'.[120]

Within days of getting the news of Frémont's ousting, Marx penned 'The Dismissal of Frémont' for *Die Presse*. The firing, Marx began, marked 'a turning point in the history of the development of the American Civil War'. Marx held that there was more to the story than Frémont's apparent conflict with Lincoln over war policy, which explained his opening thesis:

> Frémont has two great sins to expiate. He was the first candidate of the Republican Party for the presidential office (1856), and he is the first general of the North to have threatened the slaveholders with emancipation of slaves (August 30, 1861). He remains, therefore, a rival of candidates for the presidency in the future and an obstacle to the makers of compromises in the present.[121]

Marx then elaborated on his first claim with a history of Republican party presidential politics after Frémont's unsuccessful bid, specifically, the nomination – owing to his 'personal unimportance' – and election of Lincoln. Lincoln's rival for the nomination and now his secretary of state, William Seward, is who Marx had most in mind as one of the 'candidates for the presidency in the future'. Made famous in 1858 for 'the prophesying of the "irrepressible conflict" between the system of free labour and the system of slavery ... Seward manifestly regarded the post of Secretary of State as a mere preliminary step, and busied himself less with the "irrepressible conflict" of the present than with the presidency of the future ... For Seward, therefore, Frémont was the dangerous rival who had to be ruined'. Aiding him in his scheme were, as already noted, Lincoln's lawyerly disposition and 'Frémont's character'. If Douglass had tended to put a heroic shine on Frémont, Marx was more sober in his opinion of the man: 'He is manifestly a man of pathos, somewhat pompous and haughty, and not without a touch of the melodramatic'.[122]

Marx ended with a prediction. Frémont was popular in 'the states of the Northwest' where his firing was regarded 'as a personal insult'. 'Should the Union government meet with a few more mishaps like those of Bull Run and Ball's Bluff [a Union defeat on 21 October in northern Virginia] it has itself given the opposition, which will then rise up against it and smash the hitherto

---

120   DM, November 1861, p. 546.
121   Marx and Engels 1975–2004j, p. 86.
122   Marx and Engels 1975–2004j, p. 88.

prevailing diplomatic system of waging war, its leader in John Frémont'. Marx promised *Die Presse* readers an article that would look into 'the indictment of the dismissed general'.[123]

Recent scholarship doesn't confirm one way or another Marx's claims about Seward's ambitions.[124] Douglass, however, writing at almost the same time, seems to have agreed with him. 'Honest men of all parties hailed [Frémont's Proclamation] as auspicious of a speedy salvation from the evils that at present afflict us. But alas! politicians who have sometimes been mistaken for statesmen ... saw either an extinguishment of their own hopes of preferment, or some other equally important evil to result from this Proclamation; and it and its author were quietly laid aside under pretexts equally frivolous'.[125] Douglass also reprinted without comment the speech of the reception committee leader that welcomed Frémont in St. Louis upon his return there after the dismissal. 'The true causes which led to your recall are well understood and appreciated. You have risen too fast in popular favor. The policy announced in your proclamation, although hailed by the people as a political and military necessity, furnished your ambitious rivals and enemies with a welcome weapon for your intended destruction'.[126]

It is unclear if Douglass had Seward in mind when he wrote of 'politicians who have ... hopes of preferment' or when he reprinted the words of the speaker welcoming Frémont back to St. Louis. But Douglass would have certainly known that nobody among Lincoln administration powerbrokers expected to become president more than Seward, and that he would have done anything to get there including the sell-out of Frémont. In addition, Douglass had already expressed his disillusionment with Seward. In the August issue of his *Monthly*, he complained about the duplicity of the Republican party leadership.

> Take Mr. Wm. Seward for example. Standing in Corinthian Hall in Rochester [NY], speaking with a Northern tongue, he is plain, direct and to the purpose. He there proclaims the irrepressible conflict between slavery

---

123   Ibid.
124   Seward's biographer notes that he felt spurned by allies in the 1856 Republican nominating contest, opposed Frémont's appointment to an important ministerial post early in Lincoln's presidency, and supported the rescindment of Frémont's emancipation order (against his wife's vehement protests). Although he did reply to members of a 'Seward Club' in Philadelphia he was uninterested in being elected president in 1864. Stahr 2012, pp. 160–4, 254, 303–4, 311–12.
125   DM, December 1861, p. 561.
126   DM, December 1861, p. 568.

and freedom, and assures us that wherever these powers are brought into a State or Territory, that one must inevitably fall before the other. But this is in Rochester, on the borders of Lake Ontario, five hundred miles from the Capital. Listen to the same man in the Senate of the United States, and you will learn from his lips that the irrepressible conflict is quite a repressible one – that there need be no trouble between the labor States and the capital States, if slavery were not pressed into politics.[127]

Like Marx, Douglass couldn't resist an ironic dig at Seward's 1858 'irrepressible conflict' speech that made him famous. A credible case can then be made that Douglass, like Marx, did indeed have Seward in mind as the prime candidate for mover behind the scenes facilitating Frémont's removal. Whether Seward actually was influential is a separate question.[128] Marx's opinion of Seward, whatever the case, would soon take on greater significance.

Douglass also made a prediction similar to Marx's: Fremont's removal was not the last the conflagration would see of him. Douglass prefaced his prediction – more verbosely as was his tendency – as Marx had done. In a sombre and embittered tone, he deplored the way the War was going. '[D]isappointment has succeeded disappointment ... until we feel compelled to look in another direction, and to other men, to relieve the country from this direful scourge, and place it on a basis whose *quality* shall be twin brother to its *claims*. ... *In three years* the people will call for the man and his principles *to end this war*! and then they will sanction the death of slavery in *the man of their choice*. And, too, this unnatural war will render its death constitutional'. But despite Frémont's dismissal, 'Nature is remunerative, and, Phoenix-like, he shall arise from the ashes around the altar upon which he has been offered, and with the might of his unswerving purpose, destroy the monster that has, up to the present, performed all its devilish orgies in the very halls of our National Legislature,

---

127 DM, August 1861, p. 501.
128 Four months later, Marx claimed that Union General George McClellan was 'at the bottom of the highly infamous intrigue against Frémont'. Marx and Engels 1975–2004u, p. 345. Modern scholarship focuses on Lincoln's direct role and fear that an emancipation proclamation broader than the First Confiscation Act would alienate border state slaveholders, especially in Kentucky, along with the powerful Blair family who Frémont had antagonised. For details see Keith 2020, pp. 144–7, and Denton 2008, pp. 305, 310–311. Foner 2010, pp. 176–8. McPherson 2008, pp. 55–6. Blight 2018, pp. 352–3. Elizabeth Varon provides evidence that Lincoln's concerns about Kentucky Unionists' control over the state might have been unfounded and that their backlash to proclamations like Frémont's were short-lived. Varon 2019, pp. 44–5.

and made its horrid feasts upon the heart's blood of its best interests'.[129] If both Marx and Douglass predicted Frémont's return, the former did so conditionally: he'd only return 'should the Union government meet with a few more mishaps like Bull Run and Ball's Bluff'. Douglass, on the other hand, was certain it would happen because of 'Nature', a perspective that marked the difference between the revolutionary prophet and the revolutionary scientist. Time would test, indeed 'in three years', the two perspectives, the scientific possibility versus the prophetic certainty that Frémont would replace Lincoln.

Douglass, to be noted, didn't ignore the charges against Frémont but responded that those who 'live in glass houses' were in no position to criticise him. As for the misuse of funds charge against Frémont's 'extravagance', what about, Douglass countered, the Union Army of the Potomac under the feckless command of General George McClellan upon which 'money is lavished without stint'?[130] But that retort didn't address 'Frémont's character' as Marx had put it. His less than heroic but sober portrait of 'the Pathfinder', as Frémont was often called, accords with most modern opinion about him.[131] Why, therefore, could Marx, four thousand miles away, have been more accurate? Though the written record is silent on the matter, not to be forgotten is that Marx's and Engels's closest contact in the US was Joseph Weydemeyer, a member of Frémont's general staff. Weydemeyer, over the course of the War, corresponded intermittently with Engels. The available Marx-Engels correspondence is inexplicably thin between August and the end of the year, suggesting that many of their letters from that period are missing – a possible explanation for the silence in the record. Another possibility is that Marx and Engels were very cautious in their correspondence to not reveal any insider intelligence that Weydemeyer might have shared with either of them. Within a month the reasons for their circumspect behaviour regarding what their letters contained became evident.

The problems with the Union army that continued to frustrate Douglass were, Engels explained, to be expected given the country's military history, spe-

---

129 DM, December 1861, p. 563.
130 DM, December 1861, p. 563. A month before, Douglass registered his low opinion of McClellan. DM, November 1861, p. 547. Marx would reach a similar opinion three months later. Marx and Engels 1975–2004u, p. 345.
131 Many historians do not see Frémont as the revolutionary hero that Douglass made him out to be. Most sympathetic is Stauffer 2008, p. 226. Although Oakes outlines the support Frémont received in the North, he is most critical, see his Oakes 2013, pp. 153–66 and Oakes 2007, pp. 149–51. See also Foner 2010, p. 180. For the response of German-Americans to Frémont's proclamation and removal see B. Levine 2013, pp. 116–17 and B. Levine 1992, p. 260.

cifically, the absence of a well-equipped standing army. Eight months after Fort Sumter he elaborated in a local British military publication.

> ... when a civil war called forth more than a million of fighting men, the whole system broke down, and everything had to be begun at the beginning. The results are before us. Two immense, unwieldy bodies of men, each afraid of the other, and almost afraid of victory as of defeat, are facing each other, trying at an immense cost, to settle down into something like a regular organisation. The waste of money, frightful as it is, is quite unavoidable ... With ignorance and inexperience ruling supreme in every department, how could it be otherwise?[132]

Douglass, closer to the scene, could have benefitted from this historical perspective.

The article Marx promised about the charges against Frémont never appeared, possibly one of the never-published articles he wrote for *Die Presse* – pieces for which he was not compensated.[133] Marx's already precarious financial situation continued to deteriorate, threatening homelessness and, thus, taking a toll on his wife Jenny's mental well-being. Not only was she dealing with her own facial disfigurement caused by smallpox earlier in the year, but she'd also been nursing two of their daughters back to health, Jenny and Eleanor – a needed sidebar about the personal circumstances under which Marx was writing about the War.[134] Marx's own severely painful ailment, Hidradenitis suppurativa – once called 'carbuncles' or 'boils' – should not be forgotten either; this was the suffering he endured while doing research for and writing his magnum opus. Engels, of course, continued to provide financial support to the Marx household, but the resources that enabled this support were diminishing due to the Union embargo of Southern cotton meant for export to Britain. About his New Year's wish to Engels on 27 December, Marx wrote: 'If it's anything like the old one, I, for my part, would sooner consign it to the devil'.[135] Too bad that similar details about Douglass's private life are, apparently, non-existent, thus not allowing us to compare how that oh-so-essential human dimension of their personal lives may have impacted the public lives of our two protagonists.

---

132   Marx and Engels 2016, p. 85. For some reason, this article is missing in the MECW.
133   'The rotten *Presse* is printing barely half my articles'. Marx and Engels 1975–2004u, p. 338.
134   See Marx's letters to Engels, beginning on 20 November 1861, Marx and Engels 1975–2004u, pp. 321, 328, 333, 340.
135   Marx and Engels 1975–2004u, p. 338.

6   'Complications with Foreign Powers': The *Trent* Affair

Marx's first known commentary on the War, about three weeks after the firing on Fort Sumter, spoke inter alia to the logistical challenges that immediately faced the North, specifically, 'HOW TO GET THEIR FORCES TO THE SOUTH'. After discussing the problems with various landed options, 'all that remains is sea transport and naval warfare'. But those came with a liability that 'might easily lead to complications with foreign powers'.[136] Marx, again, was prescient.

The international repercussions of the War continued to have ripple effects into the fall of 1861. Douglass repeated his call: 'Let the war be made an abolition war, and no statesman in England or France would dare, even if inclined, to propose any disturbance of the blockade. Make this an abolition war, and you at once unite the world against the rebels, and in favor of the Government'.[137] Douglass's steadfast faith in the 'statesmen in England and France' was about to be tested.

In his 30 June speech, Douglass commented that 'what Louis Napoleon [Bonaparte] had to say' about the War was of import to him. He was one of the European 'statesmen' Douglass had in mind in his claim that none of them would challenge the blockade once Washington declared that the purpose of the War was to end slavery. Three months later on 31 October, Bonaparte, in league with the Palmerston government in Britain, and the Spanish government made plans to invade Mexico, to take advantage of Washington's preoccupation with the slaveholders' insurrection in order to pursue an imperialist project on its southern border. Whether Douglass blamed the Lincoln administration for the blatantly egregious move by the 'statesmen in England' and 'France' because it had yet to declare the War to be for abolition is uncertain. Not until the April 1862 issue of his *Monthly* is there any mention of the invasion.[138]

If Douglass had nothing to say about European rulers seeking to recolonise Mexico, Marx responded as soon as he learned of their nefarious plans with articles in *Die Presse* and the *Tribune*. 'The contemplated intervention in Mexico by England, France and Spain', he began his *Tribune* article, 'is, in my opinion, one of the most monstrous enterprises ever chronicled in the annals of international history'.[139] Marx labelled the internal correspondence about London's duplicity when it became public four months later as 'the most damning

---

136   Marx and Engels 1975–2004u, pp. 277–8.
137   DM, September 1861, p. 515.
138   In a reprinted speech by Gerrit Smith and without comment by Douglass.
139   Marx and Engels 1975–2004j, p. 71.

exposure of modern English diplomacy with all of its hypocritical cant, ferocity against the weak, crawling before the strong, and utter disregard of international law'. A 'minute analysis' of the documents, that Marx promised to write about in another article, offered 'irrefragable proof that the present imbroglio is of English origin, that England took the initiative in bringing about the intervention, and did so on pretexts too flimsy and self-congratulatory to even veil the real but unavowed motives of her proceedings'.[140] In the context of the US Civil War, Marx was none too happy to seize upon every opportunity to expose British ruling class duplicity.

As a pretext, the imperialist invaders of Mexico claimed they intended to end 'the anarchy' in the country owing to its own civil war between the mostly victorious reformed-minded Liberal government of Benito Juárez and the conservative clerical-supported opponents. One British organ, however, Marx noted, admitted that, 'The expedition had only one object – the satisfaction of the Mexican state's creditors in England, France and Spain'. Owing to the war, Juárez had suspended payments on Mexico's foreign debt for two years. Marx, a vigilant opponent of Bonaparte ever since his overthrow of the Second Republic in 1851 – who was always 'ready to divert the French people' – made clear his sympathies. 'The Mexican government can become solvent only by internal consolidation, but it can consolidate itself at home only so long as its independence is respected abroad'.[141]

Also at stake in the invasion of Mexico, Marx argued, was whether Europe would be allowed to violate the Monroe Doctrine that 'declared any European interference in the internal affairs of American states to be forbidden' – a policy Marx endorsed. 'The present convulsion in the United States appeared to Palmerston an opportune moment for taking up the old project in a modified form' – an opportunity, namely, to violate the Doctrine. 'Since the United States', he continued, 'for the present, must allow no foreign complication to interfere with their war for the Union, all they can do is to *protest*'. To his *Tribune* readers, especially Lincoln and the members of his cabinet, Marx was again transparent about the political allegiance of the 'occasional correspondent' in London. 'Their best well-wishers in Europe hope that they will protest, and thus, before the eyes of the world, firmly repudiate any complicity in one of the most nefarious schemes'.[142] The first troops of the Tripartite Alliance invasion of Mexico, from Spain, landed on 8 December 1861; British and French troops followed in January. There is no record of a public 'protest' from Washington.

---

140   Marx and Engels 1975–2004j, p. 172.
141   Marx and Engels 1975–2004j, pp. 67–8.
142   Marx and Engels 1975–2004j, pp. 77–8.

Not unlike his 'pusillanimity' toward the Border States at the time, Lincoln's fear of a Bonaparte-Confederacy alliance stymied him until April 1864 in declaring that the United States would never 'acknowledge any monarchical government in America, under the auspices of any European power'.[143]

Washington's official silence on the invasion of Mexico may be attributed to another 'foreign complication', one that was more pressing. On 8 November 1861 a Union ship, the *San Jacinto*, enforcing the blockade against Confederate shipments, intercepted a British mail carrier, the *Trent*, in waters near the Bahamas. After boarding the vessel, Union officials discovered two Confederate diplomats on board on their way to London to seek support for their cause. They were promptly arrested and detained. News of the boarding and arrests reached England on 27 November and then got telegraphed to the national media. An uproar ensued, prompting Engels to write to Marx immediately, 'Have the Yankees gone out of their minds, playing such a mad trick on the confederate commissioners? ... The fellows must be completely crazy to saddle themselves with a war against England'. Then some timely advice: 'If war should really break out you could send', through a circuitous route, 'your letters to New York ... [because] you'll have to take care that you're not aiding and abetting the ENEMIES of the QUEEN'.[144] This offers a reason, as noted earlier, for the inexplicable thinness in Marx's correspondence around this period; either missing or intentionally destroyed.

The Union arrest of the two Confederate officials, James Mason and John Slidell, and the reaction to it resulted in what's known as the *Trent* affair, threatening the possibility of war between London and Washington – to 'do the work of the Secessionists' as Marx later said. As Engels was writing to him, Marx, dealing with all the personal challenges to him at that moment, had already begun to compose a journal article. His 'The *Trent* Case' in the 2 December issue of *Die Presse* distilled politically the events and made a forecast. Despite the fact that 'every sound-minded Englishman went to bed [on 27 November] with the conviction that he would go to sleep in a state of peace but wake up in a state of war ... the conflict between the *Trent* and the *San Jacinto* brings no war in its train'.[145] A month later, Marx's prediction, based on a close reading of British newspaper editorial opinion, would be confirmed.

Marx rested his forecast on the distinction between 'the *legal question*' and 'the *political* aspect' of the issue. The once-trained lawyer pored over the legal

---

143   Doyle 2015, p. 129. For the unofficial assistance Washington rendered to the Juárez government and larger context, see pp. 127–8, and Chapter Five. Also, Katz 2017.
144   Marx and Engels 1975–2004u, p. 329.
145   Marx and Engels 1975–2004j, p. 89.

issues and concluded that the United States was at fault for violating a technicality rather than the substance of international law in arresting the two Confederate diplomats, an issue that could be resolved by an 'exchange of diplomatic notes'. It was the 'political aspect' that was more challenging, and for that he faulted Secretary of State William Seward, already a bête noir for Marx who he held to be culpable in the firing of Frémont. On the eve of *Trent*, Marx thought even less of him as Secretary of State. 'Read his state dispatches! What a repulsive mixture of magniloquence and petty mindedness, of simulated strength and real weakness'.[146] About one of those 'dispatches', Douglass, writing for his *Monthly*, a publication likely read by the Lincoln Cabinet – unlike *Die Presse* where Marx's biting critique of Seward appeared – exercised more tact. 'Stripped of diplomatic urbanities and circumlocutions, the recent circular of Mr. Seward, and his correspondence with Lord Lyons, have been, in our judgment, better calculated to repel than to invite the good feeling of the British government and the people ... Such behavior is very little to our credit'.[147] Marx's low opinion of Seward explains his reaction – also in *Die Presse* – to the arrest of the two Confederates. 'We regard this latest operation of Mr. Seward as a characteristic act of tactlessness by self-conscious weakness simulating strength. If the naval incident hastens Seward's removal from the Washington Cabinet, the United States will have no reason to record it as an 'untoward event' in the annals of the Civil War'.[148] The *Trent* incident sealed his contempt for Seward.

Marx employed, not unexpectedly, his first *Tribune* article on the *Trent* matter to address its 'political aspect'. If he had once appeared as a disinterested 'correspondent' – *Tribune* publisher Greeley, as noted earlier, knew better – the threat of war with England required the revolutionary communist to be unmistakably transparent about his politics, especially to an American readership that included, again, Lincoln and his Cabinet. Such honesty, from a mere 'correspondent' to now an advocate, came with the risk of losing needed income to sustain his household.

First, the 'Crown lawyers ... in my opinion, are right in their conclusion' that the captain of the *San Jacinto* did commit a 'violation in the *procedure* of' international maritime law. If 'the American Government must concede [the point], as it seems to me ... their fair fame and their interest ought alike to prevent them' – Marx the advisor – 'from nibbling at the terms of the satisfaction to be given to the injured party'. Then a sober geo-military-political reality check.

---

146 Marx and Engels 1975–2004j, p. 87.
147 DM, November 1861, pp. 545–6.
148 Marx and Engels 1975–2004j, p. 91.

They ought to remember that they do the work of the Secessionists in embroiling the United States in a war with England, that such a war would be a godsend to Louis Bonaparte in his present [domestic] difficulties, and would, consequently, be supported by all the official weight of France; and lastly, that, what with the actual force under the command of the British on the North American and West Indian stations, what with the forces of the Mexican Expedition [the Tripartite Alliance invasion], the English Government would have at its disposal an overwhelming maritime power.[149]

Marx then went after Seward, more tactfully than in the stinging language employed in his *Die Presse* articles but with the same criticism. 'As to the policy of the seizure' of the two Confederates, 'the voice not only of the English but of the European press is unanimous in expressions of bewilderment at the strange conduct of the American Government, provoking such tremendous international dangers'. A London *Times* article he cited singled out 'Mr. Seward' as the culprit.[150]

Marx ended his constructive criticism of US policy behaviour on a positive note referenced earlier. 'The people of the United States having magnanimously submitted to a curtailment of their own liberties in order to save their country will certainly be no less ready to turn the tide of popular opinion in England by openly avowing, and carefully making up for, an international blunder the vindication of which might realize the boldest hopes of the rebels'.[151]

In closing his *Tribune* article as he did, Marx sought to persuade policy makers in Washington how to advance the Union cause in England – leaving no doubt, therefore, on whose side he was in the Civil War. His penultimate *Tribune* article, six weeks away, also made clear which 'popular opinion in England' he thought decisive in that public relations campaign.

Marx appealed to the presumed political rationality of the Lincoln administration. The evidence suggests that rational self-interest prevailed – on both sides. On Christmas Day in 1861 Mason and Slidell were released from detention in a Fort in Boston and, thus, ended the crisis. As Marx had foreseen, 'a

---

149 Marx and Engels 1975–2004j, p. 99.
150 For a more sympathetic account of Seward's publication of American diplomatic correspondence and his rather moderate conduct during the *Trent* Affair and work in convincing Lincoln and his cabinet that *San Jacinto* Captain Charles Wilkes had violated international law and American principles necessitating the release of Mason and Slidell, see Stahr 2012, pp. 307–23.
151 Marx and Engels 1975–2004j, p. 100.

diplomatic note' of sorts made that possible.[152] Marx felt vindicated. He had predicted, to be recalled, as early as 2 December, '*no war*' would ensue. And to Engels on 19 December, six days before the peaceful resolution of the kerfuffle, 'I would rate the odds at 100 to 1 against' war.[153] It is impossible to know if Marx was influential in any way in the outcome of the *Trent* incident, specifically, his advice to the Lincoln administration in his *Tribune* article about how to resolve it. But for the communist, he was obligated to act as if he could have been. The imperative to act was a quality that Marx shared with Douglass. War with England, as Engels warned, would have made eventual Union victory more difficult, if not unlikely.[154]

Not until after the peaceful resolution of *Trent* did Douglass have the opportunity to make public in his *Monthly* his stance on the issue, unable, therefore, to have had any possible impact on the outcome – the advantage Marx still had of writing for daily newspapers.[155] In his first article on the incident, written before its resolution, and probably after Marx's 19 December *Tribune* article, Douglass, for different reasons, also argued for the release of the two Confederates and accused 'newspapers and orators' in the North for allowing 'the masses to suppose that we are all right ... To our mind, the capture was wrong and inexcusable on general principles, and especially so on American principles'. The United States, he argued, partly because of 'her usual tenderness towards slavery in all its forms, and her sensitive regard for the sacredness of our flag ... have contended, over and over again, that the deck of an American ship is as sacred as any part of the national domain'. In Douglass's view, the Captain of the *San Jacinto* hailed 'a British mail steamer, on her way from one neutral port to another – sends a cannon ball a few yards from her bow – boards her with armed men – demands her passenger list, and captures by force four of her passengers'. Such actions, in his opinion, were hypocritical since '[t]he practice of boarding American ships, and capturing so-called British subjects, led to the war of 1812'. While Mason and Slidell were indeed rebels, they are 'not rebels against any other than the American Government, and no other Govern-

---

152   See Doyle 2015, pp. 78–81, for details.
153   Marx and Engels 1975–2004u, p. 337.
154   Modern scholarship concurs with Engels. See Jones 2010, pp. 83, 93. See also, McPherson 1988, pp. 390–1 and Stahr 2012, pp. 308–9, 316, 318, 322–3.
155   Blight 2018, p. 359, says Douglass's article was intended 'to prevent British intervention and to enlist English abolitionists in the crusade to end slavery'. The reports in his *Monthly* on the only, apparently, public speaking Douglass did in November, on the 14th and 15th, in Syracuse, NY, make no mention of the *Trent* incident. Julia Griffiths Crofts's 6 December 1861 letter to Douglass is evidence that if not revealed in the public record, the *Trent* Affair was very much on Douglass's radar. See McKivigan 2018, pp. 322–3.

ment or people under heaven has any right to make any discrimination against them on this account ... Woe to the world', Douglass continued, 'when Governments can pursue rebels beyond their own territories, and where there shall be no longer any asylum for political offenders!' While Douglass hated the rebels 'with all the hate one man can feel ... If England demands them, GIVE THEM UP'.[156]

The peaceful end to the crisis obliged Douglass to add a new article, at the end of the prior one – again, in the same January issue of the *Monthly*. 'The Cabinet at Washington has done its duty', by releasing Mason and Slidell, 'and shown itself deaf to all vulgar and senseless clamor'. And then, as if to complement the advice Marx made to the Lincoln administration, '[w]e have done our duty, and done it under circumstances severely trying to our national pride, under a liability to be misconstrued, and having the act attributed to our sense of fear, rather than our sense of justice. We have done it promptly and gracefully'. It was as if – who knows? – Douglass applauded the Lincoln administration for following Marx's wise counsel about how to resolve the crisis. If Douglass was unable to get into print in time to advise the Lincoln administration on how to deal with the *Trent* imbroglio, then he could at least applaud them for having done the right thing – not unimportant for future relations. Then some needed chiding of the British government, a first for Douglass.

> Now, let England do hers [namely, duty]. Not by uttering complaints of the inefficiency of our blockade; not by decrying our army and navy; not by grumbling about our tariff, which the war has made necessary; not by holding out hopes of recognition to the Confederate States; not by proclaiming the inability of the North to suppress this most foul and unnatural rebellion; not by magnifying the victories of the rebel arms, and disparaging those of the loyal people; not by hints of a purpose to raise the blockade to obtain cotton for her mills; but by a whole-soul sympathy, such as one friendly nation should gladly show to a sister nation undergoing the perils of a formidable and terrible rebellion.[157]

Never before had Douglass taken the British government to task for its posture toward the War. Until this passage, Douglass had been inclined to blame Washington for London's sins. 'Of the two governments', he then pointedly noted, 'looking at all the circumstances of the [*Trent*] case, our Government stands at

---

156   DM, January 1862, p. 578.
157   Ibid.

this moment in a vastly more enviable position than that of England'. He concluded his article by looking forward. 'Let the ties of friendship between the two countries, now weakened almost to dissolution, become strong ... Let us have done with it, and now attend earnestly to the rebellion, and to slavery, its cause'.[158] Whether Marx's *Tribune* articles figured in any way in Douglass's new orientation toward England can only be a subject for speculation. It should be assumed that he did read them. Whatever the case, the *Trent* affair brought Douglass and Marx together politically unlike ever before. Three and a half years remained to see if that collaboration deepened.

In what turned out to be Marx's penultimate dispatch to the *Tribune* – domestic news about the War increasingly crowded out international affairs that correspondents like Marx supplied – he may have known that he was skating on thin ice with publisher Greeley and that his days with the organ were numbered. Thus, maybe, the decision to exit with his full agenda on display. Marx's 1 February 1862, article, 'English Public Opinion', revealed its purpose in the very second sentence:

> It ought never to be forgotten in the United States that at least the working classes of England, from the commencement to the termination of the [*Trent*] difficulty, have never forsaken them ... despite the poisonous stimulants daily administered by a venal and reckless press, not one single public war meeting could be held in the United Kingdom during all the period that peace trembled in the balance ... [S]imple justice requires to pay a tribute to the sound attitude of the British working classes, the more so when contrasted with the hypocritical, bullying, cowardly, and stupid conduct of the official and well-to-do John Bull.[159]

Marx returned to his main point in closing. 'Messrs. Mason and Slidell have done great service' to the Union cause. Those in England clamoring for a war with the United States, 'for commercial' and 'for political reasons', have been put 'to the test ... [They] failed'. The 'fury of the [slave] oligarchy has raised the suspicions of English democracy'. It has revealed 'the true character of the civil war ... to the working classes'. And 'not the least' for Marx, the whole episode taught a salutary lesson about 'the dangerous period when [Prime Minister]

---

158   DM, January 1862, p. 579. Whether this meant a fundamental reassessment of the British ruling class by Douglass remained to be seen. In DM, March 1862, p. 622, he reprinted without comment an article, 'Slaveholders and the British Aristocracy', extolling the latter and their supposedly equitable relations with the working class.
159   Marx and Engels 1975–2004j, pp. 137–8.

Palmerston rules single-headed without being checked by Parliament'. Marx, yes Marx the communist, a defender of parliamentary supremacy.

A day later Marx provided *Die Presse* readers with dramatic evidence to justify his praise of English workers in his article 'A London's Workers' Meeting'.[160] First, context. 'The misery that the stoppage of the factories and the shortening of the labour time, motivated by the blockade of the slave states, has produced among the workers in the northern manufacturing districts, is incredible and in daily process of growth'. Not only were workers in the textile industry in Northern England affected by the blockade, but others as well elsewhere in the country, Marx noted, whose livelihoods depended on exports to the blockaded South. Douglass, too, two months earlier, had lamented 'the misery' of English workers due to the blockade: '[W]e have threatened a large department of English industry with ruin, and hundreds of thousands of the British people with pangs of hunger and the desolations of famine and pestilence'. Therefore, he continued, it was to be expected that 'the British government and people should be disposed to murmur and complain' about the blockade.[161] But Marx's article, unlike what Douglass wrote, didn't conflate 'the British government and people'. That, in fact, was exactly its point.

The 'British people', specifically, the working class, did indeed have complaints, but directed not against the Union government but the newspapers of their 'natural superiors' and registered at the meeting Marx reported on. The 'great *workers' meeting*' on 27 January 1862 – two weeks after Marx penned his *Tribune* article – 'in Marylebone, the most populous district of London' was convened for the 'English people' to opine on the impending arrival to London of Mason and Slidell to promote the Confederate cause following their release from detention in Boston. 'It is the duty', said one of the speakers, 'of the working class to pronounce its opinion now, if the English government is not to believe that we regard its foreign policy with indifference'.[162] Nota bene 'its'. After a spirited discussion and debate joined by a representative of the Confederacy, the meeting voted 'unanimously' for a motion that said that Mason and Slidell 'are absolutely unworthy of the moral sympathies of the working class of this country, since they are slaveholders as well as the confessed agents of the tyrannical faction that is at this very moment in rebellion against the American

---

160   For the broader context of Marx's article and the historiographical debates on the issue, see P. Foner 1981a, Chapter Two.

161   DM, November 1861, p. 545. In some of the official labour press, there was indeed disenchantment with the blockade and to which Douglass might have been referring; see Foner 1981a, and what makes the Marylebone meeting significant.

162   Marx and Engels 1975–2004j, pp. 154–5.

republic and the sworn enemy of the social and political rights of *the working class in all countries* [emphasis added]'. Staying on the moral high ground, the meeting agreed 'that every personal insult to Mason and Slidell must be avoided during their stay in London'.

Then a second motion: given 'the ill-conceived efforts of *The [London] Times* and other misleading journals to misrepresent English public opinion on all American matters ... this meeting regards it as the very special duty of the workers, since they are not represented in the Senate of the nation [namely, Parliament], to declare their sympathy with the United States in their titanic struggle for the maintenance of the Union; to denounce the shameful dishonesty and advocacy of slaveholding on the part of *The Times* and kindred aristocratic journals'. Lastly, a third motion, also unanimously adopted: 'to forward to the American government *per medium* of [Ambassador] Mr. [Charles] Adams a copy of the resolutions framed, as an expression of the feelings and opinions of the working class of England'.[163]

Marx was forever impacted by that and similar meetings in England that followed.[164] For the first time ever a group of workers became conscious of and *acted* on the fact that the foreign policy of its ruling class was incompatible with the class interests of the proletariat – the origins of the International Working Men's Association, or First International, three years later. Whether Douglass knew about the 27 January Marylebone meeting – reported on widely in British newspapers – is uncertain. Both the February and March issues of his *Monthly* carried detailed news about the expected arrival of Mason and Slidell and other Confederate activities in England but made no mention of the historic meeting. Due to the meeting's last resolution, at least one person in the US probably knew about its proceedings and resolutions – Abraham Lincoln via his ambassador and not inconsequential as subsequent events would demonstrate.

Marx's politics, prioritising the working class and its interests, were becoming, as some suggest, increasingly indigestible for *Tribune* publisher Greeley.[165] If true, it means the severely financially strapped 'occasional correspondent in London' was willing to jeopardise a relatively secure income stream, with the consequences for his household, to advance his agenda – testament to his core

---

163   Marx and Engels 1975–2004j, pp. 155–6.
164   P. Foner 1981a, Chapters Four to Seven provide details.
165   Doyle 2015, pp. 154–5. When he lamented to Engels that he was no longer receiving the *Tribune* after March 1862, Marx called it 'a rotten trick of Greeley's and McElrath's', a co-publisher of the paper. Marx and Engels 1975–2004u, p. 362. For a useful overview of Greeley's politics in relation to Marx, see Tuchinsky 2005.

character. Marx's risk-taking may have paid off three years later – as will be seen – with regard to at least one of the habitual readers of the *Tribune*, Lincoln.

∴

Marx's 1 February 1862 *Tribune* article, 'English Public Opinion', was the last time either of our two protagonists would likely have read the other in regard to the War. While there is no reason to assume that Douglass would have read Marx's German-language *Die Presse* articles, there is also no reason to assume he would not have read the ten articles Marx wrote on the War from October to February in the *Tribune*.[166] We should assume that he did. As evidence, Douglass, beginning in the November issue of the *Monthly*, ran a quarter-page presumably paid-for ad by the *Tribune* about its pro-Union abolitionist content and its subscription rates. As for the other side of the ledger, *Douglass' Monthly*, though it had subscribers in England, it is highly unlikely that Marx read the organ. Marx – much more so than Douglass – typically cited newspaper sources he consulted, with dates, to support his arguments. There is no reason to assume he would not have done the same with the *Monthly*.

The question, therefore, is whether any of Marx's *Tribune* articles impacted Douglass. Comparative real-time political analysis also has an interest – perhaps even more so – in how political actors may influence each other as events are unfolding. There has long been speculation amongst Douglass scholars about the possible influence of Ottilie Assing on Douglass's thinking.[167] Not only an age-cohort of Douglass and Marx, Assing, the German-Jewish radical feminist, claimed to have introduced Douglass to the writings of the German materialist philosopher Ludwig Feuerbach, a figure who loomed large in Marx's conversion to communism. While the claim and its implications for a Marx-Douglass comparison are fascinating to think about, ignored so far – what this book hopes to rectify – is the opportunity Douglass had for actually reading Marx, in his own words and in original English.

The evidence reveals that Douglass was more clear-eyed about English 'statesmen' *after* the publication of Marx's first *Tribune* article on the War that

---

166 It is possible that German-language reader and associate Otille Assing did read *Die Presse* and informed Douglass about Marx's articles. A cursory reading of her articles and their notes for the period that this book addresses, Lohmann 1999, doesn't yield any references to *Die Presse*.

167 More certain is that Assing influenced and collaborated closely with Douglass during the Reconstruction years. For details see, Diedrich 1999, pp. 192–3, 294–6, 309–10 and Blight 2018, pp. 320, 512–17, 525, 529–30. For a balanced reading of Assing and Douglass, see Fought 2017.

roundly criticised the hypocrisy of the English ruling class. His *Tribune* articles that indicted British imperialism for intervening in Mexico complemented that critique. Marx's friendly criticism of Washington's handling of the *Trent* Affair probably enhanced his credibility with Douglass. The 'occasional correspondent' for the *Tribune* could be objective while being a partisan of the Union cause. The global significance of the Civil War was, unlikely for Douglass, Marx's starting point. But for Marx the communist, making clear what he opposed was insufficient. He, therefore, would have regarded his penultimate *Tribune* article, in praise of 'the working classes in England', just as if not more politically important than what he wrote that denounced the imperialist project, be it in North or Central America or, anywhere else.

One of our tasks from hereon, therefore, is to see, if possible, whether Marx's all-important claim about the English working class resonated positively in any way with Douglass. Before the publication of Marx's 1 February article in which he made his claim, Douglass, to put it charitably, had a less than favourable opinion of that layer of English society. Did that continue to be the case? Lastly, in the absence of any evidence that Marx read *Douglass' Monthly*, we can only speculate, in the Conclusion, on what impact the organ might have had on him had he read it.

Onward now to the key turning point in the War and the responses of Douglass and Marx.

CHAPTER 4

From a Constitutional to a Revolutionary Civil War: 'the Cruel and Apocalyptic War Had Become Holy'

> ... once 'Old Abe' realises ... such a turning point has been reached, he surprises friend and foe by a sudden operation executed as noiselessly as possible.
> MARX, 3 March 1862

∴

> ... that I should live to see the President of the United States deliberately advocating Emancipation was more than I ever ventured to hope.
> DOUGLASS, 25 March 1862

∴

> ... the most important document in American history since the establishment of the Union.
> MARX, October 1862

∴

> ... the proclamation ... is the most important of any to which the President of the United States has ever signed his name.
> DOUGLASS, October 1862

∴

From the very beginning of the Civil War both Douglass and Marx, from fundamentally different perspectives, contended that the future of slavery rather than the preservation of the Union was the decisive issue at stake. The months-long prelude to and the moment when the Lincoln administration came to the same realisation and then acted accordingly frames this chapter. The fate of

FROM A CONSTITUTIONAL TO A REVOLUTIONARY CIVIL WAR

America's peculiar institution could no longer be avoided. The exigencies of war taught the Sixteenth President that preserving the Union obligated him to confine the country's 'original sin' to the proverbial dustbin of history. How Douglass and Marx read, tried to impact, and reacted to Lincoln's 'crooked path', to borrow a phrase from historian James Oakes, to emancipation constitutes the substance of the chapter.[1]

Lincoln's apparent 'pusillanimity' caused Douglass to make a number of volte-faces regarding him. Marx, on the other hand, proved to be more unwavering in his faith that Lincoln, despite the contradictory signals he sent, was committed to emancipation. But Engels, his partner, and not unlike Douglass, wasn't convinced, provoking the only documented political difference between the two communists. Their differences about the prospects for the Union, which lasted for almost two years, required Marx to be at his best to make his case. Only with Lincoln's issuance of the Preliminary Emancipation Proclamation on 22 September 1862 did Douglass and Marx find themselves on the same political page. The ups and downs and sideways of 1862 that led to 1 January 1863, when the Proclamation came into full force, constitute the substance of the chapter.

1 'A *Turning Point* in the War Policy Had Been Reached'

'THE STATE OF THE WAR. We say nothing of its progress – for it has made none'. Thus began the February 1862 issue of *Douglass' Monthly*. As evidence, Union General George B. McClellan's Army of the Potomac, 'which has remained idle'. On the other hand, 'no man yet who comprehends the true nature of the rebellion and has shown the needed courage, capacity, genius and determination to put it down, receives the confidence and support of the Government'. Then a list of Union generals and officials who suffered in Douglass's opinion the same dismissive treatment that, as we noted in the previous chapter, had been meted out to General John Frémont. One of whom, General John Phelps, had denounced 'slavery as the cause of the war, and avows that slavery must be put down. He himself gets denounced as a fool for his honesty and for his moral courage'. Unwilling to fight like Phelps, there was the other problem with McClellan – his opposition to abolition, as revealed in his behaviour on 17 January towards the Hutchinson Family Singers, the country's most popular singing group. 'The Hutchinson's sing the songs of liberty by [abolition-

---

1 Oakes 2021.

ist poet John Greenleaf] Whittier to our army. They are promptly expelled by order of Gen. McClellan'.[2] Their performance of a pro-abolitionist song to Union troops stationed in Fairfax, Virginia is no doubt what McClellan most objected to – an incident, to be seen shortly, that also caught Marx's attention.[3]

Why, a frustrated Douglass asked, was the Union apparently satisfied with a 'stand-still, do-nothing policy'? Because of the 'delusive idea that the South is poor; that she is shut in from the sea; that she is now suffering untold hardships, and that if we only hold still, she will give over the struggle and come back to loyalty. The fewer the battles the better, says Mr. Seward. And the movements, or rather the immovableness of our army on the Potomac is an evidence of the power of his counsels'. Without naming it, Douglass was probably referring to the widely touted, at least in the pro-McClellan press, 'Anaconda Plan'.[4] Instituted by the now retired Union General Winfield Scott, it envisioned the strangling, as the snake could do, of the Confederacy. That involved, briefly, 'a naval blockade of the Confederate littoral, a thrust down the Mississippi, and the strangulation of the South by Union land and naval forces'.[5] But it was a deluded strategy in Douglass's view because of two problems: one, it was giving the rebels, 'busy as beavers', time to work internally to strengthen their cause; and second, every delay in a decisive defeat of the slaveholders meant keeping the blockade in place. To do so, given its negative impact on international trade, would only encourage foreign governments to grow tired of the blockade and want to end it with a recognition of the Confederacy. 'When this is done by one, it will be done by all European governments, and the war will be virtually ended' – a victory for the slaveholders. Douglass proposed an alternative to the timidity of McClellan: 'Two things now are required to save us ... The first is, fight and whip the slaveholders; and the other is, confiscate and emancipate

---

2 DM, February 1862, p. 593.
3 Fry 2020, pp. 27–8.
4 James McPherson writes that Lincoln hoped to end the Anaconda Plan with the First Battle of Bull Run after public opinion and initial success in battle by Generals Lyon and McClellan pressured him and Union leaders to strike at the Confederacy. See McPherson 2008, pp. 36–8, 50–4. Bruce Levine argues that the Anaconda Plan was instituted with the goal of not offending a presumed Unionist majority in the South. See Levine 2013, p. 110. The 'grand plan' McClellan devised to replace the Anaconda lasted one week in early August 1861 before timidity took over. McClellan certainly continued the soft war strategy of the Anaconda Plan in practice while using overestimations of Confederate forces as an excuse against engagement, to Lincoln's consternation. See also Sears 1994, pp. 14–19.
5 https://www.britannica.com/event/Anaconda-plan

the slaves'.[6] Whether or not and how soon the Lincoln administration would take Douglass up on his advice remained to be seen.

Two weeks later in a major speech given in both Boston and New York to the new Emancipation League organised by Garrison and Phillips, Douglass could still 'point to the vacillation, doubt, uncertainty and hesitation which have thus far distinguished our government in regard to the true method of dealing with the vital cause of the rebellion'.[7] 'We are without any declared and settled policy – and our policy seems to be, to have no policy'. The 'vital cause' of course meant slavery. In criticising the Lincoln administration, Douglass made the case for his patriotic and loyal bonafides as an 'American citizen', who like other Black men 'have evinced the most ardent desire to serve the cause of the country'. The biggest political obstacle to coming to grips with the question, he continued, were still 'the so-called Union men' in the Border States who were only for ending the secession and not slavery, the cause of the secession. But if Washington was slow in getting its act together, Douglass was pleased to point out that public opinion in the North was now on the side of abolition. Despite all the years of abolition movement efforts to disseminate persuasive propaganda, it was the War itself that most effectively taught Northerners the diabolical character of the slaveholding rebels. Yet, Douglass was sober about this change in Northern opinion. 'I know that national self-preservation, national safety, rather than any regard to the bondman as a man and a brother, is at the bottom of much that now meets us in the shape of opposition to slavery ... Nevertheless, I rejoice in this change, the result will be nearly the same to the slave, if from motives of necessity or any other motives, the nation shall be led to the extinction of slavery'.[8]

At least two other points deserve attention in Douglass's long and rich 'American citizen' speech, an unusual speech for Douglass because he gave, at least

---

6   DM, February, p. 593.
7   Though having been at political odds with Garrison and Phillips for more than a decade, Douglass welcomed their formation of the League, an independent organisational voice for abolition once the war had begun. A decade earlier, Marx and Engels had criticised themselves – in their 'Address of the Central Authority in March 1850' – for suspending the Communist League when the German edition of the 1848 Revolutions erupted. Douglass, too, had criticised abolition forces for putting their actions on hold once Fort Sumter exploded. The Marx party in America, interestingly, appeared to have done the same after Fort Sumter, that is, suspended its activities and dissolved itself into the Union military cause. We address that decision and its possible consequences in the Conclusion.
8   DM, March 1862, pp. 613–14. Modern scholarship debates the issue of Northern public opinion towards emancipation. Three of the most important contributions to understanding the reasons Union soldiers enlisted and fought are Gallagher 2011; Manning 2007; McPherson 1997.

in New York City, a written address. The Emancipation League organisers of both speaking engagements, which included other speakers, asked him, apparently, to address the increasingly obvious question about what to do with the former slaves after abolition. 'Leave us alone', was the gist of his answer. 'Do nothing with us, for us, or by us as a particular class'. Let us be free, he asked, to determine our own future, what 'two centuries' of slavery had never permitted. In making his case, Douglass felt obligated to explain why even sympathetic Northern opinion might not be convinced that a people who had been enslaved for so long had the wherewithal to exercise self-determination. He conceded 'the fact that the black man submits to that condition [of slavery] is often cited as a proof of original and permanent inferiority ... the argument of the Confederate states' and its spokespeople like its Vice-President Alexander Stephens of Georgia and, perhaps, the aforementioned James Hammond, from the Palmetto State. But what happened to 'the black man', Douglass went on to say, could happen to 'any race ... French, English, Irish or Scotch' that had been enslaved. He then offered an explanation for the views that fuelled doubts about Black self-determination, arguably, we think, Douglass's first elaboration of a theory of racial prejudices. His thesis asserted that

> Whenever and wherever any particular variety of the human family, having been enslaved by another, their enslavers and oppressors in every instance, have found their best apology for their own base conduct in the bad character of their victims. The cunning, the deceit, the indolence, and the manifold vices and crimes, which naturally grow out of the conditions of Slavery, are generally charged as inherent characteristics of the oppressed and enslaved race. The Jews, the Indians, the Saxons and the ancient Britons have all had a taste of this bitter experience.

He prefaced his argument with his earlier point: 'The misfortunes of my own race ... are not', he repeated, 'singular'. If twentieth- and twenty-first century opinions have become accustomed to thinking about 'the Negro problem', or 'America's original sin', as unique, Douglass would have disagreed. What existed in the United States, he argued, was a species of the same genus, namely class oppression, in which one layer of society exploits another layer. As evidence for the thesis, Douglass offered examples from European history with particular focus on the Norman conquest of England and the prejudices that came with the subordination of the conquered to justify their oppression. 'No wonder, therefore, that the colored people in America appear stupid, helpless and degraded. The wonder is rather that they evince so much spirit and manhood as they do'. In addition, he continued, the enslavement of 'the colored people in America' was exceedingly lucrative, 'their estimated value a little while ago was twenty hundred million'.[9]

> Those twenty hundred millions of dollars have all the effect of twenty hundred millions of arguments against the negro as a man and a brother ... No wonder that it has been able to bribe the press against us. No wonder that it has been able to employ learning and eloquence against us. No wonder that it has bought up the American pulpit and obtained the sanction of religion against us. No wonder that it has turned every department of the Government into engines of oppression and tyranny toward us. No nation, however, gifted by nature, could hope to bear up under such oppressive weights.[10]

Douglass, again, employed a class-based template driven by, in this instance, economic interests to explain the origins and appeal of racist ideas. Whether he forever held on to that framework remains to be seen. Nota bene Douglass's usage of 'race' and the different terms he employed to describe Blacks: a 'race', 'the black man', a 'variety of the human family', the 'colored people in America', and, 'a nation'. Caution, in other words, is advised when reading Douglass – Marx as well, we argue – through a twentieth-first century lens when it comes to the topic of race. Also noteworthy is the jibe that Douglass took at the 'American pulpit'. Marx, almost two decades earlier, had concluded that religion didn't explain anything; rather, religion required an explanation and a good place to begin was with material interests. The US had taught how religion itself could become a commodity.

Douglass's thesis about racial prejudice would have resonated with Marx and Engels. Read, for example, the description of the English and Irish working classes by the twenty-two year old, pre-communist Engels in his 1845 classic, *The Condition of the Working Class in England*. Given 'the social order', that is, the oppressed reality of the English working class, deepened by the increasing integration within its ranks of another degraded layer of British society, Irish immigrants, 'it is not surprising that the working-class has gradually become a race wholly apart from the English bourgeoisie ... The workers speak other dialects, have other thoughts and ideals, other customs and moral principles,

---

9   In the DM May 1862 issue, Douglass reprinted an article by abolitionist Gerrit Smith that made a similar argument about 'race' and 'the differences of race' (p. 648).
10 DM, March 1862, p. 615.

a different religion and other politics than those of the bourgeoisie'.[11] Whereas Douglass offered an explanation for racial prejudice, Engels, therefore, went a step further in offering an explanation for race itself, what today might be called the invention of a 'race', with its own dialect, religion and politics. Douglass, who visited England and Ireland shortly after Engels, also commented on the negative outcomes of class and national oppression on the Irish, specifically 'intemperance', but, interestingly, in a more judgemental way – Douglass identified 'temperance' as the solution to this negative social outcome.[12] Engels, on the other hand, emphasised 'the social order' in explaining working-class 'intemperance', not unlike how Douglass had explained why 'the colored people in America appear stupid, helpless and degraded'.[13]

Marx, in 1847, in his lecture 'Wage Labour and Capital', asked, pedagogically, 'What is a Negro slave?' His first answer was sarcastic: 'A man of the black race. The one explanation is as good as the other'. But, he objected: 'A Negro is a Negro. He only becomes a slave in certain relations. A cotton-spinning jenny is a machine for spinning cotton. It only becomes *capital* in certain relations'. Contrary to present-day politically correct or 'woke' readings of what Marx meant, that take his work out of historical context, Douglass, we argue, would have been in full accord with Marx. Just like Douglass, Marx was challenging the then widely accepted assumption that to be 'a Negro' is to be a 'Negro slave' with, thus, all the prejudicial baggage that came with the label. Douglass, given his self-understandings in that moment, would have had no quarrel with Marx that 'A Negro is a Negro'.[14]

The other significant point in Douglass's February 1862 speech, at least for this comparison, concerned Britain. While the *Trent* affair had seemingly disabused Douglass of any illusions about the 'statesmen' of Britain, he signalled for the first time that he had found a layer of British society that he could now embrace. Britain, he proclaimed, had undergone a fundamental change due to the victory of the Anti-Corn Law League in 1846, which effectively 'transferred

---

11   Marx and Engels 1975–2004c, pp. 419–20.
12   Bradbury 1999, p. 175; P. Foner 1950a, pp. 138–41.
13   To the Plymouth Anti-Slavery Society in 1841, Douglass declared: 'You degrade us and then ask why we are degraded; you shut our mouths and then ask why we don't speak; you close your colleges and seminaries against us, and then ask why we don't know more'. P. Foner 1950a, p. 49; Blassingame 1979, p. 12.
14   Hund 2021, p. 80, reads the monologue to mean that 'Marx recognizes only one dimension of the racism at issue; slavery is not natural. But he does not realise the other racist dimension of his deliberation; for him, race theory is valid and being a "Negro" is a natural quality, not a social relation'. We address that ill-informed criticism and similar ones in Appendix B.

the power of the landed aristocracy to the people and gave us the Brights, the Cobdens, the Wilsons and the Thompsons, and the [hitherto mentioned] William Edward Forsters, the men who represent the middle classes of England, and who are now in our days of trouble as in our days of peace and prosperity, America's best and true friends'.[15] Douglass was referring to 'the great transformation' that Marx had long been researching, that of bourgeois ascendancy in Britain. The 'middle class' or bourgeois figures that he listed did indeed, unlike the Tory 'statesmen' and their organs he had once looked to, oppose Britain's intervention in the War on behalf of the Confederacy. But so did another layer of British society that Douglass would have known about from Marx's 1 February *Tribune* article, two weeks before his speech – the 'working classes of England, from the commencement to the termination of the [*Trent*] difficulty'.[16] Neither before then or later did Douglass, unlike Marx, look positively on England's proletariat. For Marx, the historical materialist, the best the bourgeoisie had ever done was to bring into existence the gravediggers of capitalism, the working class, and the material prerequisites for eventual rule by the working class. On that all so essential point, Marx and Douglass, political allies for four years, parted ways once the War ended.

2   'At Last the Tide of Battle Seems Fairly Turned'

Thus began the opening sentence of the March issue of *Douglass' Monthly*. In full: 'At last the tide of Battle seems fairly turned in favor of the union forces'. And for the first time on the lead page appeared a battlefield balance sheet, a list of 'Union Victories' and 'Rebel Victories' for 1861 and 1862. Douglass now recognised, apparently, like Marx and Engels, that the decisive question, the end of slavery, would have to be settled on the battlefield. How to make sense of that terrain, however, could be, pardon the pun, like navigating a minefield. Ten months into the War, Douglass for the first time engaged in warfare analysis. 'The only two victories [Bull Run and Balls Bluff] which the rebels can make any show upon, are victories given them, not gained by them' owing to 'the weakness and treachery of so-called loyal officers'. He also speculated on and accurately predicted the consequences of another defeat at Bull Run (more about later). Despite having concluded, mistakenly, that recent Union victories signalled 'the failure of the rebellion as a military power', Douglass maintained

---

15   Blassingame 1985, pp. 497–8.
16   Marx and Engels 1975–2004j, p. 137.

sobriety. 'The South', with notable foresight, might now be motivated to go on 'the offensive ... and thus prolong the war to an indefinite period or till some foreign power shall step between the belligerents ... More fighting and that more desperate and terrible than any which has thus far happened may be justly apprehended'. Again, this remark indicated his remarkable foresight even though it contradicted the claim of 'the failure of the rebellion as a military power'.[17]

But then he articulated the improbable. Politically, Douglass declared, 'the rebellion with all of its losses is a decided success' in defence of 'chattel slavery'. 'The prestige and power of slavery as a political element, continues through all to be all controlling over the United States'. So much so that Douglass could entertain the possibility that 'the Government' could 'compromise with the slaveholders' and allow them 'an equal right to extend slavery outside the slave States'. And at the same time, Douglass thought he saw signs that 'it is just possible', inexplicably, 'that southern hatred of the north may outweigh southern love of slavery ... by emancipating every slave'. Admittedly, it 'would be a curious chapter in the history of human nature if this should be the turn of affairs' – indeed – 'and yet no more strange than happens elsewhere in other emergencies. Jonah was flung into the sea to save the ship, though the ship was built to carry Jonah and many precious freights have been sent to the bottom for the same reasons which may lead the southern confederacy to fling slavery overboard'.[18] Should such a 'strange' development unfold, 'the hands of many loyal soldier [sic] would fall to his side. Men who volunteered to fight slaveholders, would hesitate about striking down Emancipators'. Then, he envisioned a reconciliation of the North and the South. 'Both sections would then look at each other as friends and brethren and all cause of jealousy and suspicion would be gone'.[19]

Douglass was plainly grasping at straws to explain a highly uncertain and complex situation. As well as seeming highly improbable, Douglass's assessment rested on inconsistencies. Why would the slaveholders be willing to emancipate their slaves if, as he wrote earlier in the article, the 'prestige and power of slavery as a political element, continues through all to be all controlling over the whole United States'? On the very next page in a different article, Douglass wrote that 'the state of public sentiment respecting slavery and the necessity of its complete abolition is full of encouragement ... [T]he people are ready to sweep slavery from the country would the Government lead

---

17   DM, March 1862, p. 609.
18   Two years later, that was a real possibility. See B. Levine 2006.
19   DM, March 1862, pp. 609–10.

off or stand out of the way'. So enthused by that fact, Douglass pledged to go on a speaking tour to promote that change in public opinion. 'Every man who is ready to work for the overthrow of slavery whether a voter, or non voter, a Garrisonian or a Gerrit Smith man, black or white, is both clansman and kinsman of ours'.[20] Lastly, the claim about Northern troops fraternising with born-again southern 'emancipators' rang inconsistent. A few weeks earlier in his 12 February speech, Douglass asserted that those troops fought not for abolition but simply to maintain the Union. Why had their motives apparently changed in a couple of weeks? Douglass, as David Blight insightfully notes, 'did not yet fully grasp military campaigns, their logistics and results on the ground, thus leading him to rash statements sometimes laced with confused political sentiments'.[21] This confusion reveals his difficulty in making sense of a complex situation 'under circumstances not chosen' by him.

'President Lincoln never ventures a step forward before the tide of circumstances and the general call of public opinion forbids further delay. But once 'Old Abe' realises that such a turning point has been reached, he surprises friend and foe alike by a sudden operation executed as noiselessly as possible'. With these words, sometime in late February, Marx began an article about the complex situation that Douglass was also grappling with. Like Douglass, he and Engels, even with more military experience, were also perplexed by the situation. Yet his insight about Lincoln's modus operandi, again, four thousand miles away, proved to be remarkably predictive.

'Noiselessly' but of major significance for Marx was Lincoln's *'removal of McClellan* from his post of Commander-in-Chief of all the Union armies'.[22] The action involved a number of steps registered by Marx that included the replacement of the 'Secretary of War, Cameron, by an energetic and ruthless lawyer, Mr. *Edwin Stanton*'.[23] 'Finally, Lincoln issued some orders which he signed as "Commander-in-Chief of the Army and Navy" ... In this "quiet" manner "the young Napoleon"' – as McClellan was called – 'was deprived of the

---

20   DM, March 1862, p. 610.
21   Blight 2018, p. 366.
22   Marx and Engels 1975–2004j, p. 178. Marx's *Die Presse* article was published on 3 March 1862. Although the 'removal' wasn't made official until 11 March, Marx was probably referring to two executive orders Lincoln signed on the 27th and 31st of January 1862 – indicative of how closely and smartly he was reading intelligence about the War.
23   If Marx saw the replacement as a positive move, Douglass did not. For him, Stanton was 'a Douglas Democrat'. DM, February 1862, p. 593. Historian LeeAnna Keith disputes that reading of Stanton. According to her, Stanton advocated arming slaves even before the appointment. Also, he supported a plan to enrol former slaves into the army in the Carolina Sea Islands. Keith 2020, pp. 154–6. Whether Marx was aware of any of that history is uncertain.

supreme command he had hitherto held over *all* the armies and restricted to the command of the army on the Potomac ... The successes in Kentucky, Tennessee and on the Atlantic coast' – listed by Douglass in his *Monthly* as 'Union Victories for 1862' – 'propitiously inaugurated the assumption of the supreme command by President Lincoln'. For Marx, the removal augured well for the future. 'That [McClellan's] influence acted as a brake on the general conduct of the war, is beyond doubt'. Marx, characteristically, employed ancient history – 'Fabian's tactics' – early modern history – 'Cromwell in his speech' – and modern history – 'the Crimean War' – to deflate the Napoleon want-to-be.

Marx detailed what had been so problematic with 'the young Napoleon', beginning with his 'special order' that 'expelled the Kutchinson [sic] family of musicians from the camp because they sang anti-slavery songs'. About Douglass's assertion that the Confederate victories at Bull Run and Ball's Bluff were due 'to the weakness and treachery of so-called loyal officers', Marx provided the telling particulars. 'McClellan and most of the officers of the regular army who got their training at West Point are more or less bound by *esprit de corps* to their old comrades in the enemy camp ... In their view, the war must be waged in a strictly businesslike fashion, with constant regard to the restoration of the Union on its old basis, and therefore must above all be kept free from revolutionary tendencies and tendencies affecting matters of principle. A fine conception of a war which is essentially a war of principles' – what Douglass had been complaining about for months.[24] The 'esprit de corps' factor explained why 'McClellan covered the traitors in the Union army with his saving shield ... From General [Robert] Patterson, whose treachery determined the defeat at Manassas, to General [Charles] Stone, who *brought about* the defeat at Ball's Bluff in direct agreement with the enemy'. Then Marx provided details about how McClellan undermined the War in Missouri by putting the most aggressive Union generals on a short leash from Washington. 'President Lincoln has now restored to them the necessary freedom of action'.

Finally, a fascinating account about a reporter for the *New York Herald*, a pro-Democratic Party organ known for 'the panegyrics it continually lavishes upon' McClellan. Once Stanton was in charge, the said individual, who had had unfettered access to the inner workings of the Lincoln administration, including 'a champagne breakfast' with 'McClellan's General Staff', was unceremoniously given the boot. As reported in the *Tribune* on 11 February, he was taken 'to

---

24 The Radical Republicans who were part of the Congressional Joint Committee on the Conduct of the War, led by Senator Benjamin Wade, had a similar opinion to that of Marx. See Fry 2020, p. 31.

Fort McHenry, where, as the order of the Secretary of War expressly states, he "is to be kept under strict watch *as a spy*".[25] Marx had good reason, therefore, to believe that the end of the feckless McClellan era that so frustrated Douglass had begun. All of the rich details in Marx's 3 March *Die Presse* article indicate how much attention he had given to the War while saddled with myriad research, writing, and personal obligations. 'I admire', Engels told his partner on 28 February, 'your steadfastness, your fervour, your energy'.[26] No one knew better than Engels the significance of what Marx was doing and the sacrifices required of him.

Closer to home, it was easier for Marx to keep abreast of the British government's policy toward the War, a continuing concern for Douglass. His expert political dissection of a parliamentary debate about the legitimacy and effectiveness of the Union blockade of the Confederacy led Marx to conclude in an 8 March *Die Presse* article that 'all prospects of a breach between Britain and the United States is eliminated'.[27] Had Douglass been able to read the article, he could have been less fearful, a concern he raised in his March *Monthly*, that 'some foreign power shall step between the belligerents' to settle the conflict before the key issue, slavery, had been abolished. If Marx thought that McClellan's 'removal' was a major development, Douglass, apparently, did not. There is oddly no explicit mention of the demotion, made official on 11 March, in any of Douglass's speeches or writings, at least in that period. Because Lincoln coupled his directive with an announcement about the formation of a new unit to the west of the Potomac, the Army of the Mountain, to be headed by Frémont, Douglass along with other critics on Lincoln's left flank may have been distracted. But 'Old Abe's' stealthy modus operandi had been detected by the eagle-eyed communist four-thousand miles away.

3 Two Real-Time Assessments of 'the Tremendous Conflict'

Marx and Engels's first published balance sheet on the War were their two articles for *Die Presse* at the end of March 1862. Written between 7 and 22 March and largely by Engels, their articles entitled 'The American Civil War', 'a spectacle without parallel in the annals of military history', began with the commencement of the War through to the Union defeat at Bull Run and then

---

25 Marx and Engels 1975–2004j, pp. 179–81. See also, Marx's 3 March letter to Engels: Marx and Engels 1975–2004u, p. 345.
26 Marx and Engels 1975–2004u, p. 343.
27 Marx and Engels 1975–2004j, p. 185.

continued with the subsequent Union victories. The articles concluded with prospects for the future.[28]

The South, as both had earlier opined, was better prepared for the War owing to 'the secessionist conspiracy, patronised and supported by Buchanan's administration'. 'The North', on the other hand, 'came to the theatre of war reluctantly, sleepily, as was to be expected considering its higher industrial and commercial development. The social machinery there was far more complicated than in the South, and it required far more time to get it moving in the unusual direction'. And then they highlighted the problem that Engels had written about in December: 'The enlistment of volunteers for three months was a great, but perhaps unavoidable mistake'. Nowhere was that more evident than at Bull Run. 'It was absurd to let raw recruits attack a strong position, on difficult terrain, and having an enemy scarcely inferior in numbers. The panic which seized the Union army at the decisive moment ... could surprise no one who was at all familiar with the history of people's wars'.

In September 1861, Douglass also lamented the inexperience of Union troops and used the Bull Run disaster to push for Black enlistment. If the government continues to 'reject the Negro', Douglass wrote, they will invite 'their own social and political ruin ... this is no time to fight only with your white hand, and allow your black hand to remain tied'. Would Black men, compared to those inexperienced volunteers so far gathered in the Union Army, 'deport themselves less soldier-like on the battlefield than the raw troops'? Presciently, Douglass continued, 'such soldiers, if allowed now to take up arms in defense of the Government, and made to feel that they are hereafter to be recognised as persons having rights, would set the highest example of order and general good behavior to their fellow soldiers, and in every way add to the national power'. Take note, he pointedly added, that 'the Negroes are numerous in the rebel army [as slave labourers], and do for that army its heaviest work'. If Lincoln and his cabinet would raise 'one black regiment in such a war as this is', even if that regiment was no more brave and orderly than those organised, it 'would be worth to the Government more than two of any other'.[29]

Since the Bull Run fiasco, things had improved over the subsequent months due in no small measure to the input of the veterans of Germany's edition of the European Spring. 'Without the considerable amount of people of military experience who had immigrated to America in consequence of the European revolutionary unrest of 1848–9, the organisation of the Union army would

---

28   Marx and Engels 1975–2004j, p. 186.
29   P. Foner 1952, pp. 150–4.

have required a much longer time still' – another reason for linking America's 'second birth of freedom' to the second edition of the French Revolution.[30] Engels's imprint on the articles can be easily seen in their granularity regarding the recent Union victories. For example, note this account of how the Union army captured Tennessee: 'A single gunboat sailed boldly up the Tennessee [River] through the very heart of the State of Tennessee, skirting the State of Mississippi and pushing on as far as Florence in northern Alabama, where a series of swamps and banks (known by the name of the Muscle Shoals) prevented further navigation. The fact that a single gunboat made this long voyage of at least 150 miles and then returned, without experiencing any attack, proves that Union sentiment prevails along the river and will be very useful to the Union troops should they push forward as far as that'.[31]

The articles are replete with such details. But as Marx gently chided his partner a few months later, being in the weeds that deep, metaphorically speaking, could lead to myopia about the overall conduct of the War.

Nevertheless, Engels's expertise served the articles well. 'The leadership of the Kentucky campaign', which resulted in its capture from the secessionists, 'deserves the highest praise'. And particularly prescient, 'Halleck and Grant ... offer good examples of resolute military leadership'. But McClellan didn't garner such praise. Like Douglass, Engels and his partner also criticised 'young Napoleon's' grand strategy. 'The American papers influenced by McClellan are full of talk about the "anaconda" envelopment plan. According to it, an immense line of armies is to wind round the rebellion, gradually tighten its coils and finally strangle the enemy. This is sheer childishness. It is a rehash of the so-called *cordon system*' – whose ignominious eighteenth-century history Engels recounted.[32] Douglass would have agreed with Marx and Engels's characterisation. But unlike Douglass, they offered an alternative military strategy. Given 'the geographical shape of the secessionists' territory', an action that would split Virginia and the Carolinas from the Gulf states was imperative for the defeat of the Confederacy. The Union victories in Kentucky and Tennessee now made that possible. 'This proves', they declared with remarkable foresight, 'that *Georgia is the key to the secessionists' territory*. With the loss of Georgia the Confederacy would be cut into two sections, which would have lost all connection with one another. A reconquest of Georgia by the secessionists, however, would be almost unthinkable, for the Unionist fighting forces would be concentrated in a central position, while their adversaries, divided into two camps, would

---

30   Marx and Engels 1975–2004j, pp. 187–8.
31   Marx and Engels 1975–2004j, p. 190.
32   Marx and Engels 1975–2004j, pp. 192–3.

have scarcely sufficient forces to put in the field for a joint attack'. With a number of 'ifs', 'ands', and 'buts', they provided details for how that strategy could work.

A final 'but': 'should the anaconda plan be followed, then, despite all the successes gained at particular points and even on the Potomac, the war may be prolonged indefinitely, while the financial difficulties together with diplomatic complications acquire fresh scope'.[33] In a note to Engels on 6 March, a day before he began to pen the articles, Marx opined on the War's future:

> To me it does not seem very PROBABLE that the SOUTHERNERS will have concluded peace by July 1862.[34] When the NORTHERNERS have 1. secured the BORDER STATES – and it is upon these, in fact, that everything has centred from the start – and 2. the Mississippi as far as New Orleans and Texas, the war may well enter a 2nd phase during which the NORTHERNERS will make no great exertions of a military nature but, by isolating the GULF STATES, finally bring them to the point of voluntary RE ANNEXATION.[35]

While the Union army had made progress through March, uncertain, therefore, was whether they might rest on their laurels and continue in some fashion the all so unproductive 'anaconda plan'. Continuing that plan indicated the possibility of a much longer war which is what indeed ensued.

What became 'The American Civil War' articles in *Die Presse* were originally intended for the *Tribune*. We can only speculate as to what would have happened if they had been published there, and if Lincoln, an inveterate reader of the paper, had noticed that *'Georgia is the key to the secessionists' territory'*. Marx learned on 28 March why the *Tribune* never published the articles.[36] Charles Dana, his closest contact at the paper, informed him that domestic issues took priority in its pages owing to the War, so dispatches from London and elsewhere abroad were no longer being accepted.[37] The irony, of course, is that Marx's last submission to the paper was quintessentially domestic. To Engels a month later, 'the fellows', bemoaned Marx, 'don't even

---

[33] Marx and Engels 1975–2004j, p. 195.
[34] A day earlier Engels explained to his partner how precocious his own finances had been and improvement depended on better company sales for the next fiscal year that began in July.
[35] Marx and Engels 1975–2004u, p. 349.
[36] By then, Marx reported, the *Tribune* was publishing 'perhaps one article in 3 or none at all'. Marx and Engels 1975–2004u, p. 352.
[37] Marx and Engels 1975–2004u, p. 632.

send me the *Tribune* any more'.³⁸ 'This is a rotten trick of [Horace] Greeley's and [Thomas] McElrath's', he later added.³⁹ Evidently, a managerial shake-up had taken place at the *Tribune*, depriving Marx of not only needed income but his most important source of daily news about the War. It also revealed a key difference between Marx and Douglass – the advantage of having a loyal financial backer. Almost every issue of the *Monthly*, once the War began, included a pages-long article by the wealthy abolitionist Gerrit Smith – probably not a coincidence.⁴⁰

Three days after Marx and Engels completed their balance sheet on the War, and about a month after Marx had written his 3 March article, also for *Die Presse*, Douglass gave a speech in Rochester, New York on 25 March at Corinthian Hall. Entitled 'The War and How to End It', his assessment of the conflict covered about the same time period as Marx's analysis, making possible, therefore, a more accurate real-time comparison of our two protagonists. The important political context for the speech was Lincoln's 6 March 1862 message to Congress, a proposal for a gradual and compensated emancipation in the Border States, and the impending passage by Congress of a law for compensated emancipation in the District of Columbia. Douglass reprinted Lincoln's message in his April *Monthly*. But the news of those two historic developments didn't get to London until two weeks later and, thus 'The American Civil War' articles didn't mention them. Real-time, it may be recalled, involved a two-week delay.

Rather than commence with Lincoln's historic-making announcement, Douglass began didactically by pointing 'out a few of the leading features of the contest ... [so as to] enforce the lesson which I think they plainly teach *and the path of duty they mark out for our feet*' [our italics] – a formulation that Marx would have readily embraced and priceless evidence for why we argue that Douglass is the best that liberalism had ever offered. Making sense of the course of the 'long train of events' required knowing, Douglass began, that the North was ill-prepared for a 'civil war, the worst of all wars'. He gave as the reason that 'we misconceived the real state of the case, and misread the facts then passing before us. We were quite incredulous of the tremendous strength

---

38   Marx and Engels 1975–2004u, p. 353.
39   Marx and Engels 1975–2004u, p. 362.
40   A useful overview of the Douglass-Smith relationship can be found in McKivigan 1990, pp. 205–32. In addition to financially backing the fledgling *Frederick Douglass' Paper*, Gerrit Smith provided irregular financial contributions to help fund Douglass's paper until at least June 1863. In addition to the financial help, Douglass saw Smith as the leader of pure abolitionist political action and a friend and intellectual companion who treated him and his family as equals.

and vigor of the foe against whom we were called upon to battle ... our southern brethren'. The 'us', the 'we', and the 'our' in Douglass's claim merit their own discussion that can't be entered into here. More pertinent for present purposes are some of the examples Douglass provided of the North misreading and misunderstanding the context of the War. The North 'continued to believe in the border states', to 'dream of peace', to believe in 'a show of force rather than an exercise of force', to prefer 'to fight with dollars rather than daggers', to believe that 'the fewer the battles, the better', and finally, to sustain an 'unwillingness on our part to know the worst'. And unfortunately, he continued, 'this blindness on our part ... still lingers with us'. Douglass, in making his case, was not above playing a time worn card in the American political playbook, the 'marshaling' by 'the rebels' of 'the savage Indian to the slaughter of your sons' – almost verbatim from his beloved Declaration of Independence. And amidst the North's unpreparedness, 'Treason has become the warp and woof of the army and navy'[41] – details about which Marx had provided.

Douglas then turned to 'the physical part of this tremendous conflict' – the picture on the battlefield. That 'is at last in a hopeful way. The great armies of the North are in motion ... Brave hearts and strong hands' had made that possible. Douglass was probably referring to the executive orders Lincoln issued at the end of January that Marx pointed to in his 3 March article about the 'removal' of McClellan. Douglass then claimed that 'I knew they would from the first' – which may be correct, but after Bull Run he wasn't so certain.[42] As Engels had diagnosed back in December, the North, 'from the first', was not only ill-prepared but also unaware of what it would take to win the War. Little did Douglass know – or perhaps ever realise – that the brave volunteers he applauded eleven months earlier at their departure to the war front from Rochester, NY, along with thousands of others from elsewhere in the loyal states, would prove to be inadequate for the task at hand – 'an unavoidable' but 'great mistake' as Marx and Engels argued. Communists were obligated – this had been their practice since the 1848–9 revolutions – to evaluate past battles, including the mistakes such as utilising untrained fighters, in order to avoid them and not make virtue out of necessity for future battles – 'the lesson ... they plainly teach and the path of duty they mark out for our feet', to employ the language of Douglass.

It is not clear, again, if Douglass knew that McClellan had been demoted and why, therefore, progress was being made on the battlefield. Whatever the case,

---

41   DM, April 1862, pp. 625–6.
42   DM, April 1862, p. 626.

Douglass felt compelled to devote a portion of his speech to recent remarks by the 'young Napoleon' to 'his army'. Especially grating was McClellan having taken 'pains to compliment these [slaveholding] traitors. He is "sad" at the thought of striking them ... McClellan is careful to tell us that the Southern army is composed of foemen worthy of our steel. I do not like this. It looks bad. Instead of being foemen worthy of our steel, they are rebels and traitors worthy of our hemp', namely, our hanging ropes. No wonder then that the rebels 'are especially devoted to this "sad" reluctant General ... It is seriously doubted if he will ever try his steel upon them ... But whether McClellan ever overtakes the rebels or not, the army of the Potomac has moved, and brave men sweep both the Eastern and Western border of the rebellion'[43] – again, what Lincoln's late January executive orders made possible. What so frustrated Douglass about McClellan's kowtowing to the 'traitors' could be explained by Marx's opinion: 'McClellan and most of the officers of the regular army who got their training at West Point', again, 'are more or less bound by *esprit de corps* to their old comrades in the enemy camp'. What was incredulous for Douglass was understandable – not excusable – for Marx. Whether Douglass was aware of or ever considered that history is uncertain.

Douglass then turned to the future. Given how well the War was then going for the Union, he began with an assumption: 'having now broken down the rebel power in the secessionist States, how shall we extend the Constitution and the Union over them? ... we know how to conquer, but the question is do we know how to make peace?'[44] That unproven assumption, about having conquered the Confederates, informed virtually everything else that Douglass said in the remainder of his speech.

Douglass had good reason to feel optimistic about the prospects for abolition. In addition to Lincoln's 6 March proposal to Congress for a compensated and gradual emancipation in the Border States, and the impending enactment of a law for compensated emancipation in the District of Columbia, there was other good news on the warfront. A new law by Congress ordered that Union troops were no longer obligated to return escaped slaves to their owners. Even McClellan, as his April *Monthly* reported, 'heartily approves of this additional Article of War'.[45] And when combined, 'right on the heels of the message' of Lincoln to Congress, with the appointment of Frémont to head the Mountain Department – the general who had been fired for doing something similar –

---

43   Ibid.
44   Ibid.
45   DM, April 1862, p. 633.

Douglass could be forgiven for believing that redemption was near. His paean to Lincoln captures his mood best.

> But that I should live to see the President of the United States deliberately advocating Emancipation was more than I ever ventured to hope. It is true that the President lays down his propositions with many qualifications, some of which to my thinking, are unnecessary, unjust and wholly unwise ... A blind man can see where the President's heart is ... I see in them a brave man trying against great odds, to do right. An honest patriot endeavoring to save his country in its day of peril ... Time and practice will improve the President as they improve other men. He is tall and strong but he is not done growing, he grows as the nation grows ... He has dared to say that the highest interest of the country will be promoted by the abolition of slavery. And this, bear in mind, is not said in the bitterness of defeat, but when every morning brought news of glorious victories over the slaveholding rebels. The message comes at the call of no desperation. The time selected for sending it to Congress and the nation must be read with the document itself in order to appreciate its true significance.[46]

But for the promise of Lincoln's message to be realised, abolition and nothing less was required. Without abolition, Douglass's bottom line, peace would be a chimaera.

In a letter written a day after Lincoln's 6 March message and published in the London *Inquirer* on 29 March, Douglass declared: 'The president has presented the subject in the mildest possible terms, but all the more on that account do I trust to the radical character of his view concerning the necessity for putting away our great American abomination. I consider that we have fairly reached the turning point of the moral struggle involved in this terrible war'.[47]

Douglass's 'mildest possible terms' is reminiscent of Marx's formulation about Lincoln's executive orders at the end of January, 'executed as noiselessly as possible'. And both of our protagonists employed the language of 'turning points' to describe Lincoln's actions but with different references: for Marx, the military measures he had taken and for Douglass, his proposal for gradual and compensated emancipation. The difference is instructive.

Missing in Douglass's inspiring scenario were the details about how to abolish slavery, what it would take to do so. For Marx and Engels, on the other hand,

---

46   DM, April 1862, pp. 626–7.
47   McKivigan 2018, p. 328.

they ended their balance-sheet with a grand strategy for doing just that. Abolition, in their view, could only be achieved on the battlefield; this was why they argued that 'Georgia was the key'. That kind of grounded analysis, in the literal and metaphorical sense, was missing – at least in that moment – in the almost transcendental scenario that Douglass had sketched. Whereas Douglass made a distinction between the 'physical' struggle, that is, the military process, and the 'spiritual' or 'moral' struggle, that is, the end of slavery, these were much more interdependent processes for Marx. History would soon begin to test which of the two assessments proved to be more accurate.

What if Marx and Engels had known about the four positive developments that enthused Douglass? Would they have thought that the rebels had been conquered and, therefore, directed attention to peace? Though we can't prove it, we're doubtful. As communist veterans of a failed revolution, they had a much more informed and thus realistic view about what it would take to conquer the slave owners. That kind of battlefield perspective was simply lacking in Douglass's portrait. Their extant subsequent writings, after learning of those four developments, confirm what we claim. Nota bene that many articles that Marx had written for *Die Presse* were never published: 'out of every 4 or 5 articles, they print 1 and only pay for 1', as he told Engels on 8 March.[48] By the end of April, he was obligated for only '1 article per week', which took a toll on his finances and, thus, well-being.[49] To Ferdinand Lassalle on 29 April, to whom he was in debt, he wrote, 'it's a wonder I haven't actually gone *mad*'.[50] Forced to write only one article per week for *Die Presse*, Marx at least had more time to work on his magnum opus. 'I have now', to Engels on 27 May, '– if only out of DESPERATION – really put my nose to the grindstone and am writing away for dear life – at the political economy I mean'.[51] Immersing himself in research and writing, a revealing admission, was Marx's coping mechanism, his 'opiate' for maintaining his sanity.[52]

There is at least one sentence in Douglass's vision of post-War America that bears revisiting when we get to that moment. 'Who wants to see the nation taxed to keep a standing army in the South to maintain respect for the Federal Government and protect the rights of citizens of the United States?' No issue

---

48 Marx and Engels 1975–2004u, p. 351.
49 Marx and Engels 1975–2004u, p. 353.
50 Marx and Engels 1975–2004u, p. 356.
51 Marx and Engels 1975–2004u, p. 370. To Engels on 18 June: 'I am ... working away hard and strange to say, my grey matter is functioning better in the midst of the surrounding *misère* than it has done for years'. Marx and Engels 1975–2004u, p. 380.
52 Gabriel 2011 makes a similar point, pp. 290–1.

was more contentious after the War than the presence of Northern troops in the former Confederacy. Comparing what Douglass said in March 1862 about the matter and how he responded when it was a present reality could prove instructive.

4   Slouching Toward Redemption

A month after applauding the Union army for 'having now broken down the rebel power in the secessionist States', sobriety returned to Douglass's pen. Though heartened by emancipation in Washington, DC, on 16 April, 'there is danger that instead of making the abolition of slavery at the national Capital the beginning of the end we shall make it the end of the beginning, and our last state be worse than the first'.[53] Owing to facts on the ground elsewhere, 'we look therefore now', he wrote to the readers of the May issue of his *Monthly*, 'as at the beginning for a long war, a broad war and a most sanguenary [*sic*] war – covering the whole South with desolation and ruin and involving the North in dire calamities, in loss of property and life'. Was there an alternative to that bleak scenario? 'The answer is ready, cease to mend old garments with new cloth, cease to put new wine into old bottles, cease to court slavery. *Arm the slaves*, confiscate slave property, welcome the black man to a share in the salvation of the country, put the nation on the side of Impartial justice and universal Liberty … this alone is the way of peace out of the terrible judgment called down upon us by our manifold sins and transgressions'.[54] Prone to make, again as Blight points out, 'rash statements sometimes laced with confused political sentiments' about the battlefield, Douglass, when more thoughtful, identified the one issue that aided him to better evaluate the progress of the War – captured in the demand, 'Arm the slaves'. Lincoln too, unbeknownst to Douglass, hesitatingly inched toward the same solution.

'The English Press and the Fall of New Orleans', Marx's first publication in *Die Presse* after a month-long absence, ridiculed the pro-Confederacy British press – '"sympathisers" with the Southern "nigger-drivers"' – for initially denying what one Southern paper he quoted called 'the most serious reverse since the beginning of the war'.[55] Quoting two other Southern papers: 'It is useless

---

53   DM, May 1862, p. 644.
54   DM, May 1862, p. 643.
55   Marx and Engels 1975–2004j, p. 199. This is the first time, as far as we can tell, that Marx used the N-word either in print or in correspondence. A few weeks earlier Engels used the same expression for the first time in the English original in a letter to his partner: 'You will

to deny that the fall of New Orleans is a heavy blow', and, 'The capture of New Orleans by the Federals is the most extraordinary and fateful event of the whole war'. Two days later, in his next *Die Presse* article, Marx applauded the 'Treaty on the suppression of the slave trade concluded between the United States and Britain on April 7 of this year in Washington ... now communicated *in extenso* by the American newspapers'. He explained its significance.

> A mortal blow has been dealt the Negro trade by this Anglo-American Treaty – the result of the American Civil War. The effect of the Treaty will be completed by the Bill recently introduced by Senator [Charles] Sumner, which repeals the law of 1808 dealing with the traffic in Negroes on the coasts of the United States and punishes the transport of slaves from one port of the United States to another as a crime. This Bill does, to a large extent, paralyse the trade that the states raising Negroes (border slave states) are carrying on with the states consuming Negroes (the slave states proper).[56]

For Marx, the fall of the 'Crescent City' and the Treaty appeared to bode well for emancipation. His partner, however, wasn't so sure. Despite Union victories in Kentucky and Tennessee earlier in the year, the Peninsula campaign that began on 4 April to take Richmond, the Confederate capital in Virginia, had little to show for itself. Unlike the more direct route to Richmond from Washington that Lincoln favoured, McClellan prevailed in having his indirect and increasingly ineffective path to the Confederate capital be utilised. That decision registered for Engels, as he told Marx on 18 May, a more basic problem with the Union conduct of the War. 'What makes me lose confidence in any success where the Yankees are concerned isn't so much the military situation as such, which is what it is only as a result of the indolence and indifference apparent throughout the North. Where, amongst the people, is there any sign of revolutionary vigour? They allow themselves to be thrashed and are downright proud of the lambasting they get. Where, throughout the North, is there the slightest indication that people are in real earnest about anything?'[57] Engels's complaints were neither his first nor last expression of pessimism about Union prospects.

---

have seen in today's *Standard* (or *Morning Herald*) that General Hecker has become chief NIGGER catcher (Manhattan)'. Marx and Engels 1975–2004u, p. 361. See the Introduction for a discussion of the word for this book.
56   Marx and Engels 1975–2004j, p. 203.
57   Marx and Engels 1975–2004u, p. 364.

Engels, a week later in an article written mostly by him but co-authored with Marx, elaborated on 'the military situation'. 'McClellan has irrefutably proved that he is a military incompetent who ... wages war not to defeat the foe, but rather not to be defeated by the foe and thus forfeit his own usurped greatness ... The Confederates always escape him, because at the decisive moment he never attacks them ... A war has never yet been so wretchedly waged'.[58] McClellan's Peninsula campaign, in other words, fared poorly after five weeks. Though six weeks away, Engels proved to be prophetic. The campaign to take Richmond came to an ignominious end on 1 July, the last day of the so-called Seven Days Battle at Malvern Hill, Virginia, with McClellan's withdrawal from the battlefield after having actually bested Lee's forces. 'At the decisive moment', as Engels had so uncannily predicted, 'he never attacks them'. Incredulous when learning of the call to retreat, General Philip Kearny, McClellan's most aggressive general, declared: 'I say to you all, such an order can only be prompted by cowardice or treason'.[59] The Confederate Army of Virginia, now headed by Robert E. Lee, was not, in Engels's estimation, superior. The advantage it had was that 'it is facing a McClellan instead of a [Union General Henry] Halleck'.[60] Douglass, however, put an equal sign between the two generals – both backed by the pro-slavery Democratic Party in the north with, in his opinion, presidential aspirations.[61]

McClellan's 22 July letter to his wife is an irresistible coda. He wondered if his actions and feelings toward the Confederates would cause him to be 'accused ... of double dyed treason' because, as he told her, he had 'ordered a boat load of all such things (lemons, tea, sugar, brandy, underclothing, lint, bandages, chloroform, quinine, ice etc etc) to be sent up to Genl Lee today to be used at his discretion ...' The supplies, he hoped, would be used equally for the rebels and for the captured Union soldiers under Lee's command.[62] Marx and Engels had a name for such 'civilized niceties' of the War, the 'esprit de corps' of West Point graduates.

The fate of the Confederates, Engels held, depended on the outcome of 'a decisive battle'. And should they lose it, 'their armies will then break up into bands'. Thus, the possibility of 'a guerilla war'. But that was unlikely, he thought, because 'precisely in respect of the present war of the slaveholders it is most

---

58 Marx and Engels 1975–2004j, p. 205.
59 Browning 2017. See also Murray and Hsieh 2016, p. 188. For examples of Kearny's private laments against McClellan, see Fry 2020, p. 37.
60 Civil War historians debate the merits of Halleck; see Engle et al. 2017.
61 DM, July 1862, p. 674.
62 Sears 1989, p. 368.

amazing how slight or rather how wholly lacking is the participation of the population in it'. Examples from European history taught that successful guerrilla warfare depended on such a population. That seemed to be non-existent in the US case. Yet, Engels was aware of the preexisting class divisions within slaveholding society that could provide the kindling for post-War conflict. 'There can be hardly any doubt ... that the *white trash*, as the planters themselves call the "poor whites", will attempt guerrilla warfare and brigandage. Such an attempt, however, will very quickly transform the propertied planters into *Unionists*. They will even call the Yankees troops to their aid' to maintain law and order.[63] With an inconclusive end to the major battles phase of the War, Engels, in other words, envisioned the possibility of some kind of class warfare, without specifying the skin colours of all the combatants.[64] Douglass also raised the spectre of 'guerrilla warfare' in the aftermath of a 'decisive' routing of Confederate forces in not only Virginia. 'The defeat of the rebels ... will greatly damage the rebel cause, but will not necessarily or probably put an end to the war ... they could still carry on for a long time a fierce guerila war involving the country in hopeless debt and destruction, till a strong party at the north should rise up and insist upon measures of peace'.[65]

While the 'capture of New Orleans', Marx and Engels continued, 'is distinguished as an almost unparalleled act of valour on the part of the [Union] fleet, the "alleged burnings of cotton, etc." in and around the city portended the kind of class conflict they envisioned with an inconclusive end to the War. They were alluding to various acts of sabotage and resistance to Union General Benjamin Butler's take over of the city.[66] But such 'brigandage', they concluded, 'can only bring the dissension between the planters and the "white trash" to a head and therewith – *finis secessiae!*' – that is, the end of secession.[67] In the uncertain course of the War at that moment, speculation is all that Marx and Engels – Douglass as well – could offer. Making the situation more uncertain, as Engels noted to Marx on 4 June, 'was a colossal blunder on [Secretary of War Edward] Stanton's part, and sheer boastfulness, to put a stop to recruiting'.[68] In early

---

63 Marx and Engels 1975–2004j, p. 207.
64 The first signs of that conflict began to appear a year later. See B. Levine 2013.
65 DM, May 1862, p. 643.
66 See Marx's 'English Humanity and America', about the resistance of ruling class women to Butler's infamous – at least in their eyes – military order number 28. Marx and Engels 1975–2004j, pp. 209–12. On the capture of New Orleans and the 'tame' methods Butler used as occupier compared to other contemporary global occupations, see Murray and Hsieh 2016, pp. 161–3.
67 Marx and Engels 1975–2004j, p. 208.
68 Marx and Engels 1975–2004u, p. 373.

April 1862, Stanton had closed down recruiting offices in the belief the Union needed no more troops – 'a reasonable decision at the time'.[69] Ten days later and a month before the complete failure of McClellan's feckless plan, Marx noted that the Union would have been in a better position 'if after its victory in Tennessee, the Kentucky army had rapidly advanced on the railway junctions in Georgia'.[70]

His foresight about Virginia proved by and large to be accurate; the prediction about Georgia would be tested two years later. Military historians Williamson Murray and Wayne Wei-Siang Hsieh describe at least two Union officers on the Eastern seaboard who wanted to move against Savannah, Georgia after the capture of Port Royal, South Carolina early in the war. Murray and Hsieh indicate it was unfortunate the campaign was not supported, giving credence to Marx's real-time analysis, allowing the Confederates in Savannah to hold out until shortly before December 1864.[71]

Douglass too might have been on the same doubtful page with Engels as his point about guerilla warfare might suggest. A month before Engels's letter, late April 1862, when sobriety had returned to Douglass's pen, 'the nation', he wrote, 'awaits with breathless anxiety the war news … and any moment may herald a glorious victory, or a terrible and shameful defeat for either side'. He expressed some hope about the Peninsula campaign, though 'we doubt it', due to 'General McClellan'.[72] For sure, Engels and Marx would have agreed, and accompanied by evidence to explain why so. A month later, when Engels wrote his pessimistic letter to Marx about McClellan's plan, Douglass too may have had similar trepidations. Unfortunately, the June issue of the *Monthly*, in which he would have likely expressed such sentiment, is missing.[73] But oddly, there is no mention of the 7 April signing of the Treaty for the Suppression of the African Slave-Trade in the May issue of the *Monthly* despite the '*in extenso*' coverage it got in 'American papers'. Except, also, for a couple of articles from other newspapers in the July issue, Douglass didn't write anything about the fall of New Orleans. That might be due to Confederate rule in New Orleans having formally ended on 1 May, not giving him enough time to do so for the May issue. Douglass had

---

69 Murray and Hsieh 2016, p. 164.
70 Marx and Engels 1975–2004j, p. 212.
71 Murray and Hsieh 2016, pp. 126–9. Interestingly, Lincoln's Treasury Secretary Salmon P. Chase urged Major General George B. McClellan in an early July 1861 letter to undertake a strategic operation that bore some similarity to what Engels recommended. See Stahr 2021, pp. 343–4.
72 DM, May 1862, p. 643.
73 According to Douglass scholar John Kaufman-McKivigan, the Director of the Frederick Douglass Papers, the June issue is not in their collection.

opined prior to then that the fall of the city would 'not necessarily or probably put an end to the war'.[74] The July issue of the *Monthly* pointed out that 'we take possession of rebel cities, but not the rebel hearts' – in reference no doubt to the resistance to the Union occupation of New Orleans that Marx and Engels had commented on.[75] As for the Peninsula campaign, 'Thirty thousand loyal men have perished from disease and bullets in three months, but Richmond is not taken, and is not likely to be, unless the rebels find that they can inflict a deeper wound upon the Federal Government by a retreat than by a fight'.[76] Within days of raising that possibility, rather than Lee's army, it was McClellan's that retreated.

5 Redemption Time

As Douglass rose to address two thousand attendees at the Fourth of July celebration in Upstate New York, details of McClellan's cowardly withdrawal from Malvern Hill had yet to arrive. Prepared days in advance, Douglass's speech, 'The Slaveholder's Rebellion', to a mainly Caucasian audience, was consciously didactic. Unlike the rebellion of 1776, one in which 'Your fathers drew the sword for free and independent Government, Republican in its form, Democratic in its spirit', 'the present rebellion', as he'd been saying since its commencement, 'is found in the fact that It was conceived, undertaken, planned, and persevered in, for the guilty purpose of handing down to the latest generations the accursed system of human bondage. Its leaders have plainly told us by words as well as by deeds, that they are fighting for slavery'. Only when 'the slave holders ... saw that they could no longer control the union as they had done for sixty years before, they appealed to the sword and struck for a government which should forever shut out all light from the southern conscience, and all hope of Emancipation from the southern slave'. Blame for the War rested squarely, therefore, on the shoulders of the 'slaveholders' and not those of 'the abolitionists'.[77]

Douglass then related the history of the Slave Power, its origins in the Missouri Compromise of 1820, which gave slavery 'a new lease of life', and 'made the

---

74 DM, May 1862, p. 643.
75 DM, July 1862, p. 676. The August issue of DM reprinted an article about how 'General Butler and the federal rule are becoming exceedingly popular among the masses of peaceable citizens'. DM, August 1862, p. 699.
76 DM, July 1862, p. 675.
77 DM, August 1862, p. 690.

conflict unavoidable'. Then an innovative insight, we think, on the part of Douglass – putting the Slave Power in place required an accompanying ideology. To do that, 'lawyers, priests and politicians were at work upon national prejudice against the colored man. They raised the cry and put into the mouth of the ignorant, and vulgar and narrow minded, that "this is the white man's country," and other cries which readily catch the ear of the crowd. This popular method of dealing with an oppressed people has while crushing the blacks, corrupted and demoralized the whites'.[78] Conscious no doubt of his audience, Douglass described, in other words, the invention of the ideology of what would later be called white supremacy. Implicit in Douglass's account, and what his audience needed to know, was that such ideas did not always exist and, thus, not always held. 'This popular method' – or, maybe better, historically usual method – 'of dealing with an oppressed people' was Douglass's elaboration of his theory about racial prejudices that he first raised in his February speech in New York City, what we characterise as his class-based thesis of racism. Class oppression, as history had shown, required an accompanying ideology to rationalise oppression. White supremacy à la America was a species of a historical genus to do just that – no more, no less. We'll revisit Douglass's claim about that ideology in the Conclusion to see if it has currency today.

Douglass then did a near about-face. In almost breathtaking contrast to his paean to Lincoln in March, Douglass proclaimed that rather than the progenitors of the Slave Power, the Buchanan administration, 'today we have to deal … with … our weak paltering and incompetent rulers in the Cabinet at Washington and our rebel worshipping Generals in the field, the men who sacrifice the brave loyal soldiers of the North by thousands, while refusing to employ the black man's arm in suppressing the rebels, for fear of exasperating these rebels, men who never interfere with the orders of Generals, unless those orders strike at slavery, the heart of the Rebellion. These are the men to whom we have a duty to discharge today, when the country is bleeding at every pore, and when disasters thick and terrible convert this national festival day, into a day of alarm and mourning'. To leave no doubt for his audience to whom he was referring, 'we have a right to hold Abraham Lincoln, sternly responsible for any disaster or failure attending the suppression of this rebellion. I hold that the rebels can do us no serious harm, unless it is done through the culpable weakness, imbecility or unfaithfulness of those who are charged with the high duty, of seeing that the Supreme Law of the land is everywhere enforced and obeyed'. And then later, a little less, perhaps, strident.

---

78   DM, August 1862, p. 691.

> Mr. Lincoln and his Cabinet will have by and by to confess with many bitter regrets, that they have been equally blind and mistaken as to the true method of dealing with the rebels. They have fought the rebels with the Olive branch. The people must teach them to fight them with the sword. They have sought to conciliate obedience. The people must teach them to compel obedience.[79]

About one of Lincoln's 'rebel worshipping Generals in the field', McClellan, Douglass really unleashed his ire.

> His whole course proved that his sympathies are with the rebels, and that his ideas of the crisis make him unfit for the place he holds ... General McClellan's every movement, an apparent reluctance to strike at Virginia rebels ... From the time he took command of the Potomac army in August 1861 until now, he has been the constant cause of delay, and probably would not have moved when he did, but that he was compelled to move or be removed.

After recounting some details of his feckless Peninsula campaign, 'Gen. McClellan is either a cold blooded Traitor, or an unmitigated military Impostor'.[80] And that was before Douglass learned of his cowardly withdrawal from Malvern Hill – about a month later than Engels's uncanny prediction about McClellan. But McClellan could only do what he treacherously did because of what informed Lincoln's conduct of the War from its commencement. 'To my mind that policy is simply and solely to reconstruct the union on the old and corrupting basis of compromise, by which slavery shall retain all the power that it ever had, with the full assurance of gaining more, – according to its future necessities'.[81] Three months after Douglass had praised Lincoln, he now sang a very different tune – exactly the time it took to discover McClellan's feckless Peninsula campaign, an even grander charade.

Douglass saved his 'what is to be done' portion of the speech, with its all important political message, for the end – informed by his bottom line position.

> There is plausibility in the argument that we cannot reach slavery until we have suppressed the rebellion. Yet it is far more true to say that we

---

79 Ibid.
80 DM, August 1862, p. 692.
81 DM, August 1862, p. 693.

cannot reach the rebellion until we have suppressed slavery. For slavery is the life of the rebellion. Let the loyal army but inscribe upon its banner, Emancipation and protection to all who will rally under it, and no power could prevent a stampede from slavery, such as the world has not witnessed since the Hebrews crossed the Red Sea.[82]

But how to abolish the institution? Douglass was open to any of the ways which were being discussed in Congress and elsewhere. 'One is a stringent Confiscation Bill by Congress. Another is by proclamation by the President at the head of the nation. Another is by the commanders of each division of the army. Slavery can be abolished in any or all these ways'.[83] As for the criticism that a proclamation from the president would be 'only a paper order', he replied, 'so is any order emanating from our government ... All Laws, all written rules for the Government of the army and navy and people, are "paper orders," and would remain only such were they not backed up by force, still we do not object to them as useless, but admit their wisdom and necessity'. Compared to all other paper orders, an emancipation proclamation would possess a moral force giving it 'this self-executing power ... It would act on the rebel masters, and even more powerfully upon their slaves'.[84] Unbeknownst to Douglass, that claim would soon be put to the test in a way it had never been. Douglass's entire speech was reprinted in the August 1862 issue of the *Monthly* and, unlike any of his prior speeches, it began on the first page for about a third of the entire issue, signalling to his readers its importance for the editor.

About Douglass's near about-face on Lincoln: was it genuine or a way to pressure Lincoln to do the right thing? Douglass always worried about compromise with the slave power. As late as December 1863, Douglass, to be seen, issued such a warning after hearing Lincoln's initial reconstruction plan. While welcoming Lincoln's March 1862 message to Congress that proposed gradual and compensated emancipation in Washington, DC, McClellan still commanded the Army of the Potomac and Black men were not welcomed on the battlefield. Success in the field against Confederate troops dictated the mood of millions in the North and the failure of McClellan's Peninsular campaign in combination with no discernible move to free the slaves and enrol them in the army likely

---

82 Ibid.
83 That Douglass didn't yet mention an amendment to what he considered an abolitionist constitution isn't surprising. 'Only during the course of political struggles in late 1863 and early 1864 did the amendment emerge as the most popular of the abolition alternatives'. Vorenberg 2001, p. 2.
84 DM, August 1862, p. 693.

led to an abrupt change in Douglass's opinion about Lincoln. It is difficult to tell with certainty how much of it was genuine or strategic – probably a mixture of both.

Despite McClellan's own live and let live position on slavery, his treachery at and after Malvern Hill had unintended consequences. The outrage it provoked in the North set into motion a chain of events that would lead to the turning point in the War.[85] 'For weeks', as one Radical Republican in Congress described the perfidy, 'the army "lay in ditches, digging, drinking rotten water, and eating bad food, and sleeping in mud. Still they conquered in every fight, and still they retreated, because they were ordered to retreat"'.[86] As historian James McPherson put it, McClellan 'was defeated, even if his army was not'.[87] That's the widespread public perception that drove both Lincoln and the Congress to begin to do what Douglass had demanded of them.[88] For months, Congress had been debating another confiscation bill that Douglass had mentioned. At issue, basically, was if and how far could the Union Army go in emancipating slaves. McClellan actually thought he could be influential in the discussions to make sure that 'Military power should not be allowed to interfere with the relations of servitude'.[89] But the heretofore cornucopia of Little Napoleon's capital, after the disastrous Peninsula campaign, had evaporated.

Historian James Oakes sums up best the significance of what Congress enacted on 17 July. 'Back in mid-1861', Oakes writes, 'in the First Confiscation Act, Congress deprived masters of any slaves used in the rebellion. Almost immediately the War Department broadened emancipation's reach by freeing all slaves from rebel areas who emancipated themselves by coming into Union lines voluntarily'. Now the Second Confiscation promised to free '*All* the slaves of *all* the rebels', as Oakes puts it. In addition, the July 1862 law gave Lincoln the ability to utilise Black Americans as he believed 'necessary and proper for the suppression of the rebellion'. Even further, the Militia Act of 17 July 'removed the words

---

85 Civil War historian Gary Gallagher argues for that and other reasons – not the least the promotion of Lee to commander in chief of the Confederate Army – the Seven Days' Battles was the most consequential moment in the War. Gallagher 2012.
86 Bordewich 2020, p. 156. For instructive details to confirm the description, see Browning 2017.
87 McPherson 2008, p. 98.
88 As Elizabeth Varon writes, 'Ultimately, McClellan's reverses on the peninsula, more than any speech or editorial, vindicated the necessity of the Second Confiscation Act'. Varon 2019, p. 108.
89 Bordwich 2020, p. 158.

free and *white* from the qualifications for enrollment in the militia'.[90] While the Second Confiscation Act again promoted colonisation, it also turned every advance of Union soldiers, who had begun to see emancipation as necessary almost a year before, into an advance for emancipation. Douglass, according to David Blight, was 'at first thrilled with the Second Confiscation Act', but also realised it was 'significant or insignificant only as the President himself shall determine'.[91] Douglass's reaction was best captured, perhaps, in the short article he wrote near the end of the August issue of his *Monthly* that began: 'Mr Lincoln should be informed that the people are becoming impatient for the execution of the important laws just passed by Congress'.[92] Lincoln, in other words, had his marching orders. Marx, as we'll see, was more enthusiastic about the legislation.

Like Douglass, apparently, Engels didn't think much of the passage and enactment of the Second Confiscation Act. Prefaced with a litany of 'things are going awry in America', Engels complained in his 30 July letter to Marx that even if 'some factitious measure finally gets through Congress, the honourable Lincoln hedges it about with so many clauses that it's reduced to nothing at all' – Douglass's complaint also and why he felt the need to give the president his marching orders. Two months after Engels first raised his pessimism with his partner, he could now provide an abundance of reasons for believing so. Secretary of War Stanton was the chief culprit, owing to his order on 3 April to end recruitment, just as the Confederacy instituted a draft. In addition to shrinking 'from conscription, from resolute fiscal measures, from attacking slavery', the lack of military talent – 'one general more stupid than the other' – but most of all a 'complete absence of any resilience among the people at large which proves to me THAT IT IS ALL UP ... As I have already said, unless the North instantly adopts a revolutionary stance, it will get the terrible thrashing it deserves – and that's what seems to be happening'.[93] Engels, it seems, had thrown in the towel. Marx had his work cut out for him.

Once having received news of the enactment of the Second Confiscation Act, Marx penned in early August his 'A Criticism of American Affairs' – a title to end any appearance of a disinterested reporter. In many ways, the article was a response to the concerns that Engels had raised about the Union conduct of the War. With the conflict reaching a critical moment, Marx wanted to opine

---

90 Oakes 2013, pp. 224–5, 361. Text of the Second Confiscation Act: http://www.freedmen.umd.edu/conact2.htm
91 Blight 2018, p. 366.
92 DM, August 1862, p. 701.
93 Marx and Engels 1975–2004u, pp. 386–8.

and intervene in any way he could. Lacking his own organ, unlike Douglass, the communist was obligated to make do with what was available to him.

'The crisis', he began, 'which at the moment reigns in the United States has been brought about by two causes: military and political'. About the military factor, a bit of 'I told you so' – legitimate Monday morning quarterbacking. 'Had the last campaign been conducted according to a *single* strategic plan, the main army of the West was then bound, as previously explained in these columns, to exploit its successes in Kentucky and Tennessee to make its way through north Alabama to Georgia and to seize the railway junctions there at Decatur, Milledgeville, etc' – in other words, the *'Georgia is the key to the secessionists' territory'* strategy that he and Engels called for in March. The geopolitical reality of the United States, so unlike Europe, informed the premise of their strategy. Taking a big city, even New Orleans, or a capital like Richmond, would be inconsequential given how the population of the seceded states was dispersed. Why the Georgia route? Because the 'link between the Eastern and Western armies of the secessionists would thereby have been broken and their mutual support rendered impossible'. All that taking New Orleans did was to free up Confederate General P.G.T. Beauregard with his army in Mississippi to aid Lee in Virginia. Sarcastically, 'McClellan's generalship, already described by us previously, was in itself sufficient to ensure the ruin of the biggest and best disciplined army', namely, the Army of the Potomac.[94]

On top of that strategic mistake, there was [Secretary of War Edwin] Stanton's 'unpardonable error. To make an impression abroad' – presumably to convince foreign governments that the Union was winning – 'he suspended recruiting after the conquest of Tennessee and so condemned the army to be constantly weakened, just when it was most in need of reinforcements for a rapid, decisive offensive'.[95] And, at the exact moment of Stanton's decision, the Confederacy instituted the draft of 'every man from 18–35 years old', putting it very soon in an advantageous position. Despite all of those Union blunders

---

[94] We continue to search, without success so far, for any real-time or modern evaluations of Marx's and Engels's strategy. A potentially fruitful research project.

[95] Murray and Hsieh, as noted above, make no mention of the international factor in the decision. Stanton's recent biographer, Walter Stahr, focuses on the domestic considerations behind the decision. First, Stanton faced political pressure from Republican senators worried about the cost of maintaining a large army. Second, Stanton seemed to think, implausibly, that ceasing federal recruiting would lead state recruiting to increase. Stahr 2017, pp. 188, 194. An investigation into the Congressional Record and contemporary newspaper accounts would need to be done to see if the politicians who pressured Stanton and the newspaper editors who supported the decision had international considerations in mind.

and obstacles, Marx boldly asserted that 'the war, if not decided, had hitherto been rapidly nearing a victorious end'.[96] Of course, a victory then would have obviated the unintended consequences of McClellan's disastrous Peninsula campaign for emancipation. But that's illegitimate Monday morning quarterbacking; what no one could have known at the time.

But 'the military causes of the crisis are connected', Marx continued, 'with the political ones. It was the influence of the Democratic Party that elevated an incompetent like McClellan to the position of Commander-in-chief of all the military forces of the North'. That in turn was due to a nearly obsessive concern with the interests of the so-called '"loyal" slaveholders of the border states'. Of utmost interest to them was to make sure that 'the fugitive slave laws dictated by the South were maintained and the sympathies of the Negroes for the North forcibly suppressed, that no general could venture to put a company of Negroes in the field and that slavery was finally transformed from the Achilles' heel of the South into its invulnerable horny hide. Thanks to the slaves who do all the productive work, all able-bodied men in the South can be put into the field!' – exactly the point that Douglass had been hammering on for months.

Marx's observant eyes revealed that Lincoln had begun to rethink the free pass the Union was giving the slave owners by not depriving them of those 'who do all the productive work'. In his 12 July address to members of Congress from the Border States, Lincoln, Marx claimed, 'threatens them with inundation by the Abolition Party', meaning that 'things are taking a revolutionary turn'. Back in March, Lincoln made the offer of compensated gradual emancipation to the Border State slave owners but they declined, giving hope to the secessionists that those states were still recruitable to the slaveholding cause and, thus, prolonging the War – this at least was how Lincoln saw the implications of their refusal of the carrot he had offered them. Lincoln renewed his offer, this time with a not too disguised stick: 'If the war continues long, as it must if the object [of ending secession] be not sooner attained, the institutions in your States will be extinguished by mere friction and abrasion – by the mere incidents of the war. It will be gone, and you will have nothing valuable in lieu of it'.[97] All parties to the discussion knew the meaning of the euphemism 'the institutions of your States' and why Marx read Lincoln's message as a threat to slavery – an offer they could refuse but at their peril. Douglass reprinted Lincoln's 12 July address in the August issue of the *Monthly* but without comment. So focused on getting Lincoln to execute the Second Confiscation Act, Douglass, too close

---

96 Marx and Engels 1975–2004j, pp. 226–7.
97 Lincoln's 'Appeal to Border-State Representatives for Compensated Emancipation' can be found in Fehrenbacher 1989b, pp. 340–2.

to the scene, likely missed what Marx could better see, again, four thousand miles away – the president and Congress on the same political page.

But Marx wasn't starry-eyed about Lincoln, who was acting 'only hesitantly and uneasily'. His continuing appeal to the Border States, though now ratcheted up to a threat, was due to the 'pressure from without', the sentiment from 'New England and the Northwest', the 'main body of the army', and its determination 'to force on the government a revolutionary kind of warfare and to inscribe the battle-slogan of "Abolition of Slavery!" on the star-spangled banner'.[98] But Lincoln 'errs', Marx's advice, 'only if he imagines that the "loyal" slaveholders [in the Border States] are to be moved by benevolent speeches and rational arguments. They will yield only to force'. Then, Marx's thesis: 'So far, we have only witnessed the first act of the Civil War – the constitutional waging of war. The second act, the revolutionary waging of war, is at hand'.[99] For Douglass, the Constitution was an abolitionist document, near sacrosanct – again, a position that few abolitionists other than he adhered to. This was why, therefore, Douglass could proclaim, as he did in July 1863, 'not a sentence or syllable of the Constitution need be altered'.[100] For Marx, on the other hand, Lincoln's adherence to the document had been an obstacle for the defeat of the slavocracy. Events would soon put to the test these two alternative perspectives about the Constitution.

To prove that he wasn't engaging in wishful thinking, Marx provided evidence for his claim that 'the revolutionary waging of war is at hand' – the 'series of important measures' adopted by the just adjoined 37th Congress, details all so lacking in Douglass's article in the August issue of the *Monthly*. 'We shall briefly', he told his readers, 'summarise [them] here':

> Apart from its financial legislation, it passed the Homestead Bill, which the Northern masses had long striven for in vain; in accordance with this Bill, part of the state lands is given gratis to the colonists, whether indigenous or new-comers, for cultivation. It abolished slavery in Columbia and

---

[98] Marx saw evidence of a growing number of white Union troops, well ahead of the general public and the northern government, who were making claims regarding the centrality of slavery to their fight. Most of them, Gary Gallagher correctly emphasises, likely joined the army to defend the Union and the republic. And as Chandra Manning writes, 'Few white Northerners initially joined the Union rank and file specifically to stamp out slavery, and most shared the antiblack prejudices common to their day, especially when the war began. Yet the shock of war itself and soldiers' interactions with slaves, who in many cases were the first black people northern men had ever met, changed Union troops' minds fast'. Manning 2007, p. 12.
[99] Marx and Engels 1975–2004j, pp. 227–8.
[100] Blassingame 1985, p. 596.

the national capital, with monetary compensation for the former slaveholders. Slavery was declared 'forever impossible' in all the Territories of the United States. The Act, under which the new State of West Virginia is admitted into the Union, prescribes abolition of slavery by stages and declares that all Negro children born after July 4, 1863, are born free. The conditions of this emancipation by stages are on the whole borrowed from the law that was enacted 70 years ago in Pennsylvania for the same purpose. By a fourth Act all the slaves of rebels are to be emancipated, as soon as they fall into the hands of the republican army. Another law, which is now being put into effect for the first time, provides that these emancipated Negroes may be militarily organised and put into the field against the South. The independence of the Negro republics of Liberia and Haiti has been recognised and, finally, a treaty on the abolition of the slave trade has been concluded with Britain.

Having provided evidence to support his thesis that 'the *revolutionary* waging of war ... is at hand', Marx concluded: 'Thus, no matter how the dice may fall in the fortunes of war, even now it can safely be said that Negro slavery will not long outlive the Civil War'.[101] Douglass had yet to be convinced that was true. Only about a thousand words in length, Marx's 'Criticism' ranks with, word for word, the richest documents in what some of us call the Marx/Engels arsenal, exemplary in its combination of theory, evidence, and a course for a way forward.[102] A close reading of Engels's 30 July letter to him reveals that the article is essentially a response to the one person whose opinion he most valued. Because the two had a political disagreement, the only one documented in their decades-long partnership, Marx was obligated to respond with his best political analysis. Douglass, operating largely on his own, lacked such a worthy partner to check what could be half-baked ideas.

Marx couldn't have known it then but the Second Session of the Thirty-Seventh Congress, from January to July 1862, proved to be not only one of the most productive but also most consequential in history. Note what a recent summary of its importance says – an opportunity to compare Marx's description to that of modern scholarship.

> Its record was astonishing. Three landmark domestic acts – providing for western homesteading, the Transcontinental Railroad, and land grant col-

---

[101] Marx and Engels 1975–2004j, pp. 228–9.
[102] Written, by the way, as he was making a major theoretical breakthrough for what would be *Capital*: see his letter to Engels on 2 August. Marx and Engels 1975–2004u, pp. 394–7.

leges – would forever reshape the face of America. The series of similarly precedent-setting money bills – providing for a national tax regime, new tariffs, and the issuance of greenbacks – would lay a solid financial foundation for the war, and for the first time put the federal government in control of the nation's money supply. Another spate of bills – the abolition of slavery in Washington, D.C., the Confiscation Act, and the new Militia Act, along with acts recognizing black-governed Haiti and Liberia, permitting blacks the right to testify in federal court, and offering federal aid to states that passed their own acts of emancipation – moved the eventual destruction of slavery from the fringe of the war effort to its core.[103]

Not only of comparable quality – we find that Marx's summary is more informative. So much, therefore, for the time-worn fable that Marx didn't take bourgeois democracy seriously. He most certainly did and for good reason as Engels explained in 1892, nine years after Marx's death, to an opponent who made exactly that charge. 'Marx and I, for forty years, repeated ad nauseam that for us the democratic republic is the only political form in which the struggle between the working class and the capitalist class can first be generalized and culminate in the decisive victory of the proletariat'.[104] For the Marx party, overthrowing the Slave power and ending slavery and instituting the bourgeois republic in all of the United States was the prerequisite for 'the decisive victory of the proletariat'.

Though Marx answered Engels's pessimistic letter of 30 July with his 'Criticism' article, Marx distilled its contents to him in a 7 August reply, since the article would only appear, unbeknownst to Marx, on 9 August. Despite all the problems of the Union conduct of the War that Engel had raised, the 'North' – this is his main thesis – 'will, at last, wage the war in earnest, have recourse to revolutionary methods and overthrow the supremacy of the BORDER SLAVE STATESMEN'. Then, a sentence implicit in the *Die Presse* article but unprintable in the newspaper: 'One single NIGGER REGIMENT would have remarkable effect on Southern nerves'.[105] Though politically incorrect then and now, Marx could not have been more accurate. Finally, the 'long and the short of it is, I think, that wars of this kind ought to be conducted along revolutionary lines, and the YANKEES have so far been trying to conduct it along constitutional

---

103 Bordewich 2020, pp. 160–1.
104 Marx and Engels 1975–2004n, p. 271.
105 On the same day, 30 July, Marx for the first and only time used, in a letter to Engels, the N-word in a derogatory sense, in reference to Ferdinand Lassalle, a long-time Jewish acquaintance. See the Introduction and Appendix B about Marx and the N-word.

ones'. Marx would get his wish about six weeks later. One last and astute comment by Marx, regarding an issue that he didn't address in his 'Criticism' article – Engels's concern about how the War was being financed. Not surprising that things were 'clumsy', he pointed out, 'as, indeed, they are bound to be in a country where IN FACT taxation has hitherto been non-existent (so far as the country as a whole is concerned)'. But that and then existing related financial arrangements would 'change' – as indeed they did.[106] Whether Engels was won over by his partner's arguments remained to be seen.

If Marx eventually proved to be correct about the abolitionist course Lincoln was on, that was far from apparent to Douglass at that moment. Either strategically or by happenstance – Lincoln scholars continue to debate the issue – the president invited a small delegation of Washington, DC Black ministers to the White House on 14 August 1862 for a discussion on the contentious issue of colonisation for Blacks. Congress had authorised funds for doing so in the Second Confiscation Act and in prior legislation like emancipation in the District of Columbia that gave authority to the president to initiate such a project – Lincoln's purported rationale for having the meeting. Upon learning of what had transpired, Douglass was incensed. For almost two decades he had opposed the colonisation of Blacks in Africa or elsewhere. Douglass was able to read Lincoln's comments because the president authorised that a transcript of them be made available to the press – a fact that has fuelled much of the speculation about Lincoln's motives. For Douglass, the meeting showed that Lincoln was 'a genuine representative of American prejudice and Negro hatred and far more concerned for the preservation of slavery, and the favor of the Border Slaves States, than for any sentiment of magnanimity or principle of justice and humanity ... This address of his leaves us less ground to hope for anti-slavery action at his hands than any of his previous utterances'.[107] Already in a suspicious mood about Lincoln, as his response to the Second Confiscation Act suggested, the 14 August meeting simply justified that posture.[108]

We can't confirm one way or the other if Marx had read Lincoln's address to the meeting and whether it caused him to rethink his claims from a week earlier that Lincoln 'threatens' the Border State slave owners 'with inundation by the Abolition party', that 'the revolutionary waging of war, is at hand', and that 'it can safely be said that Negro slavery will not long outlive the Civil

---

106 Marx and Engels 1975–2004u, p. 400. See Lowenstein 2022.
107 DM, September 1862, pp. 707–8.
108 For a sample of the debate and different interpretations surrounding the meeting of 14 August, see Blight 2018, pp. 370–4; Oakes 2013, p. 310; Oakes 2007, p. 194; McPherson 2008, p. 128; Foner 2010, p. 226; Varon 2019, pp. 114–17.

War'. Lincoln's address was published in the *Tribune* that Marx faithfully read but nothing in his correspondence makes reference to it. Of particular note, however, and maybe relevant is his *Die Presse* article, 'Abolitionist Demonstrations in America' written on 22 August, a week after Lincoln's meeting with the Black delegation. Most of the article quotes a fiery speech by Wendell Phillips on 1 August in Massachusetts, 'of greater importance than a battle bulletin'. A stinging critique of Lincoln, who 'lacks backbone', for 'fighting for the preservation of slavery' because of his kowtowing to Border State slave owners, for keeping McClellan on board, and not putting 'the Confiscation Act into effect', Phillips's speech shared Douglass's critical posture. The last sentences Marx quoted are: 'Let us hope that the war lasts long enough to make men of us, and then we shall soon triumph. God has put the thunderbolt of emancipation into our hands in order to crush the rebellion'.[109] Marx ended the article without comment, giving Phillips, therefore, the last word – the only abolitionist that he ever saw the need to quote.

But Marx did know about Lincoln's colonisation option because the president tried to sell it to the representatives of the Border state slave owners with whom he met on 12 July, a month before doing the same with the Black delegation. 'Room in South America', he told them 'for colonisation can be obtained cheaply and in abundance, and when numbers shall be large enough to be company and encouragement for one another, the freed people will not be so reluctant to go'.[110] In the same address, Marx learned of another issue that caused Douglass to be suspicious of Lincoln, his revocation of Union General David Hunter's 9 May order to emancipate slaves in the coastal islands of South Carolina, Georgia, and Florida. Lincoln admitted the negative reaction his decision engendered amongst abolitionists like Douglass, 'whose support the country cannot afford to lose'. But for Marx, more significant than learning about Lincoln's colonisation option or the revocation of Hunter's order was reading his unmistakable threat to the survival of the beloved 'institution' of the slaveholders in the Border states – for Marx, the decisive evidence that Lincoln was on an abolitionist course.

Despite Phillips's no holds barred take on Lincoln, Marx continued to be optimistic. In a comradely poke to the ribs, Engels asked Marx on 9 September, 'do you still believe that the gentlemen of the North will suppress the REBELLION?' The question came after Engels had recounted the most recent Union

---

109 Marx and Engels 1975–2004j, pp. 234–5. Read Phillips's full speech in the *New York Times* online archive: https://www.nytimes.com/1862/08/06/archives/wendell-phillips-on-the-war.html
110 DM, August 1862, p. 700.

Army battlefield reverses, not least important, the second defeat at Bull Run on 28 to 30 August. Engels was all too happy to point out that it was under Union General John Pope's command that the loss was incurred, 'the lousiest of the lot'. Compared to him, 'McClellan, now strikes one yet again as being positively intelligent'.[111] In his 7 August letter to Engels, Marx asserted that 'General Pope was a man of energy'.[112] Marx took the bait and responded the very next day to Engels's obvious needling.

'I am firmly of the opinion', he wrote, 'now as before, that the North will win in the end'. Yes, along the way there would be all kinds of twists and turns but for the South to be victorious it would require 'the RECONSTRUCTION of the United States on the basis demanded by the South', namely, on the basis of slavery. 'But that is impossible and won't happen'. A peaceful conclusion for the North would entail the confinement of the South to the secessionist states hemmed in by the Mississippi River and the Atlantic Ocean, 'in which case the CONFEDERACY would soon come to a happy end'. As for Engels's complaints about the North's irresolute conduct of the War, its 'spineless goings-on', it is 'none other', Marx replied, 'than might be expected of a *bourgeois* republic where humbug has reigned for so long. The South, an oligarchy, is better suited to the purpose, especially an oligarchy where all productive labour devolves on the NIGGERS and where 4 million "WHITE TRASH" are *filibusters* by calling'. Then Marx's bottom line: 'For all that, I'm prepared' – informed by his historical materialist perspective – 'to bet my life on it that these fellows will come off worst'. It's hard to imagine Douglass saying the same.

Lastly, some comradely advice. 'It strikes me that you allow yourself to be influenced by the military ASPECT of things A LITTLE TOO MUCH'.[113] A rare correction in the Marx-Engels correspondence. Phillips's speech, 'of greater importance than a battle bulletin', and the very last sentence that Marx quoted from it, 'God has put the thunderbolt of emancipation into our hands in order to crush the rebellion', may have been what Marx had in mind in cautioning his partner and the basis for his continuing optimism – soon to be rewarded. Probably not for Engels the communist, but for Douglass the prophet, Phillips's last sentence would have resonated.

Marx and Engels's comradely exchange offers a valuable window into the nature of their partnership. It took place at a time when Marx's finances

---

111 Marx and Engels 1975–2004u, p. 415.
112 Marx and Engels 1975–2004u, p. 400. Historian Dan Welch argues that Marx would have had good reason to be positive about Pope. Welch 2021. For an in-depth study of Pope and his short-lived Army of Virginia, see Matsui 2016.
113 Marx and Engels 1975–2004u, p. 416.

were even more precarious – so much that he tried to get a job in a London railway office, albeit unsuccessfully due to his near illegible handwriting. Limited to only one article per week in *Die Presse*, if that, Marx was more dependent on Engels – whose own finances were less sure owing to the Union blockade of Confederate ports – for keeping, literally, a roof over the head of his household and food on their table. Not only was Engels's more or less weekly cheque desperately needed. An occasional hamper of wine from Manchester helped to boost family morale but also, they all thought, to improve the health of seventeen-year-old eldest daughter Jenny, whose alarming loss of weight appeared to be due to depression. That Marx could express his disagreement with the person upon whom he was so materially dependent spoke volumes about the principled character of the Marx-Engels relationship. Their difference of opinion about Union prospects lasted until mid-1864 – meaning an agreement to disagree. Unfortunately, again, such details about Douglass's private life that could have had political implications are lacking or unavailable, putting, therefore, limits on our comparison.

6   The Preliminary Emancipation Proclamation

In his 1 August speech Phillips made, in retrospect, a surprising claim that Marx quoted: 'When I was in Washington, I ascertained that three months ago Lincoln had written the proclamation for general emancipation of the slaves and that McClellan bullied him out of his decision'.[114] Whether true or not, the consensus of modern scholarship is that it was soon after Lincoln's visit on 7 July to McClellan at Harrison's Landing, Virginia, where the latter was withdrawing his troops after the feckless Peninsula campaign, that the president began to draft a proclamation. McClellan made excuses about his cowardly actions and then insisted in a letter he gave to Lincoln that the president take no steps toward emancipation.[115] Historians argue that Lincoln's road-to-Harrison's Landing moment convinced him he would have to take charge.

On 22 July, in accordance with the Second Confiscation Act, Lincoln brought a draft proclamation to a Cabinet meeting that he was prepared to immediately

---

114 Marx and Engels 1975–2004j, p. 235. Phillips's claim may have credibility owing to his visit to Washington, DC, beginning on 15 March, in which he was feted by key decision makers there including Lincoln. See, Stewart 1986, pp. 233–6 for details. For Phillips's trip in context, see Sinha 2008, pp. 177–80. Curiously, his 1 August speech is virtually absent on the radar of Lincoln scholars.

115 On the Harrison's Landing meeting, see McPherson 2008, pp. 106–7. Foner 2010, p. 217.

release. But Secretary of State Seward persuaded him to wait for a Union Army victory in order to avoid the appearance of desperation after the disastrous Peninsula Campaign. Military conditions did not improve, and even deteriorated after the second Union defeat at Bull Run. After his victory, Robert E. Lee turned his Confederate Army north and invaded Maryland. Lincoln, desperate to reorganise the army and reverse demoralisation, replaced Pope with McClellan.[116] Though having badly mismanaged the battle at Antietam, Maryland, McClellan did turn the rebels back, giving Lincoln the needed victory to issue the Preliminary Emancipation Proclamation on 22 September 1862. James Oakes writes, 'a mere eighteen months after promising never to interfere with slavery in the southern states, Lincoln committed all the military and financial might of the United States to the emancipation of millions of African Americans'.[117]

Because Lincoln kept his Proclamation secret for two months, historians argue about the motives for some of his actions during that period: especially relevant for Douglass was the 14 August meeting with the Black delegation. If Lincoln intended it, as some claim, to evoke anger from abolitionists in order to put conservative and/or racist northern opinion at ease with the executive order, then it worked in the case of Douglass. He was, as Oakes puts it, 'thrown off scent' – Phillips also.[118] But not all abolitionists, one in particular, fell for the ruse if that's what the 14 August meeting and other similar actions constituted. Despite Lincoln's colonisation offer – and the revocation of Hunter's order that also angered Douglass – Marx didn't waver in his conviction that Lincoln was on an abolitionist course. Being a historical materialist was determinant, no doubt for what proved to be Marx's accurate reading of the moment – but no guarantee for getting it right, as indicated by his partner's continuing pessimism.

'Emancipation Proclaimed', the headline column of the October issue of the *Monthly*, broadcast another reversal for Douglass. 'Common sense', his editorial began, 'the necessities of the war, to say nothing of the dictates of justice and humanity have at last prevailed. We shout for joy that we live to record this righteous decree. *Abraham Lincoln*, President of the United States, Commander-in-Chief of the army and navy, in his own peculiar, cautious, forbearing and hesitating way, slow, but we hope sure, has, while the loyal heart was near breaking with despair, proclaimed and declared' – followed by the language of Lincoln's executive order. 'But read the proclamation, for it is the most

---

116   Maybe, to be facetious, he had read Engels's 9 September letter to Marx.
117   Foner 2010, pp. 217–20. Oakes 2013, pp. 305–7, 314. McPherson 2008, p. 109. Oakes 2007, p. 196. B. Levine 2013, pp. 123–4, 126.
118   Oakes 2007, p. 188.

important of any to which the President of the United States has ever signed his name'. To Douglass's credit, he admitted to 'the loyal heart ... near breaking with despair', owing to his doubts about Lincoln ever since his paean to him in March. As for any remaining or newly minted Lincoln doubters, a now recovering one offered advice: 'Abraham Lincoln may be slow, Abraham Lincoln may desire peace even at the price of leaving our terrible national sore untouched, to fester on for generations, but Abraham Lincoln is not the man to reconsider, retract and contradict words and purposes solemnly proclaimed over his official signature'.[119] Douglass, also to his credit, could take leave of prior positions when circumstances demanded that he do so.

Douglass examined for his readers the impact the proclamation would have on the influence of the Border States versus 'the loyal North and West', European governments, the Army in the field, and the slaves themselves. 'Border State influence', Douglass argued, 'and the influence of half-loyal men, have been exerted and have done their worst. The end of these two influences is implied in this proclamation. Hereafter, the inspiration as well as the men and the money for carrying on the war will come from the North', that is, those willing to fight slavery, 'and not from the half-loyal border States'. In Europe, the executive order 'changes the character of the war'. It 'recognizes and declares the real nature of the contest, and places the North on the side of justice and civilization, and the rebels on the side of robbery and barbarism', disarming those in Europe pushing their governments to intervene on the side of the South. And in the Union Army, 'the best collateral effects' of Lincoln's proclamation will be to test the loyalty and patriotism of those who still fought for the Union as it was. 'Any man who leaves the field', because he opposes emancipation, 'will be an argument in favor of the proclamation, and will prove that his heart has been more with slavery than with his country'. Douglass expected that for every man repulsed by emancipation, 'there will be two anti-slavery men to fill up the vacancy, and in this war one truly devoted to the cause of Emancipation is worth two of the opposite sort'. In addition, 'The Star Spangled Banner is now the harbinger of Liberty and the millions in bondage, inured to hardships, accustomed to toil, ready to suffer, ready to fight, to dare and to die, will rally under that banner wherever they see it gloriously unfolded to the breeze'.[120]

Douglass then turned to abolitionists in the North. 'Now for the work', he admonished. 'During the interval between now and next January, let every friend of the long enslaved bondman do his utmost in swelling the tide of anti-

---

119   DM, October 1862, p. 721.
120   DM, October 1862, pp. 721–2.

slavery sentiment, by writing, speaking, money and example. Let our aim be to make the North a unit in favor of the President's policy'. Douglass was not alone in his joy for the proclamation. James Oakes writes that, 'Enthusiastic crowds serenaded the president' and 'loyal governors ... sped to Washington to congratulate' him. 'If there was an overarching theme to the expression of support', Oakes argues, 'it was that the restoration of the Union and the destruction of slavery were irrevocably joined'.[121] Exactly what Douglass had been fighting for.

Marx too, like Douglass, immediately put pen to paper when he learned almost two weeks later of the Preliminary Emancipation Proclamation. For 'Comments on the North American Events', *Die Presse* editors supplied an instructive preface for the first time: 'Our correspondent', after a few details of the battlefield events that preceded Lincoln's issuance of the document – 'a turning-point in the North American events' – 'whose judgement is not biased by the language of the English papers, which are almost without exception sympathetic to the South and the cause of slavery, has the following to say about the new situation in North America'.[122]

About 1,200 words, less than a third the length of Douglass's announcement of 'the good news', Marx's 'Comments' is worth reproducing, at least much of it. The historical materialist began with material reality, the battlefield. We distil that part of the article since nothing he wrote there should surprise the reader by now about his ability to read that terrain of the class struggle. Just a few nuggets, beginning with his opening thesis: 'The short campaign in Maryland', which ended with Antietam, 'has decided the fate of the American Civil War, however much the fortune of war may still vacillate between the opposing parties for a shorter or longer time'. That claim about Antietam proved to be prophetic, Gettysburg, a year later, notwithstanding. Marx then flushed out the premises for his thesis, putting the Confederate lost at Antietam in broader military context: 'One must never forget even for a moment that, when the Southerners hoisted the banner of rebellion, they held the border states', such as Maryland, 'and dominated them politically. What they demanded were the Territories. They have lost both the Territories and the border states' – and the 'Border state influence', Douglass would have added.

The loss had international consequences because 'France and England were openly preparing to proclaim the legitimacy – already recognised at home – of the slaveholders' – exactly what Douglass argued in his article. That wasn't in the cards because, for his erudite readers, '*E pur si muove*' – 'But it moves', that

---

[121] DM, October 1862, p. 722. Oakes 2013, pp. 316–17.
[122] Marx and Engels 1975–2004j, p. 395n.282.

is, the earth – what Galileo reputedly said after having been forced to recant his theory about the earth's rotation. 'Reason', Marx added – ever confident of his method – 'nevertheless, prevails in world history'.[123] The slavocracy and its cheerleaders in Britain and elsewhere in Europe represented, in other words, the pre-Enlightenment world whose final days were numbered.

Most instructive is the second part of 'Comments'. Note how Marx began. 'Lincoln's proclamation is even more important than the Maryland campaign'. No doubt in writing that sentence he had his partner in mind who had allowed himself 'to be influenced by the military aspect of things a little too much'. He then elaborated.

> Lincoln is a *sui generis* figure in the annals of history. He has no initiative, no idealistic impetus, no cothurnus, no historical trappings. He gives his most important actions always the most commonplace form. Other people claim to be 'fighting for an idea', when it is for them a matter of square feet of land. Lincoln, even when he is motivated by an idea, talks about 'square feet'. He sings the bravura aria of his part hesitatively, reluctantly and unwillingly, as though apologising for being compelled by circumstances 'to act the lion'. The most redoubtable decrees – which will always remain remarkable historical documents – flung by him at the enemy all look like, and are intended to look like, routine summonses sent by a lawyer to the lawyer of the opposing party, legal chicaneries, involved, hidebound *actiones juris*. His latest proclamation, which is drafted in the same style, the manifesto abolishing slavery is the most important document in American history since the establishment of the Union, tantamount to the tearing up of the old American Constitution.

'The most important document in American history' – almost exactly Douglass's language, '... the most important of any to which the President of the United States has ever signed his name'.

The sensibility of the one-time lawyer was also on display in these sentences. About Marx's bold claim that Lincoln's issuance of the Preliminary Emancipation was 'tantamount to the tearing up of the old American Constitution', David Blight, in a 2013 presentation, agreed: 'Dead right! ... Lincoln *was* tearing up the Constitution in a host of ways ... Lincoln is taking an authority that is not in the Constitution ... they're making up a new Constitution'.[124] Douglass continued,

---

123 Marx and Engels 1975–2004j, pp. 248–9.
124 Blight 2013.

as in his article in the December issue of the *Monthly*, to contend that the Constitution did not have to be altered for Congress to legislate on slavery in the slave states. 'We have read the Constitution carefully and often but ... found, as Patrick Henry found, when the Constitution was framed ample power given under it whereby slavery could be abolished in all the States by the Federal Government'.[125] Again, as James Oakes maintains, that was a tiny minority position in the Abolitionist movement and why, as we'll discuss later, Congress amended the document after the end of the War.

Then an irresistible swipe at Lincoln's bourgeois British press detractors.

> Nothing is simpler than to show that Lincoln's principal political actions contain much that is aesthetically repulsive, logically inadequate, farcical in form and politically contradictory, as is done by the English Pindars of slavery, *The Times*, *The Saturday Review* and *tutti quanti*. But Lincoln's place in the history of the United States and of mankind will, nevertheless, be next to that of Washington! Nowadays, when the insignificant struts about melodramatically on this side of the Atlantic, is it of no significance at all that the significant is clothed in everyday dress in the new world?

'Next to that of Washington!' How prescient. Marx never missed an opportunity to ridicule not only the British ruling class but also Europe's.

To explain what made Lincoln unique, a historical materialist interpretation of his actions immediately followed:

> Lincoln is not the product of a popular revolution. This plebeian, who worked his way up from stone-breaker to Senator in Illinois, without intellectual brilliance, without a particularly outstanding character, without exceptional importance – an average person of good will, was placed at the top by the interplay of the forces of universal suffrage unaware of the great issues at stake. The new world has never achieved a greater triumph than by this demonstration that, given its political and social organisation, ordinary people of good will can accomplish feats which only heroes could accomplish in the old world!

No better compliment to what humanity had achieved on the other side of the Atlantic – what superior political and social relations could make possible for 'ordinary people of good will'.[126] From afar, not only in distance but also in

---

125   DM, December 1862, p. 756.
126   While Marx commenting that Lincoln was 'without intellectual brilliance' may seem harsh

time, Marx could see the world-historic significance of Lincoln's actions better than those closer to the scene. Lincoln's example pleased Marx to no end. While Douglass extolled 'Great Britain' for 'preceding us ... in works of repentance and restitution', Marx was all too happy to let Europe's 'betters' know – its toilers as well – that 'a plebian', 'the son of the working class', as he later called Lincoln, did something more significant. To repeat, the advantage of historically advanced conditions for an 'average person of good will' – even 'a bourgeois republic' with all of its 'humbug'.[127]

Lastly, Marx's coda, appropriately about Lincoln's humour, prefaced with Hegel's observation 'that comedy is in fact superior to tragedy and humorous reasoning superior to grandiloquent reasoning'. 'Although Lincoln', as if in anticipation of David Reynolds's recent and insightful *Abe: Abraham Lincoln in His Times*, 'does not possess the grandiloquence of historical action, as an average man of the people he has its humour'.[128] Marx then made the point with a few details about the date he thought Lincoln chose with comedic intent to issue his Proclamation that the reader may be enticed to read in full.[129]

Marx's article, or better, essay, is a masterly and eloquent refutation of the time-worn charge that his project was all about social structures, economic ones especially, and had no room for the role of the individual in history. A recent and, in fact, most relevant example of that kind of misrepresentation is Civil War-era historian Matt Karp's charge about Marx's historical materialist reading of Lincoln quoted above. 'Rather than salute the President himself', Marx, he alleges, 'recognized that the structure of America's mass democratic institutions – more than the character of its leadership – had played a decisive role in the US road to abolition'. Karp can make such an accusation by ignoring the prior paragraphs in Marx's article. To claim that 'Lincoln is a *sui generis* figure in the annals of history', and that his 'place in the history of the United States and of mankind will ... be next to that of Washington' isn't a 'salute', then

---

to modern readers more appreciative of Lincoln's intellectual and philosophical gifts, even the *Chicago Tribune*, when endorsing Lincoln for president in 1860, noted he was 'not learned, in a bookish sense ...' Stahr 2021, p. 293.

127 Marx scholar Hal Draper, who otherwise knew the Marx corpus perhaps better than anyone, evidently missed this positive assessment of Lincoln by Marx. How else to explain Draper's generally negative view of Lincoln, "The Lincoln Myth," written circa 1970 and, apparently, influenced by the even more negative portrait of the Sixteenth president by Lerone Bennett's 1968 article. See Draper, 2005, pp. 236–41.

128 Reynolds 2020.

129 Marx and Engels 1975–2004j, pp. 248–51.

what is?[130] 'Comments on the North American Events' should be required reading for any course that advertises itself as an 'Introduction to Marxism' in order to inoculate future students of Marx against such stale nonsense.

Engels remained sceptical of Union prospects. 'What do you make of America?' to his partner on 16 October. The continued use of 'these stupid paper money measures', he alleged, portended an 'inevitable' and 'imminent' 'financial CRASH'. Then, a glimmer of optimism. 'Militarily speaking, the North may now perhaps begin to recover a bit'.[131] But no mention of the Emancipation Proclamation. Marx's response on 29 October was essentially a distillation of his 'Comments' article which, however, didn't address the financial issues Engels raised. To those concerns, Marx sketched the history of the US government finances 'from the time of the War of Independence' and concluded that the 'depreciation' of the currency was, contra Engels, 'still relatively modest'. As for the overall situation three weeks after his 'Comments' article, the 'fury with which Southerners are greeting Lincoln's acts [the Preliminary Emancipation] is proof of the importance of these measures'. Evidence for that claim, possibly, was a letter he had recently gotten from Marx party member and Union officer Joseph Weydemeyer about Border State 'slaveholders with their "black chattels" … constantly migrating to the South'.[132]

Marx reiterated his point made in a prior letter: 'I am of course aware of the distasteful form assumed by the movement of the Yankees; but having regard to the nature of a "bourgeois" democracy, I find this explicable' – what he could not have written in the liberal *Die Presse* and a reminder that Marx had to pull punches when writing for bourgeois papers like it and the *Tribune*. 'Nevertheless, events over there are such as to transform the world, and nothing in the whole of history is as nauseous than the attitude adopted toward them by the English'.[133] Marx was still unwavering, and tried to convince his partner to adopt a similar posture. About the 'nauseous … attitude' of 'the English', Douglass was putting, at that moment, pen to paper to see if he could make a difference. And for good reason, as Marx wrote in an article on 7 November: the 'English press is more Southern than the South itself … it sees everything black in the North, and everything white in the land of the "nigger"' – what Douglass sought to counter, as we'll see shortly.[134]

---

130 Karp 2019, p. 147. You can also find Karp's article online: https://catalyst-journal.com/2019/10/the-mass-politics-of-antislavery.
131 Marx and Engels 1975–2004u, p. 419.
132 Marx and Engels 1975–2004j, p. 257.
133 Marx and Engels 1975–2004u, p. 421.
134 Marx and Engels 1975–2004j, p. 260.

Engels still needed to be convinced by Marx's arguments. He agreed, in a 5 November letter, with his partner's assessment of the military advances of the North regarding the Border States like Maryland. But he failed to see any kind of commitment by the North to carry out a 'classical' bourgeois 'democratic' revolution à la 'France in 1792 and 1793'. Rather, they 'allow themselves to be beaten again and again by a force numbering ¼ of their own population and who, after 18 months of war, have gained nothing save the discovery that all of their generals are jackasses and their functionaries, crooks and traitors'. And, 'the successes of the Democrats at the polls prove that the party that is weary of war is growing'.[135] Engels elaborated on both points ten days later in another letter. 'Desirable though it may be, on the one hand, that the bourgeois republic should be utterly discredited in America too, so that in future it may never again be preached ON ITS OWN MERITS, but only as a means towards, and a form of transition to, social revolution, it is, nevertheless, annoying that a rotten oligarchy, with a population only half as large, should evince such strength as the great fat, helpless democracy'. Encapsulated here, instructively, was his and Marx's understanding of the relationship between the bourgeois democratic revolution and the socialist revolution, the former as the prerequisite for the latter – but with a clear preference for the former over the slavocracy. Regarding the elections, 'if the Democrats win in New York state, I shan't know what to make of the Yankees any more'. The election results so far had demonstrated that 'the only apparent effect of Lincoln's emancipation so far is that the North-West has voted Democrat for fear of being overrun by Negroes'. 'I am impatiently awaiting', he told Marx on 15 November, 'the STEAMER that will bring us news of the New York elections'.[136] Two days later, before the arrival of that 'news', Marx tried to calm his partner: 'It seems to me that you take too one-sided a view of the American fracas. At the AMERICAN COFFEE-HOUSE I have looked through a lot of Southern PAPERS and from them it is plain that the Confederacy is in a very tight corner'.[137] All was not lost, he cautioned.

Regarding 'the elections', Engels was referring to the gains of the Democratic Party in state and congressional elections in October and November 1862. 'Overall', Fergus Bordewich summarises, 'Democrats', with all of their anti-Black venom, 'regarded their showing as a triumph; a year and a half earlier, their party had seemed close to death. No more. The voters had delivered a clear

---

135 Marx and Engels 1975–2004u, p. 423.
136 Marx and Engels 1975–2004u, p. 428.
137 Marx and Engels 1975–2004u, p. 429.

and unmistakable message' to the Republican Lincoln administration: 'either deliver victories, or end the war' and reach a compromise with the Confederacy.[138] Marx had, once again, his work cut out for him to challenge his partner's understandable pessimism.

As soon as Marx got the news that Engels was anxiously awaiting, he penned on 18 November his analysis for *Die Presse*, 'The Election Results in the Northern States'. Soberly, his first sentences: 'The elections have in fact been a defeat for the Washington government. The old leaders of the Democratic Party have skilfully exploited the dissatisfaction over the financial clumsiness and military ineptitude, and there is no doubt that the State of New York, officially in the hands of the [Horatio] Seymours, [Fernando] Woods and [James] Bennetts [key figures in the state's Democratic Party], can become the centre of dangerous intrigues. At the same time', most importantly, 'the practical importance of this reaction should not be exaggerated'. As a student of American politics for at least two decades – as summarised in Chapter 1 – Marx then made a case for distinguishing between politics in Washington itself, between Washington and the states, and within states – allowing him to elaborate on his opening claims. Despite Democratic Party gains in the elections, 'a closer analysis' revealed that the Republicans were still in control at the national level and in a majority of the states.

Impressive was Marx's knowledge of New York state politics where the Democrats had won by 'only 8,000–10,000 votes'. Decisive there was the urban/rural divide.

> New York City, strongly corrupted by Irish rabble, actively engaged in the slave trade until recently, the seat of the American money market and full of holders of mortgages on Southern plantations, has always been decidedly 'Democratic' ... The *rural districts* of New York State voted Republican this time, as they have since 1856, but not with the same fiery enthusiasm as in 1860. Moreover, a large part of their men entitled to vote is in the field.[139]

That last fact, rural 'men ... in the field', namely, the Civil War battlefield for the North was of utmost importance for Marx – reminiscent of the worker/peasant alliance that he and Engels strove mightily but eventually unsuccessfully for in the German Revolution. An article about the elections that Douglass later

---

138   Bordewich 2020, pp. 175–6.
139   Marx and Engels 1975–2004j, p. 263.

reprinted (more about later) made a big deal about Union soldiers, owing to their being 'in the field', who were not able to vote.

Then Marx sought to explain why the Democrats made gains in Indiana and Ohio. New York City offered a reason: 'The Irishman sees the Negro as a dangerous competitor' – why they voted for the anti-Black Democratic Party. 'The efficient farmers in Indiana and Ohio hate the Negro', referring to the point Engels had raised, 'almost as much as the slaveholder. He is a symbol, for them, of slavery and the humiliation of the working class, and the Democratic press threatens them daily with a flooding of their territories by "niggers"'. Marx's explanation for Caucasian anti-Black prejudices, this time in the North, complemented Douglass's arguments about anti-Black prejudice that we discussed earlier – to be revisited in the Conclusion. Yet, for Marx, these astute observations were 'by no means the main thing' needed to explain the 1862 elections.

> At the time Lincoln was elected (1860) there was no civil war, nor was the question of Negro emancipation on the order of the day. The Republican Party, then quite independent of the Abolitionist Party, aimed its 1860 electoral campaign solely at protesting against the extension of slavery into the Territories, but, at the same time, it proclaimed non-interference with the institution in the states where it already existed legally. If Lincoln had had *Emancipation of the Slaves* as his motto at that time, there can be no doubt that he would have been defeated. Any such slogan was vigorously rejected.

Though admittedly hindsight on Marx's part, his claim about the 1860 election was undoubtedly accurate. And it was from that perspective that he viewed the election results of 1862. That the Republicans did as well as they did with the 'motto', 'Emancipation of the Slaves', was something to be applauded. The remainder of the article elaborated on his point with a state-level analysis and ended with a recommendation about how to build upon those gains. 'All that is needed now is energy, on the part of the government and of the Congress that meets next month, for the Abolitionists, now identical with the Republicans, to have the upper hand everywhere, both morally and numerically'.[140] No, pretence, again, about being a disinterested 'correspondent'.

That Engels and Marx paid close attention to elections in the US should come as no surprise to the reader of this book. The Revolutions of 1848–9 taught both of them how important elections could be for the workers' movement,

---

140   Marx and Engels 1975–2004j, p. 264.

not as an end in themselves, but as a means to an end. Marx's most insightful point about the key difference between the 1860 and 1862 elections, the different 'motto' of both campaigns – the former 'solely at protesting the extension of the slavery into the Territories', and the latter, *Emancipation of the Slaves* – recalled the kernel of wisdom of their '1850 Address of the Central Authority of the Communist League'. Elections were an invaluable tool for workers to 'count their forces and to lay before the public their revolutionary attitude and party standpoint' – thus, the importance of the 'motto'. Along with his 'Criticism' article of 9 August, Marx's 'Election Results' article should put the nail into the coffin of the time-worn fable that Marx didn't take bourgeois democracy seriously – at least we hope so. And his equally insightful points about animosity for and hatred of 'the Negro' in the latter article give lie to the oft-made allegation that Marx didn't address the racism of Caucasian toilers not just in the South but the North as well – insights that are as current now as when first penned. What makes both articles so rich, again, is that they are informed by Marx's debate with his most worthy opponent, Engels – an original insight, we claim, on our part.

Douglass never assessed, at least in his own name, as did Marx, the October/November 1862 election results. The reason, apparently – an editor's note in the December issue of the *Monthly* – was due to the lack of space given the need to reprint Lincoln's lengthy 1 December annual message to Congress. But yet, the elections did get coverage in the issue, with articles from other publications without comment – except for one – that totalled around 2,300 words, or more than three times the length of Marx's article. The reprints confirmed, by and large, Bordewich's summary of the meaning of the elections – 'a clear and unmistakable message' to the Republican Lincoln administration: 'either deliver victories, or end the war'. The one comment that Douglass added, briefly, countered a disingenuous anti-emancipation critic of the Lincoln administration.[141] We can only speculate why Douglass opted for the reprint-without-comment alternative – uncertainty about how to interpret and respond to the election results. As with Engels, the outcome demoralised sympathetic Republican voices in the North.[142] Douglass, probably, was hesitant

---

141 The December 1862 issue is not included in the HeinOnline collection we have utilised but we were able to track down a copy at the Smithsonian Transcription Center (https://transcription.si.edu/view/13242/ACM-2007.19.26_01). According to a private conversation with Professor Benjamin Fagan, a number of *Douglass' Monthly* issues are 'missing' as of August 2022, including, according to his notes, this December 1862 issue. Uncovering this issue means other 'missing' issues may be out there. For the reprinted articles on the election, see DM, December 1862, pp. 764–6.

142 Bordewich 2020, p. 176.

to echo such sentiment. It was better, what the editor of a paper could do, to reprint the varying opinions of others rather than state his own with all of the political implications that entailed – as well as avoiding the risk of being wrong, hedging, therefore, his bets. One thing for certain, none of the real-time articles Douglass reprinted were as rich as Marx's 730-word analysis – even more informed, we also contend, than what some modern scholarship has to offer.[143]

The very last sentence of Marx's 'Election Results' article asserted: 'The only danger [for the Abolitionists] lies in the retention of such generals as McClellan, who are, apart from their incompetence, avowed pro-slavery men'. No wonder the very first sentence, written six days later, for what proved to be his penultimate article for *Die Presse*: '*McClellan's dismissal*! That is Lincoln's answer to the election victories of the Democrats'. Marx's sense of vindication was palpable. Lincoln had had enough of the increasingly insubordinate opponent of emancipation beloved by the Democratic Party. Marx, notwithstanding his disdain for him, could be objective about the now deposed general. 'McClellan understood how to conceal his mediocrity under a mask of restrained earnestness, laconic reticence and dignified reserve ... McClellan possessed one single gift of the supreme commander – that of assuring himself of popularity with his army'. With pleasure, Marx ended his article with 'utterances of Lincoln' – from 'the same American papers' that brought 'the news of McClellan's dismissal' – 'that he will not deviate a hair's breadth from his proclamation'.[144]

7   The Slave's Appeal to Great Britain

Douglass would have been as elated as Marx with the firing of McClellan but lack of space in the December issue of the *Monthly* didn't permit him, he noted, to say so. For Douglass, the priority at that moment was how to challenge the phenomenon that Marx was all so familiar with: 'The English press', again, 'is more Southern than the South'. Particularly alarming were the intimations

---

143   Bordewich 2020, pp. 175–6. Bordewich's summary is what we have in mind. Bruce Levine's assessment is superior in our opinion. For example, Levine echoes Marx on the positive aspects of the elections. 'Lincoln's party that season actually suffered the smallest net loss of congressional seats by a dominant party in an off-year election in a full generation'. The Republican control of state houses allowed them to net 'six new seats in the Senate'. And so important to Marx, 'these election results failed to reflect the political opinions of the hundreds of thousands of Union soldiers whom state laws barred from voting while away from home. Those disfranchised troops included many of the administration's most fervent supporters'. B. Levine 2013, pp. 127–8.
144   Marx and Engels 1975–2004j, pp. 266–9.

of the Liberal Prime Minister William Gladstone and the *Times* of London in favour of Britain recognising the Confederacy. Douglass's 'The Slave's Appeal to Great Britain', initially published in the *New York Independent*, appeared on 20 November in newspapers across the United Kingdom with the intent to prevent that from happening.

On behalf 'of the dumb millions of my countrymen still in slavery', Douglass disputed the hypocritical and self-serving backhanded support of the British ruling class for the slaveholders. Their excuse for doing so? Because Blacks in the North were no better off than their enslaved kinsfolk in the South; that the War had nothing to do with ending slavery; and lastly, the North's prosecution of the War had been by and large feckless. Marx, a year earlier, had contested the first two pretexts in the pages of the *Tribune* (see Chapter 3), while Douglass had actually been sympathetic to the charges, especially the second, owing to Lincoln's opposition to declaring the War to be one for emancipation. As for the third charge, about the North's irresolute conduct of the War, Douglass had to admit that it too, along with the other two charges had merit. But after 22 September, Lincoln's issuance of his Preliminary Emancipation Proclamation, all of that was now history. 'From that day our war has been invested with a sanctity which will smite as with death even the mailed hands of Britain, if outstretched to arrest it'. The Union's cause now deserved unswerving support, especially from a country that 'long ago fixed the burning brand of your reprobation upon the guilty brow of the whole slave system. Your philanthropy, religion, and law, your noblest sons, living and dead, have taught the world to loathe and abhor slavery as the vilest of all modern abominations'. Any embrace of the slaveholder's government would be a heinous betrayal of that enlightened legacy. And if Britain's leaders tried to intervene on behalf of the Confederacy, the 'poorest of all the sufferers in Lancashire would hardly be willing to purchase even life itself by replunging a liberated slave into hopeless slavery'. Despite the hardships England's working classes were experiencing at the moment owing to the Union blockade of Southern cotton, they would, in other words, be unwilling to fight for the benefit of slaveholders. Douglass's 'Appeal' registered how far he had travelled politically since Fort Sumter – more sober about Britain's elite, a bit more empathetic with its toilers and, thus, in closer company with Marx.[145]

Though we can't confirm it, Marx most likely read Douglass's 'Appeal'. There is no mention of it in his correspondence or in his last submission to *Die Presse*,

---

[145] 'The Slave's Appeal to Great Britain' can be found in P. Foner 1952, pp. 299–305, in DM, December 1862, and online at https://www.tota.world/article/1103/

written on 29 November, about a week after the appearance of the 'Appeal' in Britain – after which Marx no longer had access to a venue to publish periodical writings. We suspect that Marx welcomed Douglass's intervention, though some of the 'Appeal's' language, such as the gratuitous compliments to Britain's record on slavery, no doubt caused his eyes to roll – maybe assuaged by Douglass's reference to the self-sacrificing 'sufferers in Lancashire'. Given his and Engels's disgust with the posture adopted by Britain's ruling class toward the Lincoln administration, especially after 22 September, even a liberal-worded intervention to challenge London like that of Douglass's article, and widely published, was encouraging. According to Douglass, in the January 1863 issue of the *Monthly*, his article 'has been extensively copied on both sides of the Atlantic'.[146] That former Chartist leader George Julian Harney, and close contact of Marx and Engels, made a major effort to get the 'Appeal' into the hands of the British working class, those in Lancashire in particular, would have been an added bonus for the two communists.[147]

A few days prior to New Year's Day 1863, Douglass speculated on the possibility that Lincoln might not issue the Emancipation Proclamation. In some detail, he discussed the likelihood and profound implications of such a decision in the lead editorial for the yet to be published January issue of the *Monthly*. Of relevance for our comparison was his point that for Lincoln to do so, 'would well nigh break the loyal heart of the nation, and fill its enemies North and South, with a demoniacal enthusiasm – Missouri, with its noble German population ... would fall ... '. That was the Border State where Weydemeyer and the nucleus of the Marx party had been active and effective in realising Douglass's longed for goal. Also noteworthy, the implications of the recent Union defeat at Fredericksburg, Virginia, 11–15 December: 'thus far the President is dared to do his worst, thus far the villainy of the South is a spur to the virtue of the North, and affords reason to hope that we shall have the promised proclamation of freedom to all the Inhabitants of the rebel States'. The defeat, in other words, could actually force Lincoln to be more committed to the abolition project. Before Marx learned what actually happened on 1 January, he told Engels on 2 January, '*Politically*', the defeat was a good thing. It wouldn't have done for the chaps to have had a stroke of good luck before 1 January 1863. Anything in that line might have led to a cancellation of the 'Proclamation''.[148] Marx and Douglass were both, once again, on the same political page. Along the way,

---

146 DM, January 1863, p. 771.
147 P. Foner 1981a, pp. 31–3. W.E.B. DuBois, 2016, p. 216, seemed to have thought that Marx actually read Douglass's 'Appeal'. But we have no way of confirming if he did.
148 Marx and Engels 1975–2004u, p. 440.

Douglass offered some positive reinforcement to the president for keeping his commitment – doing all he could to affect the outcome. The editorial ended by pointing out that Lincoln's silences and most recent pronouncements had 'all served to cast doubt upon the promised and hoped-for proclamation, which only the event can remove or confirm ... The suspense is painful, but will soon be over'.[149]

Whether Douglass's editorial was consequential in some way or another is probably unknowable. But on 1 January 1863 Lincoln kept his promise. Douglass gathered with a largely Black audience in Tremont Temple, in Boston, a very familiar venue, beginning at ten in the morning and waited until late in the evening for word from Washington. His talk to the crowd in the afternoon included a call for the enlistment of Black troops in the Union army – as Douglass had been doing since the commencement of hostilities. The telegraph finally brought 'the good news', and the text of the near sacred proclamation was read aloud. People sang, hugged, and cheered. Then at midnight 'the revelers', as Blight recounts, 'singing, humming, shouting, walked out onto Tremont Street into a gentle, glistening snowfall to march to what all called the "Fugitive Slave's Church"'. For Douglass, abolitionists, and the slaves who awaited the Union Army, at 'that moment, and for its duration, the cruel and apocalyptic war had become holy'.[150]

∴

It took Douglass almost a year to give the kind of detailed attention to the battlefield that Marx and Engels had given it from the commencement of the conflagration. Like them, he soon recognised the impediment to Union victory in the person of General George McClellan and did all he could through his *Monthly* to so convince the Lincoln administration. From afar, Marx's critical look at McClellan and his relationship with Lincoln proved to be more perceptive. His and Engels's balance sheet on the War, written about the same time as Douglass did the same, attests to the advantages they brought to the subject that the latter lacked as instantiated in their prescient point that 'Georgia is the key to the secessionists' territory'. Douglass made up for his inadequacies about the battlefield with what we call – and unappreciated until now – a class-based explanation of white supremacy, one with which Marx would have been in accord.

---

149   DM, January 1863, pp. 769–70.
150   Blight 2018, p. 384.

If Marx and Engels had a more accurate understanding of the facts on the ground than Douglass, they were not in accord with each other about eventual Union prospects – the only documented disagreement between the two in their four-decade long partnership. Engels's pessimism resembled very much that of Douglass. Unlike Douglass, Marx wasn't 'thrown off scent' by Lincoln's apparently contradictory actions between 22 July and 22 September 1862 when he decided on and then issued the Preliminary Emancipation Proclamation. The threat Lincoln had made to the slave owners in the Border States about the confiscation of their slaves convinced Marx that Lincoln was committed to emancipation – 'things are taking a revolutionary turn'. Douglass wasn't or couldn't afford to be as sure. And for that reason, most likely, felt that he had to cajole the administration to do the right thing. Marx read the unprecedented measures adopted by the 37th Congress as crucial evidence that 'the revolutionary waging of war is at hand'. From the other side of the Atlantic, Marx could see, better than Douglass, that both Lincoln and the Congress were on the same page, giving lie to the oft-repeated charge that Marx didn't take bourgeois politics seriously. Being able to see both in space and time allowed Marx to put Lincoln's issuance of the Preliminary Emancipation in world-historical perspective, paying, along the way, his highest compliment to the American experiment.

If Douglass appeared at times to have wavered on the Sixteenth President and felt the need to push him to an abolitionist posture, Marx kept faith in 'Old Abe'. Engels's doubts about Lincoln required his partner to be at his argumentative best and why, we argue, he proved in the end to be more accurate about him than Douglass. Lincoln's heroic actions on 22 September 1862 and 1 January 1863, nevertheless, brought Douglass and Marx closer than they ever had been – or ever would be.

CHAPTER 5

The End of the War and the Rise and Fall of Radical Reconstruction

> Slavery is not abolished until the black man has the ballot.
> DOUGLASS, May 1865

∙ ∙ ∙

> The reaction has already set in in America and will soon be much fortified if the present lackadaisical attitude is not ended immediately.
> MARX, June 1865

∙ ∙ ∙

> Why not transfer all the lands that have been abandoned, confiscated, or forfeited ... to free Negroes to cultivate independently?
> WEYDEMEYER, September 1865

∙ ∙ ∙

> Nothing will ever soften [the iron heart of slavery] save the military power of the United States.
> DOUGLASS, February 1866

∙ ∙ ∙

> The phase of the Civil War over, only now have the United States really entered the revolutionary phase.
> MARX, April 1866

∙ ∙ ∙

> ... give to every loyal citizen the effective franchise – a right and power which will be ever present, and [it] will form a wall of fire for his protection.
>
> DOUGLASS, December 1866

∴

'The short campaign in Maryland [Antietam] has decided the fate of the American Civil War, however much the fortune of war may still vacillate between the opposing parties for a shorter or longer time', declared Marx in October 1862. In hindsight he was right. Whether he knew that 'longer' could be thirty more months is unknown. But that's how long it took for the War, or at least the battlefield hostilities, to come to an end.[1]

After November 1862, Marx no longer had access to a publication for reporting on the Civil War, unlike Douglass whose *Monthly* continued to be published until August 1863. Douglass later had access to other venues, not the least important the *New York Tribune*. Though rich, Marx's correspondence with Engels about the last years of the War could not make up for the depth of his reporting in *Die Presse*. Also, unlike for Douglass, new political developments in Europe obligated Marx to devote less attention to the War. As well, the final draft for his magnum opus finally took shape in 1863 – another demand on his time. Brevity, therefore, characterises, unlike the prior chapters, the real-time comparisons we can make in this chapter. The first part of the chapter ends with the Confederate surrender at Appomattox in April 1865. From that moment until the effective end of Radical Reconstruction in 1868 constitutes the second and concluding part of the chapter.

1   The Long Grinding Road to Appomattox

'And I further declare', said Lincoln in the penultimate paragraph of his Emancipation Proclamation, 'and make known, that such persons ['the people so

---

[1] Egerton 2014 and more recently Williams 2023 characterise the post-Appomattox period as 'Wars of Reconstruction' and 'the War against Reconstruction', respectively. Downs 2015 demonstrates that war did not legally end until all representatives from rebel states were seated in Congress in 1871.

declared to be free'] of suitable condition, will be received into the armed service of the United States to garrison forts, positions, stations, and other places, and to man vessels of all sorts in said service'.[2] Douglass and the others who had gathered at Tremont Temple in Boston to await Lincoln's decision had good reason to later celebrate. From almost the very beginning of the War, Douglass urged: 'Let the slaves and free colored people be called into service, and formed into a liberating army, to march into the South and raise the banner of Emancipation among the slaves'. He now had presidential licence to realise that aspiration. Though there is no record of how Marx reacted when he got word of Lincoln's decision about twelve days later, he would have felt vindicated for his unwavering faith in the president. He had argued, as soon as the War began, that 'the North will be victorious since, if the need arises, it has a last card up its sleeve in the shape of a slave revolution'. Then later, to his pessimistic comrade on 9 August 1862 about how the North could win: 'One single NIGGER REGIMENT would have remarkable effect on Southern nerves'. All so politically incorrect and grating on modern and woke ears, but all so accurate. But the decision to recruit Black men into the Union Army was only the beginning of wisdom. To actually do so required conscious leadership – what Douglass was willing to take the lead on; arguably his finest and most consequential hour of the War.

'January', Douglass's first report to the readers of the *Monthly* following Lincoln's issuance of his Proclamation, 'has been a month of jubilee meetings ... we have travelled over two thousand miles and delivered many addresses, all the way from Boston to Chicago'. Despite the many signs of hostility to the presidential executive order that he had encountered in his travels, 'the most hopeful sign of the times is the growing disposition to employ the black men of this country in the effort to save it from division and ruin. A bill is before Congress authorizing the raising of one hundred and fifty thousand colored troops. Could this measure be adopted and vigorously put in operation we should regard the cause of the country comparatively safe'.[3] About the potential for recruitment, the 'colored men of the North', notwithstanding the rebuff in the past, 'are now waiting to be honorably invited forward ... Let the government say the word, and open the door, and we have the confidence that the colored people of the North will furnish their full proportion of soldiers for the war'. Douglass had no illusions about what awaited Black men in the Union Army

---

2 Fehrenbacher 1989b, pp. 424–5. You can also find the Final Emancipation Proclamation online: https://www.archives.gov/exhibits/featured-documents/emancipation-proclamation/transcript.html
3 DM, February 1863, p. 785.

and Navy: they 'must expect annoyance. They will be severely criticized and even insulted – but let no man hold back on this accord'. And as if in anticipation of the African American 'Double-V' campaign of the Second World War, 'we shall be fighting a double battle, against slavery at the South and against prejudice and proscription at the North – and the case presents the very best assurances of success'.[4]

Douglass printed in the February issue of the *Monthly* a letter from a Black reader who made a proposal to him:

> Now is the time for you to finish the crowning work of your life. Go to work at once and raise a Regiment and offer your services to the government and I am confident they will be accepted. They say we will not fight. I want to see it tried on. You are the one to me of all others, to demonstrate this fact.

Not for the first time – think John Brown's unsuccessful recruitment efforts – that Douglass had been asked 'to lay down the quill and take up the sword'. Because the question came from a Black volunteer in a mainly white Illinois regiment now stationed near Memphis, it had to be taken seriously. 'But our correspondent must bear with our absence from the army until our own unbiased judgement and the action of the Government shall make it our duty and our privilege to become a soldier ... Highly as we respect the motives which dictate the call from Memphis, a call from Washington requesting us to raise a regiment in the State of New York and furnishing the money to do it with, would be more respected'.[5] Consistent with what Douglass had said earlier in the editorial about the recruitment of Blacks in the North, the Lincoln administration had to take the initiative to invite Blacks like him to join the Union Army – unlike, evidently, the initiative taken by the letter-writer, or the 'contraband' who came uninvited.

Lincoln's first of January decree gave John Andrew, the abolitionist governor of Massachusetts, licence to raise a Black regiment, the famous Fifty-Fourth Massachusetts Infantry. Just over a month before, in late November 1862, Attorney General Edward Bates declared Blacks to be citizens – the last legal

---

4 DM, February 1863, p. 786. In fact, almost from the very beginning of the War, Black men had served in the Navy, yes, in mainly menial roles, but nevertheless present and at times consequential – the example of Robert Smalls. McPherson 2008, p. 158. About the 'Double-V' campaign, see Lineberry 2022; Stanton 2009, pp. 209–11. https://www.nationalww2museum.org/war/articles/double-v-victory.

5 DM, February 1863, p. 786.

impediment to their military service, and effectively, the repudiation of the odious *Dred Scott* decision.[6] 'Andrew', according to David Blight, 'called on the wealthy Boston abolitionist George Luther Stearns', John Brown's old ally, 'to direct the recruiting'. By February, Douglass, along with other black abolitionists, including 'Charles Lenox Remond, John Mercer Langston, William Wells Brown, Henry Highland Garnet, and Martin Delany', enlisted as agents with Stearns. Douglass believed fighting as soldiers 'is the colored man's way to … political and civil liberty'. Blight argues that the 'historical link between soldiering and citizenship had never before been given such an open door; Douglass's task was to convince black men to march through it'. Douglas Egerton claims that 'more than any other advocate of the Fifty-fourth, Douglass fused patriotic oratory with a rage against Confederate officials'. Douglass and others immediately engaged in the critically important, but controversial task, of enlisting Black men into the Union Army. 'No wartime issue', in the opinion of Fergus Bordewich, 'was more emotive and politically fraught, because the enlistment of blacks threatened to place Negroes on an equal plane with white men for the first time. Alarmed Democrats warned that it might well spark a white rebellion … They predicted that hundreds of thousands of Union soldiers would throw down their guns in protest'. But as Thaddeus Stevens knew, and Marx would have agreed, 'The arming of the Negroes is the only way left on earth in which these rebels can be exterminated'.[7]

2 'That the Paper Proclamation Must Now Be Made Iron, Lead and Fire'

The issuance of 'Abraham Lincoln's Proclamation of the 1st of January, 1863', declared Douglass on 6 February to an audience at the Cooper Institute in New York, 'may be called the greatest event of our nation's history if not the greatest event of the century … It shall take rank with the Fourth of July [Applause] … It will stand in the history of civilization … with that noble act of Russian liberty' – Douglass's eyes on the international situation – 'by which twenty millions of serfs … have been released from servitude [Loud cheering] Aye! It will stand with every distinguished event which marks any advance made by mankind from the thraldom and darkness of error to the glorious liberty of truth'.[8] Then, toward his wrap up:

---

6 Oakes 2013, pp. 357–61. E. Foner 2019, pp. 15–16.
7 Blight 2018, p. 391. Egerton 2016, p. 74. Bordewich 2020, p. 203.
8 DM, March 1863, pp. 804–5.

> In like manner aftercoming generations will celebrate the first of January as the day which brought liberty and manhood to the American slaves. – [Loud cheers] how shall this be done? I answer: That the paper Proclamation must now be made iron, lead and fire, by the prompt employment of the negro's arm in this contest [Great applause.] I hold that the Proclamation, good as it is, will be worthless – a miserable mockery – unless the nation shall so far conquer its prejudice as to welcome into the army full-grown black men to help fight the battles of the Republic. [Renewed applause].[9]

Douglass's accolades resonate with those Marx made five months earlier about the Preliminary Emancipation Proclamation: '… the most important document in American history since the establishment of the Union', but with a qualifier that Douglass probably would not have agreed with – 'tantamount to the tearing up of the old American Constitution'. Also, Marx's point about Lincoln: '… his place in the history of the United States and of mankind will … be next to that of Washington!' Cautious Douglass had to wait, unlike Marx, until January before offering such effusive praise. Noteworthy also was Douglass's reference to peasant emancipation in Russia and the audience reaction – as well has his. At the beginning of 1860, to recall, Marx declared, with remarkable foresight, that 'the most momentous thing happening in the world today is the slave movement … in America started by the death of [John] Brown and in Russia [with the ending of serfdom] … a 'social' movement that promises great things'.[10] With the world as his unit of analysis and theatre of *action*, Marx could be attuned to such diverse moments in the global class struggle.

'Action! action! not criticism, is the plain duty of this hour', demanded the lead editorial of the March issue of the *Monthly*, 'Men of Color to Arms!'

> Words are now useful only as they stimulate to blows … Liberty won by white men would lose half its lustre. Who would be free themselves must strike the blow. Better to die free, than to live slaves … I now for the first time during this war feel at liberty to call and counsel you to arms.

Never before had Douglas employed his organ in such fashion. The one-time pacifist had come a long way. The call was specific. Because New York had yet to make it possible to do so, 'Massachusetts', he told his New York Black male

---

9   DM, March 1863, p. 807.
10 Marx and Engels 1975–2004u, pp. 4–5.

readers, 'now welcomes you to arms as her soldiers ... I am authorized to assure you that you will receive the same wages, the same rations, the same equipment, the same protection, the same treatment and the same bounty secured to white soldiers'. After more details about the conditions under which the recruits would serve, and his credentials for making such promises, Douglass ended with instructions: 'The nucleus of this first regiment is now in camp at Readville, a short distance from Boston. I will undertake to forward to Boston all persons adjudged fit to be mustered into the regiment, who shall apply to me at any time within the next two weeks. Frederick Douglass. Rochester, March 2d. 1863'.[11] On the first page of the *Monthly*, it was now official – Douglass the recruiter.[12]

According to Douglass, his first recruit was one of his sons. 'Charley, my youngest son', he wrote in a letter, 'was the first to put his name down as one of the company'. In addition, Douglass informed Gerritt Smith, 'I have visited Buffalo and obtained seven good men. I spoke here [Rochester] last night and got thirteen. I shall visit Auburn, Syracuse, Ithaca, Troy and Albany and other places in the state till I get one hundred men'. After travelling through New York state, Douglass would go to Philadelphia to mobilise African Americans in Pennsylvania, before retracing his New York steps again. This recruiting occurred even though government policy denied Black men the possibility of promotion. 'It is a little cruel to say to the black soldier that he shall not rise to be an officer of the United States whatever may be his merits', Douglass admitted, 'but I see that though coupled with this disadvantage – colored men should hail the opportunity of getting on the United States uniform as a very great advance'. By mid-April, he reported 'I have recruited and sent forward to camp at Readville Mass. more than one hundred men for the 54th regiment', and 'I am endeavoring to raise another company'. By now a second son, Lewis, had signed up.[13]

Lincoln had 'previously opposed black recruitment and doubted blacks' military capacity'. Even after issuing the final Emancipation Proclamation, he planned to use them only in non-combat roles. In August 1862 he had told visitors that tens of thousands of Border State soldiers would throw down their bayonets if Blacks were armed – almost at the same time Marx claimed what 'one single NIGGER regiment' would do. Early in March 1863, an Illinois correspondent urged him to utilise Black soldiers, otherwise the Confederates would

---

11   DM, March 1863, p. 801.
12   Chandra Manning emphasises Douglass's recruiting as one of the main ways he 'labored to make the Union's war a war against slavery ...' Manning 2021, pp. 185, 187–9.
13   McKivigan 2018, pp. 386, 390. Egerton 2016, p. 77.

do the same; sound advice Lincoln thought. By 26 March, Lincoln would come around to what Douglass, Marx, and the Illinois correspondent had advocated. To Tennessee military governor Andrew Johnson, encouraging him to raise 'a negro military force', Lincoln wrote, 'The colored population is the great *available* and yet *unavailed* of, force for restoring the Union. The bare sight of fifty thousand armed, and drilled black soldiers on the banks of the Mississippi, would end the rebellion at once'. Very similar to – and maybe inspired by – Douglass's assertion in the February edition of his *Monthly* that whoever 'sees fifty thousand well drilled colored soldiers in the United States, will see slavery abolished and the union of these States secured from rebel violence'. Earlier in March, Black soldiers, almost all former slaves, had been successful in occupying Jacksonville, Florida under General David Hunter, certainly helping to convince Lincoln of their potential power. In a congratulatory letter to Hunter on 1 April, Lincoln said: 'It is important to the enemy that such a force [Black soldiers] shall *not* take shape, and grow, and thrive, in the South; and in precisely the same proportion, it is important to us that it *shall*'. By late spring 1863 major recruitment efforts, led by Adjutant General Lorenzo Thomas were moving forward in the Mississippi Valley. James Oakes notes that, 'the history of black enlistment in the Union army is a tale of gradual evolution as much as sudden transformation'.[14] Starting with the wildcat regiments in Kansas, Louisiana, and the South Carolina Sea Islands, the Union-saving policy of confiscation had evolved, and transformed, into the revolutionary policy of freeing the slaves, arming them, and welcoming them into the army of liberation.

On the other side of the Atlantic, revolutionary developments there brought Marx back into active politics after more than a decade of relative quiescence – the rebellion in Polish Russia on 22 January 1863. 'This much is certain, the ERA OF REVOLUTION has now fairly opened in Europe, once more ... But the comfortable delusions and almost childish enthusiasm with which we welcomed the revolutionary era before February 1848, have gone by the board'. Sobriety now informed the projections of the revolutionary veteran. 'This time', he told Engels on 13 February, 'let us hope the lava will flow from East to West and not in the opposite direction, so that we shall be spared the "honour" of the French initiative'.[15] Not the first time that Marx's algebra was more accurate than his arithmetic. There would be one last gasp of the 'French initiative' in 1871 (more about later in this chapter) and only in October 1917 would the 'lava [begin to]

---

14 Fehrenbacher 1989b, pp. 440, 443. Lincoln also encouraged Nathaniel Banks to raise Black troops in Louisiana, p. 442. DM, February 1863, p. 786. Oakes 2007, pp. 204–5. E. Foner 2010, pp. 250–1. Oakes 2013, pp. 377, 387.
15 Marx and Engels 1975–2004u, p. 453.

flow from East to West'. Marx proposed that he write a statement on the uprising for the German Workers' Educational Society in London, the organisational form of the Marx party in that era, and that both of them write a pamphlet with more details. However, serious liver and eye illness and the research and writing of *Capital* allowed for only the former to be written.

Noteworthy was Marx's follow-up letter on 17 February, signed off with 'Your Moor' for the first time to Engels, a household sobriquet, owing to his dark skin colour, at least by European standards. Perhaps not a coincidence for two reasons. The US Civil War experience is when Marx and Engels first addressed in any depth the Black American experience – 'the Moors' as they might have been called in Europe. 'Negroes' found its way into their correspondence for the first time since the beginning of the War. Also important was the content of the letter. Marx apologised to Engels for not having been sensitive enough in an earlier letter to the pain his partner was experiencing due to the sudden death in early January of Mary Burns, his two decade-long companion – the only documented strained moment in their four decade-long partnership. To have chosen the label, 'Your Moor', for the first time to Engels in a letter meant to repair their friendship indicated its significance to him. Intimacy and sincerity for Marx entailed, apparently, the signalling of an embrace of his own 'African-like' features.[16]

The Civil War still weighed, frustratingly at times, on Marx's brain: 'In the UNITED STATES things are going damned slowly', he told Engels on 13 February 1863.[17] The largely uneventful and grinding pace of the War in much of 1863 and 1864 was reflected in generally terse comments in their correspondence, the only venue Marx had for opinionating. About the Battle at Gettysburg in July 1863, all that Marx had to say was that it was 'forced on Lee by the clamour of the Richmond PAPERS and their SUPPORTERS. I regard it as a *coup de désespoir* [act of desperation]. This war, by the by, is going to be a lengthy business'.[18] He was right. Ten months later, in May 1864, some good news from Virginia that might actually enthuse his still sceptical partner:

> WHAT DO YOU SAY OF GRANT'S OPERATIONS? All that *The* [London] *Times* chooses to admire, OF COURSE, is Lee's strategy disguised as RETREATS. Says [daughter] Tussy this morning, 'IT CONSIDERS THIS VERY CANNY, I DARE SAY.' There's nothing I would be happier to see than success for [General Benjamin] Butler. It would be of inestimable value, were he to

---

16   See, again, the Introduction for more discussion on this all so vital point.
17   Marx and Engels 1975–2004u, pp. 453–4.
18   Marx and Engels 1975–2004u, p. 484.

enter Richmond first. It would be bad if Grant had to retreat, BUT I THINK THAT FELLOW KNOWS WHAT HE IS ABOUT. It is to him, at any rate, that credit is due for the first Kentucky campaign, Vicksburg and the drubbing Bragg received in Tennessee.[19]

Three weeks later, Engels replied that 'I am hoping that Grant will ... go through with the affair ... I also like the methodical pace of Grant's operations' – the first sign of optimism for Engels in almost two years.[20]

Though it would take Grant eleven months to succeed, Marx had been right to be hopeful. And his hope for Butler would have resonated with Douglass who reprinted, under the title 'Gen. Butler for the Extermination of Slavery', in the February 1863 issue of the *Monthly* a speech Butler gave in New York about how his New Orleans experience made him an ardent proponent of emancipation.[21] The reason Marx no longer had access to *Die Presse* is that some time in December 1862 he decided to part company with the Vienna organ, having grown increasingly frustrated with it for not publishing much of what he submitted – and sorely missed, not only by subsequent scholars of his project.[22] With the indispensable help of the wealthy New York state abolitionist Gerrit Smith and the indefatigable British abolitionist Julia Griffiths Crofts, Douglass still had his *Monthly* to opine in a way Marx no longer could.

One advantage in cutting ties to *Die Presse* is that it gave Marx more time to work on *Capital* and, as well, apparently, time to re-engage in face-to-face politics. Of utmost significance, Marx attended on 26 March, as he later told Engels, 'a TRADE UNIONS meeting chaired by Bright. He had very much the air of an INDEPENDENT and, whenever he said "IN THE UNITED STATES NO KINGS, NO BISHOPS", there was a BURST OF APPLAUSE. The working men themselves spoke *very well indeed*, without a trace of bourgeois rhetoric or the faintest attempt to conceal their opposition to the capitalist (who, by the by, were also attacked by papa Bright)'.[23] The advertisement for the event read:

A GREAT MEETING
of the Trade Unionists of London ...
For the purposes of expressing sympathy
with the Northern States of America,

---

19   Marx and Engels 1975–2004u, p. 530.
20   Marx and Engels 1975–2004u, p. 540.
21   DM, February 1863, pp. 795–6.
22   Draper 1985, p. 114n.60.
23   Marx and Engels 1975–2004u, p. 468.

> and in favour of
> NEGRO EMANCIPATION
> JOHN BRIGHT, ESQ., MP WILL
> PRESIDE[24]

Almost 3,000 attended the event, 'all', according to one newspaper account, 'with the exception of a few invited guests, the members of the working classes, or technically skilled laborers'. The London meeting had been preceded by other mass working class pro-Union meetings in Manchester and Edinburgh, of such size that Lincoln felt compelled to send a 19 January message of thanks that was widely publicised.[25] What Marx didn't tell Engels is that he had had a hand in organising the meeting – at least that's what Henry Adams, the son of US ambassador Charles Adams thought to be the case. According to Hal Draper's authoritative *Marx-Engels Chronicle*, Marx 'helped to organize this meeting, through [Marx party member Georg] Eccarius'.[26] Though that claim is disputed by one scholar of British labour history, the balance of evidence supports Adams and Draper.[27] Marx's initiative anticipated his so consequential actions eighteen months later; about which more below.

What Marx witnessed at the trade union meeting found its way into the promised 'Proclamation on Poland' written later in October. The document called for German working class solidarity with the Polish rebellion, 'to raise a loud protest' against both the 'German aristocracy' and the 'German bourgeoisie' for their complicity in Russia's oligarchical denial of self determination for the Polish people. Marx's task was to convince the German working class to embrace the uprising, to see how its own class interests were served by liberation for an oppressed nationality. Both the *Communist Manifesto* and a balance sheet on the Revolutions of 1848–9 had argued for proletarian internationalism.[28] But that was more aspirational than reality. What Marx needed was a living example of the realisation of that noble goal. Luckily, he had one in front of him. 'The English working class has won immortal historical honour for itself by thwarting the repeated attempts of the ruling classes to intervene on behalf of the American slaveholders by its enthusiastic mass meetings, even though the prolongation of the American Civil War subjects a million English workers to the most fearful suffering and privations'.

---

24 P. Foner 1981a, p. 59.
25 P. Foner 1981a, pp. 42–4. For Lincoln's message see, Fehrenbacher 1989b, pp. 431–3.
26 Draper 1985, p. 116n.13.
27 For details about the event, the debate about Marx's role, see P. Foner 1981a, pp. 57–8.
28 Respectively, Marx and Engels 1975–2004e, p. 519, and Marx and Engels 1975–2004h, p. 70.

Douglass wrote similarly in the March issue of the *Monthly*. 'Honor to the suffering masses of Lancashire and Yorkshire. The rebellion has fallen heavily upon them, yet they, more than all others, have stood by the cause of the Union against those who have endeavored to strike it down, although by doing so they have seemed to be prolonging their own destitution and suffering'.[29] Two subtle but not unimportant differences between the two statements. One, Marx referred to 'English workers' *subjected* to 'suffering and privations', whereas Douglass spoke of 'the suffering masses' – not unlike the difference between an enslaved person and a slave. Second, 'the enthusiastic mass meetings' that Marx drew attention to, that is, the working class organised as a class to fight. For the young Marx on the road to finding the proletariat, the thinking and fighting sufferer pointed the way forward for human emancipation. Though replete with news on middle class activities and meetings in England in support of the Union cause, those of 'the betters', never did the *Monthly* report on the trade union meetings that also took place, such as the big one on 26 March in London that Marx attended, or Lincoln's widely published 19 January message of thanks to the 'workingmen at Manchester' – foreshadowing Douglass's attitude to trade unions in post-Civil War America.

The 'Proclamation on Poland' was Marx's first party document in more than a decade and, arguably, the first that solely focused on a call for proletarian internationalism – inspired in part by the response of the 'English working class' to the firing on Fort Sumter. Everything that he had written to then on the Civil War was for a bourgeois liberal publication, be it the *Tribune* or *Die Presse*. The 'Proclamation' was pure and unadulterated communism. The actions of the 'English working class', captured in that one but rich sentence, inspired, and a year away, Marx's return, after a decade-long hiatus, to full time politics.

Aiding and abetting Marx's ability to return to active political work were the deaths of his mother Henriette at the end of 1863, and long-time Marx party member Wilhelm Wolff in May 1864 – the bequests, that is, both left to him. The latter's death hit Marx hard as revealed in a letter to wife Jenny about the funeral at which he spoke. 'It was an office by which I was much affected so that once or twice my voice failed me'.[30] Not for naught did Marx later dedicate *Capital* to Wolff. But for the first time in more than a decade, Marx could pursue both politics and 'the scientific work' without the anxiety of he and his family becoming homeless. Both bequests allowed him, despite the continuing health issues, to be more productive than he had ever been and ever would be.

---

29 DM, March 1863, p. 802.
30 Marx and Engels 1975–2004u, p. 525.

And a bit more wealthy. To his capitalist uncle Lion Philips on 25 June 1864, he revealed that he had 'made over £400' from 'speculating ... in English stocks ... It's a type of operation that makes small demands on one's time, and it's worth running some risk in order to relieve the enemy of his money'.[31] More than anyone, Marx knew – as his magnum opus would soon teach the world – that it took wealth to make wealth. Along with income from lectures and fundraising of his British supporters, wealth, that of the abolitionist Gerrit Smith, enabled Douglass to also be a full-time activist.

3   The Reality of Recruitment

David Blight paints a moving scene of Douglass seeing his son Lewis off for war as a member of the famed Massachusetts 54th Regiment, the first fruit of his recruitment efforts.

> On May 28, the regiment arrived early in the morning in Boston for their public departure for South Carolina ... Some family members and friends mingled with the soldiers at the dock as they prepared to board the big new steamer *De Molay*. Douglass himself joined the state's adjutant general, William Schouler, and a few others on board the ship and rode with the men out until it had almost cleared Boston Harbor. At nearly dusk, the father-civilian could go no farther, said his emotional farewells to his son Lewis, as well as to many other men he had recruited, and was assisted down onto a tugboat that returned him to shore. Each man on that ship had his own private joys and fears to ponder. As Frederick and Lewis Douglass watched each other fade into the harbor's dimming light, their minds and hearts swelled with the unspeakable love and dreadful anxiety that war creates in fathers and sons. The great man of words left us no statement of his thoughts that memorable night.[32]

Possibly on Douglass's mind was whether the promise he made in March to prospective Black recruits that they would 'receive the same wages ... secured to white soldiers' could actually be fulfilled. Unequal pay, however, quickly became a condition for Black participation that he and other abolitionists were unable to undo, at least then. One condition that he did agree to was that the

---

31   Marx and Engels 1975–2004u, p. 543.
32   Blight 2018, pp. 397–9.

officers of the all-Black units would be white with the hope of eventual promotion to officer status from the ranks. In the context of the times, that probably made sense. Those who had the military experience to lead those units were white. For Douglass, the priority in that moment was to get Black men like his son Lewis into action in order to have such experiences that would later lead to leadership positions not only in the military but, more importantly, in civil society as well. For Northern Blacks like Douglass, Black participation in the War as combatants, not just 'to garrison forts, positions, stations', as Lincoln put it in the Emancipation Proclamation, was essential for the 'double battle' to defeat the slavocracy *and* Northern 'prejudices' in order to achieve full citizenship.[33]

In June 1863, the War Department added unequal pay to the policy that denied promotion for Black soldiers – $10 a month with a deduction for uniforms while white soldiers got $13 without the deduction. 'As black enlistment', David Blight writes, 'moved into the border states and the Deep South, resistance to unequal pay swelled'. The Fifty-Fourth Massachusetts that son Lewis was a member of 'accepted no wages at all well into 1864' – a show of protest.[34] Douglass was working with Black recruits in Philadelphia when the New York City draft riots exploded in July – the dangerous intrigue Marx had predicted when analysing the victory of the Democrats in the New York elections of November 1862 and the most brutal example of the 'double battle' in the North.[35] Douglass would not have been surprised at the largely Irish anti-Black violence. The June issue of the *Monthly* carried a couple of articles about Irish 'ruffians' in New York attacking Blacks in the city. Marx, too, would not have been surprised. In his analysis of the Democratic Party gains in the November 1862 elections, he pointed to the 'Irish rabble' as a factor. 'The Irishman', to repeat, 'sees the Negro as a dangerous competitor'.[36] George Stearns had dispatched Douglass to Philadelphia because the recruiting efforts there were falling short. Many Blacks did not want to enlist when they would be denied bounties for joining, paid less during service, and given worse rations. Douglass's goal was to convince free Blacks to enlist anyway.[37]

---

33 The two-fold purpose of Black participation in the War is expertly distilled in McPherson 2013. For a survey of the experiences of the Black soldiers who fought in the Union Army, see Smith 2002. The classic study, which has an October 2003 edition in print, published by Vintage Civil War Library, is McPherson 1965.
34 Blight 2018, pp. 402–3. For details on the fight by the Massachusetts regiments for equal wages and treatment, see Egerton 2016, pp. 204–9, 232–4, 237–43.
35 Blight 2018, p. 404.
36 Marx and Engels 1975–2004j, pp. 263–4.
37 Blassingame 1985, pp. 590–8.

Douglass employed his 6 July speech to make a vigorous case for Black participation in the War. While acknowledging the just grievances of potential recruits in regard to the War Department's discriminatory policies regarding pay and promotion, Douglass listed what had been gained so far for making Black citizenship real for the first time. He defended his anti-slavery reading of the Constitution and championed its Second Amendment, urging his Black listeners to fight for the document and the government which defended it. With remarkable foresight about post-War developments, he argued that doing so would bring personal benefits for Blacks.

> There is something ennobling in the possession of arms, and we of all other people in the world stand in need of their ennobling influence ... Remember that the musket – the United States musket with its bayonet of steel – is better than all mere parchment guarantees of liberty. In your hands that musket means liberty; and should your constitutional right at the close of this war be denied ... your brethren are safe while you have a Constitution which proclaims your right to keep and bear arms.[38]

The one time pacifist had indeed come a long way. Whether Blacks could exercise Second Amendment rights in the post-War South proved to be an essential test in their quest for becoming full citizens for the first time.

Notwithstanding the issues of unequal pay and denial of promotion from the ranks, and the charge that by not enrolling himself in the Union Army Douglass was undermining the recruitment effort, a graver problem in his opinion had to be addressed. The failure of the Lincoln administration to take a public stance on Confederate President Jefferson Davis's response to the Emancipation Proclamation, specifically, the employment of Black troops, was more threatening to the cause. Davis declared that any Black soldiers and their white officers captured by Confederate forces would not be treated as prisoners of war but rather as insurgents who could be summarily executed or enslaved.

For Douglass, Washington's silence about Davis's threat had been deafening and, apparently, making it difficult to recruit. Douglass, sometime in late July, ran out of patience and wrote a letter dated 1 August to Stearns stating that he would stop recruiting. But by the time his letter was to be published in the August issue of the *Monthly*, he added a post-script to it saying that 'we have received assurance from Major Stearns, that the Government of the United States is already taking measures which will secure for the captured colored

---

38 Blassingame 1985, pp. 596–8.

soldiers, at Charleston and elsewhere, the same protection against slavery and cruelty, extended to white soldiers. What ought to have been done at the beginning, comes late, but it comes'.[39] Douglass was referring to Lincoln's Order of Retaliation issued on 30 July which basically threatened captured rebel soldiers with the same treatment meted out to Black Union captives. Its application, like all war measures, would depend on developments on the ground, but Douglass was satisfied and withdrew his resignation.[40] A month later, Marx noted that 'Mr. Davis ... decided to treat Negro soldiers as 'prisoners of war' – the last official order of his war secretary'.[41] It appeared that Marx also approved of Lincoln's response.

Stearns urged Douglass to go to Washington to express his concerns with the Lincoln administration which he did on 9 to 10 August. Not only did he meet with Secretary of War Stanton but, unplanned, with Lincoln also. Stanton agreed to ask Congress to end the unequal pay and denial of promotion issues. As well, Douglass agreed to Stanton's request that he go to Mississippi to help General Lorenzo Thomas to recruit Blacks but with the understanding that he'd be commissioned to do so. As for his meeting with Lincoln, Douglass left it reassured that the President would stand firm in his mission to end slavery. He quoted Lincoln as saying, 'No man can say that having once taken the position I have contradicted it or retreated from it'. In his report to Stearns on 12 August, he added: 'This remark of the President I took as our assurance that whoever else might abandon his anti slavery policy President Lincoln would stand firm to his. My whole interim with the President was gratifying and did much to assure me that Slavery would not survive the War and that the Country would survive both Slavery and the War'. The first clause, 'Slavery would not survive the War', echoed what Marx wrote a year earlier: 'no matter how the dice may fall in the fortunes of war, even now it can safely be said that Negro slavery will not long outlive the Civil War'.[42]

Douglass's newly instituted relationship with the Lincoln administration led him to make a fateful decision which he announced on 16 August in the 'Valedictory' issue of the *Monthly*: 'I discontinue my paper, because ... I am going South to assist Adjutant General [Lorenzo] Thomas, in the organization of colored troops ... [to] take some humble part in the physical as well as the moral

---

39   P. Foner 1952, pp. 367–9.
40   For Lincoln's Order of Retaliation see, Fehrenbacher 1989b, pp. 484–5.
41   Marx and Engels 1975–2004u, p. 562. The Confederacy ended its policy of executing Black soldiers, 'unauthorized' massacres and murders notwithstanding, but continued to enslave them. McPherson 2014, pp. 170–1.
42   McKivigan 2018, p. 418. Marx and Engels 1975–2004j, pp. 228–9.

struggle against slavery and urge my long enslaved people to vindicate their manhood by bravely striking for their liberty and country is natural and consistent'.[43] For the first time in sixteen years, Douglass would be without an organ to advance his ideas and programme. The expected commission, however, for whatever reason, never arrived and Douglass, at the advice of friends like Julia Crofts, did not go south. Stearns informed him at the end of August that he and not Washington would be the one to continue paying Douglass's salary – confirmation that there would be no commission.[44]

Douglass continued to have faith in Lincoln. The President's 19 November Gettysburg Address announcing a 'new birth of freedom' for the nation signalled that he and Douglass were on the same political page regarding emancipation – they would soon clash on the content of that 'new birth of freedom'. Lincoln's defence of the Emancipation Proclamation and praise of Black troops in the War was also welcomed. However, his annual message to Congress on 8 December 1863 raised alarm bells for Douglass. It sounded like Lincoln's vision of the nation's rebirth, its 'reconstruction', would be one in which Blacks would be no more than second class citizens owing to his apparent willingness to engage in that all too familiar and dreadful practice of compromise. 'Clearly', Eric Foner argues, 'Lincoln did not envision Reconstruction as embodying a social and political revolution beyond the abolition of slavery'.[45] Douglass offered an alternative, more racially egalitarian vision in his 13 January 1864 'The Mission of the War' speech at Cooper Institute in New York City, one of his 'greatest speeches', in David Blight's estimation, and 'his fullest expression of the war's meaning'.[46] The speech also revealed, more pertinent for present purposes, Douglass's thinking about his options for what would be the most consequential presidential election in US history later that year. 'Until', towards the end of the speech, 'we shall see the election of November next, and know that it has resulted in the election of a sound Anti-Slavery man as President, we shall be in danger of a slaveholding compromise'.[47] A Douglass vote for Lincoln, in other words, was not assured – it appeared that he was ready to hedge his bets for whom to support.

When Lincoln fired Frémont in November 1861 for the unauthorised confiscation of the slaves of disloyal slaveholders in Missouri, both Marx and Dou-

---

[43] P. Foner 1952, p. 376.
[44] Blight 2018, p. 414. McKivigan 2018, p. 423.
[45] E. Foner 2010, pp. 271–2. B. Levine 2013, p. 189. For Lincoln's message to Congress, see Fehrenbacher 1989b, pp. 538–54.
[46] Blight 2018, pp. 415–16.
[47] Blassingame and McKivigan 1991, p. 21.

glass raised the likelihood of him being a future protagonist in the outcome of the War. If the War was going bad for Washington, 'his dismissal', Marx held, would give those who had grown tired of 'the hitherto prevailing diplomatic system of waging war ... its leader in John Frémont'. For Douglass, Frémont was almost destined to return *'in three years'*, that is, for the next presidential election, to prominence because 'Nature is remunerative, and Phoenix-like, he shall arise from the ashes ... and destroy the monster that has ... performed all its devilish orgies in the very halls of our National Legislature'.[48] With the War not going well for the Union in the spring of 1864, and Lincoln temporising on the federal government's role in full equality for Black Americans, Douglass acted as Marx would have expected. Though he didn't attend the event, Douglas signed the call for the dump-Lincoln convention in Cleveland at the end of May organised by radicals in the Republican Party under the Radical Democracy label. Though Frémont didn't attend the event either, participants nominated him for president and John Cochrane, the nephew of Douglass's closest colleague Gerrit Smith, as his vice-presidential running mate.

At the Republican Party convention held next month in Baltimore, Lincoln was easily renominated but, at his urging, with a different running mate, the Union military governor of Tennessee Andrew Johnson.[49] Renamed the National Union Party, both changes instantiated for Douglass the inclination of Lincoln and the Republican Party to sacrifice future Black equality for the sake of reconciliation with the former slaveholders, someone, for example, like Johnson. It's not known what Douglass thought specifically about the Johnson selection. Only, apparently, Thaddeus Stevens, the radical Republican congressman from Pennsylvania, thought it wasn't a good idea – as subsequent history would tragically confirm.[50] Marx appeared to be aware of the Convention's proceedings. 'Should Lincoln', in a letter to Engels on 7 September, 'succeed this time – as is highly probable – it will be on a far more radical PLATFORM and in completely CHANGED CIRCUMSTANCES. Then the old man will, lawyer-fashion, find that more radical methods are completely with his conscience'. Marx was absolutely right about the Republican Party platform. Compared to the 1860 platform, the new one registered how far the country had travelled

---

48 See Chapter 3, pp. 143–6.
49 See Varon 2014. Heather Cox Richardson contends that Johnson's nomination was collateral damage of the Radicals' attempt to remove William Seward from the cabinet. Johnson was chosen to forestall that effort and appease Thurlow Weed and by extension Wall Street and New York businessmen. Richardson 2014, pp. 47–8, 55–6.
50 Varon 2014. Also, B. Levine 2021, p. 166. On the relative radicalism of Johnson between mid–1863 and early 1865 compared to his pre-war years and the support he received from Tennessee Blacks, see R. Levine 2021, pp. 17–25.

since then.[51] Not only did it embrace the Emancipation Proclamation but also the controversial 'measures' Lincoln took for winning the War such as the suspension of habeas corpus, and not the least, 'the employment as Union soldiers of men heretofore held in slavery'.[52] Indeed, 'radical'.

What Douglass often complained about Lincoln – Engels also – that he was too concerned with winning centrist/moderate forces, Marx attributed to the 'humbug' of American bourgeois democracy. And there was also, as Marx's aforementioned comment perceptively noted, Lincoln-the-lawyer factor – the president who didn't read the Constitution, as Douglass uniquely did, to be an abolitionist document and, thus, the need to ease 'his conscience'. But more problematic in that moment for Douglass, was Lincoln's failure – what his December address to Congress signalled – to support the right to vote for Black men after emancipation. Though the Senate approved on 8 April the new 13th amendment abolishing slavery, for Douglass, as he put it in his 'Mission of the War' speech four months earlier, the way forward was to 'destroy Slavery *and* [our italics] enfranchise the Black man … immediate and unconditional emancipation in all the States, invest the black man everywhere with the right to vote and to be voted for, and remove all discriminations against his rights on account of his color, whether as a citizen or as a soldier'.[53] Whether Marx and Engels were aware of the franchise issue at that moment isn't known since nothing in their correspondence suggests as much; within a year they and Marx party members would have something to say. We revisit the issue shortly.

Another spur to the dump-Lincoln movement were the mounting Union losses on the battlefield, the 'horrible stalemate in 1864' as Blight calls it.[54] Even Lincoln began to think that his chances for being re-elected were evaporating. For that reason, he took the unusual step of inviting Douglass to the White House on 19 August to make an extraordinary proposal to him. Disappointed that his Emancipation Proclamation had not encouraged more slaves to flee their masters, and fearful that his Democratic successor would rescind his executive order, Lincoln asked Douglass to come up with a plan that would not only inform the enslaved about the document but also with the organisational means to convince them to flee their enslavers. Douglass enthusiastically

---

51   Eric Foner argues that it was Frémont's nomination and the Cleveland Convention's platform that led Lincoln to abandon his state-by-state abolition plan and embrace the 13th amendment. E. Foner 2019, pp. 34–5.
52   The 1864 Republican Party Platform: https://www.presidency.ucsb.edu/documents/republican-party-platform-1864
53   Blassingame and McKivigan 1991, pp. 11–12.
54   Blight 2018, p. 429. For an appraisal of the situation from military historians see, Murray and Hsieh 2016, Chapter Ten, especially pp. 355, 398–9, 412.

embraced Lincoln's proposal and by 29 August put together a plan that echoed an earlier John Brown scheme and as well what Eric Foner aptly describes as 'a kind of official institutionalization of the prewar Underground railroad'.[55]

Lincoln's proposal to Douglass revealed that the Sixteenth President was willing to resort to an unusual and covert scheme to preempt the actions of his democratically elected successor in order to effectuate revolutionary change – a fact that would not have been lost on Marx and Engels had they known about his initiative. Whether it's what Marx had in mind in the very early days of the War when he predicted Northern victory because 'if need arises, it has a last card up its sleeve in the shape of a slave revolution' is uncertain.[56] Facts on the battlefield three weeks later, however, obviated its need. Also significant about Lincoln's proposal is that it convinced Douglass, more than anything to that point, that the president's commitment to emancipation was genuine and, thus, most likely, ended his flirtation with the Frémont presidential bid. Douglass, apparently favourably impressed Lincoln because the president invited him shortly after the meeting to return to have tea with him at his summer abode at the Soldier's Home in Washington, DC – an invitation Douglass was unable to accept owing to a prior commitment.[57]

But if Douglass still vacillated about supporting Lincoln's re-election after their second meeting, the Democratic Party convention in Chicago at the end of August cured him of any such hesitation. The party's nomination on 31 August 1864 of George McClellan, staunch opponent of forced emancipation, for its presidential candidate on a platform that clearly appealed to the interests of the slaveholders, left no doubt for Douglass about how to proceed. Whatever his shortcomings, Lincoln was the lesser evil. Except for Wendell Phillips and a handful of others, virtually every radical critic of Lincoln got on board with the incumbent after Chicago.[58]

In his 4 September letter to his partner, Engels, still pessimistic, opined: 'Whether Sherman will cope with Atlanta seems doubtful, but his chances are, I think, rather better ... The fall of Atlanta would be a hard blow for the South. Rome [Georgia] would fall at the same time and that's where their gun

---

55　E. Foner 2010, p. 306. Regarding Douglass's second meeting with Lincoln, see Blight 2018, pp. 435–9. See also Eaton 1907, pp. 167–76, for his role in setting up the meeting and Lincoln's interest in John Brown's methods.
56　Marx and Engels 1975–2004u, p. 277.
57　Blight 2018, p. 438. Historian Edna Greene Medford argues that by then Lincoln was seeking to befriend Douglass who had been a thorn in his political side; 'Lincoln, Douglass & Emancipation', 1 Jan. 2020, https://www.c-span.org/video/?467923-1/lincoln-douglass-emancipation, at 38:05.
58　Burlingame 2014.

foundries, etc., are; in addition, the railway connection between Atlanta and South Carolina would be lost'. Notwithstanding the uncertainty on the battlefield, Engels thought 'that Lincoln's re-election is fairly certain'.[59] Progress on the battlefield was not, evidently for Engels, inextricably linked to progress in the electoral arena. Marx, three days later, responded that

> I consider the present moment, *entre nous*, to be extremely critical. If Grant suffers a major defeat, or Sherman wins a major victory, SO ALL RIGHT. Just now, at election time, a chronic series of small CHECKS would be dangerous. I fully agree with you that, to date, Lincoln's re-election is pretty well assured, *still 100 to 1*. But election time in a country which is the archetype of democratic humbug is full of hazards that may quite unexpectedly defy the logic of events (an expression which Magnus Urquhartus [?] considers no less idiotic than 'THE JUSTICE OF A LOCOMOTIVE') ... much will depend on military eventualities.[60]

For Marx, unlike Engels, evidently, progress in the electoral arena could not be separated from the material reality of the battlefield. Their exchange here provides an invaluable window into how the two originators of historical materialism differed on how to employ their method, with Marx being more sensitive to and aware of concrete reality, in this case the role of politics, specifically, American bourgeois politics. Note also Marx's usage of 'archetype', decades before German sociologist Max Weber, and his scepticism about 'the logic of events' and, hence, his appreciation of contingency – in anticipation of the 'vulgar materialism' charge that Weber would direct toward those in Germany who claimed to be students of Marx.[61]

4 Toward Lincoln's Re-election and Union Victory

Only two weeks later would Marx and Engels learn about the fall of Atlanta on 2 September. Combined with the Union's successful Shenandoah campaign later in September and October, those victories, more than anything, ensured Lincoln's re-election. Marx and Engels, as noted above, were confident that he'd win even before then. Although Frémont officially withdrew from the presidential contest on 22 September, saying that the Democratic Party convention

---

59 Marx and Engels 1975–2004u, p. 559.
60 Marx and Engels 1975–2004u, pp. 561–2.
61 Nimtz, 2019b, p. 136.

convinced him to do so, the fall of Atlanta may have been decisive.[62] Whatever the exact motivation, there is strong evidence that the Marx party in the person of Weydemeyer played a role, if not major, in Frémont's withdrawal from the contest. Weydemeyer, who, to be remembered, had once served in Frémont's Army of the West general staff, worked to unify Missouri's radical German Republicans who had been the vanguard for the dump-Lincoln pro-Frémont Cleveland convention.[63] His candidacy, Weydemeyer argued, through his St. Louis newspaper *Die Neue Zeit* and face-to-face contacts, would only redound to the advantage of McClellan and the Democratic Party by splitting the vote and ensuring that Lincoln would not be re-elected.[64] Whether Weydemeyer was influential in some way in Frémont's withdrawal is probably unknowable. The main thing for this comparison is that the Marx party – just like it did for the 1860 campaign – did not vacillate, unlike Douglass, about supporting Lincoln. For Weydemeyer and his comrades, as long as Lincoln was willing to lead the military campaign to end slavery, communists were obligated to give him their unconditional support in what would be the most consequential presidential election in United States history.

Douglass and like-minded abolitionists, on the other hand, wanted more, a guarantee for racial equality. Regarding the fall of Atlanta and the Union victory in the Shenandoah Valley, Douglass declared, 'we rejoice with you', in the opening words of his speech to the Colored National Convention on 7 October in Syracuse, New York. The 'you' referred to Northern white Americans. Titled 'The Cause of the Negro People: An Address of the Colored National Convention to the People of the United States', Douglass quickly pivoted to a tone of sobriety and caution. Fearful about recent peace proposals that Lincoln and his Secretary of State Seward floated following the recent military victories, Douglass made an 'appeal' to 'the national conscience' that 'our race' not be forgotten, or better, sold out. In Marx's opinion, however, 'the peace proposals made by [Lincoln] are MERE HUMBUG', that is, bourgeois election eve politics.[65] But Douglass couldn't be sure about Lincoln's and Seward's motives. In his 'gloomy view', the 'hope of the speedy and complete abolition of slavery' depended on

---

62 For his withdrawal letter and that of his running mate, see https://www.nytimes.com/1864/09/23/archives/the-presidential-campaign-gen-fremont-withdraws-from-the-canvass.html. See also, Denton 2008, pp. 343–6.

63 Young 2014.

64 Obermann 1947, pp. 127–28. Abbet Sébastien isn't so sure about Weydemeyer's role but doesn't present evidence to support his scepticism, Sébastien 2016: https://www.academia.edu/30948358/Joseph_Weydemeyer_a_German_American_for_Socialism_and_Black_Rights

65 Marx and Engels 1975–2004u, p. 562.

the 'slender thread of Rebel power, pride and persistence', whether, that is, they would accept Lincoln's overtures, specifically, end their rebellion and rejoin the Union. Continuing to fight 'against the Union' only ensured that they would have 'no chance for anything but destruction. Thus the freedom of our race and the welfare of our country tremble together in the balance of events'. The proverbial ball of abolition, in other words, was in the court of the slave holders – hence Douglass's 'gloomy view'.

To deny the slave oligarchs the role of protagonists, Douglass sought to make the case for an alternative road to abolition that didn't depend on what the slaveholders were willing to do. First, the North had to make an unequivocal commitment to ending slavery. Despite having long held that the Constitution was an abolitionist document and that nothing needed to be altered in it, Douglass now insisted that Congress vote for the Thirteenth Amendment which was now being held hostage by the Democratic Party minority in Congress. If amending the Constitution was the way to abolish slavery, Douglass the pragmatist apparently concluded, then so be it and get it done.[66] Looking forward, he then offered a forceful defence of the key demand in his 1863 'Mission of the War' speech, Black male enfranchisement. The right to vote, he argued, guaranteed 'our race ... political equality', the means for 'the protection and security of human rights', and to assure that 'prejudice should be allowed no voice' with regard to 'the color of men'. Since 'two hundred thousand colored men ... are now in ... the army and the navy of the United States', the claim that Black men didn't merit the franchise because they 'were not required to perform military duty' was no longer legitimate. That Douglass could vote in New York state, owing to being a property owner, while his son Lewis, who was serving in the Union army, was disenfranchised, could not have been lost on him.

> The possession of that right [to vote] is the keystone to the arch of human liberty; and without that, the whole may at any moment fall to the ground ... If you still ask why we want to vote, we answer, Because we don't want to be mobbed from our work, or insulted with impunity at every corner. We are men, and want to be free in our native country as other men ... Let your Government be what all governments should be, – a copy of the eternal laws of the universe; before which all men stand equal as to rewards and punishments, life and death, with regard to country, kindred, tongue, or people.[67]

---

66   P. Foner 1952, pp. 415–18.
67   P. Foner 1952, pp. 420–1.

Nothing captures Douglass's liberal political core so well as these lines – and all so distinct from Marx the communist. Formal 'political equality' rather than substantive political equality is all that suffrage ensured under capitalism – the lessons of the European Spring.

The Colored National Convention where Douglass made his case and was elected president of the proceedings 'disbanded without endorsing Lincoln in the pending election'. This likely explains why Douglass made no mention of the election in his speech. The attendees, according to Elizabeth Varon, represented abolitionists who 'expressed more ambivalence and conceptualized the election as a choice between "a half-friend of freedom" in Lincoln and a "thorough partisan of slavery" in McClellan'.[68] But Douglass was on record since the publication of his 17 September letter in Garrison's *Liberator* in supporting Lincoln's re-election.[69] His 15 October letter to Theodore Tilton instructively explained why: 'When there was any shadow of a hope that a man of a more decided anti-slavery conviction and policy could be elected, I was not for Mr. Lincoln. But as soon as the Chicago convention, my mind was made up, and it is made still. All dates changed with the nomination of Mr. McClellan'. In that same letter, Douglass also revealed that he was willing to campaign for Lincoln but was not welcomed to do so because 'the Republican committees do not wish to expose themselves to the charge of being the "N – r" party'.[70] If Douglass couldn't bring himself to vote for Lincoln four years earlier, this time he would, despite being treated like a pariah by the Republican Party – a clear recognition of what was now at stake.

It isn't clear if Douglass ever reconsidered his long-held position that the Constitution was an abolitionist document, a minority position in anti-slavery circles. To demand that Congress pass the 13th amendment suggests that he had abandoned that once held view without having said so. Maybe, after all, the document wasn't an abolitionist one. On the other hand, it could be argued that getting on board the amendment bandwagon was simply a matter of expediency, the best means, as already noted, under the circumstances, to abolish slavery. But another possible reason for embracing the amendment process was the 'calamity', as he put it, of 'the platform' the Democrats adopted at their Chicago Convention at the end of August. A Democratic administration promised to end the anti-slavery policies of the Lincoln adminis-

---

68 Blight 2018, 440–1; Varon 2019, p. 368. Eric Gardner captures some of the debate over the presidential election at the convention, including a woman, Edmonia Highgate, forcefully urging support for Lincoln in his Gardner 2021, pp. 72–85, especially pp. 82.
69 P. Foner 1952, pp. 406–7.
70 P. Foner 1952, p. 424.

tration on the supposed grounds that 'the Constitution ... has been disregarded in every part, and public liberty', the suspension of habeas corpus – probably true – 'and private right alike', the liberation of slaves by the Emancipation Proclamation, 'trodden down'.[71] To make sure that the claim of a Constitutional right of property in persons could not be sustained, Douglass, whatever might have been his prior views on the matter, likely concluded – especially in that moment when the outcome of the election was uncertain – that an amendment to the document that explicitly forbade slavery was indeed needed.

How to resolve whether the Constitution was an anti- or pro-slavery document – the Republic's most contentious issue since its founding? The one-time philosophy and jurisprudence student provided a possible answer in 1843. In his densely reasoned critique of the mentor of his generation, Georg Hegel, the twenty-four year old Marx argued that constitutions are the works of 'man' and not 'the idea' as Hegel alleged. The 'man' Marx had in mind was 'the sovereignty of the people', or 'the democracy' in the parlance of that time. 'Democracy', he therefore argued, 'is the solved *riddle* of all constitutions'.[72] In the 1864 presidential election, the Republic's most contentious issue was now in the electoral arena for those eligible to opine on in a way it had never been. Three years of war had concentrated minds on the matter of slavery unlike ever before. Abolition was no longer an abstraction as it had been for most people – an informed electorate for the first time. The platforms – a time when they were taken seriously in American politics – of the National Union Party, formerly the Republican Party, and the Democratic Party offered voters an unambiguous choice for what position to take on the long contested question. Until then, only nine unelected life-long employed functionaries of the state had registered a verdict on the question – the Supreme Court's notorious 1857 *Dred Scott* decision. In the meantime, the most efficacious voting on the question was taking place, on the battlefield – largely working farmers and former slaves armed in disciplined action, imposing their will, voting with their feet. The 'democracy', in other words, was solving 'the riddle'. Only because of what was being achieved

---

71 Democratic Party 1864 platform: https://www.presidency.ucsb.edu/documents/1864-democratic-party-platform
72 Marx and Engels 1975–2004b, p. 29. In a similar vein, Salmon P. Chase wrote to newly-elected Senator John P. Hale in 1847 after losing a case at the Supreme Court – *Jones v. Van Zandt* – where he defended a white farmer against prosecution under the Fugitive Slave Act of 1793: 'If the courts will not overthrow it [the proslavery reading of the Constitution], the people will, even if it be necessary to overthrow the courts also'. Stahr 2021, p. 115.

on the battlefield could the Constitution be amended, to accurately reflect, as the twenty-four year-old Marx put it, the 'customs and consciousness of any given people'.[73]

This is the appropriate place to bring Marx and Engels into discussion on the franchise. It was the February Revolution in 1848, the commencement of the European Spring, that instituted universal manhood suffrage for the first time – certainly in any major country. In the United States it wasn't universal – exactly what Douglass sought to rectify. The commencement of the German Revolution in March 1848 prompted Marx and Engels to make universal manhood suffrage the second of the seventeen demands for realising a bourgeois democratic revolution in Germany.[74] We assume that would have been their position for the American theatre given their basic position that the democratic revolution was the precondition for the socialist revolution and, hence, their support for Black male enfranchisement. The Marx party in America, to be seen in the next part of this chapter, certainly did.

But their March 1850 self-critical balance sheet on the German Revolution, the 'Address of the Central Authority of the Communist League', drawing on its first ten months, offered a more informed and sober perspective on the electoral/parliamentary process. That workers had the right to vote for the first time, the experience taught, did not guarantee anything – contrary to what Douglass claimed. In fact, as the French experience demonstrated, that right could be taken away – as would also happen in post-Reconstruction America.[75] Rather, therefore, as an end in themselves, elections should now be treated as a means to an end for the workers' movement, 'to count their forces and to lay before the public their revolutionary attitude and party standpoint', in order to determine the moment for launching a revolution.[76] Nothing could have been as foreign to Douglass as that perspective. For him, at least at that moment, and without anything comparable to the events of 1848–9 that instructed Marx and Engels, the franchise was the 'keystone' for ensuring citizenship and, thus, 'political equality' for Black people. For Marx and Engels, only the 'Revolution in Permanence', that is, the overthrow of capitalism, could make that possible – the all so essential difference between our two protagonists. That difference goes a long way in explaining the difference between what Marx and Engels and their comrades in the United States, on one hand, and Douglass, on the other hand,

---

[73] Marx and Engels 1975–2004b, p. 19.
[74] 'Demands of the Communist Party in Germany', https://www.marxists.org/archive/marx/works/1848/03/24.htm
[75] For what happened in France, see Nimtz 2021a, pp. 39–45.
[76] See Chapter 2, p. 60.

viewed at stake in the upcoming presidential election. Only after the Democratic Party nomination of McClellan did Douglass view, for certain, the stakes as high as those of the Marx party – but, again, for very different reasons.

About the upcoming election, Marx made, without elaboration, the interesting point in his 7 September letter to Engels that Lincoln's defeat 'would probably lead to genuine *revolution*'.[77] Two months later and a few days before the election, Engels told a relative that 'I have no doubt that the war will be continued until the South is totally subjugated, irrespective of who becomes President'.[78] Both remarks are consistent with veteran Civil War historian William C. Davis's provocative but still persuasive refutation of a once popular claim that had Lincoln lost the election to McClellan, the Confederacy would have achieved independence, extending, thus, the life of slavery. To the contrary, Davis argues. Lincoln, Grant, and Sheridan were all committed to defeating the South and would have used the five-month interval between the election and Inaugural Day in March to defeat Lee at Richmond, thus presenting new president McClellan with a fait accompli. It would have been an outcome that Little Napoleon, 'the ego maniac', could not have refused. And even if he had wanted to agree to independence for the slave oligarchy, the 'outrage' and 'indignation' it would have generated in the North would not have permitted McClellan to do so – provoking perhaps the 'genuine revolution' Marx envisioned.[79] To assume that an election outcome could resolve an issue so historically and, more important, politically significant as slavery made no sense to Marx. Too much blood had been spilt for that to happen. To believe so is to be afflicted with, as one of us terms it, 'voting fetishism', the mistaken belief that what takes place in the electoral arena is the be all and end all of politics.[80]

Lincoln was re-elected with an overwhelming number of votes, and Marx had the privilege of writing a congratulatory letter to him. Owing to his involvement in organising the March 1863 mass meeting in London in solidarity with the North, Marx quickly assumed leadership of the International Workingmen's Association, the First International, as it would later be called, that issued from a 28 September 1864 mass meeting in London. After a decade-long absence, Marx was back in the saddle of party politics, this time, as he later told Engels, with '"people who really count" ... from London and ... Paris, and I therefore decided to waive my usual standing rule to DECLINE ANY SUCH

---

77   Marx and Engels 1975–2004u, p. 562.
78   Marx and Engels 1975–2004v, p. 10.
79   For the rich details of his argument, see Davis 1996, pp. 127–47.
80   Nimtz 2021b. 'Voting fetishism' is inspired by Marx's and Engels's 'parliamentary cretinism', discussed briefly at the end of this part of Chapter 5.

INVITATIONS'.[81] That the apparently obscure German political exile, living precariously in London, could be chosen by a subcommittee of the newly organised international working-class body to write the letter – in English to boot! – registered his continuing renown with and ties to what remained of the 1848–9 German Revolution. Determinant, also, in his return to active politics was the conflagration on the other side of the Atlantic and the lesson that the working class needed to have its own foreign policy in opposition to 'the pro-slavery intervention, importunities', as he put it in the letter, 'of their betters' – the layer of British society that enamoured Douglass. Thus, the rationale for founding the International Workingmen's Association.

Marx's five-hundred fifty-plus word letter, 'To Abraham Lincoln, President of the United States of America', signed by himself and fifty-four other representatives of the working class in England and other countries, consists of three parts. First, was the world-historical significance of the War, what was at stake for the European proletariat and why they embraced what they 'instinctively' understood to be an anti-slavery project. The letter, secondly, denounced the oligarchy that had 'dared to inscribe, for the first time in the annals of the world, 'slavery' on the banner of Armed Revolt', in reference to Confederate Vice-President Alexander Stephens's infamous March 1861 'corner-stone speech'. The slave oligarchs, Marx continued, had the effrontery to do so in the very land 'whence the first Declaration of the Rights of Man was issued, and the first impulse given to the European revolution of the 18th century'. Marx's praise for the 1776 project and its transatlantic significance – what partially frames our comparison – would have resonated with Douglass. Stephens held that the 'old Constitution' erroneously 'rested upon the assumption of the equality of races'.[82] That's exactly why Marx charged Stephens – continuing to quote him – in having 'glorified in rescinding 'the ... ideas entertained ... at the time of the formation of the old Constitution', and maintained 'slavery to be a beneficent institution''.[83] Admirable for Stephens about 'our new government' was that 'its corner-stone ... rests upon the great truth that the negro is not equal to the white man' – the 'corner-stone', in fact, of the notorious speech that Marx took to task.

Douglass, too, more than a year earlier, drew attention to the slavocracy's 'openly confessed and shamelessly proclaimed object of the war'. Stephens, he

---

[81] Marx and Engels 1975–2004k, p. 16. About his writing of the letter, see Marx's 2 December letter to Engels, Marx and Engels 1975–2004k, p. 49.
[82] Alexander H. Stephens, 'Cornerstone Speech', 21 March 1861: https://www.battlefields.org/learn/primary-sources/cornerstone-speech
[83] Marx and Engels 1975–2004k, p. 19.

pointedly noted, 'has stated, with the utmost clearness and precision, the difference between the fundamental ideas of the Confederate Government and those of the Federal Government. One is based upon the idea that colored men are an inferior race, who may be enslaved and plundered forever, and to the heart's content of any men of a different complexion, while the Federal Government recognizes the natural and fundamental equality of all men'.[84] For both Marx and Douglass, Stephens's speech constituted an instructive document for the Confederacy's raison d'etre and, thus, its indictment.[85]

Looking backward and forward, Marx then distilled the key political lesson of the War for the proletariat: 'While the working men, the true political power of the North, allowed slavery to defile their own republic; while before the Negro, mastered and sold without his concurrence, they boasted it the highest prerogative of the white-skinned labourer to sell himself and choose his own master; they were unable to attain the true freedom of labour or to support their European brethren in their struggle for emancipation, but this barrier to progress has been swept off by the red sea of civil war'.[86]

Marx's lines are pregnant with insight. He offered an explanation for what Douglass was long familiar with, the anti-Black 'prejudices' of many white workers and, as well, his long-held complaint about the shortcomings of American democracy. Regarding Northern workers' 'true political power', Marx was likely referring to James Hammond's provocative 1858 'King Cotton/Mudsill' speech discussed in Chapter 2. Hammond claimed, specifically, that there were also slaves in the North – the white proletariat. And unlike the slaves in the South, 'yours', to the Northern critics, 'do vote, and, being the majority, they are the depositories of all your political power'.[87] If not 'the true political power' claim, Douglass would likely have agreed with Marx's point about the 'prerogative of the white-skinned labourer'. About the second point, the singular importance of the proletariat in the realisation of democracy, that's doubtful – a matter to be revisited.

Lastly, an accolade for Lincoln. Europe's workers, the letter concluded, 'consider it an earnest of the epoch to come that it fell to the lot of Abraham Lincoln, the single-minded son of the working class, to lead his country through the matchless struggle for the rescue of an enchained race and the reconstruction

---

84   Blassingame 1985, pp. 593–4.
85   We haven't been able to determine if Douglass opined on Stephens's claim that the Constitution 'secured' the legitimacy of slavery.
86   Marx and Engels 1975–2004k, p. 20.
87   James Henry Hammond, '"Mud Sill" Speech', https://teachingamericanhistory.org/document/mud-sill-speech/

of a social world'.[88] That the newly founded organisation embraced Lincoln as one of their own should come as no surprise. Just as the mass working class meeting in Lancastershire in 1863 lauded Lincoln and to which he sent a letter of thanks, the president did the same this time through, again, his ambassador to Britain, Charles Adams. And because Lincoln's letter to the IWA was not written in the perfunctory style of his note of thanks to the bourgeois Emancipation Society, 'the betters', that also congratulated him on his re-election, the difference redounded to the new organisation's advantage. 'You can understand', Marx told Engels, 'how gratifying that has been for our people'.[89] Not to be forgotten is that it may have been 'the correspondent in London' who, in his February 1862 *Tribune* article, first alerted Lincoln to the invaluable and maybe indispensable role of the British working class in staying the pro-Confederate interventionist hand of its ruling class.

Lincoln's re-election also heartened Douglass, 'the most momentous and solemn ['Presidential election'] that ever occurred in our country or any other'. To an audience in Rochester, New York, on 13 November 1864, he explained its significance. Of major importance for Douglass was that the 'election was a peaceful one … the final test of our national fitness for self-government'. Numerous pre-election Confederate-generated rumours and machinations that Marx and Engels probably didn't know about suggested it would not be. Also, 'I hold it to be an endorsement, full and complete, of all the leading measures inaugurated by the present Administration, looking to the final extirpation of slavery from our land' – reference no doubt to the election platform upon which Lincoln was re-elected. Lastly, it 'means that the Constitution of the United States shall be so changed that slavery can never again exist in any part of the United States' – Douglass the now enthusiastic proponent of Constitutional amendments.[90]

'Yet', Douglass admitted, 'it is plain that our work is not yet done … Shall all progress cease as soon as the goading lash of military necessity is withheld from our backs? … the war is still upon us'. The outcome of the election also meant, thankfully, that 'the people … will not return the sword to its scabbard until the rebels shall disband their armies and lay down their arms'. By then, for certain,

---

[88] Marx and Engels 1975–2004k, p. 20. We address in Appendix B Wulf Hund's tendentious reading of Marx's letter: 'The black Americans were capable of being "emancipated", but, as an "enchained race", they were not seen as subjects of this process', Hund 2021, p. 87.

[89] For ambassador Charles Adams's 28 January 1865 reply on behalf of Lincoln, see Marx and Engels 2016, p. 157. Also, Marx and Engels 1975–2004v, p. 86. For details surrounding Marx's letter, see K. Anderson 2010, pp. 109–11, Nimtz 2003, pp. 120–3, and P. Foner 1981a, pp. 84–5.

[90] Blassingame and McKivigan 1991, pp. 33–6.

Douglass acknowledged that developments on the battlefield were determinant for 'progress'. Nothing could be assured until a decisive military defeat of the slave holders.[91]

As the de facto head of the fledgling international organisation, Marx could only devote limited attention to events on the other side of the Atlantic. The birth of the IWA, spawned in part by those events, signalled that the revolutionary baton had now passed back to Europe. It fell to his partner, still in Manchester, to stay on top of the course of the War. Engels's renewed correspondence with Weydemeyer, now a Colonel in the Union Army in Missouri, gave him a more accurate portrait of the War. For the first time in almost three years he sounded optimistic about Union prospects. As Engels told Weydemeyer on 24 November, 'the tide of conquest is rolling slowly but surely onward, and, in the course of 1865, at all events the moment will undoubtedly come when the organised resistance of the South will fold up like a pocket-knife'.[92] Then, as he wrote to a relative six weeks later – and presciently – 'The South has but one army left, that at Richmond. That will assuredly be quite decisively beaten in the present year, and with that the defence of the South by armies will be at an end. A guerrilla war, brigandry, etc., may then ensue and will probably do so into the next year'. Engels then commented on a proposal that Confederate president Jefferson Davis had recently made to enlist Black slaves in the Confederate army. 'If the South arms its Negroes, that will be so much the better for the North'. But, astutely, 'they will care not to. At the last moment if at all. The Negroes are not so stupid as to allow themselves to be massacred for the whip that flays their backs'.[93]

Engels proved to be essentially right about Davis's proposal. To actually carry it out would violate, as his Confederate slave-holding colleagues increasingly recognised, the very raison d'etre of their project that Alexander Stephens made so clear in his aforementioned 'corner-stone' speech. Exactly for that reason, the proposal, authorised on 23 March, 'at the last moment', was fecklessly implemented – if that – owing to the less than enthusiastic support for it by the slaveholders.[94] Two months later, Douglass seemed to have thought that

---

91   Blassingame and McKivigan 1991, p. 36.
92   Marx and Engels 1975–2004v, p. 39.
93   Marx and Engels 1975–2004v, pp. 61.
94   Davis originally opposed the idea but in November 1864 'approached the matter gingerly' and told the Confederate Congress that if he had to choose between subjugation or employing the slave as a soldier he would choose the latter. McPherson 2014, pp. 229–35. Davis 'signed and released General Order No. 14' on 23 March 1865 authorising Black enlistment in the Confederate Army. For details about 'at the last moment', see McCurry 2010, pp. 325–52; and B. Levine 2006, pp. 124–8.

the slaveholders could 'have employed the negro to fight for them' as long as Blacks were not allowed to vote.[95] But the right to vote was irrelevant, as Engels might have predicted. The Confederacy's 'at the last moment' experiment in racial equality didn't work because the 'Negroes', amongst other reasons, as the evidence suggests, were 'not so stupid as to allow them to be massacred for the whip that flays their backs'. Some slaveholders actually thought – their stupidity – they could have their overseers supervise the conduct of their slaves in battle.[96]

Lastly, an apparent mea culpa on Engels's part. 'There will certainly still be moments when things look better for the South than they do now, but we have seen that happen too often before, and I shall not be deceived by that. Such moments are merely a respite'.[97] Three years of prognosticating about the course of the War that often shortened the odds for the North had chastened Engels.

To Marx on 7 February 1865, Engels noted 'the only army the SOUTHERNERS now have is Lee's [Army of Northern Virginia]; everything depends on its destruction'.[98] And on 4 March to Engels, at the very end of a letter with details about IWA-related matters, Marx added almost incidentally: 'It seems all up with CONFEDERACY'.[99] Not quite. But Lee's defeat at Richmond and surrender to Grant at Appomattox on 9 April, almost four years to the day after the attack on Fort Sumter, marked a decisive turning point in the fight to end America's centuries-old peculiar institution.[100] When the news reached Fire-Eater Edmund Ruffin, he did the 'honorable' thing by putting the barrel of a gun into his mouth and taking his life, prompting someone to later quip that Ruffin had the distinction of firing 'the first and last shots' of the War.[101]

In the thick of the German Revolution of 1848–9, Marx and Engels coined the term 'parliamentary cretinism', a 'disorder' that inflicts its victims with the

---

95   Blassingame and McKivigan 1991, p. 85.
96   'On April 4', Bruce Levine reports, 'Confederate scout Moses Purnell Handy came upon some two dozen of those black soldiers laboring to fashion makeshift fortifications in a field. They were performing this task, the scout recalled, under the direction of several white officers and also "under the watchful eye of an overseer"'. B. Levine 2006, pp. 127–8,.
97   Marx and Engels 1975–2004v, p. 62.
98   Marx and Engels 1975–2004v, p. 82.
99   Marx and Engels 1975–2004v, p. 115.
100 Engels mistakenly thought that Lee did not surrender: Marx and Engels 1975–2004v, p. 147. Marx never made any explicit mention of Appomattox. For what Appomattox delivered and did not, see Downs 2015.
101 Maloy 2020.

mistaken belief that what takes place inside the legislative arena is the be all and end all of politics. To the contrary, they argued. Determinant in politics was what took place on the 'outside', especially on the barricades and the battlefield – a proposition we revisit in our Conclusion. Despite Lincoln's hope that his Emancipation Proclamation would motivate the enslaved to flee to Union lines, when Lee surrendered to Grant at Appomattox at least 80 percent of the enslaved were still in bondage.[102] Only when Union troops, in white and black skin, finally defeated the troops of the slaveholders, and occupied the South with soldiers, did America's peculiar institution effectively come to an end. Douglass immediately grasped its larger significance. When Richmond fell, the prelude to Appomattox, he engaged an adoring audience in Boston about the good news. '[W]hen an American', in his often catechistic style of speaking, 'asks me any questions concerning my race, what they ever did to prove their manhood ... to prove themselves entitled to liberty and protection in this Republic, my answer will be ... that the first soldiers who entered the long-beleaguered and long-desired city of Richmond, on the heels of the retreating rebels, were black soldiers. (Renewed applause)'.[103]

Neither a presidential executive order nor Congress's eventual passage of the 13th amendment could do what only armed men on the battlefield could – the arena where real power was exercised. To his credit, Lincoln admitted as much as he explained in his Second Inaugural Address a month before Appomattox: 'The progress of our arms, upon which all else chiefly depends'. And for that very reason, the War, if necessary, Lincoln added, would, in his immortal words, continue 'until every drop of blood drawn with the lash shall be paid with another drawn by the sword'.[104] Vindication, therefore, for all the ink Marx and Engels spilled, in contrast to Douglass, on the military side of the War. Their thirteen months on the barricades and battlefields of the German Revolution – the kind of experience Douglass never had – prepared them to do just that.

---

102   Oakes 2013, p. *xiv*. Gallagher 2011b. As Ed Ayers explained more than a decade ago, 'some enslaved people were able to escape to Union lines within weeks of the beginning of the War, and vast numbers remained firmly bound by slavery in 1865 as they had been in 1861'. Ayers and Gallagher 2010. Oakes examines late-stage emancipation – state emancipation, military emancipation, and the ratification of the 13th Amendment – in Oakes 2013 on pp. 476–85 and indicates that 'more slaves may have been emancipated in a single month – December in 1865 – than had been freed in the four preceding years of war'. Oakes 2013, p. 485. See also, Downs 2015, pp. 41–2.
103   Blassingame and McKivigan 1991, p. 71.
104   Lincoln's Second Inaugural Address, https://www.gilderlehrman.org/history-resources/sp otlight-primary-source/president-lincolns-second-inaugural-address-1865. Also Fehrenbacher 1989b, pp. 686–7.

5 'A Missed Revolutionary Opportunity'

Lincoln's choice of Andrew Johnson to be his running mate in the 1864 election was arguably, in hindsight, his most fateful decision – the proverbial good idea at the time. As the Union Military Governor of Tennessee during the War, Johnson dealt 'sternly' with the state's aristocratic plantation owners, a layer of Southern society he strongly disliked owing to their contempt for the white plebeians, the 'swinish multitude' as Ruffin called them, from which he originated.[105] Johnson, in a speech in 1864, had even called for the confiscation of the property of the Confederate leaders.[106] It's not clear what Douglass thought of Lincoln's choice in real-time. But after the Democratic Party convention, Douglass enthusiastically supported the Lincoln-Johnson ticket. Lincoln's assassination on 14 April 1865, which made Johnson the Seventeenth President, impacted Douglass in a major way. 'Abraham Lincoln', he wrote in a draft speech on 5 June, 'while unsurpassed in his devotion to the white race, was also in a sense hitherto without example, emphatically, the black man's President; the first to show any respect for their rights as men'.[107] Lincoln's death prompted Douglass, apparently, to unhesitatingly embrace Lincoln for the first time.

As for Lee's surrender to Grant and Lincoln's assassination, Marx, by then the de facto head of the IWA and with all the responsibilities that entailed, only had time to tell Engels on 1 May that the 'CHIVALRY OF THE SOUTH has ended worthily. In addition, Lincoln's ASSASSINATION was the most stupid act they could have committed. *Johnson* is STERN, INFLEXIBLE, REVENGEFUL and as a former POOR WHITE has a deadly hatred of the oligarchy. He will make less fuss about these fellows, and, because of the treachery, he will find the TEMPER of the North commensurate with his INTENTIONS'.[108] As is so often the case with Marx, his mistakes – in this instance about the 'poor white' – are as instructive as what he got right.

To encourage Johnson to do the right thing, Marx, on behalf of the IWMA, wrote an address to the new president, signed by Marx and thirty-seven other members on 13 May 1865. The last three sentences are instructive:

---

105 'Sternly' included raising Black regiments in Tennessee in September 1863, when slavery was still legal, exempt from the Emancipation Proclamation, and in October 1864 announcing emancipation in the state before a crowd of Black onlookers. R. Levine 2021, pp. 17, 19–20.
106 Graf and Haskins, 1983, p. 726.
107 Draft speech, June 5, 1865, Frederick Douglass Papers at the Library of Congress – Series Browse List. See also, Oakes 2007, p. 256.
108 Marx and Engels 1975–2004v, pp. 150–1. For details about Marx's IWA activities, see Nimtz 2000, Chapters Seven, Eight, and Nine.

> Yours, Sir, has become the task to uproot by the law what has been felled by the sword, to preside over the arduous work of political reconstruction and social regeneration. A profound sense of your great mission will save you from any compromise with stern duties. You will never forget that, to initiate the new era of the emancipation of labour, the American people devolved the responsibilities of leadership upon two men of labour – the one Abraham Lincoln, the other Andrew Johnson.[109]

Whether Marx actually believed that Johnson would not 'compromise with stern duties', the letter was certainly a tactful effort to get the president to do just that, namely, to deal resolutely with the former slaveholders.

On 10 May, a day after Marx had written the letter, Douglass intervened in a debate at a meeting of the Anti-Slavery Society in New York City about whether to dissolve the organisation given the impending adoption of the 13th Amendment. He argued for its continuance despite the amendment. 'Slavery is not abolished until the black man has the ballot. While the Legislatures of the South retain the right to pass laws making any discrimination between black and white, slavery still lives there (applause)'.[110] Though Douglass made no mention of Johnson, he and Marx were clearly on the same page about what needed to be done, 'to uproot by the law what has been felled by the sword ... the arduous work of political reconstruction and social regeneration'. For Douglass, the vote, again, was the only guarantee for doing that, including also the right of the former slaves to exercise the Second Amendment right to bear arms.

The new president enjoyed for about six weeks amiable relations with many African American leaders such as John Mercer Langston and once leading voices of abolition like William Lloyd Garrison and Charles Sumner. That all came to an abrupt halt – likely also for Douglass – with Johnson's issuance on 29 May of an Amnesty Proclamation for former slave-holding oligarchs who had rebelled against the federal government with essentially the only condition that they swear allegiance to the Constitution. Pardons would be granted by the president upon request, requiring Johnson's one-time 'betters' to come kowtowing to the one-time 'poor white'.[111] 'Johnson's policy', as soon as Marx learned about the Proclamation, 'likes me not', he told Engels. 'A ludicrous

---

109 Marx and Engels 1975–2004k, p. 100.
110 Blassingame and McKivigan 1991, p. 83.
111 On the Amnesty proclamation see, R. Levine 2021, pp. 54–7. On the amiable relations with African American leaders see, pp. 66–71. See also, Wineapple 2020, p. 25. https://www.presidency.ucsb.edu/documents/proclamation-179-granting-full-pardon-and-amnesty-for-the-offense-treason-against-the.

AFFECTATION of severity towards individuals; hitherto excessively VACILLAT-
ING and weak when it comes down to it. The reaction has already set in in
America and will soon be much fortified if the present lackadaisical attitude
is not ended immediately'.[112] Marx's warning proved to be tragically accurate.

Engels agreed with his partner. 'Mr Johnson's policy', three weeks later on
15 July, 'is less and less to my liking too. NIGGER-hatred is coming out more and
more violently, and he is relinquishing all his power vis-a-vis the old lords in the
South. If this should continue, all the old secessionist scoundrels', quite accurately, 'will be in Congress in Washington in 6 months time'. Engels then looked
forward to an alternative scenario.

> Without COLOURED SUFFRAGE nothing can be done, and Johnson is
> leaving it up to the defeated, the ex-slaveowners, to decide on that. It is
> absurd. Nevertheless, one must still reckon on things turning out differ-
> ently from what these barons imagined. After all, the majority of them
> have been completely ruined and will be glad to sell land to immigrants
> and speculators from the North. The latter will arrive soon enough and
> make a good number of changes. I think the MEAN WHITES will gradu-
> ally die out. Nothing more will become of this RACE; those who are left
> after 2 generations will merge with the immigrants to make a completely
> different RACE. The NIGGERS will probably turn into small SQUATTERS
> as in Jamaica. Thus ultimately the oligarchy will go to pot after all, but the
> process could be accomplished immediately at one fell swoop, whereas it
> is now being drawn out.[113]

As with his partner, what Engels didn't get right about the future is often as
instructive as what he did. Douglass, to be noted, held a similar position about
'the mean whites'.[114] Back in January, he had opined that 'that enmity will not
die out in a year, will not die out in an age', indeed, 'gradually' as Engels wrote
and history later confirmed – but not necessarily in the way the latter envisioned.[115] Nevertheless, Marx and Engels were right to argue that 'immediately',
as Marx put it, after the military defeat of the slavocracy was the time to put the
final nail in its coffin. Nota bene, also, Engels's point about the indispensabilty
of 'coloured suffrage' – exactly what Douglass was arguing for at that moment.
Marxist scholar George Novack, almost a century later, posited three stages in

---

112   Marx and Engels 1975–2004v, p. 163.
113   Marx and Engels 1975–2004v, pp. 167–8.
114   Regarding the label 'mean whites' in that epoch, see Isenberg 2016, pp. 179–80.
115   Blassingame and McKivigan 1991, p. 64.

the fall of Reconstruction. Regarding the first, '1865–66 ... marked time, and missed its most favorable opportunities'.[116] Marx and Engels would have agreed.

6 Weydemeyer's 'On the Negro Vote'

Engels, as noted earlier, was back in touch with leading Marx party member Joseph Weydemeyer and apparently convinced the now retired Lt. Col. to write a series of articles on the three issues he mentioned in his letter to Marx: Black suffrage, the future of the 'mean whites', and, most importantly, the prospect of land ownership for the former slaves. 'On the Negro Vote', the title of Weydemeyer's three articles, appeared in the German-language St. Louis *Westliche Post* of September 1865.[117] The first one addressed the big picture, six months after Appomattox. The scene was increasingly alarming. 'There are', he cautioned, 'many signs that the final struggle with slavery in this country will be even more difficult'. With all the pardons that Johnson was issuing, and the fact that the former slaves were now fully counted as part of the population rather than three-fifths of them as under the pre-War regime, the former slave oligarchs would have more political clout not only in Congress but also in the Electoral College and all that implied. Weydemeyer ended with a warning that echoed the editorial opinion of the influential Black-owned New Orleans *Tribune* which had been playing a vanguard role in the fight for racial equality.[118] 'It already appears as if the victory in the field will not be accompanied by a political victory'.[119]

As a tiny minority of the South, the former oligarchs would need the support of the 'poor whites' for maintaining their power – the subject of Weydemeyer's second article. 'Their horrifying lack of education prevents them from understanding their true interests and thus directly opposing the lords of the land ... cut off from the wider world on their poor farms, they share the prejudices

---

116 Novack 2013, p. 347.
117 Angela Zimmerman's translation of Weydemeyer's articles in her *The Civil War in the United States* (Marx and Engels 2016) is of enormous value for scholarship on the Marx party. Efford 2013, pp. 128–9, quotes a few sentences from the articles. There is no mention of them in Obermann 1947 or Obermann 1968.
118 Scores of New Orleans Blacks, including Jean Baptiste Roudanez, the punisher of the paper, petitioned Lincoln in February 1864 for the right to vote, referred to approvingly by the president in his very last speech – provoking, apparently, John Wilkes Booth to carry out his dastardly act shortly afterward. About the speech and what Lincoln actually said, see Fehrenbacher 1989b, pp. 697–701.
119 Marx and Engels 2016, p. 170.

of the slaveholders and cannot completely free themselves from their political leadership ... They have always been the most willing tools in the hands of the southern oligarchy, hunting down their slaves and fighting their battles for them, even though their only reward was poverty and contempt'.[120] Herewith, then, was Weydemeyer's explanation for the anti-Black 'prejudices' of 'poor whites'. It complemented the insights that Marx offered early in the War, specifically, 'the bait' of upward mobility for plebian white Southerners. There was, in other words, a material basis for their 'prejudices' and willingness to act on behalf of the slave oligarchs.

Douglass would probably have agreed with Weydemeyer's explanation because he continued to adhere to his thesis, first proposed in his famous 'I'm an American Citizen' speech in 1862, that such 'prejudices' were due to social circumstances, specifically, the practice of slavery. As he reiterated in January 1865, enslavement and the 'prejudices' associated with it could happen 'to any race'.[121] And in a written response to President Andrew Johnson with whom he and a Black delegation had met on 7 February 1866, Douglass engaged the president's charges about anti-white attitudes of Blacks.

> The hostility between the whites and blacks of the South is easily explained. It has its root and sap in the relation of slavery and was incited on both sides by the cunning of the slave masters. Those masters secured their ascendency over both the poor whites and the blacks by putting enmity between them. They divided both to conquer each.

Echoing Weydemeyer about the anti-Black actions of 'poor whites ... it was from this class that their masters received their slave-catchers, slave-drivers, and overseers ... Now, sir, you cannot but perceive that, the cause of this hatred removed, the effect must be removed also'.[122] In short, Douglass argued, 'prejudices' on either side were not inherent or inevitable but due to the peculiar institution. Though Johnson proved to be impervious to Douglass's argument, Marx, Engels, and Weydemeyer would have agreed with him.

So, if 'poor whites', Weydemeyer asked, could not be depended on to advance the promise of the War, namely, the abolition of slavery, then to whom to look? 'And to the Negroes?' Yes, his answer.

---

120   About 'poor whites' as understood in that epoch, see Isenberg 2016, pp. 176–86. For a superb study of poor whites in the pre-war South, see Merritt 2017.
121   Blassingame and McKivigan 1991, pp. 65–6.
122   P. Foner 1955, p. 192.

During the war they stood with the Union, gave vigorous support to our cause, and contributed their best energies to the victory of our arms. And where their interests coincided with our own they were also the interests of progress and civilization. Has the situation today so changed that President Johnson now believes he has to protect the poor whites against these same Negroes, who helped break the slaveholders' yoke, which pressed with equal weight on both of them? Let us forget the views of the president and see what the good of the country requires.[123]

Now the reader likely understood the title for Weydemeyer's series, 'On the Negro Vote'. Douglass had said almost exactly the same in January 1865 to the Massachusetts Anti-Slavery Society. 'Now, where will you find the strength to counterbalance [the 'hostile'] spirit [still prevailing in the South], if you do not find it in the negroes of the South! They are your friends, and have always been your friends'.[124] Thus, the reason Blacks merited the right to vote. 'Slavery', again, later in May, 'is not abolished until the black man has the ballot'.[125]

Weydemeyer's last article began soberly and with a view toward what is to be done. 'All reports from the South indicate that violence or the threat of violence remains necessary to convince former slaveholders that the North is serious about ending slavery and that it will not under any circumstances tolerate a return to the old conditions. To uphold the new order in this way requires the martial law exercised by the Freedmen's Bureau and an army of occupation to enforce it'.[126] Douglass, more than a year later in the December 1866 *Atlantic Monthly*, could see the need for 'the Federal government armed with despotic power' and 'a federal agent stationed at every cross-road' in order to enforce the 'general assertion of human rights'. However, he added, this 'of course, cannot be done, and ought not even if it could. The true way and the easiest way is to make our government entirely consistent with itself, and give to every loyal citizen the effective franchise – a right and power which will be ever present, and will form a wall of fire for his protection'.[127] For Douglass, therefore, the

---

123 Marx and Engels 2016, p. 171.
124 Blassingame and McKivigan 1991, p. 64.
125 Blassingame and McKivigan 1991, p. 83.
126 Marx and Engels 2016, p. 172.
127 P. Foner 1955, pp. 199–200. David Blight seemingly ignores Douglass's aversion to the federal despotism option when he writes 'Douglass advocated what he called "something like a despotic central government, to vanquish, as much as possible, the tradition of states' rights"'. Blight 2018, p. 471.

franchise, and not an army of occupation, would protect the rights won on the battlefield from the determination of their former masters to subjugate them anew.

In February 1866, Douglass had been more sober. He told an interracial audience in Washington D.C. that "the iron heart of slavery" was not "softened" by the "leniency" and conciliatory attitudes already emanating from Northern populations. "Nothing will ever soften it," Douglass explained insightfully, "save the military power of the United States."[128] By December, as the occupation of the South had weakened considerably, Douglass again looked toward universal enfranchisement as the panacea.

Yet, from the other side of the Atlantic, the foremost liberal of the nineteenth century, John Stuart Mill, agreed more with what Weydemeyer proposed. In a September 1865 letter, Mill envisioned the need for 'censorship' and a 'military dictatorship' over the recalcitrant opponents of 'freedom for the negroes' that might have to last for 'two generations' in order that 'the stain which the position of slave masters burns into the very souls of the privileged population can be expected to fade'. What about the legality of such measures, Mill asked? '[S]crupples about legality' seem 'wholly out of place ... A state of civil war suspends all legal rights, and all social compacts, between the combatants'.[129] Douglass's opposition to the measures Weydemeyer proposed were not, in other words, necessarily inherent to a liberal perspective. Or, perhaps, better, Mill proved to be more the realist than Douglass. Events on the ground would soon test these competing perspectives.

Weydemeyer didn't ignore the price of an 'occupation ... an extremely crippling influence on the growth of our prosperity'. And that price, he recognised, was increasingly seen by Northern toilers as a burden to be rid of as soon as possible. But prior occupations from the very beginning of the War revealed that 'almost everywhere we have missed the opportunity to introduce free labor into southern life'.[130] In his first article Weydemeyer addressed the point Engels had raised in his July letter to Marx, namely, that the former slaves would become 'small squatters as in Jamaica'. About that outcome, he opined: 'Nothing hindered the development of the English and French colon-

---

128 Blassingame and McKivigan 1991, pp. 109–10.
129 Nimtz 2019b, p. 79. In distinct contrast to Mill was another British liberal, Lord Acton, famous for his 1887 dictum, 'power tends to corrupt, absolute power tends to corrupt absolutely'. Before then Acton had staunchly supported the Confederacy in the War, on the grounds of states rights against the central government, and opposed Lincoln, an example of someone with too much power. See Losurdo 2011, pp. 153–4.
130 Marx and Engels 2016, p. 172.

ies more than the adherence of their planters to the old labor system, even after their governments had abolished slavery. Instead of embracing free labor without reservation', argued Weydemeyer, 'they sought out new ways to keep former slaves bound to the soil' – thus, the squatter outcome in Jamaica.[131] But that result was not inevitable, he argued in the third article, owing to the sole instance of the introduction of 'free labor into southern life' by a Union army – 'the Sea Islands of South Carolina, and there the experiment met with happy success'.[132] Union army occupation could, therefore, be remunerative for 'our prosperity'.

To make his case, Weydemeyer reproduced a New York *World* report about the 'third year of the experiment' in which the former slaves were cultivating more than 200,000 acres on 'the islands along the coast' and reaping an impressive profit – the advantages of 'free labor'. Beyond the former slaves, who else in the South might be won to support such an 'experiment'? The former oligarchs? 'Most of them cooperate only against their will and prefer to waste their time and energies on vain plans to restore the old order'. What about the 'poor whites?'

> We cannot count at all on their current generation, raised in indolence and in disdain for work. There only remains the much despised Negroes, who, along with the white craftsmen of the cities, represent practically the only workers of the South. Why not repeat the very successful Sea Island experiment in other regions? Why not transfer all the lands that have been abandoned, confiscated, or forfeited through tax default to free Negroes to cultivate independently?

An alliance of what would be a Black yeomanry and an incipient urban white proletariat was, in other words, Weydemeyer's vision for a new South.

> But this experiment can be carried out without continuing the military occupation of the South only if we also give the new representatives of free labor the political power to protect their newly acquired rights. We do not wish to deny that a certain degree of political education is necessary to exercise the right to vote independently. But it is not necessary to acquire this education from books – life is the best school for this, and the violent conflict through which the Negroes won their freedom has made

---

131   Marx and Engels 2016, p. 169.
132   Marx and Engels 2016, p. 172.

them understand their own interests more quickly than would have been possible in any other way.[133]

Douglass would have comfortably been on the same political page with Weydemeyer about suffrage for Black men, his mantra for more than two years. But his near silence – as far as we can determine – about 'the experiment' in the Sea Islands of South Carolina is deafening – and telling.[134] Like most Republicans, he opposed the confiscation and redistribution of land – what Weydemeyer proposed. Radical Republican Thaddeus Stevens was the exception to the rule. Also in September 1865, Stevens 'called for confiscating the plantations of those southerners who owned at least two thousand acres of land'. But he couldn't win his Republican colleagues to that position. Bruce Levine explains,

> The principal obstacle confronting Steven's proposals was his party's aversion to abolishing the private-property rights of plantation owners in peacetime. The challenge of treason and armed rebellion had reconciled those northern politicians to the abolition of a form of property that they already considered sinful and illegitimate – human property. But most balked at infringing upon claims to another form of property, property in land, that remained as close to their hearts as ever. And many feared that black landowners would refuse to grow cotton (a crop they associated with slavery), thereby harming New England's textile industry.[135]

Unique in the immediate aftermath of the Confederacy's surrender, it is worth noting here, is the example of former Georgia slave owner Charles Hopkins. Together with Black activist Aaron Bradley, a Boston migrant, Hopkins sought to forge an alliance of poor whites and the once-enslaved to confiscate plantation lands and redistribute them amongst the toilers themselves. Hopkins, who knew the former slave-owning class better than anyone, was prescient in November 1865 in an interview. 'Give a man a piece of land, let him have a cabin of his own upon his own lot, and then you make him free. Civil rights are good for nothing, the ballot is good for nothing, till you make some men of every

---

133 Marx and Engels 2016, p. 173. Julie Saville's *The Work of Reconstruction: From Slave to Wage Laborer in South Carolina, 1860–1870* (Saville 1994) remains the authoritative account of the 'experiment'.
134 Wendell Phillips, unlike Douglass, endorsed the Port Royal experience and used it as evidence to show that the increased leisure time the eight-hour workday would provide free labour would incentivise workers to increase their productivity. Stewart 1986, p. 262.
135 B. Levine 2021, pp. 227, 230–1. See also, Hahn 2003, p. 146. Owing to his unique position, Draper 2005, p. 235, labels Stevens as "the last bourgeois revolutionary."

class landholders'.[136] Subsequent events tragically confirmed Hopkins's forecast. Except for Stevens, and perhaps Charles Sumner in the Senate, no other liberal voices in the North, including Douglass's, championed what Hopkins and Bradley sought to realise.[137]

Weydemeyer ended his series on an optimistic note. First, in praise of 'the modern worker' whose historical task was to bring about the full industrialisation of the United States in order to produce the gravediggers of capitalism. The War had been educational in all kinds of ways, especially about the South. 'The more allies he gains for the great fight between labor and monopolizing capital, which we see organized and prepared before our very eyes, the more certain and speedy his victory. But where else in the South will he find these allies, if not among the workers themselves, regardless of what ancestry they have to thank for their skin color'. A real fight with 'monopolising capital' would have to include 'the worker who has a vote in the election of representatives', that is, Black workers. Second, in enabling the former slave holding oligarchs to return to power, Johnson hastened the day of reckoning, the necessary showdown. In anticipation of the 1866 elections, 'Congress must then choose a rapid reconstruction of Reconstruction, with the political equality of the Negro as its basis, or new disturbances and race wars a la St. Domingo [i.e. Haiti]. The newly armed [southern] aristocrat freed from military government [under the Union occupation] will quickly forget the measures forced on him, but he will no longer find the subjugated slave, unconscious of his own power, in the demobilized Negro, now trained in the use of weapons ... political equality of the Negro is the only means of permanently eliminating this danger'. As Malcolm X would say almost exactly a century later during the Second Reconstruction: 'the ballot or the bullet'.

Finally, the 'solution ... lies in the hands of the next congress, the political future of its members in the hands of the people'.[138] Weydemeyer was prescient about the Second Session of the 39th Congress. After reconvening in December 1866, it took the Reconstruction project into its own hands and out of Johnson's, instituting what became known, with good reason, as Radical Reconstruction.

---

136 Braxton, 2023, p. 89. For a full account of the Hopkins-Bradley project and outcome, see Braxton's Thesis, which is, as of this writing, being readied for book publication.
137 Eric Foner notes, 'Bradley emerged as one of the few black leaders from the North to become actively involved in freedmen's land struggles'. E. Foner 1988, p. 290. Though Wendell Phillips, as early as 1863, supported land confiscation and redistribution, that demand, in his mind, took a back seat to voting rights by the time the 15th Amendment was ratified. See Stewart 1986, pp. 247–94.
138 Marx and Engels 2016, pp. 174–5.

Seven months after Weydemeyer's articles, and nine months before the convening of the Second Session, Marx wrote to Engels: 'The phase of the Civil War over, only now have the UNITED STATES really entered the revolutionary phase, and the European WISEACRES who believe in the omnipotence of Mr. Johnson will soon be disappointed'.[139] Johnson, who came within one vote of being convicted in his impeachment trial by the Senate, had been reduced to a political nullity by the end of his presidency.[140] Perhaps Weydemeyer's last article informed Marx's accurate assessment.

Weydemeyer's articles constitute the Marx party's most detailed position on what needed to be done following the War. Being on the scene, unlike Marx and Engels, he could see what needed to be done more concretely than they could from afar. Noteworthy is the key role of the Black proletariat in Weydemeyer's vision, a social layer that only the end of chattel slavery could make possible – why, therefore, it did not figure in any of Marx's and Engels's pronouncements. Not until the twentieth century, however, would a hereditary proletariat in both white and black skin come into its own. Tragically, not only for him but also for the Marx party, Weydemeyer, at age 48, died a year later, a victim of a cholera epidemic. The party was never able to find someone with his political acumen and experience to lead their work in America – at least in that epoch.

At a large celebration on 28 September 1865 in London on the first anniversary of its founding, the IWMA, now 'known all over Europe, and ... [with] many friends in America' – one of whom was Weydemeyer – singled out 'the American people' for special honour. 'America was now free from the pollution of slavery. The South had appealed from the ballot to the bullet, and are now beaten at both'.[141] An address 'To the People of the United States of America' – unlike the May message which was addressed to Johnson – was adopted by the meeting. It began with congratulations for the victory over the slavocracy but ended with 'a word of counsel for the future' in light of the increasingly retrograde consequences for the former slaves due to the Johnson administration's reconciliation with their former masters.

> As injustice to a section of your people has produced such direful results, let that cease. Let your citizens of today be declared free and equal, without reserve. If you fail to give them citizen's rights, while you demand citizen's duties, there will yet remain a struggle for the future which may

---

139   Marx and Engels 1975–2004v, p. 269.
140   For details of Johnson's impeachment, see Wineapple 2020, pp. 175–369.
141   Marx and Engels 2016, p. 185. Marx and Engels 1992, s.1525.

stain your country with your people's blood ... We warn you then, as brothers in the common cause, to remove every shackle from freedom's limb, and your victory will be complete.[142]

The 'ballot or the bullet' – not unlike what Weydemeyer had argued only weeks earlier. It's not clear if Marx penned the message but it clearly reflected what he and Engels advocated in their correspondence.[143] Given Marx's central role in the organisation at that moment, it's unlikely the message would have been delivered without his agreement. In no uncertain terms, the organisation he effectively led 'warned' the 'American people' that if full political equality failed to be granted to the former slaves they would have a new rebellion on their hands.[144] Only in that way could the 'victory' over the slavocracy 'be complete'. Douglass would have been in full accord. Whether he would have been willing to appeal to the threat of violence is doubtful. Universal male suffrage sufficed for Douglass.

Without a newspaper to air his opinions, and in search of a 'new vocation', the paper trail for Douglass in the immediate years after the end of the War is relatively thin.[145] The first documented evidence of his discontent with Johnson came in September 1865 in Baltimore where he warned about 'the persistent determination of the present Executive of the nation ... to hold and treat us in a degraded relation'.[146] In February 1866, as already noted, he and a group of Black leaders met with the seventeenth president to air their differences in what proved to be a spectacularly unproductive encounter; thus, the reason for Douglass's aforementioned follow-up letter to Johnson.[147] Things continued to deteriorate for Blacks under the Johnson administration. The latest example was the bloody riot in Memphis at the beginning of May, when scores of Blacks

---

142 Marx and Engels 2016, p. 187. For a slightly different translation of the message, see Schlüter 2013, pp. 200–1. The 'direful results' probably refers to the notorious Black Codes of the post-War Southern governments that Johnson instituted, a way to bring in a new form of enslavement, a kind of peonage. For details on the Black Codes and what Eric Foner calls 'The Anatomy of Presidential Reconstruction' see, E. Foner 1988, pp. 198–216.

143 Although Philip Foner claims Marx's authorship of the message (P. Foner 1981a, p. 92), the editors of the *MEGA* do not include it as a writing of Marx (see 1 Bd 20). Marx, thirteen years later, seems to have confused it with his message to Lincoln, Marx and Engels 1975–2004m, p. 236.

144 On other efforts to counter Johnson policies within the German-American working class political milieu, see Nimtz 2003, p. 143.

145 Blight 2018, pp. 464–5, 468, 470.

146 Blight 2018, pp. 472–3.

147 For a transcript of the meeting, see Blassingame and McKivigan 1991, pp. 96–9.

were murdered by racist gangs – evidence that Johnson's conciliatory approach to the former slaveholders only emboldened the counterrevolution.

Marx was, thus, 'delighted', as he told François Lafargue, the father of his future son-in-law Paul – the latter with ancestral roots in Africa – on 12 November 1866, 'by the defeat of President Johnson in the latest elections … The workers in the North have at last fully understood that white labour will never be emancipated so long as black labour is still stigmatised'.[148] These were the elections that saw the defeat of Johnson's Democratic Party allies in Congress, bringing in Republican Party replacements who would institute Radical Reconstruction – what Weydemeyer hoped for fourteen months earlier. 'For the first time in American history', declares Eric Foner, 'civil rights for blacks played a central part in a major party's national campaign … More than anything else, the election became a referendum on the Fourteenth Amendment' – the Constitution's first embrace of the right of legal equality.[149]

Because the new amendment, however, did not contain the right to vote, Douglass criticised it – 'an "unfortunate blunder" on the part of Congress that created an "emasculated citizenship" for African Americans'.[150] For the umpteenth time, he reiterated his bottom line position in the January 1867 issue of the *Atlantic Monthly*: 'There is but one safe and constitutional way to banish that mischievous hope from the South, and that is by lifting the laborer beyond the unfriendly political designs of his former master. Give the negro the elective franchise, and you at once destroy the purely sectional policy, and wheel the Southern States into line with national interests and national objects'.[151] For Douglas, exercising political power took place at the ballot box; for Marx and Engels, on the barricades and battlefields – the lessons of 1848–9 and another essential difference between our two protagonists. Only because of what had taken place on the latter terrain, registered with the surrender at Appomattox, could universal suffrage become, they held, a possibility for the first time in the United States. But that conquest would take longer than they could have imagined.

---

148 Marx and Engels 1975–2004v, p. 334. More on Marx's relations with François and Paul Lafargue in Appendix B.
149 E. Foner 1988, p. 267.
150 R. Levine 2021, p. 135. P. Foner 1955, p. 204.
151 McKivigan 2021, pp. 119–20. On the class composition of those in the Black population leading the demand for suffrage both before and after the War, see E. Foner 1988, pp. 110–18.

7   Douglass and Marx on the Same Political Page – Almost

Marx's abovementioned point, communicated to the father of his future son-in law, about 'white labour' was, except for an important qualifier discussed below, drawn almost verbatim from the manuscript he was about to take to Germany to be published, the long-awaited *Capital*. 'In the United States of North America, every independent movement of the workers was paralyzed so long as slavery disfigured a part of the Republic. Labour cannot emancipate itself in the white skin where in the black it is branded'. Note the similarity between this and what he wrote to Lincoln three years earlier: 'While the working men, the true political power of the North, allowed slavery to defile their own republic; while before the Negro, mastered and sold without his concurrence, they boasted it the highest prerogative of the white-skinned labourer to sell him and choose his own master; they were unable to attain the true freedom of labour or to support their European brethren in their struggle for emancipation'. His point to Lincoln about 'white-skinned labour' being 'unable to attain the true freedom of labour', became in *Capital* 'every independent movement of the workers was paralyzed'. Marx employed the past tense in his first sentence in the *Capital* passages. But in the next sentence – 'Labour cannot emancipate itself' – he shifted to the present, referring to 1867. This suggests that Marx recognised that the battle to end the 'prerogatives of white-skinned labour', two years after Appomattox, had yet to be won. He certainly knew about the rapid backsliding of Johnson, '*a dirty tool of the* SLAVEHOLDERS', as Marx told a French member of the IWMA on 27 August 1867.[152] Not only was victory over the slavocracy still to be consolidated but white workers could use some advice – their own liberation from the exploitation of capital couldn't be accomplished at the expense or denial of the fullest equality for fellow workers of a different skin colour.

Two years later, the *New York Times* reported on a 'survey' about the attitudes of German workers toward Blacks. They were 'the only ones in the city "who appear to be really uninfluenced by this intolerant spirit of prejudice against the color of the negro" that in shops dominated by the Germans, a black worker received "fair wages – quite as much as ... a whiteman of equal skill and powers of work", and that the German workers treated the black "properly, and not simply as *the nigger*"'.[153] While there is no reason to suggest some kind of causal link between this 1869 report and what Marx published in 1867, there is

---

152   Marx and Engels 1975–2004v, p. 414. He emphasised his point for fear that the French IWMA-affiliated newspaper had illusions in Johnson.
153   P. Foner 1977 p. 374n50.

no reason not to. More certain, it teaches that white working-class anti-Black prejudices in that moment were not inevitable. Circumstances proved to be more determinant.

Worth noting here is Douglass's remarkably similar point about race and class four years earlier in his February 1863 speech at the Cooper Institute in New York City on the lessons of the War:

> The first grand error of which this war is likely to cure us is: That a nation can outlaw one part of its people without endangering the rights and liberties of all the people. They will learn that they cannot put a chain on the ankle of the bondmen without finding the other end of it about their own necks. Hitherto the white laborer has been deluded into the belief that to degrade the black laborer is to elevate the white. We shall learn by-and-by that labor will always be degraded where idleness is the badge of respectability. Whence came the degrading phrases, fast growing popular before the war, 'hireling labor', 'greasy mechanics', 'mudsills of society'. The laborer should be 'owned by the capitalists'. – Poor 'white trash' – and a dozen others of the same class: They come from Slavery. I think I never saw anywhere such contempt for poor white people as in the South. ... the war of the Rebels – is a war of the rich against the poor. Let Slavery go down with the war, and let labor cease to be fettered, chained, flogged, and branded. Let it be paid honest wages for honest work, and then we shall see as never before, the laborers in all sections of this country rising to respectability and power.[154]

If ever Marx and Douglass came close to being exactly on the same political page, it must surely be what the two had to say, initially less than two years apart, about the social class/racial slavery nexus in America. But Douglass's last two sentences explain exactly why being on the same page need not necessarily mean being in the same paragraph, literally. If the revolutionary liberal thought that the end of chattel slavery ensured that labour would be paid 'honest wages for honest work' and rise to 'power', the communist would have respectfully demurred. Those two outcomes could only be realised with the abolition of capitalist relations of production, namely, a proletarian revolution – the last thing Douglass, based on his history, would have wanted to see.

American ruling class use of race to divide and rule the toilers offered lessons, Marx soon realised, for British politics. Thus, his epiphany in 1869–70 about the Irish question.

---

154 Blassingame 1985, pp. 562–3.

> The ordinary English worker hates the Irish worker as a competitor who forces down the STANDARD OF LIFE ... He harbours religious, social and national prejudices against him. His attitude towards him is roughly that of the POOR WHITES to the NIGGERS in the former slave states of the American Union ... This antagonism is kept artificially alive and intensified by the press, the pulpit, the comic papers, in short by all the means at the disposal of the ruling class.[155]

Douglass, in the first years of the War, began to say something quite similar about white working-class anti-Black prejudices.

Ending chattel slavery for the communist project had a different end than for the liberal project, even for its revolutionary edition. It was the only way, as the run-up to the War made increasingly clear, to ensure the survival and deepening of capitalist relations of production throughout the United States and, thereby, making more visible the fundamental contradiction between labour and capital.[156] Bourgeois society, as the *Manifesto* put it, 'has simplified the class antagonisms'. Socialist revolution, however, was not, Marx understood, on America's agenda anytime soon after 1865. In the Preface to *Capital*, he noted that 'Mr. Wade, vice-president of the United States declared in public meetings that, after the abolition of slavery, a radical change of the relations of capital and of property in land is next upon the order of the day. These are signs of the times'. But the 'signs', Marx immediately added, 'do not signify that tomorrow a miracle will happen. They show that, within the ruling classes themselves, a foreboding is dawning, that the present society is no solid crystal, but an organism capable of change, and is constantly changing'.[157]

Marx was referencing 'a widely publicized speech' in early 1867 of Sen. Benjamin Wade of Ohio, the president of the Senate and next in line for presidential succession, in which he asserted that 'Property ... is not equally divided, and a more equal distribution of capital must be wrought out'.[158] On the very last page of *Capital* Marx was more explicit. While the end of the War had allowed for the 'creation of a finance aristocracy of the vilest type' – land speculation for the railroads – 'the very centralization of capital' meant that the 'great republic has therefore ceased to be the promised land for emigrating workers'. This was due to the massive exodus from Europe which 'throws men onto the labour-

---

155 Marx and Engels 1975–2004w, pp. 474–5.
156 On this point, we draw on Neil Davidson's insightful historicization of the Civil War; Davidson 2011.
157 Marx and Engels 1975–2004p, pp. 10–11.
158 E. Foner 1988, p. 309. See also Richardson 2014, pp. 72–3.

market there more rapidly than the wave of immigration to the West can wash them away' to the 'promised land'. In spite of the 'gigantic strides' in capitalist production, the process of proletarianisation 'has by no means yet proceeded so far as to reach the normal European level', Marx concluded.[159] The material conditions for socialist revolution in the United States, in other words, were not yet in place.

Marx was absolutely right about 'the foreboding' of American ruling elites about what had become possible with the end of chattel slavery. Liberal supporters of Reconstruction reacted with horror at Wade's sentiments. 'The [New York] *Times* lambasted the Radicals for desiring "a war on property ... to succeed the war on Slavery," and *The Nation* linked Wade's speech with the confiscation [of land] issue, organized labor's demand for an eight-hour day, and the rise of Fenianism among Irish-Americans as illustrations of how "demagogues" had abandoned "true radicalism" – equality before the law and equal economic opportunity – in favor of "special favors for special classes of people"'.[160] As the de facto head of the IWMA, Marx did all he could to generalise internationally 'the first fruit of the Civil War', as he called it in *Capital*, 'the demand for an eight-hour day' – to the horror of capitalists elsewhere. He also championed, in that role, self-determination for the Irish people, another irritant for the elite on both sides of the North Atlantic.

In hindsight, the 'foreboding' of American 'ruling classes' about Wade's comments that Marx foregrounded in *Capital* anticipated the beginning of the end of Radical Reconstruction. Northern state and local elections in Summer and Fall 1867 revealed declining support for that agenda, including Black enfranchisement – 'a crusher for the wild men'.[161] Symptomatic was the Democratic Party victory in Ohio for the state's senate, precluding Wade from being re-elected by that body as was the practice then. Eric Foner writes

> The results had a major impact on the balance of power within the [Republican] party, convincing moderates that issues like disenfranchisement, black voting in the North, and impeachment must be avoided at all costs ... Looming on the horizon was a new Republican self-image ... the election results marked the end of any hope that Northern Republicans would embrace a program of land distribution ... Henceforth, it appeared certain, the party would strive to bring Reconstruction to a suc-

---

159   Marx and Engels 1975–2004p, p. 760.
160   E. Foner 1988, pp. 309–10.
161   Quoted in Richardson 2014, p. 74. For a succinct description of the state elections of 1867, see Downs 2015, p. 197.

cessful conclusion rather than press it forward. And this could not but affect the balance of power within the South.[162]

Though his term of office was to end in 1869, Wade's pro-labour sympathies were enough to keep his property-conscious moderate Republican Party colleagues from garnering the sufficient votes to impeach Johnson in June 1868. While not the only issue at play for those Senators who voted to acquit Johnson, the prospect, however brief, of a Wade presidency was a spectre they could not entertain.[163]

At arguably the most critical moment in the course of Radical Reconstruction, when the possibility of land for the former slaves was posed, Douglass, as far as we can determine, was largely missing in action. Leading that fight in Congress were Radical Republicans Thaddeus Stevens and Charles Sumner, and on the outside, space normally occupied by Douglass, Wendell Phillips. Two months into the new 39th Congress, Douglass, in St. Louis, on 7 February 1867, gave one of his longest speeches in which he admitted for the first time that the Constitution was wanting and needed to be amended.[164] But nowhere in the speech, that he had been giving to audiences throughout the Northwest since December, did Douglass address the substantive failures of the Constitution regarding the citizenship of those of African origin.

More important for Douglass was the problem of a presidential republic that Johnson benefited from with his vetoes of the Congressional Radical Republican agenda. Under Britain's parliamentary constitutional monarchy, Douglass argued, such nullification could not happen; it was, by implication, a preferable political system. His silence about Stevens's proposal to confiscate the plantations of the slave oligarchs so that their lands could be parcelled up and given to

---

162   E. Foner 1988, pp. 315–16. Moderate voices also began to redbait the Radicals. 'When Butler complained of a landed aristocracy in the South, the moderate Boston *Daily Advertiser* asked, "Why a landed aristocracy? This mode of argument is two-edged. For there are socialists who hold that any aristocracy is 'fatal to the advance of the cause of liberty and equal rights' – socialists who would not hesitate to say that General Butler's large income places him in the ranks of an aristocracy … It is dangerous to prove too much"'. The conservative Cincinnati *Commercial* began to refer to Stevens and Butler as 'The Red Rads'. Benedict 1972, p. 337. Minnesota and Iowa proved to be exceptions to Northern opposition to Black suffrage, but not until 1868; see Green 1998.

163   For more on the Wade factor in the failure to impeach Johnson, see R. Levine 2021, p. 211. See also, Wineapple 2020, pp. 198, 271–4, 352, 375–8.

164   Blassingame and McKivigan 1991, pp. 149–72. Robert Levine examines Douglass's 'Sources of Danger to the Republic' speech and provides an alternative text from a Philadelphia lecture in R. Levine 2021, pp. 132–54, 237–63.

their former slaves was, again, deafening.[165] As Waldo Martin explained years ago, 'Douglass's overriding belief in the sanctity of private property ... prevented him from supporting as too radical Stevens's and Sumner's different proposals for the confiscation of large tracts of formerly Confederate land and the redistribution of this land among the freedpeople'.[166] Douglass's liberal credentials, in other words, were real. They were complemented, Martin concluded, by a larger world view. 'Douglass's belief in the fundamental soundness of the economic system impeded his comprehension of the structural reality of the economic oppression blacks endured and, therefore, the pressing imperative of fundamental economic change'.[167] On this essential point our two protagonists could not have been more different.

As for the impeachment of Johnson the next year, Douglass, it seems, at least from the paper trail, was mostly aloof, while of course supporting conviction. Two days before the fateful senate vote on 16 May, Douglass declared: 'The impeachment of the President will be a hopeful indication of the triumph of our right to vote. It will mean the negro's right to vote, and mean that the fair South shall no longer be governed by the Regulators and the Ku Klux Klan, but by fair and impartial law'.[168] Douglass's deep-held faith, once again, in the power of the ballot.

What about Marx? How did he respond to that critical moment? He alerted, as already noted, readers of his just published magnum opus in 1867 to American ruling-class anxiety about what was unfolding. But Marx had been prioritising, certainly since Appomattox, political developments in Europe, now back, in his view, on the centre stage of the global class struggle after having been sidelined for four years by the Civil War. Effectively the head of the proletariat's first international organisation, the IWMA, Marx was obligated to relegate the American theatre to the back-burner. Only with a country-wide hereditary proletariat, what the end of chattel slavery ensured, could the United States take centre stage again. To an interviewer's question in 1871 about the IWMA's prospects in the United States, Marx replied:

---

165 Only, apparently, in 1869 did Douglass declare that the 'Negro must have a right to land', not through confiscation but some kind of federal government purchase scheme. P. Foner 1955, pp. 31–2.
166 Martin 1984, pp. 71–2. More recently, Myers 2008, p. 145, makes a similar point.
167 Martin 1984, p. 282.
168 Blassingame and McKivigan 1991, p. 175. R. Levine 2021, pp. 189–204, speculates on Douglass's reaction or non-reaction to the impeachment proceedings against Johnson, and in contrast to that of his son Charles. 'Regulators' refers to other Klan-like terrorists organisations in the post-War South.

> The chief centres of our activity are for the present among the old societies of Europe. Many circumstances have hitherto tended to prevent the labor problem from assuming an all-absorbing importance in the United States. But they are rapidly disappearing, and it is rapidly coming to the front there with the growth as in Europe of a laboring class distinct from the rest of the community and divorced from capital.[169]

History proved that Marx was unduly optimistic about how long it would take for 'labor' to assume 'an all-absorbing importance in the United States'. Elegant algebra but faulty arithmetic. Usually sympathetic historian Philip Foner accused Marx of being derelict for not doing enough to head off the defeat of Radical Reconstruction. Aside from the fact that Foner didn't realise when the crucial moment for defending Radical Reconstruction occurred, between 1866 and 1868, as argued convincingly by another and related historian, Eric Foner, he either didn't know or dismissed Marx's priorities at that moment. If the latter, Foner needed to explain why he disagreed with those priorities.[170]

The 39th Congress's most notable achievement, the 15th Amendment, was ratified on 3 February 1870. Douglass spelled out its significance in a speech in Albany, NY, in late April.

> It means that the colored people are now and will be held to be, by the whole nation, responsible for their own existence and their well or ill being. It means that we are placed upon an equal footing with all other men, and that the glory or shame of our future is to be wholly our own. For one, I accept this new situation gladly. I do so for myself and I do so for you; and I do so in the full belief that the future will show that we are equal to the responsibility which this great measure has imposed upon us.[171]

In many ways, Douglass's assessment of the meaning of the 15th Amendment announced the end of his revolutionary career and the commencement of his new one, inside the system he had once severely criticised. Seven months later, 'the New York Republican Association, a political club in Washington, D.C., elected Douglass to its membership and invited him to speak at their meeting on 15 October 1870'.[172] His acceptance speech, reproduced in his new newspa-

---

169 Marx and Engels 1975–2004l, p. 606.
170 For a detailed rebuttal of Philip Foner's charges, see Nimtz 2003, pp. 171–8.
171 Blassingame and McKivigan 1991, pp. 270–1.
172 Blassingame and McKivigan 1991, p. 272.

per, the *New National Era*, captured his enthusiasm for his new-found 'vocation', as he described his quest a few years earlier. 'Gentlemen, I am a Republican, a radical Republican, a Black Republican, a Republican dyed in the wool, and for one I want the Republican party to live as long as I do. Few greater calamities could fall the country, in my judgment, at any time within the next dozen years, than the defeat and disbandment of the Republican party'.[173] Later, Douglass unapologetically described himself as a 'field hand' for the Republican Party.[174]

Unlike Douglass, Marx knew – again, the lessons of 1848 – that enacting a law or even a constitutional amendment to grant universal suffrage should not be confused with the actual exercise of that right. To do so required continued revolutionary activity – 'Revolution in permanence', as their Address of March 1850 to the Communist League argued. The slaughter of the Parisian proletariat in June 1848, the revolutionary component of France's edition of the European Spring, and for whom Douglass had little sympathy, paved the way, Marx argued in real-time, for the end of the world's first experiment in universal male suffrage after three years. A similar fate – though years longer – awaited the 15th Amendment. Alas, few figures in America saw the need for exercising real power for realising the suffrage.[175]

If there was any doubt that by 1871 Radical Reconstruction had expired, the nail in its coffin came with events on the other side of the Atlantic, once again, in France – why Marx was right to have prioritised the European political theatre. On 18 March, the Parisian proletariat not only revolted – just as they had done in 1848 – but actually seized political power, a first in the annals of the working class. Though lasting for only two and a half months, the Paris Commune, as it came to be called, was soon immortalised due in no small part to Marx. The title of his homage to and analysis of the Commune, *The Civil War in France*, written on behalf of the IWMA, demonstrated how much the American War had impacted him. The pamphlet garnered international attention for the exiled German refugee in London that he never had before and as well for the IWMA. The Commune and the attention to Marx's pamphlet also got on the radar of ruling-class elites, including those on the other side of the Atlantic. The revolt fuelled their already existent anxiety about Radical Reconstruction, fear that some version of the Commune could come to American shores, and, even more alarming, in a multi-racial working-class incarnation.

---

[173] Blassingame and McKivigan 1991, p. 275.
[174] E. Foner 1988, p. 545.
[175] Some Republicans, such as Wisconsin Senator Matthew Carpenter, were more sober than Douglass or Charles Sumner about whether force or the franchise would protect freedpeople's rights. Downs 2015, pp. 228–9.

In hindsight, America's most radical experiment with revolutionary democracy had ended by the time of the Commune. But moderate and conservative forces in the United States didn't know that. Based on a detailed survey of bourgeois newspaper opinion, historian Heather Cox Richardson argues persuasively that the Commune prompted Northern Republican elite opinion that had once supported Reconstruction to take pause.[176] That change in sentiment helped give birth to a current within the Republican Party, Liberal Republicans, who began to advocate for reconciliation with the former slave owners.

The irony is that the Republican who led that campaign was a veteran of Germany's 1848–9 Revolution. Carl Schurz was arguably the most prominent 'Forty-eighter' in the Union Army, later elected to the Senate from Missouri. Even more ironically, Schurz had crossed swords with Marx and Engels two decades earlier over the course of the German Revolution. While the two communists were advocating for the 'revolution in permanence', Schurz wanted to limit it to reformist ends.[177] Two decades later, he sought again to limit a potentially revolutionary process.[178] Marx, on the other hand, at that very moment, was doing what he could, primarily through the fledgling IWMA-affiliate in New York City, to advance independent working class political action in America, the central charge of the international, independent of not only the Democrats but the Republican party as well – also a potentially revolutionary development. Whether Schurz was aware of what his old adversary was up to and whether that motivated him in any way to put an end to Reconstruction is uncertain.[179] Whatever the case, the ironic twist was the last echo of the European Spring on the other side of the Atlantic.

Douglass, as recounted earlier, was no friend of the Parisian proletariat when it rose up in June 1848 to protest the end of the new government's jobs programs that had provided momentary relief from starvation. Two decades later, his opinion of them had not changed. At best, the Communards were 'blind and deluded tools of their leaders'. Instead of glorious or heroic, as Marx described them, they were 'deluded, ill-starred men'.[180] How Douglass responded to the Paris Commune spoke volumes about the very different course he was on from that of Marx, a story that deserves its own treatment as in Appendix A.[181] Suf-

---

176 Richardson 2001.
177 Nimtz 2003, pp. 164–7, for details.
178 Schurz 1907, pp. 331–53. E. Foner 1988, pp. 500–2.
179 Marx does appear in Schurz's *Reminiscences* (Schurz 1907), volume one, pp. 139–40, but only in the context of the German Revolution. See Nimtz 2003, pp. 164–5.
180 Douglass, 'Dark Prospects', *New National Era*, 8 June 1871.
181 See also, K. Edwards 2022.

fice it to say here that his attitude toward the Paris Commune goes a long way in explaining why the best that liberalism ever had to offer, even in its revolutionary version, could not ensure racial equality in the United States; we'll revisit the point in the Conclusion.

Five years later in 1876, Douglass, 'living in Washington, D.C., in close quarters with the Republican Party establishment', gave his well-known speech at the dedication of the Freedman's Memorial in the Capitol Hill section of the city.[182] In it, he called Lincoln 'preeminently the white man's president', which has often been interpreted, given the increasing uncertainty about Reconstruction, as Douglass's criticism of Lincoln and pessimism about the prospects for Black Americans.[183] A more convincing interpretation argues that Douglass tailored his remarks for the Washington political elite in attendance at the speech – including President Grant – who might be able to blunt the appeal of growing white supremacist ideas. Because Lincoln was 'devoted entirely to the welfare of the white man', he continued, whites had nothing to fear about what he had done for Blacks. Support for Black rights actually benefited white people – what Lincoln, he insisted, understood.[184] Along the way, Douglass traced his own, often hesitant regard for Lincoln. Taken as a whole, argues James Oakes, the speech registered 'Douglass's own journey from slave to alienated outsider and then from sceptical engagement to a full embrace of the American political system'.[185]

Ever in search of a very different audience, the working class in motion, especially in the United States, Marx and Engels took notice when the country's first general strike occurred in 1877. Most noteworthy, it 'brought together "white and colored men ... men of all nationalities in one supreme contest for the common rights of workingmen"', according to one contemporary account.[186] 'What do you think', asked Marx to Engels on 25 July, while on vacation in the seaside resort of Ramsgate, 'of the workers of the UNITED STATES? This,

---

182   Oakes 2007, p. 175.
183   For the speech itself, see Blassingame and McKivigan 1991, pp. 427–40. The most prominent recent example of that interpretation of the speech is Gates 2009, pp. l–liii.
184   Political scientist Diana Schaub (Schaub 2010) makes a similar point. Peter Myers describes the speech as 'a nation-building, nation-binding act in which Lincoln serves as a medium for bonding African Americans and white Americans to each other and to the country at large' where Douglass makes 'carefully targeted appeals to the respective interests, virtues, and sympathies of black and white Americans'. Douglass 'aims in this speech to perpetuate Lincoln's example by presenting him as an object of emulation for white Americans'. Myers 2010, pp. 209, 217, 223.
185   Oakes 2007, p. 175.
186   E. Foner 1988, p. 584 and *passim* for details about the strike.

the first outbreak against the ASSOCIATED CAPITAL oligarchy that has arisen since the CIVIL WAR, will, of course, be suppressed, but may well provide a point of departure for the constitution of a serious workers' party in the UNITED STATES'. Marx's inquiry to Engels revealed, first, his almost matter of fact recognition that capitalist relations of production would envelop the entire country following the demise of the slavocracy – what, in fact, he had hoped, namely, the incubus for the gravediggers of capitalism, a hereditary working class. Second, working class resistance to the new relations of production, while to be applauded, could not be victorious in that epoch. But, he continued, there are 'two favourable circumstances on top of that. The policy of the new President will turn the negroes, just as the big expropriations of land (EXACTLY OF THE FERTILE LAND) for the benefit of the RAILWAY, MINING, etc. companies will turn the peasants of the West – whose grumbling is already plainly audible – into militant allies of the workers. So there's a pretty fair storm brewing over there'.

Regarding 'the negroes', Marx was referring to the policy of new Republican President Rutherford B. Hayes to withdraw the last few federal troops stationed in the South, a deal struck with the Democratic Party. Though not to be, Marx presumed that decision would radicalise Southern Blacks. Coupled with the growing resentment of small white farmers to the capitalist land grab in the West, the possibility existed for a militant alliance of Blacks and white farmers. Perhaps, he added, the transfer of the IWMA headquarters to the United States in 1874 had been a good idea after all, a 'quite exceptional opportunity' for the International.[187] Engels responded that he was 'delighted by the business of the strike in America. The way they throw themselves into the movement has no equivalent on this side of the ocean. Only twelve years since slavery was abolished and already the movement has got to such a pitch!'[188]

Marx, as events revealed, was mistaken about the withdrawal and immobilisation of the last federal troops from the South prompting a militant response from Blacks. One reason is that he seems to have not known that by 1877 when the deal was struck, there were less than three thousand troops still in the former Confederacy. 'The declining number of soldiers in the South already meant that black Republicans had been in harm's way since 1870'.[189] Most troops had been sent to the West to subjugate indigenous peoples and, most recently, to suppress the 1877 general strike.[190] But that begs the question why

---

[187] Marx and Engels 1975–2004y, p. 251.
[188] Marx and Engels 1975–2004y, p. 255.
[189] Edgerton 2014, p. 316.
[190] E. Foner 1988, pp. 584–5. For more details, including informative appendices, on the rate of withdrawal of troops from the South between 1865–1871, see Downs 2015.

wasn't there Black resistance to the prior withdrawals and the anti-Black violence, as expected, that came in its wake? The answer has much to do with what Douglass represented: Black leadership that was solidly wedded to the Republican Party. The 'I am a Republican dyed in the wool' sentiment that Douglass expressed in 1870 spoke for a whole layer of Black leaders and suggests an explanation for the lack of effective resistance to the generally feckless Republican Party response to that violence, and the deals that their new found party had reached.[191] It also helps to suggest why a Black/white worker/white farmer alliance of the kind that Marx had envisioned was not likely at that moment.[192] But Black leaders were not alone in their embrace of the Republicans. 'Indeed', as Eric Foner explains, 'ordinary blacks reacted with extreme hostility to any political strategy that threatened to weaken the party of emancipation ... Thus, black political leaders had few options outside the party, since gestures toward political autonomy not only threatened their access to patronage, but undermined their credibility in their own community'.[193] It would take another seven decades for independent Black political action to emerge and, thus, Marx's vision to become a possibility.

A decade after Marx's death in 1883, regarding the American reality, a wiser and more sober Engels advised patience when Frederick Sorge, Marx party leader in the United States, lamented to him about the absence of a working-class party in the country, such as those being founded in Europe. Three obstacles in the United States, Engels replied, stood in the way. First, an electoral system inherited from England that employed the winner-take-all procedure – a disincentive to the protest vote. Second, divisions within the working class between the 'native-born and the foreign', between European immigrants, and, 'in addition, the negroes' – by which Engels no doubt meant the unfinished business of Reconstruction and all that implied. And lastly, the workers there had been 'exposed ... to a prosperity unlike anything that has been experienced for many years in Europe'. Nevertheless, Engels could envision the day when America would be 'really ripe for a socialist labour party'.[194] But less than one

---

[191] The general fecklessness of the Republican Party was punctuated by moments of genuine efforts to curb violence against the freedpeople and other southern Republicans. For example, Grant's campaign against the Klu Klux Klan in the early 1870s.

[192] See Nimtz 2003, Chapter Four, for details.

[193] E. Foner 1988, p. 545. For how this played out in South Carolina, see Saville 1994, Chapter Five.

[194] Marx and Engels 1975–2004cc, p. 236. Two years earlier, Engels told Sorge: 'I do not believe there is as yet room for a *third* party in America. ... Only when there is a race of native-born workers with nothing more to expect from speculation, shall we have firm ground beneath our feet in America'. Marx and Engels 1975–2004bb, p. 327.

year after he and Douglass both died, 1895, the United States Supreme Court gave, after a series of prior notorious rulings, its final imprimatur to the end of Reconstruction in *Plessy v. Ferguson*, the final nail of a series of Supreme Court rulings in which the Court severely restricted federal reconstruction efforts, its second most infamous decision.

Seven decades later, with a hereditary working class now in place in both white and black skin, the Second Reconstruction achieved what the First could not, political equality for the descendants of the once enslaved. At least one of the three obstacles to independent working-class political action in the United States that Engels listed for Sorge had been overcome – we elaborate on the significance of this in our Conclusion.

∴

For four years, from Fort Sumter in April 1861 to Appomattox in April 1865, Douglass and the Marx party allied in a united front. Both wanted, and *acted* to assure, the end of America's peculiar institution. With that goal achieved both protagonists went their separate ways. The reason had to do with their two very different world-historical perspectives. For Douglass the liberal, again, the abolition of chattel slavery and political equality for those of African origin in the United States was the end. For Marx the communist, the abolition of American chattel slavery was the necessary means to an end – the full realisation of American capitalism and, thus, the grave diggers of class society, namely the proletariat, not only in the United States but worldwide to achieve human emancipation. That essential difference informed their very different responses to the two bookends that frame our comparison, the European Spring and the Paris Commune. While Marx embraced the rebellious proletariat in both cases, Douglass was repelled by them. Capitalist relations of production in the United States, as Marx opined in 1852 about the nostrums of the leading American economist Henry Carey – especially, the 'harmony of interests between labour and capital' – were still too underdeveloped for subscribers to that claim like Douglass to appreciate the singularity of the proletariat for achieving human emancipation. And, most consequentially, the absence of a hereditary proletariat in the United States after the Civil War, only out of which could a class conscious fighting leadership have emerged, goes a long way in explaining the bloody counterrevolutionary demise of the country's brief experiment in racial political equality. Only in the next century would the necessary if not sufficient conditions exist for Marx's perspective to be realised.

Conclusions

If African-Americans had the right to vote, and had been exercising it for many decades, then why had their economic situation not improved? Why hadn't they been able to achieve the American dream – or, better, 'reach the Promised Land'? That's the question that perplexed Martin Luther King, Jr. by at least 1967. The African-Americans he referred to were those who had left the South decades earlier for the North in search of a better life. Their relatives left behind had only gotten the effective right to vote just two years earlier and, therefore, had no reason to expect economic improvement so soon. Thus, if the Northern experience, King increasingly realised, was the future for the just enfranchised Southern Blacks, that was disheartening, putting into question his decade-long work. In a speech to the American Psychological Association in September 1967, he even chided political scientists for questioning the efficacy of voting. But if they were right, then 'the main thrust of Negro effort has been, and remains, substantially irrelevant, we may be facing an agonizing crisis of tactical theory'.[1]

Why the vote had failed to deliver racial equality would have also perplexed Frederick Douglass had he been alive. Douglass, after all, viewed the ballot as the panacea for racial equality, 'the keystone to the arch of human liberty'.[2] But the 'riots', or, rather, the urban rebellions a century later that began in 1964 exclusively in the North, were stark and sobering evidence of the limits of the right to vote – at least for Black people, it seemed. Why? King offered an explanation via a solution: racial equality in the United States would require a 'radical redistribution of economic and political power' – a claim that he repeated on numerous occasions prior to his assassination in April 1968.

Less than a week before that fateful day, King continued to wrestle with the reason for Black socio-economic inequality.

> In 1863 the Negro was told that he was free as a result of the Emancipation Proclamation being signed by Abraham Lincoln. But he was not given any land to make that freedom meaningful. It was something like keeping a person in prison for a number of years and suddenly discovering that that

---

1 King 1968, p. 220. Find the text online at: https://www.apa.org/monitor/features/king-challenge
2 See Chapter 5, p. 238, for the full citation, as well as Douglass's comments on the 15th Amendment on p. 268.

© AUGUST H. NIMTZ AND KYLE A. EDWARDS, 2024 | DOI:10.1163/9789004706385_008

person is not guilty of the crime for which he was convicted. And you just go up to him and say, 'Now you are free', but you don't give him any bus fare to get to town. You don't give him any money to get some clothes to put on his back or to get on his feet again in life.³

Had Douglass been alive to hear King's complaint, discomfort would likely have been his reaction. After all, little did he do, if anything, to ensure that the once enslaved be 'given any land to make [their] freedom meaningful'.⁴

To return to the query that introduced this book, does a comparison of Douglass and Marx – in the period when the question of how to achieve racial equality was first posed – shed any light on the solution King proposed, a question that has even more urgency today? 'By almost every important measure', in the recent opinion of Shelby Steele, arguably Black America's leading conservative intellectual, 'educational achievement, out of wedlock birth, homeownership, divorce rates – blacks are on the losing end of racial disparities'.⁵ That's even truer if we include income and overall wealth. A 2022 RAND Corporation analysis concluded that there 'is no reason to think the wealth gap will ever close without potentially trillions of dollars in investments in Black households' – in other words, 'a radical redistribution of economic and political power'.⁶

In his final draft that Marx employed to write the *Communist Manifesto*, Engels, in the catechistic political style in vogue in 1847, posed '*Question 7*: In what way does the proletarian differ from the slave? *Answer*: The slave is sold once and for all, the proletarian has to sell himself by the day and by the hour'. After describing the implication of the difference for the quotidian realities of the two groups of toilers, Engels ended: 'The slave frees himself by abolishing, among all the private property relationships, only the relationship of slavery and thereby only then himself becomes a proletarian; the proletarian can free himself only by abolishing private property in general'.⁷ Nothing, we argue, captures better the fundamental difference between Douglass and Marx than Engels's claim about the two very different roads to freedom. No one – as a real-time comparison helps to show – better epitomised Engels's point about the limitations of a slave point of view about private property, that is, only

---

3 https://www.dc1968project.com/blog/2018/3/31/31-march-1968-mlk-speaks-at-national-cathedral
4 Douglass apparently regretted in later years his lack of action; see below, p. 296.
5 Steele 2023.
6 Irving 2023.
7 Marx and Engels 1975–2004e, pp. 343–4.

opposition to 'property in persons' and all that implied, than Douglass. Engels's 'answer', we also argue, is at the very heart of the puzzle for which King sought a solution.[8]

What follows, first, is by and large evidence for our claim that Engels's 'answer' distils the basic difference between Douglass and Marx based on what has been presented in the previous chapters. We hone in, for the sake of brevity, on only the most relevant evidence to sustain our claim – readers can revisit the chapters to see if our reading here is prejudicially selective. We conclude by returning to the question that opened this inquiry, Martin Luther King, Jr's epiphany about how to realise racial equality. What does, again, a comparison of Douglass and Marx have to offer regarding King's claim and, thus, in pointing a way forward for resolving his still so current question?

1   The Key Takeaways of the Comparison

To begin, the biographies of Douglass and Marx reveal how the two age cohorts came to hold very different political perspectives but yet could find themselves on the same political page when the Confederacy fired on Fort Sumter in April 1861. Both wanted to put an end to America's peculiar institution, chattel slavery, but for different reasons. For Douglass, it was almost obvious. As a former slave who had experienced the brutality of bondage, and one who had relatives who were still enslaved, Douglass had every reason to oppose the slavocracy. Also determinant were his exceptional and fortuitous experiences prior to Fort Sumter. Learning to read, to do public speaking as a slave, and then being recruited to the vanguard of abolitionist circles to both speak and write for the cause all prepared Douglass to be a protagonist when that fateful moment arrived.

As for the ideas that informed Douglass's abolitionist stance, the Declaration of Independence exercised the earliest influence, especially the 'all men are created equal' clause. The Enlightenment and natural law premises of the document, in defence of liberty and individual rights, such as the sanction of private property in land but not in persons, became life-time core values.

The class composition of the abolitionist movement that Douglass operated in, liberal middle- and upper-class whites in both the United States and Britain, proved to be consequential. The opportunity to collaborate politically with less well-off or working-class whites in the United States was virtually non-existent

---

[8]   For a recent take on Engels's draft on this point, see Shilliam 2015, pp. 206–7.

for Douglass. But when presented with the opportunity to do so during his first trip to Britain, he opted instead, tellingly, for the middle/upper class milieu, due, in part, to advice from his mentor William Lloyd Garrison. The trip also exposed Douglass's Anglophile proclivities. That Britain abolished slavery in its West Indian territories in 1834 meant that a constitutional monarchy might actually be superior to America's 'bastard' republic where the reprehensible practice was still in place. As a Garrisonian abolitionist, Douglass eschewed politics. But that would soon change upon his return to the United States.

For Marx, the route to anti-slavery politics was less obvious. If almost everything in Douglass's biography predisposed him to be fully attentive to the guns that fired on Fort Sumter in April 1861, the same cannot be said about Marx – apparently. In addition, however, to the French Revolution, the American experiment in liberal democracy caught the young Marx's attention almost from the beginning of his political trajectory. The all so glaring contradiction between the best that political democracy had to offer but encumbered by social inequalities that included the institution of chattel slavery – a 'defiled republic' he later said – constituted a puzzle that needed a solution.

Like Douglass, Marx too sought freedom – from Prussian monarchical rule. If the liberal enlightenment project informed Douglass's quest, Hegel's critique of liberalism, for its abstraction of the individual from social reality, informed Marx. But Hegel's solution, the constitutional monarchy, Marx argued, was bogus – it could not ensure 'true democracy'. Marx, unlike Douglass, had a low opinion of the institution. His year-long experience as a newspaper reporter and editor in monarchical Prussian-occupied Rhineland taught not only about state censorship of the press but also how the governance process privileged 'private property', particularly, 'landed property'. From the perspective of monarchical Europe, even a 'bastard' or 'defiled' republic was superior to constitutional monarchy. The millennial-old sweep of class society informed Marx rather than the relatively more recent institution of New World chattel slavery that mostly served as Douglass's starting point.

The real world of politics quickly taught Marx that the discipline in which he had been doctored had little to offer in explaining the 'defects' in Germany's governance. The study of 'actuality' seemed to be more rewarding. Also missing in philosophy, its materialist variety in particular, and of utmost importance for the road Marx would take, was the place of human intervention, namely, 'revolutionary practice'. Putting humans at the centre of society was also Marx's answer to Hegel's reliance on 'the spirit' to explain social reality. Religion, thus, for Marx did not explain anything; religion itself, rather, needed to be explained and only by beginning with humans was that possible. Thus, a fundamental epistemological difference with Douglass who looked to religion and 'providence' for doing just that. The starting point for constitutions, for example, Marx argued, should be 'man', or 'the democracy' and not Hegel's 'spirit' or 'idea'. Revolutions, the French experience taught, is how constitutions change.

Armed with those insights and a Hegelian world-historical perspective, the 'United States of North America', the most politically liberal state, proved for Marx to be especially instructive. Especially striking was how a society bereft of a feudal past had so quickly instituted social inequality, including that of chattel slavery – a society characterised by the buying and selling of everything. As in Europe, private property, landed property, especially, reproduced and explained that inequality. While Douglass blamed property in persons for America's lack of 'true democracy' and not private property per se, Marx faulted private property in general for that deficit. If the United States was the best that liberal democracy had to offer, then clearly something else, Marx concluded, was required for 'human emancipation'.

Europe taught that there was at least one layer of society that had a class interest in ridding the world of private property – the proletariat. Engels captured best – at least for our purposes – that claim in his second draft that Marx employed for writing the *Communist Manifesto*. Again, 'the slave frees himself by abolishing, among all the private property relationships, only the relationship of slavery and thereby only then himself becomes a proletarian; the proletarian can free himself only by abolishing private property in general'.[9] The slave was enchained by a species of property owners whereas the proletariat was enchained by the genus of property ownership itself upon which it depended for employment and, thus, its survival. Freedom for the proletariat required, therefore, the expropriation of the property owners, ensuring freedom not just for wage slaves but for all enchained layers of society such as debt slaves.

Douglass, the former slave, epitomised Engels's point – an adamant opponent of slave property. But only briefly did he spend time as 'a proletarian' and this was why, most likely, he could not see or agree with Marx's and Engels's call for 'abolishing private property in general'. From then on, Douglass was self-employed, someone, therefore, who had a class interest in the maintenance of private property. At about the same time, Marx and Engels decided to prioritise the emerging proletariat, the future gravediggers of private property. Ridding the world of all obstacles to the full development of the working class, such as feudalism and chattel slavery, was now their goal. Therein the basic reason why

---

9 Marx and Engels 1975–2004e, pp. 343–4.

Marx and Douglass would find themselves on the same political page when the Civil War erupted – both wanted to end the peculiar institution but, once more, for two quite different reasons.

The European Spring soon demonstrated the practical significance of Engels's slave/proletariat distinction and how it applied to Douglass and Marx. Both were heartened by the upheavals but, again, for quite different reasons. For Douglass, the 1848–9 revolutions heralded a new stage in the age-old quest for freedom. That the French edition soon resulted in the abolition of slavery in France's West Indian colonies was proof enough. The liberal provisional government that issued from the overthrow of France's last monarch deserved unconditional support. Douglass's endorsement of the new republican wave, however, was qualified. When working-class Chartists made a half-hearted attempt in London to emulate the French example, he was livid. Britain's constitutional monarchy, which had abolished slavery in its colonies in 1834 and where civil liberties existed and grievances could be aired 'within the walls of Parliament', was, Douglass charged, sufficiently democratic and, thus, no need for 'brute force or bloodshed'. While Marx and Engels hoped the London action would have a revolutionary outcome, Douglass wanted just the opposite. The two very different reactions reveal, we argue, the first real-time instance of the fundamental political differences between Marx and Douglass.

For Marx, on the other hand, the February Revolution in Paris that initiated the European Spring was only the beginning of a process and not its end. The 'bourgeois revolution', as the just published *Communist Manifesto* explained, 'will be but the prelude to an immediately following proletarian revolution'. Communists, it added, were obligated in all of the struggles to 'bring to the front, as the leading question in each, the *property* [emphasis added] question'. No wonder, then, that Marx defended the Parisian proletariat when it rebelled in June 1848 against the provisional government for ending capitalism's first jobs programme for the unemployed. Douglass, in telling contrast, lambasted the rebels as 'wild and wicked ... communists of Paris' who threatened the government he praised and, by implication, the sanctity of private property. He was in good liberal company. Tocqueville helped lead the slaughter of the rebels about which John Stuart Mill was deafeningly silent. No event before the Civil War exposed the fundamental political divide between Douglass and Marx as did the European Spring. While Douglass applauded the liberal actors in the drama, Marx extolled those who Douglass vilified. The eventual liberal betrayal of the revolutions confirmed for Marx that only the working class had both an interest and capacity in making democracy real, but ensured only by a 'proletarian revolution' – for Douglass, a horror of horrors. The two very different reactions to the June uprising reveal, we also argue, the second real-time instance of the fundamental political divide between Marx and Douglass. The European Spring, therefore, registered the key political difference between the two.

Inside the revolutionary process itself another key difference surfaced. If Douglass thought that the opportunity to act politically 'within the walls of Parliament' obviated the need to do so on the outside, Marx and Engels thought exactly the opposite. To think so, they held, was to be afflicted with 'parliamentary cretinism', the term Engels coined to describe the behaviour of like-minded liberals in Germany's first and brief experiment with parliamentary democracy in 1848–9. The plebeian street actions in Berlin, inspired by Paris a month earlier, forced the monarchy to make the concession. Should communists be enticed and take part? Marx thought so and recommended that rather than put up its own candidates for the elections to the parliament, the workers movement, too small in that moment, should endorse those of the liberal pro-democratic petit bourgeoisie. But political reality quickly revealed that the deliberations inside those bodies were increasingly irrelevant to the actual exercise of power when it came to dealing with the monarchical regime. To believe otherwise was to be a victim of 'parliamentary cretinism'.

Also instructive is that once elected, those petit-bourgeois liberals who the workers movement had supported soon ceased to advance its interests. To avoid a repeat of that, Marx and Engels issued their first self-criticism in 1850. Regardless of its size and chance for actually winning elections, the workers' movement had to run its own candidates in order to promote its ideas and determine where it had support for making a revolution – their first programmatic document on the electoral/parliamentary process. Elections for the working-class movement, to put it concisely, were not an end in themselves but rather a means to an end, for advancing the proletarian revolution. Two years later, Douglass, as part of his break with Garrisonian political abstentionist abolition, began to grapple with many of the same issues: how to use the electoral/parliamentary process for advancing the abolitionist cause. Political reality in Germany, the end to the brief experiment in parliamentary democracy, taught a sobering lesson for Marx and Engels about that process. Douglass, as events would show, would have to wait for decades to learn, if ever, that lesson. Nevertheless, in the moment, in real-time, the European Spring in its various editions registered, again, the profound political differences between Marx and Douglass.

As a protagonist in the European Spring, mainly the German theatre, Marx, through his newspaper the *Neue Rheinische Zeitung*, came to be a correspondent for the influential pro-abolitionist *New York Daily Tribune* whose readers included not only Douglass but future president Abraham Lincoln. Another reader was the leading US economist Henry Carey whose admiration for Marx owing to his *Tribune* articles indicated to the historical materialist that mid-century 'bourgeois society' on the other side of the Atlantic was 'still far too immature for the class struggle to be made perceptible and comprehensible'. Thus, the reason, as Marx noted, for Carey's mistaken belief in the harmony of interests between labour and capital. Marx's insight could have applied as well to Douglass, who too subscribed to the same thesis. Therein the fundamental difference between our two protagonists regarding political economy prior to the Civil War and about which Marx could have offered an explanation.

As with Carey, nothing in US history till then would have taught Douglass to look to the struggle between capital and labour to be the axis around which politics revolved. Though the slave economy had by then, as Marx's research revealed, been integrated into the newly global capitalist mode of production, labour, as both Lincoln and Douglass correctly understood, had yet to become fully free. Toward that end and encouraging for Marx was evidence that chattel labour had become 'conscious' of its need to be free.[10] No one epitomised that fact more than Douglass. That awakening bode well for labour's future prospects. Only with the end of chattel slavery, Marx argued, would the 'the class struggle ... be made perceptible and comprehensible'. And only then could the proletariat, in all its skin colours in the United States, become conscious of its historical task – to make a revolution.

With the demise of the 1848–9 Revolutions, many of its veterans moved to the United States, including Marx's comrades of the Communist League, the organisation he headed for the German edition of the European Spring. Marx – another key difference from Douglass – operated as part of a disciplined collective, the party that commissioned the *Manifesto* – under the threat of 'further measures would be taken' if not done – that he and Engels wrote.[11] 'Ideas', as he concluded in 1844, '*cannot carry out anything* at all. In order to carry out ideas men are needed who can exert practical force'. That insight gave Marx an advantage over Douglass who never functioned in such a fashion, rather, mostly, a one-person party within the broader abolitionist movement as suggested by his eponymous newspaper.[12] Putting forth ideas in a book, articles, a

---

10   Mark Lause conceptualises slaves as 'owned workers' in Lause 2015, p. x. Angela Zimmerman as 'enslaved black workers' in Marx and Engels 2016, p. xvi. Slaves are labour, but, as Engels teaches, they are fundamentally different from workers.
11   Nimtz 2000, p. 55.
12   Benjamin Fagan, in Fagan 2022, demonstrates that the making of *Frederick Douglass' Paper*

newspaper or in speeches, as in Douglass's case, did not ensure that they would be implemented. For that, 'men', the young Marx recognised, would be 'needed', with conscious intent, that is, a party.

The Marx party, as it came to be known, headed in the US by one-time Communist League member Joseph Weydemeyer, constituted an ersatz international party that allowed Marx to expand his reach into US politics from four thousand miles away. With minimal input on Marx's and Engels's part, but with a common programme, the *Manifesto*, and shared practical experience from the German Revolution, Marx's co-thinkers played important and consequential roles in the prelude to the Civil War. Weydemeyer took the lead in convincing German migrant workers to intervene in the debates on the Kansas-Nebraska proposal of 1854 to oppose the extension of slavery into Kansas. With Douglass of the same opinion about the proposal, he and the Marx party found themselves converging for the first time. The birth of the Republican Party shortly afterward, a product of the debates, and its presidential campaign of 1856 with candidate John Frémont, enabled that informal alliance to continue. As Weydemeyer campaigned for Frémont in the German-American community, Douglass used his paper to do the same in the abolitionist milieu.

Meanwhile, Douglass had been acting, in hindsight, most consequentially but not necessarily with the same conscious intent as had characterised Weydemeyer's actions. His public and often less than public support to John Brown's project proved to be determinant, crucial, it seems, in encouraging the failed attack on Harper's Ferry. Because Brown's post-Harper's Ferry conduct and positive Northern response to it, including Douglass's defence of Brown, did more than anything to encourage the Fire-Eaters to attack Fort Sumter, Douglass's enabling of Brown was arguably his greatest contribution to the abolition of chattel slavery. Marx and Engels, of significance, thought that the reaction to Brown's attack was of greater import than the attack itself, particularly, the apparent slave uprisings it provoked.[13]

But the slavocracy's fatal mistake, firing on Fort Sumter, depended on a firm reaction from the occupant of the White House. In that regard, the election of Lincoln was necessary. And for that cause, the Marx party was on the right side of history. Its small forces, with Weydemeyer in the lead, actively campaigned –

---

was a collective effort – 'collaboration and collectivity manifest in the pages of Black newspapers'. In Douglass's case between family members, printers, assistant editors, business managers, and interim editors, Black and white. But it is clear that Douglass always had a goal of 'singular control over the shape and content' of his newspapers. Fagan 2022, pp. 133–4.

13   We elaborate on this point in Appendix B.

unlike Douglass – for the sixteenth president. Consciously and unconsciously, the Marx party and Douglass, respectively, acted, therefore, together to set the stage for the denouement of the peculiar institution. Of our two protagonists on the eve of the Civil War, Douglass, once apolitical and a pacifist, had moved closer to the position of the other.

Once the War began, the profound political differences between Marx and Douglass dropped from view – they took a backseat to the conflagration that unfolded. The basic reason being that both of them were now, unlike in the European Spring, rooting for the same side. For Marx, as long as the bourgeoisie acted in a revolutionary way to end America's version of feudalism, he could enthusiastically embrace what Douglass wanted and forge objectively a united front with the revolutionary liberal. Thus, why our two protagonists could find themselves on virtually the same political page right after Fort Sumter – the urgent task of bringing political clarity to the conflict. Despite Abraham Lincoln's claim that the War was only about ending the secession of the Confederacy, Douglass and Marx knew better. Slavery, they argued, was the real issue. Douglass claimed at the outset of the conflict that the slave oligarchy had intended to impose the peculiar institution on the entire country. Once Marx got up to speed on the country's history, he later agreed with Douglass. As for which side would be victorious, Douglass quickly asserted that the North would win the War only if it recruited Blacks to the Union Army. The Black factor informed Marx's prediction a week or so into the War that 'in the long run, of course, the North will be victorious since, if the need arises, it has a last card up its sleeve in the shape of a slave revolution'. Douglass, however, was not as confident of victory as Marx was and, thus, his incessant call from the beginning of the War that Lincoln not wait to play that 'last card'. It needed, again, to be the 'first card'. And with Blacks in the Union Army, the War would more likely become one for emancipation and not just the end of secession.

Marx had an advantage that Douglass did not possess – the experience of having gone through a recent war, namely, the German Revolution of 1848–9. And for that reason, he quickly honed in on the minutiae, unlike Douglass, of the all-essential matter of logistics in war time, indispensable for victory. Another advantage Marx enjoyed over Douglass was to have a partner who had not only engaged in combat in the Revolution but continued afterward to do research on such matters – an asset that served him well throughout the War. Engels's assessments of Southern and Northern prospects that he supplied Marx with in the first months of hostilities proved to be remarkably prescient. To see as early as he did that Georgia would be the site where the outcome would be decided was exemplary. Though neither of us claims any kind of expertise on the military side of the War, we think a potentially fruitful research project awaits someone who does by closely examining Marx's and Engels's writings on the subject.[14]

More so than Douglass, Marx and Engels appreciated that developments on the battlefield would in the long run be determinant. Yet, as Marx would later chide Engels, military matters needed always to be seen through the lens of politics. For much of the War, Engels, like Douglass, complained about the Union Army's performance, a pessimist about its chances. Marx, contra Engels, was the optimist – the only documented long-term disagreement between the two communists. The main lesson is that having a common theoretical framework, 'the materialist conception of history', as they called it, or historical materialism, did not guarantee common conclusions. Their method, rather than a template as too often regarded by foe – Martin Luther King, Jr? – and friend alike, required deft and nuanced usage.

The challenge of how to read Lincoln tested the best of Douglass's and Marx's political acumen. Marx proved to be more adept over time. That was especially true when it came to arguably the turning point in the War, Lincoln's issuance of the Emancipation Proclamation. Marx, unlike Douglass, was confident that Lincoln was on an abolitionist course after his threat to the Border States on 12 July 1862. The president's still-debated actions in the lead-up to the preliminary executive order on 22 September threw Douglass and others like Wendell Phillips, unlike Marx, 'off-scent'. Perhaps Marx had the advantage of distance, telescopic rather than microscopic vision when it came to the Sixteenth president, being able to see beyond the daily minutiae of Washington that Douglass likely knew better than Marx. Maybe having been trained as a lawyer allowed Marx to read another lawyer, Lincoln, better than Douglass – and Engels also – again, from four thousand miles away.

Marx's earlier study and writings on constitutional law and his legal skills may explain why in the end his reading of the US constitution proved to be more accurate than that of Douglass, who contended for more than a decade that the document actually supported abolition. Within abolitionist circles, however, very few embraced that position. Lincoln certainly didn't see it that way. Marx seemed to have agreed when he told Engels just weeks before the issuance of the preliminary Emancipation Proclamation what he considered to be the main problem with Lincoln: 'wars of this kind ought to be conducted along revolutionary lines, and the YANKEES have so far been trying to conduct it

---

14   Perhaps a harbinger of forthcoming research is Winczewski 2021, pp. 207–8.

along constitutional ones'.[15] Thus, Marx's sense of vindication, no doubt, when Lincoln issued the executive order and, hence, his reaction: 'tantamount to the tearing up of the old American Constitution'.[16] Marx was 'dead right' in the opinion of David Blight.[17]

Two decades earlier, the young Marx concluded that 'democracy', the sentiments and actions of the populace, 'is the solved riddle of all constitutions', and to change them 'a real revolution has always been required'. Lincoln's extraordinary action and his move shortly afterward to constitutionalize what he had done would have all made sense to Marx. The decades-old 'riddle', whether the Constitution was a proslavery or abolition document, was now being solved on the battlefield, the only place where it could have been, by the 'democracy'. Douglass, consistent with his pro-abolition reading of the document, didn't think, however, an amendment was necessary. But he was mostly silent about the apparent inconsistency between his pro-abolition reading of the Constitution and the fact that it was now being amended. Jubilation best describes his reaction when the 15th amendment was enacted. Whether he was right or not about his reading of the document was now academic, literally.[18] But that's getting ahead of the story.

If antebellum Douglass subscribed to Providence and God's will, 'the necessities of war', as he often put it, required that he come down to earth – another instance in which he moved closer to Marx, at least epistemologically. His demand, not long after Fort Sumter, that abolitionists step up their work and not depend on Providence to ensure that the War would lead to abolition is a case in point. But without a party, Douglass could at best plant ideas, plead, and/or cajole both in print and in person rather than actually organise such efforts.

Marx party members and other Forty-Eighters, on the other hand, immediately signed on to the cause by volunteering to fight in the Union Army. Weydemeyer distinguished himself by rising to Lieutenant Colonel. The exper-

---

15   Marx and Engels 1975–2004u, p. 400.
16   Marx and Engels 1975–2004j, p. 250.
17   Blight 2013 at 48:50. Noah Feldman 2021, pp. 279–83, agrees. As well, Gregory Downs argues that the Civil War and Reconstruction constituted a Second American Revolution when '[not only] slavery but the Constitution that protected slavery had been overturned'. Downs 2019, p. 2. See also, the debate between Feldman and James Oakes on the constitutionality of Lincoln's actions: https://www.nybooks.com/articles/2022/06/23/was-emancipation-constitutional-an-exchange/
18   Constitutional scholar Akhil Reed Amar 2022, certainly no Marxist, argues that 'America's pro-democracy Constitution of 1787 was, sadly, also pro-slavery in its basic structure and foreseeable effects' (p. 39).

ience they obtained having fought in the German Revolution allowed them to take advantage of the new opportunity to advance the republican cause. That Weydemeyer had campaigned for Frémont for his presidential bid in 1856 also gave him an in when Frémont began recruiting for his officer staff. That open communists like him and others could rise to leadership positions in the Union army – a first and last in US military history – testifies to the progressive character of the War and why the label 'citizen-soldier' is apt to describe not only the rank and file but also much of the Union officer corps.[19]

But fighting in the Union Army, we should recall, was not an option for Douglass even if he had wanted to do so.[20] Only in early 1863, when Douglass was 45 years old, did Lincoln welcome Blacks into the Union Army. Douglass then actively and effectively recruited Black troops beginning with his son Charles. Marx's time-tested insight in his classic analysis of the failed French edition of the European Spring, *The Eighteenth Brumaire*, that 'men make their own history but not under circumstances of their choosing' applied all so well to Douglass. Much of his effective war-time agency depended on Lincoln's actions.

Douglass's practice during the War consisted mainly of the use of the pen and podium whereas Marx made use almost exclusively of his pen. Until Lincoln's issuance of the Preliminary Emancipation Proclamation in September 1862, Douglass mostly criticised the president for not recruiting Blacks and, most importantly, declaring the War to be one to end slavery. At times, Douglass often sounded more critical of Washington than the Confederacy. His frustration with Lincoln was palpable. The issue that most exposed the differences between Douglass and Marx had to do with European reaction to the War. For Douglass, the opinion of European elites, 'the statesmen', mattered the most, leading him to place blame on Lincoln for their backhanded endorsement of the Confederacy.

Marx, so strikingly different, took every opportunity to deride the elite, to ridicule them and poke holes in their hypocritical arguments in support of the Confederacy. The working class – dropping any pretence of class neutrality – and not the bourgeoisie deserved to be extolled for its support to Lincoln and

---

[19] Though not formally a Marx party member, August Willich, former Communist League member and later Union major-general conducted himself as if he was one, giving, on occasion, classes to his troops on such matters. After having once strongly disagreed with Marx's historical materialist perspective, Willich, by the time of the War, was in accord with Marx's views. See Easton 1966, for example. Davidson 2011, p. 50, mistakes Willich for Weydemeyer. Details about Willich's wartime activities are now, thankfully, available: Dixon 2020 and Reinhart 2006.

[20] Blacks, again, were not totally excluded in serving in Union forces as in the Navy, in integrated regiments from some Northern states or the all-Black Louisiana Native Guard.

the Union cause. The rewards of that claim would later be reaped. Obviously aware of the readership of the pro-abolitionist *Tribune*, Marx had good reason to believe that his articles would get a hearing in America. It's no accident, we claim, that Douglass's ardour for Britain's 'statesmen' markedly cooled after he had no doubt read Marx's informed, astute, and often sardonic critiques of them.

Douglass, understandably, tended to view everything through the lens of slave emancipation and gave Britain's elite too much credit for ending the detestable institution in its West Indian territories in 1834. His overestimation of Britain's bourgeoisie and underestimation of its working class – in fact, a tendency to ignore their contributions to the Union cause – went back at least to his visit there in 1846–7. Douglass's most famous speech, arguably, was provoked by Black abolitionist James McCune Smith's challenge to his claim about British enlightenment. They saw the light, as Douglass had to admit, because they felt the heat of the insurgent plebeian masses on the march, sobering evidence, indeed, that 'if there is no struggle, there is no progress'. Another fact about 1834 that Marx revealed and that Douglass had omitted: the slave owners were handsomely rewarded for seeing the light, in gold and cash.

Douglass's change of tune came just in time – for the *Trent* Affair. Had Britain intervened on behalf of the Confederacy, the eventual outcome of the War could very well have been different. Though it's impossible to prove, Marx's bona fides as a friend of the Union may have made his advice to the Lincoln administration, specifically, Secretary of State William Seward, to chill-out consequential. Whether decisive or not, Marx the communist was obligated to act, even with the limitations of pen and ink and print, as if he could have made a difference.[21] The fast-breaking events didn't allow Douglass to respond in a timely fashion in his *Monthly* in the way Marx could in the *Daily Tribune*. By the time Douglass did, he was mostly on the same political page with Marx about the 'statesmen' on the other side of the Atlantic.

Marx's possible impact on Douglass's change of heart regarding at least some of the British elite raises the interesting question if Douglass ever impacted Marx. In addition to the two important public letters published in English newspapers during the War, several of Douglass's major speeches were published in the New York *Daily Tribune*. But because Marx stopped receiving the organ around March 1862 after his services were no longer needed, only one of the speeches would Marx have likely read. Major New York papers that Marx

---

21   As far as we can tell, no one has done a thorough look at all the papers of US ambassador to the UK, Charles Adams, where an answer, possibly, awaits.

may or may not have had access to didn't start to run Douglass's speeches until February 1862. While it is possible that Marx saw those speeches there is no concrete evidence that he did.[22]

But what if he had actually read Douglass? Could he have learned something new? Possibly. The rich details in *Douglass' Monthly* about Blacks chomping at the bit to join the Union Army would have no doubt caught the eyes of both Marx and Engels, evidence for them about the North having a 'last card up its sleeve'.[23] Was there anything in the *Monthly* that might have challenged their views on the War? Maybe, but we couldn't find it. Close readers of the organ and Marx's and Engels's articles and correspondence may determine otherwise and we stand to be corrected.

One of the key revelations that came early in the comparison was to learn how much Douglass and Marx shared in common in addressing what today is called the race question, that is, racism and white supremacy. Making sense of the attitudes and behaviours of the slave oligarchs and their ideological defenders was not complicated in their opinion. Narrow economic interests motivated them, 'greed' for Douglass and the capitalist world market for Marx, in other words, what we call a class-based explanation for racism. The founding documents of the Confederacy said as much. Vice-President Alexander Stephens's 'corner-stone' speech could not have been more transparent – arguably the first official declaration of the ideology of white supremacy in service of economic exploitation.

---

22 At least two of Douglass's speeches were published in the New York *Times* in 1858. He had major speeches published in Boston, Philadelphia, San Francisco, and Rochester, New York papers during the war. In addition, in the wake of John Brown's raid, Douglass travelled to the United Kingdom and had his speeches reproduced in English, Scottish, and Irish papers. See the introductory material to speeches in Blassingame 1985 and Blassingame and McKivigan 1991. Not until 1872, it seems, did Marx first learn of Douglass, when he was nominated to be a third party vice-presidential candidate in the elections that year (P. Foner 1977, p. 374n60). Because Marx was dismissive of the Equal Rights Party's presidential candidate, Victoria Woodhull, 'middle-class humbug in America', historian Timothy Messer-Kruse (1998) insinuates that he was both sexist and racist. Marx, as it turned out, had good reason to be sceptical. Douglass never agreed to the nomination and Woodhull proved to be the charlatan that both she and her sister Tennessee Claflin had long been. See Nimtz 2003, pp. 248–50. Douglass ran into Woodhull on a trip to the United Kingdom in 1887. He did not recognise her and did not recall meeting her in the past. See Douglass's letter to Amy Post in Hanlon 2022. In fact, Douglass campaigned vigorously for Grant in 1872. See Blight 2018, pp. 533–5.

23 Almost priceless is an article about recent slaves from the Congo – yes, there was an African slave trade after 1808 – who signed up in New Orleans early in the War to fight. DM, April 1863, p. 829.

More challenging was how to explain why 'poor whites' signed on to the slave oligarchy's project. Both held that their allegiance was not innate but learned behaviour. Douglass's slave experience, especially from having worked on the docks in Baltimore, instructed him about 'the prejudices' of his white co-workers. It took the War for Marx to first offer an explanation. The 'bait', or the 'prospect one day of becoming slave owners themselves' was enough to entice them to embrace and enable the slaveocracy's inherent need to spread the peculiar institution to new territories in the United States and elsewhere. The takeaway for the Marx party was the need to abolish the institution. As long as white plebeians dreamed of upward mobility as slave owners themselves there would be no likelihood of them organising as a class to end class society.

As was common in the mid-century transatlantic world, 'race' for both Douglass and Marx was more akin to what today might be called ethnicity. And for both of them, subjugation in the form of enslavement could be the fate of any group of people regardless of skin colour. Neither had, in part, 'a theory of race' for that reason, as is often demanded, especially of Marx, by subsequent scholarship that has benefited from hindsight. In the course of the War, Douglass began to develop a set of ideas in order to think about the prospects for the former slaves after the War. Would the preexisting 'prejudices' of whites be an obstacle for racial equality? The more urgent question for Marx had to do with the 'prerogative of the white-skinned labourer', those, namely, who thought themselves superior to 'labor in black skin'. Such thinking stood in the way of their own 'true freedom' – one of the points that Marx made to Lincoln in November 1864 that later found its way into *Capital* three years later. Less than two years earlier, Douglass made, and apparently unbeknownst to Marx, almost exactly the same point in a speech in New York City. Nothing in the published record indicates that Marx said anything more significant on the race question, at least for the US reality.[24]

We contend that for those who seek to understand Marx's politics and not just his theory, there is no richer set of writings in the Marx-Engels corpus than his articles and correspondence with Engels about the Civil War.[25] They reveal why Marx could be as astute and accurate about the course of the War, specifically, the prospects for the North. Seeing how Marx tried to make sense of the 'humbug' of American politics, a process as tortuous then and now, is an added benefit. His insightful analysis of the autumn 1862 elections, for example, to see

---

24 See Appendix B, 'Marx and Engels on the Race Question: A Response to the Critics'.
25 Raya Dunayevskaya argued similarly in Dunayevskaya 1958.

if they registered support or not for Lincoln's Preliminary Emancipation Proclamation, give lie to the oft-made claim that Marx did not understand or take seriously bourgeois politics. Unlike Douglass, Marx had the advantage of debating his opinions with the only person who could best challenge him, Engels – an essential reason for Marx's acumen about the War not appreciated until now. Douglass lacked such a worthy opponent who could have possibly checked his half-baked opinions. After his partner's death, when Engels had to answer the then and still frequently made charge that their method, historical materialism, was all about socio-economic structures without room for human agency, Engels often countered by offering Marx's *The Eighteenth Brumaire* as evidence to the contrary. We propose, in addition, Marx's Civil War writings, and especially his debates with his partner. Exactly because of their more than two-year differences about the course of the War, there is no better example of real-time communist analysis of the class struggle.

Lincoln's more effusive thank you note, in the last months of the War, to the International Workingmen's Association than his more perfunctory one to the middle-class London Emancipation Society for their congratulatory messages on his re-election is significant. First, it registered that Marx, who wrote the message on behalf of the IWA, was back in the saddle doing effective disciplined collective work to advance the working class, unlike Douglass who continued to operate as a one-person party in what remained of the abolitionist movement. Second, it validated Marx's decision in his *Tribune* articles to compare more favourably the anti-interventionist stance of the English working class to that of Britain's 'betters', the crowd that Douglass looked to. Lincoln for certain read those articles. In the IWA message, Marx praised Lincoln as the 'single-minded son of the working class'; a description the president evidently appreciated. Douglass, after a lot of criticisms and doubts about him, came to laud Lincoln, in fact 'the black man's president', shortly after his assassination. But Lincoln as a 'single-minded son of the working class'? An unlikely descriptor that Douglass would have employed and soon verified by post-War developments.

If the Marx party and Douglass had been on the same page for the previous four years, they now increasingly went their separate ways after Appomattox. Weydemeyer's articles in September 1865 constituted, we argue, the party's post-War 'what is to be done' programme. On one key point both parties agreed, suffrage for Black men, the title of Weydemeyer's three articles. But Weydemeyer also called for the nationalisation of the Port Royal experience, that is, the confiscation of former slave owner plantations and making them available to former slaves upon which they and their families could make a living. For that second goal, the Marx party and Douglass objectively ended their war-time united front. Never the twain would meet.

About, first, the suffrage question. Though both our protagonists agreed that it was an essential democratic right that the former slaves should exercise, they did so for different reasons. For Douglass, the vote was 'the keystone' to eventual equality for Blacks. For Marx, on the other hand, the European Spring taught that suffrage, while an important democratic right, could only be a means to the end of social equality. More decisive toward that end, as the lessons of revolution surely demonstrated, was what took place outside the electoral/parliamentary arenas, especially on the barricades and battlefields. The best that elections had to offer, Marx and Engels concluded in their first documented self-criticism, was the opportunity for political education and determining when revolutionary forces had sufficient support to successfully make a revolution. On the way to that conclusion, Engels coined the term 'parliamentary cretinism' to sarcastically describe the belief of those who assumed that what took place in the chambers of parliament was the end all and be all of politics.

One of us, to supplement Engels's term, has coined 'voting fetishism', the mistaken belief that exercising the democratic right to vote is the actual exercise of power. To the contrary. To vote is to exercise the right to register a preference for either a candidate or a policy. Registering a preference, however, should never be confused with the profoundly different kind of action needed to exercise power.[26] To do so can be dangerous. Exhibit A is Douglass. The War provided Douglass for the first time with a road map to Black suffrage that he truly believed, to the end of his life, would guarantee full equality for African Americans – consistent with his long-held view that with suffrage 'people will cease to be subordinate to property'.[27] The real world of politics could not convince Douglass, to his peril, otherwise – in anticipation of Martin Luther King Jr.'s dilemma almost exactly a century later. That Marx did not equate elections with the actual exercise of power did not mean, however, that he dismissed them. His close reading, for example, of the Fall 1862 state and national elections testifies to how seriously he treated them. But again, not as an end but a means, in that case to determine public support for Lincoln's Preliminary Emancipation Proclamation.

It was the land confiscation issue that glaringly exposed the fundamental divide between our two protagonists. We have yet to find any mention in Douglass's corpus of his opinion of the Port Royal project, let alone any evidence of his support to what Weydemeyer proposed about generalising that example

---

26 Nimtz 2021b.
27 See Chapter 1, pp. 31, 38.

elsewhere or any such similar initiatives after the War.[28] His silence at that juncture had, we think, consequences. When the most crucial moment in the Radical Reconstruction effort occurred, Thaddeus Stevens's proposal to confiscate lands of the former slave oligarchs, Douglass, like most of the congressman's Republican colleagues, was largely missing in action. Engels's 1847 insight goes a long way in explaining Douglass's non-support for the Stevens proposal. All that could be expected of the slave, again, was opposition to property in persons. Only the proletariat, a class that Douglass only briefly belonged to, had a class interest in 'abolishing private property in general'. A bourgeois party like the Republicans, on the other hand, had no interest in undermining private property norms and, thus, their failure to support Stevens who, for whatever reason, was clearly the exception to the rule.[29] At the heart, then, of Radical Reconstruction's bloody defeat was the fundamental incompatibility of the private property requisites of capitalism and real democracy – what the demise of the European Spring taught Marx and Engels fifteen years earlier.[30] The liberal defence of private property that Douglass subscribed to, thus, aided and abetted the end to Radical Reconstruction's promise. His failure to publicly break with that ideology objectively implicated him in that all-so consequential missed opportunity – to be revisited.

If Douglass had been almost mum about the Stevens proposal in that crucial moment in Radical Reconstruction, he found his voice when the Parisian proletariat once again threatened, as it did in June 1848, capitalist property in 1871, the Commune. The one-time slave denounced them as 'deluded, ill-starred men', dupes of the 'Reds'.[31] As with the European Spring, Douglass adamantly opposed the revolutionary process becoming one 'in permanence', that is, the working class in power and, hence, the upending of capitalist property relations. The one-time slave – again, a fervent opponent of private property in persons who yet never effectively joined the working class – could never embrace any project that threatened to abolish 'private property in general'.

Douglass, like the economist Henry Carey, could be forgiven for subscribing to the harmony of capital and labour thesis, a selling-point he made for his *New National Era* newspaper earlier in 1871. Nothing in the history of the class

---

28   Another example from coastal Georgia is the subject of Robert Braxton's original research, Braxton 2023.
29   On Stevens and his motivations, see B. Levine 2021, 2021b, 2021c.
30   For details, see Nimtz 2021a. As for the class imperative in ending the postbellum experiment in political equality, Keysaar 2000, p. 114, perceptively notes: 'Ridding the electorate of blacks was a means of rendering most of the agricultural laborers of the rural South politically powerless, of restoring the "peasantry" to its pre-Civil War political condition'.
31   For details, see K. Edwards 2022.

struggle in the US would have taught him otherwise, certainly before the War. So telling for Marx about antebellum America was his employment as a correspondent by the pro-capitalist *Tribune* and the high esteem in which he was held by the country's leading economist, namely, Carey. The primitive level of capitalist relations of production and the class struggle in the country permitted, the historical materialist concluded, such an anomaly.

But after 1877, the nation's first general strike, Douglass, we contend, can no longer be excused for his disdain of an insurgent proletariat. And especially when federal troops that were supposed to protect Blacks against the terrorist violence they were being subjected to by the former slave oligarchs were sent to suppress the rebellious workers – and uncooperative Native Americans in the West. His near-silence about 1877, as far as we can determine, can only be explained by the comfortable embrace of the one-time slave by America's postbellum triumphant bourgeoisie, with all that implied for both domestic and international affairs.[32] Engels, we think again, provides an explanation – the slave/proletariat distinction.

One last point about Douglass and Reconstruction. He never seemed comfortable with what Marx, in his May 1865 letter on behalf of the IWA, advised President Johnson to carry out – 'stern duties' toward the defeated slavocracy. Likewise, it is hard to imagine Douglass agreeing with what Wendell Phillips wanted the Grant administration to do to end the mounting counterrevolutionary terror: 'I want him to go down to arrest some ex-general, who counts his acres by thousands, numbers his wealth by millions, and who stands enshrined in the loving admiration of half the South. I want to track him to his lair in the nest of assassins, and then arrest him at midnight, try him by sunrise, and shoot him before the sun is an hour high – and when it is done Georgia and South Carolina will learn unmistakably that they have a master'.[33] Even John Stuart Mill from afar, as noted, advocated a 'military dictatorship' to prevent the ensuing terror. Nor is there any indication that Douglass worked to delay the withdrawal of Union troops from the South after the War, the consequences of which became increasingly apparent, the bloody demise of Reconstruction – consequences we continue to live with.

We can only speculate on Douglass's near-silence. Perhaps his increasing integration into the upper echelons of the Republican Party gave him pause

---

32 Director of the Frederick Douglass Papers, John R. McKivigan, searched in vain for even a single mention of the Railroad Strike of 1877 in the Speeches Series. Nor could he find any mention of it in Douglass's letters – searches for which we are forever grateful. On Douglass's subsequent enabling of the US imperial project, see Blight 2018, pp. 536–45.

33 Bartlett 1961, pp. 318–19.

when it came to being critical of the Grant and Hayes administrations. The once politically independent Douglass had never failed to call-out or cajole Washington whenever he felt the need to do so – a potential lesson for twentieth-first-century equal-rights fighters who might be tempted to leave 'the streets for the suites'.

Historian Philip Foner, in general a Marx sympathiser, faults him for not doing enough to prevent Reconstruction's overthrow.[34] Perhaps it is to Foner's credit that he thought Marx had the capacity and obligation to do so. However well-intentioned, his criticism was largely beside the point, because by the early 1870s, the focus of his charges, the best that Reconstruction had to offer was history. After a detailed analysis of Foner's charges, here is what one of us wrote in 2003:

> What Foner offers is distilled by hindsight. Only if properly contextualised in the postwar U.S. reality and read within Marx and Engels's overall expectations about the American movement – along with their involvement and obligations in the international movement – can their actions or lack thereof begin to be understood. When Marx dropped everything in 1861, including the writing of *Capital*, to do what he could to affect the outcome of the Civil War, he did so because he correctly recognised that the centre of the international democratic movement, or world revolutionary process, was at that moment on the other side of the Atlantic. By 1866, the Austro-Prussian War, and certainly with the Paris Commune in 1871, the axis had shifted to Europe. That fact, more than anything, explains why, in the aftermath of the abolition of slavery, he and his partner relegated the U.S. theater to the back burner. Never, however, did they doubt that America would eventually take center stage.[35]

We stand by that response to Foner's charges.

If Foner felt compelled to call-out Marx for being derelict in defending Reconstruction, we find it odd that he didn't do the same for Douglass. Foner, after all, pioneered the collection and publication of the Douglass corpus for which we are all indebted to him. And it is in those writings that readers can learn, without too much effort, that Douglass, who, with more resources, could have been far more effective than Marx for the cause, was largely missing in action when it came to the make or break moment for America's first experiment in racial equality.

---

34 P. Foner 1977, pp. 39–42.
35 Nimtz 2003, pp. 177–8. See pp. 171–7 for a refutation of Foner's charges.

Douglass, as alluded to in the beginning of the Conclusion, seems to have had by the end of his life second thoughts about not aiding Thaddeus Stevens's land reform proposal in 1865. How to explain, he asked in his 1893 autobiography, why Reconstruction had been overthrown and the Jim Crow regime established?

> I will tell you. Our reconstruction measures were radically defective. They left the former slave completely in the power of the old master ... To the freedmen was given the machinery of liberty, but there was denied to them the steam to put it into motion ... They were called free but left almost slaves. The old master class was not deprived of the power of life and death which was the soul of the relation of master and slave. He who could say to his fellow-man, 'You shall serve me or starve' is a master and his subject is a slave. This was seen and felt by Thaddeus Stevens, Charles Sumner and leading Republicans; and had their counsels prevailed the terrible evils from which we now suffer would have been averted.[36]

By 1893 Douglass's epiphany, in uncanny anticipation of Martin Luther King, Jr's 1968 remark about the land issue for the former slaves, was too late. When radical abolitionist Wendell Phillips in 1871 called for force to deprive the 'old master class ... of the power of life and death' Douglass, again, was nowhere to be found. That same year following the Paris Commune, now made famous by his *The Civil War in France*, Marx reported 'the most important news', to a 15 August meeting of the General Council of the IWA in London, 'that Wendell Phillips, the great anti-slavery leader, had joined the ranks of the International' – an unlikely decision for Douglass.[37] How cognisant Phillips was of the IWA's programme and how active he was in its brief American incarnation is uncertain.[38] But for America's then most radical abolitionist to join the international organisation that Karl Marx effectively headed registers how pregnant that moment was with possibility if not necessarily probability. Only the class struggle and revolutionary practice, as always for Marx, could have known for sure.[39]

---

36   Gates 1994, pp. 932–3. See Foner 1955, p. 32. For the 'heavily edited' speech included as an appendix in Douglass's *Life and Times*, see Gates 1994, pp. 925–37. For the contemporaneous account of the speech and details about the version included in *Life and Times*, see Blassingame and McKivigan 1991, pp. 562–81.
37   Nimtz 2003, p. 190n46.
38   Nimtz 2003, pp. 164, 176–7, 264–5.
39   For Domenico Losurdo, the institution of the Jim Crow regime negated the significance of the overthrow of the slave oligarchy: Losurdo 2011, p. 322. Thus, the justification, appar-

Political acumen, as Engels once noted about his late partner, required knowing not only how to act but also – just as important if not more – when to act. What difference, if any, Douglass's assistance to Stevens and other 'leading Republicans' would have made will never be known. Only belatedly, again when it was too late, did Douglass come to recognise what Marx and Engels discovered a half-century earlier – the power of private property and why it needed to be expropriated by the toilers to ensure their emancipation.

For more than a decade, there has been a rich discussion amongst Douglass scholars that we end with. Most recently, as of this writing, intellectual historian Nick Bromell makes a convincing argument for what distinguished Douglass from both classical and reform liberals owing to his slave experience. Douglass had a visceral understanding of power but he 'warned that unless we have an opportunity to exercise those powers', the powers that make us human, 'we will not become conscious of them, and of the dignity and the rights that they confer' – what Marx would have fully agreed with. Compared to liberalism and natural rights philosophy, Douglass's views were 'far more relational and action-oriented' – justification, again, for our comparison with Marx.[40] Bromell, with a philosophical lens, examines Douglass's relationship to power and violence quite thoughtfully but glosses over or ignores his actual exercise of power as in enabling John Brown or recruiting Blacks for the Union army – arguably his most consequential actions. Bromell's silence is deafening, recalling the young Marx's quip: 'philosophy and the study of the actual world have the same relation to one another as onanism and sexual love'.[41] Just as one of us has long argued about Marx, the same can be said about Douglass – the need to rescue him from the clutches of philosophy – however well-intentioned it may be.

Douglass was first and foremost a political activist and his political ideas need to be evaluated on that basis – just as for Marx. We argue that Douglass's 'philosophy of reform' was a conscious alternative on his part to everything that Marx and Engels represented. That its earliest formulation came in the wake of the European Spring is no coincidence. His unsympathetic response to the slaughter of the Parisian Communards in 1871 was the other bookend to his

---

ently, of the conspicuous absence of Marx's Civil War activities amongst the many assertions Losurdo makes about him. But like the Paris Commune, America's Second Revolution was overthrown by a bloody counterrevolution upon whose ashes a *new* 'racial state' was founded and not, as Losurdo claims, the continuation of the prior one.

40   Bromell 2021, p. 197. Douglass, hence, comes close to being what political philosopher Raymond Geuss describes as a political realist. See Geuss 2008. For a critical read of Douglass's natural rights inspired notion of self-possession, see Nichols 2020, pp. 118–30.
41   Marx and Engels 1975–2004d, p. 236.

similar response to the earlier slaughter of a Parisian plebeian uprising, in June 1848. Former slave status did not, therefore, guarantee solidarity with an insurrection of the toilers. Likely more determinant, rather, was the subsequent class position of the former slave.

As for the debate amongst Douglass scholars on how to label him, we argue that it depends on which Douglass is being referred to. From the beginning of his endorsement of and material aid to John Brown's project from at least 1855 to his active recruitment of Black soldiers for the Union army, we call him a revolutionary liberal. But once he distanced himself from the Radical Reconstruction project to confiscate the lands of the former slave owners and distribute them to the former slaves, and then actively worked to advance the interests of the Republican Party, the label is inappropriate. Reform liberal is more accurate.[42]

David Blight, whose *Prophet of Freedom* was inspiration, in part, for this book, has since made the case for the 1857 Supreme Court *Dred Scott* decision being the turning point that made the War a near inevitability.[43] Resistance to the ruling, he smartly added, was also determinant. But it was the singular resistance of John Brown, Blight also needed to add, and his subsequent martyrdom that arguably did more than anything to actually start the War. The court's infamous decision may have been the necessary but not the sufficient condition for the War. And because the War, more than anything, brought about emancipation, Brown is arguably the individual who contributed more to abolition than anyone – what Engels asserted also some years later.[44] In both instances, Brown's ill-fated attack at Harpers Ferry and then his martyrdom, Douglass played a key role, possibly, therefore, his most consequential actions to end chattel slavery in America and why that moment justifies our use of 'revolutionary liberal' to label him.

Historian Matthew Karp joined the debate about labels for Douglass in order to refute Damon Root's contention that he hated socialism. 'That is a strange way', Karp objects, 'to describe an antislavery leader who devoted his life to seeking the forcible expropriation of property'. To make his point, Karp reproduced two pre-war, unpublished, articles from *Frederick Douglass' Paper* which imagined 'the economy of true equals' as he attacked land monopolies and con-

---

[42] Gregory P. Downs has coined the phrase 'bloody constitutionalist' to describe liberal revolutionaries, like Douglass, who shunned stern duties after the end of hostilities and feared the progressive march from bourgeois to proletarian revolution, that is, the revolution in permanence. Downs 2019, pp. 5–6.

[43] Blight 2022.

[44] Marx and Engels 1975–2004z, p. 77.

centrations of wealth. But Karp betrayed his own social democratic limitations. As Engels taught in 1847, being opposed to property in persons didn't make one a communist. Nor imagining an 'economy of true equals' or lambasting 'the rich' as many of Karp's persuasion are wont to do. The realisation of those worthy sentiments would require the 'abolishing of private property in general'. As well as repudiating the utopian socialism of John A. Collins, Douglass, as we've seen, disparaged the peaceful Chartist march in London in 1848 and the proletarian uprising in Paris shortly afterward, defended property in land, advocated for a harmony of interests between capital and labour, and regarded the revolutionary workers of the Paris Commune as 'blind and deluded tools' duped by 'the Reds'.[45] While one must ignore mounds of evidence to argue that Douglass should be a libertarian hero, on this point Root may be closer to the truth.

Kevin Black, an authority on transatlantic political discourses, rightly makes a case for putting Douglass in conversation with European 'contemporaries' about reform and revolution in order to fully take stock of his political ideas.[46] We wholeheartedly agree – that is what this book seeks to do. But Black is sorely mistaken to think that Montesquieu, Adam Smith, Edmund Burke, and Alexis de Tocqueville are the relevant interlocutors with Douglass when Marx is all-so present in real-time. It is as if Black went out of his way to exclude Marx from the conversation. Perhaps because it would reveal, as we argue our project has done, that however significant the contributions Douglass made in advancing the bourgeois democratic revolution, they were just that and no more. But for Marx and Engels that was fine. As Engels explained in 1892: 'Marx and I, for forty years, repeated ad nauseam that for us the democratic republic is the only political form in which the struggle between the working class and the capitalist class can first be universalised and then culminate in the decisive victory of the proletariat'.[47] Unlike for Douglass, the bourgeois democratic revolution for the two communists was, again, not an end but rather a means to an end. Deeply implicated in the protection and reproduction of private property – at its very core – that once liberatory project would be limited, at best, in the achievement of human emancipation. On full display today, in the United States and elsewhere, are the limitations of the bourgeois democratic revolution – this book's final topic.

On the eve of the publication of his *Prophet of Freedom*, David Blight fielded questions at a public presentation in 2018, the last of which – only recently

---

45 Karp 2020. Root 2017. 'Dark Prospects', *New National Era*, 8 June 1871.
46 See Black 2019 and Black 2017.
47 Marx and Engels 1975–2004n, p. 271.

discovered – asked if Douglass had a plan for Reconstruction. Not really, Blight replied. After relating some of the facts about the matter, already discussed here in Chapter 5, Blight concluded:[48]

> Douglass was not a very effective or modern economic thinker. He did not believe in property redistribution. He did not much believe in land redistribution. He wasn't an aggressive radical economic thinker at all. He believed most solutions were political. He was not a 20th-century man. You can't make him a Marxist, even if it is your life – if you put your life into it, you can't make him a Marxist. Not even close. He is the opposite.[49]

None of these emphatically made comments about the contrast with Marx, most relevant for this book, found their way, for whatever reason, into Blight's award-winning volume.[50] Nevertheless they anticipated what we discovered on our own. But Marx's and Douglass's opposition, what we uniquely demonstrate, was historically contingent and could be explained. Most importantly, our findings reveal that their differences were highly consequential for that all so pregnant moment in America's quest for social and racial equality.

2   'What Is to Be Done?' – Today

'Why I keep coming back to Reconstruction', the title of *New York Times*' columnist Jamelle Bouie's 25 October 2022 essay, is a convenient piece with which to end this book. Bouie has carved out for himself a unique place on the *Times*' op-ed pages by often interrogating present issues about race and class in the United States through the lens of the country's political history. At times, Bouie comes close to embracing some core ideas of Marx about the United States but can't quite bring himself to do so. Whether that's imposed or self-censorship is unknown. The October 2022 column is most exemplary.

At the heart of Bouie's essay is a call to take seriously W.E.B. Du Bois's explanation for the bloody overthrow of Reconstruction in his groundbreaking 1935 book *Black Reconstruction*. Basically, in Bouie's reading of Du Bois, Reconstruc-

---

48 One of the claims Blight makes is that Douglass embraced Thaddeus Stevens's Reconstruction proposals, with only minor differences. The facts, we think, especially on the crucial issue of land confiscation, say otherwise. See Chapter 5, pp. 257, 266–7.
49 Blight 2018a. Blight's reply begins at 1:30:15.
50 Blight 1991, pp. 194–5, said as much about Douglass three decades earlier. New this time, apparently, was the comparison with Marx. See also Blight 2018, pp. 426–7, 560.

tion ended owing to 'not race and culture calling out in the South in 1876', but to the fundamental incompatibility of the interests of property and postbellum democracy. 'What killed Reconstruction ... was a "counterrevolution of property" North and South' – the title of one of Du Bois's concluding chapters. 'Why is this still', Bouie asks, 'a useful framework for understanding the United States, close to a century after Du Bois conceived and developed this argument? As a concept, abolition-democracy captures something vital and important: Democratic life cannot flourish as long as it is bound by and shaped around hierarchies of status. The fight for political equality cannot be separated from the fight for equality more broadly. In other words', concludes Bouie, 'the reason I keep coming back to "Black Reconstruction" is that Du Bois's mode of analysis can help us (or, at least, me) look past so much of the ephemera of our politics to focus on what matters most: the roles of power, privilege and, most important, capital in shaping our political order and structuring our conflicts with one another'.[51]

For any close reader of this book so far or someone already familiar with basic Marx and Engels, Bouie's distillation of Du Bois should resonate. Not surprising given the origins of *Black Reconstruction* – what Bouie no doubt knows but fails to disclose.[52] That a *Times* columnist can tout a fundamental claim of Marx on its op-ed page is more significant, however, than attribution. Writing for either the *Tribune* or the liberal *Die Presse*, even Marx, we venture, would not have been so bold to do so. Thus, how to explain. We'll return to the question but first, the merits of Bouie's argument.

Because this book argues for the necessity of Marx, we are obligated to be hopeful that Bouie gets him right, even the Duboisian distilled version. Yet, Du Bois didn't always get Marx right.[53] Thus, the need to go back to the original intellectual inspiration for Du Bois's *Black Reconstruction*, as we do in this book. And even if Du Bois had always gotten Marx right, it would have strengthened his argument had he done as we do – a real-time comparison with a contemporary, specifically, Douglass. For example, in his 1933 article 'Karl Marx and the Negro', on the road to writing *Black Reconstruction*, Du Bois claimed that Marx

---

51　Bouie 2022.
52　Saman 2020.
53　Saman 2020; Oakes 2019; Kelly 2019; Barnes 2009, pp. 372–3fn 49; Novack 2013, pp. 346–54. While Barnes lauds *Black Reconstruction*'s 'rich and detailed description of what actually unfolded across the South' during Reconstruction, Du Bois's 'Stalinist exaggerations' are clear. Similarly, Novack praises Du Bois's book and says it 'remains one of the foremost contributions to American history ...' Yet, Novack offers a much more convincing analysis of the class basis and tasks of the social revolution, especially Novack 2013, pp. 353–4. For a measured yet enthusiastic endorsement of *Black Reconstruction*, see E. Foner 2013.

had to be taken with caution regarding 'Negroes' because 'he had not studied at first hand their peculiar race problem here in America'.[54] But as our comparison has revealed, in relation to Douglass's views, Marx could be remarkably insightful from four thousand miles away, offering a hitherto unknown explanation for southern white plebeian support for the slave oligarchy.[55] If Douglass's position came close to what Du Bois called a 'psychological wage' or incentive, the so-called 'wages of whiteness' thesis, Marx made the case for a material one, namely, the 'bait' of possible upward mobility.[56] Du Bois knew about Marx's closest contact in the US who helped him make sense of developments there but probably not to what extent, especially in regard to its 'peculiar race problem'. Exhibit A, Weydemeyer and his invaluable three articles in September 1865, written in response to questions and points that Engels had likely raised with him.

At the most crucial moment after the War with regard to the key issue affecting the former slaves, Weydemeyer asked: 'Why not transfer all the lands that have been abandoned, confiscated, or forfeited through tax default to free Negroes to cultivate independently?' Marx could learn more from a fellow communist than anything that Douglass had written. Being in America and in theory more aware of its 'peculiar race problem' was, in other words, no guarantee for doing the right thing when necessary.[57] Mounting a public campaign to give the new representatives of free labour the economic means, namely land, to defend their newly won political right to vote, as Weydemeyer was limited to doing in a German-language newspaper, is exactly what Douglass should have been doing with resources to do so more effectively. Being Black, therefore, as some today might presume, was also no guarantee of a greater awareness of the urgency of the land issue.

Though Du Bois did not suggest as much, for those who are prone to view social reality primarily through the lens of race rather than class, his caution is

---

54   DuBois 2016, p. 219. About the essay and another one by Du Bois on Marx in the *Crisis* that year, 'Marxism and the Negro Problem', see Saman 2020, p. 43.

55   Lacking the kind of evidence this book presents, Charles Mills mistakenly thought that Douglass had more to offer than Marx in the quest for racial equality. Mills 1997, pp. 88, 119. We revisit Mills in Appendix B.

56   Reed 2017.

57   Regarding 'in theory', we recognise that Douglass may simply have been uninformed about the land situation of the former slaves since we have yet to locate any real-time pronouncements on his part on the matter, although his son Lewis certainly informed him about the pitiful wages and lack of Black land ownership in St. Michaels, Maryland. Blight 2018, p. 448. But that begs the question, why? It simply wasn't, our assumption, a priority for him.

likely to be read that way. And, thus, be surprised to learn – as Martin Luther King, Jr would likely have been – that yes, a white male Marx party member was more attuned to the needs of Black toilers, specifically, for land, than a former Black slave, but one who defended private property relations and championed a capitalist party. Class and class orientation, in other words, matter.

With those qualifications in mind, we agree wholeheartedly with Bouie's important point about the need 'to look past so much of the ephemera of our politics to focus on what matters most: the roles of power, privilege and, most important, *capital* [our emphasis] in shaping our political order and structuring our conflicts with one another'. 'Ephemera', we think, is an appropriate word, what Marxists might call operating at the level of appearances rather than essences. But no influential daily organ of the ruling class contributes more to that ephemera than Bouie's own newspaper, the *New York Times*, the literary representative of its liberal wing. Two examples immediately come to mind and are both relevant to this book. First, what Marx called the 'humbug' of US bourgeois politics, an issue that constantly challenged Engels, and, second, the *Times'* 1619 Project. We begin with the former.

Martin Luther King, Jr., as noted in the introduction to this Conclusion, in 1967 chided political science research that questioned the efficacy of the suffrage. 'A recent major work by social scientists Matthew[s] and Prothro concludes that "the concrete benefits to be derived from the franchise – under conditions that prevail in the South – have often been exaggerated", that voting is not the key that will unlock the door to racial equality because "the concrete measurable payoffs from the negro voting in the South will not be revolutionary" (1968). James [Q] Wilson supports this view, arguing, "Because of the structure of American politics, as well as the nature of the Negro community, Negro politics will accomplish only limited objectives" (1965)'.[58] For King, again, these findings, if true, were disheartening. And because Wilson focused on northern cities, particularly Chicago, his conclusion boded ill for those who had only recently been able to vote in the South. 'If the main thrust of Negro effort has been, and remains, substantially irrelevant, we may be facing an agonizing crisis of tactical theory'.[59] Indeed, and no wonder his angst.

Exactly a decade earlier, King declared:

> Give us the ballot ... and we will no longer have to worry the federal government about our basic rights ... Give us the ballot and we will fill our

---

58 Matthews and Prothro 1966, p. 481; Wilson 1965.
59 King 1968.

legislative halls with men of good will ... Give us the ballot and we will help bring this nation to a new society based on justice and dedicated to peace.[60]

It was as if King was channelling Douglass almost a century later. But the research data did verify what King feared and someone should have told him so.[61] That no authoritative figure in the discipline of political science, as far as we can determine, ever responded to him speaks volumes about its still existent and ironical deficit – a lack of interest in politics.

King, like Douglas, was afflicted with both voting fetishism and parliamentary cretinism, the mistaken beliefs, again, that to vote is to actually exercise political power and that what takes place in the parliamentary arena is the be-all and end-all of politics. No daily organ of the capitalist ruling class is as unapologetically conscious about promoting both misrepresentations of political reality as is the *Times*, in order to make sure the class struggle is confined to both arenas, particularly the proletarian side of the struggle. As for why the suffrage hasn't delivered racial equality as King or his followers since then had hoped – and Douglass had expected – liberals now have a ready explanation: 'systemic racism', a problem baked into the country's DNA, according to the 1619 Project. But their class interests and blinders, reinforced by the daily ephemera of the *Times*, especially its devotion to the 'humbug' of bourgeois politics, prevent them from ever entertaining the real reason that Bouie has correctly distilled from Marx via Du Bois: 'Democratic life cannot flourish as long as it is bound by and shaped around hierarchies of status'. The failure of the electoral/parliamentary process to deliver racial equality stems, therefore, from the same reason that it can't deliver social equality – the fundamental incompatibility between real democracy and class society, capitalism being its latest edition. Two-hundred years before the *Communist Manifesto*, True Leveller or Digger, Gerard Winstanley, said as much – in anticipation of the bloody defeat of both the European Spring and Reconstruction.

Bouie could be called a 'diversity hire', not for his skin colour but rather his politics. The crisis of capitalism and the increasing working-class disaffection that it inevitably generates requires the *Times* editors to at least pretend to understand that sentiment and give, occasionally, a voice to it – thus, the basic reason for Bouie's column. A way to give hope to its liberal readership. But for every provocative column, the *Times* has many other columnists to drown

---

60   Charles V. Hamilton, 'Foreword' to Preston et al 1982, p. xviii.
61   Including a follow-up study to the Matthews and Prothro volume: Keech 1968.

out an occasional revolutionary insight from Bouie. And if necessary, they can recruit other system-maintenance voices to do the same, someone who might even be of the same skin colour. Witness how it opened its op-ed page at the height of the George Floyd protests in the summer of 2020 to Democratic Party leader Stacey Abrams. In a piece titled 'I Know Voting Feels Inadequate Right Now: Just Hear Me Out', Abrams pleaded with the protestors to abandon the streets and turn their attention to making sure that Donald Trump would not be re-elected – the Party's solution to police brutality. 'Voting in a democracy', she proclaimed, 'is the ultimate power'.[62] Abrams was employing a more than century-old tactic of enticing mass protest movements into the electoral arena, specifically, to her party, the graveyard of popular social movements – the populist movement in 1896 being its first victim.[63] Not for naught the quip in reply to the question, whatever happened to the Civil Rights Movement?: 'Out of the streets, into the suites'.

As for other *Times* columnists who can be relied on to counter an occasional system-threatening piece by Bouie, none is as relevant for us as David Brooks and his 2018 essay 'Understanding Student Mobists', at the beginning of the second year of the Trump presidency. Like Abrams's piece, it too was directed at youth, a plea to get them to see that societal problems, like racial inequality, are a 'mistake' rather than something more fundamental. He admitted that he would have an uphill battle in trying to convince them. To make his case, nevertheless, he urged young people

> to take two courses. The first would be in revolutions – the French, Russian, Chinese and all the other ones that unleashed the passion of the mob in an effort to overthrow oppression – and the way they ALL wound up waist deep in blood. The second would be in constitutionalism. We dump on lawyers, but the law is beautiful, living proof that we can rise above tribalism and force – proof that the edifice of civilizations is a great gift, which our ancestors gave their lives for.[64]

All so telling about Brooks's plea was how completely oblivious it was to US history, as if chattel slavery was a 'mistake' that had nothing to do with economic imperatives, and the sobering fact that an enormous amount of blood, 'waist deep', had to be spilled to get rid of it. In Lincoln's immortal words from his

---

62 Abrams 2020.
63 Novack 2013, pp. 441–53; Nimtz 2017.
64 Brooks 2018.

Second Inaugural Address about what it would take if necessary to rid the country of slavery: 'until every drop of blood drawn by the lash shall be paid with another drawn by the sword'. As for 'constitutionalism', Marx was absolutely right when he said weeks before Lincoln issued the Preliminary Emancipation Proclamation: 'wars of this kind ought to be conducted along revolutionary lines, and the YANKEES have so far been trying to conduct it along constitutional ones'.[65] For liberals like Brooks and his editors, the Civil War is a terribly inconvenient fact about American history.

No moment is as instructive in US politics as the period from March 1857 to April 1865, a moment that profoundly confirmed Marx's and Engels's insight that real politics takes place outside the electoral/parliamentary arenas. Three major decisions made under the authority of the Constitution were only *effectively* decided in an arena *unauthorised* by the Republic's founding document. We refer, respectively, to the Supreme Court's notorious Dred Scott ruling of March 1857, the contested presidential election of Abraham Lincoln in November 1860, and the passage by Congress in March 1861 of a proposed amendment to give constitutional protection to the institution of slavery in the states where it existed, and unopposed by the just inaugurated president. But it was the outcome of the Civil War, the battlefield, April 1865, that proved to be the ultimate arbiter of what took place in all three spheres of constitutional governance – what the authorised process had made no allowance for. And just as the future of chattel slavery could not be settled on authorised terrain so too will it be for the future of wage slavery – capitalism.

The first major African American experience in voting ended after a decade or two with the demise of Reconstruction. By the time all Blacks, men and women, were able to do so again, the achievement of the Second Reconstruction, capital had learned to live with the suffrage by having erected institutions to effectively wall-off capitalist property from the electorate. Chief among them and indispensable for liberal democracy are central banks whose consequential decisions for the working class on behalf of capital are not subject, by design, to popular vote. Witness, as this is being written, the actions of the US Federal Reserve Bank, created in 1913, to reduce inflation with the likely risk of a recession that will take its toll, as expected, on the working class – disproportionately on its most vulnerable layers, especially African Americans. Capitalist politicians of both parties will be able to absolve themselves of any responsibility for the Fed's actions on the supposed grounds that they had nothing to do with the recession – that too by design.

---

65   Marx and Engels 1975–2004u, p. 400.

Along with the Fed, a host of other institutions were put in place to ensure that the state could make decisions on behalf of capital without any interference of the working-class electorate, the so-called 'administrative state'. No wonder, therefore, that the 1965 Voting Rights Act and its implementation since then, despite claims of Democratic Party leaders like Abrams and President Joseph Biden that it has been eviscerated by either the Supreme Court or Republicans, has not generated the kind of bloody opposition that effectively made null and void the Fifteenth Amendment by 1900. King, therefore, had good reason to fear two years after the enactment of the Act that nothing fundamentally different would be realised. Business, that is, racial inequality, could continue as usual. We recognise, however, as history has taught, that if the capitalist rulers conclude that the walls around its wealth are no longer strong enough to hold back the toilers in all their skin colours with their pitchforks, they will suspend liberal democracy and take off their velvet gloves and let the dogs out – the fascist card.

When Barack Obama came along, one of us advised students to be sober. The metaphor employed to help them make sense of the presidential aspirant and election winner was the distinction between an operating system and an app. Obama, we said, represented a new app, with lots of bells and whistles, who was invested in by his capitalist donors only because they assumed that he would be compatible with the system that he would be downloaded into. He didn't disappoint and therein lies the fundamental reason why his two-term tenure did not result in any qualitative improvement in the well-being of African Americans. His moment in history is increasingly looking ephemeral.

The dilemma that the liberal wing of the US capitalist class has faced for some time is its inability to guarantee, as it once had, the proletarian vote. When the then head of the Delaware AFL-CIO, an African American, expressed his frustration to then Vice-President Biden about the lacklustre performance of the Obama-Biden administration on behalf of organised labour, the latter shot back: 'what are you complaining about; you know that you have nowhere else to go!'[66] Wrong, as events would show shortly afterward; workers could vote for a Republican or stay at home.

The vulnerability of the Democrats was all so visibly on display in 2016, aided and abetted by the editorial page of the *Times* – an error for which its editors have never owned up. Rather than see Bernie Sanders, a social democrat, be the Democratic Party nominee the organ was willing to risk, in Marx's all so apt words about the original Bonapartist, a 'grotesque mediocrity' in the White

---

66   Nimtz 2021b.

House, by promoting a seriously flawed nominee who personified all that was wrong for millions of workers with Washington, 'the swamp'. Rather, also, than admit to its role in getting Trump elected, and the real reason for his victory, the crisis of capitalism and the deep distrust it has generated about business as usual in Washington – again what Hillary Clinton epitomised – the *Times*' editors decided to play the race card. Therein the motivation and origins of the *1619 Project*.

The flawed facts the *Times' Project* asserts about American history – at least in its first iteration – have garnered the most attention.[67] Specifically, the claims that the arrival of the African captives in Jamestown, Virginia, in 1619 constitutes the country's true origins, and that African Americans have never been able to rely on anyone other than themselves to advance. The evidence this book presents about Douglass disputes both claims. His appearance in the *1619 Project* is at best skewed – we see only his complaints about the lack of racial equality for African Americans. Douglass, as the reader of this book now knows, was the product of the interracial abolitionist movement and continued to acknowledge that fact until the end. And of all the figures in that movement with whom he collaborated, none of them proved to be as consequential as John Brown – who too is absent in the *1619 Project*'s telling of African American history.

Also missing in the *Times*' account – conveniently in our view – is what Douglass thought about 1619. His complaints about America's shortcomings were rooted in his unshakeable contention that 1776 and 1789 were the country's true founding – not 1619. The indelible lines in the Declaration of Independence, 'all men are created equal', and in the Preamble of the Constitution, 'we the people', were Douglass's lodestar, foundational for his political beliefs. Rather than 1619, Douglass believed that what happened two centuries later birthed the 'Slave power' – the Missouri Compromise, which merits only one mention in the *1619 Project*.[68] That national ruling class decision in 1821, Douglass held, put the United States on a path-dependent course to the 'irrepressible conflict' four decades later. Recent scholarship, being collected as the *Times* was putting together its *Project*, sustains Douglass's position.[69] It makes sense that events

---

67 The *Project* first appeared in magazine form in August 2019 and, subsequently, in a book which addressed some of the criticisms engendered by some of the magazine essays, especially the opening one by *Project* editor Nikole Hannah-Jones. For both editions see: https://www.nytimes.com/interactive/2019/08/14/magazine/1619-america-slavery.html
68 For some of Douglass's pronouncements on 1619 and the Missouri Compromise, see Blassingame 1985, pp. 301–2, 324, 326–30 and P. Foner 1952, pp. 197–201.
69 Pasley and Hammond 2021.

more proximate to 1861 rather than those at the beginning of British colonial America, some two centuries earlier, would be determinant.

But as problematic as the *Times' Project* is regarding factual history, more significant in our opinion is its political agenda – a conscious effort to promote race rather than class to explain not just the Trump moment but also America's past and present. On no issue is that agenda so visible as its explanation for the overthrow of Reconstruction – a still consequential undoing, about which this book has something to say. The reason for the defeat of the country's first experiment in interracial democracy, according to Nikole Hannah-Jones, the progenitor and lead author of the *Project*, is evident: 'Tyranny is a central theme of American history ... and racial exploitation and racial conflict have been part of the DNA of American culture'.[70] More concretely, 'white rule', 'white Southerners', 'white Northerners', 'white people', and 'white owners of economic monopolies' were the culprits.[71] With that litany, beginning with a quote from a leading student of slavery taken out of context, Hannah-Jones spins a tale that occludes reality.[72] Racist animus, this book demonstrates, served rather to rationalise the triumphant bourgeoisie's post-Civil War imperative – what her last culprit at best hints at – exploitation of labour in not only Black but white skin. Capitalism, in other words, does a better job, we claim, in explaining the bloody defeat of Reconstruction rather than something called 'white'. Not for naught did we begin this section of the Conclusion with *Times* columnist Jamelle Bouie and his all so accurate point distilled from Du Bois:

> In the end, 'it was not race and culture calling out of the South in 1876; it was property and privilege, shrieking to its kind, and privilege and property heard and recognized the voice of its own'. What killed Reconstruction – beyond the ideological limitations of its champions and the vehemence of its opponents – was a 'counterrevolution of property', North and South.[73]

What our project uniquely does is to return to the real-time origins of Du Bois's insight – Marx's explanation for the overthrow of the opening act to the Second American Revolution, the European Spring – namely, the fundamental incompatibility of democracy and capitalism. Just as the 1848–9 Revolutions anticip-

---

70 Hannah-Jones et al 2021, p. 29.
71 Hannah-Jones et al 2021, p. 465.
72 Davis 2006, p. 226. Readers can verify that Davis in no way meant the comment to be his take on why Reconstruction was defeated.
73 Bouie 2022.

ated 1861 – the 'tocsin' Marx might have called them – their demise two years later foreshadowed the counterrevolution that formally commenced in 1877 on the other side of the Atlantic, and for basically the same reason.

The 1619 Project, we argue, is the liberal counterpart to the conservative Tucker Carlson Project. Both have a class interest in convincing the American public, particularly, its working-class component, that to know someone's race is more important than knowing what class they belong to. Not only Marx, but Douglass the revolutionary liberal would also, we contend, have disagreed – as his collaboration with John Brown surely demonstrated. Those who originate in the working class but have now hitched their meritocratic wagon onto the train of the capitalist ruling class have no class interest in slaying the goose that lays the golden egg upon which they comfortably feast – not unlike 'the bait' of upward mobility that Marx once diagnosed for plebeian Southern whites.

The 2020 George Floyd protests at their height registered the profound changes in racial attitudes that have taken place in the US in the last half-century owing to the Second Reconstruction. Before the anti-police brutality marches that gave rise to the Black Lives Matter movement, such actions were almost exclusively composed of African Americans. The Rodney King protests in 1992 demonstrated that it could even be dangerous for whites to be in the vicinity of such actions. The outcome of the trial of the cops who brutally beat King is also instructive. Despite video footage of the beating, a first, the all-white California jury exonerated them – in telling contrast to the half-white, all-working-class jury that voted three decades later to convict the cop who killed George Floyd, also captured on camera.

But brutality filmed, as the California trial showed, is no guarantee of outrage – attitudinal change is necessary. In the Minnesota city of Duluth, the state where Floyd was killed, ten thousand Caucasians celebrated the lynching of three Black men in 1920, many having their picture taken with the broken and mutilated bodies. Exactly a century later, thousands of the city's Caucasian residents, some no doubt descendants of the earlier celebrants, protested the killing of Floyd. How to explain the difference? Midway between both years, a mass mainly working-class African American movement, known now as the Civil Rights Movement, won the respect of the majority of white Americans and prompted positive attitudinal changes about race – registered in all kinds of ways.

Ironically, the discontent of figures like Nikole Hannah-Jones about race in the United States testifies to how much progress has been made. Their upward mobility has generated unmet and now threatened expectations. Yes, 'systemic racism' exists. It can't be otherwise in a society based on private ownership of the means of production with a history of racial slavery.[74] Equally true is that the United States is less racist than it's ever been. That bodes well for building the only kind of movement that can end racial inequality, a mass multiracial working-class movement to end social inequality, the sine qua non for racial equality. No wonder that those who have a class interest in making sure that such a movement never materialises do everything they can to play, in one disguise or another, the race card, be it the *Times*' daily op-ed page or the now-defunct Tucker Carlson Show.

We return to the question that introduced this inquiry, the one that challenged Martin Luther King, Jr. in the last year of his life: how to realise racial equality in the US for the first time, and the solution he entertained. But there will never be a 'radical redistribution of economic and political power' *without*, as Engels argued in 1847, 'the abolishing of private property in general'. Though we'll never know for sure, King, the liberal like Douglass, and conscious opponent of what Marx and Engels stood for, would likely have never agreed with Engels. Yet, two scholars recently suggest otherwise, an important intervention into the debate about King's legacy that needs, especially for this book, to be addressed.

Andrew Douglas and Jared Loggins argue that implicit in the King corpus is a critique of 'racial capitalism' that they purport to flesh out into a coherent 'critical theory' for the 'realization of a more just world'.[75] Whether they have successfully done so is beyond the immediate concern of this book.[76] More relevant for us is how they read King's reading of Marx. 'King's treatment of Marx', they write, 'was often roughshod, if not disingenuous – a fact owed partly to the pressures put upon him by the Cold War context of the 1950s and early '60s'.[77] But only in a footnote do they actually quote King regarding Marx, a passage from his 1957 autobiography *Stride Toward Freedom*. 'I read Marx as I read all of the influential historical thinkers – from a dialectical point of view, combining a partial "yes" and a partial "no". In so far as Marx posited a metaphysical materialism, and ethical relativism and a strangulating totalitarianism, I responded with an unambiguous "no"; but in so far as he pointed to weaknesses of traditional capitalism, contributed to the growth of a definite self-consciousness in the masses, and challenged the social conscience of the Christian churches,

---

74   For what's possible in a society devoid of such property relations but with such a history, see Appendix B.
75   Douglas and Loggins 2021, p. 16.
76   How they read Marx on the race question is a matter of importance that we address in Appendix B.
77   Douglas and Loggins 2021, p. 23.

I responded with a definite "yes". My reading of Marx also convinced me that truth is found neither in Marxism nor in traditional capitalism'.[78]

A decade later King, as quoted in the Introduction to this book, reiterated, and more pointedly, his rejection of Marxism, specifically its twentieth-century revolutionary leaders, in his presentation/sermon at Ebenezer Baptist Church. But nowhere do Douglas and Loggins mention those criticisms. The omission, we contend, is not accidental. To have been forthright about King's consistent anti-communism, especially his rejection of Lenin and Trotsky in 1967, would make it difficult for them to put a revolutionary veneer on him at the end of his life. As for 'abolishing private property in general', Douglas and Loggins note that 'King appeared to hold that private wealth accumulation and its legal protection could be justified insofar as it could be made to serve the public good', or that 'capital could be hemmed in by a web of regulatory constraints and made to "set aside profit for the greater good"'. Yet, they admit that these 'kinds of suggestions and insinuations cannot be easily squared with King's gestures toward a more comprehensive structural critique of capitalist production, circulation, and exchange'.[79] Marx would have been more straightforward about the contradiction. As for the proletariat, the best that Douglas and Loggins can say in King's favour is that he 'praised the dignity of labor ... a potential ally to the Black freedom struggle'.[80] Other than these points, there is no sustained discussion of either the working class or the property question in their effort to 'reconstruct King's critical theory of capitalist society', or 'racial capitalism'.[81] Despite this glaring lacuna in Douglas and Loggins's rendering of King, the Communist Party USA's *Peoples Weekly World* employs the two scholars to reinvent the Civil Rights leader, a closet communist if the organ is to be believed. Their evidence, King's criticisms of capitalism in a 1967 speech.[82]

Another recent assessment of King's politics argues that he saw himself as a 'democratic socialist'.[83] Though without citation, that characterisation comes closer, in our opinion, to the truth. Never did twentieth-century social democracy, certainly, call for 'the abolishing of private property in general'. Earlier in our book, we argued that 'bourgeois socialism', the label Marx and Engels

---

[78] Douglas and Loggins 2021, p. 98n23.
[79] Douglas and Loggins 2021, p. 45.
[80] Douglas and Loggins 2021, p. 47.
[81] A major problem Douglas and Loggins face is to hang their argument on Cedric Robinson's 'racial capitalism'. Robinson 1983, as one of us pointed out years ago (see Nimtz 1985a), was never a Marxist – was in fact an opponent – despite the title of his book *Black Marxism*.
[82] Haynes 2023.
[83] Dreier 2023. According to Keeanga-Yamahtta Taylor 2022, King was able to 'articulate and popularise a social democratic agenda'.

employed in the *Communist Manifesto* to describe social reformers who were critical of the status quo, as appropriate for describing Douglass. We think the same for characterising King's politics. 'Communists', Marx and Engels underscored at the end of the document, always 'bring to the front ... the property question' in the class struggle, 'no matter what its degree of development at the time' – all so different from 'bourgeois socialism'.

Only the proletariat, again, Marx and Engels argued, had a class interest in 'abolishing private property in general', the only way to free themselves from the chains of their capitalist oppressors. Because a hereditary working class was non-existent in the US after the Civil War, and even when Douglass and Engels died in 1895, the socialist alternative could never have been on the agenda, as Engels knew all so well. Only with a hereditary working class in place could a class conscious fighting proletarian leadership emerge. Yet Engels remained optimistic to the end that the US, like more advanced capitalist societies elsewhere, would not be the exception to the rule. What about since then? Is there evidence that warrants Engels's optimism?

By 1967 when King had his epiphany, a hereditary US proletariat had come into place, including its contingent in Black skin. No Black figure best represented and spoke in and to its interests as did Malcolm X in the last thirteen months of his life. There had been Black proletarian leaders prior to him but the vast majority of them ended up in the graveyard of progressive social movements, the Democratic Party by way of the Communist Party's Moscow-originated popular front policy. What made Malcolm X unique was his principled opposition to any kind of collaboration with or support to the Democrats, his staunch rejection of their siren call for lesser evil politics – specifically, the Democratic Party nominee in the 1964 presidential election and future president Lyndon Baines Johnson. King and other civil rights leaders, on the other hand, agreed to suspend protests in order to ensure the election of Johnson. Whether to support Democrats in opposition to Republicans continues, all so instructively, to befuddle much of the US Left.

Douglass, to be remembered and worth repeating, had to grapple with the lesser-evil issue beginning with the 1848 presidential election, after he abandoned Garrison's apolitical abolitionism, and until the 1864 contest when he briefly flirted with the Frémont nomination. And so too did Marx and Engels during the German edition of the European Spring, their first experience with elections. They concluded, also worth repeating, in a self-criticism, that it was to the long-term advantage of the working-class movement to have its own political party and candidates in elections, independently of bourgeois and petit-bourgeois parties 'even where there is no prospect whatsoever of their being elected'. Maintaining 'their independence' would allow the movement 'to count their forces and ... lay before the public their revolutionary attitude and party standpoint'. Elections for Marx and Engels, again, were not an end in themselves but rather a means to an end, to make a revolution.

Malcolm X's rejection of the Democratic Party earned him the opprobrium of the Communist Party, as well as any subsequent example of Black independent political action faithful to his course. Thus, their race-baiting charge that he hated white people. But if King reaffirmed in his last year his disdain for the communist project, after having given backhanded support to the Democratic Party nominee Johnson, Malcolm X, in the depths of the Cold War, openly fraternised with communists, spoke at their public forums, made himself available for their interviews, and endorsed their newspaper – that is, white communists who also rejected collaboration with the Democratic Party, giving lie, then, to the Communist Party's race-baiting campaign.[84] So much, also, for the Martin Luther King, Jr.-Malcolm X convergence thesis.[85] To their credit, Douglas and Loggins acknowledge that Malcolm was more of a radical than King when quoting him from his last year: '"you can't have capitalism without racism". This is a striking line from Malcolm X. King never made the connection in quite so stark a way, at least not publicly' – as per our point about the difference between the two at the end of their lives.[86]

The fight not just for racial but also social equality still suffers from Malcolm X's untimely death in 1965. Until 1966, the historical fight for equality for African Americans had largely been an interracial affair with the collaboration of Douglass and John Brown being arguably its apogee. But the decision that year of the Black leadership of the Student Non-Violent Coordinating Committee to expel its white members constituted a rupture with that tradition that's still unrepaired. In the institutionalised Black Lives Matter movement, for example, whites are relegated, if allowed to participate, to second class status in not being allowed to be in the leadership or to have equal voice in decision-making – with all that's so problematic about such a modus operandi for a movement that claims to be fighting for social equality. The figure who most inspired the SNCC leadership by then was none other than Malcolm X. The

---

84 See Appendix B, 'Marx and Engels on the Race Question: A Response to the Critics', for the historical background to this collaboration.

85 For details, see Barnes 2020, Index: Malcolm X, and Martin Luther King; and *Militant*; and SWP; and Young Socialist Alliance. For recent revelations about King's thoughts on Malcolm X, see Eig 2023.

86 Douglas and Loggins 2021, p. 9. Malcolm X made the comment at the Militant Labor Forum in New York City, sponsored by the Socialist Workers Party, the largely white communist party with whom he was collaborating. The updated source for the quote is Breitman 2020, p. 95.

exclusion decision, never, apparently, submitted to a rank and file vote, was informed no doubt by the image of Malcolm X of the Nation of Islam, that is, when he rejected any collaboration with whites.[87] Tragically, the Malcolm X of the last year of his life, fraternising openly with white communists in his principled quest for allies was unlikely known – a fact that those of us who lived through that pregnant moment could have surely benefited from knowing about.

Despite his loss, there is no reason to assume that what Malcolm X represented will not reappear in one form or another. The African American population is more proletarian than ever with even deeper class divisions, the necessary condition for birthing a revolutionary leadership of the calibre of Malcolm X. This explains why no one like him existed to effectively challenge the reformist politics of Douglass after emancipation. King, the Douglass of his era, could not be so lucky. By then, the proletarian character of Black America had been decided.

Owing, also, to the collapse of the Stalinist regimes more than three decades ago, the Communist Party USA no longer has access to the perks it once used to win proletarian Black fighters to its class collaborationist programme. Never has its influence in the working class been as diminished as it is today. It will be easier, therefore, for future working class fighters to emulate Malcolm X's example – to reject the deadly embrace of the Democratic Party that the Communist Party continues to unapologetically promote, in league with the *New York Times*.[88]

US capital, ever since the end of its post-World War II boom in the early eighties, has shown itself incapable of solving its decades-long crisis of stagnant growth and low productivity other than on the backs of the working class.[89] Ahead, then, are big labour battles in which the Black proletariat, owing to its history and place in American capitalism, will play an outsized role. Sobriety demands recognition that the best that the capitalist mode of production has to offer the world's toilers, historically unprecedented achievements and duly acknowledged by Marx and Engels in their foundational document, is behind us. As grim evidence, the deteriorating life expectancy rates of the American working class. But if the future class battles are inevitable, not so are

---

[87] For invaluable details and context, see Whitaker 2023, chapters 6 and 16.
[88] Although an import from Moscow for the CPUSA, class collaborationism has a long history in American left circles, with roots in populist and progressive movements in the second half of the nineteenth century. See Novack 2013, 'The Rise and Fall of Progressivism', pp. 441–53.
[89] For a Marxist explanation of the crisis, see Roberts 2016.

their outcomes. What the *Manifesto* promises is the class struggle, not the winners and losers – only the promise that the working class will get its shot at the title. 'Inevitable', *unvermeidlich* in the original, appears only once in the document, followed immediately by what the proletariat needs to do to win. This book unabashedly seeks to supplement those still invaluable instructions.

APPENDIX A

Douglass and Marx on the Paris Commune and the Labour Question in the United States

Kyle A. Edwards

When did Radical Reconstruction come to an effective end?[1] Historians continue to debate the issue. Heather Cox Richardson points to the Military Reconstruction Act of 1867, 'far reaching and radical', as 'the last gasp of Lincoln's Republican Party'. Richardson also argues persuasively that the reaction of liberal Republican opinion to the Paris Commune and 'the rise of labor unions' at home, was a decisive moment in the five years that followed where 'party members would abandon their commitment to equality and tie the party to big business'.[2] If true, then how did our two protagonists respond to the Commune in Paris and the rise of labour unions in the United States and what, if any, were the implications of their responses for how they viewed the way forward in the US? – the subject of this appendix.

Douglass was initially inspired by the revolutions in France in 1848. The overthrow of slavery, the institution of republican institutions, and the overthrow of the monarchy led Douglass to believe that the downfall of slavery in America might be at hand. When Chartists in England and the workers of Paris sought to enter the fray, however, Douglass denounced the mass demonstrations and violence-baited the rebellious labourers. This might suggest how Douglass would respond to insurgent workers once again in France's capital in 1871. However, world-changing events, between 1848 and 1871, along with a major shift in Douglass's political philosophy from a pacifist Garrisonian to a political abolitionist willing to endorse slave insurrection, might suggest otherwise.

In addition, between 1853 and 1855, Douglass sought to make a case for a transracial class alliance amongst US toilers in the fight against slavery. Douglass's insights about the similarities and differences of exploitation under the capitalist and the slave mode of production were remarkable, ones that Marx with his historical materialist perspective could have agreed with.

---

1 This appendix draws heavily on the research and writing from K. Edwards 2022.
2 Richardson 2014, pp. 66, 70, 93–4. Richardson 2001.

© KYLE A. EDWARDS, 2024 | DOI:10.1163/9789004706385_009

Douglass's embrace of class collaborationism, the harmony of interests between labour and capital, was most pronounced after the Civil War as he sought to convince workers through his newspaper and in the Colored National Labor Union of this thesis. As he would editorialise in 1871, 'Capital and labor meet and part as friends in these columns'.[3] In other words, Douglass staked his opposition to the idea that the interests of workers and their employers were antithetical. However, during the pre-war and war years Douglass spoke out for the need to build an alliance between white workers, slaves, and abolitionists to overthrow the slave system.

In 1853, Douglass told an interracial audience at the thirteenth annual convention of the American and Foreign Anti-Slavery Society that 'prejudice and hate are excited against' the Black worker – 'enmity is stirred up between him and other laborers'. Irish immigrants, specifically, were 'instantly taught on arriving in this Christian country to hate and despise the colored people'. Douglass was sure, though, that 'the Irish American will find out his mistake one day'. At an anti-slavery convention in Cincinnati the next year, Douglass posited 'that three millions of people in the south who own no slaves, will in time by the aid of education and enlightenment, come to see that the slaveholder's humiliation is necessary for the elevation of the slave and themselves. The intelligent working men of Virginia and Kentucky begin to understand this; they see that white slaveholders are against them as much as they are against the slaves; they are so: labor, white and black must fall or flourish together; and when laboring men fully see this, then will they stand with us on the anti-slavery platform'.[4] Douglass understood that if Black and white workers and producers did not join together to fight slavery and racial discrimination the divisions would allow for attacks on the political rights of all – no matter if they had privileged skin or not. The racism taught to workers both North and South by the slaveholders and their allies was not immutable but instead a terrain of struggle.

In his 1855 autobiography *My Bondage and My Freedom*, Douglass shared with his readers the working conditions he experienced as a slave in Baltimore, including the enmity he felt from white workers. But the brutality Douglass experienced pointed him to what would need to happen to overthrow slavery:

> That phase is this: *the conflict of slavery with the interests of the white mechanics and laborers of the south*. In the country, this conflict is not so apparent; but, in cities, such as Baltimore, Richmond, New Orleans,

---

3   'Position of the New National Era', *New National Era*, 30 March 1871.
4   Blassingame 1982, pp. 433, 474.

Mobile &c., it is seen pretty clearly. The slaveholders, with a craftiness peculiar to themselves, by encouraging the enmity of the poor, laboring white man against the blacks, succeeds in making the said white man almost as much a slave as the black slave himself. The difference between the white slave, and the black slave, is this: the latter belongs to *one* slaveholder, and the former belongs to *all* the slaveholders, collectively. The white slave has taken from him, by indirection, what the black slave has taken from him, directly, and without ceremony. Both are plundered, and by the same plunderers. The slave is robbed, by his master, of all his earnings, above what is required for his bare physical necessities; and the white man is robbed by the slave system, of the just results of his labor, because he is flung into competition with a class of laborers who work without wages. The competition, and its injurious consequences, will, one day, array the non-slaveholding white people of the slave states, against the slave system, and make them the most effective workers against the great evil. At present, the slaveholders blind them to this competition, by keeping alive their prejudice against the slaves, *as men* – not against them *as slaves*. They appeal to their pride, often denouncing emancipation, as tending to place the white working man, on an equality with negros, and, by this means, they succeed in drawing off the minds of the poor whites from the real fact, that, by the rich slave-master, they are already regarded as but a single remove from equality with the slave ...[5]

Thus, was there any likelihood that Douglass's recognition of a potential alliance between labourers of different skin colours and the conflagration of the Second American Revolution would have prompted him to change his outlook on revolutionary workers in Europe? Or would his natural rights liberal philosophy, including the near-sanctity of the rights of private property, override those history-making events and innovative ideas?

1 Reading the Commune from Two Very Different Class Perspectives

The Paris Commune emerged from the Franco-Prussian War. The abdication of Louis Bonaparte in September 1870 and the new government's anti-working-class character combined to radicalise France's working masses, especially its advanced contingents in Paris. After the Third Republic was established, the

---

5 Douglass 2014, pp. 246–7.

French Army surrendered to the Prussians and the Commune, a revolutionary workers movement and government, took power in March 1871.

No one did more to promote the Communards as heroes than Karl Marx. No one's name, as well as the International Workingmen's Association, born out of British working-class resistance to London and Paris's moves to come to the aid of the slavocracy in the United States, was more associated with the uprising. On 12 April 1871, Marx wrote from London to a colleague in Germany, 'What resilience, what historical initiative, what a capacity for sacrifice in these Parisians!' While the future of the Paris Commune was still in doubt and opportunities to consolidate the revolutionary government had been missed, Marx believed that, 'However that may be, the present rising in Paris – even if it be crushed by the wolves, swine and vile curs of the old society – is the most glorious deed of our Party since the June insurrection in Paris'.[6] To conclude his May Address of the General Council of the International Workingmen's Association, Marx wrote, 'Working men's Paris, with its Commune, will be for ever celebrated as the glorious harbinger of a new society. Its martyrs are enshrined in the great heart of the working class'.[7]

Douglass, on the other hand, saw the workers in rebellion as deluded tools of communist agitators, too dim-witted to even know what they fought for.

With Paris surrounded by Bismarck's troops after the French defeat in the siege that began in September 1870, Marx knew that any attempts on the workers' part to try to take up from where they left off in 1848–9 would be ill-advised. Through the French representatives on the General Council (GC) of the IWA, the body's executive committee, he, along with his partner Engels – who was now living in London and a member of the GC – counselled revolutionary restraint. The task of the proletariat, he instructed the representatives to tell them, was to use the new space of the Republic – declared on 4 September – to begin organising not only in Paris but elsewhere for the preparatory work needed to successfully take power. 'Let them calmly and resolutely improve the opportunities of Republican liberty', Marx advised, 'for the work of their own class organisation'.[8]

Douglass began his commentary on the Paris Commune in the 30 March 1871 edition of his newspaper and at first glance seemed to echo Marx's advice to use the newly opened space. Douglass started by explaining what he saw as the progressive results of 'the struggles which have been convulsing Europe

---

6 Marx and Engels 1975–2004x, pp. 131–2.
7 Marx and Engels 1975–2004l, p. 355.
8 Marx and Engels 1975–2004l, pp. 334–5.

of late ... the downfall of Louis Napoleon and of the Pope'. Douglass did not give France or the French people credit for declaring the Republic, but instead he claimed they had 'been freed from an odious despotism by a beneficent enemy', the armies of Prussia. With this freedom, however, 'France, indeed, offers a truly distressing sight'. For Douglass republican institutions were key, both in and of themselves and as an inspiration for other anti-monarchical fights. The task for France was 'the higher glory of demonstrating to the world not only their own capability of self-government, but the excellence of republican institutions generally'. The example of the French Republic was 'needed as a moral counterpoise to the enormous ascendency of the monarchical power in Europe, strengthened as it has been by the establishment of the German Empire'. Most importantly, France needed to become 'a true republic, resting on a solid foundation'.[9] The Republic was the culmination of the struggle for Douglass, not the most favourable terrain to continue the struggle as it was for Marx.

In one of his additions to Prosper Olivier Lissagaray's *History of the Commune of 1871*, Marx, contra Douglass, gave credit 'to the personal intervention of the people in [France's] history' for bringing down the Second French Empire. He traced the beginning of the end of Napoleon's rule to the spontaneous strikes that broke out in 1868 in France. The workers offered themselves to fight the German invaders in 1870 and then the workers 'crushed the hand that strangled him', with the institution of the Commune.[10]

Douglass hoped to see the population of France united in creating a true republic, but instead he wrote, 'we see them arrayed against each other before the German armies have evacuated the country'. Most alarming, 'Radicalism has again run mad. The Commune, the city of Paris, has risen against the country, the Provisional Government, the Constituent Assembly, in short against everything and everybody that is not emphatically and unconditionally committed to the Reds'. On 18 March, the National Guard, a civic militia composed mainly of workers, in the Parisian neighbourhood of Montmartre, refused orders of the French Army to disarm. The soldiers then fraternised for a time with the protestors and refused to attack, marking the birth of the Paris Commune. 'A few shots were fired by both sides', writes Daniel Gaido, 'but generally the soldiers ignored their officers' orders to force back the crowds. Some handed over their rifles and fraternised with the civilians'. Douglass denounced these events, writing, 'Discipline and subordination are at an end, and mob-law

---

9 'Aspects and Prospects in Europe', *New National Era*, 30 March 1871.
10 Gaido 2021, p. 24.

is supreme'. The Republic, Douglass thought, was under attack. 'The spectacle is the more disheartening and disappointing to all Republicans, here as well as in Europe, since they hailed the French republic most enthusiastically, and built great hopes on its example in Europe'.[11]

While Douglass lamented the events in Paris, Marx sprang into action in its defence. One of the immediate tasks was to counter the slanders in the bourgeois press like the *Times* of London that the Franco-Prussian War and uprising had provoked a split between the German and French sections of the International. To this end, Marx, on behalf of the GC, wrote numerous letters to the editors of newspapers in Germany, France, and England of which a number were actually published. Having beaten back one attack, Marx was then forced to respond to press insinuations that he and the GC had engineered the insurrection. He sent off another round of letters that the *Times* and at least one other London paper published, ridiculing the allegations. The GC, with Marx's encouragement, also took initiatives to win support for the Commune in England. Marx, himself, began an extensive effort to solicit aid for the insurgents from IWA sections. Six weeks after the uprising, he told Léo Frankel and Louis Varlin, two of the Commune's leaders and IWA members: 'I have written hundreds of letters on behalf of your cause to all the corners of the earth where we have branches'.[12]

In addition to Marx's letter writing campaign, he strove to gain accurate information by asking Auguste Serraillier, a GC member, to return to Paris to provide some leadership and keep the GC informed on developments; shortly afterwards Serraillier was elected to the Commune. Marx's need for accurate information was also one of the reasons that the young Russian revolutionary, Elisaveta Dmitriyeva Tomanovskaya, who the Marx family had befriended the previous summer, went to Paris and organised the Women's Union for the Defense of Paris as a branch of the IWA and eventually emerged as one of the Commune's leading socialists. Douglass, at variance with Marx, seemed to rely on the capitalist press in gathering information about events in France.[13]

The events of fall 1870 left Douglass hopeful that France would know 'this time how to form a true Republic'. The working-class movement in Paris shattered these hopes. 'It is consequently with feelings of deep regret that we look

---

11 'Aspects and Prospects in Europe', *New National Era*, 30 March 1871. Gaido 2021, p. 18. Merriman 2014, pp. 40–5. Nimtz 2000, p. 211.
12 Marx and Engels 1975–2004x, p. 149.
13 As Heather Cox Richardson writes, 'American newspapers plastered details of the Commune on their front pages, describing it as a propertied American's worst nightmare'. Richardson 2014, p. 93.

on the spectacle of disastrous failure', Douglass explained, 'and almost feel like despairing of the fitness of the French for self-government'. Douglass sided with 'the regular Government' in their attempt 'to save the Republic from the attempts of those Reds who, while honestly professing and believing themselves true republicans, evince a spirit of lawlessness and intolerance which, among us, would be considered anything but republican'. Douglass regarded the national elections that took place on 8 February 1871 as legitimate. These elections, according to Gaido, 'resulted in a reactionary majority ... and the formation of a counterrevolutionary provisional government headed by Adolphe Thiers'. While he recognised the odiousness of such a possibility, Douglass predicted 'it is quite probable that German assistance will be required for the suppression of the insurrection, since there appears to be no organised military force ready that could be trusted with the task', a consequence of troops fraternising with the Communards.[14]

Douglass described for his readers, 'A government, a constituent assembly elected by the people, and not guilty of any treasonable or tyrannical acts'. Douglass expressed his disappointment that the Thiers government 'is rebelled against; and the national guards, just those who are counted of the strongest supports of a republican government, form the strength of the insurrection'.[15] If Douglass did not think that the Thiers government did anything tyrannical to justify the insurrection of the Commune, Marx, on the other hand, laid out what he saw as the threats and actions that forced Parisian workers to revolt. In addition to the attempt of Thiers to disarm the workers of Paris on 18 March,

> Then Paris was exasperated by the frantic anti-republican demonstrations of the 'Rural' Assembly and by Thiers's own equivocations about the legal status of the republic; by the threat to decapitate and decapitalise Paris; the appointment of Orleanist ambassadors; Dufaure's laws on over-due commercial bills and house rents, inflicting ruin on the commerce and industry of Paris; Pouyer-Quertier's tax of two centimes upon every copy of every imaginable publication; the sentences of death against Blanqui and Flourens; the suppression of the republican journals; the transfer of the National Assembly to Versailles; the renewal of the state of siege declared by Palikao, and expired on the 4th of Septem-

---

14 'Adulterated Republicanism', *New National Era*, 6 April 1871. Gaido 2021, p. 17. On the elections, see also Merriman 2014, pp. 1, 32–3, 39. Nimtz 2000, p. 211.
15 'Adulterated Republicanism', *New National Era*, 6 April 1871.

ber; the appointment of Vinoy, the *Decembriseur*, as governor of Paris – of Valentin, the imperialist *gendarme*, as its prefect of police – and of D'Aurelles de Paladine, the Jesuit general, as the commander-in-chief of its National Guard.[16]

Marx more accurately saw the attacks on the republic, workers' economic situation, and the closing of political space that Thiers engaged in compared to Douglass's rosy picture of the reactionary leader.

In the same 12 April letter referenced above to Ludwig Kugelman, Marx, in order to drive home the significance of the revolt, referred him back to his *Eighteenth Brumaire* where 'you will find that I say that the next attempt of the French revolution will be no longer, as before, to transfer the bureaucratic military machine from one hand to another, but to *break* it, and that is essential for every real people's revolution on the Continent. And this is what our heroic Party comrades in Paris are attempting'.[17]

Marx also pointed to the Prussian troops, as Douglass did, as a crucial factor but in a diametrically opposed analysis to Douglass's. For Marx, it was a fortuitous set of circumstances that Prussian troops surrounded Paris. These circumstances

> ... presented the Parisians with the alternative of taking up the fight or succumbing without a struggle. In the latter case, the demoralization of the working class would have been a far greater misfortune than the fall of any number of 'leaders'. The struggle of the working class against the capitalist class and its state has entered upon a new phase with the struggle in Paris. Whatever the immediate results may be, a new point of departure of world-historic importance has been gained.[18]

Douglass attributed the current insurrection to the work of socialist agitators, acknowledged that there were such agitators in the United States, and reprinted a story from the *Pall Mall Gazette* intended to characterise the ordinary supporters of the Commune as dim-witted. To obtain a 'proper understanding of the Red movement in the French capital', Douglass wanted his readers to know that the Commune 'is the work of the Socialist agitators, who obtain supporters among the more ignorant class of workingmen by promising them

---

16   Marx and Engels 1975–2004l, pp. 319–20.
17   Marx and Engels 1975–2004x, p. 131.
18   Marx and Engels 1975–2004x, pp. 136–7.

what no community and no Government on earth can give them – a division of property and a life of ease without labor'. If anyone thought that only Europe contained radicals like this, that America was exceptional, Douglass assured his audience, 'These agitators are not unknown among us, and they will be recognised by the ingeniously suggestive platitudes' mentioned in the story printed in the *Pall Mall Gazette*. Douglass then reproduced the article where a correspondent conversed with a National Guard member stationed at a barricade intending to show that the rebellious workers did not understand the doctrines for which they were fighting.[19]

The Communard in the story related that 'the rich had everything and the poor nothing; the time has come for changing all that'. He belonged to an organisation whose programme included, 'No more imposts, no more usury, no more misery. Work for all, property for all … What is the workman? Nothing. What ought he to be? Everything'. The correspondent then attempted to exhibit his cleverness and the worker's cluelessness. The worker explained he was a cabinet-maker who earned five francs per day and demanded to share in the gains of his employer. 'But was your employer a very rich man?' the correspondent asked. The worker replied that his employer was ruined. 'Then you are agitating for the privilege of sharing his losses!' the correspondent jousted. 'He looked at me, gave a shrug, and said I didn't seem to understand the principle. He would explain it more carefully'. Douglass shared this story to place himself among the refined and intelligent while deriding militant workers of 'the more ignorant class'.[20]

In a 4 May 1871 article titled 'Dark Prospects', a title used repeatedly while covering the events in Paris, Douglass employed the nation-state as his unit of analysis rather than opposing classes. 'For weeks', he declared, frustrated, 'a struggle is carried on, in which the insurrectionists evince as much bitterness and animosity against the regular Government as they did against the victorious Germans'. This sort of conflict within the nation led him to characterise the events as the 'most distressing and heart-sickening spectacle in the world'. As for the reason for this 'heart-sickening spectacle', he pointed to 'the state of demoralization, of corruption, and mutual distrust, which lead the unfortunate people to rage more furiously and destructively against each other than any foreign enemy could do'. There was a 'spirit of distrust pervading the minds of the people'.[21]

---

19   'The Revolters Delusion', *New National Era*, 27 April 1871.
20   'The Revolters Delusion', *New National Era*, 27 April 1871.
21   'Dark Prospects', *New National Era*, 4 May 1871.

As for the claims of the Communards – 'The demand of the Commune to elect its own municipal officers is reasonable enough', Douglass wrote. John Merriman, a historian of France, points out that 'Unlike all the other 36,000 cities, towns and villages in France, Paris did not have the right to elect a mayor'. In addition, Napoleon appointed the arrondissement municipal council. Nevertheless, Douglass deplored the means used by Parisian workers to achieve their ends. 'There is, however, no cause in the world so good', Douglass wrote, 'that would not become bad when pressed by such outrages and excesses as are the order of the day: when political assassinations are openly advocated and practiced, and a despotism is exercised in the name of liberty hardly less oppressive and odious than the yoke of the Emperor'.[22] Douglass seemed to be reading news from sources friendly to the Thiers regime. Future scholarship would reveal that the bourgeois government enabled the slaughter of tens of thousands of prisoners from the beginning of hostilities, while only 66 or 68 hostages were killed by the Commune.[23]

While Douglass deplored the slaughter of prisoners by Thiers's troops during the last days of the Commune, he mistakenly reported to his readers that the brutality came from each side in equal measure. Multiple articles in the 1 June 1871 issue focused on the property destruction that occurred in Paris during the last days of barricade fighting. 'They are acts of vandalism', Douglass claimed, 'prompted by a love of destruction peculiar to the most degenerate among human brutes … The demolition of the column of the Place Vendome, the monument of bygone French glory; the burning of the Tuileries, the Palais Royal, the Hotel de Ville … will tell heavily in history against this generation of the French people'. Douglass did not examine the strategic importance of demolishing key buildings during street fighting or consider what monuments glorifying the French monarchy might mean to workers fighting for a social and democratic republic. It escaped his attention that while the Communards destroyed property as they retreated, Versailles troops carried out 'the notorious slaughter … beyond anything that Paris had seen then or since'.[24] Marx wrote later that the decree to bring down the column of the Place Vendome was 'popular, humane, profound, showing that a war of classes was to supersede the

---

22 'Dark Prospects', *New National Era*, 4 May 1871. Merriman 2014, pp. 13–14. The role of being deprived of the right to elect a mayor played in making the Commune, 'the focal point of the popular aspirations in the French capital', is contained in Marx's additions to Prosper-Olivier Lissagaray's *History of the Commune of 1871* and examined in Gaido 2021, pp. 19–20.
23 Merriman 2014, pp. 118–22, 203–24.
24 'The Last Act of the Insurrection', *New National Era*, 1 June 1871. Nimtz 2000, p. 214.

war of nations, aimed at the same time a blow at the ephemeral triumph of the Prussian'.[25] A war of classes to supersede the war of nations – something Douglass would never condone.

As if speaking directly to Douglass, Marx wrote, 'no sooner do the working men anywhere take the subject into their own hands with a will, then uprises at once all the apologetic phraseology of the mouthpieces of present society … as if capitalist society was still in its purest state of virgin innocence, with its antagonisms still undeveloped, with its delusions still unexploded, with its prostitute realities not yet laid bare'.[26]

Marx, in his *Civil War in France*, described more accurately than Douglass, who regurgitated propaganda tales of assassinations and mob rule, the violence of the conflagration. 'From the 18th of March to the entrance of the Versailles troops into Paris', Marx wrote, 'the proletarian revolution remained so free from the acts of violence in which the revolutions, and still more the counter-revolutions, of the "better classes" abound, that no facts were left to its opponents to cry out about, but the execution of General Lecomte and Clement Thomas, and the affair of the Place Vendome'. In fact, it was 'this magnanimity of the armed working men' that convinced Thiers and his generals that they could cut down thousands of prisoners with no fear of reprisals. Once Theirs had become aware 'that the Communal decree of reprisals was but an empty threat, that even their gendarme spies caught in Paris under the disguise of National Guards, that even *sergeants-de-ville*, taken with incendiary shells upon them, were spared … the wholesale shooting of prisoners was resumed and carried on uninterruptedly to the end'. Marx had the advantage over Douglass in that he had reliable sources other than the anti-Commune reporting in American papers to rely on. As mentioned above, August H. Nimtz writes that Marx and Engels 'had very close ties to some of the insurgent leaders, through whom they sought to influence its course'.[27]

The *New National Era*, in July, gave space to a view of the Commune from Civil War General Benjamin Butler that differed from its editorial line. Douglass featured a long article, taken from 'a speech at the dedication of the new town hall in Gloucester', given by the now Congressman Butler, which Phillip Katz describes as a 'campaign speech'. In the speech, Butler situated the Commune as of equal or greater importance in its effect on human liberty than the US Civil War – 'the great event which has distinguished this year, and perhaps

---

25 Gaido 2021, p. 34.
26 Marx and Engels 1975–2004l, p. 335.
27 Marx and Engels 1975–2004l, pp. 323–4, 327. Nimtz 2000, p. 213.

its effect on human liberty will distinguish this century, possibly overshadowing the great act of emancipation by which this country liberated four millions of people'.[28]

Butler seemed to reply directly to Douglass when he defended the destruction of property by the retreating Communards. He lamented the slander and misconceptions facing the defeated Parisian workers. Of the structures built 'by kings and princes' set aflame, Butler defended destroying property dedicated to the 'great deeds of the first Napoleon ... erected as an emblem of the military glory of a despot'. He explained to his audience, 'The first act of a free people was to tear it down and level it to the ground', and asked, 'Was not that in accordance with the spirit of free institutions?'[29]

Analogous to the analysis Butler gave in his speech at the town hall in Gloucester, Marx examined the fires during the last week of the Paris Commune. 'The working men's Paris', Marx wrote, 'in the act of its heroic self-holocaust, involved in its flames buildings and monuments', which dismayed Douglass. 'While tearing to pieces the living body of the proletariat, its rulers must no longer expect to return triumphantly into the intact architecture of their abodes ... The bourgeoisie of the whole world, which looks complacently upon the wholesale massacre after the battle, is convulsed by horror at the desecration of brick and mortar!'[30] While Douglass acknowledged and condemned the massacre once it became apparent to him, the destruction of the architecture of the monarchy and the bourgeoisie disgusted him.

Douglass also lent space to the reformer Wendell Phillips to defend the Communards. Phillips pointed to Paris as an example of what could happen in America if the oppression of labour continued. In May he warned, if you 'scratch New York ... you will find Paris just below the surface'. Douglass shared a speech by Phillips in the 2 November issue of his newspaper on 'theories of labor'. Phillips briefly addressed the Paris Commune in this lecture. 'The moment you make a rich class and a poor class by the cunning of corporations', he argued, 'there is no republic'. The goal of the labour movement, in Phillips's mind, was to find where poverty and misery came from and solve the problem facing millions of people. There were different methods to solve this problem. 'Paris wrote her indignation in fire and blood in opposition to wrong'. Phillips did not prefer this method, continuing, 'This is the Prussian and Italian method, and to some extent the German, but the English and American people

---

28 'General Butler on the French Situation', *New National Era*, 6 July 1871. P. Katz 1998, p. 237n40.
29 'General Butler on the French Situation', *New National Era*, 6 July 1871.
30 Marx and Engels 1975–2004l, p. 350.

do not take the sword into the council chamber'. Betraying his voting fetishism tendencies, Phillips, like Douglass, claimed, 'Our weapon is the ballot'. But unfortunately, 'The great mass of this country is verging towards a European condition of affairs as regards capital'. This is the consequence of rich men 'making vassals of our institutions ... in one half of the States there is no republic'. Phillips's remedy for these ills was discussion and voting, not the fire and blood of the Paris Commune.[31]

Even though Douglass acknowledged that Thiers 'always was a steadfast supporter of Louis Philippe', he thought 'the accusation set forth by the Commune that the Government intends to turn traitor to the Republic and to erect another monarchy on its ruins', was groundless. Instead, it was the communists who threatened the republic and opened the door to royal restoration. 'The real danger to the Republic seems rather to threaten from the Reds, who, if successful, would establish a reign of terror, bring disgrace on the very name of the Republic, and republican institutions generally, and finally open the path for another line of monarchs, either 'by the grace of God' or by the right of usurpation'.[32]

For the moment, in early May 1871, Douglass saw both opportunity and threat, writing 'there is little doubt that the Government will finally come out victorious, and that order will be restored for a while; yet the elements of trouble and discord are too powerful to hope that an era of quiet and prosperity is to follow'. He instructed his readers and the French people that, 'The only safeguard against monarchism on the one side, and the tyranny of political fanaticism and mobocracy on the other, is in that truly republican spirit which, while securing fair play, equal rights, and equal liberty, and protection to all, leaves everything else to free development, and abstains entirely from meddling with particular social and religious theories or systems, and from the attempt to force them on a people'.[33]

Two weeks later, Douglass cheered the Versailles government troops, disparaged communism in comparison with true republicanism, and contrasted class conflict in France with that in the United States. Douglass had been reading news 'with promises of the speedy suppression of the insurrection' and concluded 'that the insurrection is near its collapse'. He did not believe meritorious generalship on the part of the government had led to their success

---

31 'The May Anniversaries', *New National Era*, 18 May 1871. 'Wendell Phillips – Speech at Springfield-His Theories on Labor', *New National Era*, 2 November 1871. For another example of Phillips's voting fetishism, see Wineapple 2020, p. 75.
32 'Dark Prospects', *New National Era*, 4 May 1871.
33 'Dark Prospects', *New National Era*, 4 May 1871.

but instead cited 'the demoralization, the dessensions [*sic*], the general distrust, and the lack of discipline among the Reds', along with the fact that 'the provinces have remained quiet, instead of echoing and following the actions of the Commune'.[34]

Marx had his eye on the provinces as well – the worker-peasant alliance always at the forefront of his mind. A letter from Tomanovskaya suggests that Marx advised the Communards to do what he and Engels had long-ago concluded, based on the lessons of 1848, would be necessary for a victory in any new upsurge in Paris. In the words of the young Russian revolutionary, 'We must at all costs stir up the provinces to come to our aid'.[35]

In the first draft of Marx's *Civil War in France*, he wrote that in contrast to the French state from 1848 onwards, the Commune objectively represented the interests of the rural toilers. Hence, the reason why Versailles did all it could to prevent the realisation of its worst nightmare – a worker-peasant alliance between Paris and the countryside.[36] The lack of an alliance between the revolutionary workers in Paris and the small farmers in the rest of the country was not a nightmare for Douglass, but a development to celebrate. Douglass had worried earlier in May, 'It is true that thus far the troubles have been almost entirely confined to Paris', giving the Thiers government in Versailles the advantage, 'but since, from old times, Paris has been the representative of the intellect, the knowledge, and enlightenment of the country, and has always laid down the law for all France, we have to take the present manifestations for the expression of the spirit of the people generally'.[37] Douglass was not aware of the divide between the more religious peasants in France's rural areas whom the government drew on for fresh troops, and the anti-clerical workers in Paris and other large cities such as Lyon.

Crushing the Commune would not necessarily lead to a successful French Republic, according to Douglass. The issues at stake were too fundamental. 'The conflict between wealth and poverty, between capital and labor … and others of equal importance are at the bottom of it, besides distrust of the honesty of the government and its fidelity to the republican cause'. These issues did not inevitably lead to violent conflict. 'It is true', he argued, 'the difficulties arising from these sources do not necessitate a bloody revolution; indeed, they agitate more or less the whole civilised world, our own country as well as others … there indeed be no apprehension that they will lead to violent uprising and blood-

---

34 'No Peace in France', *New National Era*, 18 May 1871.
35 S. Edwards 1973a, p. 134.
36 Marx and Engels 1975–2004l, pp. 494–5.
37 'Dark Prospects', *New National Era*, 4 May 1871.

shed of a formidable character'. As Douglass wrote in late-March, 'Capital and labor meet and part as friends in these columns'. In the United States, Douglass thought '[f]ull liberty' would act as a safety valve. Americans were free to agitate, discuss, and experiment 'under the protection of republican institutions, taking away any need to resort to revolution'.[38]

On the contrary, there was something, Douglass alleged, about the French temperament that prevented them from acting on the same principles. They had 'the insurmountable obstacle opposed by their own unfortunate disposition, their incapacity to comprehend the very rudiments of true republican liberty'. French radicals had a 'lawless spirit, that prompts them to achieve by revolution that which ought to be left to free development, the tyrannical disposition that assumes to lay down laws, to regulate and decree in matters which concern only the choice and convictions of the individual'. This 'knowledge of the French character' impelled Douglass 'to look on the future of the French republic with as much apprehension as sorrow over the delusions of a people, which even in its errors, inspires more pity than indignation, when we remember how for ages it has been the victim of misrule and despotism'.[39]

Marx argued, contra Douglass, that the Commune actually embodied a 'true Republic'. The institutions and actions of the Commune, workingmen's wages for government officials and the replacement of the standing army by the National Guard, 'made that catchword of bourgeois revolutions, cheap government, a reality by destroying the two greatest sources of expenditure – the standing army and state functionalism … It supplied the republic with the basis of really democratic institutions'. And the secret to this, the Commune's essence, was that power was in the hands of the workers. The Commune, as Marx argued, 'was essentially a working-class government, the product of the struggle of the producing against the appropriating class, the political form at last discovered under which to work out the economical emancipation of Labour'.[40]

Marx's most important and enduring contribution to the Communards came in the immediate aftermath of their demise with the publication in mid-June 1871 of *The Civil War in France: Address of the General Council of the International Working-Men's Association*. Marx read this address to the Gen-

---

38 'No Peace in France', *New National Era*, 18 May 1871. 'Position of the New National Era', *New National Era*, 30 March 1871.
39 'No Peace in France', *New National Era*, 18 May 1871.
40 Marx and Engels 1975–2004l, p. 334. Nimtz 2000, p. 216. The 'distinguishing traits of the Commune as a workers' government' are examined in Gaido 2021, pp. 39–40.

eral Council on 30 May, two days after the Commune's fall, after writing multiple drafts throughout April and May. What Marx wrote for the GC, written in the heat of the Commune's final days, was as much a defence of the Communards as a political analysis. The political heart of the 40-page document – sandwiched between details leading up to and after the insurgency – is the fifteen-page third section which analyses the Commune itself, 'where the proletariat for the first time held political power'.[41]

After quoting from the manifesto that the National Guard's Central Committee issued to justify its actions on 18 March – 'The Proletarians of Paris ... have understood that it is their imperious duty and their absolute right to render themselves masters of their own destinies, by seizing upon the governmental powers'[42] – Marx declared: 'But the working class cannot simply lay hold of the ready-made State machinery, and wield it for its own purpose'. This was proven by the fact that the largely working-class National Guard replaced the standing army with itself.

Marx then distilled in *The Civil War* the Commune's essence:

> The multiplicity of interpretations to which the Commune has been subjected, and the multiplicity of interests which construed it in their favor, show that it was a thoroughly expansive political form, while all previous forms of government had been emphatically repressive. Its true secret was this. It was essentially a working-class government, the product of the struggle of the producing against the appropriating class, the political form at last discovered under which to work out the economical emancipation of Labor.
>
> Except on this last condition, the Communal Constitution would have been an impossibility and a delusion. The political rule of the producer cannot coexist with the perpetuation of his social slavery. The Commune was therefore to serve as a lever for uprooting the economical foundations upon which rests the existence of classes, and therefore of class rule. With labor emancipated, every man becomes a working man, and productive labor ceases to be a class attribute.[43]

---

41 How Marx and Engels expressed it in the 'Preface' to the 1872 German edition of the *Manifesto*.
42 See S. Edwards 1973b, pp. 155–6, for a longer excerpt from the statement. That the Central Committee's statement employed 'proletarians' is significant given subsequent debates about Marx's characterization of the Commune as the proletariat in power for the first time.
43 Marx and Engels 1975–2004l, pp. 334–5.

In one of Douglass's last sustained treatments of the events in France, he hoped for 'truly prominent, distinguished men' to come forward to lead, analysed and compared the morals of the French people to the people of the German Empire, while continuing his criticism of monarchists and communists alike. A main feature of the turmoil in France, according to Douglass, 'is the total absence of truly prominent, distinguished men on the stage of events'. Almost wishing for another Bonaparte, Douglass wrote, 'not one man has yet appeared to relieve the darkness of the picture, none to give promise by his patriotism, his love of liberty, and his energy to pacify the conflicting elements, of vindicating the dignity of the nation, and of making a living reality of the present sham of a Republic'. At the same time he searched for a great man, or great men, to take the helm, he warned against Bonapartism. When a population is demoralised, it is less likely that the '[m]ost honest man should obtain supreme influence, but rather the most adroit, the shrewdest plotter and intriguer, the one who will best know how to avail himself of the passions, the ambition and avarice of other plotters and intriguers, and seem to offer them the greatest advantages, the one who will besides have the gift of flattering the vanity of the masses by empty promises of future glory'. Another Napoleon would lead to another conflagration. 'A man possessed of no higher abilities and worth than Napoleon might again succeed for a while', Douglass argued, 'to be sent into exile by another revolution'.[44]

Douglass focused on what he saw as the national traits of the French and the German people when comparing them. Of the results of the Franco-Prussian War, Douglass wrote, 'Never has a nation won greater glory than the Germans, and never more crushing defeats have been seen than those suffered by the French'. The Germans did not provoke the war and went into it with 'a unanimity, and enthusiasm never surpassed in the history of nations, and going into it as a politically divided people, they came out the greatest, most powerful, most united nation in Europe'. In contrast, a 'people so deeply fallen as the French, in such a state of social and moral dissolution, one, in fact, of whose formerly so highly admired qualities hardly a shadow is left, could not possibly conquer a nation in its full mental, physical, and moral health and vigor'. Douglass blamed the Second Empire of Napoleon which acted to 'demoralize and corrupt the people more and more, yet it required the Commune and its insurrection, it required the unworthy Assembly, with all its intriguing, unscrupulous Orleanists, Bonapartists, and Legitimists, to reveal the whole depth of rottenness'.[45]

---

44 'The Coming Man', *New National Era*, 22 June 1871.
45 'The Coming Man', *New National Era*, 22 June 1871.

Marx agreed with Douglass that 'rottenness' had matured during the Second Empire, but his solution, notwithstanding his earlier counsel of revolutionary restraint, was the 'revolutionary overthrow of the political and social conditions that had engendered' the Empire, which the Commune attempted as the 'self-sacrificing champion of France'.[46] To Douglass the communists and monarchists were two sides of the same coin. The conservative assembly might have wanted to institute a terror, but if the communists were successful an era of tyranny would have followed their ascent. As Douglass put it, 'If the Assembly consists largely of plotters and conspirators, watching the opportunity to betray the Republic and erect another reign of *white* terror, like the Restoration, on its ruins, the radical Republicans are contaminated with communism and red fanaticism, and their victory would mark the beginning of an era of the most odious despotism of the mob'.[47] Without an honest man with the ability to institute on his own a true republic, Douglass called for a pox on the houses of both the monarchists and the democratic mob.

Once the horrors of the suppression of the people of Paris by the Versailles politicians, generals, and troops became apparent to Douglass, he became a severe critic of the conservative bourgeois republican government while never converting to the cause of the Commune.

Douglass implied he had not heard of the mass executions the Versailles military had been carrying out since the start of the conflict. 'For weeks the world has been the horrified spectator of the bloody deeds committed by the French insurgents, and to-day the weight of sympathy is almost reversed in consequence of the savage cruelty with which the government is wreaking its revenge on those deluded, ill-starred men'. While he believed some of the acts could be waved off as carried out by individual soldiers, he also understood that 'many, too, are the acts of cruelty by which a government calling itself republican is asserting its authority'. He recognised now that monarchists and reactionaries headed the Versailles army. 'Old politicians of the times of Louis Philippe', Douglass wrote, 'and generals of the Empire never suspected of republicanism, much less of Red republicanism, have instituted a reign of terror reminding one of the first French revolution'.[48]

---

46 Marx and Engels 1975–2004l, p. 322.
47 'The Coming Man', *New National Era*, 22 June 1871.
48 'Dark Prospects', *New National Era*, 8 June 1871. As Merriman demonstrates, Thiers had expressed support for the restoration of the monarchy in the past and 'three commanders of the army – Joseph Vinoy, Patrice de MacMahon, and Gaston Galliffet – were conservatives, Bonapartists to be sure, but who would prefer without question a monarchy to a republic'. Merriman 2014, p. 34.

Readers of the *New National Era* were given a glimpse at the criminality and barbarism that went into suppressing the Commune. While the guillotine of revolutions past was objectionable enough, 'the victims sentenced now-a-days by drumhead court-martial are slaughtered by hundreds, by means of mitrailleuses or volleys fired by whole companies'. This sort of indiscriminate firing into crowds of prisoners was not efficient, leading to 'all stages of mutilation and agony, until after repeated volleys the merciful bullet will reach them that is to give them the final blow'. Douglass admonished this 'government calling itself republican' and advised leniency, if only because the rebels were under a 'revolutionary spell'. He thought, 'it is safe to assume that by far the larger number, when looked upon from a higher stand-point, must be considered innocent, since in an insurrection of such dimensions the masses are always the blind and deluded tools of their leaders'.[49]

2 Douglass and The Labour Question in 1870–1

The Paris Commune, along with labour unrest in the United States, compelled Douglass to address the labour question throughout 1871 in various editions of his newspaper, the *New National Era*. 'The labor question', Douglass wrote in October, 'of which in this country the abolition of slavery, of property in man, was the first grand step – is not free from the evils of ignorance, passion, ambition, selfishness, and demagogism'. It was natural, Douglass thought, that working people, Chinese, Irish, or Black, felt discontent when the 'non-producers now receive the larger share of what those who labor produce'.[50]

In the 15 June edition, Douglass used a strike in Washington DC to compare the US reality to France, promote his free labour theory of labour relations, or, from a working-class perspective, class collaborationism, and offer advice to American workers. Douglass saw the strike as a danger whose worst impacts were avoided: 'A cloud no bigger than a man's hand ... its bolts were withheld'. In Douglass's opinion, this was thanks to the Territorial Governor of Washington DC, Republican Henry Cooke, appointed by President Ulysses S. Grant in late February 1871, and other politicians.[51]

Douglass reported, using language at variance with his usually sympathetic treatment of workers, that, 'A large body of muscle and of untrained mind and

---

49   'Dark Prospects', *New National Era*, 8 June 1871.
50   P. Foner 1955, pp. 264, 282.
51   'Wisdom in the Counsels of Washington', *New National Era*, 15 June 1871.

heart was in a perilous condition running loose in our streets. It wanted higher wages and fewer hours of labor, and struck for both'. Where 'pride and fury' guided Thiers and his government, 'temperance, forbearance, and wisdom' guided Cooke and the government in Washington DC. Class conflict evident in Paris was not limited to the Old World, 'riot and bloodshed' was possible 'in the streets of Washington'. Douglass warned some were 'forgetful that we might have the same [the hell of horrors enacted in Paris] here on a smaller scale'. He recognised, 'There is a terrible gulf between capital and labor constantly liable to tempests and whirlwinds'. But fortunately, 'the strike is now ended, the men are at work, good sense on both sides has prevailed, the laborers get not all they demanded, but more than they formerly received, and all goes on peacefully again'.[52]

Douglass then provided guidance to workers considering going on strike and those who would advise them to do so. Influenced, no doubt, by memories of racist white workers who had violently prevented him from working, and his sons' denial of membership in an all-white printers' union, Douglass opposed blocking strikebreakers from crossing picket lines.[53] 'It may be well and needful at times to strike', Douglass cautioned, 'but it can never be well to take the law into your own hands and undertake to prevent other men from working'. This would amount to 'despotism and anarchy' which could not 'be safely tolerated for an hour'. Workers had attempted to engage in such action and Douglass wrote, 'should the law be defied in this city by such conduct again, sterner measures of repression will doubtless be resorted to than were seen ten days ago'. Douglass, after giving cover to stern measures of repression against strikers, assured his readers that his sympathy was with labourers, and he understood their plight as a freeman and former slave. Because he empathised with their suffering, 'we are slow to favor strikes among laborers, for they almost in every instance get the worst of it'.[54]

Friedrich Sorge, a German-American Marxist and member of the International, in a report to Marx, painted a different picture of the DC strike and had different hopes for what it might lead to. There are only two explicit mentions of Black workers in International Workingmen's Association records. One is in a report that Sorge wrote in June 1871 to the GC about the state of the American labour movement. 'A great strike occurred lately in Washington amongst the colored laborers for an increase of their extremely low wages', Sorge reported.

---

52 'Wisdom in the Counsels of Washington', *New National Era*, 15 June 1871.
53 Blight 2018, pp. 91, 504. Douglass 2014, pp. 242–54, 277–80.
54 'Wisdom in the Counsels of Washington', *New National Era*, 15 June 1871.

'They were momentarily defeated by the stepping in of the white laborers. The result will probably be the emancipation of the colored workingmen from the grip of the political suckers who kept them till now almost exclusively in the ranks of the so-called Republican Party'. Did Sorge have Douglass specifically in mind with his 'political suckers' epithet? If not directly, Douglass's report on the strike, the absence of a commentary on the way race was used to break the strike – instead criticising picket lines to stop strikebreakers – and his praise of the Republican Territorial Governor made him a prime candidate. Sorge's hope, not to be fulfilled, of a major strike acting as an impetus for Black workers to break with the Republican Party echoed what Marx hoped for six years later in 1877 with the withdrawal of the last federal troops from the South. This was not to be the case in either instance.[55]

Sometimes Douglass's paper supported employers against striking workers. Other times he sounded radical as when he wrote, 'The civilization, then, looked at in its material aspect alone, which on the one hand constantly increases its wealth-creating capacities and on the other as steadily leaves out of the direct benefits thereof at least seven-tenths of all who live within its influence, cannot have realised the fundamental condition of its continuance'. The number of workers joining the labour movement would compel a hearing, Douglass thought, and could not be ignored. 'It is the duty of those who have been lifted up by this general movement, this attrition of classes, of which the coming struggle of the "proletariat" (to use a word common in European discussion, though hardly yet generally applicable to our condition) is the final and natural consequence'. Douglass's solution was to urge his readers to support a bill introduced in Congress that would set up a commission of three people to 'investigate the subject of the wages and hours of labor, and of the division of the joint profits of labor and capital between the laborer and the capitalist'.[56]

However, Douglass's prescriptions are less convincing than his insights. He believed, 'Those abuses we are outgrowing however, and not even the conservatism of monarchical Europe can stem the tide of modern ideas'. If workers decided to strike, Douglass stated he would support them 'always provided, however, that such results are achieved solely by moral persuasion, and neither violence nor intimidation are resorted to … such deeds only serve to reverse the balance of wrong, and would substitute one odious tyranny for another'.[57]

---

55 Nimtz 2003, pp. 153, 175.
56 Foner 1955, pp. 283–4.
57 'The Labor Question', *New National Era*, 26 October 1871.

Douglass's liberal worldview allowed him to argue that workers defending their picket lines were just as despicable as capitalists driving workers as beasts of burden.[58]

Nicholas Buccola argues, 'Douglass was concerned about the fundamental unfairness and legitimate discontent of the burgeoning industrial capitalist system' and his 'response to the labor question reveals that on this issue he was closer to the reform liberal view than he was to the libertarian view'. While Buccola examines Douglass's commitment 'to the institution of private property and the idea of free labor as pillars of individual liberty', and the tension between that commitment and the 'gross inequalities' of postbellum America, he avoids treatment of Douglass's criticism of labour organisations and their defence of picket lines. Douglass's defence of strikebreakers – even white scabs breaking the strike of Black labourers – and his response to the Paris Commune provide more evidence of Douglass's position 'as a member of the liberal family'.[59]

When he examined two October 1871 strikes where workers were demanding a reduction in the ten-hour work day, Douglass saw the employers as reasonable. But he also conceded that it was 'evident that ten hours' uninterrupted hard work, with the addition of the time required to commute to the factory and back, will, in the long run, reduce the laborer to the level of a beast of burden'. Douglass was able to discern cracks in free labour ideology via the proletarianization of labour. He wrote, 'the uniform, mechanical, and exhausting factory work, which keeps him busy uninterruptedly year after year, without offering him any prospect of ever becoming independent, nay, of ever achieving more than keeps starvation from his door, cannot fail either to make him desperate, or to smother all higher impulses and aspirations in him'.[60]

Waldo E. Martin Jr. explains that Douglass evinced a 'procapitalist spirit' and 'criticized trade unions for excessive hostility toward their capitalist antagonists'. Part of the reason why, as David Blight notes, Douglass did not turn to labour organisations was 'largely because of their discriminatory practices against black and Chinese workers'. Labour unions, Douglass also believed, stood in the way of workers becoming capitalists themselves. As opposed

---

58 Douglass's liberal worldview included the defence of private property, a harmony of interests between capital and labour, the end of property in man, a defence of bourgeois republican institutions, and equality before the law. Buccola 2012 and Myers 2008 are the two most recent treatments of Douglass's liberal political thought. Martin 1984 is more critical and influences this study's understanding of Douglass.
59 Buccola 2012, p. 54. See also, pp. 52–3, 135–6.
60 'The Labor Question', *New National Era*, 26 October 1871.

to workers' self-organisation, he looked to an enlightened Republican government, which had gained legitimacy in his eyes via the crusade to overthrow slavery and their proposed commissions on labour and capital. Unions, whether they were enforcing picket lines, limiting overtime, or excluding Black workers, were 'utterly incompatible with true republican principles and institutions'. Martin persuasively maintains that Douglass's contention that capital and labour were on more equal footing in the United States than in Europe 'contradicted the increasing degradation of labor as well as the overwhelming dominance of capital in the rapidly industrializing United States'. The free labour ideology of Douglass and the Republican Party made sense 'in the preindustrial world from which men like Lincoln' – and Douglass – 'came', Heather Cox Richardson explains. However, the Civil War 'had nurtured a booming manufacturing sector, with huge factories worked by hundreds of employees who never saw, let alone worked with, their employer'. Eric Foner describes this free labour social vision as 'already being rendered obsolete by the industrial revolution and the appearance of a class of permanent wage laborers'.[61]

3   Douglass and the Colored National Labor Union

Even with Douglass's support of property and wariness of labour unions which would be more fully developed in the early 1870s, he was included in the Call for the Colored National Labor Union Convention as a member of the Co-operative Executive Committee in September 1869.[62] The first meeting of the Colored National Labor Union saw few workers attend, mainly, according to Philip Foner, because they were 'too poor to come to Washington'. This led to attendees mainly composed of 'lawyers, preachers, teachers, or merchants'. The platform of this national labour union of lawyers and merchants stated, as Douglass would promote, 'capital and labor were complementary and necessary to each other, harmony between the two should be cultivated' in order to avoid strikes. Calls for land and disputes over support for a form of independent working class political action dominated parts of the proceedings, and would cause future rifts between Blacks and the National Labor Union. Douglass, and many others, would not support a move to a workers party out of genuine dedication to the Republicans, but also lesser-evilism; a victory for the Democratic

---

[61]   Martin 1984, p. 129. Blight 2018, p. 560. 'The Labor Question', *New National Era*, 26 October 1871. 'Labor in Iron – Manufactories and Workingmen', *New National Era*, 28 December 1871. Richardson 2014, p. 44. E. Foner 1988, p. 29.
[62]   P. Foner and Lewis 1978, p. 4.

Party would be disastrous and support for a labour party might have made that possible. The white leader of the National Labor Union, Richard F. Trevellick, called for unity between Black and white workers but refused to support legislation that would have allowed Black workers to enter factories and workshops. He instead focused his ire on the monetary system. Trevellick, according to Foner, asked 'the Negro to abandon the Republican Party while offering nothing meaningful in return. On the contrary, he in effect promised to do nothing himself about restrictive union practices, since he regarded them as local matters'.[63]

Douglass was later elected the CNLU's second president in January 1871. Douglass was active in writing and promoting an address to his old nemesis, the African Colonization Society, demanding they cease any propaganda among Black workers. The CNLU convention in January 1871 endorsed the *New National Era* as the group's national organ and 'several members subscribed largely to the stock of the paper' to help defer Douglass's costs.[64]

Douglass emphasised at the January 1871 gathering that he was no longer a labourer and actually held power over those now looking for work – as men from the shipyard he worked at in Baltimore came to him for assistance to find work in Washington DC.[65] In doing so he emphasised the free labour ideology that dominated the liberals and Republican Party. He denied or deemphasised the proletarianization of work in the United States and the creation of a hereditary proletariat in the working class. Given his opposition to picket lines and support of a harmony of interests between capital and labour examined above, it may be pertinent to ask – Was Douglass one of the first misleaders of American labour? By 1874, the *New National Era* was publishing editorials titled, 'The Folly, Tyranny, and Wickedness of Labor Unions', where striking miners in Pennsylvania were severely castigated while the owner of the iron works who employed the workers was praised. Foner and Lewis describe the position of Douglass and his paper as, 'The most curious position on blacks and labor unions ... Douglass's basic disposition toward unionism was hostile. In the end, the only solution seemed to be for blacks to become capitalists themselves, or convince the capitalists to obey the Golden Rule, neither of which were very constructive alternatives'.[66]

---

63   P. Foner 1981b, pp. 30–1, 36–8, 43.
64   P. Foner and Lewis 1978, pp. 82, 87, 92, 94–5.
65   'Annual Convention of the National Labor Union', *New National Era*, 12 January 1871.
66   P. Foner and Lewis 1978, pp. 140, 178–9. P. Foner and Lewis indicate that the editorials on the National Labor Union were written by Frederick's son Lewis who served as Secretary to the Colored National Labor Union.

While freedpeople were becoming more proletarianized between 1865 and 1871 after the abolition of slavery, a portion becoming wage workers and others becoming farmers, sharecroppers, or farm workers, the process was still too immature to become a proletarian movement led by anyone other than Douglass or his cohorts – 'lawyers, preachers, teachers, or merchants'. The proletarianisation of Black labour that Douglass rejected, which would make, in his words, the workers 'desperate', but, better, would organise and wake them up to their self-worth, would take decades before making decisive inroads into the union movement, and a century before the Black working class could put its stamp on what became the Second Reconstruction.

The revolutionary potential of the Black toilers would be personified in the luminary of Malcolm X – but that was a century away. When Douglass became president of the Colored National Labor Union in January 1871 only about 11 percent of Blacks were free workers[67] – so the fledgling movement could not be anything other than one of the professionals, ministers, and other middle-class layers. If only 11 percent of free Blacks were free workers that means they would have comprised a miniscule percentage of the overall proletarian population in the United States. As George Novack reminds us, 'The southern revolution was not proletarian in its character or socialist in its aims, as Du Bois believed, but plebeian and petty-bourgeois in its social basis and bourgeois in its tasks. It did not pass beyond the foundations of private ownership, production for the market, and capitalist relations'.[68] And because more than ninety percent of Blacks were still living in the south at the end of the war, the socio-political reality there inevitably determined what the Black population as a whole could do.

The practical refusal of white labour to heed Marx's call to 'to remove every shackle from freedom's limb', continued to haunt the working class. The CNLU report by the Committee on Capital and Labor, written by George Downing, severely castigated 'the unkind, estranging policy of the labor organizations of white men, who, while they make loud proclaims as to the injustice ... to which they are subjected, justify injustice ... by excluding from their benches and their workshops worthy craftsmen and apprentices only because of their color, for no just cause'. The resolution continued, illustrating the yawning gap between Black and white workers and their labour leaders, 'We say to such, so long as you persist therein we cannot fellowship with you in your struggle, and look for failure and mortification on your part'. Real unity was not possible, Foner

---

67 Du Bois 1998, p. 3. See also Allen 1937, pp. 397–8.
68 Novack 2013, p. 354.

writes, 'so long as the white trade unions refused to remove the economic barriers against black workers'.[69]

Foner takes issue with the interpretation of the election of Douglass to head the Colored National Labor Union as proof of politicisation of the movement or that the organisation looked to suffrage alone as the solution to the problems of Blacks. Foner describes interracial labour gatherings that met together under the call of the CNLU in Texas, Tennessee, Alabama, Georgia, and Missouri. He documents CNLU organisation of unions and successful strikes. These laudable actions and gains may have been in spite of Douglass and not because of his leadership. He remained focused on legislation in DC, mentioned above, supporting the appointment of a commission to investigate the condition of workers in the United States. And, in fact, 'the CNLU itself never met again after 1871'.[70]

Against 'all those who attempt to stir up hostility to wealth and encourage outrage and violence', almost certainly in response to the events in Paris, on 20 April 1871 the *New National Era* tried to convince its readers of 'The True Labor Reform'. The editorial blamed pauperism and poverty in Europe on monarchism and in the southern states on slavery, both 'faulty political institutions'. Douglass admitted that it is 'a long step from the wage system to the complete emancipation of the working people. The relation of laborer to employer is servitude for a consideration – a modified slavery entered voluntarily by the laborer himself, and terminable at his pleasure, subject to forfeiture of pay if terminated before the expiration of a specific contract'. Labour leaders, the editorial argued, 'more or less adherents of communism', attack capital and wrongly denounce it 'as the chief cause of the poverty of the laboring classes'. It is not capital or capitalism that caused poverty – 'real pauperism … can always be traced back to faulty political institutions; first of all, to monarchism with all the veils and wrongs attending it'. In the United States poverty is 'indigenous only in those States where liberty and equality have been mere mockeries until lately; where the black man was debarred by law from acquiring knowledge and wealth, and the white man who owned no slaves was the obedient tool and servant of the master of the whip'. The editorial's solution to poverty: an ill defined 'co-operation – co-operation both in production and distribution'.[71]

Douglass, or his son Lewis, editorialised in September 1870 in opposition to a labour party, encapsulating their liberal worldview, and showing the gulf that had developed between Douglass and Marx over the previous few years:

---

[69] P. Foner 1981b, pp. 40–1.
[70] P. Foner 1981b, pp. 41–3.
[71] P. Foner and Lewis 1978, pp. 171–3. Blight 2018, p. 560, credits these views to Douglass, not his son Lewis.

There is no justice or safety in any organization which seeks to specially promote the interests of any one class of citizens at the expense of others. A capitalists' party, a producers and manufacturer's party, or a working-man's party within the circumscribed meaning of these terms, would be at once a menace to all other class interests, and would not only provoke the organization of political parties or factions for the special protection of each distinctive class, but create such divisions that anarchy and violence would sooner or later become inevitable. Hence, we must not for a moment tolerate the idea of arraying the employer against the employee, the capitalist against the business man, the manufacturer and producer against the laborer, the rich against the poor, the strong against the weak, nor encourage any of the antagonisms, so freely prated about and advocated by the shallow if not vicious demagogue. We must seek rather, by just laws and efficient administration, to harmonize all these superficially antagonistic interests, justice, universal justice, and not special privileges and advantages, is what we should perpetually aim at. Equal justice will wrong no man, and give no good cause for complaint even to the most selfish.[72]

4   RTG Letter

As we have seen, Marx described the Commune as essentially a working-class government. An unambiguously anti-working class letter published on the front page of the 19 October 1871 edition of the *New National Era* provides more evidence that Douglass never would have accepted or advocated for such a government and gives insight into why he reacted to the Commune the way he did. The letter was signed by the paper's Philadelphia correspondent, RTG, likely Richard Theodore Greener.[73] While the issue opens with a disclaimer that 'The *New National Era* does not hold itself responsible for views expressed by correspondents', Douglass let Greener's attack on the Colored National Labor Union go unanswered. Marx's name was mentioned in this correspondence – the only time, from what we can tell, in any of Douglass's newspapers, writings, or speeches.[74]

After telling Douglass that he did not see land ownership as important, but rather that agriculture was 'a primitive, though to a degree a necessary

---

72 P. Foner and Lewis 1978, pp. 170–1.
73 Greener would later become 'a cantankerous intellectual nemesis of Douglass's' regarding the Kansas Exodus. Blight 2018, pp. 601–3.
74 'Communications. Letter from Philadelphia', *New National Era*, 19 October 1871.

state', Greener turned to the Colored National Labor Union. 'I notice that the [Colored] *National Labor Union*', he wrote, 'whatever that high sounding name may mean, is soon to meet in the city of Columbia, South Carolina'. Greener had followed the CNLU and found its speeches 'incongruous' and its resolutions 'indefinite'. He worried 'all of our prominent men, yourself among the number', were being attracted to the movement.[75]

What is the purpose of the CNLU? 'Is it merely another name for Communism, or La Commune under another form?' Greener asked Douglass and the readers of the *New National Era* in a set of leading questions.

> Does it propose to make labor the equal of capital – to furnish every man with a farm, or a house, and make him keep it? Or to give ten hours' pay for eight hours' work? Or is it merely a colored offshoot of the notorious *Internationale*, which now has its branches throughout the world; which ruled Paris under the name of La Commune, and proposes to overthrow stable government in England, and eventually to give us a mobocracy in America?[76]

A spectre was haunting Greener – a coloured offshoot of the International Working Men's Association, or an international, interracial alliance of workers.[77]

Greener, like many middle-class northerners, worried about what would happen after working people organised together to demand rights. 'As I have yet to read a clear statement of its object, from its high priest, Carl Marx, down to Bradleugh in England, or Phillips, Cummings, or Myers in America, I should like to know what these gentlemen propose to do with the giant they are conjuring up and assuring about his strength, after he shall have recovered all his "rights" and be monarch over capital?'[78]

What would happen to people like Greener, a trailblazing Black man who graduated from Harvard in 1870 and would go on to become a law professor in South Carolina, once working people came to power? He implied that industrial workers would come for those '*who work with our brains instead of our hands.* ... Are we to be emancipated', Greener asked,

---

[75] 'Communications. Letter from Philadelphia', *New National Era*, 19 October 1871.

[76] 'Communications. Letter from Philadelphia', *New National Era*, 19 October 1871.

[77] Without acknowledging the source of the column, W.E.B. Du Bois, in a brief comment, sees the RTG letter as evidence of a 'rivalry between the economic and political objects of the Negro'. Du Bois 1998, pp. 366–7.

[78] 'Communications. Letter from Philadelphia', *New National Era*, 19 October 1871.

who are compelled to do our eight or nine hours' work, and then work several more hours to get ready for the next day's labor? How many editors, how many ministers, how many lawyers, how many capitalists – orgres, monsters that they are! – how many professors and school teachers ... would not hasten to join this labor movement – this uprising of hard-handed toil, of sinewy workmen, and all the other glorious adjectives applied to our modern Vulcan, if he would only guarantee to us, also, eight hours' pay for six hours' work, and a chance to spend our evenings in the beer shops, or at the varieties, or in witnessing prize fights and other exhibitions laudatory of mere muscle, mere brawn, which the time-serving, tyrannical capitalist knows nothing of, and the 'aristocratic' intellectual man counts inferior in the long run to brains![79]

Appealing to that side of Douglass who had left the plantation and ship yard, Greener wrote in conclusion:

It is because I, like you, Mr. Editor, have sprung from the ranks of these myrmidons, and have shaken off the service of Vulcan, preferring to follow Minerva, even though she bid me to work fifteen hours a day, that I am anxious, yes, alarmed, lest the modern disciples of the limping god bring us back to his service. Do you long for the ship-yard again? I surely do not for the drudgery of a store with out the prospect of promotion. I prefer the rule of a judicious and sensible few to that of the mirmidons *race seconde*.[80]

It is curious that Douglass, ostensibly the President of the Colored National Labor Union Greener was attacking, would let this assault go unanswered. Curious, that is, until we understand that Douglass harboured many of the same feelings. As Peter Myers explains, 'Douglass held that the often-despised bourgeoisie, or what Locke termed the 'industrious and rational' class, in collaboration with the practitioners of modern science, represented at its best the most progressive and revolutionary class in human history'.[81]

---

79   'Communications. Letter from Philadelphia', *New National Era*, 19 October 1871.
80   'Communications. Letter from Philadelphia', *New National Era*, 19 October 1871.
81   Myers 2013, p. 135.

5   Douglass, the Paris Commune, and the Retreat from Reconstruction

The Paris Commune demanded intense scrutiny from Americans, who were in the middle of the first nationwide attempt at interracial democracy, that is, Reconstruction. This section places Douglass's views on the Commune in political context, especially amongst other liberals in the US. The reaction of many Americans to the Paris Commune – Republicans and abolitionists included – did not portend well for this first attempt, now beginning to fail, at interracial democracy. As Katz instantiates, radicals like Lydia Maria Child attacking Wendell Phillips for his support of the Parisian workers, and other abolitionists associating social change with anarchy was not a promising sign for the experiment of Reconstruction 'whose end would be hastened by association with the Paris Commune'. The Commune 'became an excuse to assert a bolder elitism, or even to retreat from Reconstruction', Katz convincingly writes.[82]

Douglass never retreated from his vision of Reconstruction as a project to win equal citizenship for Black Americans, especially the right to vote, but he was unwilling to defend the only coalition that could have made it a reality – the multiracial working class, Caucasian wage workers and farmers, immigrant and native born, along with the freed people – with the eventual goal of instituting a state that not only represented the interests of the producing classes for the first time but also defended those interests. His platform of free men, free soil, free speech, a free press, the ballot for all, education for all, and fair wages for all was tenuous in the hands of northern and southern capitalists.[83]

'The growing American tension over workers and the nature of the nation's political economy heightened dramatically with the establishment of the Paris Commune', explains Heather Cox Richardson. By this time, Douglass certainly counted himself among the propertied Americans terrified by the Commune and opposed what he saw as the turmoil of the mob in power. Douglass's commentary on the outbreak of strikes and the labour question seemed to indicate he was one of the many Americans Richardson describes who were too nervous about workers using force to defend their interests to offer them true solidarity. Events after the Civil War fed Republican fears that workers would try to gain

---

[82]   Katz 1998, pp. 93, 117.
[83]   This platform comes from the 'Position of the New National Era', *New National Era*, 30 March 1871.

property through collective action. Republicans, liberals, and even radical abolitionists formed part of a group 'that clung to the idea that the true American system depended on a harmony of interest between labor and capital'.[84] The editorial position of Douglass's *New National Era*, as well as its analysis of strikes and labour organisations, clearly placed him among this group. While Douglass expressed sympathy with striking workers, he opposed effective defences of their picket lines and their drive to affect their working conditions through their own organisations.

6   Great Railroad Strike of 1877

While we have yet to uncover any extant views from Douglass about the Great Railroad Strike of 1877, we feel there is enough evidence from earlier periods to speculate.[85] Nothing in his past indicates he would have supported the 'general railroad strike' that 'developed into a national conflagration that brought the country closer to a social revolution than at any other time in its century of existence except for the Civil War', as Philip Foner put it.[86]

Douglass had just entered the Rutherford B. Hayes administration as the marshal of the District of Columbia. The office 'helped run the federal court that once adjudicated fugitive-slave cases', ironic evidence of the progress made through the social revolution brought on by the Civil War, by posting bankruptcies and holding prisoners as they moved between jail and the courts.[87] As Hayes withdrew troops from the southern states, leaving freedpeople to the mercy of accelerating and deepening white supremacy, it is more likely Douglass would have supported the moves of law and order to restore tranquillity and crush the strikers.

He had warned of a cloud withholding its bolts when a strike of labourers did not develop into a wider conflagration back in 1871. Editorials against independent working class political action, strikes, and the defence of picket lines regularly materialised in the paper he owned and edited, the *New National Era*. The milieu he operated within as evidenced from the RTG letter, even as he was

---

[84]   Richardson 2001, pp. *xii–xiii*, 24, 44, 85–6, 89, 94.
[85]   As noted in our conclusion, we are appreciative of the effort John McKivigan put into a fruitless search. Historian Nikki M. Taylor writes that Peter H. Clark was 'the only African American on record in the nation to speak publicly about the Great Railroad Strike of 1877'. Taylor 2013, p. 147.
[86]   P. Foner 2002, p. 8.
[87]   Blight 2018, p. 583.

elected president of the National Colored Labor Union, reinforced Douglass's bourgeois outlook. Why would we expect Douglass, now established in a presidential administration, would have acted any differently in this instance?

Marx and Engels, on the other hand, were sympathetic to the general strike but sober about its chances, likely to 'be suppressed'. More importantly, it pointed the way forward for them, 'a point of departure for the constitution of a serious workers' party in the' US for the first time. Also propitious in Marx's opinion, it took place when the new President Hayes administration was withdrawing Union troops from the South, and thus likely to provoke an angry response from Blacks, while small farmers in the West were being squeezed out by the capitalist monopolies. Both developments, Marx anticipated, would turn the Blacks and small farmers 'into militant allies of the workers'.[88] Though not to be, 'Marx could not have been more correct about the alliance of social forces that would have to be at the centre of a successful revolution in the United States – the working class, toilers who are Black, and exploited farmers'.[89]

7 Conclusion

Speaking on 4 July 1862, Frederick Douglass, praising the American revolutionaries of 1776, told an audience that 'rebellions are quite respectable in the eyes of the world, and very properly so. They naturally command the sympathy of mankind, for generally they are on the side of progress. They would overthrow and remove some old and festering abuse not to be otherwise disposed of, and introduce a higher civilization, and a larger measure of liberty among men'. However, not all rebellions were created equal. For example, the slaveholding rebels waging war against the United States fought 'for the guilty purpose of handing down to the latest generations the accursed system of human bondage'.[90]

Peter Myers writes that 'Douglass aligned himself with revolutionary movements everywhere they arose to vindicate the principle of equal rights or equality in liberty against a prevailing order of entrenched inequality'.[91] But there

---

88 Marx and Engels 1975–2004y, p. 251.
89 Barnes 2020, p. 366. There was, in fact, a considerable amount of Black participation in the strike, including the socialist Peter H. Clark in Cincinnati. See P. Foner 2002, pp. 154–8 and the entry 'Blacks' in Index. For more on Clark and Great Railroad Strike see Taylor 2013, pp. 143–7.
90 Blassingame 1985, pp. 526–7.
91 Myers 2013, p. 122.

was at least one 'revolutionary movement' that repulsed Douglass which in essence did seek to 'vindicate the principle of equal rights in liberty against a prevailing order of entrenched inequality'. Without social equality, the chief lesson of capitalism's first century or less of existence, 'equality in liberty' for the proletariat would be a chimaera – a lesson not lost on the Parisian proletariat. Douglass's negative reaction to the Communards of March 1871 and the concurrent fledgling labour movement in the United States betrayed his classical liberal sensibilities and its free labour assumptions about the presumed harmony of interests between capital and labour, its solution for addressing the needs of the proletariat. Contra Douglass, Marx portrayed the Commune as 'the idea' and 'the workers' government is the fact in which the 18th of March culminates'. While the revolutionary party in Paris was too disorganised and immature to succeed, the struggle was a 'prelude' – 'an unforgettable example of initiative, boldness and courage. If it did not triumph, at least it showed the way'.[92] No one instantiated that forecast better than Lenin for whom the lessons of the Commune served as essential reading for his playbook for the October 1917 Revolution.

Consistent with his analysis of the European Spring in 1848, Douglass denounced and criticised the attempt of workers in Paris to take history into their own hands after the institution of republican structures. He accepted the accounts of mob-rule and anarchy promoted by the Thiers government and printed in American newspapers. While he opposed the Second Empire of France, Douglass concluded that communism tainted French republicanism and formed just as much an antithesis to true republicanism as the restoration of the monarchy. Marx believed a true republic required real democratic institutions in the hands of working people – what the Commune briefly realised, notwithstanding Douglass's less flattering portrait. Douglass's reaction to the Paris Commune exposes the limitations of his liberal political thought to take on an internationalist analysis of class conflict and labour struggles.

The Paris Commune and the labour upsurge coming out of the Civil War in the United States pressured Douglass to spend time and space in his newspaper analysing the labour question. While he expressed sympathy with workers attempting to improve their lives, he advocated for conciliation between capital and workers while condemning labour organisations and their picket lines. Further investigation into Douglass's writings in the *New National Era* on work-

---

92   Gaido 2021, pp. 37–8.

ers, unions, the Depression of 1873, the National Labor Union and the Colored National Labor Union would be fruitful, confirming or complicating this finding.

Douglass relied on the newly consolidated Republican-led capitalist government, rightly credited with crushing the Confederacy and enactment of the Reconstruction Amendments to the Constitution, to mediate between workers and their bosses with the goal of finding a harmony of interests.[93] Douglass did not agree with the claim that only the working class, in all its skin colours and other identities, has a class interest in ridding the world of social inequality. He resisted any move to independent working-class political action through a labour party, as those calls came from white workers insufficiently opposed to organising workers of all colours into their unions. The vast majority of Blacks, not only Douglass, were unwilling to break with the Republican Party. The eventual downfall of Reconstruction constituted the worst setback in the history of the American working class because workers and producers were forcibly divided along racial lines by Klan violence while solidarity was crippled and Jim Crow oppression enshrined.[94]

To make an ironclad case that Douglass contributed to Reconstruction's failure is probably impossible. However, the views he expressed about the Paris Commune, until now unexamined, and his opposition to effective labour organisation after the Civil War dovetailed with the views of other northern liberals that historians, such as Heather Cox Richardson, have identified as playing a significant role in the retreat from Reconstruction. As white supremacist redemption, terror, and violence increased, liberals in the North, frightened by a surging labour movement, retreated from their original embrace of Reconstruction. As David Montgomery teaches, Radical Republicans's goal was equality before the law within a unified nation. 'But beyond equality lay demands of wage earners to which the equalitarian formula provided no meaningful answer, but which rebounded to confound the efforts of equality's ardent advocates. Class conflict, in other words, was the submerged shoal on which Radical dreams foundered'.[95]

Marx would have been in agreement with Douglass that the American labour movement's 'first grand step' toward the emancipation of labour was

---

93 As David Blight writes, 'To [Douglass], the Republican Party had been the author of emancipation, the embodiment of Union victory, and the custodian of black citizenship'. Blight 2018, p. 532.
94 On the defeat of Radical Reconstruction as 'the worst setback' for the American working class in history, Dobbs 2009, p. 69.
95 Montgomery 1967, p. x.

'the abolition of slavery, of property in man', as Douglass put it in October 1871. In November 1864, Marx, on behalf of the International Workingmen's Association, congratulated Lincoln on his re-election. He took the opportunity to remind the president that as long as 'the working men, the true political power of the North, allowed slavery to defile their own republic; while before the Negro, mastered and sold without his concurrence, they boasted it the highest prerogative of the white-skinned labourer to sell himself and choose his own master; they were unable to attain the true freedom of labour or to support their European brethren in their struggle for emancipation, but this barrier to progress has been swept off by the red sea of civil war'.[96]

Three years later in *Capital*, published in 1867, Marx returned to his pregnant insight that still has currency. 'In the United States of North America, every independent movement of the workers was paralysed so long as slavery disfigured a part of the Republic. Labour cannot emancipate itself in the white skin where in the black it is branded'.[97]

Both Marx and Douglass wholeheartedly backed the abolition of slavery and the Union cause in the Civil War – the 'first grand step' – but Marx saw the reconstructed bourgeois republic as an indispensable means to an end, more favourable terrain to organise for power in the hands of the working class, and not the end in itself, as Douglass did.

---

96   Marx and Engels 1975–2004k, p. 20.
97   Marx and Engels 1975–2004p, p. 305.

APPENDIX B

Marx and Engels on the Race Question: A Response to the Critics

August H. Nimtz

In the Introduction to her 2016 collection *The Civil War in the United States: Karl Marx & Frederick Engels*, Angela Zimmerman raises what she calls 'shortcomings' in Marx and Engels with regard to race, racism, and white supremacy, limiting, she claims, 'their ability to analyze the Civil War'. Because Zimmerman has performed an invaluable service for Marxist scholarship in republishing the Richard Enmale 1937 collection of the Marx and Engels writings on the War, and translating and adding to the collection the all so important Weydemeyer articles, her criticisms have to be taken seriously.[1] An entire book or two could be devoted to other less friendly critics of Marx and Engels on the topic. This appendix addresses only those whose criticisms are relevant to this book's project, beginning with Zimmerman.[2]

Marx's and Engels's usage of the n-word, an issue addressed in our Introduction, is the 'shortcoming' Zimmerman begins with. But they 'used this term', to repeat, 'ironically … to highlight a racism that they criticized rather than endorsed. Marx and Engels opposed racism at every turn, and the communist movements that they inspired have remained some of the most powerful and consistent anti-racist and anti-imperialist forces in the world, including the United States'. We are largely in agreement with Zimmerman, given what I wrote on the matter in 2003 that we reproduced above. Again, 'Marx began to use "nigger" during the Civil War as he was familiarizing himself with the US reality. In published writings he always employed quotation marks; in letters often without. Only once, it seems, did he use it in a derogatory sense' (more about this later).[3]

The next 'shortcoming' Zimmerman raises has to do with a comment Marx made to Engels in an 1853 letter. 'When Marx remarked, in 1853, that US blacks

---

1 Enmale 1937; Zimmerman 2016, p. xxvi. Except for an article or two in the MECW, the only thing missing is an index, given the richness of the materials.
2 For a defence of Marx on the broader topics of "Nationalism, Imperialism, and Race," see, most recently, Miéville 2022, pp. 113–30.
3 Nimtz 2003, pp. 131–32n35.

who were born into slavery were not "freshly imported barbarians" from Africa but rather "a native product, more or less Yankified, English speaking, etc., and hence capable of being emancipated" (document 104 [in the Zimmerman collection]), he did not only denigrate African cultures; he also blinded himself to the many African and African American political traditions that contributed to the defeat of slavery in the Americas'.[4]

From Zimmerman, that's a serious charge because it suggests that Marx would have been unprepared and, therefore, have missed any 'African and African American' initiatives in the lead up to and during the Civil War; a real shortcoming for the revolutionary that Marx purported to be. Is that true?

But first, what did Marx actually say to Engels? Zimmerman's point refers to what Marx thought about the just published *The Slave Trade, Domestic and Foreign* by America's leading economist Henry Carey, a fan of Marx, as previously discussed, to whom he had gifted a copy.

> The only thing of definite interest in the book is the comparison between Negro slavery as formerly practiced by the English in Jamaica and elsewhere, and Negro slavery in the United States. He demonstrates how the main STOCK of Negroes in Jamaica always consisted of freshly imported BARBARIANS, since their treatment by the English meant not only that the Negro population was not maintained, but also that ⅔ of the yearly imports always went to waste, whereas the present generation of Negroes in America is a native product, more or less Yankeefied, English speaking, etc., and hence *capable of being emancipated* [italics in original].[5]

'Barbarians' seems to have bothered Zimmerman. But Marx was quoting what was in the original as the editors of the *Marx-Engels Collected Works* customarily indicate with the small capitalization. 'In the islands', Carey wrote, 'the slave was generally a barbarian, speaking an unknown tongue … [whereas] Here [the U.S.], he was generally a being born on the soil, speaking the same language with his owner'. Further on, according to Carey: 'In the islands, everything looked toward the permanency of slavery. Here, every thing looked toward the gradual and gentle civilization and emancipation of the negro throughout the world'.[6]

---

4 Zimmerman 2016, p. xxvi.
5 Marx and Engels 1975–2004s, p. 346. See also, Slack 2023.
6 https://www.gutenberg.org/cache/epub/8000/pg8000-images.html. Foster et al 2020 convincingly argue, contrary to some claims, that Marx was well-read on the slavery question before Carey's book.

Given what Carey wrote, we read Marx's 'capable of being emancipated' to mean no more than that the prospects for the enslaved would be improved by those of them who had mastered English. Douglass, it seems to us, epitomised Marx's point, his usage of English to advance the cause for abolition was exemplary. As David Blight puts it, 'Douglass was a man of words; spoken and written language was the only major weapon of protest, persuasion, or power that he ever possessed'.[7] Manisha Sinha emphasises that Douglass's first autobiography, his narrative, made 'the slave's indictment of slavery the most effective weapon in the abolitionist arsenal and for popularizing the genre'.[8] That Douglass spoke and wrote English so powerfully certainly gives credence to the claim that American slaves were capable of being emancipated.

Why what Marx underscored translates, as Zimmerman charges, into the denigration of 'African cultures' or being 'blinded ... to the many African and African American political traditions that contributed to the defeat of slavery in the Americas' is not clear. By bringing Douglass into the picture, as our book does, that lack of clarity is exposed – what comparisons can reveal as Marx pointed out to Engels.

Once the War began, Zimmerman finds problematic Marx's initial comment about Union prospects in May 1861, her chief complaint about Marx and Engels: 'When he called "slave revolution" the "last card up its [the Union] sleeve," he attributes agency to the white Northern leadership who might play this card rather than to enslaved black workers themselves'. The bookend to that comment for Zimmerman is Marx's oft-quoted sentence in his 1867 magnum opus: 'When Marx wrote in *Capital* that "Labor cannot emancipate itself in the white skin where in the black it is branded," he connected the struggles of white and black workers, but also suggested that they were separate'. The crux of Marx's and Engels's problem, according to Zimmerman, is that they 'missed ... the largest worker rebellion of all at the heart of the Union victory and the Civil War: the determination of great numbers of the four million enslaved black workers to withdraw their labor from their erstwhile masters, to transform the war for the Union into a war against slavery, and to throw their collective intelligence, capacity for labor, and armed might behind the Union'.[9] Quite a claim and indictment.

---

7 Blight 2018, p. xvii.
8 Sinha 2016, p. 426.
9 Zimmerman 2016, pp. xxvi–xxvii. Zimmerman previewed her main complaint a year earlier in 'Marxism, the Popular Front, and the American Civil War'; Zimmerman 2015. For a persuasive refutation of her claim that Marx and Engels regarded the War not as a 'bourgeois revolution but a workers' revolution', p. 317, see Kelly, 2019.

Despite Zimmerman's criticisms, she ends on a positive note. If Marx and Engels didn't fully appreciate the enslaved as a Black proletariat, their comrades in the War – Weydemeyer in particular, who 'worked with, and fought alongside' them – did. 'All this suggests' the lesson 'that the fight against racism is not a matter of white people perfecting their own "un-racist" ideas but rather develops through interracial political solidarity'. We wholeheartedly agree, wisdom that today's virtue-signalling social justice warriors could surely benefit from.[10]

But was it true that 'the largest worker rebellion', that is, the withdrawal by the enslaved of 'their labor from their erstwhile masters', brought down the slavocracy and that Marx and Engels failed to recognise that fact? These are two interrelated but separate claims. While historian James Oakes gives credence to the first one, he and other Civil War historians soberly point out that when Lee surrendered to Grant at Appomattox in April 1865, at least eighty percent of the enslaved were still in bondage.[11] Freedom for them, as had been true from the beginning of the War, depended on the battlefield progress of Union troops as in Galveston, Texas on 19 June 1865 – the now celebrated Juneteenth. Resistance, to employ Lenin's point four decades later in the context of Russia's 1905 Revolution, could take either an active or a passive form; preferable was the former.[12] While the quotidian resistance of their chattel slaves still bounded to the plantation no doubt corroded the slave oligarchy's infrastructure and undermined eventual victory for them, only an organised and disciplined Union Army, finally welcoming Blacks and former slaves alongside European immigrants and native-born white toilers, could actually bring them to heel – what Appomattox registered.

As for Zimmerman's charge that Marx and Engels were derelict in not crediting Black toilers with agency and underappreciating their role in the defeat of the Confederacy, let's bring Douglass into the conversation – something that our comparison can uniquely do. Real-time analysis requires examining events as they actually unfold.

The actual record reveals that Marx, if anything, overestimated the 'agency' of the enslaved beginning with the John Brown raid. Although Engels later said that Brown 'did more than anyone else in the abolition of slavery',[13] a *white* abolitionist, in other words – the advantages of hindsight no doubt – in real-time he and his partner thought the raid's significance was the spark it lit for a

---

10   As in Ryan Grim's painfully revealing 'The Elephant in the Zoom', *Intercept*, 13 June 2022, https://theintercept.com/2022/06/13/progressive-organizing-infighting-callout-culture/
11   Oakes 2013, p. xiv. See also Chapter 5, p. 248 of this book.
12   Nimtz, 2019a, p. 91.
13   Marx and Engels 1975–2004z, p. 77.

slave rebellion. For a brief moment that looked like a real possibility, but it soon proved not to be the case. Douglass serves as the best real-time voice for assessing Zimmerman's suggestion that Blacks were in a position to set the agenda for emancipation. As Marx might have said, they could indeed exercise free will but not 'under self-selected circumstances', that is, of their own choosing.

From the very beginning, Douglas made that clear. In his first comment about how to respond to the slave oligarchy's attack on Fort Sumter in April 1861, he wrote: 'Let the slaves and free colored people be called into service and formed into a liberating army'. Douglass's 'be called' speaks to the reality in that moment; the Union government was calling the shots. Nine months later, he reported that he had 'been often asked since the war began why I am not in the South battling for freedom'. The reason, with apparent frustration, was that the government 'does not yet rank me or [nota bene] my race with men'.[14] Douglass's agency for participating in the war, in other words, was limited by decisions and actions of the Lincoln administration. Two years later, after Lincoln had just issued the final Emancipation Proclamation, Douglass wrote on the front page of his *Monthly*, 'The colored men of the North have remained silent ... now waiting to be honorably invited forward ... Let the government say the word'.[15]

What about the enslaved in the Confederacy? Did they have more agency as Zimmerman suggests? And were Marx and Engels derelict for not appreciating that fact? Our excavation of their corpus, to briefly recapitulate, reveals three antebellum Marx utterances of possible relevance. First, Marx's first reference to slaves in 1842 and his implicit assumption that they were capable of being educated in ways that their slave masters feared and, thus, the need to censor what they might read. Exhibit A, Douglass. Second, in 1847, Marx's lecture in which he disputed the assumption that being 'a Negro' was equivalent to being 'a slave'. To know someone's social status did not necessarily say anything about who they actually were and capable of doing – a lecture to be revisited. And third, about 1857, a slave, like a proletariat, was also capable of being 'conscious' about what it meant to be free; think Douglass. Marx, in other words, should in theory have been primed to quickly recognise Black agency once the slavocracy fired on Fort Sumter in April 1861.

When we get to the Civil War, the consensus of the literature, again, is that the proximity of Union troops was determinant. Douglass recognised that fact in his coverage of the escape, weeks into the war, of the three slaves to the

---

14   Blassingame 1985, p. 467.
15   DM, February 1863, p. 785.

Union's Fortress Monroe in Virginia. The problem Douglass thought paramount in the early months of the war was Confederate use of slave labour to shore up its prospects. Not until the issuance of the preliminary Emancipation Proclamation at the end of September 1862 could Douglass happily report for the first time on large numbers of former slaves fleeing to Union lines. But again, flight depended on the progress of Union troops and in the end on Lee's surrender to Grant in April 1865.

Only when Lincoln made it official in early 1863 that Black men would be welcomed into the Union army did one-time slaves effectively ensure Union victory. What Zimmerman fails to grasp, or perhaps agree with – a fundamental premise of Marx and Engels's perspective – is that to be enslaved was to be unfree to exercise self-determination in a way that a worker could. Unlike a slave, a worker – Marxism 101 – could choose their exploiter and all that implied, such as being able to sign up for the Union army when the opportunity presented itself. In the real world of the Civil War, the enslaved had to wait for the arrival of that army – which included after mid-1863 former bondsmen – to exercise choice. If agency for Zimmerman refers to the enslaved deciding to flee to Union lines when their forces got close enough, then we have no quarrel with her.[16] And if 'the largest worker rebellion' means for Zimmerman an alliance of small white farmers, white and recently created Black workers that brought down the Slave Power, we are in complete accord with her.[17] Nothing we know of in Marx's and Engels's commentary would be in disagreement. Unlike Zimmerman, evidently, we read her astute point that 'their comrades,' like Weydemeyer, 'who served in the Union Army ... worked with, and fought alongside, formerly enslaved African Americans ... gained a better understanding of the importance of black workers in the conflict' to be a compliment to the Marx party, the advantages of organised collective work – the ersatz party that Douglass lacked. Until the end, Weydemeyer considered that he was carrying out a line that his two comrades in England would have agreed with. If Zimmerman thinks otherwise, she should say so.

A telling coda. Two decades later, Marx again overestimated Black agency when he mistakenly thought that new Republican president Rutherford B. Hayes's withdrawal of federal troops from the South in 1877 would spark a

---

16   As Oakes argues, 2019, the 'transfer of the labor services of half a million black workers from the masters who owned them to the Unionists who employed them as wage laborers, was the essence of the revolution we call emancipation, a revolution that was indispensable to Union victory'.

17   Most recently, Oakes 2019. Also, Novack 2013, pp. 345–57 and Barnes 2009, pp. 157–69, 370–4.

militant Black response. Douglass, like many other leading middle-class Blacks now in bed with the Republican Party, knew better – circumstances not of Marx's choosing.[18]

One last point about Zimmerman's criticisms, a bit ironic in our opinion. W.E.B. Du Bois's masterful *Black Reconstruction*, she correctly notes, stands on the shoulders of Marx's and Engels's Civil War writings. His notion of the 'general strike', the means by which 'these black workers transformed the war between the Union and the Confederacy into a revolution against slavery', in fact inspired her claim about 'the largest worker rebellion of all at the heart of the Union victory'. Marx's and Engels's writings, in other words, and despite Zimmerman's charge about their myopia regarding Black toilers, inexplicably inspired subsequent analysts to see Black agency, including, by way of Du Bois, Zimmerman herself. That apparent contradiction explains, perhaps, why we can regard Zimmerman as a friendly critic of 'Marx and Engels on Race'.

We can't say the same when it comes to Wulf Hund, in fact, a disingenuous critic in our opinion. We begin with him in his own words, from the abstract to his 2021 article, 'Marx and Haiti: Note on a Blank Space'.[19] Marx, according to Hund, 'ignored the history of the revolution in Haiti' because of his

> deficient analysis of contemporary racism. This is made clear in relation to 1) his acceptance of the biological meaning of race, 2) his involvement in two main racisms of his time, anti-semitism and colonial racism, and 3) his differentiation and (de)gradation of historical subjects. The consequences were dramatic not because of Marx's involvement in the racist zeitgeist but insofar as his learning process with regard to the relevance of anti-colonial movements and his awareness of negative societalization as well as its significance were not reflected in a theory of racism. This was to prove a debacle for subsequent attempts at a Marxist analysis of racism and has had effects that are still evident today.[20]

The focus here is only on Hund's claims about Marx as they relate to this book. Let's begin with what we think is obvious. If Hund is to be believed, Marx

---

[18] Frederick Sorge, Marx's and Engels's next closest contact in the US. after Weydemeyer's death in 1866, indicated to them in June 1871 that the Republican Party's hold on Blacks was a major political obstacle to Black/white working class unity. Nimtz 2003, p. 153. Apparently, Marx didn't fully appreciate Sorge's point.

[19] Hund 2021.

[20] Hund 2021, p. 76. For Charles Mills, Marx is one of the major political philosophers who is of 'limited use in theorizing' about the polity of 'white supremacy'. See Mills 1998, p. 126.

should have been missing in action in responding to modernity's first major step in eradicating the 'racist zeitgeist', the abolition of chattel slavery in the US. Because he lacked 'a theory of racism', Marx – this is implicit in Hund's rendering of him – would have been incapable of being on the right side in that history-defining moment. Hund's critique is only implied, I argue, because he knows exactly how Marx responded to the slave oligarchy's attack on Fort Sumter in April 1861. He read, in fact, what I wrote in 2003 about that response, in many ways a preview of this book. Rather than directly contest Marx's own anti-racist credentials – revealed in action and not in theory – Hund, therefore, faults Marx for the sins of those who later claimed to speak in his name on the topic of race; an issue to be revisited.

Hund's first charge, Marx's alleged 'acceptance of the biological meaning of race', refers to the aforementioned passage in his 1847 'Wage Labour and Capital' lecture that begins with 'What is a Negro'. Here's the entire text:

> What is a Negro slave? A man of the black race. The one explanation is as good as the other. A Negro is a Negro. He only becomes a *slave* in certain relations. A cotton-spinning jenny is a machine for spinning cotton. It becomes *capital* only in certain relations. Torn from these relations it is no more capital than *gold* in itself is *money* or sugar the *price* of sugar.[21]

Here is what I wrote in 2003 about the passage:

> Marx was, as it might be called in some academic settings today, deconstructing the concept of 'Negro.' By the mid-nineteenth century, in Western Europe at least, Black identity had become increasingly synonymous with servitude. This was especially true in the United States where – especially in slave states – with each succeeding decade of the nineteenth century the laws and courts made the condition of 'free Blacks' increasingly impossible. Marx, therefore challenged the racist conclusions about Blacks that derived from their oppression and exploitation.[22]

For Hund, on the other hand, Marx's response to his opening question, 'A man of the black race', is irrefutable proof that Marx subscribed to a 'biological meaning of race'. And for me to have written, Hund charges, that Marx was 'deconstructing the concept of "Negro"' was to be 'uncritical and disguises the

---

21 Marx and Engels 1975–2004g, p. 211.
22 Nimtz 2003, p. 52.

problem contained in Marx's statement ... Marx recognizes only one dimension of the racism at issue; slavery is not natural. But he does not realize the other racist dimension of his deliberation; for him, race theory is valid and being a "Negro" is a natural quality, not a social relation'.[23] But is that true?

Hund certainly knows that Marx, like so many others of that era, including Frederick Douglass, employed 'race' most often to refer to what today is usually called ethnicity and/or nationality. For example, their frequent references to the English, the German, the Russian, the Irish, etc 'races'. At the same time, Douglass would certainly have agreed with Marx calling him 'a man of the black race' as in the aforementioned self-described 'of my race'.[24] Would Hund then accuse Douglass, like Marx, of 'involvement in the racist zeitgeist' of that era? What conclusions, if so, are to be drawn from such a usage? Given its then different meanings, does Hund know for sure what Marx meant by 'race' in that passage, before social Darwinism and its biological connotations of race had become de rigueur in intellectual circles? Hund, at least, owes it to his readers to inform them about the then various usages of the term.

If Hund is accusing Marx of not knowing what science later revealed, that race is an invention, a social construction without any kind of biological justification, then he's right and why he can appear to be smarter than not only Marx and Douglass but virtually anyone else from that era to at least the middle of the twentieth century regarding race. More meaningful is the 'so what' question when it comes to Marx, the quintessential revolutionary. Did his understanding of 'race' impede or advance his revolutionary project? Once again, the overthrow of pre-capitalist modes of production like chattel slavery for Marx was indispensable for the full development of capitalist relations of production. With the latter came the proletariat, the first oppressed layer in the history of class society that had a class interest in the abolishment of private property, the material basis of social inequality and, hence, racial inequality. Whatever his understanding of 'race', Marx and his comrades in the US single-mindedly did all they could to put an end to America's peculiar institution, the most effective anti-racist work of the nineteenth century. Compared to any contemporaries, including Douglass, Marx was exemplary.

---

23 Hund 2021, p. 80.
24 Also instructive is what Douglass said to a largely white audience in October 1864: 'My white fellow-citizens: Let me defend you from your friends. You belong to the best branch of the Indo-caucasian race; you belong to the Anglo-Saxon branch of the great human family. The world is rocked by your power, and filled with your achievements. To the civilization of the nineteenth-century, your race is the main spring'. Blassingame and McKivigan 1991, vol. 4, p. 47.

We suspect that Hund, as academics like him all too often do, reads Marx in his own image, primarily a theory-maker and not as a revolutionary activist. 'Ideas', the young Marx concluded in 1844, 'cannot carry out anything at all. In order to carry out ideas men are needed'.[25] Three years later, Engels tried to explain to an opponent what he and his partner stood for: 'Communism is not a doctrine but a movement, it proceeds not from principles but from facts ... Communism, insofar as it is a theory, is the theoretical expression of the position of the proletariat in this struggle ['between proletariat and bourgeoisie'] and the theoretical summation of the conditions for the liberation of the proletariat'.[26] We suspect, also, that they fault him for not having a 'theory of race', or, of nationalism, or perhaps gender, because they fundamentally disagree with his communism and its proletariat-centric explanation for ending social inequality – and are disingenuous in not being forthright in saying so.[27] We take our lead from Engels, the person who knew him best. 'Marx was', as Engels put it at his partner's funeral in 1883, 'before all else a revolutionist'.[28] For the Civil War, the longest revolutionary moment that Marx ever lived through, the primary task was to do all he could to ensure the military defeat of the slave oligarchy and, thus, the birth of a hereditary proletariat throughout the US for the first time. Marx assumed from the beginning that the North would be victorious because, if needed, Lincoln had a 'last card up his sleeve ... a slave rebellion'. But an unknown factor that could delay or even prevent that victory would be the response of 'poor whites' in the South to the oligarchy's pro-slavery war.

Long before the War began Marx knew about the ideas that rationalised racial slavery. *Marie, or Slavery in America*, the 1835 novel about an ill-fated interracial romance by Tocqueville's travel companion, Gustave de Beaumont, was probably his first detailed introduction to the topic. Subsequent reading helped to explain the prevailing mid-nineteenth-century belief in much of the trans-Atlantic world that to be 'a Negro slave' was to be 'a man of the black race' – exactly what he contested in his 1847 'Wage Labour and Capital' lecture. Never for a moment did Marx doubt that America's peculiar institution was a quintessentially class institution, that is, one in which one layer of society lived off the uncompensated labour of another. That the exploited came exclusively in black skin and that the exploiters, beginning with the three-hundred thousand slave owners, employed racial claims to sustain and defend

---

25 Marx and Engels 1975–2004c, p. 119.
26 Marx and Engels 1975–2004e, pp. 303–4.
27 A recent example of this kind of treatment of Marx, excessive in fact, and for this topic is Sorentino 2019.
28 Marx and Engels 1975–2004m, p. 468.

the practice didn't make it any less a class institution. The slave oligarchy's foundational documents like Hammond's 1858 'mudsill speech' and Confederate Vice-President Alexander Stephens's December 1860 speech, both with which Marx was familiar, made that fact all so clear. No 'theory of race', in other words, was needed to explain why the slave oligarchs actively played the race card – it was in their class interests to do so, or, as Douglass often put it, it was due to 'greed'.

But, again, what about 'poor whites', the 'white trash' as the oligarchs contemptuously called them? Why did they embrace the slave oligarchy's racial agenda? Why would it have been, that is, in their class interest to do so? Our close reading of Marx reveals an explanation he offered, one either underappreciated or unknown until now. For Marx, it was, again, 'the bait' or 'the lure' of upward mobility for white plebeians in the South that explained their embrace of the slave oligarchs' expansionist agenda, the possibility that they too could one day become slave owners. And embracing that agenda entailed the embrace of its racist ideology. Douglass had, as a slave, personally experienced the anti-Black 'prejudices of "poor whites"', specifically, white co-workers on the docks in Baltimore, many of Irish origin. He didn't think, however, that those ideas were inherent, but learned behaviours, probably a later realisation after his first visit to Ireland in 1845 when he discovered that anti-Black attitudes were non-existent there. Marx likely knew the same owing to his familiarity with the German immigrant experience to America. But Marx offered a material reason for the embrace of the racist ideas. Douglass's explanation came closer, it seems to us, to what W.E.B. Du Bois would call in *Black Reconstruction* 'a sort of public and psychological wage' used by the Jim Crow ruling class to compensate the white working class, 'because they were white'.[29] But behind the 'psychological wage' for Marx – if that's the appropriate label – was, again, the enticement of the material perks that came with 'whiteness'.

Whether Marx's explanation constitutes 'a theory of racism' for Hund or other similar critics is for them to decide. For Marx the revolutionary, the issue of Southern white plebeians possibly breaking with the slavocracy was enormously important in that moment. His detailed attention to the secession votes in the slave-owning states was driven by that question. That secession, he concluded, was largely an elite affair without the consent of 'poor whites' was instructive for Marx. Trying, in other words, to understand what motivated the latter was an elementary communist obligation: Southern prospects depended on the recruitment of white plebeians. As it turned out, the increasing alien-

---

29   Du Bois 1998, p. 700. Also, Reed, Jr., 2017.

ation of 'poor whites' from the 'rich man's war' proved to be consequential in the Confederacy's defeat – maybe as important as the passive resistance of the enslaved.[30]

If Marx didn't have 'a theory of race', he certainly had a theory about social inequality: it rested on private property. Only the proletariat, unlike a slave for example, had a class interest, he held, in ending private property, the prerequisite for its own emancipation. Getting rid of all obstacles, therefore, to making the proletariat the ruling class, such as feudalism and chattel slavery, was the number one task of communists. That's the basic assumption, the theory, that informed Marx's practice and that of his comrades in the United States and elsewhere, the Marx party, both prior to and after Fort Sumter.

A theory of race has to begin with the fact that 'race', like nationality, is a moving target – an invention or social construct, as it is sometimes called today. More apprehensible is the inherently exploitative reality of class relations once class society came into existence about ten thousand years ago. Its most recent edition, capitalism, birthed a new exploited class, the proletariat, who could only survive by selling its labour to owners of private property and, hence, again, could only liberate itself by ending private property. If that claim makes Marx a class fundamentalist, as some might charge, we're confident that he would have pleaded guilty, especially if the alternative was some kind of race, national, or maybe gender fundamentalism, to name only a few current candidates. Even when it came to his magnum opus *Capital*, Marx in 1877, a decade after its publication, advised caution about how to read his theory. Regarding his chapter on 'Primitive Accumulation', he faulted a critic for wanting 'to metamorphose my historical sketch of the genesis of capitalism in Western Europe into a historical-philosophical theory of general development, imposed by fate on all peoples, whatever the historical circumstances in which they are placed'.[31] For the same reason, it is hard to imagine Marx wanting to have some kind of 'theory about race' that could be applicable to different realities in both place and time. That ruling elites, be they slave oligarchs or capitalists, employed ideas to divide the toilers is probably the most that Marx might have ventured about the theory of race, as in his 1869–70 comments about the similarities between anti-Irish and anti-Black attitudes amongst respectively English and American white workers – an issue to be revisited. As to why the latter two groups of workers bought into such ideas, Marx, we suspect, would have been satisfied with his lure-of-upward-mobility explanation.

30 For the best account of the class divisions in the Confederacy and their significance, see B. Levine 2013.
31 Marx and Engels 1975–2004m, p. 200.

Before turning to Hund's claim that Marx's lack of a 'theory of racism' proved to be 'a debacle for subsequent attempts at a Marxist analysis of racism and has bad effects that are still evident today', we briefly address some of his other criticisms of Marx.

As for Hund's charge that Marx's failure to say anything in detail about the Haitian Revolution registered his buy-in to anti-Black attitudes then in vogue, our response, again, is that it is Hund who is derelict – for not acknowledging Marx's revolutionary response to the nineteenth century's decisive moment in the struggle against racism. Whatever was lacking in Marx's oeuvre on Haiti clearly was not to his disadvantage in doing the right thing when the slave oligarchy attacked Fort Sumter – probably the reason for Hund deafening silence about Marx's practice during the Civil War. It would be easy to dismiss Hund's complaint for that reason alone, but what he raises about the Haitian Revolution offers an opportunity to gain a better appreciation of Marx's communist project on the eve of the Civil War.

There was a very consequential actor in the lead up to the War who had studied the Haitian Revolution in detail. Probably no one in the US knew as much about modern history's first successful slave revolt as did John Brown. The autodidact read everything he could about the Revolution as preparation for his project.[32] But did it make Brown more effective as Hund's complaint about Marx might suggest? That would be a dubious claim. For Marx and Engels, again, the significance of Brown's failed attack was the likelihood that it sparked a slave uprising, a development, if Hund is to be believed, about which Marx would have been dismissive. The 'most momentous thing happening in the world today', Marx told Engels at the beginning of 1860, 'is the slave movement – on the one hand in America, started by the death of Brown, and in Russia, on the other'.[33] Brown, I argue, would have been better off reading the *Communist Manifesto*. But, as in the case of the economist Henry Carey and Douglass, the absence of a hereditary proletariat in the US would have likely made the document incomprehensible to Brown. Douglass no doubt knew about Brown's expertise on the Haitian Revolution but that wasn't enough to convince him to join his attack on the armoury at Harpers Ferry. What might have made sense for Haiti in 1794 did not for America in 1859.

Hund also takes Marx to task for alleged anti-Semitism. His first evidence, Marx's 1843–4 articles, 'The Jewish Question'. We referenced them in the first chapter of this book because of what they taught about Marx's trajectory

---

32   Reynolds 2005, pp. 107–10. Especially p. 108: 'The society of blacks that was by far the greatest inspiration for John Brown was the one created in Haiti by Toussaint L'Ouverture'.
33   Marx and Engels 1975–2004u, p. 4.

toward communist conclusions, specifically the lessons from America about the buying and selling of everything. For Hund, the articles betray Marx's subscription to en vogue anti-Jewish stereotypes. We disagree and still find persuasive Hal Draper's detailed retort to that long-made accusation.[34] Hund, in search of evidence for his anti-Marx thesis, misses the significance of the articles. If the United States, again, was the best that liberal democracy had to offer, then clearly something else was required to end its social inequalities, including that of chattel slavery, perpetuated and deepened by its market mania, in order to realise 'true democracy', or 'human emancipation'. That conclusion helps to explain why Marx could be ready to aid and abet the abolition of America's peculiar institution when the opportunity presented itself.

More damaging in Hund's opinion is Marx's characterisation of Ferdinand Lassalle in a letter to Engels in 1862: 'The Jewish NIGGER Lassalle … is descended from the negroes who accompanied Moses' flight from Egypt (unless his mother or paternal grandmother interbred with a NIGGER) … The fellow's importunity is also niggerlike'.[35] This is the comment I was referring to when I wrote in 2003 about Marx's usage of the n-word: 'only once, it seems, did he use it in a derogatory sense, in a diatribe against Ferdinand Lassalle'. I added that any of his and Engels's comments 'in personal correspondence that were unambiguously racist, sexist or anti-Semitic must be seen in context in relation to their entire corpus of writings and actions'.[36] To be considered alongside that disparagement of Lassalle is what Marx told his wife Jenny upon learning that Lassalle was mortally wounded two years later, the result of a duel about an embarrassing love affair: 'We were genuinely dismayed by the news since, whatever one may say L[assalle] is too good to go under in this way'.[37] The Marx-Lassalle relationship was obviously complicated and can't be reduced to a one-off comment that Marx made in rage about someone he felt to be 'too good' to meet an ignominious end.[38] Nor is it certain, contrary to Hund, what meaning Marx assigned to 'nigger', 'negro' or 'niggerlike'. To repeat what I wrote in 2003: 'For what it's worth, Marx was fondly known by close friends and family as "Moor" owing to his dark features and had a son-in-law, Paul Lafargue, a mulatto, who was also fondly called in family circles, "African", "Negro" and "Negrillo"'. This suggests that one should be cautious and not rush to judgment

34 Draper 1977a. More recently, see Avineri 2019, pp. 41–54.
35 Marx and Engels 1975–2004u, pp. 389–90.
36 Nimtz 2003, p. 132n35.
37 Marx and Engels 1975–2004u, p. 556.
38 See also, Stedman Jones 2016, pp. 165–7, 444; Sperber 2013, pp. 409–14.

based on the vapid criteria of 'political correctness'. I stand by that assessment. The issue of anti-Semitism merits a revisit.

Marx's above-mentioned comments in the April 1870 letter about the similarities between anti-Black and anti-Irish attitudes by respectively 'poor whites' and 'English workers' draws Hund's final critique of Marx. Here's the actual passage that is the target of Hund's ire:

> The ordinary English worker hates the Irish worker as a competitor who forces down the STANDARD OF LIFE. In relation to the Irish worker, he feels himself to be a member of the *ruling nation* and, therefore, makes himself a tool of his aristocrats and capitalists *against Ireland*, thus strengthening their domination *over himself*. He harbours religious, social and national prejudices against him. His attitude towards him is roughly that of the POOR WHITES to the NIGGERS in the former slave states of the American Union.[39]

Hund – whose transcription of the passage doesn't include the small capitalisation that indicates terms in the original English – criticises the remark by saying that it's an inappropriate comparison, apples and oranges, mixing race and class categories, and in so doing Marx deprecated the Irish by comparing them to 'the niggers'. But with his focus on theory-making, Hund missed or, perhaps, ignored the real story – Marx's correction of his prior position on the Irish struggle. Contrary to Hund's charge, he now elevated 'the Irish question'. Five months before the April 1870 letter with the passage that Hund inadequately quotes, Marx explained to Engels his change of opinion:

> For a long time I believed it would be possible to overthrow the Irish regime by ENGLISH WORKING CLASS ASCENDANCY. I always took this viewpoint in the *New-York Tribune*. Deeper study has now convinced me of the opposite. The English WORKING CLASS will *never accomplish anything* BEFORE IT HAS GOT RID OF IRELAND. The lever must be applied in Ireland. This is why the Irish QUESTION is so important for the social movement in general.[40]

As the effective head of the IWA, Marx's task, he told Engels, was to convince the English labour leaders on the General Council of the IWA of his new position –

---

[39] Marx and Engels 1975–2004w, pp. 474–5.
[40] Marx and Engels 1975–2004w, p. 398.

'the thing now', to another correspondent, 'is to drum this conviction into the English working class' – a goal that proved elusive owing largely to the attitudes of the labour aristocracy from which virtually all of those leaders originated.[41]

The background to this change of position was the new upsurge in the Irish struggle for self-determination and the support it was winning in England itself. A mass demonstration for amnesty for Irish political prisoners in London on 24 October 1869 that his youngest daughter Eleanor insisted that her parents attend seems to have made the difference. She had recently returned from an extended visit with Engels and his Irish nationalist wife Lizzie Burns in Manchester and came back to London an ardent defender of the Irish struggle. Thus, it was the agency of the Irish struggle itself that convinced Marx to change his position, the communist obligation to learn from the real movement as Engels once explained in 1847. The significance of Marx's correction can't be overstated and about which there is not even a hint of in Hund's narrative. One of only three corrections in my reading of his and Engels's corpus – the other two being the self-criticism of the 1850 Address about how communists should participate in elections (see Chapter Two) and, the new 1872 preface to the *Communist Manifesto* owing to what the Paris Commune had taught about the state – it would have enormous importance for his followers in the twentieth century.[42] Hund, on the other hand, uses the passage from the April 1870 letter and the one from *Capital* about 'Labour in white skin' to accuse Marx of not giving agency to Blacks, similar to Zimmerman's charge that I've already addressed.

Time now to turn to what happened to Marx's project with regard to the race question after his death. Did Marx and Engels bequeath their followers enough kernels of wisdom with which to be creative when the real movement of history demanded that they be so – as communists, and not as academic theory-makers? Or did the project lead, as Hund claims, to a 'debacle' for his followers owing to his failure to not have bequeathed them a 'theory of racism' – Hund's main charge? Again, and not to beat a dead horse, Marx, according to Hund's logic, should have flunked the most important test of his lifetime on the race question because he lacked a 'theory of racism'. No wonder, then, the deafening silence in his account about Marx's practice during the US Civil War. To have recognised in any sustained way what Marx did would render null and void his claim, beginning with Marx himself. Only at the end does Hund actually address his primary argument about the lacuna in Marx's oeuvre.

---

41   Marx and Engels 1975–2004w, p. 390.
42   Regarding the lessons of the Commune, see Nimtz 2000, pp. 215–16.

> This had lasting impacts on the handling of racism within the wing of the labor movement that was based on Marxist ideas and not least on the Marxist theory itself. Even if we assume the existence of various Marxisms, their exponents either viewed racism as a subordinate problem or did not bring the debate on the relationship between class and race to a consensual conclusion; in addition, they did not bring the analysis of two of the main racisms of modernity, antisemitism and colonial racism to a common denominator.[43]

But for such a sweeping claim Hund ends with at best five hundred words for evidence. Titling his critique a 'note' doesn't absolve Hund from providing something more substantive. What does the actual record reveal about the 'lasting impacts'?

Marx didn't live long enough to witness the bloody overthrow of Reconstruction. Even when Engels died in 1895, the United States Supreme Court had yet to make the defeat official with its infamous *Plessy v. Ferguson* decision the following year. The lack-of-theory complaint by Hund and others, we suspect, is about the racist counterrevolution, an outcome that the critics seem to think that Marx and Engels should have anticipated. But even Douglass, as we document, more intimately familiar with what was underway, had difficulty explaining that outcome.

The complaint in our view is the wisdom of hindsight. Real-time analysis, rather, is the best test of theory and perspective. Not for naught did Du Bois, in his 1933 article in the NAACP's *Crisis* magazine, 'Karl Marx and the Negro', end on a note of regret. 'It was a great loss to American Negroes that the great mind of Marx and his extraordinary insight into industrial conditions could not have been brought to bear at first hand upon the history of the American Negro between 1876 and the World War'.[44] Explaining the overthrow of Reconstruction, in other words, would have surely benefitted, Du Bois believed, from Marx's real-time examination.

Du Bois sought to make up for Marx's missing analysis with one of his own, his 1935 magisterial *Black Reconstruction*, inspired by many of Marx's insights. Because of the volume's renown, Hund is forced to admit, contrary to his argument, that students of Marx like Du Bois could theorise on race even though their mentor hadn't left them anything, apparently, upon which to do so. Hund, unsurprisingly, can't resist finding something deficient in Du Bois's tome: 'he

---

43 Hund, 2021, p. 89.
44 Du Bois 2016, p. 219.

never expanded these deliberations [based on 'his reading of Marx'] towards a general theory of racism (including anti-semitism and other forms of racist exclusion not based on color racism)'.[45] Frantz Fanon, who also looked to Marx, is guilty of the same failing because he 'never expanded on both deliberations [the similarities between anti-Black and anti-Jewish prejudices] towards a general theory of racism'.[46] Nothing less than a unified field theory of race for all places and time can satisfy Hund. His protests to the contrary, Hund comes close to naturalising – in fact arguably naturalises – something called 'race', about which there can be 'a general theory'.

Another student of Marx also challenges Hund's claim that his racial 'blind spot' incapacitated them for saying anything meaningful not only about the race/class nexus but also the Haitian Revolution. Marxist historian C.L.R. James is a particularly inconvenient figure for Hund's thesis. His still influential 1938 analysis of the Revolution, *The Black Jacobins: Toussaint L'Ouverture and the San Domingo Revolution*, was inspired by rather than handicapped by Marx's analysis, especially, his *Eighteenth Brumaire* and its opening thesis: 'Men make their own history, but they do not make it as they please; they do not make it under self-selected circumstances, but under circumstances existing already, given and transmitted from the past'.[47] Until the end of his life James considered himself to be a Marxist revolutionary. For that reason, most likely, Hund could not bring himself to include James's book in the main text of his article but instead deeply buries it in a footnote.[48] And as with his treatment of Du Bois's tome, Hund had to take a hit to James's *Black Jacobins*, his failure to 'debate the "blank space" ... in the oeuvre of Marx (and Engels), nor ... discuss their insufficient analysis of racism as the background of this peculiar silence'.[49] Only a critique of Marx, as well as a 'general theory of race', it seems, will satisfy Hund.

And then there is the heroic and also inconvenient example of Abram Leon. A devoted student of Marx, Leon titled his signature essay after his mentor's 1843–4 *Zur Judenfrage* articles that Hund accuses of being anti-Semitic. Leon's 250-page manuscript *The Jewish Question: A Marxist Interpretation*, completed two years before his death in the gas chambers at Auschwitz in 1944, does exactly what Hund claims a Marxist could not do. Leon's findings after a deep dive into ancient and medieval history question Hund's argument that 'a gen-

---

45 Hund 2021, p. 89.
46 Hund 2021, p. 90.
47 Marx and Engels 1975–2004i, p. 103.
48 Hund 2021, p. 98.
49 Hund 2021, p. 98n102.

eral theory of racism' must incorporate an explanation for both anti-Black and anti-Jewish prejudices. Owing to the almost caste-like role to which they were assigned for managing medieval finances, especially money-lending, Jews could uniquely serve capital as it emerged as the dominant mode of production in the second half of the nineteenth century in Europe – as scapegoats for its sins. No other ethnic/racial group has ever been labelled a secret cabal that runs the world – conveniently deflecting attention away from the multi-racial, multi-national and multi-gendered ruling class that actually does run the world today. Leon's conclusion that 'there is no way to resolve the Jewish question independent of the world proletarian revolution' is as valid today as when he asserted it eight decades ago – a conclusion which Hund would no doubt find unpalatable.[50] Some of us, nevertheless, find Leon's thesis to be a valuable teaching tool to help youth of all skin colours and creeds understand how a most ancient prejudice operates in today's capitalist world and why it is dangerous, its benign as well as its malignant manifestations.[51]

None of Marx's students was as consequential as, of course, Lenin. Is he relevant to this discussion? Indeed, what the above-mentioned comment about the significance of Marx's correction on the Irish struggle alluded to. More informed about Marx's and Engels's corpus than any of their students, he corrected Rosa Luxemburg in his 1914 polemic 'The Right of Nations to Self-Determination'. Contrary to her claim that independence for oppressed nationalities in empires such as Ireland would not be 'practical', Lenin seized upon Marx's revision of his position on the Irish struggle in 1869. He quoted exactly the above-cited passage that Marx wrote to Engels on 10 December about his change of opinion along with other exchanges between Marx and Engels on the matter such as Marx's campaign inside the General Council of the IWA: 'I have done my best to bring about this demonstration of the English workers in favour of Fenianism [the ideology of Irish self-determination]'. Then Lenin's distillation:

> At first Marx thought that Ireland would not be liberated by the national movement of the oppressed nation, but by the working-class movement of the oppressor nation ... Marx reconsidered his view and corrected it. 'What a misfortune it is for a nation to have subjugated another'. The English working class will never be free until Ireland is freed from the English yoke. Reaction in England is strengthened and fostered by the enslave-

---

50   Leon 2020, p. 41.
51   Nimtz 2019c.

ment of Ireland (just as reaction in Russia is fostered by her enslavement of a number of nations!) ... The policy of Marx and Engels on the Irish question serves as a splendid example of the attitude the proletariat of the oppressor nations should adopt towards national movements, an example which has lost none of its immense *practical* importance.[52]

Lenin's enthusiastic embrace of Marx's correction on the Irish question came to be one of the key programmatic differences that distinguished the Bolsheviks from other currents in the Socialist or Second International. The right of oppressed nations to self-determination became de rigueur for them not only for the Russian Revolution itself but for other anti-colonial movements. Marx's correction would also have an echo inside the United States.

Until the Bolshevik Revolution, socialists in the United States tended to view the struggle for Black equality in the same manner that Marx had once viewed the Irish struggle in Great Britain, secondary to and/or dependent on the struggle of the proletariat, mainly, that is, the white working class. Just as Rosa Luxemburg evidently didn't know about Marx's revision, the same was true for American socialists – if they were attentive at all to Marx's project. And had they known Marx's change of opinion on the 'Irish Question', they may not have made any connection with the 'Negro Question'. In the opinion of Socialist Party leader Eugene V. Debs, 'We have nothing special to offer the Negro, and we cannot make separate appeals to all the races. The Socialist Party is the party of the whole working class, regardless of colour – the whole working class of the whole world'.[53] Though always appreciative of Debs's historical importance to the American theatre of the global class struggle, Lenin and the Bolsheviks had a different opinion.

To American radicals who were inspired by Russia's history-defining moment, the Bolshevik leaders sought to impress upon them what was 'special' about the fight for equality for Black Americans. Lenin, in his 'Theses on the National and Colonial Questions' for the Second Congress of the recently organised Communist International in 1920, was unequivocal: 'all Communist parties must directly support the revolutionary movements among the nations that are dependent and do not have equal rights (for example Ireland, the Negroes in America, and so forth), and in the colonies. Without this last, especially important condition, the struggle against oppression of the dependent nations and colonies and recognition of their right to a separate state remain a

---

52 Lenin 1977, pp. 437–42.
53 Barnes 2020, p. 243.

dishonorable facade, such as we see in the parties of the Second International' with whom the Socialist Party had been affiliated. Nota bene 'Ireland' and 'the Negroes in America' – echoes of Marx's 1870 point about the similarities of Irish and Black American oppression that Hund dismisses as incomparable. For Lenin, in other words, the struggle for Black equality included the right to self-determination. Just as Marx had wanted 'to drum ... into the British working class' support for Irish self-determination, Lenin sought to do the same for those who claimed to be the communist vanguard of the American working class with regard to the Black struggle.

Lenin added to his directive. 'The fight against ... the most deeply rooted petty-bourgeois, nationalist prejudices (which are expressed in all possible forms, such as racism, national chauvinism, and anti-Semitism) must be given all the more priority as the question becomes more pressing of transforming the dictatorship of the proletariat from a national framework ... into an international one'.[54] The fight against scourges like racism was, in other words, indispensable for the international dictatorship of the proletariat, that is, the working class becoming the global ruling class, requiring, therefore, special attention. Also noteworthy is Lenin's inclusion of 'anti-Semitism' along with the other hateful prejudices in his draft – supposedly absent, according to Hund, in Marxist discussions of the issue. Lenin obviously didn't feel that he was incapacitated in fighting against racism by not having been bequeathed, contrary to Hund, a 'general theory of race' from Marx. But was he effective?

Given American radicalism's history of not lending special attention to the 'Negro question', it should come as no surprise, as James P. Cannon, one of the founders of the American Communist Party later admitted, 'it took time for the Americans ... to assimilate the new Leninist doctrine. But the Russians followed up year after year, piling up the arguments and increasing the pressure on the American communists until they finally learned and changed, and went to work in earnest. And the change in the attitude of the American communists, gradually effected in the twenties, was to exert a profound influence in far wider circles in the later years'.[55] Cannon, himself, to be seen shortly, tested the patience of the Russian comrades.

With Lenin incapacitated from March 1923 to his death ten months later, the stage was set for Stalin's ascent and the effective end to the best that the Russian Revolution had to offer the fledgling communist parties around the world still inspired by the October Revolution. It fell to Trotsky, Lenin's second

---

54   Riddell 1991, pp. 286–7.
55   Barnes 2020, p. 247.

in command of the Russian Revolution, to maintain continuity with his programme. In forced exile, he counselled aspiring revolutionaries from all parts of the world, including the United States – the 'profound influence ... in the later years' that Cannon alluded to. Especially relevant for purposes here were his meetings with American comrades in 1933 and later 1939.

For the first meeting, in Turkey, the key issue was whether his co-thinkers in America should promote, as the Stalinists there were doing, the slogan of self-determination for Black Americans or rather equal rights. He agreed with them that the slogan was opportunistic, having originated in Moscow and not from within Black America itself. Rather than criticising the demand, on the grounds that it led away from the class struggle, Trotsky countered that it was the racism of the white workers – 'ninety-nine point nine percent of the American workers are chauvinists; in relation to the Negroes they are hangmen as they are also toward the Chinese, etc.' – that would be the blame should significant separatist sentiment emerge amongst Blacks. His American co-thinkers, he continued, should be open to the idea of Blacks, especially the proletariat, making self-determination their demand because its logic had revolutionary implications. 'It is very possible that the Negroes will proceed through self-determination to the proletarian dictatorship in a couple of giant strides, ahead of the great bloc of white workers. They will then be the vanguard. I am absolutely sure they will in any case fight better than the white workers. That, however, can happen only provided the communist party carries on an uncompromising struggle not against the Negroes' supposed national prepossessions but against the colossal prejudices of white workers and make no concession to them whatever'.[56] Like Marx and Lenin before him, Trotsky too sought 'to drum this conviction', namely, support for self-determination for oppressed nationalities, into the vanguard of the American working class.

To the end, Trotsky campaigned for special attention to the 'Negro Question' and defended the right of self-determination for African Americans. A year before his assassination in Mexico in 1940 at the hands of one of Stalin's many agents, Trotsky met with the aforementioned C.L.R. James who was now a member of the American Socialist Workers Party to discuss its perspectives for the struggle for Black equality there. He took issue with James's characterisation of 'self-determination' for African Americans as 'reactionary ... as a step backward so far as a socialist society is concerned'.[57] For Blacks, Trotsky replied, to 'fight for the possibility of realizing an independent state is a sign of great

---

56   Barnes 2020, p. 265.
57   Barnes 2020, p. 281.

moral and political awakening. It would be a tremendous revolutionary step'. In a letter to party leader James Cannon about the meeting, Trotsky wrote that what James presented at the meeting was a 'very good statement' but

> I do not accept his categorical rejection of self-determination (an independent state) for the American Negro. As a party, we do not enter into the making of the decision, either one way or the other. We say to the Negroes, 'You must decide whether or not you wish the separation. If you decide in the affirmative, we as a party will help you with all of our power to realize; and in this way the separation of states will assure the brotherhood of workers of both colors. This is what we want above all'.[58]

More important for Trotsky about the meeting with James and the two other party members in attendance was the opportunity it gave him to chide the party for not prioritizing the 'Negro question', especially in the recruitment of Black workers. 'Many times I have proposed that every party member, especially intellectuals, who cannot win a worker-member to the party over a six-month period should be demoted to sympathiser, and the same in relation to winning Negro members. It is a question of the vitality of the party – of whether the party is transformed into a sect or is able to find its way to the most oppressed part of the working class'.[59] His patience wearing thin, he wrote to Cannon in the same 10 April 1939 letter that 'the party ... cannot postpone this extremely important question any longer'. To the end, again, Trotsky sought 'to drum' the urgency of the Black question into the vanguard of the workers movement in the United States. Not for naught did Cannon write two decades later: 'Everything new and progressive on the Negro question came from Moscow, after the revolution of 1917, and as a result of the revolution – not only for the American communists who responded directly, but for all others concerned with the question'.[60]

The communist perspective on the right of oppressed nationalities for self-determination that began with Marx's correction on the Irish question and that Trotsky bequeathed to his followers in the US paid major dividends for the Socialist Workers Party – what Cannon likely referred to regarding the 'profound influence *in far wider circles* in the later years' that resulted from the drumming of the Bolsheviks. When the Black struggle took the form of Black

---

58 Trotsky 1974, pp. 298–9.
59 Barnes 2020, p. 295.
60 Cannon 1962, p. 233.

nationalism in the 1960s, the party was theoretically equipped to advantageously respond to the opening. The communists with whom Malcolm X collaborated in the last year of his life, as we noted in our Conclusion, were precisely members of the party. Even before he broke with the Nation of Islam and its Black separatist course, SWP members were able to see the revolutionary implications of his discourse for a proletarian agenda and came to his defence against the race-baiting of the Stalinists and the violence-baiting of the government.

That Malcolm X's widow entrusted Pathfinder Press, the SWP's publishing arm, with keeping his speeches in print not only testifies to the fraternal relations that existed between him and the SWP at the time of his assassination but ensures that future fighters for racial equality can know what Malcolm X stood for in his own words. They'll be able to learn about his trajectory from a Black nationalist separatist to his political convergence with communists – a development that should have been impossible if Hund is to be believed. It is the same Pathfinder Press, by the way, that keeps in print not only the public declarations of Malcolm X in his final year, those of Trotsky and the record about how he convinced at least one Marxist current to prioritise the 'Negro question', but also the first book-length Marxist analysis of anti-Semitism, Leon's *The Jewish Question*. There is, therefore, at least one of the 'various Marxisms', as Hund calls them, that promotes theoretical clarity for a set of complementary issues that Hund accuses Marxists of not addressing.

Another critique of Marx on the race question appeared the same year, 2021, as Hund's. Andrew Douglas's and Jared Loggins's *Prophet of Discontent* seeks to make a case for Martin Luther King Jr's revolutionary credentials. But to do so, the two scholars feel compelled to downgrade those of Marx on the grounds, according to the authorities they cite, that 'when it comes to race, Marx missed the mark'. Also, 'Marx relegated "as subsidiary the very things which should have been the center of his study"'.[61] Though at best a secondary theme in their essay, the critique of Marx plays a vital role in their effort to elevate King to revolutionary status because he apparently, unlike Marx, prioritised race in his liberatory project. We addressed Douglas's and Loggins's claims about King in our Conclusion and were not persuaded. Not only did King, as they themselves instantiate, reject the solution Marx and Engels proposed for ending social inequalities, namely, the abolition of private property, but also the entire programme of the two founders of modern communism and those of their most capable students Lenin and Trotsky. The most that Douglas and Loggins can

---

61 Douglass and Loggins 2021, p. 6.

say, to repeat, about that rejection is that 'King's treatment of Marx was often roughshod, if not disingenuous – a fact owed partly to the pressures put upon him by the Cold War context of the 1950s and early '60s'.[62] But that's apologia. Malcolm X wasn't deterred by that same context from collaborating with communists in his last year. The basic problem with Douglas and Loggins regarding Marx is the same one with Hund, as well as other academic critics: the tendency to treat him in their own self-image, as a scholar. That they reduce him to 'the center of his study' rather than to the centre of his practice says it all.

What Hund, Douglas and Loggins all have in common in their critique of Marx is a reliance, to one degree or another, on Cedric J. Robinson's 1983 *Black Marxism: The Making of the Black Radical Tradition*, much more explicitly in the case of the latter two. Robinson's tome was the first book-length indictment of Marx and Engels for their supposed deficit regarding the race question.[63] Owing much to the accolades of historian Robin Kelley, Robinson's critique has gotten the kind of attention that it never had when he was alive.[64] Robinson's solution to Marx's failing, the alternative to their mode of analysis, was the notion of 'racial capitalism' – this is what King sought to give content to, according to Douglas and Loggins. Because Robinson never defined 'racial capitalism', scholars who have since employed the concept have given their own meaning to it.

This response to Zimmerman, Hund, and Douglas and Loggins is in many ways an update of my 1985 critical review of *Black Marxism* written at the request of the editors of the short-lived but influential London and Accra-based *Journal of African Marxists*.[65] Some of my above-discussed criticisms of all four were previewed in that essay. Subsequent research permitted me to address in another article the all-too-frequent Eurocentric charge against Marx and Engels made not only by Robinson.[66] Missing in both essays, however, are any of the rich details about Marx's and Engels's practice regarding the Civil War – another reason to fault Robinson's book. A revisit to *Black Marxism* reveals what Hund probably has in mind regarding the 'debacle for subsequent attempts at a Marxist analysis of racism' and '[its] ... effects that are still evident today' – namely, what both Social Democracy and Stalinism did in the names

---

62 Douglass and Loggins 2021, p. 23.
63 Oliver Cox's 1948 *Caste, Class and Race*, an example of the Black radical tradition for Robinson, could be argued to have been the first. Critiquing Marx, or better, correcting him, is, however, at best, unlike for Robinson, a minor theme with Cox.
64 Kelley 2017.
65 Nimtz 1985a.
66 Nimtz 2002.

of not only Marx and Engels but Lenin as well. Much of the target of Robinson's ire is the 'opportunism' of both currents as he calls it, and rightly so, that is, the betrayal of the Black struggle. But to lay those crimes, as Hund and Robinson do, at the feet of Marx and Engels betrays their own theoretical shortcomings when it comes to understanding politics. Lenin and Trotsky remain the best analysts of why those two tendencies fell far short of what Marx and Engels's original programme sought to accomplish.[67]

There is another omission in *Black Marxism* – an almost glaring one. For a book that claimed to be an exposition of the 'Black radical tradition', the absence of Malcolm X – less than two decades after his assassination – is remarkable. He didn't even rate a mention in Robinson's list of post-World War II Black revolutionaries.[68] That Malcolm X was publicly fraternising with communists in the last year of his life, white ones to boot, no doubt was a very inconvenient fact for Robinson – what his footnotes suggest that he knew about.[69] Neither, it should be noted, does Fredrick Douglass make an appearance in Robinson's account; testimony to the definitional problems with his 'Black radical tradition'. Was Douglass, the one-time Black slave, not a radical? If not a 'Black Marxist', certainly, then at least, as we characterise him, a revolutionary liberal. Had Robinson been truly interested in testing the merits of Marxism against Black political thought, why didn't he even consider what this book does – a return to the foundational moment of Marxism and the best, arguably, that Black political thought then had to offer, that is Douglass, and see what a comparison taught?

The late political philosopher Charles Mills exemplified the academic reading of Marx – almost exclusively at the level of ideas rather than politics. He too, not surprisingly, employed Robinson to charge Marx and Engels with 'a clear Eurocentricity in their writings about non-white people'.[70] And Mills, to the end, unapologetically defended his apolitical reading – not unlike Robinson – of Marx.[71] Never would it have occurred to him to examine Marx's politics,

---

[67] A good place to begin with for Lenin, real-time analysis, is his 1907 critique of German social democracy on the colonial question. Lenin Collected Works, vol. 13, pp. 82–93. As for Stalinism, Trotsky's 1936 classic, *The Revolution Betrayed*, remains the best explanation for the Stalinist counterrevolution in Russia. Trotsky 1972.

[68] Robinson 1983, p. 450.

[69] Robinson 1983, p. 389, reveals that he certainly knew about C.L.R. James's discussion with Trotsky and the account published by the SWP's publishing arm, Pathfinder Press.

[70] Mills 1998, pp. 36–7.

[71] Hear the interview that Michael Dawson did with Mills that was aired on April 2022: https://www.centerforthehumanities.org/programming/the-life-and-work-of-charles-mills

as we do in this book, to see if his practice informed his ideas about morality, justice and race – all wanting in Marx according to Mills.[72] 'Where is', Mills indignantly once asked, 'Karl Marx and Frederick Engels's outraged *Political Economy of Slavery*'?[73] Mills, owing to his earlier embrace of 'Marxism', likely knew better but by then had consciously chosen not to acknowledge the political Marx – 'a missed opportunity', as one scholar aptly puts it, to really engage Marx, to test the validity of his propositions, again, as we do here.[74]

The real world of politics may best explain Mills's subsequent apolitical rendering of Marx owing to what Hund, as noted earlier, gratuitously faults Marx for – the Social Democratic and Stalinist misrepresentations of Marx and Engels's project. Those of us who had the good fortune to know Trotsky's explanation of Stalinism were at least theoretically – if not emotionally with regard to the first event – prepared to make sense of the 1985 counterrevolution in the Caribbean nation of Grenada and the collapse, five years later, of the Stalinist regimes in Russia and Eastern Europe.[75] For many, like for Mills, both developments – especially the tragedy in Grenada – were demoralising and disillusioning. He then sought refuge in the world that the young Marx parted company with. As the two new converts to communism proclaimed in *The German Ideology*, 'One has to "leave philosophy aside" ... one has to leap out of it and devote oneself like an ordinary man to the study of the actuality, for which there exists also an enormous amount of literary material, unknown, of course, to the philosophers'.[76] Whether known or not to him, Mills simply wasn't interested in the rich materials this book has presented to determine if Marx had anything of significance to say about the *'Political Economy of Slavery'* or 'non-white people'. Lenin, one might argue, did something similar due to the Guns of August of 1914, his deep dive into Hegel to explain Social Democracy's betrayal of proletarian internationalism. But for Lenin that philosophical detour, unlike for Mills, was a means to an end – revolutionary practice.

If Marx and Engels did not have a theory about race, they did have one about social inequality of which racial oppression is one of its species. That theory was captured all so pedagogically in Engels's question and answer number seven in his final draft that Marx employed to write the *Manifesto*.

---

72 See Slack 2020 for a most informed critique of Mills.
73 Mills 1997, p. 94.
74 We are indebted to Igor Shoikhedbrod for this insightful point.
75 Mills 1990, pp. 23–46. Also, Nimtz 1985b.
76 Marx and Engels 1975–2004d, p. 236.

> In what way does the proletarian differ from the slave? ... The slave is sold once and for all, the proletarian has to sell himself by the day and by the hour ... The slave frees himself by abolishing, among all the private property relationships, only the relationship of slavery and thereby only then himself becomes a proletarian; the proletarian can free himself only by abolishing private property in general.[77]

For Marx and Engels, in other words, private property was the material basis for social inequality and only the proletariat had a class interest *and* capability in ending it and, thus, ensuring 'human emancipation'.

Is there any evidence, then, that the fight to end class inequality advances the struggle for racial equality? More specifically, what happens when a society with roots in racial inequality begins to abolish private property? What are the consequences for racial inequality? Again, any evidence? There is, I argue – from our own hemisphere; if not conclusive, certainly suggestive.

Racial slavery has long been the place to begin to explain the persistence of structural or institutional racism – before they came to be called racial capitalism or systemic racism – in societies where the 'peculiar institution' was in place. The Western hemisphere was unique with that iniquitous practice. The three countries where the institution marked the entire societies and prevailed the longest, in that order, are Brazil, Cuba and the United States, respectively, 1888, 1884, and 1865. What if we compare outcomes regarding racial inequality for the three countries? What can we learn?

Comparing so different a group of societies is fraught with all kinds of methodological issues, especially, the apples and oranges or false equivalency problem. Yet, I argue, there is – to take advantage of a topic on the brains of many as this is being written – something of importance and meaning that can be said with confidence. The probability of someone with visible roots in Africa losing their life in an encounter with the police is qualitatively greater in, first, Brazil and, second, the United States than in Cuba. The difference between the first two and the latter is one that did not always exist. Prior to the first of January 1959, the rankings were probably Brazil, Cuba, and the United States in that order without qualitative differences between the three countries. In other words, what a difference a proletarian revolution makes.[78]

What ensued on that historic date was the beginning of the end to all the perks that came with private ownership of the means of production in the

---

77 Marx and Engels 1975–2004e, pp. 343–4.
78 Nimtz 2020.

Caribbean country, including those of racial privilege. The only way that the Cuban proletariat with roots in Africa could ensure itself of secure employment for the first time was to abolish private property – exactly what the new government that issued from the island-wide general strike on that date began doing, the first time anywhere in the Americas.

What the comparison reveals is that history is not destiny as proponents of the *New York Times 1619 Project* are prone to believe. How else to explain why Cuba is the outlier of the three societies where racial slavery long existed if not for its revolution? A detailed comparison for other social indicators such as life expectancy, infant mortality, educational attainment, homelessness would likely yield similar results, and especially if the comparisons are made with Cuba's Caribbean neighbours – Puerto Rico, a colony of the United States, being the most appropriate cohort. The abolition of private property, to wit, has life and death outcomes for the toilers, and especially its most oppressed as Marx and Engels would have predicted.[79]

What took place in Cuba also had consequences for the world-wide fight against racial oppression – what a theory of race would also have to incorporate. As Nelson Mandela famously remarked when he visited Cuba in 1991, a year and a half after his release from twenty-seven years of prison in South Africa: 'the defeat of the racist army at Cuito Cuanavale has made it possible for me to be here today'.[80] Largely at the hands of Cuban troops, the South African regime suffered a major military reversal in Angola in 1988 that proved to be critical in ending apartheid – what's possible in the fight against racism when the proletariat has state power.[81]

As the Cuban Revolution has come under increasing pressure from its 'neighbour' to the north, world capital's most ardent and effective defender of private property, to carry out 'reforms', namely, to grant space to private property, social behaviours that were once rare in revolutionary Cuba have reared their ugly heads. By no means to the degree that it exists ninety miles away but a fact nonetheless – evidence about the inequalities and anti-social values and conduct that come with private property even with all the limits on it that continue to exist in Cuba. The future of the Cuban revolution depends on the proletariat elsewhere emulating its example, not the least important being its cohorts to the north. As Engels, again so pedagogically, put it in his last draft

---

79 A comparison of how Cuba and the United States dealt with the natural phenomena of hurricanes in the summer of 2005, specifically, Hurricane Katrina, offers further evidence to verify this claim. See Nimtz 2006.
80 Mandela and Castro 1991, p. 20.
81 For the authoritative account, see Gleijeses 2013.

that Marx employed for the final document: 'will it be possible for the revolution to take place in one country alone? No ... the communist revolution will ... be no merely national one ... It is a worldwide revolution and will therefore be worldwide in scope'.[82] Little wonder that Washington continues its six-decade-long bipartisan campaign to try to confine the Cuban revolution to the dustbin of history.

A return to Martin Luther King Jr's 1967 epiphany is the appropriate ending for this book's reply to Marx and Engels's critics on the race question. Despite the best efforts of Douglas and Loggins to make him into a revolutionary, most telling is the virtual silence that has since greeted the insight upon which they seek to reinvent him. How to explain why the refrain, 'I have a dream', is far more likely to be quoted than 'a radical redistribution of economic and political power'? For we 'class fundamentalists', the answer is elementary. The beneficiaries of the Second Reconstruction – I include myself in that category – now have a class interest in defending private property and this is why they, especially its meritocratic layers, prefer to talk about race rather than class – this is their way to defend recently acquired class privileges. Only the proletariat, to beat the drums again, has a class interest in the abolition of private property. A theory about race that doesn't begin with a theory about class is an ideology, that is, a misrepresentation of social reality.

---

[82] Marx and Engels 1975–2004e, pp. 351–2.

Bibliography

Newspapers

Douglass, Frederick, *Douglass' Monthly*, Rochester, NY, https://www.readex.com/products/african-american-newspapers-series-1-and-2-1827-1998; https://heinonline-org.ezp3.lib.umn.edu/HOL/Index?index=slavery/dougmo&collection=slavery; cited as DM.

Douglass, Frederick, *New National Era*, Washington DC, https://www.readex.com/products/african-american-newspapers-series-1-and-2-1827-1998

References

Abrams, Stacey 2020, 'I Know Voting Feels Inadequate Right Now', *The New York Times*, 4 June 2020: https://www.nytimes.com/2020/06/04/opinion/stacey-abrams-voting-floyd-protests.html

Achorn, Edward 2023, *The Lincoln Miracle: Inside the Republican Convention that Changed History*, New York: Atlantic Monthly Press.

Allen, James S. 1937, 'The Struggle for Land during the Reconstruction Period', *Science & Society*, Vol. 1, No. 3 (Spring, 1937), pp. 378–401.

Amar, Akhil Reed 2022, 'Founding Myths', *Myth America: Historians Take On the Biggest Legends and Lies about Our Past*, New York: Basic Books.

Anderson, Bonnie S. 1998, 'The Lid Comes Off: International Radical Feminism and the Revolutions of 1848', *NWSA Journal*, 10:2, 1–12.

Anderson, Kevin 2010, *Marx at the Margins: On Nationalism, Ethnicity, and Non-Western Societies*, Chicago: The University of Chicago Press.

Anderson, Kevin 2017, 'Marx's intertwining of race and class during the Civil War in the United States', *Journal of Classical Sociology*, vo. 17(1), 24–36.

Ayers, Edward L. and Emory Thomas, '1861: Issues Leading to War', (lecture, Fort Sumter-Fort Moultrie Historical Trust, Charleston, SC, 11 April 2011): https://www.c-span.org/video/?299027-1/american-leaders-issues-1861

Ayers, Edward L. and Gary Gallagher 2010, 'The Geography of Emancipation', (lecture, Society of Civil War Historians, Richmond, VA, 17 June 2010): https://www.c-span.org/video/?294120-1/geography-emancipation

Aptheker, Herbert 1983, *American Negro Slave Revolts*, New York: International Publishers.

Avineri, Shlomo 2019, *Karl Marx: Philosophy and Revolution*, New Haven: Yale University Press.

BIBLIOGRAPHY

Balfour, Lawrie 2011, *Democracy's Reconstruction: Thinking Politically with W.E.B. Du Bois*, New York: Oxford University Press.

Bartlett, Irving 1961, *Wendell Phillips: Brahmin Radical*, Boston: Beacon Press.

Barnes, Jack 2020, *Malcolm X, Black Liberation & the Road to Workers Power*, New York: Pathfinder Press.

Battistini, Matteo 2021, 'Karl Marx and the Global History of the Civil War: The Slave Movement, Working-Class Struggle, and the American State within the World Market', *International Labor and Working-Class History*, no. 100, 158–185.

Benedict, Michael Les 1972, 'The Rout of Radicalism: Republicans and the Elections of 1867', *Civil War History* 18:4, 334–344.

Bennett, Jr., Lerone 1968, "Was Abe Lincoln A White Supremacist?" *Ebony* (February).

Berlin, Ira, Barbara Fields, Thavolia Glymph, Joseph Reidy, and Leslie Rowland (eds.) 1985, *Freedom: A Documentary History of Emancipation, 1861–1871, Series 1 Volume 1: The Destruction of Slavery*, New York: Cambridge University Press.

Berquist, James M. 1966, 'The Political Attitudes of the German Immigrant in Illinois, 1848–1860', PhD diss., Northwestern University.

Black, Kelvin C. 2017, 'Democracy's False Choice: The Reform-Revolution Dilemma', *Journal of Nineteenth Century Americanists*, 5:2, 382–388.

Black, Kelvin C. 2021, 'Politics', in Michaël Roy (ed.), *Frederick Douglass in Context*, Cambridge: Cambridge University Press.

Blackburn, Robin 2011, *An Unfinished Revolution: Karl Marx and Abraham Lincoln*, London: Verso.

Blassingame, John W. (ed.) 1979, *The Frederick Douglass Papers: Series One: Speeches, Debates, and Interviews Volume 1: 1841–1846*, New Haven: Yale University Press.

Blassingame, John W. (ed.) 1982, *The Frederick Douglass Papers: Series One: Speeches, Debates, and Interviews Volume 2: 1847–1854*, New Haven: Yale University Press.

Blassingame, John W. (ed.) 1985, *The Frederick Douglass Papers: Series One: Speeches, Debates, and Interviews Volume 3: 1855–63*, New Haven: Yale University Press.

Blassingame, John W. and John R. McKivigan (eds.) 1991, *The Frederick Douglass Papers: Series One: Speeches, Debates, and Interviews Volume 4: 1864–80*, New Haven: Yale University Press.

Blight, David W. 1991, *Frederick Douglass' Civil War: Keeping Faith in Jubilee*, Baton Rouge: LSU Press.

Blight, David W. 2013, 'Ending Slavery in America', (lecture, German Historical Institute, Washington, D.C., 5 September 2013): https://www.c-span.org/video/?314870-1/legacy-emancipation

Blight, David W. 2018, *Frederick Douglass: Prophet of Freedom*, New York: Simon & Schuster.

Blight, David W. 2018a, 'Frederick Douglass at 200,' (lecture, Maryland Historical Society, Baltimore, MD, 7 February 2018): https://www.c-span.org/video/?440811-1/frederick-douglass-bicentennial

Blight, David W. 2021, 'Frederick Douglass & the Constitution', (lecture, James Madison Memorial Fellowship Foundation, Arlington, VA, 2 July 2021): https://www.c-span.org/video/?513108-1/author-david-blight-constitution

Blight, David W. 2022, 'Was the Civil War Inevitable?', *The New York Times Magazine*, 21 December 2022.

Borden, Morton 1957, 'Some Notes on Horace Greeley, Charles Dana, and Karl Marx', *Journalism Quarterly*, December, vol. 34, no. 4.

Bordewich, Fergus M. 2020, *Congress at War: How Republican Reformers Fought the Civil War, Defied Lincoln, Ended Slavery, and Remade America*, New York: Alfred A. Knopf.

Bouie, Jamelle 2022, 'Why I Keep Coming Back to Reconstruction', *The New York Times*, 25 October 2022: https://www.nytimes.com/2022/10/25/opinion/reconstruction-civil-war-du-bois.html

Bradbury, Richard 1999, 'Frederick Douglass and the Chartists', in Alan J. Rice and Martin Crawford (eds.), *Liberating Sojourn: Frederick Douglass & Transatlantic Reform*, Athens: University of Georgia Press.

Brands, H.W. 2020, *The Zealot and the Emancipator: John Brown, Abraham Lincoln and the Struggle for American Freedom*, New York: Doubleday.

Braxton, Robert 2023, 'Revolution and Counterrevolution in Georgia, 1865–1870: Charles Hopkins, Aaron Bradley, and the Union Leagues', M.A. Thesis, Georgia State University.

Breitenwischer, Dustin 2021, '"An Impeachment of the existing order of things": Revisiting Frederick Douglass' Philosophy of Reform', *Amerikastudien/American Studies*, 66:4, 567–584.

Breitman, George (ed.) 2020, *Malcolm X Speaks*, New York: Pathfinder Press.

Bromell, Nick 2021, *The Powers of Dignity: The Black Political Philosophy of Frederick Douglass*, Durham: Duke University Press.

Brooks, Corey M. 2016, *Liberty Power: Antislavery Third Parties and the Transformation of American Politics*, Chicago: The University of Chicago Press.

Brooks, David 2018, 'Understanding Student Mobbists', *The New York Times*, 8 March 2018: https://www.nytimes.com/2018/03/08/opinion/student-mobs.html

Browning, Judkin 2017, 'Lectures in History: Civil War's Peninsula Campaign and Seven Days' Battles', (lecture, Appalachian State University, Boone, NC, 28 February 2017): https://www.c-span.org/video/?423972-1/civil-wars-peninsula-campaign-days-battles

Buccola, Nicholas 2012, *The Political Thought of Frederick Douglass: In Pursuit of American Liberty*, New York: New York University Press.

Buccola, Nicholas 2018, 'The Human Heart Is a Seat of Constant War', in Neil Roberts (ed.), *A Political Companion to Frederick Douglass*, Lexington: University Press of Kentucky.

Burlingame, Michael 2014, 'Radicals, Abolitionists and Lincoln's Reelection', (lecture,

Lincoln Group of the District of Columbia, Washington, DC, 8 November 2014): https://www.c-span.org/video/?322673-5/radicals-abolitionists-lincolns-reelection

Burlingame, Michael 2021, *The Black Man's President: Abraham Lincoln, African Americans, & the Pursuit of Racial Equality*, New York: Perseus Books.

Cannon, James P. 1962, *The First Ten Years of American Communism: Report of a Participant*, New York: Lyle Stuart.

Clark, Christopher 2023, *Revolutionary Spring: Europe Aflame and the Fight for a New World, 1848–1849*, New York: Crown.

Clark, Steve and Terry Evans 2023, 'Socialist Workers Party leadership sets course ahead', *The Militant*, 10 July 2023. https://themilitant.com/2023/07/01/socialist-workers-party-leadership-sets-course-ahead/ (accessed 3 July 2023).

Clinton, Catherine 2005, *Harriet Tubman: The Road to Freedom*, New York: Back Bay Books.

Cook, James H. 1999, 'Fighting with Breath, Not Blows: Frederick Douglass and Antislavery Violence', in John R. McKivigan and Stanley Harrold (eds.), *Antislavery Violence: Sectional, Racial, and Cultural Conflict in Antebellum America*, Knoxville: University of Tennessee Press.

Cova, Antonio Rafael De la 2007, *The Moncada Attack: Birth of the Cuban Revolution*, Columbia: University of South Carolina Press.

Cox, Oliver 1970, *Caste, Class and Race*, New York: Modern Reader.

Davidson, Neil 2011, 'The American Civil War Considered as a Bourgeois Revolution', *Historical Materialism*, 19:4, 45–91.

Davis, David Brion 2006, *Inhuman Bondage: The Rise and Fall of Slavery in the New World*, New York: Oxford University Press.

Davis, William C. 1996, *The Cause Lost: Myths and Realities of the Confederacy*, Lawrence: University of Kansas Press.

Denton, Sally 2008, *Passion and Principle: John and Jesse Frémont, the Couple Whose Power, Politics and Love Shaped Nineteenth-Century America*, New York: Bloomsbury.

Derfler, Leslie 1991, *Paul Lafargue and the Founding of French Marxism, 1842–1882*, Cambridge: Harvard University Press.

Detzer, David 2002, *Allegiance: Fort Sumter, Charleston, and the Beginning of the Civil War*, New York: Harcourt.

Diedrich, Maria 1999, *Love Across Color Lines: Ottilie Assing and Frederick Douglass*, New York: Hill and Wang.

Dixon, David T., 2020, *Radical Warrior: August Willich's Journey from German Revolutionary to Union General*, Knoxville, Tennessee: University of Tennessee Press.

Dobbs, Farrell 2009, *Revolutionary Continuity: The Early Years, 1848–1917*, New York: Pathfinder Press.

Douglas, Andrew J. and Jared A. Loggins, 2021, *Prophet of Discontent: Martin Luther King Jr and the Critique of Racial Capitalism*, Athens: University of Georgia Press.

Douglass, Frederick 2014, *My Bondage and My Freedom: Introduction and Notes by David W. Blight*, New Haven: Yale University Press.

Downs, Gregory P. 2015, *After Appomattox: Military Occupation and the Ends of War*, Cambridge: Harvard University Press.

Downs, Gregory P. 2019, *The Second American Revolution: The Civil War-Era Struggle over Cuba and the Rebirth of the American Republic*, Chapel Hill: The University of North Carolina Press.

Doyle, Don H. 2015, *The Cause of All Nations: An International History of the American Civil War*, New York: Basic Books.

Draper, Hal 1977, *Karl Marx's Theory of Revolution, Volume 1: State and Bureaucracy*, New York: Monthly Review Press.

Draper, Hal 1977a, 'Marx and the Economic-Jew Stereotype', https://www.marxists.org/subject/marxmyths/hal-draper/article.htm

Draper, Hal 1985, *The Marx-Engels Chronicle: A Day-by-Day Chronology of Marx and Engels' Life and Activity*, New York: Schocken Books.

Draper, Hal 1986, *Karl Marx's Theory of Revolution, Volume 3: The 'Dictatorship of the Proletariat'*, New York: Monthly Review Press.

Draper, Hal 1990, *Karl Marx's Theory of Revolution, Volume 4: Critique of Other Socialisms*, New York: Monthly Review Press.

Draper, Hal 1994, *The Adventures of the Communist Manifesto*, Berkeley: Center for Socialist History.

Draper, Hal and E. Haberkern 2005, *Karl Marx's Theory of Revolution: Volume 5: War & Revolution*, New York: Monthly Review Press.

Dreier, Peter 2023, 'A True and Visionary Radical, Martin Luther King, Jr. was no Moderate', 17 January 2023, *Countercurrents.Org*. https://countercurrents.org/2023/01/a-true-and-visionary-radical-martin-luther-king-jr-was-no-moderate/

Du Bois, W.E.B. 1998, *Black Reconstruction in America, 1860–1880: Introduction by David Levering Lewis*, New York: The Free Press.

Du Bois, W.E.B. 2016, 'Karl Marx and the Negro', in Zimmerman, Angela, ed. *The Civil War in the United States, Karl Marx and Frederick Engels*, New York: International Publishers.

Dunayevskaya, Raya 1958, *Marxism and Freedom: From 1776 Until Today*, New York: Bookman Associates.

Easton, Loyd D. 1966, *Hegel's First American Followers: The Ohio Hegelians: John B. Stallo, Peter Kaufmann, Moncur Conway, and August Willich, with Key Writings*, Athens: Ohio University Press.

Eaton, John 1907, *Grant, Lincoln, and the Freedmen: Reminiscences of the Civil War with Special Reference to the Work for the Contrabands and Freedmen of the Mississippi Valley*, New York: Logmans, Green, and Company.

Edwards, Kyle A. 2022, '"Those Deluded, Ill-Starred Men": Frederick Douglass, the *New National Era*, and the Paris Commune', *New North Star*, 4, 1–19.

Edwards, Stewart (ed.) 1973a, *The Communards of Paris, 1871*, Ithaca: Cornell University Press.

Edwards, Stewart (ed.) 1973b, *The Paris Commune, 1871*, Chicago: Quadrangle Books.

Efford, Alison Clark 2013, *German Immigrants, Race, and Citizenship in the Civil War Era*, New York: Cambridge University Press.

Egerton, Douglas 2010, *Year of Meteors: Stephen Douglas, Abraham Lincoln, and the Election That Brought on the Civil War*, New York: Bloomsbury Press.

Egerton, Douglas 2014, *The Wars of Reconstruction: The Brief, Violent History of America's Most Progressive Era*, New York: Bloomsbury Press.

Egerton, Douglas 2015, 'The Slaves' Election: Frémont, Freedom and the Slaves Conspiracies of 1856', *Civil War History*, 61:1, 35–63.

Egerton, Douglas 2016, *Thunder at the Gates: The Black Civil War Regiments That Redeemed America*, New York: Basic Books.

Eig, Jonathan 2023, *King: A Life*, New York: Farrar, Straus and Giroux.

Engle, Stephen et al. 2017, 'Panel Discussion on Controversial Generals of the Civil War', (lecture, Pamplin Historical Park and National Museum of the Civil War Soldier, Petersburg, VA, 22 October 2017): https://www.c-span.org/video/?435570-3/panel-discussion-controversial-generals-civil-war

Enmale, Richard, ed. 1937, *Karl Marx and Friedrich Engels, The Civil War in the United States*, New York: International Publishers.

Evans, Terry 2023, 'What is road to unify, strengthen working class?', *The Militant*, 24 July 2023. https://themilitant.com/2023/07/15/what-is-road-to-unify-strengthen-working-class/ (accessed 16 July 2023).

Fagan, Benjamin 2014, '"The North Star" and the Atlantic, 1848', *African American Review*, 47:1, 51–67.

Fagan, Benjamin 2018, *The Black Newspaper and the Chosen Nation*, Athens: University of Georgia Press.

Fagan, Benjamin 2021, 'Journalism', in Michaël Roy (ed.), *Frederick Douglass in Context*, Cambridge: Cambridge University Press.

Fagan, Benjamin 2022, 'The Collective Making of *Frederick Douglass' Paper*', *Civil War History*, 68:2, 131–146.

Fehrenbacher, Don E. 1989a, *Abraham Lincoln: Speeches and Writings 1832–1858: Speeches, Letters, and Miscellaneous Writings; The Lincoln-Douglas Debates*, New York: The Library of America.

Fehrenbacher, Don E. 1989b, *Abraham Lincoln: Speeches and Writings 1859–1865: Speeches, Letters, and Miscellaneous Writings Presidential Message and Proclamations*, New York: The Library of America.

Feldman, Noah 2021, *The Broken Constitution: Lincoln, Slavery, and the Refounding of America*, New York: Farrar, Straus and Giroux.

Feldman, Noah, reply by James Oakes, '"Was Emancipation Constitutional?": An

Exchange', *The New York Review*, 23 June 2022 issue: https://www.nybooks.com/articles/2022/06/23/was-emancipation-constitutional-an-exchange/

Finkelman, Paul, 'Manufacturing Martyrdom: The Antislavery Response to John Brown's Raid', in *His Soul Goes Marching On: Responses to John Brown and the Harpers Ferry Raid*, edited by Paul Finkelman, Charlottesville: University of Virginia Press.

Finley, James S. 2020, 'Frederick Douglass in the United Kingdom: From the Free-Soil Principle to Free-Soil Abolition', *New North Star*, 2, 45–60.

Fleche, Andre M. 2012, *The Revolution of 1861: The Civil War in the Age of Nationalist Conflict*, Chapel Hill: The University of North Carolina Press.

Foner, Eric 1988, *Reconstruction: America's Unfinished Revolution, 1863–1877*, New York: Harper & Row.

Foner, Eric 2010, *The Fiery Trial: Abraham Lincoln and American Slavery*, New York: W.W. Norton & Company.

Foner, Eric 2013, 'Black Reconstruction: An Introduction', *The South Atlantic Quarterly* 112, no. 3: 409–418.

Foner, Eric 2015, *Gateway to Freedom: The Hidden History of the Underground Railroad*, New York: W.W. Norton & Company.

Foner, Eric 2019, *The Second Founding: How the Civil War and Reconstruction Remade the Constitution*, New York: W.W. Norton & Company.

Foner, Philip S. 1950a, *The Life and Writings of Frederick Douglass Volume 1: Early Years, 1817–1849*, New York: International Publishers.

Foner, Philip S. 1950b, *The Life and Writings of Frederick Douglass Volume 2: Pre-Civil War Decade, 1850–1860*, New York: International Publishers.

Foner, Philip S. 1952, *The Life and Writings of Frederick Douglass Volume 3: The Civil War, 1861–1865*. New York, International Publishers.

Foner, Philip S. 1955, *The Life and Writings of Frederick Douglass Volume 4: Reconstruction and After*, New York: International Publishers.

Foner, Philip S. 1975, *The Life and Writings of Frederick Douglass Volume 5 (Supplementary Volume) 1844–1860*, New York: International Publishers.

Foner, Philip S. 1977, *American Socialism and Black Americans*, Westport: Greenwood Press.

Foner, Philip S. 1981a, *British Labor and the American Civil War*, New York: Holmes & Meier.

Foner, Philip S. 1981b, *Organized Labor and the Black Worker, 1619–1981*, New York: International Publishers.

Foner, Philip S. 2002, *The Great Labor Uprising of 1877*, New York: Pathfinder Press.

Foner, Philip S. and Herbert Shapiro (eds.) 1994, *Northern Labor and Anti-Slavery: A Documentary History*, Westport: Greenwood Press.

Foner, Philip S. and Ronald L. Lewis (eds.) 1978, *The Black Worker, Volume 2: The Black*

Worker During the Era of the National Labor Union, Philadelphia: Temple University Press.

Foster, John Bellamy, Hannah Holleman and Brett Clark 2020, 'Marx and Slavery', *Monthly Review*, July/August 2020 (72:3)

Fought, Leigh 2017, *Women in the World of Frederick Douglass*, New York: Oxford University Press.

Fox-Genovese, Elizabeth and Eugene D. Genovese, *Slavery in White and Black: Class and Race in the Southern Slaveholders' New World Order*, Cambridge: Cambridge University Press.

Fry, Zachery A. 2020, *A Republic in the Ranks: Loyalty and Dissent in the Army of the Potomac*, Chapel Hill: The University of North Carolina Press.

Gabriel, Mary 2011, *Love and Capital: Karl and Jenny Marx and the Birth of a Revolution*, New York: Back Bay Books.

Gaido, Daniel, 'The First Workers' Government in History: Karl Marx's Addenda to Lissagaray's *History of the Commune of 1871*', *Historical Materialism*, 29:1, 1–64.

Gallagher, Gary 2011a, *Union War*, Cambridge: Harvard University Press.

Gallagher, Gary 2011b, 'Emancipation During the Civil War', (lecture, U.S. Capitol Historical Society, Washington, DC, 5 May 2011): https://www.c-span.org/video/?299485-1/emancipation-civil-war

Gallagher, Gary 2012, 'The Civil War Seven Days' Battles', (lecture, Virginia Historical Society, Richmond, VA, 11 July 2012): https://www.c-span.org/video/?306880-1/civil-war-days-battles

Gardner, Eric, 'A Word Fitly Spoken: Edmonia Highgate, Frances Ellen Watkins Harper, and the 1864 Syracuse Convention', in Gabrielle Foreman, Jim Casey, and Sarah Lynn Patterson (eds.), *The Colored Conventions Movement: Black Organizing in the Nineteenth Century*, Chapel Hill: The University of North Carolina Press.

Gates, Henry Louis (ed.) 1994, *Frederick Douglass: Autobiographies*, New York: The Library of America.

Gates, Henry Louis (ed.) 2009, *Lincoln on Race and Slavery*, Princeton: Princeton University Press.

Geuss, Raymond 2008, *Philosophy and Real Politics*, Princeton: Princeton University Press

Gleijeses, Piero 2013, *Visions of Freedom: Havana, Washington, Pretoria, and the Struggle for Southern Africa, 1976–1991*, Chapel Hill, N.C.: University of North Carolina Press.

Graf, Leroy P. and Ralph W. Haskins, eds. 1983, *The Papers of Andrew Johnson, vol. 6, 1862–1864*, Nashville: The University of Tennessee Press.

Green, William D. 1998, 'Minnesota's Long Road to Black Suffrage, 1849–1868', *Minnesota History*, Summer 1998, 69–84.

Grim, Ryan 2022, 'Elephant in the Zoom: Meltdowns Have Brought Progressive Advocacy Groups to a Standstill at a Critical Moment in World History', *The Intercept*,

13 June 2022: https://theintercept.com/2022/06/13/progressive-organizing-infighting-callout-culture/

Gronowicz, Anthony 1998, *Race and Class Politics in New York City Before the Civil War*, Boston: Northeastern University Press.

Hahn, Steven 2003, *A Nation Under Our Feet: Black Political Struggles in the Rural South from Slavery to the Great Migration*, Cambridge: Harvard University Press.

Halberstam, David 1967, 'The Second Coming of Martin Luther King', *Harper's Magazine*, no. 1407 (August 1967), 39–51.

Hamilton, Thomas 1833, *Men and Manners in America*, 2 Volumes, Edinburgh: William Blackwood.

Hanlon, Patrick 2022, '"Persons with whom I am acquainted": Frederick Douglass's Encounters with Americans in Europe in 1887, and Maybe Jack the Ripper', *New North Star*, 4, 91–94.

Hannah-Jones, Nikole, Caitlin Roper, Ilena Silverman, Jake Silverstein, eds. 2021, *The 1619 Project*, New York: One World.

Haynes, Khadija, 'A communist view: let's reject falsehoods about Dr. Martin Luther King', *Peoples's Weekly World*, 19 January, 2023.

Heinrich, Michael 2019, *Karl Marx and the Birth of Modern Society*, New York: Monthly Review Press.

Herriott, F.I. 1928, 'The Conference in the Deutsches Haus Chicago, May 14–15, 1860', *Transactions of the Illinois State Historical Society for the Year 1928*, 35, Illinois State Historical Library.

Holzer, Harold 2014, *Lincoln and the Power of the Press*, New York: Simon & Schuster.

Honneck, Mischa 2011, *We Are the Revolutionists: German-Speaking Immigrants & American Abolitionists after 1848*, Athens: University of Georgia Press.

Howard-Pitney, David 2004, *Martin Luther King Jr., Malcolm X, and the Civil Rights Struggle of the 1950s and 1960s: A Brief History with Documents*, Boston: Bedford/St. Martin's.

Hund, Wulf 2021, 'Marx and Haiti: Note on a Blank Space', *Journal of World Philosophies*, 6 (Winter 2021), 76–99.

Irving, Doug 2023, 'What Would It take to Close America's Black-White Wealth Gap', *Rand Review*, 9 May 2023.

Isenberg, Nancy 2016, *White Trash: The 300-Year Untold History of Class in America*, New York: Viking.

Jackson, Kellie Carter 2019, *Force and Freedom: Black Abolitionists and the Politics of Violence*, Philadelphia: University of Pennsylvania Press.

Jackson, Kellie Carter 2021, 'Abolition', in Michaël Roy (ed.), *Frederick Douglass in Context*, Cambridge: Cambridge University Press.

Johnson, Walter 2013, *River of Dark Dreams: Slavery and Empire in the Cotton Kingdom*, Cambridge: Harvard University Press.

Jones, Howard 2010, *Blue and Gray Diplomacy: A History of Union and Confederate Foreign Relations*, Chapel Hill, N.C.: University of North Carolina Press.

Joseph, Peniel E. 2020, *The Sword and the Shield: The Revolutionary Lives of Malcolm X and Martin Luther King Jr*, New York: Basic Books.

Karp, Matt 2019, 'The Mass Politics of Slavery', *Catalyst*, 2:3, 131–178.

Karp, Matt 2020, 'Frederick Douglass Railed Against Economic Inequality', *Jacobin*: https://jacobin.com/2020/02/frederick-douglass-railed-against-economic-inequality

Katz, Jamie 2017, 'Why Abraham Lincoln was Revered in Mexico', *Smithsonian Magazine*: https://www.smithsonianmag.com/history/why-mexico-loved-lincoln-180962258/

Katz, Phillip M. 1998, *From Appomattox to Montmartre: Americans and the Paris Commune*, Cambridge: Harvard University Press.

Keech, William R. 1968, *The Impact of Negro Voting: The Role of the Vote in the Quest for Equality*, Chicago: Rand McNally

Keith, LeeAnna 2020, *When It Was Grand: The Radical Republican History of the Civil War*, New York: Hill and Wang.

Kelly, Brian 2019, 'Slave Self-Activity and the Bourgeois Revolution in the United States: Jubilee and the Boundaries of Black Freedom', *Historical Materialism*, 27:3, 31–76.

Kelley, Robin D.G. 2017, 'What Did Cedric Robinson Mean by Racial Capitalism?', *Boston Review*, 12 January, 2017.

Kendrick, Paul and Stephen Kendrick, *Douglass and Lincoln: How a Revolutionary Black Leader and a Reluctant Liberator Struggled to End Slavery and Save the Union*, New York: Walker Books.

Keysaar, Alexander 2000, *The Right to Vote: The Contested History of Democracy in the United States*, New York: Basic Books.

King, Martin Luther 1967a, 'MLK Talks "New Phase" of Civil Rights Struggle, 11 Months Before His Assassination', *NBC News*: https://www.youtube.com/watch?v=2xsbt3a7K-8

King, Martin Luther 1967b, 'When Jesus Says Love He Means It: Excerpts from Martin Luther King Jr.'s 1967 Frogmore speech on its 50th Anniversary', *Kairos Center for Religions, Rights & Social Justice*: https://kairoscenter.org/mlk-frogmore-staff-retreat-speech-anniversary/

King, Martin Luther 1968, 'The Role of the Behavioral Scientist in the Civil Rights Movement', *Journal of Social Issues*, 74:2, 214–223.

Kloppenberg, James 2016, *Toward Democracy: The Struggle for Self-Rule in European and American Thought*, New York: Oxford University Press.

Kulikoff, Allan, 2018, *Abraham Lincoln and Karl Marx in Dialogue*, New York: Oxford University Press.

Lampe, Gregory 1998, *Frederick Douglass: Freedom's Voice, 1818–1845*, East Lansing: Michigan State University Press.

Lause, Mark A. 2015, *Free Labor: The Civil War and the Making of an American Working Class*, Urbana: University of Illinois Press.

Lenin, Vladimir I., 1977, *Collected Works*, Moscow: Progress Publishers.

Leon, Abram 2020, *The Jewish Question: A Marxist Interpretation*, New York: Pathfinder Press.

Levine, Bruce 1992, *Spirit of 1848: German Immigrants, Labor Conflict and the Coming Civil War*, Urbana: University of Illinois Press.

Levine, Bruce 2005, *Half Slave and Half Free: The Roots of Civil War, Revised Edition*, New York: Hill and Wang.

Levine, Bruce 2006, *Confederate Emancipation: Southern Plans to Free and Arm Slaves During the Civil War*, New York: Oxford University Press.

Levine, Bruce 2013, *The Fall of the House of Dixie: The Civil War and the Social Revolution that Transformed the South*, New York: Random House.

Levine, Bruce 2021, *Thaddeus Stevens: Civil War Revolutionary, Fighter for Racial Justice*, New York: Simon & Schuster.

Levine, Bruce 2021b, 'Thaddeus Stevens', (lecture, National Archives and Records Administration, Washington, D.C., 11 March 2021): https://www.c-span.org/video/?509864-1/thaddeus-stevens

Levine, Bruce 2021c, 'Thaddeus Stevens: Bourgeois Revolutionary', *Against the Current*, Sept/Oct. 2021.

Levine, Robert 2021, *The Failed Promise: Reconstruction, Frederick Douglass, and the Impeachment of Andrew Johnson*, New York: W.W. Norton & Company.

Liedman, Sven-Eric 2018, *A World to Win: The Life and Works of Karl Marx*, New York: Verso.

Lineberry, Cate 2022, 'The Greatest Generation', *New York Times*, 16 October 2022.

Littlefield, Daniel C., 'Blacks, John Brown, and a Theory of Manhood', in Paul Finkelman (ed.) 1995, *His Soul Goes Marching On: Responses to John Brown and the Harpers Ferry Raid*, Charlottesville: University of Virginia Press.

Lohmann, Christoph (ed.) 1999, *Radical Passion: Ottilie Assing's Reports from America and Letters to Frederick Douglass*, New York: Peter Lang.

Losurdo, Domenico 2011, *Liberalism: A Counter History*, New York: Verso.

Lowenstein, Roger 2022, *Ways and Means: Lincoln and His Cabinet and the Financing of the Civil War*, New York: Penguin.

Magness, Phillip W. 2009, 'Tariffs and the American Civil War', *Essential Civil War Curriculum*: https://www.essentialcivilwarcurriculum.com/tariffs-and-the-american-civil-war.html

Maloy, Mark 2020, 'Fort Sumter & First Shots of the Civil War', (lecture, Emerging Civil War Blog, Spotsylvania, VA, 8 August 2020): https://www.c-span.org/video/?474620-8/fort-sumter-shots-civil-war

Mandela, Nelson and Fidel Castro, 1991, *How Far We Slaves Have Come! South Africa and Cuba in Today's World*, New York: Pathfinder Press.

Manning, Chandra 2007, *What This Cruel War Was Over: Soldiers, Slavery, and the Civil War*, New York: Alfred A. Knopf.

Manning, Chandra 2021, 'The Civil War', in Michaël Roy (ed.), *Frederick Douglass in Context*, Cambridge: Cambridge University Press.

Martin Jr., Waldo 1984, *The Mind of Frederick Douglass*, Chapel Hill: The University of North Carolina Press.

Marx, Karl 1989, *A Contribution to the Critique of Political Economy: Edited with an Introduction by Maurice Dobb*, New York: International Publishers.

Marx, Karl and Friedrich Engels 1975–2004a, *Collected Works*, Volume 1, New York: International Publishers.

Marx, Karl and Friedrich Engels 1975–2004b, *Collected Works*, Volume 3, New York: International Publishers.

Marx, Karl and Friedrich Engels 1975–2004c, *Collected Works*, Volume 4, New York: International Publishers.

Marx, Karl and Friedrich Engels 1975–2004d, *Collected Works*, Volume 5, New York: International Publishers.

Marx, Karl and Friedrich Engels 1975–2004e, *Collected Works*, Volume 6, New York: International Publishers.

Marx, Karl and Friedrich Engels 1975–2004f, *Collected Works*, Volume 8, New York: International Publishers.

Marx, Karl and Friedrich Engels 1975–2004g, *Collected Works*, Volume 9, New York: International Publishers.

Marx, Karl and Friedrich Engels 1975–2004h, *Collected Works*, Volume 10, New York: International Publishers.

Marx, Karl and Friedrich Engels 1975–2004i, *Collected Works*, Volume 11, New York: International Publishers.

Marx, Karl and Friedrich Engels 1975–2004j, *Collected Works*, Volume 19, New York: International Publishers.

Marx, Karl and Friedrich Engels 1975–2004k, *Collected Works*, Volume 20, New York: International Publishers.

Marx, Karl and Friedrich Engels 1975–2004l, *Collected Works*, Volume 22, New York: International Publishers.

Marx, Karl and Friedrich Engels 1975–2004m, *Collected Works*, Volume 24, New York: International Publishers.

Marx, Karl and Friedrich Engels 1975–2004n, *Collected Works*, Volume 27, New York: International Publishers.

Marx, Karl and Friedrich Engels 1975–2004o, *Collected Works*, Volume 28, New York: International Publishers.

Marx, Karl and Friedrich Engels 1975–2004p, *Collected Works*, Volume 35, New York: International Publishers.

Marx, Karl and Friedrich Engels 1975–2004q, *Collected Works*, Volume 37, New York: International Publishers.
Marx, Karl and Friedrich Engels 1975–2004r, *Collected Works*, Volume 38, New York: International Publishers.
Marx, Karl and Friedrich Engels 1975–2004s, *Collected Works*, Volume 39, New York: International Publishers.
Marx, Karl and Friedrich Engels 1975–2004t, *Collected Works*, Volume 40, New York: International Publishers.
Marx, Karl and Friedrich Engels 1975–2004u, *Collected Works*, Volume 41, New York: International Publishers.
Marx, Karl and Friedrich Engels 1975–2004v, *Collected Works*, Volume 42, New York: International Publishers.
Marx, Karl and Friedrich Engels 1975–2004w, *Collected Works*, Volume 43, New York: International Publishers.
Marx, Karl and Friedrich Engels 1975–2004x, *Collected Works*, Volume 44, New York: International Publishers.
Marx, Karl and Friedrich Engels 1975–2004y, *Collected Works*, Volume 45, New York: International Publishers.
Marx, Karl and Friedrich Engels 1975–2004z, *Collected Works*, Volume 46, New York: International Publishers.
Marx, Karl and Friedrich Engels 1975–2004aa, *Collected Works*, Volume 47, New York: International Publishers.
Marx, Karl and Friedrich Engels 1975–2004bb, *Collected Works*, Volume 49, New York: International Publishers.
Marx, Karl and Friedrich Engels 1975–2004cc, *Collected Works*, Volume 50, New York: International Publishers.
Marx, Karl and Friedrich Engels 1992, *Gesamtausgabe* [MEGA], 1 Band 20 (Apparat), Berlin: Dietz Verlag.
Marx, Karl and Friedrich Engels 2016, *The Civil War in the United States: Edited and with an Introduction by Angela Zimmerman*, New York: International Publishers.
Mason, Matthew 2013, 'Internationalizing the Civil War,' *History: Review of New Books*, 41, 3: 51–53.
Matsui, John H. 2016, *The First Republican Army: The Army of Virginia and the Radicalization of the Civil War*, Charlottesville: University of Virginia Press.
McCurry, Stephanie 2010, *Confederate Reckoning: Power and Politics in the Civil War South*, Cambridge: Harvard University Press.
McDaniel, W. Caleb 2015, *The Problem of Democracy in the Age of Slavery: Garrisonian Abolitionists and Transatlantic Reform*, Baton Rouge: LSU Press.
McFeely, William S. 1991, *Frederick Douglass*, New York: W.W. Norton & Company.
McGinty, Brian 2009, *John Brown's Trial*, Cambridge: Harvard University Press.

McKivigan, John R. 1990, 'The Frederick Douglass-Gerrit Smith Friendship and Political Abolitionism in the 1850s', in Eric J. Sundquist (ed.), *Frederick Douglass: New Literary and Historical Essays*, New York: Cambridge University Press.

McKivigan, John R. 2008, *Forgotten Firebrand: James Redpath and the Making of Nineteenth-Century America*, Ithaca: Cornell University Press.

McKivigan, John R. (ed.) 2009, *The Frederick Douglass Papers: Series Three: Correspondence Volume 1: 1842–1852*, New Haven: Yale University Press.

McKivigan, John R. 2013, 'Frederick Douglass and the Abolitionist Response to the Election of 1860', in A. James Fuller (ed.), *The Election of 1860 Reconsidered*, Kent: The Kent State University Press.

McKivigan, John R. (ed.) 2018, *The Frederick Douglass Papers: Series Three: Correspondence Volume 2: 1853–1865*, New Haven: Yale University Press.

McKivigan, John R. (ed.) 2021, *The Frederick Douglass Papers: Series Four: Journalism and Other Writings Volume 1*, New Haven: Yale University Press.

McKivigan, John R. and Jason H. Silverman 1999, 'Monarchial Liberty and Republican Slavery: West Indies Emancipation Celebrations in Upstate New York and Canada West', in John R. McKivigan, ed. *History of the American Abolitionist Movement: A Bibliography of Scholarly Articles*, New York: Garland Publishing, Inc.

McPherson, James M. 1965, *The Negro's Civil War: How American Negroes Felt and Acted During the War for the Union*, New York: Pantheon Books.

McPherson, James M. 1988, *Battle Cry of Freedom: The Civil War Era*, New York: Oxford University Press.

McPherson, James M. 1997, *For Cause and Comrades: Why Men Fought in the Civil War*, New York: Oxford University Press.

McPherson, James M. 2008, *Tried by War: Abraham Lincoln as Commander in Chief*, New York: Penguin Press.

McPherson, James M. 2013, 'African American Soldiers and Emancipation', (lecture, Frederick Community College: Catoctin Center for Regional Studies, Frederick, Maryland): https://www.c-span.org/video/?311266-1/african-american-soldiers-emancipation

McPherson, James M. 2014, *Embattled Rebel: Jefferson Davis and the Confederate Civil War*, New York: Penguin Books.

Medford, Edna Greene, Harold Holzer, and David W. Blight 2020, 'Lincoln, Douglass, and Emancipation', (lecture, New York Historical Society, New York City, NY, 11 January 2020).

Matthews, Donald R. and Prothro, James W., 1966, *Negroes and the New Southern Politics*, New York: Harcourt, Brace and World.

Merriman, John 2014, *Massacre: The Life and Death of the Paris Commune of 1871*, New Haven: Yale University Press.

Merritt, Keri Leigh 2017, *Masterless Men: Poor Whites and Slavery in the Antebellum South*, New York: Cambridge University Press.

Messer-Kruse, Timothy 1998, *The Yankee International: Marxism and the American Reform Tradition, 1848–1876*, Chapel Hill, N.C.: The University of North Carolina Press.

Miéville, China 2022, *A Spectre Haunting: On the Communist Manifesto*, Chicago: Haymarket Books.

Mill, John Stuart 1985, *The Collected Works of John Stuart Mill, Volume XXI – Essays on Equality, Law, and Education*, Toronto: University of Toronto Press.

Mills, Charles 1990, 'Getting Out of the Cave: Tension between Democracy and Elitism in Marx's Theory of Cognitive Liberation', *Social and Economic Studies*, 39: 1 (March 1990).

Mills, Charles 1997, *The Racial Contract*, Ithaca, N.Y.: Cornell University Press.

Mills, Charles 1998, *Black Visible: Essays on Philosophy and Race*, Ithaca, N.Y.: Cornell University Press.

Montgomery, David 1967, *Beyond Equality: Labor and the Radical Republicans, 1862–1872*, New York: Alfred A. Knopf.

Montgomery, Scott L. and Daniel Chirot 2015, *The Shape of the New: Four Big Ideas and How They Made the Modern World*, Princeton: Princeton University Press.

Moses, Wilson Jeremiah 2004, *Creative Conflict in African American Thought: Frederick Douglass, Alexander Crummell, Booker T. Washington, W.E.B. Du Bois, and Marcus Garvey*, New York: Cambridge University Press.

Mounk, Yascha 2023, *The Identity Trap: A Story of Ideas and Power in Our Time*, New York: Penguin Press.

Murray, Williamson and Wayne Wei-Siang Hsieh 2016, *A Savage War: A Military History of the Civil War*, Princeton: Princeton University Press.

Myers, Peter C. 2008, *Frederick Douglass: Race and the Rebirth of American Liberalism*, Lawrence: University of Kansas Press.

Myers, Peter C. 2010, '"A Good Work for Our Race To-Day": Interests, Virtues, and the Achievement of Justice in Frederick Douglass's Freedmen's Monument Speech', *American Political Science Review*, vol. 104, no. 2 (May 2010), 209–225.

Myers, Peter C. 2013, 'Frederick Douglass on Revolution and Integration: A Problem in Moral Psychology', *American Political Thought*, vol. 2, no. 1 (2013), 118–146.

Nadel, Stanley 1990, *Little Germany: Ethnicity, Religion, and Class in New York City, 1845–80*, Chicago: University of Illinois Press.

New York Times, 2019, *The 1619 Project*, https://www.nytimes.com/interactive/2019/08/14/magazine/1619-america-slavery.html

Nichols, Robert 2020, *Theft is Property! Dispossession and Critical Theory*, Durham: Duke University Press.

Nimtz, August H. 1985a, 'Marxism and the Black Struggle: The "Class v. Race" Debate Revisited', *Journal of African Marxists*, No. 7, 75–89.

Nimtz, August H. 1985b, 'The Making and Unmaking of a Revolution: Some Lessons from Grenada', *The African Review* [Dar es Salaam], 12:2.

Nimtz, August H. 2000, *Marx and Engels: Their Contribution to the Democratic Breakthrough*, Albany: SUNY Press.

Nimtz, August H. 2002, 'The Eurocentric Marx and Engels and other related myths', *Marxism, Modernity, and Postcolonial Studies*, eds. Crystal Bartolovich and Neil Lazarus, New York: Cambridge University Press.

Nimtz, August H. 2003, *Marx, Tocqueville and Race in America: The 'Absolute Democracy' or 'Defiled Republic'*, Lanham: Lexington Books.

Nimtz, August H. 2006, 'Natural versus Social Phenomena: Cuba and the Lessons of Katrina', *The Black Scholar*, Winter, 36:4.

Nimtz, August H. 2016a, 'Violence and/or Nonviolence in the Success of the Civil Rights Movement', *New Political Science*, 38:1, 1–22.

Nimtz, August H. 2016b, 'Marx and Engels on the revolutionary party', in Panitch, Leo and Greg Albo (eds.), *Socialist Register 2017*, London: The Merlin Press.

Nimtz, August H. 2017, '"The Bolsheviks Come to Power": A New Interpretation', *Science & Society*, 81:4, 478–500.

Nimtz, August H. 2019a, *The Ballot, the Streets, or Both? From Marx and Engels to Lenin and the October Revolution*, Chicago: Haymarket Press.

Nimtz, August H. 2019b, *Marxism versus Liberalism: Comparative Real-Time Political Analysis*, Cham: Palgrave Macmillan.

Nimtz, August H. 2019c, 'From a Constituent of Congresswoman Ilhan Omar on Anti-Semitism: What It Is and Why It's Dangerous'. *Tikkun*, 8 May.

Nimtz, August H. 2020, 'Why there are no George Floyds in Cuba', *Legal Form*, 17 June. https://legalform.blog/2020/06/17/why-there-are-no-george-floyds-in-cuba-august-h-nimtz/

Nimtz, August H. 2021a, '"Putting weapons into the hands of the proletariat": Marx on the contradiction between capitalism and liberal democracy', in Paul O'Connell and Umut Özusu (eds.), *Research Handbook on Law and Marxism*, Cheltenham: Elgar Publishers.

Nimtz, August H. 2021b, 'The Trump Moment: Why It Happened, Why We "Dodged the Bullet", and "What Is To Be Done?"', *Legal Form*, 24, February 2021: https://legalform.blog/2021/02/24/the-trump-moment-why-it-happened-why-we-dodged-the-bullet-and-what-is-to-be-done-august-h-nimtz/

Novack, George 2013, *America's Revolutionary Heritage*, New York: Pathfinder Press.

Oakes, James 1982, *The Ruling Race: A History of American Slaveholders*, New York: Vintage Books.

Oakes, James 2007, *The Radical and the Republican: Frederick Douglass, Abraham Lincoln, and the Triumph of Antislavery Politics*, New York: W.W. Norton & Company.

Oakes, James 2013, *Freedom National: The Destruction of Slavery in the United States, 1861–1865*, New York: W.W. Norton & Company.

Oakes, James 2015, 'Lincoln's AntiSlavery Politics', (lecture, Lincoln Group of the District of Columbia, Chevy Chase, MD, 8 July 2015): https://www.c-span.org/video/?326989-1/lincolns-antislavery-politics

Oakes, James 2019, 'Du Bois's "General Strike"', *NONsite.org*, No. 28, May 10.

Oakes, James 2021, *The Crooked Path to Abolition: Abraham Lincoln and the Antislavery Constitution*, New York: W.W. Norton & Company.

Obermann, Karl 1947, *Joseph Weydemeyer, Pioneer of American Socialism*, New York: International Publishers.

Obermann, Karl 1968, *Joseph Weydemeyer: Ein Lebensbild*, Berlin: Dietz Verlag.

Pasley, Jeffrey L., and John Craig Hammond, eds. 2021, *A Fire Bell in the Past: The Missouri Crisis at 200, vols. I and II*, Columbia, Missouri: University of Missouri Press.

Potter, David M. 2011, *The Impending Crisis: America Before the Civil War: 1848–1861*, New York: Harper Perennial.

Preston, Dickson J. 2018, *Young Frederick Douglass: The Maryland Years*, Baltimore: Johns Hopkins University Press.

Preston, Michael B., Lenneal J. Henderson, Jr., and Paul Puryear, eds. 1982 *The New Black Politics: The Search for Political Power*, New York: Longman.

Reed Jr, Adolph 2017, 'Du Bois and the 'Wages of Whiteness': What He Meant, What He Didn't, and, Besides, It Shouldn't Matter for Our Politics Anyway', 29 June 2017, *NONsite.org*.

Reinhart, Joseph R. (ed.) 2006, *August Willich's Gallant Dutchmen: Civil War Letters from the 32nd Indiana Infantry*, Kent, Ohio: Kent University Press.

Reynolds, David S. 2005, *John Brown, Abolitionist: The Man Who Killed Slavery, Sparked the Civil War, and Seeded Civil Rights*, New York: Alfred Knopf.

Reynolds, David S. 2020, *Abe: Abraham Lincoln in His Time*, New York: Penguin Books.

Richardson, Heather Cox 2001, *The Death of Reconstruction: Race, Labor, and Politics in the Post-Civil War North, 1865–1901*, Cambridge: Harvard University Press.

Richardson, Heather Cox 2014, *To Make Men Free: A History of the Republican Party*, New York: Basic Books.

Riddell, John (ed.) 1991, *Workers of the World and Oppressed Peoples, Unite!: Proceedings and Documents of the Second Congress, 1920, Vol. One*, New York: Pathfinder Press.

Roberts, Michael 2016, *The Long Depression: How It Happened, Why It Happened, and What Happens Next*, Chicago: Haymarket Books.

Roberts, Neil 2015, *Freedom as Marronage*, Chicago: The University of Chicago Press.

Roberts, Neil (ed.) 2018, *A Political Companion to Frederick Douglass*, Lexington: University Press of Kentucky.

Roberts, Timothy Mason 2009, *Distant Revolutions: 1848 and the Challenge to American Exceptionalism*, Charlottesville: University of Virginia Press.

Robinson, Cedric J. 1983, *Black Marxism: The Making of the Black Radical Tradition*, London: Zed.

Root, Damon 2016, 'Frederick Douglass on Capitalism, Slavery, and the "Arrant Nonsense" of Socialism,' *Reason*, 28 August 2016: https://reason.com/2016/08/28/frederick-douglass-on-capitalism-slavery/

Root, Damon 2017, 'Frederick Douglass Hated Socialism', *Reason*: https://reason.com/2017/03/12/frederick-douglass-hated-socia/

Rosenblatt, Helena 2018, *The Lost History of Liberalism: From Ancient Rome to the Twenty-First Century*, Princeton: Princeton University Press.

Rossi, Matteo M. 2019, 'Protecting America: Order, Nation and Exception in Henry Carey's Social Science', *USAbroad Journal of American History and Politics*, 2, 1: https://doi.org/10.6092/issn.2611-2752/8542

Saman, Michael 2020, 'Du Bois and Marx, Du Bois and Marxism', *Du Bois Review*, 17:1, 33–54.

Sandefur, Timothy 2018, *Frederick Douglass: Self-Made Man*, Washington, D.C.: Cato Institute.

Saville, Julie 1994, *The Work of Reconstruction: From Slave to Wage Laborer in South Carolina, 1860–1870*, New York: Cambridge University Press.

Schaub, Diana 2010, 'Lincoln and Frederick Douglass', (lecture, Washington and Lee University, Lexington, VA, 5 March 2010): https://www.youtube.com/watch?v=vmiLpi1IgPQ

Schurz, Carl 1907, *The Reminiscences of Carl Schurz Volume 1, 1829–1852*, New York: The McClure Company.

Schlüter, Herman 1913, *Lincoln, Labor and Slavery*, New York: Socialist Literature Co.

Sears, Stephen W. 1989, *The Civil War Papers of George B. McClellan: Selected Correspondence, 1860–1865*, New York: Ticknor & Fields.

Sears, Stephen W. 1994, 'Lincoln and McClellan', in *Lincoln's Generals*, edited by Gabor S. Boritt, New York: Oxford University Press.

Sébastien, Abbet 2016, 'Joseph Weydemeyer: A German American for socialism and Black rights', Historisches Seminar: *Atlantic Migrations: 15th–20th Century*: https://www.academia.edu/30948358/Joseph_Weydemeyer_a_German_American_for_Socialism_and_Black_Rights

Shilliam, Robbie 2015, 'Decolonizing the *Manifesto*: Communism and the Slave Analogy', in Terrell Carver and James Farr (eds.), *The Cambridge Companion to The Communist Manifesto*, New York: Cambridge University Press.

Shoikhedbrod, Igor 2020, *Revisiting Marx's Critique of Liberalism*, New York: Palgrave Macmillan.

Shoikhedbrod, Igor 2023, 'Revisiting the "Jewish Question" and Its Contemporary Discontents', *Historical Materialism* [forthcoming]

Sikafis, Stewart 1988, *Who Was Who in the Civil War*, New York: Fact on File Publications.

Sinha, Manisha 2008, 'Allies for Emancipation?: Lincoln and Black Abolitionists', in *Our Lincoln: New Perspectives on Lincoln and His World*, edited by Eric Foner, New York: W.W. Norton & Company.

Sinha, Manisha 2016, *The Slave's Cause: A History of Abolition*, New Haven: Yale University Press.

Slack, Gregory 2020, 'From Class to Race and Back Again: A Critique of Charles Mills' Black Radical Liberalism', *Science & Society*, vol. 84, no. 1, January 2020, 67–94.

Slack, Gregory 2023, 'Did Marx Defend Black Slavery? On Jamaica and Labour in Black Skin', *Historical Materialism*, 31.3.

Smith, John David (ed.) 2002, *Black Soldiers in Blue: African American Troops in the Civil War Era*, Chapel Hill: The University of North Carolina Press.

Sorentino, Sara-Maria 2019, 'The Abstract Slave: Anti-Blackness and Marx's Method', *International Labor and Working Class History*, No. 96, Fall 2019.

Sperber, Jonathan 2013, *Karl Marx: A Nineteenth Century Life*, New York: W.W. Norton & Company.

Stahr, Walter 2012, *Seward: Lincoln's Indispensable Man*, New York: Simon & Schuster.

Stahr, Walter 2017, *Stanton: Lincoln's War Secretary*, New York: Simon & Schuster.

Stahr, Walter 2021, *Salmon P. Chase: Lincoln's Vital Rival*, New York: Simon & Schuster.

Stampp, Kenneth M. 1990, *America in 1857: A Nation on the Brink*, New York, Oxford University Press.

Stanton, Fred (ed.) 2009, *Fighting Racism in World War II*, New York: Pathfinder Press.

Stauffer, John 2002, *The Black Hearts of Men: Radical Abolitionists and the Transformation of Race*, Cambridge: Harvard University Press.

Stauffer, John 2008, *Giants: The Parallel Lives of Frederick Douglass and Abraham Lincoln*, New York: Twelve.

Stedman Jones, Gareth 2013, *Karl Marx: Greatness and Illusion*, Cambridge: Harvard University Press.

Steele, Shelby, 2023, 'Reparations Are No More Than a Dream of Privilege', *Wall Street Journal*, 17 June 2023.

Stevens, Alexander H. 1861, 'Cornerstone Speech', *American Battlefield Trust*: https://www.battlefields.org/learn/primary-sources/cornerstone-speech

Stewart, James Brewer 1986, *Wendell Phillips: Liberty's Hero*, Baton Rouge: LSU Press.

Taylor, Nikki M. 2013, *America's First Black Socialist: The Radical Life of Peter H. Clark*, Lexington: The University Press of Kentucky.

Taylor, Keeanga-Yamahtta 2022, 'It's Called Capitalism: Naming the System Behind Systemic Racism', *Spectre Journal*, 1 June 2022.

Trotsky, Leon 1972, *The Revolution Betrayed: What is the Soviet Union and where is it going?* New York: Pathfinder Press.

Trotsky, Leon 1974, *Writings of Leon Trotsky, 1938–39*, New York: Pathfinder Press.

Tuchinsky, Adam-Max 2005, '"The Bourgeoisie Will Fall and Fall Forever": The New York Tribune, the 1848 French Revolution and American Social Democratic Discourse', *Journal of American History*, 92:2, 470–497

Valverde, Sergio 2017, 'A Speculative Theory of Politics: Logic of the Party Form', PhD diss., University of Minnesota.

Varon, Elizabeth 2014, 'Confederate View of 1864 Election', (lecture, Lincoln Group of the District of Columbia, Washington, DC, 8 November 2014): https://www.c-span.org/video/?322673-2/discussion-confederate-view-1864-election&event=322673&playEvent

Varon, Elizabeth 2019, *Armies of Deliverance: A New History of the Civil War*, New York: Oxford University Press.

Vorenberg, Michael 2001, *Final Freedom: The Civil War, the Abolition of Slavery, and the Thirteenth Amendment*, New York: Cambridge University Press.

Wallace, Maurice O. 2021, 'Religion', in *Frederick Douglass in Context*, edited by Michaël Roy, Cambridge: Cambridge University Press.

Washington, James Melvin (ed.) 1991, *A Testament of Hope: the Essential Writings and Speeches of Martin Luther King, Jr.*, San Francisco: Harper Collins.

Welch, Dan 2021, 'Fallen Leaders: Union General John Pope', (lecture, Emerging Civil War Blog, Spotsylvania, VA, 6 August 2021): https://www.c-span.org/video/?513962-2/fallen-leaders-union-general-john-pope

Weyland, Kurt 2012, 'The Arab Spring: Why the Surprising Similarities with the Revolutionary Wave of 1848', *Perspectives on Politics*, 10, 4: 917–934.

Whitaker, Mark 2023, *Saying It Loud: 1966 – The Year Black Power Challenged the Civil Rights Movement*, New York: Simon & Schuster.

Williams, Kidada E. 2023, *I Saw Death Coming: A History of Terror and Survival in the War against Reconstruction*, New York: Bloomsbury Publishing.

Wilson, James Q. 1965, *Negro Politics: The Search for Leadership*, New York: Free Press.

Wineapple, Brenda 2020, *The Impeachers: The Trial of Andrew Johnson and the Dream of a Just Nation*, New York: Random House.

Winczewski, Damian 2021, 'Engels's Military Thought: Historical Materialism and Modern Warfare', *Socialism and Democracy*, 35:2–3, 193–213.

Young, Patrick 2014, 'Lincoln Wins the 1864 Election With Immigrant Votes', *Long Island Wins*, 10 December 2014: https://longislandwins.com/columns/immigrants-civil-war/lincoln-wins-the-1864-election-with-immigrant-votes/

Zimmerman, Angela 2015, 'From the Second American Revolution to the First International and Back Again: Marxism, the Popular Front, and the American Civil War', in Gregory P. Downs and Kate Masur, eds. *The World the Civil War Made*, Chapel Hill, N.C.: University of North Carolina Press.

Zimmerman, Angela (ed.) 2016, 'Introduction', *The Civil War in the United States, Karl Marx and Frederick Engels*, New York: International Publishers.

Index

1619 Project   6, 303, 304, 308–10, 380
1776 project   6–7, 54, 68, 71, 243
1848–49 European Revolutions   12, 14, 55–56, 59, 71, 103, 111, 115–16, 261, 309, 317
    proletarian uprising in Paris and   59–60, 63, 68, 81, 106, 269, 270–71, 317 (*See also* European Spring; Paris Commune)

abolition and abolitionists   22–25, 27, 30, 53, 53*n*110, 57, 63, 63*n*26, 68, 70, 74, 77, 80, 84, 92, 94, 98, 101–02, 105, 109, 113, 116, 118, 121, 123, 126, 131, 138, 153*n*155, 178, 180, 185, 188, 193, 197, 200–01, 203–04, 209, 211, 214, 219, 223, 225, 228, 232, 234, 237–40, 248, 250, 253, 257, 264, 274, 277, 281–83, 285–86, 288, 291, 295–96, 308, 317–18, 335, 341, 346, 351
    in France/French colonies   63–64, 280
    in the UK   32, 63, 79, 126, 133, 133*n*87, 213
Abrams, Stacey   305, 307
Adams, Charles Francis   142*n*117, 157, 226, 245, 245*n*89
Adams, Henry   226
Adams, John Quincy   24, 138
'Address of March 1850 of the Central Authority of the Communist League' (*see also* Communist League)   60, 120, 163*n*7, 210, 241, 269, 281, 313–14
African Americans (*see also* Black people)   1, 23, 108, 200, 219, 222, 250, 250*n*111, 261, 271*n*184, 275–76, 292, 306–308, 310, 314–15, 347*n*85, 353–54, 357, 373
African Colonization Society   340
African Methodist Episcopal Zion Church (AMEZ)   22, 105, 107–109, 116, 119, 121
Agassiz, Louis   94
Amar, Akhil Reed   286*n*18
American Anti-Slavery Society   25
American and Foreign Anti-Slavery Society   318
American Psychological Association   275
American Revolution   12, 19
Amerikanische Arbeiterbund (American Workers' League)   73, 74*n*62, 88, 94
Anaconda Plan   162, 162*n*4, 173, 174

Andrew, John   219–220
Anglo-American Treaty of 1862   181, 184
Angola   380
Anthony, Aaron   18
Antietam, Maryland   200, 202, 217
anti-semitism   34, 40*n*85, 364–66, 369–70, 372
Anti-Slavery League (Great Britain)   32
Appomattox   12, 14, 217, 247, 247*n*100, 248
April 10, 1848   London protest 65, 65*n*30, 299
Arab Spring   55
Assing, Ottilie   106*n*2, 113*n*29, 158, 158*n*166
Atlantic Monthly   117, 252, 261
Auld, Anthony   18
Auld, Hugh   20
Auld, Sophia   17
Auld, Thomas   20–21
Avineri, Shlomo   11*n*32, 40*n*85
Ayers, Edward L.   248*n*102

Ball's Bluff, Battle of   143, 146
Banks, General Nathaniel   223*n*14
Barnes, Jack   301*n*53, 314*n*85
Bates, Edward   219–20
Beaumont, Gustave de   40, 49
Biden, Joseph   307
Black Codes   260*n*142
Black Jacobins (*see* C.L.R. James)
Black, Kelvin   3*n*9, 299
Black Lives Matter   314
Black Marxism (*see* Cedric Robinson)
Black people   5, 18, 21–24, 26, 35, 40, 49–50, 70, 75, 78–79, 86–87, 89, 98, 101, 106, 108, 110, 120, 124–25, 127, 130, 136, 163–66, 172, 180, 186, 188–89, 193*n*98, 195–96, 212, 218–20, 222, 229–30, 232–33, 275, 315, 339–41, 346, 348, 350
Black Reconstruction (*see* W.E.B. Dubois)
Black Union soldiers   108, 117, 189, 214, 219, 222–23, 228–29, 231–32, 234, 238, 248, 249*n*105, 287, 357
Black workers   258, 262, 282*n*10, 318, 336–42, 350–51, 354, 357, 357*n*17, 358, 374
Blair, Montgomery   142
Blassingame, John W.   9

INDEX

Blight, David W.   3, 15, 17–18, 21, 84–87, 93, 153n155, 169, 180, 190, 203, 220, 228–29, 232, 234, 254n127, 298, 299–300, 300n48, 338, 354
bloody constitutionalist   298n42
Bloody Kansas   74, 118
Bonaparte, Louis Napoleon   59, 63, 121, 148–49, 151, 319–21, 326, 333
   December 1851 coup and 59   71, 149
Bonapartism   119, 333, 334n48
border states   109, 115, 117, 132–33, 136, 139–40, 145n128, 150, 175, 197, 222
Bordewich, Fergus   207–08, 210, 211n143, 220
Bouie, Jamelle   300–01, 303–05, 309
bourgeois socialism   81
Bradley. Aaron   257–58, 258n136, 258n137
Brazil   379
Braxton, Robert   258n136
Bright, John   225–226
British West Indies   32
Bromell, Nick   3n8, 113n29, 297
Brooks, David   305–06
Brown, John   68, 70, 74–75, 77, 84–85, 88, 90, 92, 98, 102, 106–07, 219–20, 235, 298, 310, 364
   armed underground railroad and   84, 86, 235
   execution   84, 88–89, 97, 102
   Pottawatomie Creek   85, 85n97
   provisional constitution   86
   role in abolition of slavery   91, 102, 298
   Tubman, Harriet and   87
Brown Jr., John   112
Brown, William Wells   220
Buccola, Nicholas   3n8, 32, 338, 338n58
Buchanan, James   77–78, 84, 97, 114
Bull Run/Mannassas, First Battle of   137–38, 138n101, 143, 146, 162n4
Bull Run/Mannassas, Second Battle of Second Bull Run   198, 200
Burke, Edmund   299
Burns, Lydia and Mary   46, 224
Butler, Benjamin   112, 183, 183n66, 224–25, 266n162, 327–28

Canandaigua, New York   33, 78
Cannon, James P.   372, 374
Capital   4, 7, 10, 12, 44, 46, 47n97, 61–62, 82, 114, 117, 147, 179, 217, 224–25, 227–28, 262, 264, 265, 267, 290, 295, 351, 354, 363, 367
capitalism   41, 44, 46, 49, 58–59, 82, 85, 108, 167, 239, 241, 258, 272, 274, 280, 293, 301, 303–04 306–09, 311–12, 314–15, 342, 349, 363
capitalists/bourgeoisie   10, 43, 56, 58, 60, 66, 72, 76, 76n70, 82, 96, 142, 165–67, 226, 263, 265, 284, 287–88, 294, 309, 328, 338, 340, 343, 345–46, 361, 363, 366
Carey, Henry   58, 58n15, 62, 274, 282, 293, 353–54, 364
Carson, Tucker   310
Cassius Clay   27
Castro, Fidel   87
Chartists   27, 31–32, 45, 46, 53, 62–64, 65, 280, 299, 317
Chase, Salmon   75, 110n17, 240n72
Child, Lydia Maria   346
Chinese   373
Civil Rights Movement   1, 305
Civil War   1–3, 5–7, 12–14, 54–55, 68, 70, 84, 90, 105, 107–08, 111–12, 114–17, 121–22, 125, 129, 131, 134, 137–38, 142, 145, 149, 154, 158, 160, 217, 224, 229, 234, 240, 249, 259, 265, 267, 272, 274, 280, 282–84, 286n17, 290, 295, 306, 313, 318, 327, 339, 341, 346–347, 350
   military matters and   5, 7, 105, 109–10, 115n34, 137, 234–237
The Civil War in France (Marx)   269–70, 296, 327, 330–32
The Civil War in the United States: Karl Marx & Frederick Engels   352
Clark, Christopher   56n4
Clark, Peter H.   347n85, 348n89
class and race   186, 344, 348, 350, 361–62, 368, 381 (*see also* race and class; Appendix B)
class collaborationism   59n17, 124, 315n88, 318, 335, 339
class struggle   58, 61, 71, 81, 91, 123, 131–32, 202, 336, 350
Clay, Henry   74
Clement Thomas, General Jacque Leon   327
Clinton, Hillary   308
Cluss, Adolph   62
Cochrane, John   233
Coffin, William   23

Collins, John A.   23, 25–26, 32, 39, 52, 299
colonisation   23, 190, 196–97, 200, 340
Colored National Labor Union   318, 339–40, 340n66, 341–45, 348, 350
Columbian Orator   19
Committees for Communist Correspondence   51–52
communism/communist movement   43, 52–53, 56, 61, 76, 176, 227, 344, 361
Communist Club (US)   96, 96n142, 97
Communist International   371
The Communist Manifesto (Marx and Engels)   50, 52, 56, 60, 72–73, 85, 226, 264, 276, 304, 313, 316, 364 (*see also Manifesto of the Communist Party*)
Communist League   52, 56–57, 60–62, 88, 282 (*see also* Address of March 1850 Central Authority)
Communist Party USA   312–15, 315n88, 372
comparative analysis   2, 4, 6, 8–9, 11–13, 120, 158, 175, 276, 301, 355, 368
Compromise of   1850 68, 70–71, 75, 118
The Condition of the Working Class (Engels)   45, 165
Confederacy/Confederates   13–14, 55, 110–11, 114–15, 124, 128, 131, 138, 150–54, 156–57, 162, 162n4, 164, 167–68, 170–71, 173, 177, 180–84, 188, 189n85, 190–91, 198–200, 202, 207–08, 212, 217, 220, 222, 230, 231n41, 242–44, 246–47, 249, 257, 267, 272, 277, 284, 287–89, 350, 355–58, 362–63
Confederate emancipation   246, 246n94, 247
Confiscation Act, First   138–39, 145n128, 189
Confiscation Act, Second   189, 189n88, 190, 190n90 192, 195–97, 199
Congress   24, 68, 70, 73–74, 85, 94, 119, 137, 175, 177–78, 188–90, 192–94, 196, 204, 209–10, 215, 217n1, 218, 231–32, 234, 238–39, 248, 251–52, 258, 261, 266, 306, 337
    Thirty-Seventh   194, 215
    Thirty-Ninth   258, 268
constitutional monarchy   27, 29, 31, 37, 51, 63
Cooke, Henry   335–36
cotton production   48, 83, 91, 98–99

Covey, Edward   20–21, 21n17
Crisis (New York)   368
Critical Race Theory   6–7
Cuba   379–81

Dana, Charles   58, 174–75
Davis, Jefferson   132, 230–31, 246, 246n94
Davis, William C.   242
Dayton, William L.   75
Debs, Eugene V.   371
Declaration of Independence   6, 6n17, 7, 23–24, 36, 71, 176, 243, 277, 308
Delany, Martin   220
democracy   8, 38, 55, 74, 301, 304, 309, 346
Democratic Party   75, 77, 88, 96, 122, 170, 182, 192, 207–209, 211, 220, 235–240, 242, 249, 265, 272, 305, 307, 313, 315, 339–340
Democracy in America (Tocqueville)   40, 66
Deutsches Haus conference   94–95
dictatorship of the proletariat   142, 372–73
District of Columbia   101, 114, 121, 137, 175, 177, 180, 188, 193–94, 196, 199n114, 235, 335–36, 340, 342, 347
Divine Providence   17–18, 20, 51, 81, 112–113, 123, 141, 279, 286
Douai, Adolph   94–96, 99–100, 101n156
Double V Campaign   219, 219n4
Douglas, Andrew   311–12, 314, 375–76, 381
Douglas, Stephen A.   73
Douglass, Anna   111n21
Douglass, Charles   222, 287
Douglass, Frederick   345
    1848 presidential election and   70
    4 July   1852 speech and 71–72
    1852 presidential election and   75n65, 92–93
    1856 presidential election and   75–76, 92–93
    1860 presidential election and   92–93, 95–96, 93n125, 237
    1864 presidential election and   232–33, 235, 239, 242, 245
    3 August   1857 speech and 78–81, 91–92, 133
    4 July speech 1862, 'the Slaveholder's Rebellion,'   185
    13 January 1864 speech 'The Mission of the War'   232, 238

INDEX

abolition, role in   102–103, 163, 188–89, 201–02

the abolitionists and   24–27, 53, 77, 112–13, 138, 163, 164m 169, 185, 228, 237, 250, 288, 308, 318

Assing, Otille and   106*n*2, 113*n*29, 158, 158*n*166

autobiographies   5, 9, 17, 26–27, 34, 77, 84, 124, 296, 318, 354

Black enlistment/arming of Blacks and   108, 110, 117, 138, 214, 218, 221, 223, 238, 248, 356

Black military recruitment and   218–22, 222*n*12, 228–32, 284, 287*n*20

Black suffrage and   234, 238, 241, 250–51, 254–55, 257, 260–61, 275, 342, 346

Bonaparte's coup and   71

border states and   115, 133, 139–40, 163, 175–76

Brown, John and   68, 70, 74, 77, 84–87, 89–90, 97–98, 102–03, 219, 283, 297, 314, 364 364*n*32

Butler, Benjamin and   112, 225

Chartist demonstration, April   1848 64–65

China and   72

civil liberties   141–42

class collaborationism   59*n*17, 282, 293, 299, 318, 330–31, 335, 337–38, 338*n*58, 339–40, 342–43, 347, 349–50

class conflict   330, 336–37, 342

Colored National Convention and   1864 237–39

Colored National Labor Union and   318, 339–45, 348

communists (Reds) and   66, 320–21, 323–24, 329–30, 333–34, 342, 349

Compromise of   1850 and 70, 118

Confederate emancipation and   246–47

Confiscation Act, First and   139, 188

Covey, Edward and   20–21

Declaration of Independence and   176, 185, 277

early years   17–22

early years and Marx   34, 35, 36, 39, 43, 53, 277–80

elections and   61, 63, 68, 70, 92–93, 245, 313, 323, 326

emancipation and   168, 188, 218, 221, 317

Emancipation Proclamation and   200–01, 212–14, 218, 220–21

emigration and   101, 105–06, 106*n*2

Engels on the Civil War and   161

English/European response to the War and   121–22, 126, 128–29, 134, 148, 151, 154–56, 156*n*161, 158–59, 166–67, 212, 227

English middle class and   166–67, 227, 242

English working class and   156–57, 159, 167, 212, 213, 227, 280

Equal Rights Party and   289*n*22

European history and origin of racial prejudices   164–65

European Spring and   55–68, 103, 106, 269–70, 317, 349

expansionism of slavery and   107–08, 132, 135, 137

Feuerbach, Ludwig   158

Fifthteenth Amendment and   268

Fifty-Fourth Massachusetts Infantry and   220, 222, 228

Fourteenth Amendment and   261

Free Soil Party and   70, 70*n*46, 75*n*65, 93

Frémont, John C. and   75, 143–46, 161, 177, 232–33, 235, 313

Frémont's proclamation and   139–44, 232–33

force/violence and   20–21, 24, 26–27, 30–31, 65, 67, 67*n*38, 68, 74, 77, 80, 84–85, 90, 97–98, 103, 126, 180, 230, 317, 326, 330–31, 337

Fugitive Slave Act and   70–71, 74, 97

fugitive slaves and   111–12, 116

Great Britain visit   27, 45, 63, 278

Haiti and   364

Indians and   164, 176

Irish/Irish Americans and   27–30, 45, 124, 164, 229, 318, 335

Johnson, Andrew and   249–50, 253, 260, 266–267

Kansas-Nebraska Act   74

labour and   335–42, 346, 349

liberal   3, 3*n*8, 43, 66–67, 69, 239, 255, 258, 267, 274, 280, 293, 311, 338, 340, 342, 348–49

Liberty Party and   70, 75

INDEX

Lincoln, Abraham and   54–55, 93, 100–01, 107, 115, 121, 139–40, 154, 163, 172, 178, 186–88, 196, 200–01, 214, 219–20, 230–35, 239, 245, 249, 271, 271n184
McClellan, George and   146, 146n130, 161–63, 176–77, 186–87, 188–89, 214, 235, 239, 242
Marshall of the District of Columbia   347
Marx on the Civil War and   169, 173, 177, 178–79, 203–04, 212–14, 261, 267, 274, 277, 284–90, 300
military analysis and   116–18, 138, 138n101, 167–68, 169, 170, 172, 175–77, 179, 185, 214, 237, 245–46, 248
Missouri Compromise and   73
moral suasion and   24–26, 57, 74n64, 80, 337
natural rights/law and   6, 19, 36, 49, 51, 81, 238, 277, 297, 297n40, 319
New Bedford and   22–23
New York Daily Tribune and   58, 62, 117, 158
northwestern states and   118–19
pacifism   30–31, 32, 65, 67, 67n38, 68, 80, 85, 90, 98, 103, 107, 221, 230
Paris Commune and   81, 223, 270–71, 293, 297, 299, 317, 320–26, 328–30, 333–36, 338, 343, 346, 349–50
Paris uprising June 1848 and   269, 270, 298
peasant emancipation in Russia and   91, 220–21
philosophy of reform   79, 79n80, 80–81, 297–98
poor whites and   108, 125, 135, 251, 319
Port Royal, South Carolina and   257 292–93
post-abolition   164, 179–80
property and   22, 25–26, 28, 31, 50, 50n124, 51, 69–70, 79, 111, 141, 180, 267, 293, 300, 319, 324–26, 335, 338, 346
race and class and   4, 83–84, 99, 124–25, 127, 135–36, 263, 317–19, 337–38, 346, 350
race and race prejudice   12, 124, 134–35, 135n91, 164–65, 166n13, 186, 244, 248, 251, 253, 263–64, 290, 318–19, 360n24, 362

Radical Abolitionist Party   75, 77
Radical Democracy Convention and   233
Reconstruction and   82, 217, 254–55, 257, 266–67, 276, 293, 295–96, 298, 300, 302n57, 346, 350
reform liberal   298, 338
religion and   19–20, 39, 165
republicanism/republican institutions and   3n8, 28–29, 67, 321–23, 329–31, 333–35, 338n58, 339, 349
Republican Party and   75–76, 93, 144, 233, 239, 268–69, 271, 273, 294–95, 298, 335, 339, 350
revolutionary liberal   3, 14, 81–82, 87n106, 180, 263, 284, 298, 298n42, 310, 377
secession   97–99, 102, 104, 107, 120, 132
Second Amendment and   230, 250
Seneca Falls and   67
Seward, William and   144–45, 151, 162
"The Slave's Appeal to Great Britain"   211–12
slavery and   2, 4, 13–14, 17, 19, 21, 24–29, 29n41, 30, 32–33, 36, 39, 41, 43, 49, 53, 57n10, 63–64, 67n38, 69, 71–76, 78n75, 79, 82–83, 90, 93, 100, 106–09, 113, 116–17, 125–26, 128, 135, 137–38, 141, 144–45, 148, 153, 153n155, 155, 164, 167–69, 171, 178–80, 185–88, 196, 201, 204, 212, 219, 222n12, 223, 231–32, 234, 237–40, 245, 250, 296, 317–18, 335, 342, 348
slavery as the cause of the Civil War   106–09, 128, 135, 137, 155, 185–86, 187–88, 243
strikes and   335–40, 342, 346–47, 349
tariff   121, 126
Thirteenth Amendment and   238–40, 250
trade unions and   227, 336, 338–40, 347, 349
Trent Affair and   153, 153n155, 154–55, 159, 166
Turner, Nat and   70, 80, 117
United States Constitution and   69–71, 78, 78n75, 106, 111, 141, 204, 230, 238–40, 243, 245
white plebeian support for slavery and   125, 318–19

white workers and   21, 84, 108, 119, 124, 127, 130, 263, 277–78, 318–19, 336, 346, 350, 362
writ of *habeas corpus* and   141
(*see also, Narrative of the Life of Frederick Douglass*)
Douglass, Lewis   222, 228–29, 238, 302n57, 340n66, 342, 342n71
Douglass' Monthly   9, 93, 100, 105, 108, 111, 115–117, 120, 125, 137–138, 138n101, 139, 139n108, 140, 144, 148, 151, 153, 153n155, 154, 157–158, 161, 167–68, 170, 175, 177, 180, 184–85, 188, 190, 192, 193, 200, 204, 210, 210n141, 211, 213, 217–19, 221–23, 225, 227, 229–31, 356
Downing, George   341
Downs, Gregory   217n1, 247n100, 265n161, 269n175, 272n190, 286n17, 298n42
Draper, Hal   9, 10n29, 11n32, 40n85, 205n127, 226, 365
Dred Scott v. Sandford   68, 78, 78n76, 84, 86, 101, 220, 240, 209, 306
Du Bois, W.E.B.   213n147, 300–01, 301n53, 302–03, 304, 309, 341, 358, 362, 368–69
Duluth, Minnesota   310
Dunayevskaya, Raya   6n16, 290n25

Eccarius Georg   226
The Economist   121, 123, 125–26, 128
Edwards, Kyle A.   15, 317n1
Egerton, Douglas   92n124, 217n1, 220, 229n34
The Eighteenth Brumaire of Louis Bonaparte (Marx)   59, 66, 68, 72, 287, 291, 324, 369
elections   6, 24, 60–62, 68, 75, 84, 92, 119, 241, 244, 322–23, 323n14, 326 (*See also* suffrage)
  1848 presidential election   70
  1852 presidential election   75n65, 76
  1856 presidential election   75–77, 92, 96, 143
  1860 presidential election   92, 103, 237
  1864 presidential election   232, 235–37, 239–40, 242, 249
Electoral College   77, 252
Emancipation League   163–64
Emancipation Proclamation   12, 14, 136, 200–02, 206, 212–15, 217–18, 221–22, 229–30, 232, 234, 240, 248, 249n105, 275, 285, 287, 291–92, 306, 356–57
Emerson, Ralph Waldo   88
Engels, Frederick
  1862 congressional election and   207
  1864 presidential election and   236, 245
  anti-Irish prejudices and   165–66
  armed struggle and   59
  Black suffrage and   251–52
  Brown, John and   91, 283, 298, 355–56
  Chartist demonstration, April 1848 65
  Confederate emancipation and   246–47
  Douglass on the Civil War and   161, 173, 190, 215, 276–77
  early years   43–46
  early years and Douglass   50
  elections   61, 292, 313–14
  Georgia, military significance   173–74
  German Americans and   172–73
  Great Railroad Strike of 1877 and   272
  Harpers Ferry and   91
  International Workingmen's Association and   320
  Jamaica and   251, 255
  Johnson, Andrew and   251
  King Jr., Martin Luther and   4–5
  Lincoln, Abraham and   190
  Marx disagreements   136, 193–94, 196, 197–99, 203, 207–08, 214–15, 285
  Marx partnership and   7–8, 43–45, 62, 67, 90, 105, 114, 147, 198–99, 224, 290–91
  military analysis   7, 109, 114–15, 117, 137–38, 146–47, 171–74, 181–83, 187, 235–36, 242, 246–47, 247n100, 248, 284–85
  n-word and   10, 91, 251
  Negroes and   224, 273
  parliamentary cretinism   61, 65, 242n80, 247–48, 281, 292
  party work and   51
  pessimism   7, 181–82, 184, 190, 200, 206–07, 210, 215, 234–35, 247, 303
  poor whites and   183, 251
  proletarian internationalism and   45
  property and   50, 297, 313, 379
  race and its invention   166
  secession and   99, 101, 119
  slave agency and   91, 99, 283

slave/proletariat difference   50, 69, 276–77, 279–80, 293–94, 299, 311, 378–79
suffrage   234, 241, 251
Trent affair and   150, 153, 153*n*154
U.S. labour party and   273–74
'white trash' and   183
Willich, August   88
world revolution and   381
England   27, 30, 32–33, 36, 38, 44–46, 55, 65, 89–90, 92, 99, 121–22, 127–29, 148–59, 164, 166–67, 202, 212, 227, 243, 273, 317, 322, 344, 357, 367, 370
Enmale, Richard   9*n*25, 352
European Spring   5, 8, 12–13, 16, 52, 55, 57, 59, 63, 66–68, 71–72, 111, 142, 172, 239, 241, 269–70, 274, 280–82, 284, 287, 292–93, 297, 304, 309, 313, 349 (*see also* 1848–49 European Revolutions)
The Examiner   121, 126

Fagan, Benjamin   64, 210*n*141, 282*m*12
Fanon, Frantz   369
Federal Reserve Board   306–07
Feldman, Noah   286*m*17
Feuerbach, Ludwig   4, 46–47, 47*n*97, 51, 113*n*29, 158
Fifteenth Amendment   258*n*137, 268–69, 275*n*2, 286, 307
Fifty-Fourth Massachusetts Infantry   219–20, 222, 228–29
Floyd, George   305, 310
Foner, Eric   78*n*75, 138–39, 232, 234*n*51, 235, 258*n*137, 260*n*142, 261, 265, 273, 339
Foner, Philip S.   9, 18, 260*n*143, 268, 295, 339–42, 347
Forster, John   128, 167
Fort Monroe   112, 141, 357
Fort Sumter   13, 43, 49, 89, 99–100, 102, 104–07, 110, 113–14, 119, 125, 147–48, 163*n*7, 212, 227, 247, 274, 277–78, 283–84, 286, 356, 359, 363–64
Fourteenth Amendment   261
France   33, 36, 38, 51, 55–56, 59, 63–64, 67, 69–71, 90, 148–49, 152, 202, 207, 317, 321–22, 326, 329–30, 333–35, 349
Franco-Prussian War   319–22, 324, 333
Frankel, Léo   322
Frederick Wilhelm IV   51

Fredericksburg, Virginia   213
Freedmen's Bureau   254
freedom of speech   65, 91, 141, 346
freedom of the press   27, 36, 38, 65, 91, 142*n*115
free labour   24, 82–83, 96, 100, 133, 143, 255–56, 257*n*134, 302, 335, 338–40, 349
Frémont, John C.   75–76, 92–93, 96, 117, 139–44, 144*n*124, 145, 145*n*128, 146, 146*n*131, 147, 151, 161, 171, 177, 232–33, 234*n*51, 235–37, 283, 287, 313
French Revolution   2, 33, 38, 45, 55, 63, 173, 207
French Third Republic   319–23
Fugitive Slave Act (1793)   192, 240*n*72
Fugitive Slave Act (1850)   70–71, 74, 74*n*64, 97, 126, 192
Fugitive Slave Clause   24, 70

Gaido, Daniel   321, 323, 326*n*22
Gallagher, Gary   112*n*26, 189*n*85, 193*n*98
Galveston, Texas   355
Garibaldi, Giuseppe   98, 114
Garnet, Henry Highland   26, 86, 220
Garrison, William Lloyd   8*n*19, 23–26, 28–31, 47, 51, 63, 69, 75, 88, 113, 118, 163, 163*n*7, 239, 250, 278, 313
Garrisonian   23–25, 27, 32, 46, 53, 57, 57*n*10, 63, 68, 80, 169, 278, 281, 317
General strike of   1877 271–72, 294, 294*n*32
Genovese, Eugene D.   134*n*90
Genovese, Elizabeth Fox-   134*n*90
Georgia   24, 164, 173–74, 179, 184, 191–92, 197, 214, 235, 284–85, 293*n*28, 294, 342
German Americans   18, 89, 94–97, 100–01, 118, 129, 133–34, 136, 146*n*131, 172–73, 213, 237, 260*n*144, 262–63, 336
The German Ideology   39, 47, 378
Germany   33–34, 36, 40, 44, 51, 56–57, 59, 61, 73, 129, 236, 241, 262, 278, 281, 320, 322
Gettysburg, Battle of   202, 224
Gettysburg Address   54, 67, 71, 232
Geuss, Raymond   297*n*40
Gladstone, William   211
Grant, Ulysses S.   173, 224–25, 236, 242, 247–49, 271, 273*n*191, 289*n*22, 294–95, 335, 355, 357
Great Britain   5, 27, 29, 29*n*41, 63, 121, 126, 133, 205, 212, 280, 371

Great Railroad Strike of 1877 347
Greeley, Horace 58, 151, 155, 157, 157*n*165, 175
Green, Shields, 87
Greener, Richard Theodore (RTG) 343–45, 347
Grenada 378
Griffiths (Crofts), Julia 153*n*155, 225, 232

Haiti 89, 105–106, 106*n*2, 109, 111, 194–95, 358, 364, 364*n*32
Haitian Revolution 55, 63, 258, 358, 364, 364*n*32, 369
Hale, John 240*n*72
Halleck, General Henry 173, 182, 182*n*60
Hamilton, Thomas 41–43, 49
Hammond, James 83–84, 91, 99, 124, 134, 164, 244, 244*n*87, 362
Hannah-Jones, Nikole 308*n*67, 309–10
Harney, George Julian 65, 213
Harpers Ferry 84, 87, 87*n*106, 88–91, 91*n*122, 92, 97, 99, 102, 283, 298, 364
Hayes, Rutherford B. 272, 295, 347–48, 357
Hegel, Georg 4, 35–39, 43, 47*n*97, 48–49, 63, 78, 205, 240, 278–79, 378
Hess, Moses 34–35
Highgate, Edmonia 239*n*68
historical materialism 7, 136, 141, 200, 236, 282, 285, 287*n*19, 291
The Holy Family (Marx and Engels) 40*n*85, 40*n*87, 44, 47
Homestead Act 94, 94*n*131, 193
Hopkins, Charles 257–58, 258*n*136
Hsieh, Wayne Wei-Siang 183*n*66, 184, 191*n*95, 234*n*54
human emancipation 40–42, 44, 46, 53, 67, 69, 81, 83, 92, 102, 227, 274, 279, 299, 365, 379
Hund, Wolfgang 11*n*35, 50*n*102, 166*n*14, 245*n*88, 358–70, 375, 376
Hunter, General David 197, 200, 223
Hutchinson Family Singers 161–62, 170

Independent working-class political action 60–61, 262, 270, 274, 339, 347–48, 350–51
Inquirer (London) 178
International Workingmen's Association 10, 157, 242–243, 245–247, 249, 259–60, 262, 265, 269, 272, 291, 296, 320, 322, 336, 344, 351, 366–67
Ireland and the Irish 27–30, 32*n*53, 46, 124, 166, 362, 366–67, 370–72
Irish Americans 12, 18, 96, 124, 133–134, 208–09, 229, 265, 318, 362

Jamaica 62, 251, 255–56, 353
James, C.L.R. 369, 373–74
The Jewish Question (Marx) 40–41, 364–65, 369
Johnson, Andrew 13, 124, 223, 233, 233*n*49, 233*n*50, 249–54, 258–59, 259*n*140, 260, 260*n*142, 260*n*144, 261–62, 262*n*152, 266, 266*n*163, 267, 267*n*168, 294
Johnson, Lyndon Baines 313–14
Johnson, Walter 99*n*148
Joseph, Peniel E 4*n*13
Journal of African Marxists 376
June uprising in Paris 1848 59–60, 65–67, 81, 269–270, 280, 293, 298, 320

Kansas-Nebraska Act 68, 73–75, 84, 122, 283
Kant, Immanuel, 36
Karp, Matt 205–06, 298–99
Katz, Phillip 327, 346
Kearny, Philip 182, 182*n*59
Keith, LeeAnna 169*n*23
Kelly, Brian 354*n*9
Kentucky 27, 115, 115*n*34, 133, 139, 145*n*128, 170, 173, 181, 184, 191, 225, 318
King, Martin Luther, Jr. 1, 2, 1*n*1, 4–5, 7, 275–76, 277, 292, 296, 303–04, 311, 313, 375–76, 381
   Douglass and 275, 304, 311, 315
   Abraham Lincoln and 275
   Malcolm X and 314
   Marx and 4–5, 311–12
Kriege, Hermann 52, 73, 94*n*131
Kugelman, Ludwig 324
Kulikoff, Alan 18*n*8

labour 13–14, 82, 133, 135–36, 250, 262–63, 318, 328, 331, 335, 339, 351
labour movement 328, 336–37, 345, 349–51, 368
labour unions 225–27, 317, 338–39, 341–42
Lafargue, François 261
Lafargue, Paul 11, 261, 261*n*148, 365

land reform   14, 52, 94*n*131, 257–58, 266, 296, 298, 303, 339
Langston, John Mercer   220, 250
Lassalle, Ferdinand   11, 11*n*32, 179, 195*n*105, 365–66
Lawson, Charles   20
League of the Just   46, 52
Lecomte, General Claude   327
Lee, General Robert E.   182, 185, 189*n*85, 191, 200, 224, 242, 247, 247*n*100, 248–249, 355, 357
Lenin, V.I.   3*n*11, 4, 61*n*20, 312, 349, 355, 370–73, 375, 377, 377*n*67, 378
Leon, Abram   369–70, 375
lesser evil/splitting the vote conundrum   61, 93, 95, 235, 237, 313, 339–40
Levine, Bruce   131*n*77, 146*n*131, 162*n*4, 168*n*18, 183*n*64, 211*n*143, 247*n*96, 257, 293*n*29, 363*n*30
Levine, Robert S.   250*n*111, 266*n*163, 266*n*164, 267*n*168
liberals/liberalism   2–3, 3*n*8, 8–9 14–15, 31, 33–34, 38, 41, 43, 45, 53, 56, 60–61, 63, 66–67, 69, 71*n*49, 79–81, 84*n*94, 122, 175, 239, 304, 307, 310, 319, 338, 346, 350
Liberator   29–30, 239
Liberty Party   24–25, 70, 75, 110*n*17 (see also Radical Abolitionist Party)
Life and Times of Frederick Douglass   296*n*36
Lincoln, Abraham   351
    1860 presidential election and   13, 55, 92–97, 95, 123, 209, 283
    14 August   1862 meeting with Black ministers 196–97
    1864 presidential election and   10, 233–34, 236–37, 239–40, 242, 245, 249, 351
    6 March   1862 speech 175, 177
    Anaconda Plan and   162*n*4
    assassination   124, 249
    Black soldiers and   108, 110, 180, 189, 218, 222–23, 223*n*14, 232, 287
    civil liberties and   142, 142*n*115, 234
    Columbian Orator   19
    Confiscation Act, First   138–39
    Dred Scott and   101
    Emancipation Proclamation and   136, 199–206, 212–14, 217–20, 222, 229, 232, 234, 248, 285, 287, 291–92

expansionism of slavery and   108, 108*n*10, 128, 135
First Inaugural   101–02, 107
Frémont, John C.   117, 143–44, 146
Frémont's proclamation and   139–40, 142, 145*n*128, 232–33
fugitive slaves   111–12
Gettysburg Address   54–55, 67, 71, 232
Hammond, James and   83
invasion of/intervention in Mexico (Tripartite Alliance invasion) and   148, 150
Johnson, Andrew and   249–50
letter of thanks to English trade unions 19 January 1864 226–227, 245
letter to the International Workingmen's Association   245, 291
New York Daily Tribune   58–59, 153, 158, 174, 291
Order of Retaliation   230–31
Reconstruction and   188, 317, 232–33
republican internationalist   55
secession and   97, 100–102, 102*n*161, 103, 107, 284
Second Inaugural   77, 248, 305–06
Trent affair   152*n*150, 153–54
Lissagaray, Prosper Olivier   321
Locke, John   36, 50*n*104, 345
Loggins, Jared   5*n*14, 311–12, 312*n*81, 314, 375–76, 381
London Emancipation Society   291
London Times,   121–122, 128, 152, 157, 212, 224, 322
Lord Acton   255*n*129
Lord Palmerston   65, 128, 129*n*72, 148–49, 156
Losurdo, Domenico   43*n*91, 80*n*83, 296*n*39
Louis-Philippe   51, 52, 55, 64, 328, 334
Lovett, William   32, 32*n*51
Luxemburg, Rosa   370–71

McClellan, George   145*n*128, 146, 146*n*130, 161–62, 162*n*4, 169–71, 173, 176–77, 181–82, 182*n*59, 184, 184*n*71, 185, 187–89, 189*n*88, 192, 197–200, 200, 211, 214, 235, 237, 239, 242
McCurry, Stephanie   120, 246*n*94
McKivigan, John R.   9, 29*n*41, 71*n*49, 106*n*2, 175*n*40, 184*n*73, 294*n*32, 347*n*85

INDEX

McPherson, James 162*n*4, 189, 229*n*33
Malcolm X 80*n*81, 258, 313–14, 314*n*86, 315, 341, 375–77
Manchester, England 44–46, 62, 90, 99, 119, 199, 226–27, 246, 367
Mandela, Nelson 380
Manifesto of the Communist Party 56, 69, 76, 80–81
Manning, Chandra 193*n*98, 222*n*12
Marie, or Slavery in the United States (Gustave de Beaumont) 40, 361
Martin, Jr. Waldo 3*n*8, 267, 338*n*58, 338, 338*n*58, 339
Massachusetts 22–24, 26, 85, 197, 219, 221, 228–29, 229*n*34, 254
Marx, Eleanor "Tussy" (daughter) 110, 147, 224, 367
Marx, Henriette 227
Marx, Jenny (wife) 51, 111*n*21, 147, 227, 365
Marx, Jenny (daughter) 51, 111*n*21, 147, 199
Marx, Karl
  1848–9 revolutions and 55–60, 64, 66, 68, 71, 103, 111, 142, 223, 226, 241–243, 247–48, 261, 280–81, 292–93, 309, 320, 330
  1856 presidential election and 143
  1860 presidential election and 96–97
  1862 congressional election and 207–10, 229, 290–92
  1864 presidential election and 233, 236, 242
  abolition and 52–53, 57, 116, 126, 136, 181, 192, 194, 209, 265, 350–51
  alienation and 82
  Black enlistment and 195, 218, 220, 223–24, 284
  border states and 109, 132–33, 136, 139–40, 174, 192, 196, 197, 202, 215
  Brown, John/Harpers Ferry and 90, 91–92, 99, 221, 355–56
  Chartist demonstration, April 1848 65, 280
  chattel slavery and 5, 53
  civil liberties and 69, 141–42, 152
  Civil War and 2, 5, 6*n*16, 105, 109–10, 114–15, 121–22, 125, 128–29, 132–33, 137–38, 143, 147–49, 151–52, 155, 159, 191–92, 217, 224, 226–27, 231, 235–36, 243–44, 247, 253, 259, 264–65, 284–90, 351
  class struggle and 58, 80–81, 131–32, 221, 282, 326–27, 332
  Congress, Thirty-Seventh 193–95, 215
  constitutions and 37–38, 69, 74, 78, 132, 134, 140, 193, 240–41, 306, 332
  Democratic Party and 192, 208–09, 211
  democracy/democratic movement and 8, 38, 40, 42–43, 57, 60, 155, 236, 240, 278–79, 286, 331
  Douglass on the Civil War and 169, 171, 176–77, 178–79, 192–93, 196–98, 202–03, 203–05, 215, 261, 274, 276, 277, 284–91
  Dred Scott 78
  early years 3, 33–34, 67
  early years and Douglass 34, 35, 36, 37, 39, 41, 43, 47, 48–49, 51, 53, 277–80
  elections and 60–62, 120, 122, 130*n*76, 143, 207–10, 236, 241–42, 261, 281, 313–14
  Emancipation Proclamation and 14, 202–05, 209, 215, 218, 221
  Engels disagreements 136, 193–94, 196, 197–99, 203, 207–08, 214–15, 285
  Engels partnership and 7–8, 43–45, 62, 67, 90, 105, 114, 147, 198–99, 224, 290–91
  English/European response to the War and 121–22, 125–28, 134, 149, 152, 155–57, 171, 225–27, 287–88
  expansionism of slavery and 123, 131–33, 137
  Feuerbach, Ludwig and 4, 46–47, 47*n*97, 51, 113*n*29, 158
  free trade and 126
  Frémont, John C. and 143–44, 145*n*128, 145–47, 151, 171, 232–33
  Frémont's proclamation and 139–40, 143, 232–33
  Garibaldi, Giuseppe 114
  Great Railroad Strike of 1877 and 348
  Grundrisse 82
  historical materialism 7, 58, 64, 127, 136, 141, 202, 204, 205–06, 236, 285, 317
  International Workingmen's Association and 157, 242–43, 245–47, 249, 260, 262, 267, 291, 294, 296, 320, 322, 331–32, 351
  invasion of/intervention in Mexico (Tripartite Alliance invasion) and 148–49, 152, 159

Irish question and   263–64, 366–67, 370–71, 372, 374
Irish Americans and   208–09, 229
Jamaica and   353
his Jewishness   33–34
Johnson, Andrew and   249–51, 259, 261–62, 294
Kriege, Hermann,   51–52, 73
land confiscation and   14, 292
letter to Lincoln on his re-election   242–45, 245n89, 262, 290, 351
Lincoln, Abraham and   6, 122–23, 127, 130, 139–40, 143, 149, 151–54, 161, 169–70, 171, 192–93, 197, 200, 203–06, 214–15, 218, 221, 231, 233, 235–36, 242–45, 249–50, 262, 285–88, 290, 351
London trade union meeting   26 March 1864 225–27, 242, 245
McClellan, George and   145n128, 169, 169n22, 170–71, 189, 192, 211
May (1871) Address of the General Council of the IWA   320
Memphis and   260–61
military analysis   109–10, 115, 117, 137–38, 143, 148, 170–71, 191–92, 217–218, 224–25, 236, 248 (see also Douglass, Engels, Marx, military matters)
Negro/Negroes and   166, 192, 207, 209, 224, 229, 262, 272, 340, 351, 372
'n-word' and   11, 180, 195, 195n105, 198, 206, 209, 239, 365–66
newspaper writings   10, 58, 62, 106, 111, 114, 117, 121, 127–29, 131, 133–34, 136, 139, 142–44, 147, 147n133, 148–52, 155–56, 158–59, 167, 174–75, 217, 227, 301 (see also *New York Daily Tribune*, *Die Presse*)
northwestern states, role of   118–19, 123, 143, 209
Paris Commune and   14, 320–24, 326–28, 330–32, 334, 343, 349
party work and   51–53, 94, 282–83 (See also Marx party)
peasant emancipation in Russia and   90–92, 221
Peninsular campaign and   181–82, 185
Phillips, Wendell and   197, 296

philosophy   39–40, 44–46, 278, 297
Polish uprising 22 January 1863 and   223–24, 226
poor whites and   124–25, 125n62, 129–31, 183, 198, 249, 253, 264, 290, 362, 366
press censorship and   36, 59, 120
Proclamation on Poland   226–27
proletarian internationalism and   226–27
property and   38, 39, 69–70, 82, 279, 297, 313, 363
race/racism and   40, 49–50, 108, 124–25, 134–36, 186, 209, 210, 243–44, 253, 262–64, 273, 289, 341, 250, 289, 310, 317, 351, 358–63, 370
Reconstruction and   251–52, 267–68, 291, 295, 348, 368
religion and   39, 41
Republican Party and   122–123, 143, 233, 283
revolutionary restraint and   320
secessionist movement and   104, 119–120, 123, 126, 128, 131–32, 139
Seward, William and   143–45, 151–52, 152n150, 237
slave agency and   83, 91, 99, 221
slave insurrection/revolution and   110–11, 116, 126, 218, 235
slavery and   4, 35–36, 39, 43, 43n91, 48, 48n98, 49, 49n99, 62, 69, 76, 79, 82–84, 94, 99, 101, 121–23, 125, 127–28, 131–34, 139, 141, 143, 192, 195, 231, 243, 265, 353, 356
slavery and capitalism and   48, 79, 82–83, 98, 108, 141, 282
slavery as the cause of the Civil War   122, 131–32, 139
suffrage and   38, 119, 234, 239, 241, 269, 292
Taiping Rebellion and   72
tariff and   126, 154
Trent affair and   150–53, 155, 159
Union military strategy and   110, 117–18, 184
United States Constitution and   203–04, 221, 240–41243, 285–86
U.S. history and   36, 43, 117–19, 122–23, 132, 203, 206, 271–72, 279, 294

INDEX 413

U.S. politics and   36, 38–39, 40, 42–43, 96–97, 119, 122–23, 129, 143, 152, 236–37, 241, 244, 251, 268, 272, 303
Wade, Benjamin and   264
white plebeian support for slavery and   83–84, 123–24, 129–31, 198, 310
white workers and   244, 262, 273, 290, 354, 363
Willich, August and   88, 89n113
worker-peasant alliance and   208, 273, 330
visit to England   46
(see also *Capital*)
Marx-Engels Collected Works   9, 9n23, 10, 353
Karl Marx and Frederick Engels: The Civil War in the United States   9n25, 10
'Marx party'   52, 56, 59, 62, 76, 84, 93, 96, 99–100, 103, 108, 116, 130, 131n77, 163n7, 195, 206, 224, 226–27, 234, 237, 241–42, 252, 252n117, 259, 273–74, 283–84, 286, 287n19, 290–91, 303, 324, 357, 363 (see also Communist League)
Mason, James   150, 152, 152n150, 153–57
materialist conception of history   7, 48–49, 53, 136, 285, 363
Matthews, Donald R, and Prothro, James W,   303, 304n61
Medford, Edna Greene   235n57
Men and Manners in America (Thomas Hamilton)   41
Merriman, John   323n14, 326, 334n48
Messer-Kruse, Timothy   289n22
Mexico   28, 28n38, 148–50, 159, 373
invasion of/intervention in Mexico (Tripartite Alliance invasion)   148–50, 152
Mexican-American War   28, 68, 70
Military Reconstruction Act (1867)   317
Militia Act of   1862 189–90, 195
Mill, John Stuart   3, 8, 35, 66, 71n49, 122, 255, 255n129, 280, 294
Douglass and   255, 294
Mills, Charles   71n52, 302n55, 358n20, 377, 377n71, 378, 378n72
Missouri   70, 73–74, 86, 90–91, 117–18, 139, 142, 170, 185, 213, 232, 237, 246, 270, 308, 308n68, 342

Missouri Compromise   70, 73–74, 185–86, 308, 308n68
Monroe Doctrine   149
Montesquieu, Charles Louis   3n9, 299
Montgomery, David   350
moral suasion   24–26. 57, 74n64, 80, 84, 337
Morrill Tariff   126
Murray, Anna   22, 111n21
Murray, Williamson   183n66, 184, 191n95, 234n54
My Bondage and My Freedom   17, 77, 84, 87n106, 124, 127, 318
Myers, Peter   3n8, 50–51, 267n166, 271n184, 338n58, 345, 348
'n-word'   10–12, 17, 91, 251, 352, 365–66
Narrative of the Life of Frederick Douglass   26, 26n33, 27, 47

National Labor Union   339–40, 340n66, 350
Native Americans   12, 29, 40, 164, 176, 294
The Nation   265
Negro   11, 17, 27–28, 34–35, 48, 48n98, 49, 62, 73, 94, 106, 112, 124–25, 132–34, 164–66, 172, 181, 192, 194, 196, 207, 209–10, 220, 224, 229, 243, 246–47, 302, 302n54, 303, 319, 340, 351, 359–60, 373–74
Neue Rheinische Zeitung (NRZ)   57, 57n10, 58–59, 63, 66, 281
Die Neue Zeit   237
New National Era   59n17, 268–69, 293. 327, 335, 340, 342–44, 347, 349
New Orleans   174, 180–81, 183, 183n66, 184–85, 191–92, 225, 252, 252n118, 289n23, 318
New York Daily Tribune (NYDT)   9, 58–59, 62, 78, 83, 90, 90n120, 99, 106, 111, 114, 117, 121, 127–29, 131, 134, 142, 148–49, 151–52, 155–59, 167, 174–75, 197, 217, 227, 245, 281–82, 288, 291, 301
New York City draft riots   229
New York Herald   170
New York Independent   212
New York Times   6–7, 90, 139, 197n109, 262, 265, 289n22, 300–01, 303–04, 305, 307–09, 311, 315, 322, 380
New Yorker Demokrat   96, 100
Nimtz, August H.   3n10, 10n29, 15, 295, 327, 359–60
The North Star   50, 63, 66

Novack, George   12, 17, 251–252, 301*n*53, 315*n*88, 341

O'Connell, Daniel   28–29
Oakes, James   69, 93, 115*n*34, 134*n*90, 138, 146*n*131, 161, 189, 200–01, 204, 223, 248*n*102, 271, 286*n*17, 355, 357*n*16
Obama, Barack   307
Ohio   75*n*65, 118, 209, 264–65
Pall Mall Gazette   324–25

Paris Commune   5, 14, 81, 269–271, 295–96, 317, 319–36, 338, 344, 346, 349
parliamentary cretinism   61, 65, 242*n*80, 247–48, 281, 292, 304
Pathfinder Press   375, 377*n*69
Peninsula campaign   181–82, 184–85, 187–89, 189*n*88, 192, 199–200
People's Weekly World   312
Phelps, General John   161
Philips, Lion   111, 228
Phillips, Wendell   32, 53*n*110, 113, 163, 163*n*17, 197, 107*n*109, 198–99, 199*n*114, 200, 235, 257*n*134, 258*n*137, 266, 285, 294, 296, 328–29, 329*n*31, 344, 346
Plessy v Ferguson   274, 368
poor whites   108, 123–25, 129, 129*n*74, 130–31, 131*n*77, 135, 183, 198, 249–50, 252–53, 253*n*120, 254, 256–57, 263–64, 290, 319, 361–63, 366
Pope, General John   198, 198*n*112, 200
popular sovereignty   73–74, 77, 84
Port Royal, South Carolina   184, 256–57, 257*n*134, 291–92
presentism, fallacy of   6, 11
Die Presse   9, 10, 114, 128*n*70, 129, 131, 133–34, 136, 139, 143–44, 147, 147*n*133, 148, 150–52, 156, 158, 158*n*166, 169*n*22, 171, 175, 179, 180–81, 197, 199, 202, 206, 208, 211, 212, 217, 225, 227, 301
proletarian revolution   60–61, 66, 72, 142, 263, 280–281, 198*n*42, 327, 370, 379
proletariat   42, 44–46, 50, 53, 59, 66, 69, 72, 81, 84, 122, 142, 157, 167, 195, 227, 243–244, 256, 258 262, 265, 271, 274, 279, 287–88, 312, 313, 315, 320, 328, 332, 337, 340–41, 349, 354, 361 (See also working class)

property   26, 28, 42, 50, 69–70, 134*n*90, 141, 257, 297, 301, 312–13, 324–26, 328, 346, 379–81
Prophet of Freedom   3, 15, 298–99, (*see also* David Blight)
Proudhon, Joseph   48–49, 51
Puerto Rico   380

race   6, 12, 27, 49–50, 74, 77, 83–84, 94, 98, 108, 125, 133–34, 135*n*91, 136, 164–165, 165*n*9, 166*n*14, 237–38, 243–44, 245*n*88, 249, 251, 253, 258, 273*n*194, 289–90, 301, 308, 311*n*75, 314, 337, 358
  in America   40–41, 165, 248, 251, 300, 302, 311
  class and   37, 124, 134, 134*n*90, 136, 166–67, 262–63, 289, 300, 302, 309–11, 381
  presentism and   6
  invention of   166, 359–60
  (*see also* Appendix B   352–81)
racial capitalism   311–12, 312*n*81, 361, 376, 379
Radical Abolitionist Party   75, 77, 77*n*74, 85, 93
RAND Corporation   276
Reconstruction   158*n*167, 188, 198, 217*n*1, 232, 252, 258, 260*n*142, 265, 270–71, 273–74, 286*n*17, 294–96, 300–01, 301*n*53, 304, 306, 309, 309*n*72, 346, 350, 368
  Radical   14, 82, 217, 257–59, 261, 265–66, 268–69, 274, 293, 198, 300–01, 317, 350*n*94
Redpath, James   106*n*2
Remond, Charles Lenox   26, 220
republicanism/republican institutions   3*n*8, 19, 27–29, 40, 43, 49, 55–56, 59–60, 63–64, 67, 321, 324. 326, 328–29, 331, 351
Republican Party   58*n*15, 75–76, 92–96, 110*n*17, 122–23, 125–26, 142–44, 233–34, 239–40, 257, 265–66, 270, 273, 317, 335, 337, 339–40, 346–47, 350, 358, 358*n*18
Revolution and Counter-Revolution in Germany (Engels)   59–60
revolution in permanence   60, 241, 269–70, 298*n*42
Reynolds, David   88*n*111, 102, 364*n*32
Rheinische Zeitung   34–36, 38
Rhode Island Anti-Slavery Society   50
Ricardo, David   36

INDEX

Richardson, Heather Cox   233*n*49, 270, 317, 322*n*13, 339, 346, 350
Roberts, Neil   3*n*8, 87*n*106
Robinson, Cedric   312*n*82, 376, 376*n*63, 377, 377*n*69
Root, Damon   26*n*31, 298–99
Roudanez, Jean Baptiste   252*n*118
Ruffin, Edmund   102–03, 106–07, 107*n*5, 120, 123–24, 247, 249
Ruge, Arnold   40, 47
Russell, Lord John   121, 128, 128*n*70

Sandefur, Timothy   3*n*8
Sanders, Bernie   307
The Saturday Review   121, 204
Schurz, Carl   270, 270*n*179
secession   96–100, 102, 104, 107*n*5, 113, 119–20, 123, 126, 128, 130–32, 139, 163, 183, 192, 284, 362
    as reaction to Harpers Ferry   88*n*111, 89, 91, 101
    Mississippi Ordinance of   98–99
    slavery's role in   98
Second American Revolution   286*n*17, 309, 319
Second Reconstruction   80*n*81, 258, 274, 306, 310, 341, 381
Seneca Falls Convention   67
Serraillier, Auguste   322
Seward, William   143–44, 144*n*124, 145, 151–52, 152*n*150, 162, 200, 233*n*49, 237, 288
Sherman, General William   235–36
Sheridan, General Philip   242
Shoikhedbrod, Igor   36*n*66, 36*n*68, 40*n*85, 378*n*74
Silesia weavers strike   46
Sinha, Manisha   26, 26*n*31, 32*n*51, 74*n*62, 199*n*114, 354
slave insurrection/rebellion   26, 77, 81, 87, 89–90, 91*n*122, 99, 110, 112, 116–17, 126, 317, 356, 361, 364
slave labour   18, 48*n*98, 82–83, 100, 126, 172, 357
slave power   17, 75, 100, 105, 110, 113, 123, 131–32, 135–38, 185–86, 188, 195, 308, 357
slave oligarchy/slavocracy   13, 22, 28*n*38, 69–70, 75–77. 89, 96, 98–99, 101, 103, 105, 108, 115–16, 119, 121–26, 131–32, 134–36, 141–42, 155, 193, 203, 207, 229, 238, 242–43, 249–51, 259–60, 262, 272, 277, 283, 294, 320, 355–56, 362
slavery   4, 19, 24, 28, 39, 64, 71, 74–77, 79, 82–83, 88–90, 92, 94–96, 98–100, 106–09, 113–14, 117, 122, 125, 127–28, 131, 135, 137, 139, 141, 143–44, 153, 155, 160–61, 163–64, 167–69, 171, 178–80, 185, 187–90, 192, 194–98, 200–04, 209–10, 212–13, 219, 225, 231–32, 234, 237–39, 242, 248, 248*n*102, 249*n*105, 250, 252–57, 262, 272, 276, 280, 284, 286*n*17, 287, 295, 317–18, 335, 339, 341–42, 351
    as cause of the Civil War   106–07, 122, 131, 137, 139, 161, 186, 188
    chattel slavery   2–3, 5, 13, 17, 26, 28, 35, 43, 49*n*99, 53, 63–64, 70, 72–73, 76, 83–85, 99, 108–09, 134, 136, 168, 259, 263–65, 267, 274, 277–79, 282–83, 298, 305–06, 359–60, 363, 365
    racial slavery   7, 14, 43*n*91, 263, 311, 379–80
    wage slavery   64, 69–70, 73, 127, 134, 244, 306, 342
Slidell, John   150, 152, 152*n*150, 153–57
Smalls, Robert   219*n*4
Smith, Adam   3*n*8, 36, 299
Smith, Gerrit   7–8, 8*n*19, 70, 75–76, 85, 93, 93*n*125, 148*n*138, 165*n*9, 169, 175, 175*n*40, 222, 225, 228, 233
Smith, James McCune   79, 79*n*79, 288
social democracy   56, 65, 299, 312, 312*n*83, 376, 377*n*67, 378
Socialist Party (USA)   371–72
Socialist Workers Party   314*n*86, 373–75
Society of Fraternal Democrats   46
Sorge, Frederick   273, 358*n*18
    Washington DC strike and (1871)   336–37
South Carolina   1*n*1, 24, 83, 97–99, 101, 105, 117, 120, 126, 131, 184, 197, 223, 228, 236, 256–57, 273*n*193, 194, 344
The Spectator   127
Stalin, Joseph   34, 372–73
Stalinism   142, 301*n*53, 315, 373, 375–76, 377*n*67, 378
Stauffer, John   86, 139*n*107, 146*n*131
Stanton, Edwin   169, 169*n*23, 170–71, 183–84, 190, 191, 191*n*95, 192, 231

415

Stearns, George Luther   220, 229–32
Steele, Shelby   276
Stephens, Alexander   122, 124–25, 164, 243–44, 244n85, 246, 289, 362
Stevens, Thaddeus   220, 233, 257, 257n135, 258, 266, 266n162, 267, 293, 293n29, 296–97, 300n48
Still, William   86
Stowe, Harriet Beecher   122
Stride Toward Freedom (Martin Luther King, Jr.)   311
Student Non-Violent Coordinating Committee   314
suffrage   27, 31–32, 38, 42, 45, 64, 69, 204, 239, 241, 251–52, 257–58, 260–61, 261n151, 266n162, 269, 291–92, 303–04, 306, 342 (*See also* elections; Weydemeyer "On the Negro Vote")
Sumner, Charles   181, 250, 258, 266–67, 269n175, 296

Taney, Roger   78
tariff   121, 126
Taylor, Keeanga-Yamahtta   312n83
Taylor, Nikki M.   347n85, 248n89
Ten Days That Shook the World (John Reed)   44
Tennessee   139, 170, 173, 181, 184, 191, 223, 225, 233, 233n50, 249, 249n105, 342
Thiers, Adolphe   323–24, 326–27, 329–30, 334n48, 336, 349
Theses on Feuerbach (Marx)   46–47
Thirteenth Amendment   234, 234n51, 238–39, 248, 248n102, 250
Thomas, General Lorenzo   223, 231
Tilton, Theodore   239
Tocqueville, Alexis de   3n8, 8, 40–41, 41n87, 42–43, 66, 280, 299, 361
Tomanovskaya, Elisaveta Dmitriyeva   322, 330
Trent affair   13, 141, 149–52, 152n150, 153, 153n155, 154–55, 159, 166–67, 288
Trevellick, Richard F.   340
Tribune (New Orleans)   252
Trotsky, Leon   4, 312, 372–75, 377, 377n67, 377n69, 378
Trump, Donald   6n17, 305, 308–09
Tubman, Harriet   87
Turner, Nat   70, 80, 117

Union Army   112, 116–17, 138, 146, 170, 172–74, 180, 200–01, 214, 218–20, 223, 229n33, 230, 238, 246, 256, 270, 284–87, 289, 297–98, 355, 357
  fugitive slaves and   112, 114, 138–39
  role in emancipation   112, 112n26, 189, 248, 248n102, 284, 355
United States Constitution   6–7, 24–25, 36–37, 69–71, 74, 78, 78n75, 97, 100–01, 106, 111, 132, 140–41, 177, 188n83, 193, 203–04, 221, 230, 234, 238–41, 243, 244n85, 245, 250, 261, 266, 285–86, 286n17, 286n18, 306, 308, 350
United States Supreme Court   1, 68, 70–71, 78, 85–86, 101, 108n10, 240, 240n72, 274, 298, 306–07, 368

Valverde, Sergio   47n97
Varlin, Louis   322
Varon, Elizabeth   115n34, 130, 145n128, 189n88, 239
Vesey, Denmark   117
Vinoy, Joseph   324, 334n48
Virginia   7, 42, 70, 80, 86, 89–90, 102, 112, 117–118, 137, 141, 143, 162, 173, 181–184, 187, 191, 199, 213, 224, 308, 318, 357
voting fetishism   242, 242n80, 292, 304, 329
Voting Rights Act of 1965   1, 307

Wade, Benjamin   170n24, 264–66, 266n163
Wage Labour and Capital (Marx)   49, 166, 359, 361
Washington, George   204–05
Watts, Los Angeles   1
Weber, Max   3n11, 236
Weed, Thurlow   233n49
Westliche Post (St. Louis)   252
Weydemeyer, Joseph   58–59, 61–62, 73–74, 74n62, 94, 94n131, 95, 96n142, 108, 117, 130, 131n77 146, 206, 213, 237, 237n64, 246, 252, 252n117, 253–61, 283, 286–87, 287n19, 291–92, 302, 352, 355, 357, 358n18
  1852 presidential election and   76
  1856 presidential election and   76, 93
  1860 presidential election and   93–94, 96–97
  1864 presidential election and   237
  Douglass and   254–55, 257, 302

Frémont, John C. and   76, 93, 117, 146, 237
   Kansas-Nebraska Act and   73
   Marx party and   259, 283
   "On the Negro Vote"   253–59, 291, 302
   poor whites and   252–53, 256
   Port Royal, South Carolina and   256–57, 291
   Republican Party and   76, 94, 237
Whig Party   74
white workers   21–22, 84, 108, 124, 130, 130n76, 134, 244, 262–63, 273, 318, 336, 340–42, 346, 350–51, 354, 363, 373
Willich, August   88–89,   89n113, 95–96, 100–01, 101n156, 287n19
Wilson, James Q.   303
Winstanley, Gerard   304
'woke' sensibility   6, 166, 195, 218
Wolff, Wilhelm   227

Women's Union for the Defense of Paris   322
Woodhull, Victoria   289n22
working class   5, 12, 27, 30–32, 44–46, 50, 53, 55, 63, 65, 67, 70, 81, 84n94, 89, 127–28, 132–35, 155–57, 159, 165–67, 195, 205, 209, 212–13, 226–27, 242–45, 263–64, 269–74, 277, 279–81, 287–88, 291, 293, 299, 304, 306–07, 310–13, 315–16, 320, 322, 324, 331–32, 335, 339–41, 343, 346–48, 350, 350n94, 351, 358n18, 362, 366–67, 370–74, (*see also* proletariat)
Writ of *habeas corpus*   141, 234, 240

Zimmerman, Angela   9n25, 10–12, 252n117, 282n10, 352–54, 354n9, 355–58, 367, 376

Printed in the United States
by Baker & Taylor Publisher Services